# Centuries of Trial

## A History of Ireland under English Rule until 1922

## Volume 2

## 1692 - 1922

MICHEÁL MAC SEIRIDH

Published by *ÉIRE DUISIGH PRESS*

© *ÉIRE DUISIGH PRESS 2023*

www.centuriesoftrial.ie

Centuries of Trial Volume 2
A History of Ireland Under English Rule Until 1922
Volume 2, covering the years 1692 until 1922.

All photos courtesy of Wikimedia Commons except for pages 73, (copyright H Mc Loughlin) 234, (Thanks to Joe Hogan) and 469 (OPW)

ISBN 978-1-7394367-1-1

© MICHÉAL MAC SEIRIDH 2023

MICHÉAL MAC SEIRIDH asserts the moral right to be identified as the author of this work.

All rights reserved. No part of this publication may be reproduced, stored in a retrieval system, or transmitted in any form or by any means, mechanical, electronic, recording, photocopying or otherwise, without the prior permission of the publisher.

Jacket Image – The ruins of Cork following the burning of the city centre by British Crown Forces, December 1920.

Jacket and book design by the author.

"Centuries of brutal and often ruthless injustice...have driven hatred of British rule into the very marrow of the Irish race."

- David Lloyd George

"It has pleased the English people in general to forget all the facts in Irish history. They have been also graciously pleased to forgive themselves all those crimes."

- Daniel O'Connell

"If history is deprived of the truth, we are left with nothing but an idle unprofitable tale."

- Polybius

# Do cum glóire Dé agus Onóra na h-Éireann[I]

---

[I] For the glory of God and the honour of Ireland

# Contents
|  | Page |
|---|---|
| Map of Ireland | 28 |
| A Note on the Title | 29 |
| Author's Note | 31 |
| Foreword by Fr. Eóghan Monaghan | 33 |
| Introduction | 37 |
| Part 3 – Cross Upon Cross | 44 |
| Part 4 – Freedom? | 381 |
| Afterword | 661 |
| References | 665 |

## Part 3 – Cross Upon Cross

### Chapter 1 – Perfidious Albion

At the Mercy of England — 45
- The Disposal of Forfeited Estates
- Ireland at the Mercy of England
- Catholics Barred from Parliament
- Lord Lieutenant Capel and his Parliament
- The Return of Priest Hunting

The Penal Code — 53
- The Change of Monarch
- "A Bill For Preventing the Further Growth of Popery"
- "The Sacramental Test"
- The Bill is Enacted

The Penal Laws — 56
- Property
- Public Life
- The Catholic Faith

| | |
|---|---|
| Conversion and Perversion | 61 |
| The Protestants Triumphant | 62 |
| The Penal Laws and an Irish Town | 63 |
| Impact of the Penal Code on Catholic Landowners and Tenants | 65 |
| Catholics Barred From Practicing Law | 67 |
| "Protestant Horses" | 68 |

## Chapter 2 – The Pearl of Great Price

| | |
|---|---|
| Penal Days in Ireland | 69 |

- The Mass House
- The Registration of Secular Clergy
- 1709 – The Oath of Abjuration and the Mass Rock
- The "Relatio" of Bishop MacMahon
- The Priest Hunter
- "I will go unto the Altar of God"
- The Persecution Continues
- The Penal Laws Mark II
- The Trial and Execution of Fr. Nicholas Sheehy

## Chapter 3 – The Hammer and the Anvil

| | |
|---|---|
| The Governance of Ireland until 1800 | 83 |
| The "Irish" Parliament | 84 |

- The Composition of the Parliament
- Corruption Within the Political System

| | |
|---|---|
| The Restriction of Trade | 88 |
| Life in Ireland during the Eighteenth and Early Nineteenth Centuries | 90 |

- "A Destitute and Poverty Stricken People"
- The Hearth Tax
- The Tithe

- "A Levy on all Papist Households"
- The Landlord
- The Great Famine of 1740-41

Education     97
- The Charter Schools
- The Charter School Nurseries
- Hedge Schools

The Rise of Secret Societies     105
- "Whiteboys" and "Rightboys"

The Founding of The Orange Order     108
- The Charter Toast of the Orange Order
- From Bad Feeling to Violence
- "Drive out the Catholics"
- Lord Gosford Intervenes

## Chapter 4 – The Protestant Nation

The Irish Colonists Fight for Parliamentary Independence     113
- "The Patriot Party"
- The Decline of The Penal Code
- The Protestant Volunteers
- "Free Trade for Ireland"
- The Dungannon Convention

The Protestant Nation     119
- An Illusory Independence
- The Act of Renunciation
- The Foiled Duel
- The Corn Laws

The Anti-Climax     123
- The Failure of Parliamentary Reform
- The Demise of The Volunteers
- English Resentment

The Catholic Convention     125
- The Catholic Committee

- "An Unconstitutional Proceeding of the most Alarming, Dangerous and Seditious Tendency"
- His Majesty's Catholic Subjects
- A Few Concessions

## Chapter 5 – Theobald Wolfe Tone and The United Irishmen

The Society of The United Irishmen     130
- The French Revolution
- The Founding of The Society of The United Irishmen
- The United Irishmen Are Forced Underground
- Wolfe Tone Leaves Ireland

"England's Closest Escape Since The Armada"     136
- Wolfe Tone Comes to France
- The Beginning of the Road Towards the Act of Union
- The Insurrection Act
- "Esto Perpetua"?
- The French at Bantry Bay
- The Battle of Camperdown

## Chapter 6 – The 1798 Rebellion

The Drift towards Insurrection     146
- Martial Law in Ulster
- A Brief Setback for English Plans
- Religious Tensions Within the Leadership of The United Irishmen
- Fanning the Embers of Rebellion
- The Bridge Street Raid
- The Death of Lord Edward Fitzgerald

The Rebellion     154
- The Rising is Launched

- The Rising in Leinster excluding Wexford
Wexford before the Rebellion   158
  - The Arrival of The North Cork Militia
  - A Reign of Terror – Wexford Goaded into Rebellion

The Rising in Wexford   161
  - "Better for us to die like Men than to be Butchered like Dogs"
  - The Days of Victory
  - The Battle of Tubberneering Rock
  - New Ross
  - Massacre of English Prisoners in Wexford Town
  - Vinegar Hill – The End of the Rebellion in Wexford
  - Mass Murder in Kilcumney, Carlow
  - The Death of Fr. Murphy

The Rebellion in Ulster   173
  - Henry Joy McCracken and the Battle of Antrim Town
  - The Rising in North Down

The Testimony of Lord Cornwallis   175
  - "If a priest is put to death, the greatest joy is expressed by the whole company"

The Amnesty   177

"The French are in the Bay"   178
  - The French at Killala
  - "Ireland Forever"
  - Crown Forces Routed at Castlebar

The Rising in Longford   181
  - Humbert's Odyssey
  - Battle and Massacre at Ballinamuck

Killala – The Last Land Battle   183

Tory Island – The Naval Battle of the 1798 Rebellion   184

- The Capture of Wolfe Tone
The Trial and Death of Theobald Wolfe Tone     186
- "A Common Criminal"
- The Trial
- Sentence and Suicide

## Chapter 7 – Union and Insurrection
The United Kingdom of Great Britain and
Ireland     191
- The Plan
- The Union is Formally Proposed
- Palm Greasing and Graft on an Unknown Scale
- The Maiden Speech of Daniel O'Connell

The Act of Union     198
- January 15th 1800
- The Passage of the Act
- Robert Pitt Fails to Keep his Word

Robert Emmett and the Insurrection of 1803     203
- "Croppies Lie Down"
- Robert Emmett Attempts to Revive the Cause of Irish Freedom
- "We war against English Dominion"
- The Insurrection
- "No Man Can Write My Epitaph"
- The Resignation of Sir William Wickham

## Chapter 8 – A New Moses
The Early Life of Daniel O'Connell     212
- Ireland at the Turn of the Century
- Youth and Education of Daniel O'Connell

The Catholic Board     214
The Duel     218
- The Sectarian Corporation

- "The Beggarly Corporation"
- The Challenge
- The Duel
- The Aftermath

Fighting the Anti Catholic Bias — 221
The Road to Catholic Emancipation — 223
- The "Distracted and Unsettled state of Ireland"
- The Catholic Association
- So Near
- The 1826 Election

An Incident in the Struggle against Landlord Tyranny — 231
- The Battle of Magheracloone

A Catholic Member of Parliament for Clare — 235
- The Clare By-election
- "They must either crush us or conciliate us"

The Granting of Catholic Emancipation by the British Government — 238
- The Passage of The Bill
- The Irish Electorate is Reduced by 87%
- King George IV Curses Daniel O'Connell
- English Vindictiveness in Defeat
- "The Little Ark"

"The Member for All-Ireland" — 245
- Early Battles For Repeal of the Union
- The Carrott and the Stick

The Tithe War — 247
"A Starving Race of Fanatical Slaves" — 250
The Balance of Power — 251
"Abandon Hope All Ye That Enter Here" — 253
The Repeal Association — 254
- One Last Try
- The Emergence of The Young Ireland Movement

- The Repeal Courts
- The Monster Meetings

The End of the Repeal Movement ... 261
The Decline ... 262
- The Split with Young Ireland

The Death of Daniel O'Connell ... 265
- "If you do not save Her, She cannot save herself!"
- "Do not let them bury me until I am dead"

## Chapter 9 – The Great Starvation

The Irish 'Land System' ... 269
Potatoes and Rent ... 272
Poverty ... 274
The Devon Commission ... 277
The Coming of the Potato Blight ... 279
- The Recollection of Jeremiah O'Donovan Rossa

Recommendations to the Government on Arresting the Starvation ... 282
The Exportation of Irish Food during The Great Starvation ... 284
- England's Necessity

The Course of The Great Starvation ... 288
- Autumn 1845 – Summer 1846
- The Repeal of the Corn Laws and the Change of Government
- Summer 1846 – Summer 1847
- August 1847 – "The End of The Famine"

"We are Starving! – Give us something to Eat" ... 301
- Report on the Starvation in Connacht by W.G. Foster
- The Testimony of Irish Lawyer and Historian A.M Sullivan

| | |
|---|---|
| The Starvation Continues | 304 |
| Private Charity during the Starvation | 307 |
| Mass Eviction in the Wake of Starvation | 309 |

- Rates and the Change in Agricultural Practice
- The "Encumbered Estates Act"
- Evictions in Co. Clare – The Testimony of Captain Arthur Kennedy, Poor Law Inspector May 7th 1849

| | |
|---|---|
| Emigration and Coffin Ships | 312 |
| The Failure of The Act of Union | 313 |

## Chapter 10 – The Irish Republican Brotherhood

| | |
|---|---|
| 1848 – The Young Ireland Rebellion | 315 |

- A Different Path
- Sedition and Treason Felony
- The Rebellion

| | |
|---|---|
| The Irish Republican Brotherhood | 319 |

- The Founding of the I.R.B and The Fenians
- The Funeral of Terence MacManus
- "The Irish People"

| | |
|---|---|
| 1867 – The Republic is Declared | 323 |

- Dublin Castle Moves Against The I.R.B Leadership
- "The Invasion of Canada"
- Colonel Kelly assumes leadership of The I.R.B
- The 1867 Insurrection

| | |
|---|---|
| "God Save Ireland" | 328 |

- The Rescue
- The Trial
- The Executions

| | |
|---|---|
| "The Clerkenwell Outrage" | 333 |

## Chapter 11 – The Land War

| | |
|---|---|
| "The Felon" | 335 |
| The Tenant Right League | 336 |
| Ireland – "The Only Real Danger to the Noble Empire of The Queen" | 337 |
|    - The Effect of the Clerkenwell Explosion on British Opinion and Policy | |
|    - The Disestablishment of The Church of Ireland | |
|    - The 1870 Land Act | |
| The Introduction of the Secret Ballot | 342 |
| The Home Government Association of Ireland | 343 |
|    - To Preserve the Link with England | |
|    - The Formation of The Home Rule Party | |
|    - Despised at Westminster | |
| The Irish National Land League | 346 |
|    - 1877 / 79 - The Return of the Potato Blight | |
|    - The Formation of The Irish National Land League | |
| The Campaign against the Landlords | 349 |
|    - "A Sort of Moral Coventry" | |
|    - Captain Charles Boycott | |
| The 1881 Land Act | 351 |
| Parnell Imprisoned | 353 |
|    - The "No Rent" Manifesto | |
|    - The "Kilmainham Treaty" | |
| The Irish National League | 355 |
| The Plan of Campaign | 356 |
|    - "The Landlord League" | |
| Selling the Land of Ireland to the Irish People | 358 |
| The Land Purchase Acts | 359 |
|    - The Ashbourne Act | |
|    - The Balfour Act | |

- The Wyndham Act

## Chapter 12 – Home Rule for Ireland?

| | |
|---|---|
| "Coercion Plus" | 362 |
| - The Phoenix Park Murders | |
| - The Repression Act of 1882 | |
| Dublin Castle – Centre of English Rule in Ireland | 364 |
| The First Home Rule Bill | 366 |
| - The 1885 Election | |
| - The "Hawarden Kite" | |
| - The Introduction of The First Home Rule Bill | |
| The Piggott Forgeries | 371 |
| The Adultery Scandal | 373 |
| The Split within The Irish Parliamentary Party and The Death of Parnell | 374 |
| The Second Home Rule Bill | 375 |
| Killing Home Rule | 376 |
| - The Congested Districts Board | |
| - The Local Government Act | |
| The Visit of Queen Victoria | 379 |

# Part 4 – Freedom?

## Chapter 13 – Gaelic Awakening

| | |
|---|---|
| The Steady Decline of Gaelic Culture | 383 |
| "Shoneens" | 385 |
| The Gaelic League | 385 |
| - Douglas Hyde | |
| - Patrick Pearse | |
| The Gaelic Athletic Association | 389 |

| | |
|---|---|
| The Anglo Irish Literary Revival | 390 |

## Chapter 14 – The Home Rule Crisis

| | |
|---|---|
| The Death of Queen Victoria | 392 |
| Sinn Fein | 393 |
| - Arthur Griffith | |
| - The Founding of Sinn Fein | |
| The Reforming of The Irish Republican Brotherhood | 396 |
| Continued Sectarianism within Government | 397 |
| An "Instalment" of Home Rule Rejected | 398 |
| The Third Home Rule Bill | 399 |
| - Curbing the Power of the House of Lords | |
| - Unionist Opposition | |
| - Sir Edward Carson | |
| - Forming a Unionist "Sinn Fein" | |
| - The Third Home Rule Bill | |
| The Solemn League and Covenant | 405 |
| - Reaction in Ulster to the Home Rule Bill | |
| - "Ulster Day" | |
| - Prime Minister Asquith Deceives the Irish Parliamentary Party | |
| The Ulster Volunteers | 408 |
| Southern Volunteers | 409 |
| - The Dublin Lockout and the Irish Citizen Army | |
| - The Irish Volunteers | |
| The Home Rule Bill Passes Unaltered | 413 |
| "The Curragh Incident" | 414 |
| Gun Running | 415 |
| - The Larne Gun Running | |
| - The Howth Gun Running | |
| Bachelors Walk | 418 |

Home Rule "...rendered a nullity"  419

## Chapter 15 – For the Defence of Small Nations
The Split in The Irish Volunteers  420
England's Difficulty – Ireland's Opportunity  421
Roger Casement in Germany  423
The Funeral of Jeremiah O'Donovan Rossa  425
- "The fools, the fools, the fools!"
Planning an Insurrection  427
- A Date Decided
- The 'Kidnapping' of James Connolly
- The Plan
- The Imperative
The Eve of Rebellion  433
- "The Aud" Departs Lubeck
- A Change of Plan
- Plans Discovered
- The Scuttling of The Aud
- The Capture of Roger Casement
- "Danger Averted"
- Manoeuvre Orders "Rescinded"
- "Orders from the Captain"
- A Parade for Irish Freedom

## Chapter 16 – "In the Name of God and of the Dead Generations"
The Proclamation of The Irish Republic  443
The Rebellion in Dublin  446
- The First Military Casualties of the Rising
- Crown Forces Dispatched to Dublin
- Mount Street Bridge
- The Destruction of the City Centre
- The South Dublin Union and St. Stephen's

- Green
- Twenty Six Against Five Hundred
- Final Hours in the G.P.O
- Number 16, Moore Street
- Surrender

The Rebellion Outside Dublin   460
- Galway
- North Dublin and Meath
- Wexford

Crown Forces Atrocities   464
- North King St.
- Guilty but Insane

## Chapter 17 – Dying For Ireland

The Court Martials   470
Lessons in Dying   473
- May 3rd, Patrick Pearse
- May 3rd, Thomas MacDonagh
- May 3rd, Tom Clarke
- May 4th, Edward (Ned) Daly
- May 4th, Willie Pearse
- May 4th, Michael O'Hanrahan
- May 4th, Joseph Mary Plunkett
- May5th, John MacBride
- May 8th, Sean Heuston
- May 8th, Eamonn Ceannt
- May 8th, Michael Mallin
- May 8th, Con Colbert
- May 12th, James Connolly
- May 12th, Sean MacDiarmada

The Trial and Execution of Thomas Kent   481
- The Battle of Bawnard House
- The Execution of Thomas Kent

The Trial and Execution of Roger Casement   482

- "Hanged on a Comma"
- Speech from the dock
- Conversion and Execution

## Chapter 18 – After the Battle
Mass Imprisonment 488
"A Nefarious Scheme" 487

## Chapter 19 – A Changing Political Landscape
The First Prisoners are Released 490
Electoral Victories for a New Force in Irish Politics 491
Lloyd George Announces a National Convention 493
DeValera is Elected to the British Parliament 494

## Chapter 20 – The Emergence of a Republican Political Movement
The Killing of Thomas Ashe 497
A New Sinn Féin and a New National Leader 500
- Making a Start on the Undermining of British Rule

The End of Lloyd George's Convention 503
Fighting Conscription 504
- "The German Plot"
- "Crush the National Movement"

The End of the Great War 510

## Chapter 21 – "Citizens of A Free and Gaelic Ireland"
The Establishment of Dáil Eireann 511
- A National Plebiscite on the Way Forward

- The First Dáil Convenes
"We are now done with England"     515
- The Declaration of Irish Independence
- The Paris Peace Conference

"For the Benefit of the Irish People"     518
- The Democratic Program of Dáil Eireann

The Government of the Republic     521
- Escapes and Releases
- DeValera's Cabinet
- Fund Raising for the Republican Government
- Republican Courts

## Chapter 22 – An Approaching State of War

The Irish Republican Army     525
- Arming the IRA

Soloheadbeg and Knocklong     529

The Choice     534

An Escalating Situation     535
- The Formation of "The Squad"
- A Modern Version of an Old Policy
- The Suppression of Dáil Eireann
- A Failed Assassination Attempt
- Lloyd George Introduces a Partitionist Home Rule Bill

## Chapter 23 – A Fight For Irish Freedom

The British Government's Irish Policy     543
- War and Politics

The Municipal Elections     545
- Ulster
- Sinn Fein Victorious
- A Dramatic Increase in Repression

The Assasination of the Lord Mayor of Cork     549

The War from Spring to Autumn of 1920          551
- The Assassination of Judge Alan Bell
- "I Loathe the Country…and its people"
- Hunger and Other Strikes
- "Tans" and "Auxies"
- Council Elections and Pogroms
- "The more you shoot the better I will like it"
- "A Race of Treacherous Murderers"
- Mass Resignation Among the Judiciary
- The IRA at War
- An Act for the Restoration of Order in Ireland
- "There can be no Truce with the Powers of Hell"
- The Pogroms Continue
- The Ulster Special Constabulary
- The Destruction of Irish Industry
- The Internment Camps
- "In the Highest Traditions of the Service"

## Chapter 24 – Ambush and Atrocity

| | |
|---|---|
| Bantry, Co. Cork | 587 |
| The Capture of General Lucas | 587 |
| Templemore, Co. Tipperary | 588 |
| Galway City | 588 |
| Balbriggan, Co. Dublin | 589 |
| Rineen, Co. Clare | 591 |
| Mallow, Co. Cork | 593 |
| Tralee, Co. Kerry | 593 |
| Granard, Co. Longford | 594 |
| Dublin City, November 21st 1920 | 595 |

- The IRA Strike Against British Intelligence
- Bloody Sunday at Croke Park
- Murder in the Guardroom
- "Kill him! Kill him!"

| | |
|---|---|
| Camlough, Co. Armagh. – December 12th 1920 | 599 |
| Co. Cork; Nov28th – Dec 15th 1920 | 600 |

- Kilmichael
- The Destruction of Cork City Centre
- Murder in Dunmanway
- "We took a Sweet Revenge"
- The Intervention of Bishop Colahan

## Chapter 25 – The War in 1921

| | |
|---|---|
| Martial Law and Official Reprisals | 609 |
| Torching the Big Houses | 612 |
| The Resignation of Brigadier General Frank Crozier | 613 |

- "A Heavy and Hidden Hand"
- Trim and Drumcondra
- "You can have a KBE in June"

| | |
|---|---|
| Death of a General | 616 |
| Crossbarry – The Largest Battle | 617 |
| The Burning of the Custom House | 620 |

## Chapter 26 – Treating with the Enemy

| | |
|---|---|
| Peace Moves | 622 |
| Partition Accomplished and Peace Offered | 625 |

- The Second Dail
- Options
- The King in Belfast
- A Letter from Lloyd George

| | |
|---|---|
| The Truce | 629 |
| Dublin and London – July to October 1921 | 631 |

- DeValera in London
- Irish Rejection of the British Offer
- Letters

- An Invitation
## The Treaty Negotiations 637
- The London Conference
- A Defining Day
- Concern Among Members of the Irish Delegation
- Griffith Agrees with Lloyd George's 'Technical Manoeuvre'
- Irish Proposals Resubmitted
- "You will split Ireland from top to bottom!"

## The Treaty is Signed 647
- New Irish Proposals
- Griffith Breaks his Word to the Republican Cabinet
- Hans Place
- The Treaty is Signed

## The Bloody Aftermath 655
- "If it's good enough for Mick Collins, it's good enough for me"
- The Provisional Government of Southern Ireland
- "No Other Law!"

## Afterword – The Unfinished Revolution 661
## References 665

"Already the curse is upon Her,

and strangers Her valleys profane;

They come to divide – to dishonour,

And tyrants they long will remain.

But onward! – the green banner rearing,

Go, flesh every sword to the hilt;

On our side is virtue and Erin,

On theirs is Saxon and guilt."


Excerpt from;

"The Song of O'Rourke, Prince of Brefnie"

by

Thomas Moore, "The Bard of Erin"

1779 - 1852

Ireland

## A Note on the Title

The title of this book is taken from a phrase in the Preamble to The Irish Constitution. The Preamble declares:

"In the Name of the Most Holy Trinity, from Whom is all authority and to Whom, as our final end all actions both of men and States must be referred,
We, the people of Éire,
Humbly acknowledging all our obligations to our Divine Lord, Jesus Christ, Who sustained our fathers through **centuries of trial**,[1]
Gratefully remembering their heroic and unremitting struggle to regain the rightful independence of our Nation,
And seeking to promote the common good, with due observance of Prudence, Justice and Charity, so that the dignity and freedom of the individual may be assured, true social order attained, the unity of our country restored, and concord established with other nations,
Do hereby adopt, enact, and give to ourselves this Constitution."

---

[1] This passage is based upon a phrase in the Irish Declaration of Independence as read to the assembled members of Dáil Eireann on January 21st 1919: "We humbly commit our destiny to Almighty God, Who gave our fathers the courage and determination to persevere through long centuries of a ruthless tyranny..."

## Author's Note

The story of these two volumes of Ireland's "Centuries of Trial" under English rule began in May of 2018 following Ireland's abandonment of the unborn child.

I have been passionate about history ever since I can remember and this has given me the habit of viewing modern events in an historical light. In the Summer of 2018, following the referendum which overturned the right to life of the unborn child in Ireland, my mind was filled with thoughts of what our forefathers, who sought to free our country from a different tyranny would think of this crime against God and against our own people and nation.

Once more I immersed myself in the history of our land, seeking a way of escape from what I would regard as being the lowest point in our history. I finally felt compelled to record Ireland's historic struggle against English tyranny for the current generation. This history of Ireland under English rule, divided into two volumes is the result.

The sources which I have used in these two volumes are a mixture of primary and both ancient and modern secondary sources. To the authors of all sources, both living and dead, I owe a great debt of gratitude.

At every point I have attempted to sacrifice political correctness for accuracy. Events from English history which impacted on the English rule of Ireland are also recorded.

Rather than being an academic work, this is instead a popular history.
Buiochas le An t-Athair Eóghan Monaghan, Maire, Peadar, Diarmuid, Joe, agus mo Chlann.

# Foreword

# Patrick's Coming

In a pagan land far to the north, the druids and witch doctors were nervous. The prophets had foretold the coming of a strange religion with a strange God.

"Pole-headed shall come from over the sea,
His staff crook-headed, his garment hole-headed,
His servants shall sit in the east of his house,
And they shall say Amen, Amen."

"Pole headed" was Patrick; the "crook-headed staff" was his crosier; the "hole-headed garment" was his chasuble.[I] Little did they know! The hand of God was moving and the days of the Scotti worshipping the sun and sacrificing their children to Crom on the Fields of Slaughter[II] would soon be numbered. The worldly nephew of St. Martin had been taken prisoner and enslaved on Mount Slemish. He had been drawn to the desert. "And he watched over me before I knew him... and consoled

---

[I] Chasuble – outer vestment worn by the priest during the offering of the Holy Sacrifice of the Mass
[II] Numerous Irish townlands derive their origin from the title "Fields of Slaughter" where pagan sacrifices took place before the coming of Patrick.

me as a father would his son"[1] he wrote. He found God in Ireland. Then he escaped from Ireland determined never to go back...
Then, one night, Patrick saw a man coming as if from Ireland with innumerable letters... "and he gave me one of them, and I read the beginning of the letter: "The Voice of the Irish', and as I was reading the beginning of the letter I seemed at that moment to hear the voice of those who were beside the forest which is near the western sea, and they were crying as if with one voice: 'We beg you, holy youth, come back and walk among us once more."

Just a dream? Then Pope Celestine sent him back.

The pagan priests were ready, they saw the fire, they knew its meaning. "Unless that fire is extinguished tonight," they said, "it will never again be extinguished in Ireland."
Nor was it. For Patrick had brought the light of Christ to the end of the Earth "where they never had any knowledge of God but, always, until now, cherished idols and unclean things."

"They are lately become a people of the Lord, and are called children of God, the sons of the Irish and the daughters of the chieftains are to be seen as monks and virgins of Christ."

The Island of Saints and Scholars, the cradle of re-Christianised Europe...until the English invaded, and then apostatized. What of Ireland now, would it remain faithful? It did.
And the heretical English conquered the world for earthly glory – even as far as the ends of the earth. And wherever the English went, they were followed by the sons of Patrick.They brought the light of Christ they had received, and the Holy

---

[1] All quotations in the Foreword are from "The Confession of St. Patrick"

Sacrifice was offered, and sins were forgiven, and souls were saved.

And now? When the Irish worship the sun once more and sacrifice their children to devils on the fields of slaughter? Now, it remains for us to be faithful.

"For this sun which we see, by God's command rises daily for our sakes, but never will it reign, nor will its splendour last; but all those who worship it shall go in misery to punishment. But we who believe in and worship Christ the true Sun, who will never perish, nor will anyone who doeth His will, but he will abide for ever, who reigneth with God the Father Almighty, and with the Ghost before the ages now and for ever and ever. Amen."

                Fr. Eóghan Monaghan

36

# Introduction to Volume 2

This introduction gives a brief synopsis of Centuries of Trial Volume 1, a history of Ireland under English rule from 1171 to 1691. If you have read Volume 1, then this introduction can be dispensed with.

Deposed for his crimes in the Spring of 1166, the King of Leinster, Diarmuid Mac Murrough, escaped from Ireland and made his way to England and then France, where after offering his allegiance to King Henry II of England, he returned to Ireland with a Norman warrior band to retake his Kingdom. In 1171, King Henry II followed and found a country where the majority of regional kings were happy to offer him their allegiance as Overlord, but not the governance of their lands.

Henry II agreed to accept their allegiance on those terms but afterwards embarked on a savage war of conquest, conducted by Barons he had appointed with the task of taking Ireland. The Irish now did their utmost to defend themselves. For Henry's armies, progress was slow. As a land of regional kingdoms, whose armies were well used to war, not by one or many great battles could the invader bring Ireland to submission despite their well used policy of 'divide and conquer'.

After a century and a quarter, this first phase of English invasion was at its height and saw the invader in control of the eastern seaboard, and great swathes of Connacht and Munster. By 1350, thanks to an Irish / Scottish military campaign led by Edward and Robert Bruce, coupled with the after effects of the 'Black Death', English power in Ireland was in decline. Not only were the Irish reasserting control over their native land but many Anglo-Irish, (who were descendants of the original English invaders, and were now viewed and treated with suspicion by London) were now casting aside their loyalty to England.

In 1367, the English Crown responded with a new legal code known as 'The Statute of Kilkenny'. This Statute sought not only to legalise the English land grab but also forbade the Anglo Irish to have any contact with the native Irish, now referred to as "Mere Irish" or "The King's Irish Enemies". As such the Irish as a nation were cast out from legal protection and regarded as non-persons.

Throughout the English 'War of the Roses', during the second half of the fifteenth century, the Gaelic resurgency continued, reaching its height in 1500 when English power and control was at its lowest point since the first decades of the invasion. At this stage, even powerful Anglo-Irish families such as the Fitzgeralds of Kildare straddled a thin line between their loyalty to the King of England and their friendship with some of the Gaelic Princes. Others such as the Fitzgeralds of Desmond, without formally renouncing their loyalty to London had little time for the King of England, following the execution by the Crown of their leader, Thomas Fitzgerald.

When King Henry VIII became King of England, he viewed Ireland and her resources with great interest. How could he succeed where so many before him had failed? After successfully ridding himself of the powerful Fitzgeralds of Kildare, a new scheme was put into operation whereby the

Irish Kings would be offered peace and the security of their lands in return for accepting Henry as King of Ireland and, following his schism with Rome, Supreme Head of the Church in Ireland. For the Irish it was to be a poisoned chalice, for after accepting English title, the Crown would with all methods at its disposal seek to supplant them.

Throughout the remainder of Henry's reign and the reign of Edward VI the scheme took hold, but the religious reforms of Edward's reign proceeded slowly due to the unswerving loyalty of the Anglo Irish (or 'old English') to every aspect of the Catholic faith which they firmly held to.

When Mary Tudor became Queen of England, the Catholic religion was restored both in England and Ireland. However it was in Mary's reign that a new policy was first tried, which was to become the cornerstone of English policy in Ireland in the centuries that followed. This policy was 'plantation' or the banishment of the Irish from their ancestral lands and their replacement with loyal English.

When Henry's daughter Elizabeth, became Queen of England in 1558 following Mary's death, she quickly renounced her Catholic faith and embraced Protestantism. In Ireland both the Old English and the native Irish remained faithful to the Catholic faith. Elizabeth I would now use this loyalty to Catholicism to her advantage and her Irish Wars would become a war of religion.

In Ireland, the Gaelic Princes realized the error of their fathers in accepting the policy of 'Surrender and Regrant' and English title. Elizabeth's footsoldiers quickly sought to overthrow Gaelic rule in Ireland. Opposition and revolt were provoked and then crushed. Extermination of the native Irish was the order of the day. More Plantations followed.

Ulster now remained as the last Gaelic stronghold, but the persistent persecution conducted by the English now provoked another rebellion.

But when an Irish captain, Hugh O'Neill whom Elizabeth had nurtured and appointed as 'Earl of Tyrone' rebelled against her and allied himself with his nation in 1595, a war launched by the Ulster Chieftains in 1594 developed into a national war and struggle for freedom for both Catholicism and the Gaelic way of life. Armies sent over from England were repeatedly defeated until eventually the English resorted to scorched earth and mass murder of the native Irish in order to secure victory.

When O'Neill finally surrendered in 1603, Elizabeth was dead and had been replaced by King James I (King James VI of Scotland) who passed an Act of Oblivion and restored the Ulster princes to their ancient patrimony. This was short lived however, for the powers of state in London quickly gained control of James. Following a government plot against Hugh O'Neill, he fled Ireland in 1607 with many of the Gaelic leaders in what became known as 'The Flight of the Earls'.

King James's renunciation of the Act of Oblivion quickly followed. The way was now clear for James and the London government to seize Ulster and enforce a mass plantation of the English and Scots in Ulster. The native Irish were cast out "to depart with their goods and chattels into whatever part of the realm they pleased." Those who could fled to the mountains, there to remain until a new Gaelic resurgency might be launched. Meanwhile, in the rest of Ireland, the persecution and seizure of land continued unabated.

However bad things were for the Irish people under the rule of the British monarchy, under the rule of the English parliamentarians they promised to be worse. When King Charles I, who was under severe pressure from Parliament at home, placed the Parliamentarian Judges, Borlase and Parsons, at the head of his Irish administration, plans promising the extirpation of the Irish and the Catholic faith were published. The aim was to drive the Irish into rebellion and complete the seizure of Irish land. A great Gaelic rebellion against English rule was launched towards the end of 1641.

The Catholic 'Old English' who professed undying loyalty to King were also being persecuted and finally agreed to make common cause with the native Irish in defence of the Catholic Faith, forming an alliance known as "The Confederation of Kilkenny"

After initial military successes by the Confederacy, the King's chief soldier in Ireland, The Duke of Ormond, finally succeeded in undermining the alliance by creating division between the two parties.

By the time Cromwell had defeated the King's forces in England in 1648, the Confederacy was broken and Ireland was ripe for Cromwell's bloody conquest during which great massacres were committed. The chapter of Cromwell's rule was one of murder, persecution and banishment to England's slave colonies. Landowners were driven from their lands into unfertile lands in Connacht.

Following the dissolving of Cromwellian rule in England and the return of the monarchy, Catholic persecution in Ireland abated. But King Charles II who preferred his former enemies over the Irish would not alter Cromwell's 'Irish land settlement'.

Following the death of Charles II, his Catholic brother James II became King. When James forbade Catholic persecution in England those whose families had profited by it became uneasy. When a son was born to James's Queen, Mary, James's enemies invited a Dutch Prince, William of Orange to come to England and overthrow their monarch. James fled to Ireland and gathered an army composed of both Irish and Anglo Irish to defend the country against invasion. Seeing in James their only hope, the Irish flocked to his standard. An Irish Parliament assembled and King James II agreed to overthrow 'the Cromwellian Settlement' in its entirety.

On June 11th 1690, William landed at Carrickfergus with a huge English and continental army in tow. When battle was joined at the River Boyne at the beginning of July, James's army was defeated and he fled Ireland for France leaving his army to try and secure victory for him. A year of war followed before the Irish were decisively beaten at The Battle of Aughrim and driven back to their final stronghold of Limerick.

The Irish army finally surrendered their fortress at Limerick after securing a treaty from the English which guaranteed the right to profess the Catholic faith and security of property. The first of what became known as 'The Wild Geese', most of the Irish army chose to leave Ireland for France and join the ranks of the French King, Louis XIV, in order to continue their fight against the English.

# Part 3

# Cross Upon Cross

# Chapter 1

# Perfidious Albion

### At the Mercy of England

"That Treaty was totally violated by the British government, the moment it was perfectly safe to violate it. That violation was perpetrated by the enactment of a code, of the most dexterous and atrocious iniquity that ever stained the annals of legislation." – Daniel O'Connell

As soon as the Jacobite army had departed Ireland, the English began breaking the articles of the Treaty of Limerick. Soldiers of the Jacobite army, who had chosen to remain in Ireland and return to their homes, had no sooner arrived when magistrates ordered that they be dispossessed of their land and have their weapons removed, both measures in direct contravention of the Treaty's terms. The land of all those Jacobites who had been killed in the fighting or had gone to France was also seized including the estate of the former Lord Mayor of Dublin Simon Luttrell, who had been particularly mentioned in the treaty and guaranteed the preservation of his estate as he was in France at its signing.

Very soon the Dublin Lord Justices who had signed the treaty were inundated with complaints from those who claimed the Treaty's protection. Whilst a declaration was issued by the government regarding the upholding of the Treaty, this was a dead letter as no effective action was actually taken to uphold it. Vast numbers of those Irish Jacobites who had chosen to remain in Ireland now changed their minds, and decided to go to France after all preferring exile instead of remaining in Ireland to face dispossession, poverty and abuse.

Both in Ireland and England, the Protestants denounced the Treaty of Limerick as being too lenient and the Protestant pulpits resounded with the cry that the treaty should not be kept because of the "sin of keeping faith with the Papists". In the Irish House of Lords, the Protestant Bishop of Cork preached so vociferously against the Treaty that the Lords "voted the thanks of the House to be given to him for his sermon, with their desire that he should print it"[1]

## The Disposal of Forfeited Estates

Immediately following the conclusion of the war,[1] acts of outlawry and attainder against almost 4,000 Irish Catholic landowners, merchants and persons of wealth, who had remained loyal to King James II after his usurpation by William of Orange were passed by the English Parliament. King William, by now fully aware of the vindictiveness of his

---

[1] The Irish politician Edmund Burke (1729- 1797) described the outcome of the War of the Two Kings as follows; "The ruin of the native Irish and in a great measure too, of the first races of the English was completely accomplished. The new interest was settled with as solid a stability as any thing in human affairs can look for. All the penal laws of that unparalleled code of oppression, which were made after the last event, were manifestly the effects of national hatred and scorn towards a conquered people whom the victors delighted to trample upon, and were not at all afraid to provoke. They were not the effects of fear but of their security. They who carried on this system looked to the irresistible force of Great Britain for their support in their acts of power. They were quite certain that no complaints of the natives would be heard in England with any sentiments other than those of contempt and indignation. Their cries served only to augment their torture. Indeed at that time in England the double name of the complainants, Irish and Papist- it would be hard to say which was most odious – shut up the hearts of every one against them."

English parliament towards the Irish[I] promised to reverse these Acts but his promise came to nothing and he instead turned his attention to Protestant dissenters in Ireland, granting to Ulster's Presbyterian ministers who had preached against King James, a "Regium donum" (Royal Gift) of £1,200 annually. He also prevented discriminatory measures against non conformists (such as the "Clarendon Code") from being extended to Presbyterians in Ireland.

King William III of England

While it was a long time since the native Irish had any real influence in the affairs of Ireland, these acts and the mass dispossession of the Catholics now signalled the end of the Old English as a body with any power in the affairs of Ireland. Thereafter the Old English Catholics became more or less as one with the native Irish, as they were now as much despised as the native Irish by what came to be known as the "The New Interest" or "The Protestant Ascendancy".

The vast majority of the land of Ireland (over 90%[II]) now passed into the hands of Protestants, among them Dutch and German allies of William of Orange, who liberally granted vast

---

[I] William of Orange showed himself to be equally vindictive with regard to Scottish Catholics. After the Scottish resistance in favour of the Jacobite King James II came to an end following the defeat of the Jacobites in Ireland, the Catholic Clan Mac Donald surrendered and were afterwards massacred in the Pass of Glencoe on William's orders on February 13th 1692.

[II] Following the vast appropriation of land by King William and the English government, 14% of land was still in Catholic hands. The penal laws that followed the Williamite victory reduced this figure to around 4%.

estates to his favourites including de Ginkell, Keppel and Ruvigny.

In this series of land acts 1,060,792 (further) acres were vested in the Crown and by these acts a Commission for the Sale of Forfeited Estates was formed which saw the emergence of the despicable and verminous Irish Landlord system which was to ravage the country and feed on the body of the Irish people for the following two centuries.[1] Indeed, such was the amount of Irish land available to William that his former mistress, Mrs.Elizabeth Villiers (whom he also created Countess of Orkney) was granted almost 100,000 acres in Tipperary.

The confiscations in their entirety were summed up by the Lord Chancellor, Lord Clare during a speech in Dublin: "…the whole of your island has been confiscated, with the exception of five or six families of English blood…and no inconsiderable portion of the island has been confiscated twice, or perhaps thrice in the course of a century. The situation, therefore, of the Irish nation at the revolution stands unparalleled in the history of the habitable world…The whole power and property of the country have been conferred by successive monarchs of England upon an English colony, composed of three sets of English adventurers, who poured into this country at the termination of three successive rebellions. Confiscation is their common title; and from their first settlement they have been hemmed in on every side by the old inhabitants of the island, brooding over their discontent in sullen indignation"[2]

---

[1] Between 1700 and the Great Starvation which commenced in 1845 there would be twenty seven man made famines in Ireland. This was because of the dependence of the Irish people on the (often diseased) potato crop and the fact that all other crops had to be used to pay the rack rents of the landlords.

In 1700 King William, (who was not well liked by Parliament[1] due to the brake which he attempted to put on the worst excesses of the anti- Catholics) saw most of his grants undone when the House of Commons passed a "Resumption Bill" which vested the stolen land of Ireland in a Parliamentary board and thus opened the granting of vast estates to the highest bidder.  Naturally Catholics were excluded, being barred from purchasing any amount of land greater than two acres and the estates were taken up in the main by a variety of wealthy English aristocrats, businessmen and merchants. By the early 1700s Ireland was in the firm grip of a government / landlord pact which had absolutely no interest in the welfare of the ordinary Irish people. This abominable pact would now suck the country dry of its every resource while its people descended into a sucking mire of poverty which was the worst of any country in Europe.

Catholics Barred from Parliament
Following the "Glorious Revolution", the English Parliament had immediately passed acts which barred Catholics from being members.  After the Williamite victory these acts were extended to Ireland.
When the new Lord Lieutenant, Lord Sydney, called an "Irish" Parliament in 1692 the few Catholics members that remained were barred unless they would swear that "…there is no transubstantiation of the elements in the Lord's Supper…"[3] and that "…the sacrifice of the Mass is damnable and idolatrous…"[4] As the Catholics eligible to participate in the parliament would not deny their faith, they could not enter.

---

[1] King William lived in a well founded and constant fear of assassination. He took numerous precautions for his personal safety and for the majority of his reign lived in isolation outside London.

## Lord Lieutenant Capel and his Parliament

In 1693 Lord Sydney was recalled and Henry Capel (Baron Capell of Tewkesbury) was appointed to replace him. An avowed anti Catholic he embarked on a program of legislation in direct contravention of the Treaty of Limerick[1]

Lord Sidney Capel

In 1695 he summoned a parliament in Dublin. In the wake of the Jacobean war the aim of the government would not be to govern the Irish but to suppress them. When parliament assembled Capel introduced an act that he had the audacity to call "A Bill for the Confirmation of Articles Made at the Surrender of the City of Limerick".[5] The small print read "so much of them as may consist with the safety and welfare of his Majesty's subjects."[6] Naturally, very few of the acts of the Treaty were found to conform with the safety of the New Interest and most of the acts were interpreted in the narrowest way possible or dismissed altogether including the article which allowed Catholics the same freedom to practice the faith which they possessed under Charles II.

Further acts, all contrary to the first article of The Treaty of Limerick were also passed in the same parliament. There were

---

[1] To this day, Dublin's "Capel St." remains named in honour of this man, one street among a host of others in the capital of the Irish Republic that are to this day named after the men who served the Crown of England during one of the darkest chapters in Ireland centuries of trial. (Others include Molesworth, Grafton, Cumberland, Bolton, Pembroke, Northumberland and Dorset.)

laws for "restraining foreign education", (which also forbade children to be instructed in the Catholic faith by "any Popish person") "for better securing the government by disarming the Papists", "for banishing all Papists exercising any ecclesiastical jurisdiction, and all regulars of the Popish clergy out of the Kingdom", and for "the prevention of Protestants intermarrying with the Papists".  When a petition was presented to the parliament by Robert Cusack Esq and Captains Segrave and Eustace (who were Catholic) asking that they might be heard before the acts passed into law the Dublin House of Commons unanimously rejected it.

During the parliament, its members, all of the Protestant ascendancy, a grouping that England had long sought to establish and nurture in Ireland also sought legislative independence from England but the English parliament would have none of this and went to King William asking him "to take all necessary care that the laws which directed and restrained the parliament of Ireland should not be evaded"[7]

As a punitive measure against their fellows in Ireland, the English parliament enacted legislation against the colonist run wool trade that was undermining the wool producers of England.  Such exorbitant tariffs were imposed on wool produced in Ireland as to kill off the trade completely.  As a result thousands of native Irish who produced the wool were left destitute.

## The Return of Priest Hunting
"They bribed the flock, they bribed the son
  To sell the Priest and rob the sire
Their dogs were taught alike to run
  Upon the scent of wolf and friar" – Anon, 17th century

It was set down in Capel's act that by May 1st 1698, all Bishops, Jesuits, Monks, Friars and any priest exercising any sort of jurisdiction were to have departed Ireland[1], leaving behind only so-called "secular clergy" or parish priests. As priests were forbidden from entering the country it was hoped that the priests left behind would eventually die out, resulting in the eventual demise of the Catholic religion in Ireland.

Even before this date, large numbers had already departed because of acts of violence against them and by the date in question around half of the country's clergy and religious had left the country.

Those who were earmarked by the government for departure and remained behind, were, if caught, imprisoned until they could be transported to the penal colonies. Any who departed and then returned were guilty of high treason and were liable to be executed. A system of branding with a hot iron was used on some of the clergy forced to depart in order to determine if any of them returned.

In the act, measures were also introduced imposing exorbitant fines on anyone who sheltered those ordered to depart. Offenders faced a fine while repeat offenders had their "lands, goods and chattels" confiscated. These were to be divided between the King and the informer. Informing was encouraged. It was proclaimed that "informing against Papists is an honourable service to the government",[8] while persons in authority who did not "exert themselves"[9] in this regard were warned that they were "betrayers of the liberties of the Kingdom"[10].

Rewards for the "discovery" of a bishop were greatly increased compared to previous acts. In Cromwell's time it had been £10, but this now rose to £50. The price for reporting the presence of a monk in the country went from £5 to £20. There

---

[1] "...if any of them remain after that day, or return, the delinquents are to be transported, and if they return again to be guilty of high treason and to suffer accordingly."

was also a new category. For the discovery of a "Popish Schoolmaster" £10 was offered.

Initially English soldiers took it upon themselves to make some extra money by apprehending Catholic clergy, but they were soon outclassed by professional priest-hunters who used cunning methods such as disguising themselves as priests in order to track down clergy proscribed under the act. The "profession" of Priest Hunting attracted even those from abroad and one of the most successful in this regard was a Portuguese Jew named Garcia.

## The Penal Code

"I must do it justice. It was a complete system, full of coherence and consistency, well digested and well composed in all its parts. It was a machine of wise and elaborate contrivance, and as well fitted for the oppression, impoverishment, and degradation of a people and the debasement in them of human nature itself, as ever proceeded from the perverted ingenuity of man" – Edmund Burke

"The Penal Laws form a code which every tyrant might study, and find his knowledge of the surest means of producing human wretchedness extended. He would see at once a terrible engine made perfect with all the science of political mechanism, for those who, with devilish malignity, would reverse the end of government, and instead of improving the well being of the community, deliberately set about the destruction of a race" – Mac Knight.

"It would be difficult in the whole compass of history to find another instance in which such various and such powerful agencies concurred to degrade the character and to blast the prosperity of a nation." – William Lecky

"Upon the whole, the Irish may justly blame themselves...for whatever they have or shall suffer in the issue of this matter, since it is apparent that the necessity was brought about by them, that either they or we must be ruined." – William King, Protestant Archbishop of Dublin

## The Change of Monarch

On February 26th 1702, King William fell off his horse and broke his collarbone. The horse (whose name was Sorrell) had been confiscated from the Jacobite officer, Sir John Fenwick. It had stumbled on the entrance to a mole's burrow and William had been thrown.[1] Pneumonia followed as a complication of the broken bone and on March 8th, William died, age 52.

Upon the accession of Queen Anne[II], (daughter of James II) to the throne of England, the Englishmen sitting in the Dublin Parliament felt that the final restraints had been removed from them in their efforts to crush the Catholics of Ireland, for once and for all. They already possessed the land and wealth of the country and the natives were in a state of utter subjection, but this was not enough. Too many times before the Irish had risen up like a phoenix from the ashes, but this time, the English, already possessing all, were determined that it should never ever be taken away from them.

---

[1] Following the incident, the toast "To the little gentleman in the black velvet waistcoat" became popular among Jacobites.

[II] After Anne became Queen, a Bill of Succession was passed in parliament which excluded Catholics from being monarchs of England. The act was aimed at the son of James II who had been recognized as the legitimate King of England (King James II) by Louis VIV of France following the death of his father on September 16th 1701. During Anne's reign (in 1706) the United Kingdom was formally established following the union of England and Scotland.

### A Bill "For Preventing the Further Growth of Popery"
In 1703, James (the second and last) Duke of Ormond was appointed by London as Lord Lieutenant of Ireland. Upon his arrival at the Dublin House of Commons, he found the members of the house waiting on his presence with a bill entitled "For Preventing the Further Growth of Popery" more popularly known as "The Penal Code". The members[1] presented the Bill to him and with some vehemence entreated him to take the Bill to England and use all his influence to ensure that it received the royal seal.

### "The Sacramental Test"
In England, the bill was viewed by some Tories as being too harsh, but they had neither the courage or conviction to work against it, and the bill was approved and returned to Dublin after a clause known as "The Sacramental Test" was added to it, by which all persons who refused to receive communion in an Anglican church would be barred from public office. By the addition of this clause, which was aimed at the Presbyterians and other Protestant dissenters (who were among the most vocal in promoting the Penal Code) London hoped that the Dublin parliament might think twice about enacting the Bill as it would gravely affect many influential members of Parliament who were Presbyterians.

### The Bill is Enacted
As London expected, the addition of "The Sacramental Test" to the Bill was viewed with hostility by the Protestant dissenters in the Dublin Parliament, but at length they accepted the assurances of their fellow members who told them that they

---

[1] A few members who disapproved of the Bill, did not oppose it but rather resigned their seats and new members who approved the Bill took their places.

would ensure that only the Papists were affected. After the Presbyterians in the House withdrew their opposition, the Bill passed unopposed and received the royal assent on March 4th 1704.

However in 1707, the Sacramental test was indeed extended to the Presbyterians and until 1775, they were also barred from public office and the holding of the King's commission. Initially the other measures of the Penal Code did not affect them but in 1715 further measures barring intermarriage between Anglicans and Presbyterians and forbidding Presbyterian ministers from giving instruction to children were enacted in the Dublin Parliament. Thus, the Presbyterians suffered a little of what they had earlier meted out to the Catholics.

On March 17th a motion was passed in the House of Commons that all government officials who did not uphold all measures contained in the Bill to the fullest extent betrayed the public liberty and in the years that followed especially during the reigns of Anne and George I, further acts augmenting and strengthening the Penal Code were passed

## The Penal Laws

The measures contained in the "Act for Preventing the Further Growth of Popery" and the individual pieces of legislation passed both before and after this legislation by the House of Commons are collectively known as "The Penal Laws". For many years these laws were tinkered with and further refined, the most notorious proposed change to the laws being in 1723 when The Privy Council in Dublin submitted a request to London that unregistered priests should be castrated, but this was too much for London and was not permitted.

Any Catholic found guilty of breaking the law was liable to be fined, jailed or banished to a penal colony.

The laws may be summarised as follows;

1. Property
- Upon the death of a Catholic landowner, his land was to be divided among all his sons thereby reducing in size estates owned by Catholics. If one son became a Protestant he inherited everything. This was known as the "Gavelkind Act"
- Any son of a Catholic landowner, on becoming a Protestant was entitled by law to dispossess his father of all his property.
- If a Protestant suspected another Protestant of holding property in trust for a Catholic, he was allowed to file a bill against the trustee and seize his property.
- If a Catholic inherited land, he could be dispossessed by his closest Protestant relative. Furthermore children of Catholics sent abroad were not allowed to inherit property anywhere within the Realm.
- Catholics were forbidden to own a horse valued at more than five pounds. Any horse could be seized from a Catholic simply by paying him £5.[1]
- The Protestant Militia were entitled to seize from Catholics wagons and horses for the use of Her Majesty's forces.
- Catholics were forbidden to have firearms.
- No Catholic was allowed to take out a lease on a piece of land for longer than thirty one years. Aside from the rent paid to the Landlord, the terms of the leasehold included such measures as a certain number of days of forced labour, and the supply of poultry and other commodities to the landlord. It was a vastly different system from that of England where landlords leased complete farms with outbuildings and a furnished

---

[1] The Act read "No Papiest shall be capable to have or keep in his possession, or in the possession of any other, to his use or at his disposition, any horse, gelding or more of the value of £5 or more"

house. The description of an English member of the House of Lords was "In England the landlords let farms, in Ireland land"[11]

2. Public Life
- Catholics were banned from voting and from taking part in all political activity.
- Catholics were forbidden from living within the walls of provincial or county towns
- No Catholic was allowed to be a member of a jury or to be a barrister.
- Mixed marriages between Catholics and Protestants were forbidden. Progeny of such a marriage (if discovered) were by law to be brought up as Protestants.
- Catholics were forbidden to be guardians of orphans or executors of wills.
- Catholics were forbidden from taking court cases as they were not recognised as persons under the law, neither did the law of "Habeas Corpus" extend to them. As late as 1760 a declaration was made by the Lord Chancellor of Ireland and thereafter repeated by the Chief Justice that the laws of the Kingdom "did not suppose any such person to exist as an Irish Papist"[12]
- Protestants were forbidden to hire Catholics for remunerative employment.
- Catholics were forbidden from all public office or any office of trust.
- All orphans or wards of court were to be brought up as Protestants.
- A Catholic employer was forbidden to hire more than two apprentices except in the linen weaving industry.
- Catholics were forbidden to travel more than five miles from their houses.

- No Catholic was allowed to employ a Catholic teacher to educate his children
- Catholics were forbidden from joining the army. This measure could be relaxed in time of war, but only for the ranks of the enlisted. No Catholic was permitted to hold the King's commission.
- Catholics were forbidden from printing or selling newspapers or books.[1]

3. <u>The Catholic Faith.</u>
- The teaching of the Catechism or any Catholic doctrine was forbidden.
- Two justices of the Peace were allowed to summon any Catholic man before them and request him to abjure the Catholic religion. If he refused, his property could be passed to his next of kin. They could also ask him various questions regarding infractions of the penal code (i.e. any knowledge he possessed regarding the holding of secret Masses etc.). If he refused to answer these questions to their satisfaction he could be imprisoned.
- All Bishops and regular clergy, friars and those holding any form of ecclesiastical authority were banished.
- Any Catholic Bishop, priest, etc upon entering the country was to be arrested and could be hanged.
- Heavy fines were imposed for not attending the Sunday Protestant service.

---

[1] To circumvent this law, numerous books in Gaelic by Irish exiles were published on the continent and smuggled into Ireland. Books were also published in French for the use of exiles including a History of Ireland by the chaplain to the "Wild Geese" in French service, Fr. James MacGeoghegan. Entitled "Histoire d'Irlande", it is one of the sources for these two volumes.

- Any four judges could summon a man who refused to attend Protestant Service and summarily sentence him to be transported to a Penal Colony.
- Catholic chapels were not allowed to have steeples or crosses.
- Priests had to register with the government. Registration could only take place if a layman paid the authorities £50 as a surety for the good behaviour of the priest. They were not allowed to say Mass outside their own parishes. They were forbidden from wearing cassocks or other priestly clothing or vestments in public. At any time a registered priest could be summoned for questioning regarding the locations where he said Mass or a range of other questions regarding infractions against the penal code. Failure to give satisfactory answers resulted in imprisonment.
- Priests were forbidden from administering the sacraments outside their parish.
- One secular priest was allowed per parish. If he fell ill or died it was forbidden to replace him.
- Pilgrimages to holy places (especially Lough Derg) were forbidden

There were two Irelands. Pre-eminent was the Ireland of the minority "Protestant Ascendancy.[1] They 'owned' the land and controlled the country and viewed it (like many English colonists in other parts of the world) as theirs. They cared not a jot for the Irish except that they should pay their rents, do the menial tasks and not cause any trouble for them. The other

---

[1] The term "Protestant Ascendancy" was first used during debates in the Dublin parliament during the late 1790's. It is a term which encompassed all Protestants of the "new interest"; landowners, lawyers, merchants, clergymen, aristocracy and their families.

Ireland was that of the Irish. Dispossessed disenfranchised and denied every human and in many cases spiritual comfort they sought to eke out a living among their English overlords.

## Conversion and Perversion

An aspect of the Penal Code that is often overlooked is the effect that they had on those Protestants who converted to Catholicism. Severe penalties were prescribed in the Code for such offenders who were thereafter considered as enemies of the state.

In 1748, Mr. George Williams from Wexford was found guilty in the local court "of being perverted from the Protestant to the Popish religion"[13] and was sentenced to be "out of the King's protection"[14] while his "lands, tenements, goods and chattels"[15] were declared to be "forfeited to the King and his body to remain at the King's pleasure"[16] (imprisonment). Two years following this case a registered Tipperary priest, Fr. John Hely was summoned to appear on the charge of "perverting a dying Protestant". When he failed to appear, the court sentence him to be punished as befitted "a tory, robber and raparee of the Popish religion in arms and on his keeping"[17]

For those Protestants who married Catholic women the effects were no less severe. During the election of 1760 any Protestant gentleman who had a Catholic wife, had his vote disqualified, while by act of parliament, any solicitor, attorney or barrister who married a Catholic was barred from their profession. If a Protestant woman married a Catholic, her property or inheritance went to her nearest Protestant relative. If any child of a mixed marriage was baptised a Catholic, the Protestant parent was classified as a Papist, heavily fined and imprisoned. Such a fate befell the Protestant father of the former Catholic Bishop Young of Limerick who upon his release from prison "perverted to the Popish faith"

## The Protestants Triumphant

Apart from the restrictions placed on access to the sacraments, the Penal Code was not particularly directed at those in the lower classes of Irish life as they had long since lost whatever privileges they possessed upon the demise of Gaelic Ireland.

However in Ulster, the ordinary people had to suffer more than most. That this was the case was made clear by the Catholic Bishop of Clogher Dr. Hugh Mc Mahon in 1714 when he wrote: "Although all Ireland is suffering, this province is worse off than the rest of the country, because of the fact that from the neighbouring country of Scotland, Presbyterians are coming over here daily in large groups of families, occupying the towns and villages, seizing the farms in the richer part of the country and expelling the natives... The result is that the Catholic natives are forced to build their huts in mountainous or marshy country"[18] The huge influx of families from the Scottish lowlands (counties of Scotland which border England) was also attested to by the Protestant Primate, Archbishop Synge, who estimated in 1715 that not less than 50,000 families had arrived in the province of Ulster between 1689 and 1715.[1]

In some towns Catholics were almost completely driven out. In the town of Hollywood, Co. Down the only Catholic left in the area was the coach driver for a certain gentleman named Mr.Isaacs. As his carriage was driven through the town the people would come to their doors to "have a look at the Papist"[19]

As Ulster was the most heavily planted part of the country, Protestant tenants in Ulster enjoyed lower rents and a practice that became known as "The Ulster Custom" which gave the tenant extra rights (similar to tenants in England) and allowed the tenant to sell his tenancy with the custom intact.

---

[1] Cardinal Patrick Moran of Syndney wrote in his history of the period that "...everything worth having passed into their hands..."[1]

Unlike Elizabethan times the Protestants showed no great appetite for attempting the conversion to Protestantism of the Irish people, being satisfied that they had placed enough temptation in the way of those well off Catholics who desired to advance in the world. This was enunciated by Lord Drogheda when he stated "I shall be very glad to see the Protestant religion strengthened; but what shall we do for hewers of wood and drawers of water, for labouring men to plough our lands and thresh our corn."[20]

The laws were in the main directed at what remained of the educated Catholic middle and upper class, which now consisted in the main of the Old English. Their ruin was seen by the Protestants as a great victory.

## The Penal Laws and an Irish Town

Galway was one of the many Irish cities and towns where the Penal Code was rigorously enforced. In 1703 the council passed a bye-law forbidding Catholics from purchasing a house or tenement within the city. Any Catholic already residing in the city was forced to find a Protestant who would vouch for their good behaviour or face expulsion. Furthermore Catholics could only sell goods on market day, with all goods being sold by them subject to a special "Popery tax".

In 1708, the law regarding the presence of Catholics in the city was changed to one of banishment for all Catholics residing there. By special order of the council some priests were arrested and flogged as a warning to all priests to stay clear of the city. Following the execution of this special order the government secretary in Dublin Castle wrote to the Mayor of Galway John Gibbs expressing the hope that "...you would continue your endeavours to banish the priests out of the town and cause those whom you have apprehended to be prosecuted at law with the utmost vigour"[21.]

In order to bring more Protestants into the city and region, in 1717, the Dublin Parliament passed a law called the "Galway Act" whereby any foreign Protestant, no matter what Protestant sect he belonged to would be welcome in the city or its surrounds so long as they would swear the required anti Catholic oaths. This idea was not a new one for French Huguenots had already been tempted to Ireland, and in 1709 a great deal of land belonging to extirpated Catholics in Limerick was made available to a colony of over 700 Protestant German families from an area of Germany known as The Palatine. Huge sums were made available by the government to subsidise this settlement that took place mostly around Rathkeale in Co. Limerick. Regarding the Palatine Settlement, Arthur Young (the English Agriculturalist who visited Ireland in 1776) wrote how they "…had houses built for them, plots of land assigned to each at a rent of favour, were assisted in stock, and all of them with leases for life from the head landlord…the Irish are rarely treated in this manner; when they are they work much greater improvements than are common among those Germans"[22.]

In Galway however, the scheme for the importation of Protestants was a complete failure, as most of those who took up the offer had no interest in the development of the area. The eminent historian William Lecky recorded the result; "Enterprise in every form had died out; the corporation, being narrowed to the utmost in order to keep the control of the city in the hands of a few Protestants, became even more corrupt than others in Ireland. The whole aspect of the town became one of ruin and desolation. About the middle of the century the fortifications were entirely out of repair, the gates were falling from their hinges, the main wall of the city was full of holes made by smugglers for the convenience of their trade"[23.]

Around the middle of the century, Galway's military governor was Governor Eyre. By this stage the law allowing Catholics within the city walls had been relaxed, more out of necessity than governance. A series of martial laws were still in force against the Catholics, and Governor Eyre used these laws to keep the city gates closed until afternoon, a measure which prevented those Catholics in the city from going to Mass, as by necessity this was generally offered in the countryside away from the city in the early morning. This measure of keeping the gates closed contributed greatly to the ruin of trade in the city and was finally overturned on the orders of Dublin Castle after complaints by Protestant merchants and the Galway Corporation.

In spite of Governor Eyre's best efforts, Protestantism within the city continued to decline especially towards the latter end of the eighteenth century. In a letter to Dublin Castle he wrote of a Protestant Grammar School which had been forced to close for want of pupils and of: "...several old Protestants and the children of such who have been perverted to the Popish religion...from the fullness of my soul I acquaint you with this; I grieve to see the decline of the few poor Protestants that are here, or rather fear an entire extermination of them."[24]

## Impact of the Penal Code on Catholic Landowners and Tenants

As a direct result of the Penal Code the land ownership of Catholics in Ireland was reduced to less than 4%. This occurred for a number of reasons;
- Due to land seizures by the government or Protestants because of real or alleged infractions of the Penal Code,
- Numbers of the Catholic gentry were unwilling to sacrifice all that was demanded of them and so "turned over" (apostasized) so as to avoid loss in social status or because they wished to enter one of the professions from which Catholics were barred.

- Sometimes a son "took advantage" of the measures and "turned over" in order to dispossess his father or did so after his death so that he could inherit the land in its entirety instead of sharing it with his brothers.
- A further factor in the reduction of the amount of land owned by Catholics was that no land that came up for sale could be purchased by them.

It is reckoned that up until 1789 over 5,000 Catholics "turned over" either to gain land or admittance to one of the barred professions. The most notable "turning over" was that of Alexander McDonnell, (thereafter Earl of Antrim) in 1734.

In 1739 it was reckoned in a petition to parliament that "two thirds of the business of the Four Courts consists in Popish discoveries...by idle and wicked vagrants informing against (Popish) leases and tenements."[25]

Even Catholics who converted to Protestantism for material advantage could also fall foul of the Penal Code. On November 26th 1741 a Catholic man by the name of Farrell from Longford, "turned over" and declared himself a Protestant but did not receive communion in the Protestant church until May 16th 1742. Around ten years later Farrell, whose progress as a Protestant was being closely watched by a local Protestant named Tomlinson purchased land which Tomlinson thereafter claimed as his own, because Farrell had not kept the letter of the law that "no one conforming to the Protestant religion shall be deemed a Protestant unless he receive the sacrament with the space of six lunar months after his declaration of conformity."[26] The case went to court and in 1759 the common law judges upheld that "Tomlinson as the first Protestant discoverer, was, by virtue of the Popery Acts entitled to the benefit of the purchase made by the defendant"[27] and that Farrell had to pay the costs of the lawsuit. Farrell appealed and the case went to the House of Lords in London who also found in Tomlinson's favour. Farrell was subsequently financially ruined as the entire costs of the case were awarded against him.

## Catholics Barred From Practicing Law

Initially the penal laws did not prevent Catholics practising as solicitors.

However, in 1724, a number of descendants of old Irish families who had been dispossessed by Cromwell, decided to band together and petition the crown to have their rightful property restored. When word of the proposed petition reached the ears of a member of the Dublin House of Commons, he raised the matter in parliament after which an address to the Crown was passed stating that "nothing could enable them to defend the King's right and title to his crown so effectually as the enjoyment of those estates which have been the forfeitures of the rebellious Irish and then in possession of his Protestant subjects"[28] and praying the King to renounce "all applications or attempts that should be made in favour of such traitors or their descendants so dangerous to the Protestant interest of the kingdom"[29]. The King replied to the House that such a petition on behalf of Irish Catholics would most certainly not be entertained.

As some Catholic solicitors had been involved in the drawing up of the petition, the House now moved against them and drew up and passed a bill barring all Catholic solicitors.

As the bill went before the House, some of the solicitors determined to try and appeal the measure, and launched a collection, the entirety of the amount gathered never amounting to more than £5. When news of the collection became public, the House of Commons described it as a collection for the "bringing in of the pretender"[30] (the Jacobite, Bonnie Prince Charlie). All documentation pertaining to the collection was ordered seized and in a report to the House of Commons it was reported that "great sums of money had been collected, and a fund established by the Popish inhabitants of the kingdom, through the influence of the clergy, highly detrimental to the Protestant influence and of imminent danger to the present happy establishment"[31.] The House then adopted an address to the Lord Lieutenant encouraging him "put the laws against popery into execution"[32.]

## "Protestant Horses"

When drawing up a deed of lease for his Catholic tenants, the Protestant Landlord included various clauses regarding the prohibition of Popish Worship on the property, the prohibition of "sub letting to Papists" and often the requirement to stable what was termed in the lease as "Protestant Horses" for the cultivation of the land.

Those Catholics who could afford a good horse frequently had their horses appropriated from them as the law allowed. In a recorded case in Mullingar, Co. Westmeath, a Catholic landowner by the name of MacGeoghegan was driving into the town in a cart pulled by two horses when he was stopped by a Protestant who proffered £10 and told him that he was taking them. Contrary to the law, Mac Geoghegan held a brace of pistols, which he now produced and used to shoot the horses dead before the Protestant could intervene. Following this incident MacGeoghegan's carriage was pulled by two oxen.

A similar incident in Mullingar occurred when a Catholic horse-owner of "old English" lineage named Barnewall also had his horse appropriated. As the new "owner" was about to ride away, Barnewall grabbed hold of the bridle and told him that he had no entitlement to the saddle or bridle. When the Protestant laughed and tried to ride away, Barnewall stretched him out on the ground with blows from his whip. Later, in the dock of the court for assault, Barnewall was acquitted by the Magistrate on the plea that the complainant had tried to steal his riding accoutrements.

# Chapter 2

# The Pearl of Great Price

## Penal Days in Ireland

### The "Mass House"

Following the introduction of the Penal Code, those secular priests who were allowed to remain in the country were generally expelled from urban areas, thereafter finding refuge either in back streets or in the countryside. In Waterford city, three chapels had been shut down since The Battle of the Boyne and following the enactment of the Penal code the city council shut down the last chapel which was located in a backstreet using the excuse that its "dirt and nastiness had become a public nuisance"[33], while in Cork the Protestant Bishop Dr. Downes wrote "The Popish Priest, called Daniel Sullivan …celebrates Mass generally in a ditch, sheltered with a few bushes and sods and sometimes in a cabin."[34]

In 1704, after the measure compelling priests to register with the authorities was introduced it was permitted that those parish priests that registered were allowed to offer Mass in a "Mass House" in their parishes. Keeping the Mass from going underground served the authorities well, as spies could keep an eye both on the content of sermons and the identity of the parishioners in case there were any soldiers or public officials present.

## The Registration of Secular Clergy

Only those priests who registered in 1704 were allowed to say Mass and administer the sacraments. Once the period for registration closed, it was the intention of the government that no further registrations would ever take place and as no priest could be replaced so that over time the number of Catholic clergy in the country would dwindle. By depriving the people of priests, it was hoped that the people would eventually lose the faith. In order to further reduce the number of priests, the government offered an incentive; to any priest who would apostatise and renounce the Catholic faith an award of £40 was given. The total number who did so during the penal days of the eighteenth century was twelve.

In the early eighteenth century the average life expectancy in Ireland among the Irish was less than 40 while the average age of the priests who registered in 1704 was 54. By eighteenth century standards the priests were all advanced in age and so the authorities were confident that within a generation Ireland would be almost devoid of Catholic clergy.

Priests who registered needed a layperson to pay £50 as surety for their good behaviour. In areas of abject poverty for Catholics such as parts of Ulster which had been heavily planted with lowland Scottish Presbyterians, many priests could not be registered which resulted in priests who were able to register doing so for multiple parishes. Whilst the Catholics were denied churches and the priests lived in as much poverty as their parishioners, during the first decade of the eighteenth century the measures had no serious effect on the ordinary people or the secular clergy, most of whom remained steadfast in their apostolate.

## 1709 - The Oath of Abjuration and the Mass Rock

In 1709, a law obliging all registered priests to take the Oath of Abjuration was passed. The oath was directed against the

Jacobite heir to the throne, James III, but as it obliged the taker to acknowledge albeit indirectly the jurisdiction of the English monarchy over the "…estate ecclesiastical and spiritual and abolishing all foreign power repugnant to the same…"[35] the Pope forbade the clergy to take it.

Any priest who did not take the oath associated with the Act by March 25th 1710 was liable to be arrested and deported. As the date approached many priests went into hiding and as such were now fair game for the red-coated soldier and Priest-hunter alike.

Now without church or chapel, the priests, writes Fr.Augustine, (the priest who ministered to some of the 1916 leaders before their execution) "went forth to the valleys, the hills and the mountains, to the caves and caverns of this Irish soil…there is scarcely a large district in Ireland in which cannot be found some Irish name that crystallises a poignant but glorious story, a great and stirring poem, on the Irish devotion to the Mass…Carraig an Aifrinn – The Mass Rock"[36]

In his history of the period, Fr. Augustine writes that once the oath was made obligatory "The pace of persecution was quickened. The government became more cruelly active; espionage was perfected into a system at home and abroad and informing against a priest was declared by the Irish parliament to be an honourable act deserving the nation's gratitude"[37]

## The "Relatio" of Bishop MacMahon

In 1705 two bishops remained in the country; the infirm Bishop of Cashel who was housebound and the Bishop of Dromore, who was in prison. However in spite of the banning of bishops numerous prelates in disguise attempted to enter the country to take charge of the diocese to which they had been appointed. One such bishop was Dr. Hugh Mac Mahon who, in 1714 as Archbishop of Armagh recorded an account of his initial experiences as Bishop of Clogher which is most illustrative of the condition of the Catholic faith in Ireland during the penal days of the eighteenth century.[1]

Appointed to the See of Clogher in 1707, MacMahon left Rome some time afterwards and travelling by a circuitous route, entered Ireland in disguise early in 1710 finally arriving in his diocese in March of that year just as the deadline for signing the Oath of Abjuration approached. He relates that upon his arrival in his diocese he found waiting for him "…neither ring, nor mitre, nor cross, nor any of the pontifical vestments nor even a chalice or missal."[38] Travelling around in disguise under an assumed name he met individually with his priests, none of whom had abjured. He wrote that "…from that time the open practice of religion either ceased entirely or was considerably curtailed according as the persecution varied in intensity…"[39] After meeting his priests and assuring himself of their loyalty and faithfulness, he organised conferences or mini retreats for them in out of the way houses, or on a mountainside. His priests had no fixed abode but rather travelled from house to house staying a night here and two nights there.

The danger of discovery or being reported for saying Mass by a member of the congregation was always present, and as a means of lessening the risk somewhat, Sunday mass was generally said as early as 2 or 3 am on Sunday morning even in the midst of winter, with confessions being heard and baptisms being performed beforehand. Bishop MacMahon relates how many of his priests "…in order to prevent being identified by any in the congregation celebrated Mass with veiled faces. Others again shut themselves into a closet with the Mass server

---

[1] Between the years 1707 and 1749, three MacMahons in succession were Bishops of Clogher and Archbishops of Armagh. These were Hugh McMahon and two of his nephews Bernard and Ross MacMahon, who were brothers. When Hugh died in 1737, Bernard was appointed to the See of Armagh. Ross replaced him as Bishop of the Diocese of Clogher.

The Mass Rock

alone, and apertures were made or a small hole by means of which the people outside could hear the voice of the celebrant but could not recognise it, or at all events could not see him…not uncommonly one would come across men and women with their hands joined in prayer – having got the signal that Mass was begun – and thus united themselves in spirit with those who, afar off, were praying on bended knees although they could not see the priest. It often happened to myself when saying Mass by night that not a soul was present except the man of the house and his wife – not even the children, for they could not be trusted with the secret."[40] Mass was seldom said at the same place two Sundays in a row.

Those who sheltered a priest or bishop or allowed them to celebrate Mass in their houses faced serious penalties if caught. For a first offence it was a fine of £20 and for a second offence, a fine of £30 and one year in prison.

Travelling around in secret, Bishop MacMahon attempted to carry out his duties. In 1712 he was almost caught by the notorious Priest Hunter, Edward Tyrell who was on his track. Noting the poverty of his people and their inability to spare even a little for the support of their priests, the Bishop wrote "the remuneration of their pastors is necessarily small and altogether insufficient…A more regrettable feature of the situation is that some priests have to celebrate Mass in soiled and tattered vestments – they cannot provide better. There are hardly any chalices made of gold or silver in the diocese. Most are made of tin, not gilt even on the inside"[41]. In spite of the persecution and hardships the Bishop noted that there were many men in the diocese who wished to become priests, but could not because of poverty. This matter he attempted to address with money bequeathed him by his Uncle on the continent, establishing a fund for the foreign education of priests for the dioceses of Clogher and the neighbouring diocese of Kilmore. In 1714 (the year in which he wrote his account) his work in the diocese came to the attention of the local magistrate, Mervyn Archdale and orders were issued for the arrest of many of his priests but the outcome of the crackdown is not recorded. In 1731 the authorities recorded that there were nine Mass Houses in the diocese while Mass was celebrated at 50 Mass Rocks in "ye open fields"[42]

## The Priest Hunter

Following the requirement and failure of the Catholic priests to take the Oath of Abjuration, priest hunting resumed with greater intensity. Due to the substantial rewards offered, the "profession" of priest hunting did not only attract Protestants but also the odd Catholic apostate, who, if not widely known as such was the least suspected and so their efforts at capturing or killing priests invariably met with much greater success. One of the most notorious priest hunters of the period was a Mayo man from Ballintubber by the name of John O'Mullowny – better known as "Séan na Sagart" or "John of the Priests" who lived from 1690 to 1726.

Described as "arrogant and cunning"[43] John was also an alcoholic. Shortly before the law requiring priests to take the Oath of Abjuration was enacted he had turned to horse thievery to obtain money to fund his "fondness for a strong drink".[44] Arrested as a horse thief, he was convicted and sentenced to death by hanging, but the night before his execution, he was visited by Bingham, the local Sheriff, who promised him his life if he would become a Protestant, Priest Hunter and spy in the service of the Crown, which he readily agreed to.

Following the introduction of the Oath of Abjuration, John excelled at priest hunting and was responsible for the capture or death of many priests. One of his favourite techniques in ensnaring them was to pretend that he was seriously ill and close to death. He would summon help from an unsuspecting local and in Connacht Irish ask the person to find a priest for him so that he could confess his sins before dying. If a priest came, Mullowny would either kill him with a knife hidden under the bedclothes or capture him. On another occasion he led a party of redcoats to Pulnathacken Mass-rock where a hunted priest by the name of Fr. Andrew Higgins was saying Mass. When the lookout raised the alarm the congregation broke up. Fr. Higgins made for a waiting currach and managed to escape but Mullowny rode his horse into the sea after the little boat and shot Fr. Higgins dead.

Despised by his countrymen he killed many priests during his "career" until finally he attacked a priest named Fr. Burke at a funeral. In the struggle that followed a local homeless man named McCann produced a knife and attacked Mullowney in the priest's defence. In the ensuing fight Mullowney was killed. Wherever Mullowny was, the redcoats were not far behind and so Fr. Burke, McCann and everyone else quickly dispersed. The following day the redcoats discovered his body and buried it in the graveyard at Ballintubber Abbey[1]

---

[1] On account of the fact that he was an apostate who had been killed while trying to knife a priest, the locals exhumed him and threw his body in a local lake. However Fr. Burke told them to rebury the body in the graveyard.

### "I Will Go Unto the Altar of God"[1]

During the Autumn of 1712, the priest hunter Edward Tyrell traversed the length and breadth of the country in search of his prey after which he presented a petition to Dublin Castle complaining that the implementation of the new laws was not uniform across the country and that some magistrates showed a lack of zeal in their application. Whenever such complaints were made, the Castle issued censures against the offending magistrates. Ironically, numbers of bishops who were being sought by the authorities in the countryside took refuge in the city of Dublin relying on the old adage "the closer to danger, the further from harm".

In an attempt to gain information on their quarry the government passed a new law obliging any "popish person" who might be summoned to appear before two magistrates for examination on when and where they last heard Mass, if they knew the identity of the priest and any other questions they might care to ask

In spite of all these measures priests continued to be ordained in significant numbers within the country after which they went abroad to study, thereafter returning to the lion's den. Around 1730 the Protestant Archbishop of Tuam reported to the House of Lords that "…young men are often ordained, and

---

Catholics are buried facing the east and the rising sun "to face Christ who will come again in glory from the east" but the locals reburied Mullowny facing the north. Following his burial an ash sapling grew on his grave and when it became a tree it split his grave in two. The tree is still there today on his grave and is known as the "Séan na SagartTree".

[1] "Introibo ad Altare Dei" -Quotation from the opening prayers of theTridentine Latin Mass used during the penal days in Ireland and in various slightly diverging rites from the early centuries of the Catholic Church until the introduction of a new "ecumenical" Mass in English at the end of 1969 which sought to align the mass with the service of Anglican worship. This came about following the liberal reforms of the second Vatican council which was held between 1962 and 1965.

then go into foreign countries to prosecute their studies and back as missionaries, whereby the number of priests is greatly increased".[45] The necessity of their being ordained before going to the continent was due to the hardships and privations on the continent, which awaited those students who had no means. Once ordained, the student was often able to gain a chaplaincy position in a college on the continent with payment being the monies necessary for his training and board. In time bursaries were established for the training of priests for Ireland by Irishmen abroad. In Lisbon, Seville and Cadiz, the Irish merchants agreed to put a small tax on every cask of wine that they exported, the money to be used in the training of Irish students. Ironically, the wines supped by English Lords and gentlemen may have helped in the training of Irish priests!

While the willingness of these young priests to return to Ireland in the knowledge that they might be killed baffled the English authorities, it also infuriated them. This infuriation led in 1723 to the drafting of the barbaric proposal that any priest caught entering the country would be castrated. This proposal, which was refused by London, seems to be the high watermark of the persecution as following its refusal by London more magistrates were willing to turn a blind eye to Catholic activity so long as the Mass and the priests remained out of sight. According to Fr. Augustine, the "...desire to say Mass is the real explanation of the mystery that puzzled and baffled so many that were not of the household of the faith". In his history of the period he quotes the example of Fr. Sweeney of Macroom, an old priest who had refused to take the oath and had ended up in jail. Old and infirm he requested parole, which was refused, the magistrate who refused it being a certain Captain Hedges. Hedges wrote to Dublin Castle regarding Fr. Sweeney's case; "...if he comes out he will say Mass, so that I mean not to make any request for him"[46.]

Bishops were being consecrated in secret. On April 4th 1714 Dr. Francis Burke was consecrated Archbishop of Tuam on the Connemara mountains. Friars were also returning to their country and reforming in secret. As early as 1715 the Grand Jury in Co. Galway informed the Judges at the Lent Assizes that "Friars were retuning to the neighbourhood of their old abbey in great numbers, to Ross near Wexford, to Athenry and other places". Bishops writing to their clergy or addressing homilies or letters to their flock, in place of their address, finished their letters "ex loco refugii"[47] or "from his place of refuge."

### The Persecution Continues

In 1731 the House of Lords in Dublin ordered all magistrates and Protestant Bishops to make a report to them regarding the state of Catholicism in the various dioceses. The report from the Diocese of Cloyne reported that there are "seventy Mass houses in the diocese of Cloyne. These Mass-houses are generally mean thatched cabins, many, or most of them, open at one end. Some new Mass-houses have been attempted to be raised about three years ago, particularly at Cloyne and Charleville, within view of the churches of those towns, and where no Mass-houses were before. But the finishing of the same has been hitherto prevented by the care of the respective magistrates of these places."[48]

As the years progressed the authorities became weary of their lack of success in breaking the practice of the Catholic faith. It seemed to them that in spite of the numbers of priests who were being caught, imprisoned, exiled or killed that there were always more to replace them. In 1744 the already huge sums offered for the capture of unregistered Catholic clergy were increased yet further when the authorities let it be known that they would pay £150 for a bishop, £50 for a priest and £20 "for the discovery of persons who, being in the possession of a certain amount of property, had nevertheless been guilty of entertaining, concealing, or relieving a priest"[49.]

Shortly after the reward was increased, the Bishop of Raphoe, James O'Gallagher was almost captured while on a visit to the parish of Killygarvan. Upon hearing that the authorities were on his track he quickly left the home of the parish priest Fr. Hegarty. Shortly afterwards, the local magistrate whose name was Buchanan arrived from Milford along with the dreaded redcoats at Fr. Hegarty's cabin and were enraged to find the Bishop gone. Seizing Fr. Hegarty, they were in the act of carting him off to Milford when a huge crowd gathered demanding the priest's release whereupon Buchanan shot the priest dead and threw his body from the cart onto the road.

The Duke of Devonshire who as Lord Lieutenant was responsible for this initiative was apparently shocked at the huge loss of life, and the large number of atrocities committed by the priest hunters following the introduction of the higher rewards and after less than a year the rewards were reduced in size.

## The Penal Laws – Mark II

By the 1750s the Dublin Parliament was only too well aware that their aim of eradicating the Catholics faith had not been realised. In an attempt to re-launch a modified campaign against the Catholic faith, a new bill was proposed which on the face of it appeared to offer a measure of compromise to the clergy, but in reality was a renewed attempt by the government to prepare the way for the demise of Catholicism. The government proposed to officially recognise many of the priests who were then illegally in the country and register them for the country's parishes. However once again, all friars and bishops were to be excluded from this toleration and were to be tracked down and killed or arrested for deportation. The parliament readily assented to the bill but when the registration period was opened, not one priest registered. Meanwhile, as with all legislation passed in Dublin, the bill also had to be approved by London. However when the bill was sent to England for assent, the government felt that such a measure might prove unwise and refused it.

This was not to be the only time when London would quieten the anti-Catholic zeal of the colonists. In 1787 the Rightboys (the reformed "Whiteboys", who engaged in violent acts against the landlords and their property in order to win tenant rights) held a number of meetings outside churches. When word of this reached the Attorney General in Dublin, he introduced a bill in the Dublin Parliament that proposed that whenever such meetings were held outside churches that the authorities would "pull down, level and prostrate any Popish Chapel"[50] where such a meeting was held. The bill duly passed all stages in Dublin, but on its referral to London, it was refused and so never came into force.

Shortly after the Bill failed, a Protestant gentleman in Dublin by the name of Mr. Lawrence Saul was prosecuted for giving asylum in his household to a Catholic girl who was being pressurised by her Protestant friends to conform. It was at his trial for "preventing Papists from embracing Protestantism"[51] that the Irish Lord Chancellor uttered the memorable phrase: "The laws of the land do not presume that an Irish Papist exists in the Kingdom, nor can they breathe here without the connivance of the government"[52.]

Mr. Saul was found guilty and heavily fined after which he decided to leave the country for France. In a letter to the notable Catholic advocate, Charles O'Conor of Belanagare, Co. Roscommon, he outlined his reasons: "I am an utter stranger to what our people here are doing...I was then made to understand from the mouth of no less a person than the Lord Chancellor, that the law did not presume a Papist to exist here, nor could they breathe without the connivance of the government...and now my dear friend since there is not the least prospect of such a relaxation of the Penal Laws as would induce one Roman Catholic to tarry in this house of bondage, who can purchase a settlement in some other land, where freedom and security of property can be obtained, will you condemn me for saying that , if I cannot be one of the first, I will not be one of the last to take flight...these trials may perhaps be intended for our greater benefit to show us that we are not to expect any real happiness in this life"[53.]

## The Trial and Execution of Fr. Nicholas Sheehy

Of the many cases and instances of persecution that occurred during the Penal Days of the eighteenth century, the trial of Fr. Nicholas Sheehy stands out for its notoriety.

Fr. Sheehy was parish priest of Clogheen in the Diocese of Waterford. During his ministry he had been arrested and questioned regarding infringements of the Penal Code but had been subsequently released. However he became a thorn in the side of the local authorities as he constantly spoke out regarding the iniquity of the Protestant tithe and the methods of the tithe gatherers. When the tithe proctors had tried to enforce the payment of the tithe in the parish of Newcastle, where there was no Protestant church or minister, Fr. Sheehy, advised the people to stand firm against the unjust payment.

In 1764 a warrant was issued for his arrest under the charge of high treason and a reward of £300 was offered for his capture. Fr. Sheehy, who was innocent of the charges of which the government accused him (involvement with a Secret Organisation known as "The Whiteboys"), wrote to the government in Dublin, offering to surrender himself on condition that his trial would not take place in Clonmel, where the local magistrate and authorities had pledged to convict and hang him, but rather in a Dublin court. His condition was accepted and he surrendered himself to the authorities after which he was tried in Dublin and acquitted of the charges laid against him, as the witnesses for the prosecution could not provide evidence acceptable to the jury.

As soon as the trial was over, Fr. Sheehy was re-arrested on a charge of murder as one of the witnesses for the prosecution (John Bridge) had mysteriously disappeared and was presumed murdered by The Whiteboys.

Now on trial for the charge of murder Fr. Sheehy was returned to Clonmel where the case was heard before those who had initially sought his arrest and the witnesses were none other than those who had been discredited in Dublin.

On the evening in question when Bridge was supposed to have been murdered Fr. Sheehy testified that he was in the company of Mr. Keating, a property owner and a man who was well respected by all in the community. When Mr. Keating entered the court room to give evidence corroborating what Fr. Sheehy had testified, a local Protestant Minister named Hewetson stood up in the court and after consulting some paper in his possession accused Mr. Keating of involvement in the murder of two soldiers in Newmarket. Immediately and without having had the chance to give evidence Keating was arrested and transported to Kilkenny jail and Fr. Sheehy, thus left without any alibi, was now at the mercy of his enemies.

Fr. Sheehy was subsequently convicted on the charge of having murdered Bridge and was hanged in Clonmel on March 15th 1766, aged 38. His head remained spiked on the porch of Clonmel Jail for over twenty years after his death. In due course Keating was also tried on the charge of murder and found innocent as there was not a shred of evidence against him for having been involved in the murders in Newmarket.

# Chapter 3

# The Hammer and the Anvil

"A Government, a prey to every vice; and a country a victim to every wrong...a nursery for young tyrants was formed in the very bosom of the legislature" – Wyse.

> "So to effect his monarch's ends,
> From hell a Viceroy devil ascends,
> His budget with corruption crammed,
> The contributions of the damned,
> Which with unsparing hand he strows
> Through Courts and Senates as he goes,
> And then at Beelzebub's black hall,
> Complains his budget is too small" – Swift

## The Governance of Ireland until 1800

Following the end of the Jacobean war, it might be assumed that the system of governance imposed on Ireland would incorporate the changes that "the Glorious Revolution" of 1688 had brought to England. This was not to be the case. While England had a prime minister whose government, along with the country's revenues and judicial system were all subject to a parliamentary majority and a parliament of fixed duration, Ireland, which in spite of English domination was still an independent kingdom, remained under the control of an appointed Lord Lieutenant and his secretary (both Englishmen) who reported to the English Secretary of State for Home Affairs.

Great powers were also vested in the Chief Justices, who in England's interest bribed, pensioned and granted offices to members of Parliament in order to ensure that the English interest took precedence over local concerns. The most prominent of the Chief Justices during the eighteenth century was the Protestant Primate and Archbishop of Armagh, Dr. Hugh Boulter who was appointed as Lord Justice no less than thirteen times. A "pure bred" Englishmen, he had a certain disdain for Protestants born in Ireland and was determined to fill all governmental posts and bishoprics with men of pure English blood like himself. Adept at bribery and the packing of governmental posts, Boulter was famous for never allowing Christian ethics to interfere in his political life

## The 'Irish' Parliament

The Composition of the Parliament

As there were no specific political parties in the Colonist Dublin Parliament, members of parliament in general allied themselves (with their own interests in mind) with the interests of a powerful Lord who sat in the Dublin House of Lords.

Shackled by Poynings Law (which meant that all legislation appearing before the parliament had first to be approved in London) the Irish parliament served merely as a rubber stamp of approval from the colonisers for the measures that England wished to impose on the colony for its own benefit. Its powerlessness was further confirmed when in 1719, the dependency of the Dublin legislature upon the English parliament was confirmed by London with the statute known as "The Sixth of George I", following the property suit of "Sherlock v Annesley".[1]

Until the Octennial Act, (which limited the duration of the Irish Parliament to eight years) was passed in 1768, the Irish Parliament sat for the duration of the life of the English monarch or until it was dissolved. King George II reigned for thirty-three years, and during this time the Irish Parliament sat continuously without an election.

The Parliament consisted of 300 members and its constitution was as follows: There were fourteen citizens from seven cities, 220 Burgesses from 110 boroughs, 64 members from 32 counties and two members from Trinity College. Of this entire number only the 64 members who were elected by the Protestant "forty shilling freeholders" had any claim to represent a substantial numbers of voters.[II]

Of the 110 boroughs, 86 were the property of wealthy Landlords and peers. These "sold" the seats of their boroughs to the highest bidder. In many boroughs the number of those on the electoral register did not exceed 10 while in the Boroughs of Bannow and Harristown there was no one on the electoral register!

---

[1] Following the court case between Sherlock and Annesley, the Irish Court of Exchequer found in Annesley's favour. Sherlock appealed to the Irish House of Lords who overturned the earlier ruling. Annesley, then appealed to the English House of Lords who overturned the ruling of the Irish House of Lords. Following the case, and to make its binding superior power over the Irish Parliament absolutely clear a decree was issued (6 Geo., c,5): "That the King's Majesty, by and with the advice and consent of the Lords spiritual and temporal and Commons of Great Britain in Parliament assembled had, hath, and of right ought to have, full power and authority to make laws and statutes of sufficient force and validity to bind the people of Ireland".

[II] As a parliament which represented only the Protestants, the "population" was vastly overrepresented. For example, Co. Longford had ten members of parliament for a protestant population of 700!

All told 116 parliamentary seats "belonged" to 25 owners who generally rented them to the government in return for pensions, titles and governmental or other postings. With difficulty His Majesty's opposition in the Dublin Parliament might muster eighty votes. The opposition benches often consisted of those who had resisted the touch of money and the offer of a government post.

This "system" continued into every part of the country's local administration. The Landlords were the lynch pin of the system and generally appointed entire town councils and even city corporations. The impunity with which the Landlords, their agents and indeed the entire civil administration treated the Irish is easily understood for aside from the fact that no Catholic could take a court case, the Landlord generally filled the shoes of the local magistrate.

## Corruption within the Political System

With a parliamentary composition and government majority arrived at in such a manner, a corrupt system of governance was the natural result. To go through the statistics for pensions awarded by parliament is illustrative of the endemic corruption that pervaded the colonist parliament of the ruling elite.

In 1723 the cost of pensions to the exchequer was £30,000 per annum. Ten years later this amount had more than doubled to £69,000. In 1763 the pension's budget included an "addition" of £75,000 to pay the pensions for the officers of ten regiments that were disbanded before their actual formation ever took place! At the outbreak of the American War of Independence in 1776 the amount spent on pensions by the Dublin parliament exceeded that spent on the entire civil administration and by 1790, it was more than £100,000. However, some of these pensions were ordered paid by the English Privy Council, which more than once ordered a pension paid as a bribe to a member of His Majesty's opposition.

The Irish exchequer also had to pay exorbitant amounts towards the "quartering" of King's mistresses and the progeny of His Majesty's extramarital liaisons. Among the mistresses to whom vast amounts were paid by the Irish exchequer were £5,000 to Catherine Sedley, £1,500 to Lady Darlington, £3,000 to Madame deWalmoden and £3,000 to the Duchess of Kendal who was also awarded the contract for Irish copper coinage worth over £100,000 in 1724. After being awarded the contract, the Duchess hired the English Ironmonger William Wood to make the coins from base metal for £60,000 intending to share the £40,000 "profit" with Wood and others involved in the scheme. However, the affair was discovered by the Dublin Protestant clergyman, Jonathan Swift who managed through his anonymous "Drapier's Letters" to create such uproar that the government was forced to cancel the contract.

King George I

Various English nobles were also awarded pensions "for services rendered to the Irish people." These included the Duke of Cumberland who was awarded £3,000, Princess Augusta £5,000, Princess Amalie £1,000 and the Duke of Gloucester £5,000. The services they rendered are not recorded! The madness continued to such an extent that eventually the Irish pension list exceeded, not in relative terms but in actual cost that of the pension list of the English parliament.

Such corruption was called out – most notably by the Editor of "The Citizen's Journal" Charles Lucas. For attacking parliament and similar crimes, the Irish House declared him "an enemy of his country"[54] and he was forced to leave Ireland in 1749 in order to escape arrest. As mentioned above, Swift also called out the corruption through his many clever texts and his "Drapier's Letters" but through his anonymity and the refusal of many in government or parliament to have any part in his chastisement, he escaped censure.

## The Restriction of Trade

"Ireland is the only kingdom I ever heard or read of, either in ancient or modern history, which was denied the liberty of exporting their native commodities wherever they pleased" – Jonathan Swift

When the English monarchy was restored after Cromwell's death, various measures such as the "Navigation Act" of 1660 were introduced prohibiting the export of goods from Ireland to England's other colonies, while in 1666 cattle exports from Ireland to England were torpedoed by the government. Following the Treaty of Limerick, further measures were put in place against Irish goods so that English manufacturing would not suffer in any shape or form.

During the reign of Charles I, Irish wool exports had been taxed so heavily that the trade became unviable. However, manufacturing of wool and cloth picked up again towards the close of the seventeenth century and so in 1699, the English parliament banned the export of wool from Ireland to all markets except England.

In order to protect the English market, the Dublin Parliament (acting on instructions from London) introduced an export tax of four shillings on every pound of fine woollen cloth and two shillings for cloths of lesser quality while the number of ports from which cloth could be exported from in Ireland and to which it could be imported into in England was also heavily restricted. The sum total of the measures crushed the trade and aroused the indignation of the ordinary colonists who felt betrayed by their mother country. As a result many Protestants who controlled and ran the trade in Ireland emigrated to America. These were later joined by large number of northern Presbyterians who were anxious to escape the despised tithe due to the state church, the high rents on land and the lack of official recognition for their pastors who since 1710 had been denied the "Regium donum" granted to them by William of Orange (although this was to be partially restored in the early years of the reign of George I).

This exodus alarmed the Protestant clergy. The Archbishop of Dublin, William King wrote in 1718 "…no papists stir…the Papists being already five to six to one you imagine in what condition we are like to be in"[55], while Boulter, the Protestant Primate wrote "…the worst is that it affects only Protestants…"[56] Boulter also lamented that many of the descendants of Cromwell's Catholic hating soldiers who had remained in Ireland after his conquest had converted: "…We lose many of ours, the descendants of Cromwell's officers and soldiers here having gone off to Popery."[57] [1]

The Catholics of Ireland might well have looked with envy upon them and wished they could go too, however they had neither the funds, nor the offer of fine land when they got there as Catholics were not welcome in the new colonies. This movement of Ulster Presbyterians to the new world would eventually see considerable numbers of Catholics able to move down from the mountains and boglands to the plains below and successfully re-establish themselves, this time as tenant

---

[1] Many of the descendents of Cromwell's soldiers also could not speak English. In 1697, Robert Molesworth wrote: "…how many there are of the children of Oliver's soldiers who cannot speak one word of English."

farmers with superior rights to their neighbours further south, thanks to the "Ulster Custom".

A "black market" now arose in the Irish wool trade and in spite of the export ban many merchant ships clandestinely carried wool, apparently manufactured for the home market, from Ireland to markets abroad.

Following on from these measures against textiles, almost every other industry (beer making, glass, ironmongery, silk, gunpowder,etc) had similar although less restrictive taxes imposed on them.

In the early eighteenth century, there was also a steady growth in the number of families supported by fishing. Along the Eastern seaboards many men took to the waters of the Irish Sea in order to catch herrings for which there was a steady demand in England. However in the fishing towns of England, the arrival of fish from Ireland was a source of irritation and petitions were presented to the parliament in London from Folkestone and Aldborough that the arrival of fish from Ireland would be stopped whilst other petitions were sent that all fishing in the Irish sea would be prohibited except in boats "built and manned by Englishmen"[58]

## Life in Ireland during the Eighteenth and early Nineteenth Century

A Destitute and Poverty Stricken People

In 1718 a new Protestant Bishop of Derry named Dr. Nicholson was appointed. Having arrived in Dublin from England, a guard of dragoons was appointed to escort him to Derry in case his carriage should be held up. After his arrival in Derry he recorded what he saw on the way; "...I travelled in great security through the country said to be infested with a set of barbarous and pilfering Tories. I saw no danger of losing the little money I had; but was under some apprehension of being starved, having never held such dismal marks of hunger and want as appeared in the countenances of most of the poor creatures I met on the road. The poor wretches lie in reeky sod-hovels and have generally no more than a rag of coarse blanket to cover up a small part of their nakedness. Upon the strictest inquiry I could not find that they are better clad, or lodged in the Winter season. These sorry slaves plough the ground to the very tops of their mountains for the service of their lords, who spend truly rack-rents in London"[59]

As the years went by, and the population increased, poverty and destitution among the Catholics was rampant. The peasant farmer grew to rely on the potato as a cheap and easily grown staple with which to feed his family while all other crops were sold to pay his rent. Many peasant farmers only had a one-year lease on their holding. When this ran out the landlord could rent the property to someone else who was willing to pay a higher rent and as a consequence the rent for a small-holding climbed year after year. There was no incentive for a tenant to make improvements to a property or even to reclaim a piece of boggy ground as this raised the value of the property and consequently the rent.

The poverty in cities and towns was just as bad, but made worse by overcrowding and the lack of clean water for drinking. While the upper class luxuriated in their wealth and lavish lifestyle the poor, according to a Protestant cleric lived in a "degree of filth and stench inconceivable"[60] in severely overcrowded dwellings in areas of towns and cities close to rivers that were often prone to flooding during the Autumn and Winter months. There was no sanitation whatsoever and the back streets of the urban centres abounded with rubbish and filth that in turn led to infant mortality, illness and very low life expectancy among the poor.

Two unjust taxes served to worsen an already dire situation for the poor namely the Hearth Tax and the mandatory Protestant tithe.

## The Hearth Tax

The Hearth tax was a tax on every fireplace or hearth within a dwelling. This tax had been in force in England up until the reign of William and Mary who had revoked it as being "not only a great oppression to the poorer sort, but a badge of slavery upon the whole people."[61] In spite of its abolition in England, the government saw fit to maintain it in Ireland. The tax was a deplorable imposition on a people already mired in poverty, and the inability of many Irish peasants to pay the amount required for even one fireplace forced them to do without. In effect this meant that when lighting a fire in their cabin, the tenant would light it on the floor close to the open door, or to create a hole in the roof of the cabin so that the smoke could escape. As a result cabins would be filled with smoke which was the cause of many respiratory ailments and blindness in infants. The Hearth Tax would remain in force until it was finally revoked in 1793.

## The Tithe

By means of a "tithe" (a "tenth part"), everyone, be they Protestant or not, had to contribute to the established Protestant Church and the upkeep of its English ministers and bishops.

Once the tenant had paid his rent, which generally consisted of the vast majority of his income, 10% of the remainder had to be paid to the local Protestant clergyman, In many cases the clergyman sold his tithes to a "Tithe Proctor" who in order to make his investment pay, was most assiduous in their collection. When the Tithe Proctor and his assistants called to collect the Tithe, the tithe was forcibly collected in kind if the family had no money. Items such as potatoes, vegetables or whatever else the tenant possessed was seized in lieu of the amount owed. The removal of these items contributed in no small part to the extreme poverty of the people.

Whilst content to burden Catholics and Protestant dissenters with the bill for supporting their clergy, the Landlords who generally belonged to the established Church of Ireland looked for, and found a way out of paying the full level of the tithe themselves. In 1735, a grotesque piece of legislation was passed in the Dublin parliament that exempted all pasturelands from the tithe, which effectively meant that the monetary support given by the Landlords to their own Church was reduced to a fraction of what it had been. In order to maximise on their savings, many landlords evicted large numbers of their small tenant farmers so that more land could be converted to pasturage.

A Levy on all Papist Households
In the event that a Protestant had his property stolen or damaged and the culprit was not apprehended, all Catholic households in the district had a levy placed on them so that the Protestant's loss would be recompensed. This was the case as the authorities worked on the assumption that all criminal acts were perpetrated by Papists.
In his "Relatio" (on which I have written a paragraph in the previous chapter), Bishop MacMahon of the Diocese of Clogher (Monaghan) writes about this with specific reference to Ulster; "If any injury is done to the property of the planters, compensation is levied on the neighbouring Catholics, and the priest is thrown in jail until the amount is paid. There are instances when the Presbyterian planters swear to some pretended injury done to them, and have the compensation levied as usual on the Catholics. When, subsequently, however the fraud becomes known, and even officially proved, the Catholics seek in vain to have the exacted fines refunded to them."[62]
An example of this completely unjust levy was quoted in the Dublin Parliament in 1782 whereby a Protestant gentleman in

Kilkenny from whom some property had been stolen was compensated by a tax levied on local Catholics. Some time afterwards the thief was caught and found to be a Protestant but no restitution was made to the Catholics who had been fined after the incident. Mr Bushe M.P, who brought up the matter in the Dublin Parliament added that: "it is a rule with the magistrates that if the thief is heard to speak with an Irish accent, this is sufficient proof of his being a Papist"[63]

## The Landlord

"A great cause of this nations misery is that Egyptian bondage of cruel, oppressing, covetous landlords; expecting that all who live under them should make bricks without straw; who grieve and envy when they see a tenant of their own in a cart, or able to afford one comfortable meal in the month; by which the spirits of the people are broken and made fit for slavery." – Jonathan Swift

Between 1778 and 1780, the noted English Agriculturalist Arthur Young, toured Ireland and recorded his observations in a two volume work entitled "A Tour of Ireland".

Regarding the tyrannical rule of the landlords he wrote: "A landlord in Ireland can scarcely invent an order which a servant, labourer, or cottar dares to refuse to execute. Nothing satisfies him but unlimited submission. Disrespect or anything tending towards sauciness, he may punish with his cane or his horsewhip with the most perfect security. A poor man would have his bones broken if he offered to lift a hand in his own defence...I have heard anecdotes of the lives of people being made free with, without any apprehension of the justice of a jury...it must strike the most careless traveller to see whole strings of cars whipt into a ditch by a gentleman's footman to make way for his carriage; if they are overturned or broken in pieces no matter, it is taken in patience. Were they to complain they would perhaps be horsewhipped...they know their situation too well to think of it; they can have no defence..."[64]

The general term that Young used to describe the landlords of Catholic estates was "despot", as he: "yields in obedience...to no law but that of his own will" Possessing supreme power in his local district, the landlord along with his brother landlords and the Church of Ireland clergy ruled the councils and corporations of counties, towns and cities.

## The Great Famine of 1740-41

The mid eighteenth century saw Ireland (and much of Europe) experience two of the worst winters that have ever occurred since the ending of the Ice Age. Still reeling from the effects of the Winter of 1740, the country fell victim to an even worse winter the following year thanks to widespread famine and disease.

The Winter of 1739-1740 was quite unremarkable until around the middle of January 1740, when an artic weather system moved down over Ireland. This weather system remained over the country almost until the end of March during which time the ground froze along with rivers, lakes and ports.

The first casualty of the severe weather was the potato stores. As the ground froze ever deeper, the straw covered potatoes that were buried in pits in the ground or stored in the cabins of the tenant farmers turned into a watery inedible mush, destroying not only the potatoes for eating but also the seed potatoes for the next year's crop. As yet not wholly reliant on the potato, many ordinary people survived on a reduced diet of oats. As the arctic spell continued all manner of farm animals perished and were used to augment the food supply.

When the freezing temperatures finally abated, the deep frosts had done great harm to the land, a factor that was not helped by the total lack of Spring rains. Many animals which had survived the "Great Frost" now succumbed due to a lack of grass, while that year's crop of cereals died in the ground for want of rain, resulting in a much smaller harvest during the Autumn of 1740, an Autumn during which one storm quickly succeeded another. The storms continued right into December, and then quite suddenly the arctic weather of the previous January returned, repeating the effects of the winter before.

Already weakened by hunger, thousands of people now fell ill from fever and typhus that quickly spread in the urban centres that at least benefited from localised charity provided by the wealthy. In the countryside the people died from hunger and disease in their thousands. In Monaghan, the Protestant clergyman, the Rev. Philip Skelton recorded how: "the dead have been eaten in the fields by dogs for want of people to bury them...whole thousands in a barony have perished, some of hunger and others of disorders occasioned by unnatural, unwholesome, and putrid diets."[65]

It is reckoned that in 1739 the population of Ireland was less than 2.5 million souls. By the end of the two calamitous winters of 1740 and 1741, the population was just above 2 million.

In the aftermath of the catastrophe, large numbers of landlords who had made a loss due to the failure of almost all crops sought to divest themselves of the direct responsibility for their holding. There was a large growth in the number of absentee landlords who leased their estates to middle-men who subdivided it. A shortage of beef and dairy products in England around 1750 (which was caused by the deaths of large numbers of cattle by disease) resulted in the restrictions upon the entry of Irish produce into the English market being overturned. Some landlords made the decision to adopt beef and dairy farming completely, the result of which was that evictions increased during which many other tenants found themselves homeless when their short leases were not renewed.

# Education

## The Charter Schools

Since the reign of James I, a number of Protestant schools had emerged in various parts of the country. Whilst some were specifically for the education of Protestants, others, such as those founded by Erasmus Smith and the Protestant Bishops Foy in Waterford and Popcoke in Kilkenny had as their aim according to Popcocke "to bring up young Irish papists to Protestantism."[66] However these schools lacked the destructive nature of the educational scheme founded by Archbishop Boulter and the Protestant Bishops of Ireland in 1730.

Archbishop Boulter

Under the penal code, the Irish were forbidden to have their children educated by a Catholic teacher. The eradication of Catholic teachers was seen by the government as a priority, and in the penal code their importance was equated to that of the Catholic clergy.

Taking advantage of this situation, an educational program was designed by the Protestant hierarchy which promised "manifold material blessings to the Irish people"[67]

The "Charter Schools", (so called as they were provided for under royal charter) were founded in 1730 specifically for Catholics, after a petition "praying" for a charter of incorporation signed by Lord Chancellor Wyndham, Archbishop Boulter and 15 other Protestant Bishops among others was presented to the King.

The wording of the petition enumerated how: "...in many parts of the kingdom there are great tracts of mountainy and coarse land...almost universally inhabited by Papists...(who)...appear to have very little sense or knowledge of religion, but what they implicitly take from their clergy...among the ways proper to be taken for the converting and civilizing of these poor deluded people and bringing them in time to be good Christians and faithful subjects, one of the most necessary, and without which all others are likely to prove ineffectual, has always been thought to be, that a sufficient number of English Protestant schools be erected and established wherein the children of the Irish natives might be instructed in the English tongue and the fundamental principles of true religion"[68].

To the Protestant Bishop of London, Boulter wrote: "The great number of Papists in this kingdom and the obstinacy with which they adhere to their own religion occasions us trying what may be done with their children, to bring them over to our Church."[69]

Once founded, and for the following 100 years, nothing which money could buy was lacking to this project, as once the King's recommendation and significant annual donation was secured, huge numbers of English landed gentry contributed to this "benevolent" project. After the first school was opened on land donated by the Earl of Kildare at Castledermot, the number of schools grew swiftly so that by the 1780's there were over 40 schools and four nurseries.

Underlying the apparent educational advantages to be derived by the impoverished youngsters of Ireland was the system of forced conversion to Protestantism, as all Catholics entering the school had to be educated as a Protestant. On entry the pupil had to take a new name, so that they would lose their former identity. New pupils were moved to a school far from their home area, and afterwards to different locations on a regular basis. In spite of these precautions many children were tracked down and rescued either by their parents or relatives. In 1747, in a report sent to London on the "state of the Popish religion in Ireland" the author voiced: "the hope…that the Charter Schools (and) the due execution of the laws against the Popish clergy will in the next age root out that pestilent, restless and idolatrous religion"[70]

In order to increase the number of entrants, in 1749 the Dublin parliament passed a law allowing all poor Catholic children found begging to be seized and forcibly entered into the Charter Schools.

Once the age of understanding was attained, all were taught catechisms prepared especially for these schools, which not only laid out the Protestant faith but also derided the Catholic faith in every aspect.

Children were apprenticed to Protestants, and once the apprenticeship was complete, a dowry of £5 was awarded to them on the strict condition that they should marry a Protestant.

When George III became king in 1760, the Earl of Halifax, who was Lord Lieutenant, reinforced the importance of the project during a special session of the Dublin Parliament, saying that: "There is no object more worthy of your attention than the Protestant Charter Schools. Notwithstanding the peaceable demeanour of the Papists in this kingdom, it must always be your duty and interest to divert from error by every effectual though gentle method the deluded followers of a blind religion."[71] This mantra was taken up by successive Lord Lieutenants on their arrival in 1777, 1781, 1783 and 1785 when the Duke of Rutland thanked the government for the "liberality which they have shown to the Protestant Charter Schools"[72]

The Catholic Church was unable to actively combat the system but it nevertheless foundered, not only due to lack of entrants but also because of the corruption of those tasked with the schemes success. Of its failure, the English historian James Froude writes: "the industrial training in these schools degenerated by negligence into a system in which the children became the slaves of the masters and grew up in rags and starvation...the masters and mistresses plundered the funds, starved the children, and made the industrial system an excuse for using the children as slaves to fill their own pockets."[73] When the prison reformer, Howard, visited the schools in 1784, his report was damning, so much so that a parliamentary inquiry was ordered. Describing the schools as a "disgrace to the kingdom"[74], he gave examples of children who had been inmates for five years. While a few could read, not one could write and the children were either "half starved and clothed in rags...and in all respects shamefully neglected...(and a)...disgrace to all society".[75] Far from promoting Protestantism he described the condition of the schools as being so; "deplorable as to disgrace Protestantism and to encourage Popery in Ireland"[76]

The result of the parliamentary enquiry was not to discipline or reprimand those responsible for this disastrous state of affairs, but rather to increase its patrimony to The Charter Schools.

Following the Act of Union, during a debate in the English House of Lords, Lord Byron brought up the subject of the Irish Charter Schools during which he castigated the vicious anti Catholic rhetoric contained in the Schools Catechism, and accused the authorities of training up children that "...they may issue forth filthy and venomous, to sting the Catholic...better it would be to send them (the children) to those islands in the south seas where they might more humanely learn to become cannibals; it would be less disgusting than they were brought up to devour the dead than prosecute the living. Schools do you call them? Call them rather dunghills"[77]

When in 1819, an official government inspection took place, the inspector, Rev Mr. Lee concluded that many children were "stunted in body, mind and heart"[78] while a later report on Irish education lamented that: "there is no form or shade of conceivable vice that did not abound in these infamous proselytising institutions"[79]

## The Charter School Nurseries

Collectively known as "The Foundling Hospital", these nurseries were a subsidiary part of The Charter Schools and like the Charter Schools were funded by grants and had no less than 300 Peers and gentlemen as governors. The main nursery was located in Dublin (on the campus of the current St. James's Hospital).

Around 2,000 Catholic infants were brought to the institution every year, and when they were old enough, they were transferred to the Charter Schools as the Foundling Hospital's aims were identical to those of the Charter Schools.

For around 50 years The Foundling Hospital carried out its work until finally in 1791, as the result of persistent and terrible rumours regarding the institution an enquiry was ordered by the Dublin parliament.

After the inquiry was launched, evidence was collected on oath and registered and recorded in the Journals of the Irish House of Commons. What the inquiry discovered was so shocking as to be almost beyond belief. During the year preceding the inquiry the statistics for the Foundling Hospital were as follows: In the year 1790, 2,187 children entered the institution, but the enquiry found that only 100 of them were still living. During the preceding ten years over 19,000 children had entered the Foundling Hospital but of this vast number only a little over 2,000 were still alive. The inquiry concluded that the majority of deaths were due to mistreatment, finding that after the infants were collected in various parts of the country, they were generally brought to Dublin in baskets, around 12 infants to a basket. The baskets were transported on a horse and cart so that when the destination was reached, generally half of the infants were already dead from bruising, asphyxiation and other injuries after which the bodies were then thrown into a pit and covered with quicklime. The inquiry also found that sick or injured infants within the institution did not have recourse to medical attention. Sick infants were given a "medicine" which acted as a slow poison resulting in their deaths. During the parliamentary debates on the findings of the enquiry, one M.P. attested that the evidence collected by the enquiry was the most horrible and ghastly that he had ever heard.[80]

Following the enquiry and debate no action was taken as a means of reforming The Foundling Hospital. When the issue was raised in parliament again in 1797, it was found that of 540 children admitted during the first three months of 1796, only 67 were still alive, the remainder having succumbed as before to ill treatment and negligence. During the debate in 1797 one M.P stated that he had personally visited the Foundling Hospital in Dublin and found eighteen sick infants in a room all together where they were left to die.[81] Of all the children who died or were killed only a handful had their deaths officially recorded.

It was to be a further three decades, when finally, as a result of public outrage both The Charter Schools and The Foundling Hospital were wound up in 1830.

### Hedge Schools

As the authorities wished to force those Catholic families who wanted to educate their children to convert to Protestantism, the banning of Catholic teachers had a hugely detrimental effect on the education of Irish children. Nevertheless many Catholic teachers were determined to act in the same manner as the Catholic clergy and formed underground schools. These teachers, acting more or less independently, created an almost nationwide system of clandestine and illegal schools.[1] Called "Hedge Schools" as education often took place out of doors, the teachers of these schools determined to pass onto their pupils not only the rudiments of reading, writing and maths but also Latin, Greek, history and home economics. During these days, young scholars progressed from the rudiments to sometimes translating from Latin and Greek into Gaelic, not only the works of Cicero and Demosthenes but also the poetry of Virgil and Homer.[II] By the 1820s, the government reckoned that upwards of 400,000 children were being educated in these schools.

Parallel with the Hedge Schools, there was also a foundation of minor seminaries by the Catholic Church, who desired to impart to those youths who wished to enter the religious life the basics of education before they would leave Ireland's shores for foreign seminaries. When these schools were organised, the students moved to a particular area where the school was based, lodging and working for a farming family. When classes took place the students came together at the appointed time to the secret location to receive instruction. From the mid eighteenth century the teachers in these schools were often highly qualified having received doctorates in theology on the continent. In some cases their priest teachers had been offered teaching positions in seminaries on the continent, which they turned down so that they could return to Ireland to teach in the "Hedge Seminaries", the end result

---

[1] In 1899, in his "Literary History of Ireland" Dr. Douglas Hyde wrote: "I doubt if a single college survived into the eighteenth century to come under the cruel law which made it penal for a Catholic to teach a school"

[II] "Many of the common people speak Latin fluently and I accidentally arrived at a hut, in a very obscure part of this country, where I saw four lads reading Homer..." – Arthur Young, "Tour of Ireland" (1776)

being that some students received the training necessary for the priesthood without having to travel abroad.

During a debate on the penal laws in the Irish House of Commons in 1764, James Caldwell M.P vehemently encouraged the government not to relax the laws on education. He complained that the hedge schools were already doing a lot of harm as the children were "...all taught Latin in the hedge schools, which were scattered throughout the southern part of the kingdom, in order to qualify for foreign service."[82]

Finally in 1782 the penal law forbidding Catholic teachers was relaxed, with a law being passed permitting Papists to teach "Papist children only". However in order for a Catholic school to open, permission had to be obtained from the local Protestant bishop who could if he so desired deny permission. In 1792, the law was relaxed further. Catholic schools were permitted to open on condition that the prescribed oath of allegiance was taken by the school's founder. By this stage the permission of the local Protestant Bishop could not be refused but still had to be obtained by the school's founder.[1] After 1800 many formal Catholic schools began to appear after Edmund Ignatius Rice established two religious congregations whose primary aim was to be the education of Catholic children. These were the Presentation Brothers and the Christian Brothers.

---

[1] In 1801 permission was granted to the superior of the Presentation Convent in Kilkenny to open a school. The permission from the Protestant bishop of Ossory read in part: "...Whereas you are sufficiently recommended to unto us as proper person to keep school within our said Diocese for the education of Papists or persons professing the Popish Religion. We do therefore by these presents give and grant unto you full leave and licence to keep and teach a school within the said parish during our will and pleasure only, for the education and instruction of children of Popish parents only, you having first produced to us a certificate of your having taken the oath of allegiance..."

## The Rise of Secret Societies

The tithe, the rack-rents, and the hearth tax all contributed to the sense of injustice felt by tenants. Following the exemption of pasture-lands from the Protestant tithe, landlords started evicting tenants and claiming for themselves large areas of waste land known as "commonage" which had always been available to tenants as one of the few means of raising an animal to pay their rent. The sense of long-suffering and injustice felt by tenants coupled with endless humiliations by those who had taken their lands finally turned to outrage in 1761 when evictions increased due to an increasing demand for beef in Britain and the desire of the landlords to turn the acres of their tenants into extra pasture land.

### "Whiteboys" and "Rightboys"

A secret oath bound society emerged, initially in the Munster counties of Cork, Limerick, Waterford and Tipperary. Known as "Whiteboys" (as they hid their identity with white garments which also served to identify friend from foe on a dark night) the movement initially restricted itself to tearing down the fences erected around common pasturage (for which they were called "Levellers" by the authorities) but they quickly moved onto more drastic measures including the destruction of the landlord's crops and the disabling of his cattle by hamstringing. Threatening letters were sent to landlords, agents, ministers and tithe proctors, from "Captain Moonlight" ordering them to lower rents or desist in the collection of tithes. To ignore such a warning could mean a visit from "Captain Moonlight" who might kidnap the person concerned and according to Arthur Young "...(bury) them up to their chin in a hole filled with briers, not forgetting to cut off one of their ears"[83]

The reaction of the authorities to the Whiteboys was both violent and extreme. Although neither religion or rebellion had any part to play in the actions of the Whiteboys, the government very quickly labelled their actions "a Popish Rebellion". Furthermore, various landlords falsely claimed (in order to alarm the government) that their agents had seen French soldiers landing and that these soldiers were training the Whiteboys, so that the return of Jacobite heir might be effected  Large areas were combed by soldiers during "pacification actions" which resulted in the summary execution of "suspects". Naturally these indiscriminate and murderous sweeps resulted in the deaths of many innocent bystanders to such an extent that the Lord Lieutenant, Lord Halifax called on the authorities to rein in their repressive measures as "…in several places the majority of the inhabitants have been struck with the utmost consternation and have fled to the mountains, in so much that at this season, from the almost general flight of the labouring hands, a famine is not without reason apprehended".[84]  The former Lord Deputy, Lord Chesterfield was more pragmatic in his summation of the situation:  "If the military force had killed half as many landlords as it had Whiteboys, it would have contributed more effectually to restore quiet"[85].  From Tipperary, the Dublin Journal reported on the terror felt by the populace from the scourge of the Light Dragoons who combed the county in search of 'suspects'.

Halifax, in an official report on the matter to London on April 17th 1762 also tried to put the record straight regarding the actions of the "Whiteboys" being labelled as a Popish Rebellion: "Protestants as well as Papists have been concerned in these tumults; one or two of the most considerable of those we have hitherto detected are Protestants; these outrages have fallen indiscriminately on persons of both persuasions, and I cannot yet find that any matter of state or religion had been mentioned at their meetings".[86]  The government made no attempt to address the injustices that had triggered the outrages but instead further reinforced the Landlords who claimed that the entire Protestant establishment was at stake. Aside from the indiscriminate actions of soldiers in repressing the Whiteboys, not to mention the high number whose end was the scaffold, a coercion act was passed in the Dublin parliament which prescribed the death penalty for those who administered illegal oaths or were caught in groups of more than five during the hours of darkness.

In 1787 the Whiteboys reformed, this time as the "Rightboys". As the regime of tithes, rates and rack-rents continued unabated, some of those affected now determined to take justice into their own hands. Attempts were made in the Dublin parliament to raise the issue of the widespread abuses of the Landlords and a case was quoted of a tenant farmer in Munster who was forced to pay £6 for an acre of ground used for planting potatoes for which the tenant had to pay the landlord by working for him at the rate of sixpence a day. However, no action was taken by parliament and as before the actions of the Righboys generally ended on the scaffold

The example of the Whiteboys was taken up by the Presbyterians in Ulster, who formed many different secret societies with differing aims in mind. The "Hearts-of-Oak boys" campaigned to suppress unpaid road repairing duties for which tenants were enlisted as part of their tenancy agreement while the aims of the "Hearts-of-Steel boys" was the reduction of the "rack rents" exacted by the middlemen and also the high rents charged for bogland. Here, the actions of the government were very different. A commission of enquiry was formed to address the grievances of the Presbyterians and following a campaign lasting a little over two months the Oakboys were able to claim that the injustices done to them had been addressed.

# The Founding of The Orange Order

## The Charter Toast of the Orange Order

"To the glorious, pious and immortal memory of the great and good King William the Third, not forgetting Oliver Cromwell, who saved us all from Popes and popery, knaves and knavery, slaves and slavery, brass money and wooden shoes. And all that refuse to drink this toast may they be rammed, stammed, crammed and dammed into the great gun of Athlone to be blown over the hills of damnation. May their teeth be converted into paving stones to pave the way of the Croppies[1] into hell, and their blood into train oil to light their souls to damnation. May I be at the end of a gun with a fiery flambeau to send them burring round the earth, the moon, the stars and the sea; may they be blown against the rocks of blastation, and come down in a shower of innumerable pieces, and may those pieces be picked up and made into sparables to mend the souls of the Orangemen's boots to walk on the 12th of July" – The Charter Toast of the Orange Grand Jurors of Ulster (all implied even if the toast is shortened to "Our Charter Toast")[87]

## From Bad Feeling to Violence

Seeking a better life, and full freedom and recognition for their form of Protestantism, many Presbyterians had emigrated from Ulster to the New World. In many cases Catholics were in a position to outbid other Protestants for the tenancy of farms which came on the market following their departure.

This influx of Catholics from the boglands and uplands grew as the penal codes lapsed and relief bills for Catholics were introduced. The Catholics also proved themselves able weavers, resulting in their capture of a share in a market that had heretofore been the exclusive domain of the Protestants.

---

[1] "Croppies" – a derogatory term for Catholics or members of "The United Irishmen."

Bad feeling among the Protestants, against the Catholics, quickly turned to violence, especially in Co. Armagh. Under the pretence that the Catholics were planning outrages against them, the Protestants organised themselves into groups and attacked the houses of Catholics under the pretence of searching for weapons. These raids invariably resulted in the rough handling of the inhabitants and their smashing of their looms, furniture and household objects, with the intention that the Catholics might abandon their tenancy. As the raids were carried out at dawn, the disparate groups became commonly known as the "Peep o' Day Boys", but also as "Wreckers" and "Protestant Boys".

Different Catholics groups were organised for protection against these outrages, becoming collectively known as "The Defenders" and sectarian unrest became common with Protestants and Catholics groups meeting each other in pitched battles. However, in the battles that took place between the two groups, the Protestants possessed most of the guns, which were handed out to them by both landlords and magistrates and the Defenders, who had few such weapons, suffered heavy loss of life. As the authorities were squarely on the side of the Protestants, Protestants were acquitted whenever they appeared before the magistrates while the Catholics were severely punished. When the situation deteriorated further, the government sent in the military volunteers (Militia) to restore order, but, in Armagh especially, these units were nothing more than Peep o' Day Boys in army uniform. In a situation that would find its echo in the mid twentieth century, these volunteers committed "legal" acts of murder and atrocity. Whilst priests sought to reign in the excesses committed by Catholics, some Protestant ministers poured fuel on the flames. In a sermon given at Drumcree Parish Church outside Portadown, during July 1795 the minister, Rev. Devine "...so worked up the minds of his audience, that upon retiring…(they fell)…upon every Catholic they met, beating and bruising them without provocation or distinction, breaking the doors and windows of their houses, and actually murdering two unoffending Catholics in a bog"…"[88]

"Drive out the Catholics"
On September 21st 1795, around 30 Defenders were shot dead by the Peep o' Day Boys in the village of Loughgall, Co.Tyrone. Numbers of those Protestants who had taken part in the "battle" went to the House of James Sloan to celebrate their victory. During the meeting at Sloan's the Orange Order was founded, afterwards growing into an association of lodges with a ceremony of initiation, rules, regalia, passwords and signals along Masonic lines. At their meetings the extreme anti Catholicism of Cromwellian days was rekindled, and according to one of its earliest members, William Blacker, "…a determination was expressed of driving from this quarter of the country the entire of its Roman Catholic population…a written notice was thrown into or posted upon the door of a house warning the inmates in the words of Cromwell, to betake themselves 'to hell or Connacht'"[89]

During the months that followed the Order's foundation, a massive campaign of "ethnic cleansing" of Catholics by Protestants was undertaken.[I] In what became known as "The Armagh Outrages", an estimated 7,000 Catholics were driven from their homes and livelihoods by wholesale attacks upon homes, chapels and businesses along with many murders and other outrages. During a speech on the Outrages in the Dublin Parliament, Henry Grattan, the M.P for Charlemont, said that

---

[I] The notable nineteenth century Presbyterian historian, the Rev William Killen has written "Nothing can be more evident that the original Orangemen were the very scum of society and a disgrace to Protestantism." Lord Gosford denounced the initial foundation of the Orange Order as an "ungovernable mob"

their object was "the extermination of all the Catholics of that county", describing it as "a persecution conceived in the bitterness of bigotry" by men who had "committed, with greater audacity and confidence the most horrid murders, and had proceeded from robbery and massacre to extermination"[90.] Regarding the inactivity of the magistrates, Grattan added: "From all the inquiries that I could make, I collect that the Catholic inhabitants of Armagh have been actually put out of the protection of the law; that the magistrates have been supine or partial; and that the horrid banditti have met with complete success; and from the magistrates with very little discouragement"[91.]

Lord Gosford Intervenes
In an attempt to try and enforce the law, the Governor of Co. Armagh, Lord Gosford, addressed the magistrates of Co. Armagh on December 28th 1795 regarding the outrages: "It is no secret that a persecution, accompanied with all the circumstances of ferocious cruelty, is now raging in this country. Neither age nor sex, nor even acknowledged innocence as to any guilt in the late disturbances is sufficient to excite mercy, much less to afford protection. The only crime which the wretched objects of this ruthless persecution are charged with is a crime, indeed, of easy proof, it is simply a profession of the Roman Catholic Faith. A lawless banditti have constituted themselves judges of this new species of delinquency; and the sentence they have denounced is equally concise and terrible. It is nothing less than a confiscation of all property and an immediate banishment. It would be extremely painful, and surely unnecessary to detail the horrors that attend the execution of so rude and tremendous a proscription – a proscription that certainly exceeds, in the comparative number of those it consigns to ruin and misery, even that ancient and modern history can supply…this is no

exaggerated picture of the horrid scenes now acting in this county."[92]

# Chapter 4

# The Protestant Nation

## The Irish Colonists Fight for Parliamentary Independence

"The Patriot Party"

Since the parliament of 1693, there had invariably been a grouping in the Dublin Parliament that had advocated freedom of action for the Irish colonists from the restrictions placed upon them by London. The earliest leader of this group or "party" had been William Molyneux who in 1698 had published his treatise on "The Case of Ireland being bound by Acts of Parliament made in England".[93] London found his treatise to be of "a dangerous tendency"[94] and ordered it burnt for "denying the authority of the King and Parliament of England to bind the kingdom and people of Ireland"[95]

Following the Statute "The Sixth of George I" in 1719, those who advocated Dublin's independence from London now retired into abeyance until the arrival of Henry Flood as an M.P in 1759. Led by Flood the newly reformed "Patriot Party" successfully contested the attempt of the Privy Council in London to originate money bills for Ireland. To the scandal of the rest of the group, Flood was shortly afterwards neutralised when he accepted the bribe of "Office of Vice Treasurer" at the rate of £3,500 per annum. Thereafter for the best part of a decade he kept his mouth shut about freedom of action for

Dublin and the Patriot Party retreated into the shadows once more.

For the Patriot Party, 1775 was an important year. Henry Grattan, who was to be the key figure in the Patriot movement for the following decade, took his seat as M.P for the constituency of Charlemont and the American War of Independence began.

Henry Flood

After the outbreak of war, almost all English soldiers stationed in Ireland were sent to fight the American colonists who denied the right of London to pass laws affecting them and the right to levy taxes without their consent. This action of the American colonists was not lost on the Irish colonists, many of whom not only sympathised with their aims but also wished, in some respects, to emulate them. The ire of the Patriot Party was further aroused when shortly after the war with America began, the government imposed a total embargo on all Irish exports to English colonies.

## The Decline of the Penal Code

In October 1777, at the height of the American War of Independence, the 6,000 strong English army of General Burgoyne surrendered to the American General Gage at The Battle of Saratoga. This massive defeat for English arms at the hands of the American colonists was the catalyst for the British Prime Minister Lord North to try and achieve a greater sense of unity among Englishmen in the face of growing international support for the American rebels. As well as making plans to repeal some of the laws against Catholics in England, he encouraged the Dublin Parliament to relax the penal laws against the Catholic majority. However his plea fell on deaf ears, as the majority of members remained in favour of unrestricted Catholic persecution.

Early the following year, after some reforms in favour of Catholics were introduced in England, the Irish M.P Luke Gardiner (later Lord Mountjoy) who desired a repeal of the more severe penal laws, introduced a bill into the Dublin parliament in May 1778. However in spite of Government pressure on the house the bill was rejected. Undeterred, Gardiner persisted, and finally after a total of eight votes and much rancorous debate, the measure was finally passed by nine votes. As a result of the legislation Catholics were now entitled to lease property for up to 999 years and a Catholic child who later became a Protestant was no longer able to inherit the entire estate of his father. Furthermore the clauses of the penal laws allowing for the hunting of priests and Catholic teachers were repealed.

## The Protestant Volunteers

In early 1779, the Secretary of State sent reports to Belfast that naval raids might be expected on the city from among others, the famous Scottish American privateer, John Paul Jones. As the city was without any sort of armed protection against a sea-borne assault, a volunteer corps was formed. Catholics were naturally excluded. The idea quickly spread and soon all the gentlemen of the Protestant ascendancy throughout the land were forming corps of Protestant volunteers in their areas to replace the absent army. The government were uneasy at this turn of events but acquiesced, and at the behest of the Dublin Parliament agreed to supply 16,000 muskets to the volunteers.

As the numbers of armed men in these units swiftly grew, Henry Grattan, along with some of his colleagues in the Patriot Party thought that they might know how to use this newly acquired military power best.

## "Free Trade for Ireland"

Following the speech of the Lord Lieutenant at the opening of Parliament in October 1779, Henry Grattan got to his feet. After outlining the disastrous state of trade in the country, he moved an amendment calling for a free export trade for Ireland. After the amendment was altered to "free trade for Ireland" by Hussey Burgh M.P it was voted on and almost unanimously carried. When the speaker carried the resolution from the parliament, he had to walk through long lines of volunteers to Dublin Castle to obtain the signature of the Viceroy to the amendment. Two artillery pieces with placards reading "Free Trade or This" were placed on College Green in front of the statue of King William of Orange. When the British Prime Minister, Lord North, received news of what had taken place, he decided that he did indeed prefer free trade to "this" and gave way, thereafter introducing free trade legislation for Ireland in the English parliament.

All the while the size of the volunteers increased rapidly, so much so that by the beginning of 1780 their number was over 40,000. Afraid of their power, the government longed to disband them but were afraid to as they dreaded the consequences if they attempted such a measure.

Determined that the "Patriot Party" should not have the last word following the introduction of free trade, the English government applied pressure to those MPs who had agreed to support the government, and in a number of votes which occurred in the period following the admission of free trade, the Patriot Party was defeated by the government's usual majority of 134 to 67. However the government's corrupt majority had an Achilles heel. When public opinion was swayed by the powerful oratory of a noble man untouched by the power of money such as Henry Grattan, the government's vacillating parliamentary majority were sometimes induced to follow him. A master orator, Grattan often spoke with a "fervid and thrilling eloquence".[1]

A sure sign that the tide was turning in the Patriot Party's favour came when Henry Flood, having made a tidy sum in his career as a government official, decided to sacrifice place to principle and return once more to the ranks of the Patriot Party who welcomed him with open arms.

Watching the parliamentary impasse from the sidelines, the efforts of the Patriot Party on the one side and the government on the other, with their bribery and corruption desperately trying to hold back the demands of the Patriot Party, were the Ulster Volunteers, who now decided that it was high time that they take a hand in affairs.

## The Dungannon Convention

On December 28th 1781, a meeting of all the officers of the southern battalion of the first Ulster regiment of Volunteers was held in Armagh, at which it was decided to hold a convention of the Ulster Volunteers.

The following February 15th 1782, the convention of the 143 corps of the Ulster Volunteers was held in the Presbyterian meeting house in Dungannon. With Colonel William Irvine presiding over the assembly of 242 delegates, twenty one resolutions were adopted including most notably:

---

[1] One of his most memorable speeches occurred on April 19th 1780. It included the lines"...I will never be satisfied as long as the meanest cottager in Ireland has a link of the British chain clanking to his rags. He may be naked, he shall not be in irons...though great men should apostatise, yet the cause will live..."

"That the claim of any body of men other than the King, Lords, and Commons of Ireland, to make laws to bind this Kingdom is unconstitutional illegal and a grievance"[96]

"That the powers exercised by the Privy Councils of both Kingdoms, under colour or pretence of the law of Poynings, are unconstitutional and a grievance"[97]

"That therefore, as men and as Irishmen, as Christians and as Protestants, we rejoice in the relaxation of the penal laws against our Roman Catholic fellow subjects"[98]

However in this last resolution, the Convention, while content to see the abolition of the purely penal aspects of the law were divided over whether Catholics should be allowed to vote, and still further divided over their admittance into parliament.

### The Declaration of Parliamentary Independence

The pressure applied by the combined Ulster Volunteer Corps had the desired effect. Up and down the country, similar Volunteer conventions followed suit, adopting similar resolutions to the Ulster Convention. With the military power of the Volunteers at its back the Patriot Party now focused on gaining their primary objective – legislative independence from England.

On April 16th 1782, when parliament assembled, Volunteers as far as the eye could see had formed up in front of the Parliament building, their bayonets gleaming in the morning sun. When Henry Grattan arrived, he walked through their ranks on his way into the building. After the Secretary of State, John Hutchinson had read the legislative address, Grattan stood up and proposed an amendment: "…that the Crown of Ireland is an imperial Crown inseparably annexed to the Crown of Great Britain, on which connection the interests and happiness of both nations essentially depend: but that the kingdom of Ireland is a distinct kingdom, with a Parliament of her own – the sole Legislature thereof. That there is no body of men competent to make laws to bind this nation except the King, Lords, and Commons of Ireland; nor any other Parliament which hath any authority or power of any sort whatever in this country save only the Parliament of Ireland."[99.]

When the amendment was voted upon, it was unanimously carried.

## The Protestant Nation

Following the vote, Grattan addressed the Dublin parliament in which "not one member of the ancient Irish nation was present"[100] and four fifths of the Irish people were not represented:

"I am now to address a free people. Ages have passed away, and this is the first moment in which you could be distinguished by that appellation...I found Ireland on her knees; I watched over her with an eternal solicitude; I have traced her progress from injuries to arms and from arms to liberty. Spirit of Swift! Spirit of Molyneux! Your genius has prevailed! Ireland is now a nation! In that new character I hail her! And bowing to her august presence, I say Esto perpetua!"[101] [I]

However England had yet to give her consent to this declaration of parliamentary independence by the Dublin Parliament. She had already lost one colony, and if She refused the demands of the Dublin Parliament, armed conflict with the sizeable volunteer corps beckoned and perhaps the loss of another colony.

England, now under the newly formed administration of the Marquis Rockingham, was not in a position to argue, but preferred to bide her time. For decades the Dublin Parliament had been rank with corruption, its members easily affected by

---

[I] "Esto perpetua" – "May it be forever"

the touch of money – what had worked before could work again when the time was right.

On May 27th, after an adjournment of almost a month, Portland who had been appointed as Viceroy to replace Carlisle addressed the parliament and announced the repeal of the "Sixth of George I" by the English parliament along with numerous other concessions including the abolition of the sacramental test for Presbyterians and other Protestant dissenters. (Methodists, Baptists, etc.) From now on they were eligible for election to parliament and for government office.

An Illusory Independence

After Portland's announcement, almost the entire House was in awe of Grattan, and promptly voted to award him £50,000 so that he might buy a large estate and mansion for himself.

Henry Grattan

However in spite of the fact that some members of the Dublin Parliament now considered Ireland to be a "Sister Nation" with England, the "English Connexion" would still remain almost as strong as ever. Apart from the King who would veto any Irish bill if advised to do so by the English Prime Minister, the Dublin Parliament still had to contend with the power of the viceroy and his ministers of state who actually formed the government and introduced the majority of the bills into parliament. When William Pitt became Prime Minister, he fully realised the importance of keeping the independent Irish Parliament in check and lavished peerages and pensions on the un-elected members to copper fasten their support for the government and make sure that the Patriot Party would remain a minority faction.

## The Act of Renunciation

The euphoria of independence was short lived. Almost immediately a row developed between Flood and Grattan over what exactly London had actually given the Dublin Parliament. Flood maintained that the simple repeal of the Sixth of George I did not legally give Dublin Parliamentary independence while Grattan was content that it did. While parliament listened to Grattan, the Volunteers agreed with Flood, and contrary to Grattan's wishes Flood campaigned for the express renunciation by London of the right to legislate for Ireland. Once more England gave way and passed a "Renunciation Act" sooner than face a possible showdown with the Volunteers. The Act of Renunciation by London laid down "...the right claimed by the people of Ireland, to be bound only by laws enacted by his Majesty and the Parliament of that kingdom, and to have all actions and suits at law...decided in his Majesty's courts therein finally and without appeal..."[102] With the repeal of the Sixth of George I now apparently copper-fastened by Flood's campaign, his popularity went from strength to strength while Grattan's declined.

## The Foiled Duel

Relations between Flood and Grattan were now at an all time low. During October 1783, harsh words passed between them during a debate on public expenses in the Dublin House of Commons. Following the debate a duel was arranged between the two men. It is most likely that Flood challenged Grattan as during the debate, Grattan had launched a personal attack on Flood telling him: "Sir, your talents are not so great as your life is infamous. You might be seen hovering about the Dome, like an ill omened bird of night, with sepulchral notes, a cadaverous aspect, and broken beak, ready to swoop and pounce upon your prey. The people cannot trust you; the ministry cannot trust you: you deal with the most impartial treachery to both. I therefore tell you in the face of your country, before all the world; nay to your beard, you are not an honest man!"[103.]

However the police got to hear of the impending duel and both men were arrested on the way to their mutual appointment and afterwards bound to the peace.

## The Corn Laws

Following the allowance of free trade and the declaration of parliamentary independence, there was a marked growth in Irish agriculture, as the Dublin parliament, eager to flex its independent muscle, not only endowed but also sought to protect those industries which it nurtured. This, the colonists felt, was their country and freed from the shackles of Mother England, full advantage should be taken of the new situation. In 1706, exports from Ireland stood at a mere £550,000. By 1796 this had increased to over £5,000,000, the majority of the increase following on from the declaration of free trade.

Agriculture was now greatly encouraged by the Dublin parliament. As England embarked upon an industrial revolution the need for food in English cities was a need that the Dublin Parliament felt that it could answer. In 1784, Foster's Corn Law offered grants for the growth of corn. As foreign corn was by law excluded (until 1846) from England, Ireland now became the arsenal of British food, growing tillage for export to feed the industrial revolution.

In order to enable the passage of goods from the country at large to the capital, from where they could be shipped abroad, a number of canals were constructed.

Labour was now required in large numbers, and vast numbers of native Irish who lived on little more than potatoes worked for a pittance in order to feed the hungry mouths across the Irish Sea. For the lords and landlords however, it was a time of abundance. Great corn mills were built across the length and breadth of the country and from their profits and taxes, mansions and huge edifices in the capital gave Dublin the title "The Second City of the Empire"

## The Anti-Climax

<u>The Failure of Parliamentary Reform</u>

One would assume that Grattan and Flood should have been united on the question of parliamentary reform, but this was not the case. Flood now championed parliamentary reform while Grattan, although not altogether opposing it, remained curiously mute on the subject.

During the Autumn of 1783, Flood drew up a bill of parliamentary reform and brought it before a grand convention of the Volunteers held at the Rotunda in Dublin. After he gained their support he immediately brought it before Parliament. The bill extended the franchise to less well off Protestants and sought to redefine "rotten boroughs" by redrawing the map of boroughs to include adjacent towns or other areas of high population. It also withdrew the right to sit in parliament from Crown pensioners and required those members who accepted government posts to be re-elected in a by-election. Perhaps its most defining clause was that after an election it required all the newly elected members to take an anti bribery oath. As the government was unequivocal in its opposition to Flood's bill it was defeated by 157 votes to 77. Thereafter measures for parliamentary reform often came before the house being introduced on many occasions by George Ponsonby M.P., and were always rejected by the customary government majority.

## The Demise of the Volunteers

Having made good use of the Volunteers in his efforts to gain Parliamentary independence, following the Act of Renunciation, Grattan, (along with many others in Parliament) now saw them as a threat and a source of intimidation to the parliament, and loudly voiced his opinion in this regard telling his fellow members that the Volunteers: "had originally been the armed property of the kingdom; were they to become the armed beggary?"[104.]

Cowed, the United Volunteers Convention adjourned their deliberations, never to resume them. As the American war was at an end, the size of the army stationed in Ireland was once more increased, Parliament (including Grattan) now voted for a grant of £20,000 for the establishment of a territorial force composed in its officer corps entirely of the ascendancy, landlords and gentry. This force known as "The Militia" was to be the iron hand that would enforce the will of parliament against any threat against it that would arise within the Protestant nation.

## English Resentment

In spite of its inherent corruption, the Dublin Parliament, by its declaration of parliamentary independence had ushered in the high period of Ireland as a nation controlled and elected by the colonist Protestant minority. Exports flourished. Dublin, which ever since its founding had been the city of the foreigner, grew larger and larger, its public architecture easily rivalling that of London due to the large building projects undertaken by the Ascendancy. As Dublin flourished its progress was jealously watched by the English upper class and by their leader, the new English Prime Minister William Pitt the Younger.[1] Dismayed, not only by the loss of the American

---

[1] Referred to as "The Younger" in order to distinguish him from his father.

colonies, but by the Irish Colonists bid for freedom, he now set himself the task of the recovery of the control of Ireland and also of the extension of English power globally.

## The Catholic Convention

<u>The Catholic Committee</u>

In the year 1757, a small group of leading Irish Catholics led by Charles O' Conor, of Belangare, the historian Dr. Charles Curry and a certain Mr. Wyse of Waterford met together at the Globe Coffee House in Essex St. Dublin. Calling themselves the Catholic Committee, their object was to try and put forward the Catholic interest both in the public domain and at the highest levels of government.

In government quarters their efforts were treated with contempt and when any member of the committee received words of encouragement there was always an ulterior motive such as to try and cause a split within the group or encourage the group to distance itself from the resistance of the bishops and priests. However the group did succeed in bringing the plight of Irish Catholics before the British public by the publication of anonymous works by both Charles O'Conor and Dr. Curry.

For years and by different means the group tried and failed to bring the predicament of Irish Catholics before the government, but it was not until 1793 that their efforts met with partial success. That some success was achieved was due in small part to the most virulent and strident of their enemies in the Dublin parliament, the M.P.s Boyle Roche, Latouche, Toler and the Lord Chancellor, John Fitzgibbon who was also Earl of Clare.

In 1790, the group, now led by the Dublin Merchant John Keogh submitted a petition to parliament asking that Catholic grievances might be enquired into. However not one member of parliament would agree to present it. In 1792 they again prepared a petition to be presented before the Dublin Parliament and this time they succeeded in persuading the M.P for Sligo to put the petition before the House. When the petition was presented uproar ensued in the House and the insolence of the Catholic Committee, that they would dare to presume to present such a petition, was castigated. Torrents of abuse were heaped upon the Committee, especially by the members mentioned above. After a verbal drubbing the petition was voted down by a majority of 185.

## "An Unconstitutional Proceeding of the Most Alarming, Dangerous, and Seditious Tendency"

Following this failure, John Keogh refused to give up the project. Instead, he undertook a re-organisation of the group along the lines of the Volunteers Convention. Two representatives from each county along with one from each city joined the executive in Dublin to form a new group called "The Catholic Convention". In Dublin, two young Protestant barristers, Theobald Wolfe Tone and Simon Butler offered their service to the Convention. Their input was decisive, for they were able to give the Convention much needed advice regarding the legal niceties to be observed while encouraging them to be more forthright in the language of their petitions.

When news of the formation of the Convention reached the ears of the members of parliament, their rage reached almost apoplectic levels, with Lord Chancellor Fitzgibbon leading the charge. He declared the formation of the Convention to be treason against the Crown. Throughout the land, the grand juries assembled and followed suit. The Catholic Convention was declared to be "an unconstitutional proceeding of the most alarming, dangerous, and seditious tendency"[105] with the resolution being taken by both parliament and the grand juries "to maintain at the hazard of everything most dear to us the Protestant interest of Ireland"[106].

Such was the torrent of abuse heaped upon the Catholic Convention that the effect achieved by the Protestant Ascendancy was quite the opposite to that which they desired. The entire Catholic population of Ireland backed the convention and as the Parliament were quite clearly acting in opposition to a reasonable request of the Catholic majority the decision was made by the executive to travel to London and attempt to petition the King directly. In this matter the advice of Wolfe Tone was decisive.

### "His Majesty's Catholic Subjects"

This episode occurred just after the Battle of Valmy, when the government of the newly declared French Republic had defeated an alliance of foreign powers. England was by this time at war with France and was fearful of the consequences if it ignored the Catholic Convention completely, as the Convention had quite obviously the support of the majority of the Irish people. It also feared the effect that the French revolution was having on Ireland for already the example of the French rebels was being lauded and celebrated in some quarters. Another factor was England's need for Irish Catholic men to help fill the regiments of her armies. This was an opportune moment for London to remove the bar on Irish Catholics serving in the officer ranks of the British Army, (the ban on enlisted men having already been earlier removed.) By appearing to be magnanimous to the Catholics of Ireland in the face of opposition from the Dublin Parliament, England could also serve her own interests.

After the delegation from the Catholic Convention reached London, they were received with respect by the government and given an audience with the King on January 2nd 1793 in spite of the repeated petitions of the parliament in Dublin that they would be completely ignored. After the meeting it was announced that the King had "graciously accepted their petition"[107].

When the Irish Parliament assembled on January 10th 1793, the many anti Catholic members of Parliament braced themselves for any reference the Lord Lieutenant might make regarding the Catholics. For the first time since the reformation, the speech of the Lord Lieutenant to the Dublin Parliament, contained a paragraph recommending the condition of "His Majesty's Catholic subjects to its serious consideration"[108].

As the King had spoken through his Lord Lieutenant, the Dublin Parliament had little option but to follow London's instructions. A bill was introduced and passed the House of Commons which extended the vote (which was limited to a fraction of the seats in the Dublin Parliament) to large Catholic freeholders along with a few other concessions including the holding of a King's commission in the army and navy. When the bill was introduced in the Irish House of Lords, Fitzgibbon remained obstinate in his opposition to any further concession to the Catholics. He called on Parliament "to guarantee once and for ever, intact and inviolate, the principles of Protestant Ascendancy, that is to say a Protestant King, a Protestant Parliament, a Protestant Hierarchy, Protestant electors and government, the bench of justice, the army and the revenue, through all their branches and details, Protestant!"[109].

## A Few Concessions

London had spoken and the parliamentary placemen and the members London's pay now felt compelled to accquiess with London's wishes. By the end of March 1793 the bill had become law. Although the measures granted were by any measure contemptible as the legal position of Catholics was altered only in minor ways, it signalled the effective end of the more draconian measures of the penal laws.

All Ireland knew that the relief measures which passed through the Dublin parliament had emanated from London. Aside from the other considerations which affected London's decision to introduce the measures, they were specifically designed by Pitt, ever the master tactician, to appear that the beneficent English father was the only one who would give some measure of relief to the ordinary Irish and to prepare the minds of the great mass of the Catholic Irish for the Act of Union, so that the Irish people would believe that when the Act of Union finally came, it would give them total emancipation.

That the Dublin Parliament should appear anti-Catholic, while he, Pitt, appeared magnanimous served his purpose wonderfully.[1]

A further measure of concession came in 1795, when in the wake of the French revolution and the subsequent policy of de-Christianisation undertaken by the new French government, Irish students for the priesthood were no longer able to receive seminary training in France and the government agreed, following a request from the bishops, to allow and partially fund the construction of a Catholic Seminary at Maynooth. However, it was quite some time before any monies were actually paid over to the church authorities due to the amount of "red tape" which parliament now placed in the Church's way.

---

[1] That Pitt was "Janus faced" cannot be doubted. As we shall see, having offered concessions to the Irish Catholics for his own ends, he would also attempt to incense religious feeling in Ireland for his own ends and then let loose on the unarmed Irish the cruel and fanatical Protestant militia also for his own ends – the fomentation of rebellion and the achievement of the Union of Britain and Ireland.

# Chapter 5

# Theobald Wolfe Tone and The United Irishmen

## The Society of The United Irishmen
### The French Revolution
To accurately trace the origins of the United Irishmen, it is necessary to write a few lines on the French Revolution, as it was the inspiration not only for the founding of the United Irishmen but also for the growth of the republican movement in Ireland which Theobald Wolfe Tone helped to establish.

By the late 1780's the greater portion of the French upper and middle class had been captivated by the teachings of the philosophers Voltaire and Rousseau. Using his clever wit and literary genius, Voltaire had attacked the entire established order in France which included revealed religion, Christian culture and Catholicism in particular. Rousseau very ably preached rationalism, local democracy, liberalism and equality (the end of hierarchy and kingship coupled with political and social equality for all). The ideas of these men gained widespread credence, a credence that the French Freemasonic lodges hoped to capitalise on.

When France suffered a severe financial crisis in the late 1780s, the King was finally forced in 1789 to summon the nationwide council known as "The States General" in order to raise money. The situation is comparable to that of King Charles I, who by summoning parliament let loose a power he could not wield. Those who followed the ideas of Voltaire and Rousseau now saw their chance for change, and The States General rapidly turned into a forum where the new ideas were expressed – reform, equality, and the end of the privileged classes, the monarchy and the Catholic Church. In order to help change along, the people of Paris rose up "spontaneously" in the Summer of 1789 and stormed the Bastille, and from this the French revolution began. By the Autumn of 1792, the King had been executed and the new National Convention had declared France a republic. Furthermore the Convention issued an "Edict of Fraternity" to all oppressed peoples and launched a crusade for the spread of its principles abroad.

## The Founding of "The Society of the United Irishmen"

Since the turn of the decade, the English upper class and the Anglo Irish ascendancy were transfixed in horror at what was happening in France. Since 1789 France had been convulsed by a revolution that had increased in ferocity from year to year and which had ripped asunder the established order throwing aside both monarchy and church.

Fear grew among the Anglo Irish, knowing that their authority had its foundations in the subjugation of the native Irish. By maintaining a firm grip not only on power but on seized lands they were determined that any such parallel movement in Ireland would not be allowed to flourish.

As the Catholic Convention was composed of both Catholics and liberal minded Protestants and dissenters, it presented a perfect target for the ire of parliament. Theobald Wolfe Tone was one of these liberal minded Protestants. Influenced by the French revolution and its motto of "liberty, equality and fraternity" he not only offered his services to the Catholic Convention but also decided that he would try to do more to promote and foster a common fellowship between all classes and creeds and work for the abolition of privilege and the official corruption which consumed both government and parliament.

It was with this object in mind that he accepted the invitation to visit the volunteer club in Belfast in October 1791.whose leading members, Samuel Neilson, Thomas Russell and Robert Simms were all of common mind with Tone. Their meeting passed a number of resolutions:

"That the weight of English influence in this country is so great as to require a cordial union among all the people of Ireland, to maintain the balance which is essential to the preservation of our liberties and the extension of our commerce."[110]

"That the sole constitutional mode by which this influence can be opposed is by a complete and radical reform of the representation of people in parliament."

"That no reform is just which does not include every Irishman of every religious persuasion."[111]

Following the adoption of these resolutions, the first club of a new organisation was established with Samuel Neilson as founder and Wolfe Tone as organiser. It was given the name "The Society of the United Irishmen" and adopted the following membership oath: "I, A.B, in the presence of God do pledge myself to my country that I will use all my abilities and influence in the attainment of an impartial and adequate representation of the Irish nation in parliament; and as a means of absolute and immediate necessity in the establishment of this chief good of Ireland, I will endeavour, as much as lies in my ability, to forward a brotherhood of affection, and identity of interests, a communion of rights and union of power among Irishmen of all religious persuasions without which every reform in parliament must be partial, not national, inadequate to the wants, delusive to the wishes and insufficient for the freedom and happiness of this country"[112].

On his return to Dublin, Tone met with among others, his fellow barrister for the Catholic Convention, Simon Butler and with the Quaker merchant and former member of the volunteers James Naper (called "Napper") Tandy. At the meeting, the decision was taken to establish the Society in the capital with the same resolutions being adopted and with Napper Tandy as Secretary.

To the casual observer, this was no revolutionary society, but was in many respects similar to the many political clubs that existed especially in England. Whilst Tone and Tandy especially were far more republican in their ideas than they would have admitted to the other members, they did not openly espouse anything other than monarchical principles, and the aims of the movement remained restricted to those mentioned above. However to his diary, Tone revealed his true intentions in assisting in the formation of the new society: "To break the connection with England, the never failing source of all our political evils, and to assist the independence of my country – these are my objects"[113]

## The United Irishmen Are Forced Underground

In the same parliament in which the "Catholic Relief Bill" was passed "The Convention Act" was also introduced. By this measure which was also contained in The King's Speech and therefore could not be ignored by the emancipated Dublin Parliament, the Prime Minister of England William Pitt the Younger, using the war with France and the security of the realm as pretext, sought to abolish any movement in Ireland that acted contrary to the government interest by placing a complete prohibition on the assembly of representative delegations. When the bill was introduced, Grattan protested in vain: "If this bill had been law, the independence of the Irish Parliament, the emancipation of the Catholics and even the English Revolution of 1688 could never have taken place."[114]

The member for Trim, Major Wellesley called the measure "...the boldest step that ever yet was made to introduce military government."[115]

Overnight the Catholic Convention found itself dissolved while The United Irishmen were on notice not to engage in any activity that might be considered against England's interest.

When in February 1793, following a meeting of the United Irishmen in Dublin, an address against the secret committee of the House of Lords was published, the Chairman of the Leinster Convention of the Society, Mr. Butler, and the Secretary, Mr. Bond, were summoned and both men were fined and imprisoned. The same occurred in January 1794, when after a meeting of the United Irishmen, an address to the Volunteers delivered by Archibald Hamilton, came to the notice of the Irish Parliament. Despite a robust defence at his trial, the packed jury found him guilty of seditious libel and he was sentenced to two years imprisonment and a fine of £500.

Events leading to the Society's effective suppression came to a head in April 1794, when an emissary from the French Convention, the Rev. William Jackson (an English Protestant clergyman), arrived in Ireland with his legal advisor, John Cockayne. Having lived in France for many years, and embraced the revolution, he had been sent to Ireland by the French National Convention to find out how a French invasion of Ireland would be received by the people. Unbeknownst to Jackson, Cockayne had betrayed his mission to the English government and had been instructed by Pitt to accompany him and find out all that he could about the people he met and what was discussed. When Jackson met Wolfe Tone, Hamilton Rowan and some of the other leaders, he did not gain their full confidence as they were unsure of his credentials, and they refused to commit themselves to anything in front of Cockayne.

Days after the meeting, Jackson was arrested after which Hamilton Rowan went on the run, but Tone stood his ground. On May 4th, the Tailor's Hall in Dublin was raided while a meeting of The United Irishmen was in progress, and all documentation that the police could get their hands on was seized. When news of the raid spread, many more prominent members of the Society went underground as did the Society which now assumed a new character, that of a secret society. From this moment French aid and military force became hot topics for the leadership of the society. The original oath too was changed to take account of the new circumstances. The phrase "equal representation of the people in parliament"[116] was altered to "a full representation of all the people of Ireland"[117] with the word "parliament" being completely omitted. The Society now also sought to drill down into the grassroots of Irish society. Committees were formed in baronies, counties and all the provinces. Each committee delegated one member to the higher committee which finally formed the executive directory of five people elected by ballot. However in spite of all precautions, from the very beginning all the proceedings of this secret society were betrayed to the government by informers. Numerous gentlemen and ordinary folk were either employed by the government to join the Society as government spies or turned informer. Having wormed their way into the upper echelons of the society, these men betrayed to the government every scrap of information that came their way, receiving good pay and government pensions in return. The most notorious of these informers were the Society's Barrister Leonard Mc Nally, Thomas Reynolds of Kildare who was a Landlord and the husband of Wolfe Tone's sister, John Hughes from Belfast and a Militia Captain by the name of Armstrong from Down.

## Wolfe Tone Leaves Ireland

On April 23rd 1795, the Rev William Jackson went on trial for treason. The chief witness against him was John Cockayne. Before he was due to take the stand, Jackson took arsenic, his motive being to avoid a guilty verdict, and so preserve the money he had saved for his wife and children which would be automatically confiscated by the government once a guilty verdict was reached.

Content that the new secret organisation of The Society had a firm foundation, Tone prepared to depart Ireland for America.

Theobald Wolfe Tone

Even though he had been implicated by Cockayne's evidence, the links between himself and Jackson remained tenuous at best and through the influence of powerful friends he was allowed to depart the country for exile in America. Before he left Ireland, he promised Napper Tandy and his other intimate friends that shortly after his arrival in America, he would re-cross the Atlantic and go to France where he would put the case for a French invasion of Ireland before the National Committee.

## "England's Closest Escape since the Armada"
### Wolfe Tone Comes to France

On February 1st 1796, Wolfe Tone arrived at the French port of Le Havre, after which he journeyed to Paris. Despite the fact that the only references he had with him were two letters of thanks from the Catholic Committee in Dublin and his certificate of membership for the Belfast Volunteers, he quickly became friends with the American Ambassador, after which he was introduced to the influential physicist and politician, Count Lazare Carnot. Carnot, impressed with Tone, immediately gave him a commission in the French army and brought him into the upper echelons of the French revolutionary leadership. If anything, since he had left Ireland, Tone's attitude had hardened. He now confided to his diary: "The truth is I hate the very name of England, I hated her before my exile, and I will hate her always"[118.]

In May of 1796, Tone was joined in France by two other men seeking French help for Ireland, both of whom were unaware of Tone's presence there. They were Arthur O'Connor M.P and Lord Edward Fitzgerald, both of whom had recently joined the United Irishmen. Fitzgerald was already known to the French leadership as he had been in France a few years earlier. As a result of this earlier visit he had lost his commission in the British army after it had been reported back to London that he had drunk a toast to the "…speedy abolition of all hereditary and feudal distinctions"[119.]

### The Beginning of the Road Towards the Act of Union
"The day Lord Fitzwilliam arrived, peace was declared throughout all Ireland. The day he quitted it, she prepared for insurrection." – Sir Jonah Barrington M.P.

Fitzgerald and O'Connor had come to France as the result of the immediate fallout of the recall of the liberal Viceroy Lord Fitzwilliam who served as Viceroy between early January and late March 1795.

Towards the end of 1794, the English Prime Minister, William Pitt made it known that he had had decided to adopt a policy of conciliation towards Ireland, and to this end he recalled the serving Viceroy Lord Westmoreland and appointed in his place Lord Fitzwilliam, who was known as being in favour of far reaching parliamentary reform and full freedom for Catholics.

After his appointment, Fitzwilliam arrived in Ireland on January 4th 1795 and wasted no time in immediately advancing his program. In his brief tenure he sought to advance both Catholic emancipation and parliamentary reform. Furthermore, he proceeded to take steps against corruption in the Dublin administration relieving John Beresford as Commissioner of Customs along with Undersecretary Cooke. For the Catholics of Ireland, his first weeks in office heralded the turning of a page, the beginning of a new era where the long established anti Catholic, anti Irish system of apartheid would at last be tackled head on. If his tenure had continued undisturbed, the appeal of The Society of the United Irishmen for Catholics and moderate Protestants could well have abated as his first steps promised a squaring of accounts with the venal and corrupt members of parliament.

However by appointing Fitzwilliam, William Pitt was in fact gravely misusing the art of statecraft. Ever since the heady days of 1782 when the Dublin parliament had gained independence from London thanks to the rattling of Volunteers sabres, Pitt had considered the complete union of Ireland with England to be of paramount importance in order to extinguish the danger of an independent Ireland for all time. Now that he held the reins of power he was not only actively considering it, but preparing for it. Despite his patronage towards the Irish M.Ps he remained concerned that at some time in the future the Dublin Parliament might decide to embark upon its own independent path. This danger was exposed to him, when, during the temporary madness of King George III at the end of 1788, the Dublin Parliament had offered the Regency of Ireland to the Prince of Wales only for the King to regain his sanity before the deed was accomplished.

The governance of Ireland was now at a crossroads. Pitt had the power to lead the ascendancy on a path of reformation and full Catholic emancipation or he had the power to shut the door on reform and reinforce the old order for his own ends. Determined to eliminate any danger of a truly Irish parliament, Pitt chose the latter.

After the Act of Union was complete, Henry Grattan commented on Pitt and the path on which he now led Ireland: "His devil went forth. He destroyed liberty and property: he consumed the press: he burned houses and villages: he murdered..."[120]

As Fitzwilliam's policies might bring the country to contentment, instead of the widespread discontentment that Pitt knew was required for his project of parliamentary union, Pitt now brought Fitzwilliam's tenure as Viceroy to a swift conclusion before he could achieve anything substantial. After raising the expectations of the Catholic majority he shattered them, callously calculating that the reaction of the Catholic majority would make the Protestant minority more eager to accept the termination of their colony and the complete protection of Mother England.

In this act he was encouraged by King George III, who had been convinced by the sacked Beresford that Fitzwilliam was trying to undermine Protestantism and the Protestant Ascendancy, and at the King's insistence Beresford was given his old job back after Fitzwilliam's recall.

William Pitt had no strong objection to allowing some English Catholics to sit in an English parliament, but in Ireland the stakes were much higher. In Ireland the Catholics were in the majority, while in England the number of Catholics in parliament could never amount to more than a few. Knowing that parliamentary reform meant the end of the "rotten boroughs" and that with full emancipation Catholics must be allowed to take parliamentary seats, by abolishing the Dublin

Parliament he calculated that Irish Catholics would never at any time in the future be in a position to recover the governance of their country even if that governance remained under the restraints of the English Crown.

Pitt also felt that allowing Catholics to take seats in parliament was an "ace in the hole" with which he could persuade the Catholic majority of Ireland that union with England was in their best interests, as they would now be freed of the shackles imposed upon them by the Ascendancy parliament in Dublin. However after union with England, Irish Catholic politicians would only be a tiny minority in the English parliament capable of achieving little or nothing.

King George III

After Lord Fitzwilliam was recalled, numerous addresses and resolutions were submitted to London appealing for the decision to be reversed but to no avail. On March 25th 1795, Fitzwilliam left Dublin. Large crowds were in attendance openly grieving at his departure. This grief would shortly turn to anger and resentment, an anger and resentment that would eventually end in bloodshed.

The Insurrection Act

With the departure of Lord Fitzwilliam, Ireland was on a trajectory towards war, a trajectory that would only be encouraged by the actions of William Pitt and the Dublin government and Parliament.

As a replacement for Fitzwilliam, and with the intention of re-establishing the old rotten order (for the time being) and provoking a set of circumstances which would put the country in a state of ferment bordering on rebellion, Pitt now appointed a willing triumvirate to conduct governmental affairs in Ireland. Earl Camden was secretly instructed to oppose both reform and emancipation and appointed as Viceroy. Robert Stewart (Viscount Castlereagh) who was a former advocate of reform (now bribed), was appointed to the Irish Executive, and General Henry Luttrell[1] (Lord Carhampton) was placed in command of the army.

The willing accomplices of the English government in this new chapter of coercion were the majority of members in the Dublin Parliament who, after pocketing their bribes, towed the line given them. The cruel disappointment of Fitzwilliam's recall and the harsh policies which followed drove not only many Catholics but also numbers of moderate Protestants towards rebellion.

In 1796, the government suspended the Habeas Corpus Act and passed The Insurrection Act that gave the government such powers of repression as had not been seen in Ireland since Cromwell. Power was given to magistrates to proclaim martial law in any part of the country considered to be in a state of disturbance. This allowed houses to be entered by Crown Forces, and the residents seized and imprisoned without any form of trial. Even before the act had passed all stages in the Dublin Parliament over 1,000 people had already been incarcerated without trial. As Commander of the army, Carhampton encouraged his commanders to carry out their duties with ferocity and indiscretion. In an attempt to

---

[1] General Henry Luttrell was the grandson of Henry Lutrell who had betrayed his brother Simon and the Jacobite cause in 1691.

supplement British military power in Ireland, the militia was reinforced with a yeomanry corps (local defence dragoon units) consisting in the main of well to do and lower class loyalists who were eager to maintain the established order at any price. On the eve of the 1798 rebellion the Crown Forces numbered 50,000 yeomen, 18,000 militia and 15,000 regulars.

The Act also made the administering of an oath such as that administered by the United Irishmen punishable by death. In order to free up prison space for the expected influx of United Irishmen and other malcontents, Castlereagh ordered the prisons cleared of existing petty prisoners by transferring them almost wholesale into the navy as ratings. The parliament now firmly refused any further measures brought forward in favour of Catholics by Henry Grattan and any effort to promote any reform whether parliamentary or otherwise was voted down. Everything was done to increase discontentment within the country and nothing was done to allay it.

For centuries it had been England's policy in Ireland to provoke rebellion for her own ends. Now, well aware that members of the United Irishmen were in France trying to persuade the French Directory to send troops, the government desperately fanned the burgeoning revolt by deciding to officially consider Ireland as being in a state of "smothered rebellion" so that any rebellion would be prematurely launched and crushed before French troops might arrive.

### "Esto Perpetua"?

In spite of the return of "business as usual" to the Dublin parliament, Henry Grattan along with a number of colleagues persisted in their efforts to achieve some sort of meaningful reform in parliament and in the country, so as to calm the rising tensions.

However as a result of government policy and parliamentary acquiescence, Grattan finally felt he could do no more.

Already his bill for further reforms in favour of Catholics had been rejected and when parliamentary reform looked like being voted down for the umpteenth time Grattan finally told the House in May of 1797: "We have offered you our measure- you will reject it; we deprecate yours - you will persevere; having no hopes to persuade or dissuade, and having discharged our duty, we shall trouble you no more, and after this day shall not attend the House of Commons"[121.]

The French at Bantry Bay
In France meanwhile, Fitzgerald, O'Connor and Tone entered into negotiations with the French Republican Directory. The French were not slow to see the opportunities that Ireland offered in their war against England, and the negotiations between the two parties finally led to the planning of a large scale French invasion of Ireland.

General Hoche

On December 16th 1796, a powerful French naval force consisting of 43 ships, 17 of which were the larger ships of the line, set sail from the port of Brest bound for Ireland. Aboard different ships were Generals Hoche, Grouchy, and the newly appointed Adjutant General Wolfe Tone who sailed aboard the "Indomptable". In case he should be captured he had now adopted the name Smith. Also aboard ship were 15,000 troops with their weapons, artillery, supplies and 30,000 additional muskets for the United Irishmen and their sympathisers.

It was imprudent to say the least, to launch such a project in the depths of Winter and any fears that Wolfe Tone may have had regarding the weather quickly turned to reality. As soon as the fleet entered the open sea, a storm broke it up in smaller groups. One group of vessels, which contained the ships on which General Grouchy and Wolfe Tone were sailing, continued on towards the southern coast of Ireland while the ship which contained General Hoche lagged behind, unable to make progress in the foul weather. When Grouchy's group of vessels reached the entrance to Bantry Bay, it waited for the arrival of more ships from the convoy that never arrived. Grouchy was unwilling to land without Hoche, but Tone crossed over to his ship by boat and persuaded him to land. However the weather grew progressively worse and finally some of the ships that had arrived cut loose and set sail for France. Tone was finally left with a small number of ships containing only around 6,000 men and only a few artillery pieces. Finally, he too decided that the mission was destined to fail and turned back. On their journey across and the return journey there was no sign whatever of the British navy. Tone's verdict on the doomed invasion was that it had been "England's closest call since the Spanish Armada"

## The Battle of Camperdown
After Tone returned to France, he knew that there was little chance of further French aid in the immediate future. He now prepared himself to settle down in French exile and serve the French republic. General Hoche and Tone had become devoted friends and if it had been left to Hoche, another attempted French landing would have been organised almost immediately but Hoche's star was waning while that of another general was waxing. The rising star in the French military was now Napoleon Bonaparte.

Tone along with Hoche decided that they had one more card to play. The newly formed Batavian Republic, formerly the Dutch Republic but now a vassal of the French state, was eager to prove its mettle and its independence from its French masters. With Hoche's influence a new expedition was formed which would consist of 6,000 French troops earmarked for the invasion of England and 14,000 soldiers of the Batavian Republic. From June 1797, a new armada destined for Lough Swilly in Donegal began to collect off the Texel in the Dutch Wadden Islands, but well aware of this threat, the English sent a fleet under Admiral Duncan to blockade them until finally in the middle of October the two sides met in battle in the north sea near Camperdown resulting in the scattering of the Batavian fleet and the end of another invasion force destined for Ireland.

When Hoche died shortly afterwards, the French stage was left clear for Bonaparte.

Unlike Hoche, Napoleon was not as enthusiastic about the idea of a French invasion of Ireland and preferred the tactic of landing smaller raiding parties that would keep the British in Ireland off balance and tie down large British military resources there.

Nevertheless, in Ireland, the United Irishmen continued to hope that sooner or later there would be a French landing of some description on an Irish shore, which would act as a beacon around which they could rally. Undeterred they continued to organise for a rising.

# Chapter 6

# The 1798 Rebellion

"The Rebellion of 1798 itself was, almost avowedly, and beyond a doubt provably, fomented to enable the British Government to extinguish the Irish legislative independence and bring about the Union." – Daniel O'Connell

"The rebellion of 1798, with all the accumulated misery it entailed, was the direct and predicted consequence of His (Prime Minister William Pitt's) policy" – William Lecky

## The Drift towards Insurrection
"Poor croppies ye know that your sentence was come,
When ye heard the dread sound of the Protestant drum,
In memory of William, we hoisted his flag,
And soon the bright orange put down the green rag." - Anon

### Martial Law in Ulster
With the Insurrection Act having become law on March 13 1797, the commander of the army in Ulster General Lake declared Donegal, Derry, Tyrone, Antrim and Down to be under martial law. Having failed to deal in any effective manner with the Orange Terror and the ethnic cleansing of Catholics in Armagh, the Crown now proved itself equal to deal with the threat posed by the United Irishmen. English militia units were brought to the province and along with the

local orange yeomanry indulged in every conceivable form of outrage. Confessions were extorted by measures such as flogging, half-hanging, pitch capping and picketing. Half hanging involved the victim undergoing all the horrors of strangulation, but the sufferer was generally released while life still remained. The pitch capping of a suspect entailed molten tar being poured either directly on the head or a paper cap filled with the substance being rammed on the head. After cooling both cap and tar were ripped off with the scalp. Picketing was another hellish form of torture, long abolished, but now re-introduced. For this act of torture, a bed of short wooden stakes was made with the pointed ends upwards. The suspect was made to stand on the bed of nails until he passed out. The process could be repeated several times until a "confession" was obtained.

For many, their greatest fear was to be subject to a Crown Forces patrol. When undertaking a patrol the officers in charge of the various units would determine beforehand how many weapons the district to be searched should yield. Every house suspected of containing a weapon was not only searched but all furniture and property was removed. If no weapons were found, it mattered not. The house and all the removed contents were burnt. The process continued until the required number of weapons laid down by the officer prior to the beginning of the patrol were located. In a speech in the English House of Lords, Lord Moira sought to get the support of the peers for restrictions to be placed on the army units, telling their Lordships that: "Before my God and my country, I speak of what I myself have seen. I have seen in Ireland the most absurd as well as the most disgusting tyranny that any nation groaned under. I have seen troops set full of this prejudice, so that every inhabitant of that kingdom is a rebel to the British Government. The most wanton insults, the most cowardly oppression upon men of all ranks and conditions, in a part of the country as free from disturbances as the City of London. Thirty houses are sometimes burned in a single night, but from prudential motives, I wish to draw a veil over the more aggravated facts."[122] Lord Moira continued: "...these are not particular acts of cruelty, exercised by men abusing the power committed to them, but they form a part of our system...they are notorious"[123]

In vain Moira pleaded for a stop to be put to the outrages while also predicting that they would force the populace towards rebellion.

One incident in particular aroused public anger in Ulster and caused many Protestants to join the ranks of the United Irishmen. A well respected businessman from Carrickfergus, William Orr was found guilty before a packed jury and afterwards hanged for the crime of administering the oath of the United Irishmen to a soldier, on the testimony of the soldier alone. When Orr was sentenced to death, the soldier repented of his false accusation and swore on oath that he had perjured himself. However, the Lord Lieutenant, Lord Camden ordered that Mr. Orr's execution should nevertheless proceed. "Remember Orr" now became a watchword and recruiting slogan for the United Irishmen in Ulster.

## A Brief Setback for English Plans

In December of 1797, Sir Ralph Abercrombie was appointed Commander in Chief of the army in Ireland. The tactics of the government and the methods employed by the army, militia and yeomanry were anathema to him and shortly after his arrival in Ireland he wrote in a letter to his son which read in part "...the abuses of all kinds I find here can scarcely be believed or enumerated..."[124] Determined to do whatever he could to try and bring the army to heel, he issued orders in February 1798 which described the army as being "in a state of licentiousness which must render it formidable to everyone but the enemy"[125] He directed that the army must only act as aid to the civil power when requested to do so by a civil magistrate. He added: "(I) positively forbid the troops to act but in case of attack without my authority and the most positive orders are to be given to officers commanding for this purpose"[126]

As his orders flew directly in the face of government policy, and as he sought to calm the prevailing situation, the government council in Dublin Castle, encouraged by the Dublin Parliament, positively forbade Abercrombie's orders from being implemented. After serving less than four months in his post Abercrombie, hindered by the government in the fulfilment of his duty in every respect resigned in disgust in April 1798 and was replaced with General Lake whose actions in Ulster were exactly in line with government policy and which the government wished him to replicate nationally. The forces of the Crown now had carte blanche to hang, shoot, burn and terrorise at will.

Sir Ralph Abercrombie

## Religious Tensions within the leadership of the United Irishmen

The United Irishmen had always been predominantly Protestant in its leadership. Of its 162 leading members, two thirds were Protestant while the remaining third were Catholic. As the situation within the country grew gradually worse, and an element of desperation began to enter into the deliberations of the leaders, cracks began to appear in the leadership along religious lines – not along Protestant and Catholic lines but rather along the lines of those who publicly professed belief in God and those who did not. There was a distinct element within the leadership led by Arthur O'Connor who professed the godless atheism of the French republicans and this group were distinctly annoyed by those who laboured on the point of full freedom for Catholics and the Catholic faith as part of the principles of the society. O'Connor disliked the Catholic leaders in the organisation on account of their public professions of faith and even towards Thomas Emmett, who was a God fearing Protestant, he entertained a positive enmity on account of his religious conviction. As the country edged towards a climax, the leadership of the United Irishmen not only had traitors and spies within its ranks, but even among those who were not compromised in this way there was a distinct lack of harmony and a good deal of personal enmity over the question of public Christianity.

## Fanning the Embers of Rebellion

Following Lake's appointment, the measures that he had employed in Ulster, now became nationwide as he effectively gave carte blanche to the army units to do as they pleased. Of the period which now followed, Lord Holland (Charles James Fox) wrote at the time: "The fact is incontrovertible that the people of Ireland were driven to resistance...by the free quarters and excesses of the soldiery, which were such as are not permitted in civilized warfare...trials, if they must so be called were carried on without number under martial law. It often happened that three officers composed the court and that of the three, two were under age and the third an officer of the yeomanry or militia, who had sworn in his Orange Lodge eternal hatred to the people over whom he was thus constituted a judge. Floggings, picketings and death were the usual sentences...many were sold at so much per head to the

Prussians. Other more illegal but not more horrible outrages were daily committed by the different corps under the command of government...Dr Dickson, Lord Bishop of Down assured me that he had seen families returning peaceably from Mass, assailed without provocation, by drunken troops and yeomanry, and the wives and daughters exposed to every species of indignity, brutality and outrage, from which neither his remonstrances nor those of other Protestant gentlemen could rescue them"..."[127]

Of the months before the rebellion Lord Castlereagh later admitted that: "measures were taken by the government to cause the premature explosion (of rebellion)"[128]

## The Bridge Street Raid

With the country in a state of turmoil, a meeting of the Leinster directory of the United Irishmen was planned for the morning of March 12th 1798. It was due to take place at the house of the Dublin draper Oliver Bond, at 13 Bridge Street. The time and place of the meeting had been betrayed to the authorities by one Thomas Reynolds, and as the meeting got underway the building was stormed by the police accompanied by Chief Justice Swan who held the warrant. In all fifteen members including two members of the directory were arrested. Reynolds, who was present at the meeting was not arrested and this fact later aroused the suspicion of the other members. Robert Graham, who was the delegate for Wexford, had been delayed on his way to the meeting and so escaped arrest. Other prominent members of the society who were not at the meeting were that same morning arrested at their homes including Thomas Emmett, the Society's Head and Chief Organiser.

Arthur O'Connor was already in custody in England, having already been arrested along with a priest named Fr. Quigley while they were on their way to France. O'Connor was returned to prison in Dublin but Fr. Quigley was put on trial for treason, found guilty and hanged using evidence so inconclusive that after the trial, Lord Chancellor Thurlow declared:"If ever a poor man was murdered, it was Quigley!"[129] The authorities had expected to find Lord Edward Fitzgerald, the Society's military leader at the Bridge St. meeting but he had been tipped off regarding the round up and had avoided arrest. He was now on the run in Dublin with a price of £1,000 on his head and was staying at a safe house belonging to a Mrs. Dillon who lived beside the canal at Portobello. From this safe house he regularly travelled to other safe houses to spend a night before retracing his steps to Portobello.

With all the other main leaders either incarcerated or abroad, Fitzgerald was now more or less forced to act alone. Of those leaders who remained at large, some advised Fitzgerald that an immediate rebellion should be launched whilst others advised that it was better to wait until a French landing should take place, as even though the society's was numerically strong it was badly armed and compromised. At length, Fitzgerald, perhaps influenced by the latin motto of his friend General Hoche: "Facta - Non verba!"[1] decided that it would be folly to wait any longer and that a rebellion should be launched before the end of May.

## The Death of Lord Edward Fitzgerald

On the evening of May 17th, Fitzgerald attended a meeting of the Dublin Committee of the United Irishmen at the house of Francis Magan on Usher's Island, afterwards staying there until the evening of the 18th when he moved to another safe house. Magan, a trusted member of the Dublin Committee was one of those government informers which riddled the

---

[1] "Actions – Not words!"

Society. Unwilling to see Fitzgerald arrested at his own house, Magan informed the authorities that Fitzgerald was moving to the house of Nicholas Murphy at 153 Thomas St.

Fitzgerald was suffering from a heavy cold and around 7pm the following evening was lying on a bed in the attic of Murphy's house. Murphy had just entered the room and the two were conversing when suddenly Justice Swan, pistol in hand and accompanied by a plain clothes soldier, burst into the room. Swan shouted at Fitzgerald "You are my prisoner!" at which Lord Edward jumped up and producing a dagger ran at Swan while the soldier came to grips with Murphy. Swan fired his pistol, but missed, and was injured in the hand by Lord Edward's dagger. Swan's shouting brought a third soldier into the room, a Yeoman Captain called Ryan. Ryan jumped on Fitzgerald, but Fitzgerald wounded him with his dagger (a wound from which he later died). By this time Swan had summoned more soldiers who now entered the room and Fitzgerald was shot in the arm and restrained. As one of the soldiers was tying his hands, he wounded him very severely with his sword in the back of the neck. By the time the authorities were ushering Fitzgerald out of the building, a crowd had gathered, as had other military reinforcements. A fight ensued as the crowd attempted to rescue Fitzgerald, but the soldiers overpowered them and he was brought to Dublin Castle for questioning and from there to the nearby Newgate

Edward Fitzgerald

Prison where he died on June 4th after the wound to his neck became infected.

With his arrest, the organisation of the rebellion was now deprived of a man of military skill and proven heroism in battle who commanded not only the loyalty and respect of the organisations leaders but also of its rank and file.[1]

## The Rebellion

### The Rising is launched

Although deprived of all their prominent leaders, it was decided by those leaders still at large that the rising would nevertheless go ahead on May 23rd both in Dublin and in the country at large. On that day all mail coaches leaving urban centres were to be held up. When the mail coaches failed to arrive, this was to be the signal to the country units of The United Irishmen that the revolution had started. However by May 21st the government were in full possession of the details of the plan thanks to a planted agent named Captain John Warneford Armstrong who had over the preceding months wormed his way in the Society and in particular the confidence of the brothers, John and Henry Sheares, who since the Bond St. Raid had become members of the Directory. As a trusted confidant of the brothers and promising them that the men of Loughlinstown Army Barracks were in complete support of the aims of the United Irishmen, the brothers divulged to him all the information. By the 23rd, all loyalists in the city had been

---

[1] In the book "The Earls of Kildare and their Ancestors" Edward Fitzgerald is described as: "...about five feet seven inches in height. He had a very interesting countenance, beautiful arched eyebrows, fine grey eyes, handsome nose, high forehead and thick dark coloured hair...he was as playful and humble as a child, as mild and timid as a lady, and when necessary as brave as a lion." In his history of the United Irishmen, Madden describes him as "a sincere and ardent Christian".

informed and Dublin bristled with armed men as all members of the militia turned out for work, armed and in their uniforms. However, the city remained quiet. On the night of the 23rd numbers of the gas lamplighters who were members of the United Irishmen did not turn up for work and the upper classes were dismayed to find the city in darkness fearing that they would be killed in their houses. Some of these lamplighters were later arrested and hanged from Dublin's lampposts.

While the city escaped, the country areas outside the capital did not. At Santry there was a massacre as a large group of United Irishmen preparing to march into Dublin were attacked by a group of Yeomen led by Lord Roden. The following day scores of the dead were brought in Dublin on carts and displayed as a spectacle for the populace in the yard of Dublin Castle, while prisoners were hanged from the scaffolding at Carlisle Bridge and on lampposts.

Due to the premature and rushed nature of the rising, only those counties of Leinster in the immediate vicinity of the capital rose up and prepared to seize control in local towns, while in the countryside around the capital, the United Irishmen prepared to march on Dublin. Like proverbial lambs to the slaughter they were ill equipped, being without any sort of modern military equipment and without proper leadership and training. They now had to contend with the tender mercies of army units such as the North Cork Militia, the Armagh Militia, the German Hompesch Dragoons (a unit of German mercenaries in the service of George III) and the British Army unit called "The Ancient Britons" under the command of Sir Watkins William Wynn.

## The Rising in Leinster excluding Wexford
Everywhere the loyalist Yeomanry, militia and army conducted the repression of the rising with unimaginable

savagery and slaughter reminiscent of Drogheda and Wexford at the hands of Cromwell.

In Naas, the military under the command of Lord Gosford lost around thirty men to the rebels in an engagement in the town. Once they had gained the upper hand everyone who came within their grasp whether United Irishman or bystander suffered the same fate – hanging. The cabins were set alight and those who emerged to escape the flames nevertheless met their end.

In other parts of the county, the United Irishmen briefly gained the upper hand. In Prosperous Co. Kildare where the notorious Captain Swayne and a unit of the North Cork Militia had subjected the populace to numerous outrages including cabin burnings and pitch capping, the United Irishmen surrounded their barracks and set it on fire. Anyone escaping the flames was piked. Dr. Esmonde of the Salins Yeomanry was compelled by the United Irishmen to join in this attack for which he was later hanged from Carlisle Bridge. At Rathangan and Kilcullen the rebels also gained the upper hand but when the army returned, the rebels were repulsed and slaughtered with anyone unfortunate enough to be taken prisoner being hanged.

Outside Carlow town, a large number of rebels formed up on the lawn of the home of Sir Edward Crosbie intent on seizing the town. As they entered the town and proceeded into its centre they were met by a hail of musket fire. Having no answer to this, they took refuge in the thatched cabins of the peasants. The army stormed forward and set the thatches of around eighty houses alight. Hundreds of rebels were either killed in the flames or emerged to a fusillade of musket fire. All those taken prisoner whether rebel or not were quickly hanged, along with Sir Edward Crosbie who had nothing whatsoever to do with the United Irishmen.

Disaster followed disaster for the rebels and in Kildare a group of around two thousand rebels assembled on the Hill of Allen after which they successfully negotiated an honourable surrender with General Dundas whereby they were allowed to return home without molestation after surrendering their weapons. In imitation of this a further group of around 350 rebels, realising that their cause was hopeless assembled on the Curragh of Kildare hoping to surrender honourably to General Duffe who was making his way towards Kildare from Limerick. However Duffe would not entertain the rebels bid to surrender and instead ordered his men to attack and kill them all.

In Meath, a rebel encampment consisting of around 3,000 rebels had sprung up on the Hill of Tara preparatory to any attack by the rebels on the county town of Navan. However, before the rebels had a chance to launch any assault of their own, they were instead attacked by a force of around 400 yeomanry and militia supported by a six pounder artillery gun. In spite of being inadequately armed the rebels held their own for a period, at one stage almost capturing the six pounder, before the superior firepower of the enemy won the day. Pikes were no match for muskets and artillery firing grapeshot[1] and the rebels were forced to retreat from the hillside leaving up to one third of their number behind either dead or wounded. Masters of the battlefield the English closed in. No prisoners were taken and all the wounded were killed. That evening the United Irishmen returned to claim their dead, only to find that every last one of their slain had been disembowelled.

---

[1] Grapeshot – A projectile fired by an artillery cannon containing dozens of shrapnel bombs which look like grapes. The effect is similar to that of a cannon firing a huge shotgun cartridge. The modern equivalent is referred to as a cluster bomb.

## Wexford before the Rebellion
### The Arrival of the North Cork Militia
In the parish of Kilcormac (Boolavogue) in Co. Wexford, Fr. John Murphy[1] was, like his Bishop and many of his brother priests concerned with the rise of The United Irishmen. They considered the movement dangerous to the faith of their parishioners because of its protestant origins and its links to the French anti Catholic and Masonic revolution that had begun in Paris in 1789. While in no way unsympathetic to the movement's nationalist aspirations, Fr. Murphy knew only too well the precarious position the Catholic Church in Ireland was in at this time of heightened tension and he agreed with Bishop Caulfield as he applied Christ's words to the situation during a meeting of diocesan priests; "Render unto Caesar the things that are Caesar's and to God the things that are God's"

The United Irishmen had flourished among Wexford's Catholics despite clerical warnings. The county was home to a large number of members, including a good number of liberal minded protestant landlords and merchants who were for the most part, the organisations leaders in the county.

At Easter 1798 in order to try and avert the introduction of "special measures" by the military authorities (already introduced in other parts of the country) Bishop Caulfield and his clergy decided to do all they could to avoid their introduction including encouraging their parishioners to sign an address which would be given to the Lord Lieutenant, declaring their "attachment to his most sacred majesty King George the Third". Fr. Murphy went even further and

---

[1] "...a genius of the first order; an orator whose angelic soul spoke through every word and every look; an accomplished preacher of the word of God; an apostle in whose short life shone forth all the virtues." – Cardinal Moran of Sydney on Fr. John Murphy.

declared he would refuse the sacraments to any United Irishman who would not renounce the secret oaths he had taken.

The actions of the clergy were to no avail as the government had come into possession of a note from Lord Edward Fitzgerald that named Wexford as a possible landing ground for French troops and the letter from the Catholics of Wexford promising loyalty to Crown were disregarded. On April 27th martial law was declared in Wexford at a joint meeting of magistrates in Gorey. Just a few days before at a military parade, Hunter Gowan, the Commander of the Gorey Yeomen, had led his men through the streets holding his sword on which a human finger was impaled. That evening at dinner Gowan used the "Croppy Finger" to stir a bowl of punch.

After martial law was declared in Wexford, additional forces in the form of the North Cork Militia, with the Earl of Kingsborough commanding, were dispatched to supplement the local Wexford Yeomanry. The officers of the militia were all landed gentry and Orangemen, while the enlisted men were mainly composed of Protestants along with some Catholics. When the North Corks arrived, they were accompanied by two British army foreign regiments, the Hessian Cavalry and the Hompesch Dragoons, the latter proving themselves particularly obnoxious in the weeks that followed.

A Reign of Terror – Wexford Goaded into Rebellion

The arrival of the North Corks in Wexford signalled the commencement of an orgy of violence against the population which according to one account of the time could not be imagined by any person who did not experience it. Anyone was fair game, everyone was deemed guilty of either membership of or sympathy with the Society of the United Irishmen and with possession of information regarding their activities.

In order to persuade "suspects" to divulge information, the primary methods used were flogging with the "cat o' nine tails" to the extent that bones and even internal organs were often exposed. Hanging until the suspect lost consciousness (half hanging) and then repeating the procedure when the suspect had recovered a little was also common. However in many cases the suspect would never regain consciousness.[1] Conical paper or linen caps were made and filled with heated tar, and then rammed onto the suspect's head. Tar dripping down the face often rendered the suspect blind. Once set, the cap could only be removed by bringing the scalp with it, or the suspect could be released with the pitchcap in place, the pitchcap having been set on fire to provide entertainment for the soldiers as he danced in agony while trying to remove it. A soldier of the North Corks earned for himself the nickname "Tom the Devil" as after having sheared the suspect's hair with shears (often cutting the ears off in the process) he would then put gunpowder on the shorn head and set it alight.

The soldiers might arrive at a small tenant holding and perform one or all of the above on the menfolk of the house. One Yeoman Commander, Hamilton Jacob, never left Enniscorthy for a patrol without an executioner accompanying him. Blacksmiths as manufacturers of pikes were particularly sought after as they were suspected of possessing information regarding individuals who had requested their manufacture. Anyone with a cropped haircut, after the French fashion of the

---

[1] In carrying out this procedure, one officer, Edward Heppenstall, (of the Wicklow Militia) gained notoriety as far back as 1796 when his unit was based in Westmeath. After placing the noose around the neck of the suspect, he preferred to then drag the suspect by the rope, preferably until life was extinguished which earned him the nickname "The Walking Gallows". In command of his unit which roamed the countryside at will, Heppenstall acted as Judge, Jury, Executioner and Gallows.

time, was liable to have it "capped". (The United Irishmen were commonly referred to as "croppies")

Women were not exempt to the terror, and many were violated. The wearing of anything green before the North Corks was like the proverbial red rag to a bull and many a lady whether loyalist or not suffered ignominy or worse if anything green was seen among her garments.

As the terror progressed, the violence of the army increased. Houses were burned and people working in the fields were targeted and fired upon. As the army became more ruthless, the people became fearful of a repeat of the Armagh Outrages and so got into the habit of avoiding their homes as much as possible and found it necessary to sleep in the fields.

In the midst of all this terror, Fr. Murphy still sought to hold back the excesses of the Crown Forces and demanded of his parishioners that they surrender all weapons in order that they might be given a ticket of safe passage for doing so. Despite this the excesses continued unabated and after a month of this living nightmare, things got worse. On May 26 news broke that 28 prisoners had been executed in Carnew, on the Wexford / Wicklow border as a warning to the locals against attempting a rising. The local Protestant Rector, the Rev. Cope who was also a magistrate, had been in command of the proceedings. Word also filtered through that 34 yeomen had been executed as suspected rebels in Dunlavin, Co. Wicklow without any form of trial.

By this stage, the surrender of a pike to the authorities was a guarantee of death.

## The Rising in Wexford
<u>"Better for us to die like men than to be butchered like dogs"</u>
On the evening of May 26th, Fr. John Murphy had organised a neighbourhood watch in his parish, having received word that a night raid by the Yeomen was likely. As he was making his

rounds by moonlight with a group of local men, they ran into a group of the local Camolin Yeoman Cavalry who had just torched a nearby farmhouse and now proceeded to open fire on Fr. Murphy and his group. In the ensuing fight the Yeoman Commander, Bookey, was killed along with a greatly reviled local Yeoman called Donovan.

Fr. John Murphy

Realising that he and the parishioners who accompanied him were now little better than dead men following the killing of the local commander in his parish, Fr. Murphy immediately resolved to do what he could against the regime of terror, telling his men that "It would be better for us to die like men, than to be butchered like dogs in a ditch."[130]

### The Days of Victory

"O'Rourke the blacksmith forged the pike, and
better ne'er was made,
The ashen handle eight feet long, and four
feet long the blade.
Brave Father Murphy blessed it, one night by
Slaney side,
And Bryan Bawn caressed it, as a lover
Would his bride." Anon.

After the fight with the Yeomen, Fr. Murphy dispatched riders far and wide to rouse the countryside to action. Raids took place on the homes of loyalists in an attempt to get weapons, and everyone who was willing to fight was told to bring whatever weapons they had to the hill outside Oulart village. Those joining the rebels the following morning brought word that Fr. Murphy's chapel[I] had been burnt to the ground by yeomen, bringing a half burnt chasuble[II] with them as proof. The chasuble was now affixed to poles and thereafter used as a banner by the ad hoc group of rebels. By the following afternoon around 1,000 men had assembled with their families on the hillside at Oulart when Redcoats were spotted in the distance. It was the dreaded North Cork Militia with local yeomanry in support. Along with local yeoman Sergeant turned rebel, Edward Roche, Fr. Murphy prepared the men for battle. Thanks to high ditches on the lane up the hill, along with the ruse of placing hats on sticks the Redcoats discharged their weapons prematurely. Before they had time to reload a charge of rebel pikemen took militia and yeomen by surprise. Once their blood was up, and with the weeks of torment fresh in their memory, none that the pikemen could lay hands on survived. The rebels lost six men to the redcoats 100. The following days saw the rebels capture Enniscorthy after savage fighting and then Wexford town, which had been abandoned by the Redcoats. In Enniscorthy, the pikemen had won the day after Fr. Murphy ordered that a herd of cattle be driven into the enemy ranks ahead of the pikemen. The cattle were half mad with the noise of battle raging around them and knocked down the redcoats like ninepins after which they were then slain by the pikemen.

---

[I] During the rising in Wexford, a total of 34 Catholic chapels were burnt to the ground in Wexford County by Crown Forces. Only one Protestant church (Old Ross) was torched by either the insurgents or camp followers.

[II] Chasuble – the outer vestment worn by the priest during mass.

As the rebels contemplated their next move from their encampment outside Wexford town a contingent of the Meath Militia from Duncannon Fort determined to attack the rebel camp at "The Three Rocks" overlooking Wexford. Despite the fact that the militiamen were far better armed than the rebels their numbers were far too small and they were quickly overwhelmed by the rebels. In the exchange 70 militiamen were killed and three howitzers were captured.

By May's end the number of rebels had swollen to almost 15,000. Fr. Murphy, now a general in the rebel army, headed north towards Gorey with his division, but he was not in overall command of the ad hoc army. He shared rank with other notables in the United Irishmen such as Edward Roche, Edward Fitzgerald, John Hay and Fr. Michael Murphy. This shared leadership was to seriously hamper operations, as whenever an important decision had to be arrived at, unanimity was necessary. As Fr. Murphy headed towards Gorey other divisions moved West and South in an effort to expand their area of operations while linking up with other rebels. However in the days that followed there was to be limited success for the rebel cause. On June 2$^{nd}$ part of Fr. Murphy's division which had attacked Ballycarnew were defeated while on Sunday June 3$^{rd}$ the rebel division which had tried to break through to the west returned, having been defeated at Bunclody. After capturing the town they have stopped to celebrate and regroup instead of pursuing the enemy. Meanwhile the redcoats had quickly regrouped and attacked, successfully recapturing the town.

Away from these local action, the British General, Loftus, was heading south from Gorey with 1500 men and artillery in order to surround Fr. Murphy's division. On receiving word of this on June 4$^{th}$ from his scouts Fr. Murphy decided to attack at once towards Gorey so as not to allow his division to be in danger of encirclement. In doing this he ran into part of

Loftus's division that was led by Colonel Walpole, at Tubberneering Rock.

## The Battle of Tubberneering Rock

As Fr. Murphy advanced towards Gorey, Walpole's men were already drawn up for battle and artillery was soon raining down on the rebels advance party. Despite heavy losses the rebels managed to take cover along a ditch and were now in a position to take the enemy under fire, allowing the pikemen, who were led by Fr. Murphy to go forward. A furious battle ensued with neither side giving any quarter. A group of rebels led by Myles Byrne outflanked the main battle and overran the redcoat artillery position. Byrne and his men now threatened the redcoated artillery-men with instant death unless they fired the artillery at the ranks of the redcoats. Prodded by pikes they complied.

The losses from the artillery fire and the death of Col. Walpole who had been killed by a musket shot through the head, turned the tide of battle in the rebels favour, and before long the redcoats were retreating headlong, pursued by pikemen. Having successfully escaped Walpole's army the rebels made all possible speed to reach Gorey, knowing that as soon as news of their victory got there, the redcoats would start executing rebel prisoners who were being held in the Market House. When the pikemen arrived in Gorey, the executions were just getting under way with redcoats firing through the prison windows at the rebel prisoners inside.

Meanwhile Gen. Loftus was walking through the graveyard that was the battlefield at Tubberneering. Fearing the same fate that had overtaken Col. Walpole he determined to retreat and abandon Gorey and Arklow until a more powerful force could be brought to bear against the rebels.

## New Ross

On June 5th the rebel division commanded by Bagenal Harvey headed south and attacked the town of New Ross. After seven hours of hard fighting the town seemed to be in rebel hands. The resistance of the Redcoats was confined to only a fraction of the town, when the Redcoat General Johnson, rallied his troops and attacked back into the town taking the rebels by surprise, snatching victory from the jaws of defeat. Like Bunclody, some days previously many rebels had started celebrating their victory with alcohol while others were asleep, exhausted from a hard day's fighting. In the bloodbath that followed almost 3,000 rebels were killed and the town recaptured. No prisoners were taken and 100 rebels who were in a wooden building serving as a hospital were burnt alive when the hospital was torched by Crown Forces.

The remaining rebels retreated to their camp outside the town that was located at a large farmhouse at Scullabogue. They were horrified to find that in their absence a mob of camp followers and hangers-on who had steered clear of the fighting had set fire to a barn that had contained over 100 loyalist prisoners in revenge for the atrocities of the Redcoats. Only two prisoners managed to escape this awful death.

The rebel General, Thomas Cloney who fought in the Battle of New Ross later wrote that "...the wretches who burned Scullabogue Barn did not at least profane the sacred name of justice by alleging that they were offering her a propitiatory sacrifice. The highly criminal and atrocious immolation of the victims at Scullabogue was, by no means premeditated by the guard left in charge of the prisoners; it was excited and promoted by the cowardly ruffians who ran away from the Ross battle and conveyed the intelligence that was too true, that several wounded men had been burned in a house in Ross by the military"[131]

Following the disaster at New Ross, Bagenal Harvey was reassigned as Commander of the Town of Enniscorthy, while the overall command of his group fell on the shoulders of Fr. Phillip Roche, who placed Edward Roche in military command.

Meanwhile Fr. Murphy's division rested far too long on the laurels won at Tubberneering while debating their next move. When word reached them that Arklow had been reoccupied and that Fr. Michael Murphy[1] had been killed, they decided to attack at once but Fr. Murphy who disagreed with the move declined to take part, The rebels attacking Arklow met with little success and their attacks were repulsed by the superior firepower of the Crown forces who by now seemed to have the measure of the strengths and weaknesses of their untrained adversaries.

## Massacre of Crown Prisoners in Wexford Town

Defeated everywhere, the rebels retreated to Vinegar Hill outside Enniscorthy where they were determined to make their last stand. Around 15,000 Irishmen gathered there, where atop the hill Fr. Murphy did his best to organise the defence.

While the Irish prepared for battle in Enniscorthy, a massacre of Crown prisoners took place in Wexford town. A ship's captain named Dixon who was locally renowned for his cruelty took charge of a drunken mob and proceeded to the town jail which held many crown officers (belonging to the North Corks and various other units and Yeomanry formations), the

---

[1] The Protestant clergyman, the Rev. Mr. Gordon of Killegny, Wexford, who was at the very centre of the horrors during the rebellion later wrote down his memories of the rebellion. Regarding the fate of the remains of Fr. Michael Murphy he reported: "...some soldiers of the ancient British regiment cut open the body of Fr. Michael Murphy, after the battle of Arklow, took out his heart, roasted his body and oiled their boots with the grease which dripped from it" (History of the Rebellion, p212)

most senior there being Lord Kingsborough (who was not harmed).

After forcing an entry into the prison, the rabble took control of it and proceeded to remove the prisoners around ten at a time to the bridge at the mouth of the Slaney where Dixon who had appointed himself as judge now proceeded to hold mock trials. After the first ten had been murdered, the second ten were sent for. Finally, when around 35 people had been killed, a local priest named Fr. Corrin who had heard what was happening went to the bridge where he remonstrated with the crowd and after praying aloud that God might forgive them their heinous deed finally persuaded them to desist after which the prisoners on the bridge were returned to the prison.

## Vinegar Hill – The End of the Rebellion in Wexford

By June 20th General Lake and his armies were closing in around Vinegar Hill. Lake was in overall command of four armies totalling around 20,000 men that were commanded by Generals Moore, Loftus, Duffe and Needham. Lake's plan was to have the hill completely surrounded by the early hours of June 21st, and to launch his attack at 7am. After his artillery had done its work, the hill was to be overrun and the rebels annihilated.

As the attack got underway Lake's artillery, which was firing grapeshot, took a heavy toll of the rebels, and in spite of charging the Redcoat line several times the pikemen failed to break through. For an hour and a half the Irish line held in spite of the murderous artillery. As the redcoats advanced firing their muskets, a massacre loomed. However, all was not lost. For some unexplained reason General Needham had been delayed, leaving a gap in the English line which was unseen by the other commanders. Facing defeat and death many rebels including Fr. Murphy escaped through "Needham's Gap" leaving behind their supplies. One group joined the rebels in the Wicklow Mountains while another group with Fr. Murphy headed west towards Carlow, determined to continue the insurgency there.

After the English victory at Vinegar Hill, terrible deeds were perpetrated by the victorious soldiers in Enniscorthy. Within the town, any person believed to be a rebel straggler was killed in cold blood. The soldiers also discovered a building used by the rebels as a hospital and this was set ablaze with the sick and wounded being consumed by the flames.[1]

The people of Wexford town were also subject to atrocity once the rebels had departed. In spite of the fact that an agreement had been reached between representatives of the townspeople and Lord Kingsborough that no innocent civilian would be harmed, General Lake refused to honour the agreement unless the rebel leaders were handed over to him. When the army arrived many people were murdered and the worst deeds of the reign of terror were repeated both within and outside the town. All the male patients in Wexford hospital were also killed so that any wounded rebels among them would die. In the days that followed some of the rebel leaders including Bagenal Harvey, and Fr. Philip Roche were tracked down and hanged as was the aged Cornelius Grogan of Johnstown Castle who had been forced by the rebels to act as a Commissioner for them.

## Mass Murder in Kilcumney, Carlow

As Fr. Murphy continued with his group into Carlow, he was determined that the rebellion should continue but his hopes were illusory. Many of his men, now realising that further

---

[1] The Rev. Mr Gordon, who was the Rector of Killegny outside Wexford reported that he was told by a surgeon that the hospital was set on fire accidentally by lit musket wadding while the troops were executing the wounded United Irishmen in their beds. (Historica of the Insurrection – Hay, Cloney and Gordon)

resistance was pointless, had already departed his group, while others who had joined Fr. Murphy (coal miners from Castlecomer) had quickly abandoned him after stealing the weapons and gunpowder that remained.

On the morning of June 26, Crown forces under the command of Sir Charles Asgill were in the process of surrounding Fr. Murphy's camp at Kilcumney Hill, when the rebel group managed to break through the cordon. After this the rebels that remained intended to make their way to the mountains of Wicklow[1] but Fr. Murphy and his bodyguard James Gallagher became separated from the main group in the early morning fog.

Sir Charles Asgill

Meanwhile in Kilcumney, Co. Carlow, Sir Charles Asgill and his men (Downshire and Wicklow Militia, Queens County Yeomanry and Leighlinbridge Yeomanry) found that Fr. Murphy and his men had evaded them. They now embarked on an orgy of murder and destruction in the parish of Borris during which around 150 innocent people were murdered in cold blood. Those who were murdered had their houses robbed and then torched. Around 500 children were made orphans by their actions. As

---

[1] This small party became worthy successors of the Raparees of a century earlier. They were led by the "brave and true" Michel Dwyer, whose exploits challenged the authority of the Crown Forces until he was finally captured in December 1803, after which he was transported to the penal colony at Botany Bay, dying there in 1826.

the atrocities were being carried out, a regiment of the King's Cavalry were following behind Asgill's army but did nothing to prevent the atrocities.

## The Death of Fr. Murphy

Alone with James Gallagher, Fr. Murphy determined to make his way to the Wicklow mountains by a circuitous route and so hopefully evade those Crown forces who were searching for rebel fugitives. At various stops along his planned route, the two men who were travelling on horseback received hospitality and rest, including at the home of Protestant farmers; George and Anne Keppel. After offering Mass for the last time at the home of the Jordans of Coolnasneachta, Fr. Murphy and James Gallagher continued to the south west of Tullow where they sought refuge with the O'Tooles during those hours of daylight of July 2$^{nd}$ when it was too dangerous to continue. As the men slept in a hay loft, the O'Tooles were working on the land saving hay with two horses in halter. Suddenly Yeomen approached them and demanded the two horses for the army. In an outburst of anger, Mrs. O'Toole shouted at the Yeomen "Why not take the strangers' horses that are in the yard over there?" On further investigation the Yeomen found two horses tied in the yard with their horseshoes nailed on back to front.

Dead to the world with exhaustion, Fr. Murphy and James Gallagher were roused by the Yeomen.and unceremoniously brought to Tullow and the headquarters of General Duff.

In Tullow, around 20 officers including General Duff assembled to question the two men. When they were searched nothing was found on Gallagher but on Fr. Murphy they found a stole, a small crucifix, a vial for holy oils and a pyx.[1] As it

---

[1] Pyx – a sacred vessel in the form of a small metallic box lined with gold, used for the transportation of the Blessed Sacrament for administering to the sick and dying.

was obvious that Fr. Murphy was a priest, he was immediately subjected to insults and jibes by Major Hall who had been appointed as the chief interrogator. The two men were then subjected to repeated questioning but neither man would answer. As they would not offer any defence they were pronounced as rebels and handed over to the Yeomen to be put to death.

Delivered into the hands of the Yeomen, Fr Murphy and James Gallagher were brought to the Market Square of Tullow. Gallagher was the first to die. After being tied to the whipping post he was flogged and then questioned but still refused to talk. After being half hanged and revived he again refused to talk. Once more he was hanged, and this time he was left to die.

After James Gallagher was dead, the Yeomen proceeded to flog Fr. Murphy with five hundred lashes[132] but he refused to cry out or answer any questions. Once the five hundred lashes had been administered, the yeomen were infuriated by the fact that Fr. Murphy still lived. They immediately hanged him until he was dead after which his body was burned in a barrel of pitch in front of the house of a Catholic family, the Callaghans. When his body was set alight, the yeomen entered the Callaghans house and opened all the windows so that the family could "enjoy the smell of a roasted priest".

Fr. Murphy's corpse was later beheaded and his head carried in procession by the yeomen to the Sessions House where it was impaled.[I] It was finally removed after the repeated protests of a local Protestant woman and laid to rest in Mallawn graveyard with the rest of his remains.

---

[I] Fr. Murphy died without the Yeomen knowing who he was. The venom and hatred they directed towards him was due to his being a Catholic priest. Their treatment of him ties in with the testimony of Lord Cornwallis (below).

## The Rebellion in Ulster
### Henry Joy McCracken and the Battle of Antrim Town
As with other parts of the country, in Ulster the organisation and planning for a rebellion was seriously compromised owing to the large number of spies and infiltrators that pervaded the United Irishmen. The net result was that the rebellion in Ulster was not only delayed but was small in size and was confined to the east and south east of the province.

On June 7th, a large group of around 4,000, insurgents, (which included many members of the "Catholic Defenders") under the command of the youthful Presbyterian, Henry Joy McCracken, attacked Antrim Town where a meeting of magistrates was taking place. After an hours fighting, the Crown Forces retired from the town in order to regroup while the rebels prepared the town's defences for the military's return. It wasn't long before the Crown Forces reappeared with large reinforcements from the nearby army base at Lisburn

Henry Joy McCracken

and after offering stiff resistance, the United Irishmen were forced to abandon the town. Following the days fighting and the overwhelming strength of the military, the majority of McCracken's men returned to their homes. Along with around 50 more stalwart comrades, McCracken fled up Mount Slemish in order to await developments and hopefully effect an escape. He remained at liberty until the beginning of July when he was captured by Crown Forces and brought to Belfast. In short order he was brought before the magistrates, tried and sentenced to death, being hanged on July 17th.

## The Rising in north Down

In north Down, the rebellion was much larger than that which took place in Antrim. The local leader of the United Irishmen was a man of Scottish descent, Henry Munro, a linen trader who after assembling his army at Saintfield on June 7th successfully repulsed an attacking Crown Forces cavalry unit. From there he led his men to Ballynahinch, setting up encampment on Windmill Hill outside the town where he awaited developments.

On June 12th a sizeable army of Crown Forces, both militia (from Monaghan) and English regulars (Argyleshires) converged on Munro's position and the town of Ballinahinch. After occupying the town they spent the evening on the rampage. While the army were in Ballinahinch, Munro's men could hear their drunken looting and burning but Munro refused to launch a night attack, saying that it would be un-gentlemanly. His misplaced chivalry caused anger among his men that the advantage was not taken and a large numbers of his men departed.

On Windmill Hill, Munro had skilfully emplaced his men and few artillery pieces to cause maximum damage to the enemy. A prolonged engagement followed the next day after which Munro successfully entered the town and looked like recapturing it. The rebels had almost won the day, when panic spread after it was falsely reported after bugle blowing was heard that the Crown Forces were preparing for a massed charge. In an instant, Munro's men started falling back. Their retreat quickly turned into a panicked and disorderly rout which Munro or his officers were unable to stop. Having gained the upper hand the English were quick to capitalise on it. Munro was pursued and surrounded again at Ednavaddy, but by this time the majority of his men had either been slaughtered or had abandoned him. The few that were left agreed to surrender but Munro escaped through the cordon to the mountains along with a soldier named Kane. Early on June 15th, after apparently being betrayed, Munro and Kane were surrounded. Munro was removed to Lisburn and immediately tried by court martial. After being found guilty he was brought to his own house where a gallows had been set up outside his door and hanged. His wife and sisters were forced to watch his execution, but Munro remained calm. After having prayed, he uttered his final words: "Tell my country I deserved better of it"

When the execution was over, his house and property were completely destroyed by the soldiers.

## The Testimony of Lord Cornwallis

"If a priest is put to death the greatest joy is expressed by the whole company"

Appointed as the new Viceroy and Commander in Chief of the army, Lord Cornwallis arrived in Ireland on June 20th 1798. Three weeks later he wrote letters to the Duke of Portland and to General Ross concerning not only the rebellion but also the prevailing attitude of the Protestant Ascendancy to the Catholic Irish. His testimony is very important as it lays bare the bigotry and hatred of the ascendancy party for the native Irish and also dispels any accusations of exaggeration relating to the many accounts of the cruelty of Crown Forces during the period. His words, although powerful, are doubtless inadequate in expressing the actual state of things as felt by the people who suffered them. Cornwallis wrote: "The Irish militia are totally without discipline, contemptible before the enemy when any serious resistance is made to them, but ferocious and cruel in the extreme when any poor wretches, either with or without arms come within their power; in short murder appears to be their favourite pastime. The principal persons of this country, and the members of both houses of parliament, are in general, averse to all acts of clemency, and although they do not express and are much too heated to see the ultimate effects which their violence must produce, would pursue measures that could only terminate in the extirpation of the greater number of the inhabitants, and in the utter destruction of the country. The words papists and priests are forever in their mouths and by their unaccountable policy they would drive four fifths of the community into irreconcilable rebellion and in their warmth they lose sight of the real cause of the present mischief".

Lord Cornwallis

Describing the feelings of the Ascendancy he continues: "The minds of the people are now in a state that nothing but blood will satisfy them, and although they will not admit the term, their conversation and conduct point to no other mode of concluding this unhappy business than that of extermination. I am much afraid that any man in a brown coat who is found near the field of battle is butchered without discrimination. The violence of our friends and their folly in endeavouring to make it a religious war added to the ferocity of our troops who delight in murder and most powerfully counteract all plans of conciliation. We are engaged in a war of plunder and massacre. Our war is reduced to a predatory system in the mountains of Wicklow"

Cornwallis then refers to the horrors entailed when a district is declared as being under martial law and adds: "…but all this is trifling compared to the numberless murders that are hourly committed by our people without any process or examination whatever...The conversation of the principal persons of the country all tends to encourage this system of blood and the conversation at my table where you will suppose I do all I can to prevent it, always turns on hanging, shooting, burning etc. And if a priest has been put to death the greatest joy is expressed by the whole company. So much for Ireland and my wretched situation."[133]

## The Amnesty

By the beginning of July, the rebellion appeared to be over. What remained were a few disparate bands, such as that of Michael Dwyer, determined to carry on the fight, even in defeat and so follow the example of the Raparees. In much of the country, bands of Crown Forces continued to traverse the country engaging in murder and mayhem. In an effort to bring to an end the criminal actions of the Crown Forces, Cornwallis issued a proclamation on July 3rd that all insurgents who had not killed any member of the Crown Forces would be granted protection if they surrendered, but in spite of this the killing continued.

An amnesty was offered to some of the incarcerated leaders such as Arthur O'Connor, Thomas Emmett and Samuel Neilson. The terms of the truce were that if they divulged everything they knew regarding the insurrection under oath they would be allowed to go into exile. However many leaders such as the Sheares brothers were excluded. As negotiations between the prisoners' legal representatives and the government regarding their inclusion in the amnesty continued they were preparing for their hanging. At the last moment, the amnesty was extended to them but when the court representative arrived at the prison they were already dead. Another twenty leaders were imprisoned in Fort George in Scotland until 1802 when they were released following the signing of the Peace of Amiens.

## "The French are in the Bay"

### The French at Killala

It had often been Ireland's fate that in her centuries-old struggle against the English, that foreign aid arrived too late. This had occurred during the second siege of Limerick in 1691 when French aid arrived just after the Treaty of Limerick had been signed and also in 1601 when Spanish aid had arrived in Kinsale after the Gaelic insurgency had been extinguished in most of the country. 1798 was to be no different, for on the 22$^{nd}$ August, when the rebellion had been completely suppressed a French force of around 1,100 men under the command of General Humbert (who was accompanied by Wolfe Tone's brother Matthew and another United Irishman Bartholomew Teeling) landed in Killala Bay to the north of Ballina in Co. Mayo. This was no French invasion, but was rather in line with the policy of Napoleon Bonaparte of keeping the British on edge. Napoleon's policy was full of peril for the Irish who would gladly flock to this paltry force and take up arms in their support, only to be overwhelmed and cut down like dogs while the French received the correct treatment due to prisoners of war, followed by repatriation.

### "Ireland Forever"

After seizing control of Killala, the French hoisted a green flag on which was written the Gaelic motto "Erin go bragh" or "Ireland Forever" and declared that they had arrived to establish an Irish Republic. As the news of what the Irish imagined was the long awaited French landing spread around the area, many local men rallied to the flag and after receiving muskets and rudimentary training joined the ranks of the new arrivals.

After consolidating his position at Killala, Humbert moved inland and captured Ballina on the 25th August after overcoming stiff resistance. After Ballina, Humbert prepared to move against Castlebar.

Meanwhile, news of the French landing had reached Dublin. Vast numbers of Crown Forces were quickly mustered and immediately departed for the West of Ireland.. Around 7,000 men under the command of Generals Hunter and Moore marched to the line of the river Shannon, while General Lake proceeded into Connacht and onto Castlebar with about 6,000 men to reinforce the Connacht army of Major General Hutchinson.

## "An Ignominious Defeat for English Arms"

At dawn on August 27th 1798, the English commanders received word that the French and Irish were preparing to attack the town of Castlebar. The alarm was sounded and the English formed up with their artillery to the north of the town ready to defend against the imminent attack. The attacking force was a fraction of their size – around 800 French soldiers accompanied by 1,500 Irish recruits.

As the French and Irish formed up for the attack, the sizeable English artillery force opened up on them causing heavy casualties in their ranks. Having no answer to this weapon, General Humbert decided to call off the attack and retreat back towards Ballina in the hope that a more favourable opportunity might arise. In order that the retreat would not turn into a rout, Humbert ordered General Surrazin to conduct a spoiling attack against the British flank in order to divert English attention and allow him safely retire with the bulk of his men.

When Sir Ralph Abercrombie described the Crown Forces as being "in a state of licentiousness which must render it formidable to everyone but the enemy" he had been forced to resign. Now his prophecy came to pass. When Surrazin launched his attack, panic seized the enemy ranks and the Crown Forces immediately retreated in the expectation that the French were trying to turn their flank.

General Lake

Seeing this completely unexpected reaction, Humbert quickly changed his plan and immediately launched an all out attack against the English Line. Retreat quickly turned into rout and Lake's vastly superior force literally melted away. The French and Irish successfully captured the army's entire artillery, vast quantities of small arms and ten regimental colours. English losses were extremely high, but Lake would only admit to 350 men lost. The rout, termed "The Races at Castlebar" continued until General Lake had reached Tuam in Co. Galway.

Following this stunning victory, Humbert issued a decree on August 31st appointing John Moore as Republican President of the Government of Connacht.

## The Rising in Longford

"Oh then tell me Seán O'Farrell, Tell me why you hurry so?
Hush, a bhuachaill, hush and listen,
and his cheeks were all a-glow.
I bear orders from the Captain, get you ready quick and soon.
For the pikes must be together at the rising of the moon."

- John Keegan Casey

<u>Humbert's Odyssey</u>

Following news of the disaster at Castlebar, Cornwallis rushed to Athlone to take personal command of the situation. Humbert, who expected more help from France, stayed in Castlebar for a few days, but then decided he must act or face being surrounded. Encouraged by assurances of help from the United Irishmen, who promised him the people would rise wherever he marched, Humbert decided to go into Ulster. His march took him from Castlebar to Foxford and from there onto Swinford. Crossing into Sligo he went through Bellaghy and onto Tubbercurry, but at Colooney he encountered a force of British army regulars under the command of Colonel Vereker. After having defeated them, Humbert, feeling that Vereker's force must be an advance guard of a large army changed his plan and decided to go into the midlands instead via Granard where it had been reported to him that there was an uprising of the United Irishmen. As Humbert traversed Mayo, Sligo and then Leitrim, an English army of 20,000 men led by General Lake accompanied by

General Humbert

Colonel Crawford shadowed them, while Cornwallis was further back with 15,000 men determined to prevent any breakout into the midlands.

## Battle and Massacre at Ballinamuck

Humbert, doubtless aware that the odds of victory were very heavily stacked against him, nevertheless continued to elude his pursuers.

On September 7th, news reached him that the rebels who had been fighting in Longford and Westmeath, whom he had been on his way to help had been defeated and slaughtered at The Battle of Wilson's Hospital School, just outside Multyfarnham near Mullingar in Co. Westmeath while in a further battle at Granard lasting around 5 hours the United Irishmen had been defeated with the loss of 150 killed while a further 150 were hanged after the battle. General Humbert now decided that he could no longer achieve anything of significance, but he was not prepared to surrender.

After he had crossed the Leitrim border into Longford on the morning of September 8th 1798, his army took up positions at Shanmullagh, just outside the village of Ballinamuck. By this time Humbert's force consisted of around 850 French and 800 Irish. As Lake's army took up position, it became obvious to the French how impossible the odds were. After the first English attack, around two hundred of the French troops laid down their weapons, but in spite of this Humbert held the English at bay for almost an hour. When Lake launched a massed charge, Humbert had no choice but to surrender, and the English accepted the surrender of 96 French officers and 748 enlisted men.

Knowing that there would be little mercy for them, around 500 of Humbert's Irish auxiliaries tried to escape the battlefield but were pursued. Most of those captured were slaughtered while some were taken to Ballinalee, the location of a Crown Forces encampment. When the Crown Forces departed Ballinalee, every sizeable tree in the area had Irishmen hanging from them.

On the battlefield itself, around three hundred Irishmen had successfully surrendered along with the French after which the English extricated all the Irish from the ranks of the French and murdered them in cold blood.

A few prisoners, other than the French still remained alive – Tone, Teeling and a Galwayman, Richard Blake. Matthew Tone and Teeling were dispatched to Dublin for questioning and afterwards hanged while Blake, who had previously been a British Cavalry officer was hanged for treason.

In the weeks that followed, those Irish that had joined Humbert's army and escaped his final battle were ruthlessly pursued and swept up by Crown Forces along with anyone deemed to be of interest. A number of these men were taken to the courthouse at Carrick-on-Shannon for "trial". They were all made to draw lots in the form of pieces of paper from a hat. Those who drew a piece of paper with the word "death" were immediately hanged in the precincts of the courthouse.

## Killala – The Last Land Battle

After Humbert had surrendered, the town of Killala remained the last stronghold of the United Irishmen in the West. The rebels who were under the command of four French officers[1] were left in control of the town for a fortnight after Humbert's surrender, until finally on the 22nd a British army of around 1,200 heavily armed men with artillery, under the command of Major General Trench was reported to be approaching. Refugees from the surrounding area began streaming into the town, reporting that Trench's men were laying waste the entire countryside as they advanced.

---

[1] Boudet, Truc, Ponson and Charoust

On their approach to Killala, the English proceeded to envelop the town in a pincer movement and after a brief but furious battle on the Ballina side of the town, the English broke through to the town proper. On entering the town, all the United Irishmen who could be found were killed to the number of about 400. In their enthusiasm, Trench's men also killed civilians, including loyalists who had thus far not been harmed either by the French or the United Irishmen. Scouring parties were also sent into the surrounding areas in the hunt for fugitives. In the days that followed a further 75 people in Killala and 110 in Ballina were tried for treason with the sentences handed down being either hanging or transportation to Botany Bay.

## Tory Island - The Naval Battle of the 1798 Rebellion

As far as the French were concerned, the gallant Humbert was still holding his own against the English and deserved to be supported. With this in mind, a French fleet under the command of Admiral Bompart, carrying a larger French army consisting of around 2,200 men under the command of General Jean Hardy attempted to set sail from the port of Brest on September 20$^{th}$ but were blockaded by the British fleet and did not succeed in slipping through the blockade until October 6$^{th}$.

There were eleven ships in Bompart's fleet, the largest being the flagship "Hoche" which had 74 guns, along with 8 frigates and two schooners. When the fleet finally left Brest the English were fully aware of the French plans including the fact that Wolfe Tone was aboard the Hoche.[134] Plans were laid and a "reception committee" under Admiral Warren lay in wait for the French fleet.

Aboard the Hoche in the company of Admiral Bompart, Wolfe Tone was determined that if the expedition should not succeed he would not return to France but would rather remain in Ireland come what may.

When the French fleet sailed up the west coast, it was spotted by two English frigates. Shortly afterwards, Admiral Warren's fleet were on their track and Bompard, in an effort to avoid the English, detoured out into the Atlantic, before turning back for Donegal and his destination – Lough Swilly. With Warren in pursuit, the French fleet began to split up, so that by the time the Hoche was nearing the Donegal coast only three other ships were with her. Already damaged during the voyage, the Hoche seemed doomed as Warren closed in with his battle group. According to Wolfe Tone's son: "During six hours, she (the Hoche) sustained the whole fire of the fleet till her mast and rigging were swept away, her scuppers flowed with blood, her wounded filled the cockpit, her shattered ribs yawned at each new stroke, and let in five feet of water in the hold, her rudder was carried off, and she floated a dismantled wreck on the waters"[135]

## The Capture of Wolfe Tone

During the entire action, Wolfe Tone commanded one of the ship's gun batteries. Standing aloft, he remained at his post, seemingly impervious to the cascade of death being poured onto the ship. The Hoche's final moments arrived after she struck rocks and began to sink. One of the French Schooners managed to come alongside the foundering ship and Tone was offered a place on her, with her captain saying that he would bring Tone to France and freedom, but Tone refused.

After the Hoche surrendered, her officers including Tone were transferred by the English to the ship "Robuste" which was supposed to bring them to Portsmouth. High seas and storms prevented this however, and after being battered at sea for two weeks, the Robuste could not fulfil its original mission, and instead entered Lough Swilly, arriving at Buncrana at the end of October. Of the eleven French ships that had sailed for

Ireland, only three managed to return to their home port, the rest being either destroyed piecemeal or captured.

## The Trial and Death of Theobald Wolfe Tone
### "A Common Criminal"

When Tone stepped ashore at Buncrana on November 3rd, he made no effort to hide his identity. Among the members of the Crown Forces at the landing ground, there stood Colonel Sir George Hill of the militia, who was a magistrate and member of Parliament for "Londonderry". Tone had been a member of the bar with Hill and on exiting the boat immediately addressed him. Of the meeting Hill later wrote to Edward Cooke of Dublin Castle: "The first man who stepped out of the boat habited as an officer was T.W. Tone; he recognised and addressed me instantly with as much sang froid as you might expect from his character".[136] Viewed as an arch-traitor who had betrayed his king and country, Tone was brought to the headquarters of Major General Richard Lambart, the Earl of Cavan, where he remained for two days before being sent to Derry where he was imprisoned and chained like a common criminal in spite of the fact that he was a French citizen and had high rank in the French army. Assuming that there must be some mistake, Tone wrote to Lambart: "Under the circumstances I address myself to your Lordship as a man of honour and a soldier; and I do protest in the most precise and strongest manner against the indignity intended against the honour of the French army in my person; and I claim the rights of privilege as a prisoner of war"[137] to which Lambart replied: "I looked on you and you have proved yourself a traitor and rebel to your sovereign and native country, and as such you shall be treated by me...I lament as a man, the fate that awaits you".[138] General Hardy then interceded for Tone with Lambart, describing him as a: "...French citizen, member of the French army, prisoner of war, and for each of these reasons he should be treated with consideration and respect"[139] but was told: "Wolfe Tone is only known to his excellency (Lambart) as a traitor..."[140]

## The Trial

Still bound in irons, Tone was sent to Dublin and incarcerated in what he described as the "pestilential"[141] Provost Prison of the Royal Barracks located in the Dublin Castle complex. The general feeling was that he was destined to die but nevertheless the very able John Philpot Curran was engaged to represent him.

A week to the day after he had landed in Buncrana his trial at the Royal Barracks began. Dressed in full French uniform, with a large French tricolour cockade on his hat, Tone pleaded guilty to the charges of treason laid against him but begged to be allowed to account for his actions. The court acquiesced, and Tone read a prepared statement which included in part: "The great object of my life has been the independence of my country; for that I have sacrificed every thing that is most dear to man...I have submitted to exile and to bondage; I have exposed myself to the rage of the Ocean and the fire of the enemy; after an honourable combat that should have interested the feelings of a generous foe...Whatever I have said, written or thought on the subject of Ireland I now reiterate; looking upon her connexion with England to have been her bane I have endeavoured by every means in my power to break that connexion; I have laboured in consequence to create a people in Ireland by raising three millions of my countrymen to the rank of citizens...I have laboured to abolish the infernal spirit of religious persecution by uniting the Catholics and the Dissenters; to the former I owe more than can ever be repaid; the services I was so fortunate to render them, they reward munificently but they did more; when the public cry was raised against me, when the friends of my youth swarmed off and left me alone, the Catholics did not desert me; they had the virtue even to sacrifice their own interests to a rigid principle of honour; they refused though strongly urged to disgrace a man who whatever his conduct towards the Government might have been, had faithfully and conscientiously discharge his duty towards them, and in so doing though it was in my own case, I will say they sowed an instance of public virtue and honour of which I know not whether there exists another example…I have attempted to follow the same line in which Washington succeeded and Kosciusko failed; I have attempted to establish the independence of my country; I have failed in the attempt; my life is in consequence forfeited and I submit; the court will do their duty and I will endeavour to do mine."[142]

After concluding his statement, Tone asked for a soldier's death – by firing squad; "…from a respect to the uniform which I wear and the brave army in which I have fought"[143] but was told that it would be the Lord Lieutenant's decision.

## Sentence and Suicide

The trial was brief, for Tone had pleaded guilty and there could be no doubt of the sentence. Having being returned to his cell without definite word of his fate, Tone busied himself with last letters. To his wife he wrote in part: "…Adieu, dearest Love, I find it impossible to finish this letter…remember that you are now the only parent of our dearest children, and that the best proof you can give of your affection for me will be to preserve yourself for their education – God Almighty bless you all, Yours ever, T.W. Tone"[144]

On the evening of Sunday November 11th, Tone was dismayed to find out that he was to be hanged publicly at Newgate Prison at 1.P.M the following day. His plea for a soldier's death had been refused. That night, he apparently cut his throat either with an open razor left by his brother or a penknife, almost severing his windpipe. After he was discovered at 4 am by the sentry, surgeons were called and they successfully stabilised him to make him "fit for the hangman". But that was not to be his fate. At 11 am that morning, a last minute appeal was lodged by Curran challenging Tone's sentencing by a military court. Legal opinion was in support of Curran and a stay was put on Tone's execution pending a hearing. When Curran asked that Tone be allowed to receive further medical attention, his request was denied. As the week progressed, Tone, who was now constantly guarded and in a strait jacket, got weaker. His wound became infected with the result that his lungs became inflamed, and he died the following Monday morning. Following his death, three surgeons conducted an autopsy.

Lord Clare

They found that lung inflammation had been the direct cause of death. A Coroner's Inquest was held, at which the surgeons gave testimony and a verdict of death by "self murder"[145] was returned.

In Dublin Castle and London, where Fitzgibbon (Lord Clare) was busy planning the accomplishment of the Union, the English government were delighted with Tone's death, for the prospect of a lengthy court case that would receive widespread public attention and in which Tone would be endlessly referred to, did not appeal to them. On November 15th, Fitzgibbon wrote to Lord Auckland: "We had got into a little scrape by bringing up Mr. Tone for trial to Dublin by a court-martial, sitting by the side of the

Court of King's Bench. We shall probably get out of it by the death of Mr. Tone who was suffered to cut his throat[1] on the day appointed for his execution".[146]

---

[1] By this comment it may be inferred that the government suspected that Tone would try and commit suicide in the event that a sentence of death by hanging was handed down and colluded in this. (It also must be remarked that throughout the centuries the English possessed remarkable "form" in the "disposal" of Irish leaders - Shane O'Neill, Hugh Roe O'Donnell, Donal O'Sullivan Beare etc. The author is not prepared to rule out that Tone met "an English fate" as It most certainly would have been in English interests to avoid his public hanging which would ot only have created a martyr for Irish freedom, but would have further inflamed French animosity towards England as Tone was a French officer and citizen.)

# Chapter 7

# Union and Insurrection

### The United Kingdom of Great Britain and Ireland
"I know of no blacker or fouler transaction in the history of man than the making of the Union between England and Ireland" – William Gladstone

"The Union was inflicted on Ireland by the combined operation of terror, torture, force, fraud, and corruption." – Daniel O'Connell

"If it must be called a union, it is the union of a shark with his prey" – Lord Byron

<u>The Plan</u>
After the last battles of the 1798 Rebellion had been fought, the Crown Forces remained in a state of war against the Irish people. As late as November 16th of that year the Lord Deputy Lord Cornwallis laid the blame not only for the rebellion but also the ongoing tumult squarely at the door of the ascendancy when he wrote to his friend General Ross: "The vilest informers are hunted out from the prisons to attack, by the most barefaced perjury, the lives of all who are suspected of being or of having been disaffected; and indeed, every Roman Catholic is in great danger. I attempt to moderate that violence

and cruelty, which has once driven, and which if tolerated, must again drive this wretched country into rebellion."[147]

If Cornwallis was Prime Minister William Pitt's "Useful Idiot" for the passage of the Act of Union then Pitt had picked well, for Cornwallis was a humane sort and seemed genuinely convinced that in the absence of Parliamentary reform in the Dublin legislature, a complete union with England that would eliminate the Irish Parliament might actually save the Catholic Irish people from the eternal wrath of the Colonist Assembly.

Lord Castlereagh

Cornwallis could not understand how the Rebellion had come to be framed by the ascendancy as "A Catholic Rebellion" when out of 162 leaders in the Society of The United Irishmen 106 of them were Protestant and his correspondence with General Ross clearly outlined his distaste for the goings on in Governmental and official circles in Dublin. He felt that the sooner London was in complete control of Irish affairs the better for all concerned. In the aftermath of the rebellion he devoted himself wholeheartedly to the project determined to stop at nothing (including bribery – which he found particularly distasteful) to achieve it.

Pitt on the other hand, along with the Chief Secretary, Lord Castlereagh (Robert Stewart) and the Chancellor, Lord Clare (John Fitzgibbon) were only concerned with the eternal preservation of the Unionist and Protestant governance of Ireland, an Ireland that would be, if they achieved their wish, forever chained to England. Pitt was determined that now was the time to achieve this.[I] The ascendancy must be persuaded, cajoled and bribed to the opinion that permanent union with England would be their salvation.

## The Union is Formally Proposed

On September 25th 1798, Cornwallis wrote to Pitt: "The principal people here are so frightened that they would, I believe, readily consent to a union; but then it must be a Protestant union; and even the Chancellor (Lord Clare) who is the most right-headed politician in the country will not hear of the Roman Catholics sitting in the united parliament"[148.]

On January 22nd 1799, the union of Britain and Ireland was raised by Cornwallis in his legislative speech.  Expecting something of the sort, those members of the ascendancy who did not wish to see their parliament terminated immediately took up the gauntlet and launched a debate on the matter. Most vociferous for the preservation of their parliament were the speaker John Foster, Prime Sergeant Fitzgerald, the Chancellor of the Exchequer, John Parnell and the MP for Tuam Jonah Barrington.[II]  A motion was moved that "a

---

[I] If David Lloyd George is considered as 'the father of Irish partition' then William Pitt the Younger must necessarily be considered as 'the grandfather of Irish partition'.

[II] Regarding the 1798 rebellion, Jonah Barrington was under no illusions as to where the blame lay when he wrote: "Mr. Pitt's end was answered. He raised the Catholics to the height of expectation, and by suddenly recalling their favourite viceroy, he inflamed them to the degree of generating the commotions he meditated, which would throw the Protestants into the arms of England for protection, whilst the horrors would be aggravated by the mingled conflict of parties. Having sent Lord Fitzwilliam to Ireland with unlimited powers to satisfy the nation, Mr. Pitt permitted him to proceed until he had unavoidably committed himself, both to the Catholics and to the country, when he suddenly recalled him. The day Lord Fitzwilliam arrived peace was proclaimed throughout all Ireland. The day he quitted it she prepared for insurrection. Within three months Lord Clare had got the nation into full training for military execution. Mr. Pitt decided upon forcing a premature insurrection for a particular object and did not calculate the torrents of blood that would be shed,

resident and independent legislature should be maintained" and after an all night sitting the motion was voted upon. The result was regarded as a defeat for the government – 106 votes on each side. Shortly afterwards both Fitzgerald and Parnell were dismissed from office for their opposition to the Union.

Despite the fact that the measure had been defeated, Pitt was not for turning. He made it clear that the Dublin parliament would vote again and again on the Act of Union until it agreed to dissolve itself. In February of 1799, the Act of Union was introduced in the English parliament and approved. Once this occurred, the government in Dublin went into overdrive. The Act was to be introduced in the Dublin Parliament in the next session and no effort was to be spared to ensure that it would gain assent.

## Palm Greasing and Graft on an Unknown Scale

As the government prepared for the vote on the Act of Union in the Irish Parliament, it invoked any and every measure at it disposal. All office holders (commonly referred to as "Placemen" as they were un-elected members of parliament) that showed any inclination whatever against the Act of Union were dismissed so that they could not vote against it.

As we have seen, only around one third of MPs actually represented a proper constituency while the remaining 200 seats were assigned to members who sat for ("rotten" or "pocket") boroughs that "belonged to" and were sold by the landlords to the highest bidder. In order to ensure the support of those who held these seats for Union, £8,000 per vote was offered or an appointment worth £2,000 per year. The actual "owners" of the boroughs also needed to have their support bought to compensate them for the loss of their boroughs

---

and the inveterate hatred that might be perpetuated against the British government".

whose seats would disappear in the new united parliament. They were offered between £14,000 and £16,000 each.

£1,275,000 was spent in the purchase of the boroughs with a further £1,000,000 being spent in the direct bribing of those members who held representative seats, the entire total of the bribes being added to the national debt of Ireland. In order to garner the "support" they required, the government showered appointments on MPs and Lords who wanted them in return for their support. Twenty peerages were immediately created along with ten bishoprics. These new appointments now swamped the Irish House of Lords in time for the vote. Baronetcies, judgeships, and commissionerships abounded. Appointments as high-ranking army and naval officers were two a penny. 140 MPs along with their bribes were later identified. The highest price demanded for a "patronage" seat was given to Lord Downshire who received £52,500. Lord Claremorris first offered himself for sale to the anti Unionists, but when they could not satisfy him he negotiated with the government and received £23,000. James Cuffe MP demanded that his father be made Lord Tyrawley in return for his support. Hugh Howard MP was made Postmaster General. In 1799, William Hancock MP was composing songs and ditties against the union which he sang at dinner parties. By the following year after he had been bribed, he was looking forward to being created Lord Castlemaine and was composing songs and ditties in the union's favour.

Cornwallis felt not a little uncomfortable in his role of courting and bribing MPs and Lords. Corresponding to his friend and confidant General Ross he wrote: "My occupation is now of the most unpleasant nature, negotiating and jobbing with the most corrupt people under heaven. I despise and hate myself every hour for engaging in such dirty work, and am supported only by the reflection that without a union the British empire must be dissolved...sincerely do I repent that I did not return to

Bengal…I trust I shall live to get out of this most cursed of all situations, and most repugnant to my feelings. How I long to kick those whom my public duties oblige me to court…the nearer the great event (the vote on the Act of Union) approaches the more are the needy and interested senators alarmed at the effects it may possibly have on their interests, and the provision for their families, and I believe that half of our majority would be at least as much delighted as any of our opponents if the measure could be defeated"[149] Cornwallis also related to Ross that he often recited to himself the lines composed by Swift (which you will find at the start of chapter 3).

While Cornwallis was busy with the MPs and Lords, Chief Secretary Castlereagh[1] and Lord Chancellor Clare got to work on the barristers as it was felt that their support was essential. As they only had limited success here, Clare was forced to create additional positions on the Bar in order to satisfy his needs.

### The Maiden Speech of Daniel O'Connell

The Irish too, although bottom of the list, were not completely ignored. Not for them the palm greasing, bribery and graft of the ascendancy, but promises regarding Catholic emancipation which Pitt could not and would not fulfil.

---

[1] After the Union had been passed Lord Castlereagh wrote to Chief Secretary Cooke who was in London regarding how the Union had been accomplished: "…it will be no secret what has been promised and by what means the union has been carried out…disappointment (of those MPs who did not receive as much money as they wanted for their vote) will encourage, not prevent disclosures and the only effect of such a proceeding on their part will be to add the weight of their testimony to that of the anti-unionists in proclaiming the profligacy of the means by which the measure has been accomplished."

Although one of Pitt's aims was to forever deny the Irish, the governance of their own country, many were persuaded that the union was in their interest for after the united parliament of Britain and Ireland was a fact, Catholics, according to Pitt would be admitted to full citizens rights and complete Catholic emancipation – for only in a united Parliament would Catholic emancipation cease to be a threat to English hegemony in Ireland.  Pitt also made it clear that the intolerable situation regarding enforced tithing to the established Church of Ireland would be addressed.

The Catholic bishops, having received guarantees regarding church freedom and government support acquiesced with the government's plan, but not so the laity.  At a meeting of prominent Catholic laymen in Dublin, Pitt's scheme was recognised for what it was – the giving away of Ireland's independence by the colonists so that the native Irish might never ever get their hands on it.  Although the Dublin Parliament was corrupt and served only the interests of the colonisers, it was nevertheless an Irish parliament, which if reformed could be transformed into a real representative body of the Irish people and could in time be the vehicle by which greater freedom and perhaps eventually independence could be wrested from England by Irishmen.

One speaker at the meeting was a young Catholic barrister called Daniel O'Connell who passionately declared that: "...the Catholics are incapable of selling their country; they will loudly declare, that if their emancipation were offered for their consent to the measure – even were emancipation after the Union a benefit – they would reject it with prompt indignation...let every man who feels with me proclaim that if the alternative were offered him of Union , or the re-enactment of the whole penal code in all its pristine horrors, that he would prefer without hesitation the latter, as the lesser and more sufferable evil; that he would rather prefer the reintroduction of the penal laws against the faith than the loss of the parliament".[150]

Far sighted as O'Connell's objections were, no one could have predicted that William Pitt, with his Act of Union was laying not only the foundation stone of Irish partition but also of The Great Starvation of 1845-52 as during this great crime the Irish would be completely subject to the ineffective measures of the London Parliament instead of having a parliament of their own that would have more effectively dealt with the failure of the potato crop and the evil "land system"

Also (initially) opposed to the Union were the Orange Order who feared that Pitt's promises of Catholic emancipation in the united parliament of Great Britain and Ireland would be honoured. But they need not have worried.

## The Act of Union

"Thus was the legislative independence of Ireland extinguished. Thus was the greatest crime ever perpetrated by the English Government upon Ireland consummated"[1] – Daniel O'Connell

<u>January 15th 1800</u>

On January 15th 1800, the final session of the Dublin Parliament opened. For all to see it was business as usual as in the Viceroy's speech there was no mention of the Act of Union. In spite of this, the opposition MP Lawrence Parsons moved an amendment to the speech: "that the House should maintain intact the Constitution of 1782, and that Ireland should retain its absolute right of self-government for ever."[151] Having thrown down the gauntlet to the government party, an all night debate on the Union ensued until finally at 7am the following morning, the newly elected member for Wicklow,

---

[1] The Act of Union of 1800 would finally lead to the partitioning of Ireland in 1921.

Henry Grattan, clad in the uniform of the Volunteers of 1782 entered the House. Although ill, Grattan injected new life into the debate. For two hours Grattan spoke, telling the members in part: "...I have done with the pile which the Minister batters. I come to the Babel which he builds, and as he throws down without a principle so does he construct without a foundation. This fabric he calls a Union. It is no union, for it excludes the Catholics. It is an extinction of the Constitution and an exclusion of the people. He has overlooked the people as he has overlooked the sea"[152.]

At 10am, a vote on the amendment to the Viceroy's speech took place. There were 96 votes in favour and 138 against, a majority of 42 for the government.

### The Passage of the Act

The very absence of a Bill proposing the Act of Union from the Viceroy's speech gave rise to gossip and various theories. The only delay was most likely due to the fact that the government was garnering the support of borough owners who were overseas. However on February 5th, Lord Castlereagh read to the House of Commons a formal note from the Viceroy proposing that The Act of Union be brought before the House. The House was now required to vote on whether it would allow the note (and so the legislation) to be admitted. The vote was 158 in favour and 115 against, while 27 members were absent. In the House of Lords, where Lord Clare introduced the measure, the vote in favour of the government's proposal was much greater – 75 to 26.

Thereafter the act passed all stages but not without incident. Lord Castlereagh had organised a "Shooting Club" among the bribed members whereby all oratory against the Act of Union was to be heckled and shouted down. In one such exchange, Corry, the Chancellor of the Exchequer repeatedly heckled Grattan who replied: "I have returned to protect that constitution of which I was the parent and the founder from the assassination of such men as the right honourable gentleman and his unworthy associates. They are corrupt, they are seditious, and they at this moment are in a conspiracy against their country...I dare accusation. I defy the honourable gentleman. I defy the government. I defy their whole phalanx. Let them come forth. I tell the Ministers I will nether give them quarter or take it."[153] Corry, feeling slighted, challenged Grattan to a duel following the debate and the following morning at dawn the rivals met, the outcome being that Corry ended up with a bullet through his hand.

On August 1st 1800, The Act of Union was given the royal assent. Aside from laying down the letter of the law regarding representation for Ireland in the House of Commons in London (Ireland was to have a representation of 100 MPs out of 660), it tied Irish industry and commerce and all others facets of Irish life into the English system which ensured that England's interest was once more pre-eminent.[I] Within a very short time the advantages and employment that had been gained due to the re-emergence of the wool trade following 1782 had been lost. The Act also burdened Ireland with an enormous proportion of Britain's debt from the 1st January 1801 onwards.[II] The position of the Protestant Church was once

---

[I] Following the Union, England became more and more dependent on livestock and agricultural produce from Ireland in order to feed the workers of her industrial revolution. An example of this may be found in the exportation of cattle and sheep from Ireland to England. Between 1799 and 1884 the number of livestock exported to England increased from 14,000 to 715,843 while the number of sheep increased from 800 to 533,285.

[II] In 1793 Ireland's national debt was almost £2.5 million. On the eve of the union less than seven years later it was almost £28 million. The expenses of the Crown Forces who were first employed to provoke the rebellion and then to suppress it amounted to £16,000,000 of this debt. The rest of the debt was incurred through compensation claims by Loyalists after the rebellion, the bribery and graft associated with the act of union, secret service monies and the

more reinforced so that it would be, according to the Act, "continued forever and to be united with that of England". This was a move dear to Castlereagh's heart, for to him the Protestant bishops were the "Ecclesiastical Aristocracy of Ireland". Even the Presbyterians had their "Regium Donum" (government stipend) increased from £3,000 in entirety to almost £100 per minister. Only the Catholic Church – the Church of the Irish was ignored in the Act.

### Williamt Pitt Fails to Keep his Word

In the aftermath of the Act's passage Pitt's promises to the Catholics regarding Catholic emancipation following Union and that a government stipend for the support of Catholic priests were not honoured, the excuse being that the King would not assent to them. However, if Pitt had been in earnest, he would certainly have known this when the promises were being made. Whatever the King may or may not have felt, the reality (as we have seen from Cornwallis's testimony) was that most members of the Dublin parliament who voted for the union would not countenance

William Pitt

---

removal of departments to London.. By 1817 Ireland's debt was almost £113 million as since the union Ireland had to accept 13% of the total debt incurred by "The United Kingdom of Great Britain and Ireland." When Lord Castlereagh committed suicide in 1822, Daniel O'Connell remarked that: "...the only wonder was that Ireland was not charged for the knife with which he had slit his throat".

the presence of Catholics in the united parliament and so an oath framed in order to exclude Catholics from parliamentary seats remained as part of the Act of Union.

Shortly after the new united parliament of Great Britain and Ireland was formed an official document was leaked by Lord Cornwallis that outlined to the Catholics what was to be given them after the Union. When the House of Commons got wind of it there was uproar. One MP called Grey outlined the situation: "If Catholic freedom were offered to the Irish as the price of their support of the Union, if the faith of the Government were pledged on that occasion, it forms the highest species of criminality on the part of the Ministers; because I am confident if such were the case, it was so pledged without the authority of the King; for I know that his Majesty is superior to the idea of swerving in the slightest degree from the observance of his word. This, then, was a crime of the highest denomination in Ministers, and calls for inquiry. I ask if such promises were made, were Lord Clare and the Protestant Ascendancy Party made acquainted with it? If so, they were a party to the delusion of 'having' in the words of the promise 'so many characters' of eminence (Pitt and his officials) 'pledged not to embark in the service of Government except on the terms of the Catholic privileges being obtained.'"[154] Pitt denied all knowledge of the promises made to the Irish but nevertheless resigned as Prime Minister only resuming office in 1804 after promising the King that Catholic emancipation would never be mentioned again.

When all was said and done it amounted to this – as with The Treaty of Limerick a century earlier, the Irish had once more been deceived by the English.

# Robert Emmett and The Insurrection of 1803

## "Croppies Lie Down"

In the aftermath of the 1798 rebellion, one of the most popular songs among the Protestant Ascendancy in Ireland was "Croppies Lie Down" by George Watson Taylor. Following the 1798 rebellion it was ceremoniously played on an annual basis on Dublin's College Green before the statue of William of Orange. It included the lines;

> "Oh croppies ye'd better be quiet and still
> Ye shan't have your liberty, do what ye will
> As long as salt water is formed in the deep
> A foot on the necks of the croppy we'll keep
> And drink, as in bumpers past troubles we drown,
> A health to the lads that made croppies lie down
> Down, down croppies lie down"

## Robert Emmett Attempts to Revive the Cause of Irish Freedom

A member of the Protestant Ascendancy, Robert Emmett was the younger brother of Thomas Addis Emmett, who had been intimately involved in both the organisation of the United Irishmen in Dublin and the planning of the 1798 rebellion. Of like mind with his brother, Robert had been expelled from Trinity College in early 1798 on account of his political opinions.

By 1803, many Protestants, having initially supported the United Irishmen, reverted to Unionism in the realisation that any future Irish Parliament must be dominated by Catholics. This however did not deter Robert Emmett. In spite of the failure of the 1798 rebellion, he was determined that while he was still at liberty, the cause of the United Irishmen was not a lost one. If anything his determination was redoubled by the passage of the Act of Union.

After visiting his incarcerated brother at Fort George, Scotland, Robert Emmett travelled to Paris where he visited his brother's family. In Paris, there still existed a United Irishman network with government links and Emmett was received by Napoleon who promised French help if rebellion should break out again in Ireland He also confirmed to him the likelihood of renewed hostilities between France and England. Emmett was well aware that Napoleon would like to see rebellion in Ireland for his own ends and was not taken in by his promises.

In October 1802, Robert Emmett secretly returned to Dublin and attempted to undertake a re-organisation and revitalisation of the remnants of the United Irishmen in the capital. Upon his return he learned of a failed conspiracy undertaken by an Englishman and United Irish sympathiser, Colonel Despard. Despard had dispatched an agent named Dowdall from London to try and find out what the chances were for an insurrection in the capital in the wake of the Act of Union but upon his arrival Dowdall had acted in anything but a clandestine manner and Despard and his associates quickly became known to the authorities. Within a short time Despard was arrested, court martialled and hanged for treason along with nine others. Dowdall managed to avoid capture and escaped to Paris.

Following the death of Despard and his associates, Emmett had no second thoughts regarding his intentions. In spite of the brutality with which the '98 rebellion had been crushed and the fact that the Act of Union was now an accomplished fact he remained determined in his intention – regroup, rearm and rise.

Robert Emmett had recently received £2,000 in his deceased father's will (his father had held the prestigious appointment of personal physician to the Viceroy) and put the money to use by setting up a number of clandestine workshops in the capital for the manufacture of pikes, grenades, and rudimentary mines powerful enough to fell a cavalry charge. Old contacts were re-established and envoys (James Hope and Thomas Russell) were dispatched into Ulster to try and reunite the republicans there. Emmett also successfully contacted the remnants of various groups who had continued to fight a guerrilla war following the 1798 rebellion such as that of Michael Dwyer in Wicklow and others in Wexford and Kildare.

### "We War Against English Dominion"
Amidst the planning for an insurrection in which Emmett hoped to seize Dublin Castle and The Pigeon House Fort (after which he hoped that the country would rise in support), Emmett found time to pen a very lengthy proclamation to the Irish people and his army to be issued after the capital had been seized. It was headed: "The Provisional Government to the People of Ireland" and began: "You are now called upon to show the world that you are competent to take your place among the nations; that you have a right to claim their recognizance of you as an independent country, by the only satisfactory proof you can furnish of your capability of maintaining your independence – your wresting it from England with your own hands."[155]

### The Insurrection
As Emmett's preparations continued, the authorities in Dublin appeared unaware that anything out of the ordinary was afoot. However on July 16th 1803, a small explosion took place at one of Emmett's workshops on Patrick St. and the fire brigade were summoned by a passer by. When they arrived at his Patrick St. depot Emmett's men refused them entry and after they departed without having investigated the cause of the explosion it was feared that the police would be called and the plot discovered. Emmett decided not to wait any longer and

fixed the date for his insurrection – it would take place one week later, on Saturday July 23rd.

In spite of all his preparations, Emmett had overlooked any sizeable procurement of muskets, a fact that only came to light when the men from Kildare arrived in the capital on the morning of the 23rd and asked to be armed. Upon seeing that Emmett had only around 20 muskets along with pikes and rudimentary explosive devices for them, they advised him to call off the insurrection but Emmett refused, after which some of the Kildare men returned home. During the afternoon Emmett dispatched a number of his followers to buy guns for the men who were supposed to ride into the courtyard of Dublin Castle aboard coaches and seize the Viceroy and the castle but only six blunderbuss shotguns were procured. The Wicklow men arrived and were accommodated in stables and warehouses. They were to stand by for a rocket signal that would be released when Dublin Castle had been secured.

Robert Emmett

In the evening, one of Emmett's lieutenants –Ned Conlon, was sent to hire and bring six carriages that were to be loaded with men for the assault against the Castle. After hiring the coaches, Conlon was returning, when the convoy of carriages was stopped by a soldier. Conlon panicked and shot him at which the carriage drivers scattered. taking their carriages with them.

Emmett remained determined – he would seize Dublin Castle on foot. With less than a hundred men he set forth, but many of his men doubtless realising the futility of their escapade and the certain death that awaited them now abandoned him. With defeat now assured, Emmett told the remaining men to go home at which he himself left the city to return to his home in Rathfarnham. Behind him he had left groups of armed men, without a commander who were determined in spite of Emmett's order not to go home without a fight.

A number of the Capital's streets were seized and held by the rebels including St James's St. and Thomas St. At the barricade at Thomas St. a coach arrived. Inside the coach was the Chief Justice of Ireland, Lord Kilwarden, his daughter and his nephew, Rev Richard Wolfe. Kildwarden had been at his home in the country and had returned to the city after hearing reports of disturbances and a possible rebellion. With his coach surrounded, Kildwarden shouted: "It is I, Kilwarden, Chief Justice of the King's Bench"[156] at which one of the men at the barricade answered "You are the man I want".[157] Kilwarden, possibly the most honourable and humane of all the Judges then serving the Crown in Ireland, was pulled from the coach and murdered.[1] His nephew attempted to escape but was also killed. His daughter, by then in a state of terror was taken from the coach and escorted by the rebels to a nearby house.

For a few hours of darkness, some streets of the capital remained in possession of the rebels but by the following morning, the insurrection was over. By the time the soldiers arrived at his Rathfarnham home, Emmett had already left and gone into hiding. His housekeeper Anne Devlin was tortured and half hanged in order to get her to divulge Emmett's whereabouts.

---

[1] In some accounts which the author has read of the incident, it is stated that the men at the barricade believed that the so called "Hanging Judge" Lord Norbury was the occupant of the coach.

After two days Emmett left the city and could have secretly left the country like many of those involved in the insurrection. Instead he returned to the city, ostensibly to bid farewell to his fiancee, Sarah Curran who was the daughter of the MP and barrister John Philpot Curran,[1] who had defended many of the leaders of the 1798 Rebellion at their trial. Due to Emmett's acquaintance with Sarah Curran, John Philpot Curran was also arrested and questioned after which he was released without charge.

After hiding out in the capital for over three weeks, Robert Emmett's hiding place at Harold's Cross was betrayed and Major Sirr who had arrested Edward Fitzgerald apprehended him there on August 25th.

## "No Man Can Write My Epitaph"

On September 19th, a special commission headed by "The Hanging Judge" Lord Norbury convened for Emmett's trial. Emmett was "defended" by the barrister Leonard McNally, a government infiltrator and spy who had betrayed many a United Irishman and then "defended" them at their trial. Before the trial McNally had agreed to accept a payment of £250 and a pension from the government so that he would present an ineffectual defence. However, McNally's assistant, Peter Burrowes would not entertain any attempts to bribe him and did his utmost to effectively represent Emmett.

During the trial, the Judges heard the damning evidence of some of those who worked for Emmett in his munitions workshops after which Emmett was asked for his defence. Making no excuses for his actions, Emmett sought rather to

---

[1] Curran had done his utmost to keep the pair apart. After being arrested and released following the insurrection he could not bring himself to defend Emmett at his trial. In the aftermath of the trial his disowned his daughter, Sarah. She died of Tuberculosis five years later.

clarify certain false accusations that had been made against him. Amid repeated interruptions from Lord Norbury, Emmett dismissed the charge that he was an agent of France: "...I did not wish to deliver up my country to a foreign power, and least of all to France. I am charged with being a conspirator! I am and have been engaged in a conspiracy, of which the whole object is the disenthrallment of my beloved country...I appeal to the Immaculate God! I swear by the throne of heaven before which I must shortly appear; by the blood of the martyred patriots who have gone before me, that my conduct has been, through all this peril and through all my purposes, governed only by the convictions which I have uttered, and by no other motive but the emancipation of my country from the oppression under which she has too long and too patiently travailed."[158]

Despite being heckled by the Judge, Robert Emmett assured him that his cause would not die with him on the scaffold: "You say that in cutting me off, you cut off its head, and destroy the germ of future conspiracy and insurrection. It is false! This conspiracy will exist when I am no more. It will be followed by another more strong, and rendered still more formidable by foreign assistance...(interruption from the Judge)...I who fear not to approach the Omnipotent Judge to answer for the conduct of my whole life - am I to be appalled and falsified by a mere remnant of mortality here? By you, too, who if it were possible to collect all the innocent blood that you have shed during your unhallowed ministry into one great reservoir, your lordships might swim in it...my lamp of life is nearly extinguished. My race is finished, and the grave opens to receive me. All I request at my departure from this world is the charity of its silence. No man can write my epitaph. And as no man who knows my motives dares to vindicate them, so let no man who is ignorant of them with prejudice asperse them. When my country takes her rank amongst the nations of the earth, then only can my epitaph be written and then alone can my character be vindicated. I have done."[159]

The trial concluded, Robert Emmett was sentenced to be hanged and beheaded.

The following day, September 20th, twenty five year old Robert Emmett was hanged on a large gallows erected in Thomas St, after which he was cut down and clumsily beheaded. Holding up his head the executioner declared "Behold the head of the traitor, Robert Emmett" – but Emmett had not betrayed Ireland.

Of the large numbers who had been arrested in the wake of the rising, eighteen were to follow Emmett on the gallows walk.

Although an utter failure both in its planning and execution, Robert Emmett's insurrection was important, not on account of what he had achieved but on account of his having attempted it at all, in the face of such overwhelming odds as to seem like madness. Together with his idealism, spirit of self sacrifice and his oratory, he was to provide the generations that followed with an example which would be told and retold to the generations that followed, an example which others would emulate and one which would finally bear fruit. His death had not been in vain.

## The Resignation of Sir William Wickham

One of the most interesting aspects of Emmett's insurrection and death was the resignation in December of 1803 of the Chief Secretary for Ireland Sir William Wickham.

On the night before his execution, Emmett wrote a letter to Wickham in which he thanked him for the fair treatment that he had experienced. In his letter Emmet also outlined to Wickham the necessity of his rebellion. The letter had such a profound effect on Wickham that it prompted him to resign. By way of explanation to his friends regarding his resignation, Wickham told them that after reflecting on the contents of

Emmett's letter over a period of time "no consideration on earth can induce me to remain in my post,"[160] and that he could not continue to serve a government that imposed upon Ireland such "unjust, oppressive and unchristian"[161] laws.

Wickham went even further: "If I had been an Irishman I should most unquestionably have joined him"[162]

Describing Emmett's letter as his "constant companion" Wickham was to keep it on his person until his death in 1840.

Following the death of William Pitt at the beginning of 1806, Wickham (who was still an MP) was appointed as Lord of the Treasury in the government formed by Lord Grenville. The following year he resigned both from government and politics saying that he could no longer serve in a government that excluded Catholics from parliament.

# Chapter 8

# "A New Moses"

"He infused the spirit that keeps the pulses of Irishmen in all parts of the globe beating to one measure. He took the cause of independence out of the hands of a faction and made it the life of a country" – W.A. O'Connor

## The Early Life of Daniel O'Connell
### Ireland at the turn of the Century
In the wake of the Act of Union Ireland remained in a state of veritable siege with 100,000 soldiers either on patrol or in garrisoned reserve. Habeas Corpus remained suspended and the Convention Act, barring the formation of any group or association remained in force.

The English, having finally neutralised the Colonist Parliament had taken for themselves complete and total control of Irish affairs. They now had the chance to prove that a London parliament would treat Ireland better than a Dublin parliament but instead so called "Coercion Acts" were passed year after year which ensured that burgeoning protests against continually rising rents and tithes (an issue which the government had promised to deal with at the time of the Act of Union) would be dealt with without either mercy or redress.

With regard to the Catholic question, the British government, although appearing to be outwardly sympathetic were only too happy to use the excuse that the mentally unsound King George III would not entertain such a proposal.

### Youth and Education of Daniel O'Connell
Born in 1775 to the wife of a poor mountain herdsman near Cahersiveen in Co. Kerry, Daniel O'Connell had been adopted by his unmarried wealthy uncle Maurice with the idea that he would be his heir. In the event his uncle struck him from his will after he married his penniless distant cousin Mary instead of a woman of means. Thereafter his uncle split his property between his three brothers and in this way his uncle's house along with part of his land was finally to come into Daniel O'Connell's possession.

Living in the wilds of southwest Kerry, Maurice "Hunting Cap" O'Connell was one of a very small number of Catholics in the entire country who had managed to retain the title to the family land during the penal times. In Maurice's case it was thanks to the very remoteness of his property and the fact that the leases to his land had been well established by the time the Treaty of Limerick had been signed. In the wake of the restrictive trade laws imposed during the early part of the eighteenth century, Maurice O'Connell of Derrynane took full advantage of his coastal location by engaging in the smuggling of wool and other commodities to the continent and the importation of fine cloth and wine much of which he sold to the local ascendancy who turned a blind eye to his activities. Having made his fortune in this way, Maurice O'Connell longed to buy additional land but as a Catholic in penal times could not. As a way of circumventing the law he persuaded his Protestant cousin, Hugh Falvey (who had apostatised from the Catholic faith so that he could become a barrister) to sign the deeds and swear that the lands which Maurice had bought were his own. This continued until finally Falvey wrote to him: "I regret that I am too near my end to perjure myself any more, even for so old and valued a friend as yourself"[163].

As a boy, Daniel O'Connell attended the local hedge school before being sent to school in Queenstown (Cobh) after the relaxation of the penal laws. His uncle then sent him abroad to France to complete his secondary education but the French Revolution interfered and after a few years he was forced to return home after the army of the French Republic surrounded Douay.

O'Connell had little sympathy with the French revolutionaries who had killed their king and waged war on the Catholic faith. On his return trip, in the carriage bound for Calais, republicans who shouted abuse at the occupants had surrounded the conveyance several times but finally Calais was reached. On the ship for England O'Connell was joined by two young Irishmen who produced a blood stained handkerchief. In Paris they had been present at the execution of the King and had bribed a soldier to dip it in the King's blood as one of them explained: "For the love of the cause."[164] It transpired that they were the Sheares brothers from Dublin who were years later executed for their part in the 1798 rebellion. Back in Ireland O'Connell was as aghast as any at the disastrous recall of Lord Deputy Fitzwilliam in 1795 and felt that what had happened in France might well be brought home to the Ascendancy in Ireland also.

Due to changed circumstances because of the French revolution, upon his return to Ireland Daniel O'Connell was able to study to become a lawyer. As a law student he honed his later legendary speaking techniques and in 1798 he was one of the first Catholics to be called to the bar.

## The Catholic Board

With a gift for oratory, Daniel O'Connell gradually rose to prominence in the wake of the Act of Union, delivering speeches on both Catholic Emancipation and The Repeal of Act of Union whilst still declaring his unswerving loyalty to the Crown later maintaining that: "...the only chance of doing any good for the people was by affecting ultra loyalty"[165.] As a Catholic barrister, he was denied being called to the inner chamber of the bar or being promoted to the bench as a Judge while as a prominent Catholic he could never be an M.P. O'Connell quickly realised that without repeal of the Union emancipation was of limited value, but the door to repeal was firmly shut while the door to emancipation gave the impression that eventually it might yield.

In spite of the "Convention Act", O'Connell was involved in the re-formation of the "Catholic Committee" in 1809, becoming its acting secretary in 1810. Ever fearful of being closed down by the government the Committee carefully guarded its language, for while Protestants could say as they liked on any topic, Dublin Castle was ever watchful of the Catholics and the group was hounded by police magistrates who at one meeting appeared to put Lord Fingal under arrest and then denied that they had done so. With O'Connell increasingly in charge, Dublin Castle found it difficult to ensnare the organisation as O'Connell[I] guided it through the intricacies of the law. At the end of 1811, under O'Connell's recommendation the name "Catholic Convention" was changed to "Catholic Board" in order to appear more benign to the government.

In June of 1813, as Henry Grattan made another (failed) attempt to secure Catholic emancipation in the English

---

[I] Dublin Castle were taken aback by the adroit leadership which O'Connell gave to the Catholic cause. As a renowned barrister who preferred to defend, he quickly gained fame throughout the country. On one occasion he managed to get a woman who was accused of stealing a cow acquitted when he pointed out to the judge that as the animal was dead when it had been stolen the charge should have read: "...for the stealing of beef..."

parliament, Daniel O'Connell addressed a public meeting in Dublin on the topic in which he digressed onto a different topic: "...your enemies accuse me of a desire for the independence of Ireland. I admit the charge; and let them make the most of it. I have seen Ireland a kingdom; I reproach myself with having lived to behold Her a province. Yes, I confess it; I have an ulterior object. It is the repeal of the Union, and the restoration of old Ireland to her independence...".[166.] In spite of repeated refusals by Westminster to grant emancipation, O'Connell's efforts as head of the Catholic Board continued unabated as he strove to garner more and more Protestant support for the Catholic emancipation campaign. When a twenty four year old rising star by the name of Robert Peel (who had taken Westminster by storm) was appointed as Irish Secretary under the administration of The Earl of Liverpool, Robert Jenkinson, O'Connell decided to throw caution to the wind and began making speeches designed to bring both himself and the movement to the attention of Dublin Castle once more. From the beginning O'Connell's speeches (which were widely disseminated) were designed to annoy Peel – which they did. Nicknaming him "Orange Peel" because of his anti Catholic bias[1] he said of him: "...this raw youth squeezed out of the working of I know not what factory in England...was sent over here before he got over the foppery of perfumed handkerchiefs and thin shoes – a lad ready to vindicate anything – everything..."[167]

It was at this point that a new effort for emancipation by a minister in Jenkinson's government named Canning took hold. He proposed that if emancipation were granted to the

---

[1] After dinner, Peel frequently rose and took up the traditional pose for giving the Orange toast – standing on his chair with one foot on the table, after which he would propose the notorious Orange Toast.

Catholics the government would have a veto on the nomination of Catholic bishops as in the Anglican Church. Grattan accepted the proposal, and a few of the Catholic Bishops of Ireland along with most of the English bishops secretly acquiesced after which a bill for Catholic emancipation steadily made its way through parliament.

However, once the matter of the veto became public knowledge, it was roundly condemned at a meeting of the Irish bishops, who along with the priests and people condemned it. O'Connell castigated the very idea of an English government veto over the appointment of Catholic Bishops: "Does anyone imagine that the Catholic religion will prosper in Ireland if our prelates, instead of being what they are at present, shall become the servile tools of the administration? They would lose all the respect for themselves, all respectability in the eyes of others. They would be degraded to the station of excisemen..."[168] and on another occasion he told his audience: "How very dismal the prospect of liberty would be if in every Catholic diocese there was an active partisan of the Government and in every Catholic parish a priest as an active informer"[169]. It was clear to O'Connell that both the Catholic priests and the people were in his words: "...totally repugnant to allow the crown any power to nominate the Catholic Bishops of Ireland"[170] To the annoyance of many of the English Catholic bishops and lobbyists the bill collapsed thanks to O'Connell's intervention. In front of an excited meeting of the Catholic Board, O'Connell complained that Grattan had shown himself unworthy to be their spokesman as he had not taken them into his confidence from the beginning with regard to the veto. After the final defeat of Napoleon in 1815, any desire within the British government to give Catholic emancipation collapsed. In spite of the fact that the efforts at Catholic emancipation would now recede for a time O'Connell was not downcast: "I for one, most readily and heartily offer to postpone emancipation in order to promote the cause of our country"[171].

## The Duel

Amid the reverberations of Grattan's failed attempt at a compromised emancipation for the Catholics, there occurred one of the most important episodes in O'Connell's life – an episode that left him with both a lifelong regret and a detestation of violence which was to impact on his future decisions

### The Sectarian Corporation

At the turn of the century, when Prime Minister Pitt had been determined to force through his policy of union between Britain and Ireland, Dublin Corporation, realising the detrimental effect of such a policy had stood firmly opposed to Pitt. However by the beginning of the second decade of the nineteenth century, in the realisation that repeal of the union would see Catholics control the corporation, the members were now firmly in favour of the union and opposed to Catholic emancipation except for one member, Alderman John D'Esterre, who supported the Catholics at the Corporations deliberations. By the end of 1814 the recently married D'Esterre was heavily in debt and was hoping to be elected as a Corporation Sheriff in order that he might earn enough money to pay his debts.

### The "Beggarly Corporation"

Annoyed by the Corporation's volte face in favour of the Union and their continual opposition to Catholic Emancipation in any form, in January of 1815 Daniel O'Connell openly referred to the Corporation in a speech as "...the beggarly Corporation of Dublin..."[172].

While most members of the Corporation had paid little heed, this reference had greatly annoyed D'Esterre on several accounts – as a Protestant supporter of emancipation, and after O'Connell's reference he felt his chances of being appointed as a Sheriff were greatly reduced. Furthermore as a member of the Corporation and as a heavily indebted man he resented the term "beggarly". Incensed, and determined to recover what he felt was his loss of esteem among the other Aldermen of the city he wrote a public letter to O'Connell condemning him for the remark to which O'Connell replied: "I deem it right to inform you that from the calumnious manner in which the religion and character of the Catholics of Ireland are treated in that body, no terms attributed to me, however reproachful, can exceed the contemptuous feelings I entertain for that body in its corporate capacity, although doubtless it contains many valuable persons whose conduct as individuals I lament must necessarily be confounded in the acts of the general body."[173] O'Connell concluded his letter with the expression that he had no interest in further correspondence on the subject.

### The Challenge
Unhappy that O'Connell had secured the moral high ground, D'Esterre was determined to pursue the matter. Knowing that O'Connell as a Catholic was opposed to duelling, D'Esterre felt certain that he could regain the high ground if he forced O'Connell to challenge him to a duel or at least apologise publicly for the remark. In the days that followed D'Esterre (a former naval officer and a crack shot with a pistol) sent further letters to O'Connell insulting him personally. Furthermore he appeared at the Four Courts with a whip telling anyone that would listen that he was looking for O'Connell in order to teach him a lesson. With O'Connell unwilling to challenge D'Esterre to a duel or apologise, D'Esterre now challenged him to a duel with pistols which O'Connell reluctantly accepted.

Normally on learning of an impending duel, the forces of the law would act to prevent it. However in Dublin Castle the authorities rejoiced and waited for D'Esterre to do his work and rid Ireland of the man they regarded as a danger to the security of the status quo.

### The Duel

On the afternoon of February 2nd 1815 at Bishop's Court in Co. Kildare, the ground was virgin white from a recent snowfall. Arriving at the appointed rendezvous an hour before D'Esterre, O'Connell spent the time in prayer. As duelling was a mortal sin, no diocesan priest could be on hand to administer the last rites but O'Connell had enlisted the help of a family friend, Fr. Mullane who was suspended from his faculties after a row with his bishop. Fr. Mullane waited in a nearby cabin lest O'Connell should be fatally wounded.

When D'Esterre arrived (with the deputy surgeon from Dublin Castle who was to attend to him if injured) the light was fading and the duel got underway at once. When the handkerchief was dropped D'Esterre quickly stepped to one side and fired, his round hitting the ground at O'Connell's feet. O'Connell who had fired at almost the same instant hit D'Esterre in the thigh and although the wound was not believed fatal the round had in fact lodged in his stomach.

Rejoicing that no one had been killed, O'Connell returned to Dublin where his family were overcome with joy at his safety. O'Connell quickly penned a note to Archbishop Murray expressing his regret for having been forced to fight the duel. The Archbishop replied: "Heaven be praised! Ireland is safe!"[174]

### The Aftermath

When O'Connell heard the following morning that D'Esterre was in fact seriously ill, he was distraught. When he died of his wound the next day (after taking full responsibility for the duel on his deathbed) O'Connell considered himself a murderer. The episode was destined to haunt him for the rest of his days and would make him opposed to violence in any form for the rest of his life. Until the end of his days he always approached the altar rails to receive Holy Communion wearing a white glove on his right hand as a sign of his penitence.

Attempting to make restitution he contacted D'Esterre's widow and offered to share his income with her, which she declined. However he did pay an annuity to D'Esterre's daughter for the next thirty years and when some years later he heard that Mrs. D'Esterre was appearing as plaintiff in a court case which she greatly desired to win, O'Connell offered his services for free and won the case for her.

Following the duel and with a heavy heart and conscience he once more turned his attention to Irish affairs.

## Fighting the Anti-Catholic Bias

Ever since the majority of the penal laws had been repealed, Catholics had nevertheless continued to suffer from an anti Catholic bias that began at the very highest levels of government. Even after emancipation it was the continual practice of the Crown when conducting prosecutions to continually challenge the presence of Catholic jurors until it had assembled for its own ends a jury either with a Protestant majority or a totally Protestant jury if so required.

In the second decade of the eighteenth century, the Attorney General, William Saurin, who was an anti Catholic Hugenot, was adept at gathering Protestant juries for Crown trials. In one such case, taken by the Crown against John Magee of the Dublin Evening Post, Saurin was the prosecutor. In this case O'Connell deliberately offered his services to the defence in order to expose the modus operandi of the Crown. Magee was charged with publishing an article contrary to the good name of the retiring Viceroy Lord Richmond, accusing him of contributing in no small way to a regime of state oppression and murder and of being no better than the worst of his predecessors.

The Jury as usual was Protestant, and O'Connell knew he could and would not win. Saurin opened the case and set the tone of the proceedings by addressing the Judges with the melodramatic statement: "My Lords, you will be shocked, to hear that the defendant is indicted with charging His Grace of Richmond with being a murderer!"[175]

Daniel O'Connell

Nevertheless, at the trials conclusion, in a speech lasting four hours O'Connell won the high ground. Addressing the jury he told them: "It is a cheerless, a hopeless task to address you..."[176] he then pointed out, not for their benefit but for the benefit of the press the repeated bigotry and inconsistency with which the Crown wielded her sword of justice, the number of times Protestant papers had escaped even reproach never mind court when they abused Catholics and incited violence against them.

Turning to the issue of how the jury were there, hand picked so that they would do Saurin's bidding whether or not the defendant should be innocent or guilty, O'Connell attempted to prick their conscience: "Gentlemen, he thinks he knows his men – he knows you...will you allow him to draw you into a perjury out of zeal for your religion...will you violate the pledge you have given to your God to do justice, in order to gratify your anxiety for the ascendancy of what you believe to be His Church?"¹⁷⁷

Although the jury were unmoved, and Magee found guilty, O'Connell's speech in which he faced full-square the bigotry of Dublin Castle and the "packed" nature of the Irish justice system received national acclaim and earned for him the vituperation of both Saurin and Peel.

## The Road to Catholic Emancipation
### The "distracted and unsettled state of Ireland"

Since the act of Union, anguish, despair and discontent had seized Ireland. The rebellion of '98 had failed. Since the completion of the Act of Union, whatever hope there had been that England might undertake measures to improve the lot of the Irish people had rapidly diminished.

Following the Union, Dublin, once the second city of the empire, had become a provincial backwater. An exodus had taken place of M.P.s, Lords, department officials etc. while many landlords who were renting large estates from the bigger landlords had decided to sell up. These landlords had traded places with a new breed of landlord who were more determined than ever to make their investment pay. As the prices for commodities (cereals, agricultural produce, flax etc) had increased during the years of the Napoleonic wars, rents for small holdings had become exorbitant.¹ Agrarian discontent was also rife as many landless labourers attempted to rent small holdings but were priced out by larger tenant farmers. When the threat of Napoleonic domination disappeared in 1815, the price of commodities fell but the rents did not. Many tenants who now found themselves unable to

---

¹ On the Skeagh Estate in Co. Cavan (Bailieborough amd Knockbride) where Sir Robert Hodson was Landlord, rents had increased by 257% between 1806 and 1812.

pay the exorbitant rent were evicted. From the British government's point of view, Ireland, once more seized by universal discontent and widespread violence was in a "state of insubordination".[178] Determined to either prevent their evictions or gain revenge for evictions already perpetrated, groups such as "The Whiteboys" and "Captain Rock's Men" carried out attacks on landlords and land agents. One notable example was in Co. Clare, when the Courtenay Estate was cleared of its tenants by the Land agent and his men. Deprived of any means to house and care for their families, some of the dispossessed men turned to revenge and assassinated those who had evicted them. Large numbers of the dispossessed who engaged in these or lesser activities invariably ended up in a hangman's noose or on a prison ship destined for a penal colony at the other side of the world.

In 1821 the troubled situation in the country was made worse by a partial failure of the potato crop on which the native Irish were almost wholly dependent. (This dependence on the potato will be examined more closely in the next chapter.) Because of the shortage of potatoes, the price of this commodity had increased by over 300% so that when people had consumed their own reduced crop, those potatoes that were available were unaffordable. By May of 1822 almost the whole of Connacht along with parts of Munster was in a state of starvation. Most people considered themselves fortunate if they could have one small meal of porridge soup in the day, while some resorted to consuming the precious seed potatoes that they had preserved for planting the following summer. In the most badly affected areas the dreadful spectre of typhus appeared.

The government reaction was not to prevent the removal of the tillage crops from the country[I] or to allay starvation and want but instead to reinforce law and order. In 1822 a new Irish Constabulary was formed by Robert Peel[II] whose aim was not only to maintain law and order, but to monitor and target dissent at a local level.

## The Catholic Association

In 1811, King George III had become insane and this time would remain so until his death. His vice-ridden eldest son George,[III] now became Prince Regent.and succeeded him as King George IV after the death of George III on January 29th 1820.

Prior to the Act of Union, in 1797, George, then Prince of Wales, had been in favour of limited Catholic emancipation and it was hoped by all Catholics that his reign would herald full emancipation for them. However in spite of visiting Ireland for the month of August 1821, where he was assured by the Catholic bishops of the loyalty of the Catholics of Ireland, the new King (having been greatly influenced by his anti Catholic mistress Lady Hertford) became if anything more hard-line than his father in his anti Catholic attitude and

---

[I] "…we know the food is there; for since this famine has been declared in Parliament, thousands of quarters of corn have been imported every week from Ireland to England." – William Cobbett, English Historian and Agriculturalist, July 1822.

[II] A Police force known as "The Peace Preservation Force" had existed before this. The new Irish police force were nicknamed "Peelers" after their founder.

[III] "Is it madness or meanness that clings to thee now?
   Were he God – as he is but the commonest clay,
   With scare fewer wrinkles than sins on his brow
   Such servile devotion might shame him away." – Byron on George IV

avowedly expressed his intention that he would never sign any document in favour of Catholic emancipation.

In the Spring of 1823, when it appeared that there was no sign that emancipation would be granted for the foreseeable future, Daniel O'Connell founded "The Catholic Association." By not claiming to be a representative body, and by throwing open its membership to anybody who wanted to join, O'Connell managed to sidestep the Convention Act. In effect the Association was in modern terms, nothing other than a Catholic trade union, formed to fight and win for Irish Catholics by peaceful means the rights due to them as citizens of their native land.

The Association held regular meetings in Dublin and by the hard work of its organising committee who undertook a census of the Catholic population; it first gradually and then rapidly spread throughout the country where it gained the universal support of the Catholic clergy. Every parishioner, no matter how poor, was able to join the association by contributing the so-called "Catholic rent" of one penny per month. By 1825, many of the Catholics of Ireland were members and were unified in this common cause of their religious freedom as never before. In almost every locality the parish priest acted as the representative of the Association and collected the "rent". Soon £500 a week was being contributed to the Association by the Catholics of Ireland. The monies collected allowed the association to fund a newspaper and to defend the common man in court with barristers and attorneys against the non-payment of the tithe to the Protestant Church of Ireland. The Association also took legal action against landlords for their acts of blatant injustice. Grants were given to fledgling Catholic schools. All the while O'Connell maintained a high profile and regularly addressed mass meetings of tens of thousands of people.

Alarmed by the rapid rise and power of this "association" which in spite of the extreme poverty of its members was not lacking in funds, the government decided to take action and declared its intention to introduce a bill in parliament to ban The Catholic Association, in spite of the fact that since it had become all powerful in the country, crime had greatly decreased. When the government's intentions were made public O'Connell issued a warning to them during a speech: "I warn the British minister against either intimidating or coercing the people of Ireland. They are a brave and a chivalrous race, whose valour the history of all Europe attests. If ever they shall be driven to the field to vindicate their liberties they may not want another Bolivar[1] to animate their efforts".[179] The government was incensed by this fighting talk and as Robert Peel (now Home Secretary in London) had already given the instruction that O'Connell was to be punished on the first possible pretext it was decided to prosecute him but Peel was foiled when a grand jury found that O'Connell had no case to answer.

Peel nevertheless could still proceed with the suppression of The Catholic Association, and as the Old Convention Act was not sufficient for its suppression; "A Bill for the Suppression of Unlawful Associations in Ireland" was quickly drafted and presented to the House of Commons.

## So Near

In early 1825, O'Connell travelled to London where a reconciliation took place between himself and the English Catholic lobbyists. Quite taken by O'Connell's enthusiasm, magnetism and oratory powers, O'Connell now became the

---

[1] This was a reference to Simon Bolivar who had just led Colombia to freedom from Spanish rule.

spokesman for the unified group and thanks to pro emancipation M.Ps and Peers in the parliament; negotiations were opened once more between the Catholics and the government during which O'Connell agreed to the dissolution of the Catholic Association. Such was the progress in London that O'Connell was sure that this time his efforts for emancipation would meet with success. In a letter to his wife he wrote: "Call my children together – tell Danny to fling up his cap for old Ireland. I have now no doubt but that we shall be emancipated…we have won the game"[180]. That very same day the Prime Minister, Lord Liverpool met a delegation of Tory M.Ps to discuss the mechanics of Catholic emancipation.

However one month later, as the bill for Catholic emancipation was being drafted, the Duke of York and heir presumptive Prince Frederick (who only a few weeks before had received and entertained O'Connell with great friendliness) made a passionate speech in the House of Lords which torpedoed the project: In a voice full of emotion he told the Lords: "The Roman Catholics will not allow the Crown or the Parliament to interfere with their Church. Are they nevertheless to legislate for the Protestant Church in England? I have been for five and twenty years ever since the question has been agitated, advocating the cause of Protestant ascendancy. I have been brought up in these Protestant principles, and from the time when I began to reason for myself, I have entertained them from conviction; and in whatever situation I may be placed in life, I shall maintain them, so help me God!"[181]

With the bill's collapse, the immediate danger was now for the Catholic Association which was about to be suppressed by Robert Peel, but there was a loophole in Peel's bill which O'Connell now intended to make use of – one which allowed for Catholic organisations which engaged in charitable works.

When the bill banning the association had passed all stages, "The Catholic Association" was officially dissolved, and almost immediately a new body called "The New Catholic Association" appeared as an association formed for "charitable purposes"[182] and to "promote concord between all classes of Irishmen"[183], but the real work of the Association continued as before. Having saved the Association and beaten "Orange Peel" once more, O'Connell could be forgiven for boasting: "I can drive a coach and six through any act of Parliament!"[184]

During the mid 1820s The New Catholic Association continued to grow from strength to strength. By 1826, the membership of The Association was such that the half penny membership per month amounted to £1,000 per week. But how could the Catholic Association actually force the government's hand?

## The 1826 Election

When the vote had been granted to the forty shilling freeholders in 1793, they had since that time become unwilling hostages to their landlord, who they had to vote for if he was seeking election, or if not, vote for the candidate which the landlord "recommended" or face punishment or eviction from the landlord or his agents. This was due to the system of "open ballot" where every voter had to declare to the clerk in front of anyone who was present who he was voting for. Invariably, an agent of the landlord was there making notes during the voting.

During the election campaign of 1826 O'Connell was taken pleasantly by surprise when a suggestion emanating from Waterford was put to him, that a Catholic emancipation candidate should be put forward in that county to challenge the sitting M.Ps, Lord George Beresford and the Duke of Devonshire (both of whom "owned" the county between them) and that the Catholic forty shilling freeholders should be instructed to vote for the emancipation candidate.

O'Connell was delighted with the proposal and a Protestant candidate in favour of Catholic emancipation was decided on;

Mr. Villiers Stuart. When Stuart's candidacy was announced the establishment were appalled and the local Protestant newspapers took up the charge in favour of the landlords. Villiers Stuart was accused of "encroachment on the rights of private property"[185] while the Duke of Devonshire said that: "...he refused as a peer to interfere with the votes of his £50 freeholders but expected of course that his 40 shilling freeholders would abstain from giving their vote to either of the rival candidates"[186].

In their anger at the audacity of the move, the Beresfords protested in their election leaflet that the Catholic Association and the local priests were trying to set the populace against the landlords who were their "natural protectors"[187] and that "...a few itinerant orators emanating from a scarcely legal body called the Catholic Association, aided by a portion of the Roman Catholic clergy subservient to its views, claim a right to impose a representative upon the legitimate electors of the county."[188]

At the official nomination meeting, Daniel O'Connell attended and employed a clever tactic to make a speech to the large audience outlining the issues at stake. By getting one of Beresford's oldest tenants, a man named Casey to nominate him for the seat, O'Connell spoke for two hours before declining the nomination and asking his supporters to vote for Villiers Stuart.

When the votes were counted, Stuart was easily elected to the detriment of Beresford who lost his seat. The ascendancy party throughout Ireland and the establishment in England were aghast for it seemed that before their very eyes a crack had appeared in the established order. The Irish Croppies had dared to stand up. In Dublin, The Evening Post announced "Let it be proclaimed throughout the Empire! The Mighty are down before the breath of the people"[189]

Before the election concluded in the few other constituencies which were still voting, the Association attempted to repeat its Waterford success and managed to get pro-emancipation candidates elected in Monaghan, Louth and Westmeath.

For the forty- shilling freeholders who had defied their landlords, there was a dreadful price to be paid. Where "great" men such as George Beresford or his kind were defeated or had a close run thing, revenge followed in the form of wholesale evictions, where tenants were cast out and the land turned over to cattle grazing.¹⁹⁰ In the case of tenants who were evicted while still in arrears with their rent, they were imprisoned.

## An Incident in the Struggle against Landlord Tyranny

On the Shirley estate in the district of Farney, South Monaghan, the Landlord, Evelyn John Shirley, who up to this period had been regarded as one of the more fair minded landlords, now turned on his tenants who had failed to vote as he had instructed in the election of 1826.[1]

When Shirley's Land Agent Humphry Evatt died shortly after the election, Shirley replaced him with Sandy Mitchell who now became one of the most feared and hated men in Co. Monaghan.

Mitchell, who became leader of the local Yeomanry, now examined all leases and raised all rents by at least one third. Local bogland which the tenants had used to harvest peat to heat their cabins had up to this point been "free" for tenants but Mitchell now imposed a rent on bogland of up to £8 an

---

[1] Shirley's tenants had voted for him, but he had also instructed them to vote for his running mate Colonel Leslie who like Shirley was against Catholic emancipation. The tenants had decided to "cast one vote for their landlord and one for their Faith" and had elected Shirley's opponent, the pro emancipation Westenra instead of Leslie.

acre and divided up the bog into ridiculously small lots forcing even the smallest tenants to "rent" multiple lots at exorbitant prices.

In the local Catholic schools which were on "Shirley land" Mitchell insisted on Protestant instruction and the use of the King James Bible. A standoff quickly developed, and eviction followed for the many tenants who withdrew their children from the schools.

Between 1829 and 1843, Mitchell was as a "devil incarnate" to the tenants of one of the largest estates in the county which consisted of over 20,000 acres. In 1843, while attending the spring court session in Monaghan town, Mitchell dropped dead during an apoplectic fit. When this news reached Farney, bonfires were lit all over Carrickmacross and the surrounding district that night, partly in joy and relief that the the people had been delivered from this man and partly in the hope that Mitchell would be replaced by someone better, as it was felt by some of the tenants that E.J. Shirley was not a party to every evil deed that Mitchell committed.

The tenants were shortly to be disabused of this notion, for Shirley now appointed William Steuart Trench as his Land Agent, and acting on Shirley's instructions, Trench now proceeded to increase both rents and bog payments. Trench informed the tenants that from now on rents would be collected in money or in kind "at the point of a bayonet".

The general tenantry were now unable to pay their rent and those who could do so refused until their grievances were addressed.

In 1589, the Gaelic ruler of Farney, Hugh Roe MacMahon had been tried by an English Kangaroo Court and hanged outside his own door by Lord Deputy Fitzwilliam on a charge of cattle driving (or distraining) in order to collect outstanding rents. Following this, Monaghan had been "confiscated" becoming "the property of the Crown". Now, two and a half centuries later Shirley attempted to use this same method to collect his outstanding rents. As Shirley's men roamed the estate in search of cattle, his tenants (who were expecting such a move) reacted quickly and withdrew all livestock into their cabins where Shirley was forbidden to follow without a warrant. To shouts and hoots of derision Shirley's cattle drivers returned to Carrickmacross with one small calf that they had found trapped in a ditch,

Shirley was not prepared to let his tenants have the last word in the matter. With the Royal Irish Constabulary as backup, Shirley now employed a private army to seize goods and evict and arrest all tenants against whom decrees had been obtained at the Monaghan assizes. In response many of the menfolk among the tenants banded together into a "Whiteboy" group called "The Molly Maguires". Dressed as women and with their faces smeared, the process servers, bailiffs and cattle drivers in Shirley's army were ambushed, knocked up and ordered to resign from Shirley's service lest some greater evil should befall them. In response, Shirley now decided upon the eviction of many of his tenants.

### The "Battle of Magheracloone"

In order to evict a tenant, Shirley's Land Agent, Trench, was required by law to post the notice of eviction on the wall of the dwelling. Trench now applied to Dublin Castle for a "Substitution of Notice" meaning that he could post a list of those to be evicted on any building which the person or persons to be evicted frequented. Trench chose the door of the local Catholic chapel.

On June 5th 1843 a Stipendiary Magistrate and a company of troops supplied by Dublin Castle arrived in the area. Accompanied by Shirley's baliff they marched towards the Chapel of Saints Peter and Paul in Magheracloone to post the notice detailing all those who were to be evicted. Met near the church by a large crowd intent on stopping the posting of the notice, the troops were ordered to fix bayonets. The magistrate was told by Trench to proceed to the Chapel and post the notice. However on attempting to do so he was met by a volley of stones, none of which hit him. He retired and the soldiers were ordered to advance. The advancing troops were now met by a shower of stones after which they were ordered to halt and fire their weapons into the crowd. Six or seven men

fell under the volley. The troops advanced once more but the crowd charged them, and using a variety of weapons (sticks, farm implements and stones forced the soldiers to flee.

Outside the chapel, most of those hit by the musket balls had only been injured but one – Peter Agnew from Lisnaguiveragh had been killed. At the inquest the jury found that at no time had the lives of the troops been in danger.

The incident now became widespread knowledge and was finally raised in the House of Commons, bringing Shirley unwanted media attention. Forced to draw in his horns,

Shirley decided not to proceed with the evictions and for a short time at least, relative peace returned to Farney.

## A Catholic Member of Parliament for Clare

The Clare By-election

When the (Dublin born) anti Catholic Duke of Wellington Arthur Wellesley became British Prime Minister with Robert Peel as his Home Secretary in January of 1828, it appeared that the chance of Catholic emancipation becoming a reality was as far away as ever. However in June of that year, the M.P for Clare, Vesey Fitzgerald accepted Wellington's appointment as President of the Board of Trade and was by law forced to undergo re-election. In appointing Fitzgerald, Wellington felt sure that his re-election could not be jeopardised by the Catholic Association as he was in favour of emancipation and was also very popular in his constituency.

It was at this juncture that one of O'Connell activists, a Protestant named David Roose came up with the same plan that brought to O'Connell's mind the words uttered years before by the Catholic activist John Keogh - that a Catholic, even though barred from sitting in Parliament should nevertheless put himself forward for election, and if elected, present himself before parliament so that he could be excluded. By being excluded, those who had elected him would be excluded and Keogh felt that denying a Catholic the right to represent his constituency would cause such a tumult that emancipation would follow or in Keogh's words "...until John Bull's instinctive respect for Parliament had been so shocked that the barriers would be removed"[191.]

O'Connell himself now took the decision to stand for election, against Fitzgerald. Attacking the anti Catholic oath (which elected M.P.s were required to take in order to sit in parliament) was almost the entire thrust of O'Connell's short campaign. In an address to the voters of Clare he did not mince his words: "It is true that as a Catholic I cannot, and of course never will, take the oaths at present prescribed to members of Parliament; but the authority which created these oaths can abrogate them, and I entertain a confident hope that, if you elect me, the most bigoted of our enemies will see the necessity of removing from the chosen representative of his people an obstacle which would prevent him from doing his duty to his King and Country. The oath at present required by law is – "That the Sacrifice of the Mass and the invocation of the Blessed Virgin Mary and other saints as now practised in the Church of Rome are impious and idolatrous." – Of course, I will never stain my soul with such an oath. I leave that to my opponent, Mr. Vesey Fitzgerald. He has often taken that horrible oath; he is ready to take it again and asks your votes to enable him so to swear. I would rather be torn limb from limb than take it. Electors of the County Clare! Choose between me, who abominates that oath and Mr. Vesey Fitzgerald who has sworn it full 20 times! Return me to Parliament, and it is probable that such a blasphemous oath will be abolished for ever. As your representative, I will try the question with the friends in Parliament of Mr. Vesey Fitzgerald. They may send me to prison. I am ready to go there to promote the cause of the Catholics, and of universal liberty. The discussion which the attempt to exclude your representative from the House of Commons must excite, will create a sensation all over Europe, and produce such a burst of contemptuous indignation against British bigotry in every enlightened country in the world, that the voice of all the great and good in England…being joined to the universal shout of the nations of the Earth, will overpower every opposition and render it impossible for Peel and Wellington any longer to close the doors of the constitution against the Catholics of Ireland."[192]

## "They must either crush us or conciliate us"

When the result of the election was announced before an ecstatic crowd of 60,000 people Daniel O'Connell had won the seat by a majority of two to one. Setting out for Dublin almost immediately, his carriage was greeted in every town by large crowds. Upon his arrival in Dublin, O'Connell told his audience: "What is to be done with Ireland? What is to be done with the Catholics? They must either crush us or conciliate us. There is no going on as we are; there is nothing so dangerous as going on as we are...if Wellington be not the madman he is said to be, if Peel be not the driveller I think he is, let them recollect that two years ago they obtained concessions which I would rather die upon the scaffold than yield to them now..."[193]

In London both Wellington and Peel were in shock. King George IV was furious and demanded that an election be called, during whose campaign the cry of "No Popery" should resound within Britain from end to end. Wellington was more practical. Under the present political system, Ireland could no longer be considered a stronghold of the Protestant ascendancy – the game was up. After a row with George IV, Wellington, tears streaming down his face left the King convinced that he would have to resign as Prime Minister.

Peel wrote: "All the great interests broke down and the desertion has been universal"[194] Already 80% of the British army was stationed in Ireland but still Peel felt powerless, realising that he could not repeat the butchery of old as for one thing the ordinary garrisoned soldier who happily fraternised with the Irish Catholic would not stomach it.

When all was said and done, both the King and Wellington decided that there was no option but to grant emancipation and in the King's speech of 1829 it was announced that the laws that imposed civil disabilities on Catholics were to be considered by his majesty's government.

Preparatory to this momentous change in policy, Peel as Home Secretary felt that he had no option but to resign his Oxford University seat and ask his electors to re-elect him with the mandate for a free hand in dealing with the issue of Catholic emancipation. However when he went before his electorate he was heavily defeated.[1] Faced with the ignominy of Peel's absence from parliament, the government quickly found a pocket borough named Westbury in Wiltshire where there was an election in the offing. Even here, Peel was stoned in the streets as he canvassed and later admitted his election was only due to the fact that his rival for the seat arrived late for the nomination meeting or: "…it is highly probable that I should have fared no better at Westbury than I did at Oxford…"[195.]

## The Granting of Catholic Emancipation by the British Government

"Wellington and Peel – blessed be heaven – we defeated you. Our peaceable combination, bloodless, unstained, crimeless, was too strong for the military glory." – Daniel O'Connell.

### The Passage of the Bill

On March 5th 1829, the British Home Secretary Robert Peel introduced the Catholic Emancipation Bill in the House of Commons. For over four hours Peel explained to the members why the government felt that it had no choice but to grant equal rights to Catholics. Henceforth Catholics could be granted appointment to all military and civil posts but they were still to be excluded from a number of high offices. A new

---

[1] One of those heavily involved in the campaign against Peel's re-election as the M.P for Oxford was a young Oxford don by the name of John Henry Newman who was determined to preserve the rights of Protestantism. He was to later convert to Catholicism and eventually became a Cardinal of the Catholic Church.

oath had been formulated which allowed a Catholic to give his allegiance to the King without denying the most sacred doctrines of the Catholic faith. After an often stormy debate the Bill was carried by a majority of two to one after which it was introduced into the House of Lords by the Prime Minister, the Duke of Wellington. Here the bill faced stiff opposition, for to their Lordships, the exclusion of Catholics was an article of faith and to vote in favour of it was something akin to an act of treason. However, the King wanted it so and when Wellington warned the house that a refusal to endorse the bill might well result in civil war, the House yielded. On April 13th 1829 the Emancipation Act was placed on the Statute Book.

Robert Peel

### The Irish Electorate is reduced by 87%
However the bill had a sting in the tail for the Catholics of Ireland, one that O'Connell foolishly agreed to as a precondition for the introduction of the bill. Knowing full well that at the next election, Catholics would win the majority of the Irish seats Wellington and Peel sought to take back with the left hand what they had given with the right and protect the ascendancy establishment as much as they could. In Ireland as in England all forty-shilling freeholders had been entitled to vote, but following the passage of the Act the Irish franchise was increased to £10 while it would remain at 40 shillings in England. In one fell swoop the number of men able to vote in Ireland fell from 200,000 to 26,000. The vast majority of Irish

Catholic voters had been disenfranchised. The situation was only made worse by the parliamentary reform bill of 1832 that saw the franchise further reduced in Ireland while it was extended in England.

Furthermore the government also passed a law that banned The New Catholic Association which had already been disbanded by O'Connell. In spite of this disbandment, the government proceeded with the legislation, called "The Act for the Suppression of Illegal Associations" as they wished to ensure that O'Connell would never again be able to repeat the harm he had done to the establishment.

When the Emancipation Bill became law[1] it was not retrospective, meaning that as O'Connell had been elected as M.P for Clare before the Act became law, he could not legally take his seat in the House of Commons. However it was widely felt that in a spirit of generosity and magnanimity the government would make a special provision for him and allow him to take his seat by taking the new oath. O'Connell himself was of this opinion as he felt that the government would be keen to show Ireland that in the wake of the often acrimonious battle for emancipation a new page had been turned, and that he, as the de facto Irish leader would be welcomed into the Commons.

## King George IV Curses Daniel O'Connell

As was the custom for new members of parliament, Daniel O'Connell was obliged to present himself before King George

---

[1] Following the passing of the Emancipation Bill, O'Connell wrote: "The from of persecution is altered – the spirit remains the same. Those who heretofore would have used the dagger, or the knife of the assassin, employ now only the tongue, or the pen of the calumniator – and instead of murdering bodies exhaust their energies in assassinating reputation. Calumny has been substituted for murder, and the faction which has so long rioted in Irish blood, consoles its virulent and malignant passions by indulging in ever varying, never-dying falsehood and truculent slander."

IV at the Royal Levée. Intending to utter words of loyalty O'Connell approached the King, who appeared to be already speaking to him. However by the time he had arrived at the throne the King had stopped talking. O'Connell then proceeded to kiss the King's hands as was required of him and then moved away.

In the days that followed the Royal Levée there were rumours about the coldness of the King's reception to him and when a Scottish newspaper contained an article that reported that the King had actually cursed O'Connell, he spoke about the matter to the Duke of Norfolk who told him: "Yes, you are the person alluded to. The day you were at the Levée his Majesty said as you were approaching, "There is O'Connell. God damn the scoundrel"[196].

### English Vindictiveness in Defeat

After the King's harsh reception, O'Connell now doubted that the government would allow him take his seat under the new oath. He was correct. When he presented himself before the House he was offered the old Oath of Abjuration. After claiming that he should be allowed to take the new oath he was informed by the speaker that the act was not retrospective after which O'Connell bowed and departed.[1]

One pro emancipation M.P, Henry Brougham succeeded in carrying a motion that O'Connell's case should be heard at the bar of the House during which O'Connell outlined the reasons why he should not be asked to take the old oath but to no avail.

---

[1] By this time, the first English Catholic M.P, The Earl of Surrey (son of the Duke of Norfolk) had already been elected to the House. Instead of supporting O'Connell's bid to take his seat, Surrey remained mute. This was in line with the "gratitude" of English Catholic peers who alienated O'Connell and sneered at him. When O'Connell was "put up" for membership of the Catholic "Cisalpine Club" located in London, he was "blackballed" or refused membership because of an objection by one or more existing members of the Club.

On May 19th, for the second time he was again presented with the old oath by the speaker before a packed House. After studying the paper he spoke in a voice full of defiance: "I see in this oath, one assertion as to a matter of fact which I know to be false; I see in it another assertion as to a matter of opinion which I believe to be untrue. I therefore refuse to take that oath."[197] Once more O'Connell bowed and departed the House. But the vindictiveness in defeat of both Crown and government did not end here. On a personal level, with the passage of the Emancipation Bill, O'Connell had every expectation that as the most senior barrister then practising on the Irish circuit he would be now appointed to the so called "Inner Bar" and made a Senior Counsel or King's Counsel, but this was not to be until after the death of King George IV and the overthrow of Wellington. Furthermore, in spite of the act, Irish Catholics were still to a greater degree excluded from "The Club". As they were not "good chaps" or "one of us" many government appointments which had technically opened up to Irish Catholics under the act, did not open up to them in fact.[I]

Very soon it was clear to O'Connell that the "government contemplated no real change"[198] in favour of the appointment of Irish Catholics to positions which they were now both eligible for and even entitled to.

Furthermore by barring Catholics from the very highest governmental offices in Ireland, (Lord Chancellor and Lord Lieutenant) the substance if not the outward appearance of the Protestant ascendancy remained.[II]

---

[I] By 1890 after 60 years of "emancipation", the number of Protestant Judges in Ireland was 3,826 while the number of Catholic Judges was 1,229.

[II] In the decade following Catholic emancipation, the British Government of the day undertook various reforms in both the Parliamentary and Corporate

Preparatory to another by-election in Clare, Daniel O'Connell left London and returned to Dublin where he received a tumultuous reception. Back in Clare the Protestant gentry including William Smith O'Brien (soon to be leader of the Young Ireland Movement) were opposed to O'Connell's re-election to the seat but such was his popularity that no candidate put their name forward against him and he was elected unopposed on July 30th 1829.

## The Little Ark
Not only was Catholic emancipation not being enforced at a national level, it was also not being enforced even at a more local level. Landlords who had thus far refused to allow a Catholic chapel or Mass-house on their estates could continue to do so with impunity. One such landlord was Marcus Keane, a virulent anti-Catholic who refused to allow the construction of a Mass House on his estate of 150,000 acres which he rented from a Mr. Westby on the Loop Head peninsula of West Clare. Keane swore that any of his tenants who allowed a priest to offer Mass in their cabin would be immediately evicted, while any family who gave assistance or shelter to an evicted family would also be evicted in their turn. Keane also engaged in the pressurising of his tenants to renounce the Catholic faith by offering them food and better conditions if they complied.

Whilst the parish priest of Kilbaha attempted to minister in such conditions, in the late 1830's, a younger and more active priest, Fr. Michael Meehan was appointed to the parish. After much struggle and hardship in the parish, in 1851 Westby was approached by the Bishop who appealed to him to relent and allow the construction of a chapel but Westby refused to over-rule Keane.

---

spheres. Among Scotland and Wales, Ireland received the lowest increase in representation per head of population, the least amount of franchise extension and the least amount of reform.

The following year Fr. Meehan came up with the idea of offering Mass on the beach in a small cabin on wheels, just large enough to enclose the altar, and a few elderly parishioners. As the beach was technically not part of Keane's estate, it was assumed he could not interfere. However Keane continued to make life difficult and brought Fr. Meehan to court on a charge of causing an obstruction on the roadway to the beach, a case which Keane lost. On one occasion Keane's men burnt down a tenant's house while the family attended Mass on the beach, burning to death the baby of the family who had been left asleep in its cradle.

For many years, the people of Kilbaha flocked to the beach on Sunday's at low tide in all kinds of weather to attend Mass at "The Little Ark". The beach was also the scene of weddings, christenings and funerals. The situation was brought to prominence by visitors to the area who were both amazed that a quarter of a century after "emancipation" such conditions existed and also at how highly the people valued the Mass, enduring great suffering and hardship in order to attend it.

Finally in 1856, Keane offered Fr. Meehan a piece of land on which to construct a church. Fr. Meehan refused as it was a piece of bogland on which no building could be constructed. The following year Keane was forced to give way. The Bishop of Killalloe had decided to take the matter to court in Dublin and Mr. Westby fearing the bad publicity from the court case and the possibility of questions in the House of Commons forced Keane to give way, instructing him to allocate a piece of ground for a Catholic Church. The church which was named "Our Lady Star of the Sea" is still known locally as "The Church of the Little Ark[1]"

---

[1] "The Little Ark" remains housed in the parish church of Kilbaha on Loop Head.

## "The Member for All-Ireland"[1]

### Early Battles for Repeal of the Act of Union

For O'Connell, Catholic emancipation had always been a secondary consideration to the repeal of the Act of Union. Now as an independent Irish Catholic M.P he realised all too clearly that his voice for the Irish majority was lost in Westminster and that his speeches and lobbying fell on deaf ears. Furthermore in Westminster, he was regarded with hostility even at social events where "the great and the good" turned their backs on him.

With repeal of the Union firmly in his sights, O'Connell knew full well that a repeal movement had to be started in Ireland before the question would gain the attention of the government. At every turn, the government immediately sought to close him down, and every organisation that he formed was immediately proscribed.

Nevertheless in spite of the best efforts of Dublin Castle, O'Connell proceeded with his attempts to evade the intricacies of the law announcing weekly breakfasts at Holmes's Hotel declaring that if the government banned them, he would: "...resort to a political lunch. If the luncheon be equally dangerous to the peace of the great Duke (Wellington) we shall have political dinners. If political dinners be proclaimed down, we must, like certain sanctified dames resort to tea and tracts..."[199]

### The Carrot and the Stick

In London meanwhile the administration of Wellington and Peel was in its last days. The Tory Party that had resisted

---

[1] This was the name given to Daniel O'Connell by the prominent English agriculturalist and campaigner William Cobbett. As he was initially the only genuine representative of the native Irish people at Westminster, O'Connell came to be known by this name all over Europe.

Catholic emancipation at every turn was replaced at the end of November 1830 by what O'Connell felt would be a more Irish friendly administration under Earl William Grey who reappointed the pro-emancipation Lord Anglesey as Viceroy. Whereas the previous administration had treated O'Connell as a pariah, he was now vigorously courted by the government. Almost immediately he was appointed as a King's Counsel and offered the post of High Court Judge. Furthermore Anglesey made it clear to him that no high ranking legal position (such as Master of the Rolls or Attorney General) would be denied him if he would but join the government and give up his unceasing agitations. As soon as it became clear to O'Connell that the new government had no intention of applying the new emancipation at a practical level, he told Anglesey: "Then it is war between us."[200]

On his return to Ireland, the people were already fearful that O'Connell had been bought by the government but they need not have worried. O'Connell told a huge gathering in Merrion Square: "They wanted me to join them. They asked me what I wished to have done for myself. Like a true Irishman I answered their question by asking another. Tell me, said I, 'What are you going to do for Ireland'?"[201]

Having made clear his unwillingness to cooperate with the government, Anglesey and his new chief secretary Lord Derby stopped at nothing in their attempts to prevent O'Connell from organising repeal meetings or political discussions in any form even going so far as to proscribe a group formed by O'Connell called "A Body of Persons in the Habit of Meeting Weekly for Breakfast at a place called Holmes's Hotel". Every time O'Connell formed a group, the government banned it, until finally the government issued a declaration banning outright the meeting of any party, body, society or association no matter what its title or aim. Unimpressed by the government's determination to silence him, O'Connell held a breakfast at

Hayes's Hotel after which he was arrested and charged under the Act for the Suppression of Illegal Associations. However, in London the government realised how foolish they would look all over Europe if O'Connell was convicted for holding a public breakfast.[I] The case was postponed and finally dropped. O'Connell however was not conciliated and with all else having failed now decided to use his Westminster platform to good effect.

## The Tithe War

Since Catholic Emancipation had become law the government had failed to implement the law in Ireland in any meaningful way. Furthermore, in spite of the fact that the country was at peace, the government had completely closed down the public forum[II] and introduced in 1833 one of the most severe coercion bills yet seen. It was as if England was once more trying to drive Ireland into rebellion in order to punish it for having forced the emancipation issue.

Addressing the government benches at Westminster at the beginning of 1833, O'Connell did not mince his words: "I call upon you to conciliate Ireland if you would preserve the connection with England…recollect that the sword of desolation has swept over her, as when Cromwell sent eighty thousand of her people to perish in the West Indies; that you have burdened her with grinding penal laws, despite of treaties and in violation of every compact; and that you have neglected to fulfil the promises you held out to her at the Union…we know you as yet but in our sufferings and in our

---

[I] O'Connell was now an international figure and had even been nominated in Belgium as a candidate in their monarchical election.

[II] Writing to his friend Edmund Dwyer, O'Connell expressed his determination to fight "…the atrocious attempt to extinguish public liberty with which Ireland is menaced."

wrongs and you are now kind enough to give us as a boon this (Coercion) Act which deprives us of trial by jury and substitutes court martial; which deprives us of the Habeas Corpus Act, and in a word imposes on a person the necessity of proving himself innocent…we hoped then that you would afford us a redress of our grievances…and you give us instead an Act of despotism."[202]

Getting nowhere with his campaign for repeal of the union, O'Connell now felt that the only avenue left open to him was to put his weight and experience behind the long running struggle for the abolition of the tithe to the established Church of Ireland which had to be paid by all in spite of the fact that the membership of the Protestant Church in Ireland was but a tiny percentage of the population. As if the tithe wasn't enough, a separate tax known as the "Church-rate"[I] was also levied on all Catholics for the repair and upkeep of Protestant Churches.

In Ireland in the early 1830's, when Catholic emancipation had been granted, the injustice of the tithe, as a tax on the Catholic people for which nothing was given in return was bravely resisted, resulting in loss of life when the Yeomanry and the newly formed Irish constabulary were drafted in to enforce its collection. In spite of the overwhelming forces of "law and order", people up and down the country stood firm in resisting the tithe and paid for it with their lives. On May 22nd 1831, seventeen people were killed in Castlepollard, Co. Westmeath when police opened fire on a crowd at a fair at which distrained animals[II] were for sale. At Newtownbarry in Co. Wexford on June 18th 1831, thirteen people who resisted the

---

[I] Popularly called the "Cess Tax"

[II] Distrained animals refers to animals seized from those who refused to pay the tithe (or rent).

enforced seizure of their livestock in lieu of the tithe were shot dead. Following this incident, the Catholics became more organised and church bells were used to warn people of the approach of the police. On December 14th 1831, at the Battle of Carrickshock in Kilkenny thirteen policemen were ambushed and killed while trying to remove livestock and property. In the aftermath of this ambush, Daniel O'Connell spoke at a mass meeting of around 200,000 people that was held in support of those who had defended their property from being forcibly removed. For all of 1832, this "Tithe War" continued unabated. The forcible removal of property by the forces of the Crown was answered by robbery, cattle maiming, assault and burning. In Westminster O'Connell repeatedly raised the issue, but knowing that in the current climate, there was no chance that the government would abolish the tithe, O'Connell pleaded not for its abolition but for its reduction.

Here at least O'Connell met with a little success as the injustice of the tithe was so blatantly indefensible that the government were once more forced to act. In 1833 the church rate was abolished and the number of Protestant bishops in Ireland was slightly reduced. Furthermore, a commission was set up to examine the tithe, a move that caused Chief Secretary Stanley (Lord Derby) to resign. In spite of these sops, the people's resistance to the unjust tax continued with great loss of life. Just before Christmas 1834, a small body of police, accompanied by around 90 soldiers of the 29th Worcestershire Regiment of Foot killed twelve and wounded almost 50 after stones were thrown at them as they attempted to "collect" a tithe of around 50 shillings from a widow named Ryan in the parish of Gortroe, Co. Cork.

Finally in April 1836, an Irish Tithe Bill was introduced in the House of Commons that lowered the rate of the tithe by 25%. The specific collection of the tithe was also to be abolished as it was proposed that the tithe would instead be added to the rent paid to the landlord who would then make the payment. This was a move by the government which guaranteed the payment of the unjust tax by a population held hostage, because if the tithe was not paid in full, eviction by the landlord / tithe proctor would be the likely result.

Before the new bill would become law in 1838, the Protestant clergy and their tithe proctors engaged in feverish efforts to "collect" all outstanding tithes "due" from the Catholics of Ireland.

## "A Starving Race of Fanatical Slaves"

In 1835, the London media was consumed with a public row between O'Connell and a young Jewish conservative named Benjamin Disraeli who later became British Prime Minister for two terms. In 1832 O'Connell had publicly supported Disraeli at Disraeli's own request when Disraeli was standing for election as a Radical candidate. By 1835 Disraeli had become a conservative and now paid O'Connell back for his help. During his campaign to be elected in the constituency of Taunton, Disraeli labelled O'Connell as "an incendiary and a traitor"[203] and accused him of having a "bloody hand".[204]

Having previously gone out of his way to help him, O'Connell was furious at his ingratitude and in a speech told his audience: "...he calls me a traitor. My answer to that is he is a liar...England is degraded in tolerating or having upon the face of her society a miscreant of his abominable, foul and atrocious nature...(he) possesses just the qualities of the impenitent thief who died on the cross...for aught I know the present Disraeli is descended from him..."[205.]

Disraeli was not prepared to let O'Connell have the last word, He published a public letter to him that by its barely concealed loathing for him, the Irish people, and the Catholic Church made the young Disraeli the toast of the Conservative Party and launched him on his path to prominence and the position of Prime Minister. In his letter Disraeli wrote in part:"it is clear that the 'hereditary bondsman'[1] has already forgotten the clank of his fetters. I know the tactics of your Church– it clamours for toleration, and it labours for supremacy…with regard to your taunts as to any want of success in my election contests…no threatening skeletons canvassed for me…I an not one of those public beggars that we see swarming with their obtrusive boxes in the chapels of your creed, nor am I in possession of a princely revenue arising from a starving race of fanatical slaves."[206]

Beniamin Disraeli

## The Balance of Power

In the King's speech of 1834, the already bolted door to repeal of the Act of Union was further barred when in the King's speech it was declared that the union of Britain and Ireland would be upheld "…at the utmost cost and with all the power of the state…"[207.]

---

[1] A reference to the lines of Byron often quoted by O'Connell during the fight for emancipation: "…hereditary bondsman, know ye not; who would be free himself must strike the blow."

Following the general election of 1835, O'Connell's party of 36 M.Ps possessed the balance of power in Westminster between the Tories and the Whigs"[I] The anti repeal rhetoric from both sides was so strong that O'Connell decided to abandon the topic of repeal for the present, much to the dismay of many of his supporters. Following a meeting with the Whig leader Lord Melbourne at Lichfield House in St. James Square, London, an agreement was reached whereby O'Connell, in return for certain concessions, declared that he would support the Whigs in parliament.[II]

In return for joining the Whigs in an uneasy alliance O'Connell was allowed to put forward candidates for the legal appointees of the Irish administration. Both sides were ready to pounce on him if the repeal question were raised, but the Whigs were at least prepared to grant some concessions to O'Connell, such as a local government bill. Even here the government was especially careful to retain the appointment of all county sheriffs by Dublin Castle instead of allowing them to be elected by the town councils as in England. The reason for this was that if the sheriffs were elected, the long established practice of the "packing" of Irish juries would become impossible.

Nevertheless, in spite of everything, by the time Victoria became Queen of England in 1839, O'Connell had at least some reason to feel that the alliance with the liberals had achieved an

---

[I] The "Whigs" became the Liberal Party after 1850.

[II] Following this agreement which was known as the "Lichfield House Compact" the London Times bitterly criticised the move and a vitriolic poem about O'Connell was published which ran: "Scum condensed of Irish bog!, Ruffian – coward – demagogue!, Boundless liar – base detractor!, Nurse of murders – treason's factor!, Of Pope and priest the crouching slave, While thy lips of freedom rave; Of England's fame the vip'rous hater, Yet wanting courage for a traitor, Ireland's peasants feed thy purse, Still thou art her bane and curse."

easing in the harshness of the governance emanating from Dublin Castle. He proclaimed to his detractors that he was prepared to make: "...this one experiment...if we shall be deceived, we can fall back on our own resources."[208]

## "Abandon Hope all Ye that Enter Here"

Despite the fact that he and his M.Ps held the balance of power, the Whig government were often in a position to ignore O'Connell, especially when there was cross party support for a piece of legislation. In 1837, an investigation was commissioned by Lord John Russell into the dire state of poverty and destitution in Ireland from which emerged The Nichols Report of 1838. The reasoning behind the commissioning of the report was not concern for the welfare of Her Majesty's Irish subjects, but rather concern at the steady stream of destitute Irish who were making their way to England in search of a better life. This much was admitted to by George Nichols who later drafted the Irish Poor Law when he wrote regarding the Irish: "...who crossed the channel in search of the means of living...make it (an Irish Poor Law) a matter of policy"[209].

Among its conclusions, the report found that one quarter of the population of Ireland were dependent on charity for six months of the year and that the earnings of an average labourer was the paltry sum of two shilling and sixpence per week from which he had to pay his rent and tithe, and feed and clothe his family.

After the report emerged, Russell introduced the Poor Law Extension Bill (for Ireland) and, in spite of O'Connell's violent opposition that vast sums of money were to be spent in the erection of buildings and the implementation of a totally inadequate system where the cure might be said to be worse than the disease, the bill passed all stages and the "Poor Law" was officially established in Ireland along English lines (no clerical or religious involvement).

Sooner than tackle the evil landlord system with their rack-renting, the government had introduced an Act that allowed only for limited eligibility as those wishing to enter the Poor House had to be completely destitute. In order to avail of the government relief which was to be funded by the collection of commercial rates and general taxation a person was obliged to enter a workhouse where they would be engaged in extremely strenuous work in exchange for an amount of food which was barely life supporting.

## The Repeal Association

<u>One Last Try</u>

By the late 1830's Daniel O'Connell regarded his public life to be in a state of decline. Having repeatedly refused high office, he was almost bankrupt and totally reliant on the charity of his now dwindling supporters as many in the country now regarded his career as over. As late as June 1838, he had refused the high position of "Master of the Rolls" telling his friend P.V. Fitzpatrick; "I do not intend to nail my colours to the mast while Ireland is so totally unredressed...I am perhaps a fool but I have not the heart to desert Ireland – Ireland that has never yet had a steady friend."[210] By mid 1839, following the death of his beloved wife Mary, he was contemplating a complete withdrawal from public life. Once more confiding in Fitzpatrick he wrote: "...I think of giving up my income, save an annuity of a small sum to myself and my two sons, and going, if I am received to Clongowes (Jesuit College and Monastery) to spend the rest of my life there. I want a period of retreat to think of nothing but eternity."[211] However by the following Spring, the dying embers within him had been rekindled and he determined to make one last great effort to win the repeal of the Act of Union. His enthusiasm was in no small part due to an effort by the government to reduce the number of Irish voters once more, so much so that the Bill would almost cancel entirely the paltry effect of emancipation. In a public letter to his followers from London he wrote: "We are treated as if we were Helots.[1] Let the Irish rally with me for Repeal...My struggle has begun...I will terminate it only in death or repeal"[212.]

As many of his former chief activists now had busy careers O'Connell took much of the organisation of "The Loyal National Repeal Association of Ireland" upon his own shoulders. After the campaign was launched, O'Connell did not focus entirely on repeal but also addressed many other issues that oppressed the people and pronounced that the disestablishment of the Protestant Church of Ireland was a parallel aim of the movement. Realising that he was in earnest, the people rallied to his banner. The crowds at his meetings grew rapidly as people flocked to hear the man whom many had previously regarded as a spent force and the new Repeal Association flourished.

As the general election of 1841 approached, O'Connell, ever the pacifist, realised how much his speeches had inflamed public discontent. To his friend Fitzpatrick he confided: "Repeal and the Repeal alone is and must be the grand basis of all future operations...the people will take nothing short of that...I bitterly regret to tell you that the popular excitement is of so exasperated a character that they will rush into insurrection unless my influence checks and controls them"[213.]

Thanks to the recently passed Irish electoral bill, the native Irish electorate had been reduced to a minimum, making the emancipation bill almost inconsequential. Even O'Connell lost

---

[1] In Roman times, the Helots were a body of serfs (neither slave or citizen) from Sparta in Greece.

his seat in Dublin, but at the last minute managed to get himself nominated and elected in Cork. He no longer commanded the balance of power. In London, the Tory party had swept to power with his old foe Robert Peel as Prime Minister.

In spite of being hamstrung by the system at the general election, O'Connell's party fared extremely well in the corporation and municipal elections where the number of Catholic voters had been increased thanks to the measure of local government reform that he had won from the Whigs. Using this new power to good effect, the Corporations of Dublin and Cork along with many other towns successfully passed resolutions calling for the repeal of the Act of Union. For the first time since the reign of James II, a Catholic – Daniel O'Connell – became Lord Mayor of Dublin, an office which he discharged with such fairness and decorum that not even the worst of his detractors could find anything to complain about.

### The Emergence of the "Young Ireland" Movement

Shortly after Daniel O'Connell had undertaken the renewal of his movement for repeal of the Union, a meeting took place in Trinity College at which the long dormant College Historical Society was reconvened. As Catholics were now allowed to attend Trinity College, the reformed society contained both Catholics and Protestants. The most prominent among the attendees were Thomas MacNevin (who was elected President), John Dillon, John Mitchell and Thomas Davis. From the meetings of the society a new group or organisation called "Young Ireland" gradually emerged whose aims were the re-awakening of the national consciousness by the publication of articles on Irish history and the spirit of Irish Republicanism as espoused by Tone and Emmett.

Once the Young Ireland Organisation came into being, other members joined, one of the most prominent being the Monaghan journalist Charles Gavan Duffy. The members of the society all recognised in Daniel O'Connell the spearhead of the fight for repeal of the Union and most of them, if not already members of O'Connell's Association, joined it. By the spring of 1841 both Thomas Davis and John Dillon were on the central organising committee of the Repeal Association, but the fledgling Young Ireland movement also formed their own newspaper called "The Nation" which first appeared in late 1842. "The Nation" was chiefly a collaboration between Davis, Dillon and Duffy but Davis, a man of great intellect, quickly developed a flair for editorials which delighted the paper's fast growing readership. In the first issue of the paper, he outlined its aims, the first of which was the awakening of a sense of Irish nationality: "…which will not only raise our people from their poverty…but inflame them and purify them with a heroic love of country…"[214.] Other aims included raising; "…our people from their poverty, by securing to them the blessings of a domestic legislature".

Thomas Davis

The marriage of "The Nation" newspaper with the Repeal Association's campaign proved to be a great success, as through Davis's fine prose, the clamour for Repeal reverberated throughout the land. In "The Nation" Davis eloquently described the shortcomings of emancipation and the necessity of repeal: "Emancipation made it possible for

Catholics to sit on the judgement seat; but it left a foreign administration which has excluded them save in two or three cases...it left the local judges – those with whom the people had to deal – as partial, ignorant, and bigoted as ever; while repeal would give us an Irish code and Irish-hearted judges in every court...emancipation dignified a dozen Catholics with a senatorial name in a foreign and hostile legislature. Repeal would give us a senate, a militia, an administration all our own. The penal code, as it existed since 1793 insulted the faith of the Catholics, restrained their liberties and violated the public Treaty of Limerick. The Union has destroyed our manufactures, prohibits our flag, prevents our commerce, drains our rental, crushes our genius, makes our taxation a tribute, our representation a shadow, our name a by-word...it were nobler to strive for repeal than to get emancipation".[215]

However from the beginning, there was disquiet among the Young Irelanders at some of O'Connell's more measured statements, especially when he stressed before Dublin Corporation that although he sought complete repeal, he would in fact accept an Irish parliament subordinate to London if it were offered.[1] Furthermore, the Young Ireland movement did not appreciate O'Connell's unwillingness to accept their help and leadership at the highest levels of the repeal movement while their suggestions as to how repeal could be achieved went unheeded by O'Connell – the old campaigner who felt that he could not be taught anything new.

## Repeal Courts

As O'Connell's movement grew so did the concern of the British Prime Minister Robert Peel. Previously O'Connell had

---

[1] O' Connell said: "I will never ask for or look for, any other save an independent Legislature; but if others offer me a subordinate Parliament, I will close with any such authorised offer and accept it"

successfully backed the government into a corner over the issue of Catholic emancipation but on the issue of the union, Peel and his government, not to mention the whole British establishment were of one mind – there would be no compromise.

In May of 1843, Daniel O'Connell, along with any magistrate involved in the organisation of the Repeal Movement were dismissed from their positions as judges because of their involvement in a "seditious movement". If Peel had intended that this move would drive away numbers of the chief organisers for the movement, he was much mistaken – for his move was to have consequences which would find their echo almost eighty years later.[1] Out of disgust at Peel's punitive measure many other magistrates on the Irish circuit, both Protestant and Catholic resigned their appointments and offered their services to O'Connell, the most prominent among the Protestants being James Grattan (son of Henry Grattan) and William Smith O'Brien.

In Peel's move, O'Connell quickly saw an opportunity. Knowing that he had the full support and confidence of the people, he announced the setting up of "Repeal Courts", asking the people of Ireland to boycott the ordinary courts. The move was an immediate success, and once which struck at the heart of direct rule from Westminster, as O'Connell was effectively demonstrating an advantage of repeal – a fairer and more sympathetic judicial system that did not have packed juries and English judges.

When Peel saw, not only how his move had failed but also backfired upon him he issued a veiled threat to O'Connell and his campaign from Westminster, telling the House of

---

[1] So successful was O'Connell's strategy that it was imitated by Sinn Fein during the war of independence by the setting up of the Dáil or Sinn Fein Courts in 1919 and 1920.

Commons that:" deprecating as I do all war, especially civil war there is no alternative which I do not think preferable to the dismemberment of this Empire."[216]

## The Monster Meetings

From the Spring of 1843, both the number and size of the repeal meetings grew rapidly. Their rapid growth can in no small measure be ascribed to the disenfranchisement of the Irish people which O'Connell himself had foolishly agreed to as part of Catholic emancipation, the only replacement for disenfranchisement being mass action.

Every week found Daniel O'Connell travelling to a different part of the country to attend mass or "monster" meetings where for hours he would extol to the people the virtues and benefits of an Irish Parliament. This however was not his only topic, for O'Connell was adamant that the meetings and the movement would be completely free of disturbance, drunkenness or violence of any description and he often gave long speeches to the people on the benefits of teetotalism, encouraging them to either become members of, or adhere to the principles and promises of the Temperance Association founded by the Cork Capuchin Fr. Matthew, which in a few short years had achieved remarkable results in reducing the level of alcohol abuse among a poverty stricken population which sought to escape it's woes in cheap liquor.

In May of 1843 O'Connell addressed a meting of 150,000 people in Mullingar, Co. Westmeath, where he told the crowd: "...Peel is the merest man of words that the world ever produced...Boys, take my word for it, Peel is the very man that will repeal the Union".[217] Nothing could have been further from the truth for during the fight for emancipation, Peel was the very man who had wanted Wellington to stand firm and not give an inch. Once more Peel declared his intention not to shrink from civil war if the Union was in danger, and was much gratified by O'Connell's pleas to his followers not to arm themselves or engage in any activity contrary to the law: "In the midst of peace and tranquillity they are covering our land with troops...there was no House of Commons on Thursday, for the Cabinet were considering what they should do, not for Ireland, but against her. But, gentlemen, as long as they leave us a rag of the constitution we will stand by it. We will violate no law, we will assail no enemy; but you are much mistaken if you think others will not assail you."[218]

As O'Connell's rhetoric grew, so did Peel's resolve never to bend on the question of Home Rome for Ireland, for not only was Peel convinced that it would herald an eventual declaration of Irish independence but he knew for a fact that Parliament and England would back him in not giving into to O'Connell a second time. Surely, Peel reasoned, O'Connell must know this too?

## The End of the Repeal Movement

For the entire Summer and early Autumn of 1843, O'Connell, spoke, roused and excited audiences up and down the country, assuring them that victory was at hand. In August, a crowd so large that its size could not be reckoned gathered at the seat of the ancient high kings of Ireland at Tara, in Co.Meath. The London Times reported that one million people were present. Finally, to bring the season of meetings to a conclusion, it was announced that an even larger meeting would take place at the beginning of October at the site of King Brian Boru's victory over the Danes – Clontarf in Dublin.

An English view of O'Connell at Tara

By this time, Ireland, already awash with British troops, had been sent sizeable reinforcements in order to quell any insurrection – but O'Connell had given the government no excuse for action. When the Clontarf meeting was announced, the government decided that with or without insurrection the time for action had come.

As if trying to provoke a reaction, Dublin Castle did not reveal its intentions until the preparations for the great Clontarf meeting were complete. The day before the meeting was due to take place – Sunday October 8$^{th}$, a proclamation was issued banning the meeting. With warships in Dublin Bay and artillery on the approaches to Clontarf, O'Connell quickly arrived at his decision telling his committee that the Proclamation: "…must be obeyed"[219.]

Having suffered that end which all men suffer who desire an end but do not want the means, O'Connell nevertheless felt that victory might yet come and that the masses were content to trust his judgement. However Peel followed up with another blow. The following Saturday, Daniel O'Connell was among a group of repeal activists and newspaper editors to be arrested on charges of undermining the constitution and exciting disaffection in the army. In order to ensure a conviction, Peel instructed Dublin Castle to use every tried and tested method at its disposal. All Catholics were to be removed from the jury list, and the jury handpicked. A guilty verdict was assured and was duly delivered with sentence postponed. When sentence was finally delivered the following May, O'Connell and the other defendants were to be imprisoned for one year, along with a fine of £2,000 for O'Connell.

## The Decline

It was during the trial that O'Connell's closest advisors began to notice both his physical and mental decline as his court speeches lacked their usual electric quality. For O'Connell, prison was almost a relief from his unending toil. He was well treated and housed in the governor's quarters with servants while his family were allowed to freely come and go. While O'Connell himself was reluctant to appeal, an appeal against his sentence was nevertheless launched by the Repeal Committee and succeeded in London before Lord Chief Justice Denman on the grounds of jury packing.

Now freed from prison much to the chagrin of Peel and the government, everyone waited to see what O'Connell's next move would be. However by this time Daniel O'Connell, burnt out from a life of campaign and struggle was a spent force no longer capable of the action of earlier years. In spite of the fact that Peel had lost face over O'Connell's release from prison, he had nevertheless defeated the Repeal movement and the fight for repeal of the Act of Union gradually collapsed.

## The Split with Young Ireland

Daniel O'Connell now became increasingly alien to some of those in the Young Ireland movement who acted as his lieutenants in the repeal movement. A damaging break between the two sides now occurred over the issue of Catholic education.

At the end of 1844, Robert Peel proposed to establish in Ireland three "Queen's Colleges" which would provide higher education for Catholics. This move was part of a series of conciliatory public relations measures in the wake of the O'Connell case to show the Irish people that without a home rule parliament, England would indeed take care of its Irish subjects. The move proved to be divisive from the outset as Peel proposed that the colleges should be non denominational, which meant that they would not have a Catholic ethos. While O'Connell echoed the criticism of Archbishop McHale and the Catholic bishops over the establishment of "godless teaching"[220] in a Catholic country, the Young Ireland movement (which had a high percentage of Protestants among its leadership) took the opposite view, and maintained that the colleges should not be opposed. Still the unity between Young Ireland and the Repeal Movement endured in spite of an outburst by O'Connell against his protégé Thomas Davis for which O'Connell afterwards heartily apologised.

Just as the life and death struggle against starvation was about to break, many Irish people were both shocked and saddened to learn of the death from scarlet fever in September of 1845 of Thomas Davis, who through the organ of "The Nation" had become renowned for his eloquent writings and poetry. When his place as editor was taken by John Mitchel, the tone of "The Nation" became more forthright, and did not shy away from the question of using physical force to obtain freedom for Ireland. By mid 1846 O'Connell was under pressure to disassociate himself from the Young Ireland movement. O'Connell decided instead that he would demand of them a pledge to use only peaceful means. At a meeting of the repeal association in July 1846 (at which O'Connell was not present) the issue was raised and after a heated discussion in which no common ground could be found the Young Ireland Movement and the Repeal Association parted company.[1]

By the Summer of 1846, repeal of the Act of Union was not a priority for O'Connell's followers – the ordinary people of Ireland. A much greater struggle – for life and death - was continuing in the country, as the failure of the potato crop of 1846 coupled with the removal of the rent crops and

---

[1] It was at this discussion that a very young Thomas Francis Meagher (of which more will be told) asserted: "Be it for the defence or the assertion of a nation's liberty I look upon the sword as a sacred weapon". Thereafter he became known as "The Sword Meagher"

agricultural produce from the country spelled imminent disaster.

As Ireland starved, O'Connell commended the generosity of the British people towards Ireland, a generosity that was lacking among the government. He wrote: "If individual generosity could save a nation, British generosity would do so now; but it is impossible without the bountiful hand of parliament, and the disposition to bounty of the parliament appears to be extremely limited...How different would the scene be if we had our own parliament taking care of our people, of our own resources!"[221]

## The Death of Daniel O'Connell
"If you do not save Her, She cannot save Herself!"

As the people of Ireland sank every deeper into the all encompassing horrors of The Great Starvation, Daniel O'Connell health began to fail, a failure added to in no small measure by the suffering of his country. In December of 1846 he wrote: "The nation is starving and to the all-prevalent famine are now super-added dysentery and typhus. What is to be done? What is to be done?"[222] In February of 1847, he wrote to his friend Fitzpatrick: "...there's every reason to despond of efficient succour (from the government).[223]"

As his strength failed he made one supreme effort, and returned to the House of Commons for one last time to plead with the members of parliament to save Ireland. In a whisper he told the Prime Minister Lord Russell and the other members of the Commons: "Ireland is in your hands, in your power; if you do not save her she cannot save herself. I solemnly call on you to recollect that I predict with the sincerest conviction that one fourth of her population will perish unless you come to her relief."[224]

### "Do not Let them Bury me Until I am Dead"

Advised by his doctor to travel to Italy where it was hoped that the warmer climate might help to restore him, O'Connell left London in March 1847 accompanied by his friend and chaplain Fr. Miley. After travelling to France, O'Connell seemed to improve, but when the country was swept by a resurgence of Winter weather, he quickly declined. By the time Italy was finally reached in early May, O'Connell's health had completely broken down. Fr. Miley recalled: "His face had grown thin and his look proclaimed an inexpressible sadness, the head hung upon the breast and the entire person of the invalid, formerly so imposing was greatly weighed down".[225] By mid May it became increasingly apparent that he had a bleeding brain tumour that caused bouts of delirium during which he would shout: "Waken me if there is a division…I have the repeal!"[226] Afraid of lapsing into a coma he warned Duggan, his valet: "Do not let them bury me until I am dead".[227]

On May 15th, his last day, he was fully conscious when he received the last rites of the Church, after which he did nothing but pray until he finally closed his eyes.

# Chapter 9

# The Great Starvation

"We adopt the English expression and call those years the 'famine years' but there was no famine in the land. There is no famine in any land that produces as much food as will support the people of that land – if the food is left with them. But the English took the food away to England, and let the people starve...they cried out that there was a famine in Ireland, and they appealed to the nations of the earth to help the starving people...ships laden with food were sent from America...and while these ships were going into the harbours of Ireland, English ships laden with Irish corn and cattle and eggs and butter were leaving the harbours, bound for England. Ireland during those three years of '45, '46, and '47, produced as much food as was sufficient to support three times the population" – Jeremiah O'Donovan Rossa

"The horrors of the Irish famine have never been exceeded in the annals of human woe. To die of hunger in catastrophes of nature or military sieges is one thing; to perish miserably in the midst of plenty, which one has created, and is forbidden to touch in the name of political economy is quite another. It was the consumption of food by rent, instead of by the people that produced the famine. All through the famine Ireland was the greatest food-exporting country in the world." – John Morrison Davidson

"It must be clearly understood that the Irish Famine was not due to a lack of food. It was due to that impoverishment of the Irish race which had fallen upon them when their land was taken from them by force in the seventeenth century. There was plenty of food in Ireland; there was even the export of food during the famine itself: the failure of the potato crop destroyed only the food of the poorest, and had money been provided by a sufficient loan, or better still by a direct levy upon the whole resources of Great Britain, to furnish a minimum of purchasing power, the Irish could have been fed until the crisis was past. Partly, from false economic theory, partly from the errors inherent to all governments which have no experience of the governed, more from an indifference to the fate of Ireland, more still from religious animosity, in some degree from an obscure feeling that the weakening of Ireland would always be the strengthening of England, the tragedy was allowed to go its way." – Hilaire Belloc

"Ireland produced quite enough of corn to feed the people of the whole country; but day after day it was exported in shiploads while the people were dying of hunger." – P.W Joyce M.A

"It is true also, that Government did, to a certain small extent, speculate in Indian corn, and did send a good many cargoes of it to Ireland, and form depots of it as several points; but as to this; also, their mysterious intimation had led all the world to believe they would provide very large quantities, whereas, in fact, the quantity imported by them was inadequate to supply the loss of grain exported from any one county; and a Government ship sailing into any harbour with Indian corn, was sure to meet half a dozen sailing out with Irish wheat and cattle. The effect of this, therefore, was to blind people to the fact that England was exacting her tribute as usual, famine or no famine. The effect of both combined was to engender a dependent and pauper spirit...A landless, hungry pauper cannot afford to think of the honour of his country" – John Mitchel

## The Irish "Land System"

"Returning nothing to the soil, they (the landlords) consume its whole produce, minus the potatoes strictly necessary to keep the inhabitants from dying of famine" – John Stuart Mill

Following the War of the Two Kings (1688-1692, Ireland had become the domain of English landlords[I] and Protestant farmers who existed independent of the landlords. The native Irish Catholics were to all intents and purposes forbidden to hold any land, and in order to survive were forced to rent a plot of land from the landlord who regarded his estate as a source of income from which he tried to extract as much revenue as possible. As a direct result of this system the Irish people descended into a state of incomparable poverty.

Landlordism in Ireland was a hierarchical system. The Landlord who had been granted a vast estate by the crown often divested himself of all responsibility to his tenants by letting the estate to one or more middlemen sometimes in perpetuity and elected to live and spend his rent in England or on the continent.[II] This system evolved so that by the time of

---

[I] Sometimes referred to as "The Garrison Class" by the Irish

[II] When the English historian and Agriculturalist William Cobbett visited Ireland in 1834, there were six thousand higher ranking Irish landlords who did not live in Ireland. One of these landlords was Lord Middleton who received around £30,000 annually from his estate. In 1842 alone, around £6,000,000 in rent left Ireland to be spent abroad.

the famine, most estates had been divided and let to middlemen who then subdivided their holding and re-let them until finally there were 4, 6 and sometimes even 8 middlemen between the original landlord and the tenant.  With each subdivision (45% of Irish farms were of less than five acres) the amount of profit derived grew smaller and smaller meaning that rents, which were already twice that what they were in England, were increased at every opportunity.  If any improvement was made to the land, if bog was reclaimed or drained, or if the tenant was deemed to be "wealthier" than he should be, the middleman landlord often seized on the opportunity to increase the rent.  The lower ranking middleman in an effort to maximise his profit often split his land into smaller and smaller holdings in order to create more lots which could be rented to casual labourers (jobbers) or tradesmen for one season only at a very high rent. This system was known "Conacre". These men worked at their trade to pay the rent and grew as little as half an acre of potatoes to feed their family.[1]

A further measure that placed the tenant at the mercy of the landlord was the hanging rent, better known as the "hanging

---

During his visit to Middleton's estate, Cobbett recorded the state of the tenant's houses: "They all consisted of mud-walls, with a covering of rafters and straw...I took particular account of the first (house) that I went into...the floor, the bare ground. No fireplace, no chimney, the smoke going out a hole in the roof. No table, no chair, one window the glass broken half out. No bed, no mattress, some large flat stones, to keep the bodies from the damp ground; some dirty straw and a bundle of rags were all the bedding.

[1] It must be noted that it was the system itself that was evil. Numbers of the lower ranking landlords (which since the relaxation of the Penal Laws included a small number of Irish) had rented fifty or a hundred acres at an exorbitant rate and in many cases were themselves hard pressed to pay their rents to the landlord above them. The totality of the higher ranking landlords were either English or from the Protestant Ascendancy

gale". As almost all tenant farmers lived a 'hand to mouth' existence, there was no money with which the landlord could be paid until after the first harvest, which meant that many tenants were constantly a year in arrears with their rent – money that the landlord could demand at any time

Even aside from the fear of the "hanging rent" the majority of tenants had no security whatsoever in their tenancy. Known as "tenants at will", they were without a formal lease and could remain on their holding only at the landlord's pleasure. Furthermore, if evicted, after the notice period had elapsed they were not compensated in any way for improvements which they had made to their holding, meaning there was no incentive to conduct improvements, and spend what little they had on something that could be taken away from them on the morrow. However in Ulster, the tenants enjoyed what was known as the "Ulster Custom" which was a jealously guarded grant of tenant rights originally given to the planters so that they could have the same rights as British tenants. Any attempt in parliament to extend this custom to the rest of the country was thrown out as the Landlords maintained that in Ireland: "Tenant right is landlord wrong", a sentiment echoed by the majority of M.Ps and a totality of Lords.

In Ulster, tenant farmers improved their holdings in the sure knowledge that they would be adequately compensated if they moved on, meaning that farms in Ulster were generally more prosperous than those in the other provinces.

According to Sir John Burgoyne: "the possession of a bit of land was the one and the only thing absolutely necessary, (for survival) the rent consequently was high and generally well paid, being the first demand on all money received in order to secure that essential tenure; and only what remained became applicable to other objects"[228.]

For those families unceremoniously evicted from their holding, which was generally accompanied by the "tumbling" of their dwelling, it was "tantamount to a sentence of death by slow torture"[229] the House of Commons was informed in April 1846.

## Potatoes and Rent

Potatoes - "Food for the contented slave, not the hardy and the brave" – The Economist Newspaper.

Rent - "The corn crops were sufficient to feed the island. But the landlords would have their rents in spite of famine and in defiance of fever. They took the whole harvest and left hunger to those who raised it. Had the people of Ireland been the landlords of Ireland not a single human creature would have died of hunger, nor the failure of the potato been considered a matter of any consequence" – James Fintan Lalor

In 1845, the majority of the Irish people were divided into two classes; those who farmed and those who laboured. For both, the potato was equally important, providing either the only or the main source of nourishment for them and their families.

For those who farmed, the money to pay their annual rent was derived mainly from the sale of their crops, which occupied the majority of their land. For most the crops that paid the rent were cereal crops such as barley, oats and wheat. This was the case even in the inland areas of counties such as Galway and Mayo. Although it is hard to imagine now, no county was without a number of mills that converted the crops into saleable commodities. However those who rented land that was exposed, boggy or mountainous could not grow cereal crops and grew potatoes both as a rent crop and as the food on which they survived. Farmers who rented better land, paid much higher rents and therefore had to grow a crop which offered a better financial return.

The paying of the rent, was generally an annual event, and took first place on whatever income the tenant farmer could accrue. Any additional income which the farmer could derive, either from a high yield on the cereal crops or from the sale of other agricultural produce or poultry was necessary for the procurement of seed and to ward off hunger during the Summer months before the next year's potato crop was ready. Ever since the Irish had out of necessity, become totally dependent on the potato the Summer months had always been months of hunger, as once the old potato crop was exhausted there was often no regular or dependable food source until the new crop was ready. June, July and August were known as "meal months" as the purchase of corn was essential for survival. Other essentials such as clothing and farm implements could often not be afforded and were often fashioned by hand from whatever was available.

The tradesman or "Jobber" rented a very small plot of land on which he constructed his cabin. Land for the growing of the potato crop to feed his family was often rented in a separate location. As already noted, the land was rented for a season at a very high price (conacre) on which he grew a crop of potatoes to feed his family as these offered a higher yield at a lower cost. His was a precarious existence, for when there was less income among the farmers people tried to do without extra labour on the land or neglected essential maintenance to their thatch, footwear or clothing.

In 1845 the Irish population was around 9,000,000 souls, and may have been even much higher, as many rural areas had not been properly surveyed in the census of 1841. Of this great number around 3,000,000 were entirely dependent on the potato while a further 2,000,000 relied on it as their main source of food. In the west and north-west dependence on the potato was higher than anywhere else in the country with around 90% of people being completely reliant on it.

Many have maintained that the country was overpopulated. However this is only true in the respect that the great majority of the Irish people relied upon and were expected to rely upon a single root crop, the potato, for their entire diet and source of food.

Ireland was in fact heavily cultivated with around 75% of her soil providing crops of all varieties,[230] which meant that in the event of the failure of the potato there would be more than enough food in the country.

## Poverty

"In a climate soft as a mother's smile, on a soil fruitful as God's love, the Irish peasant mourns. Consider his griefs! They begin in the cradle; they end in the grave. Suckled by a breast that is supplied from unwholesome or insufficient food and that is fevered with anxiety; reeking with the smoke of an almost chimneyless cabin; assailed by wind and rain when the weather rages; breathing when it is calm, the exhalations of a rotten roof, of clay walls, and of manure which gives his only chance of food – he is apt to perish in his infancy" - Thomas Davis.

"How long will the landlords be suffered to plunder and impoverish people to whom they have no sympathy and on whose behalf they have never taken a single step. Sacred Heavens! Is it not horrible to think that in their fertile land millions of human creatures able and willing to work are doomed to pine and want and drag out a life more horrible than death itself when their taskmasters are enjoying all the luxuries life can afford" – The Sligo Champion newspaper (July 1840).

"The blacks have a proverb, If a nigger were not a nigger, the Irishman would be a nigger" – John Walter M.P and proprietor of the London Times (speaking in the House of Commons).

When a landlord let a plot of land to a small tenant farmer, it was devoid of anything that might assist him in the establishment of a farm. Most farmers who were starting out on a new holding raised a one roomed windowless mud cabin in which his family was housed. The census of 1841 found that half of Irish houses were of this variety while west of the Shannon the proportion was much higher. Those fortunate enough to have long-term tenancies progressed to a stone cottage.

When a family had paid the rent due on their plot of land (into which the tithe to the Protestant Church was now incorporated) almost all available income was exhausted, meaning that people had little or no money to spend on the other necessities of life. According to the report of Patrick McKye, a National School teacher in Donegal the people who lived in Gweedore had almost none of the necessities of life. In a district that was home to 9,000 people, even proper farm implements were almost non-existent, meaning that the planting and tending of crops had to be accomplished with the most rudimentary tools. In 1837, in a letter to the Viceroy, Constantine Phipps, McKye stated that in the entire region (which may be considered typical of any area along the western seaboard) there was a total of twenty shovels, sixteen harrows, one cart and one plough. Within the mud cabin homes, furniture or any semblance of comfort was almost non-existent. One bed for the entire family was the norm. The mattress consisted of: "green and dried rushes or mountain bent: their bed clothes are either coarse sheets, or no sheets and ragged filthy blankets"[231] Many children had no clothing while those that did wore: "filthy rags, most disgustful to look at."[232]

Food was in short supply, for when the potato crop did not partially fail, it ran out before the next year's crop was ready due to the limited amount of ground which was available for it as for the small tenant farmer almost all land was devoted to the growth of rent crops. In 1838 McKye found the people: "full of grief, hunger, debility and dejection"[233] while their children were: "crying and fainting with hunger (and) likely to expire in the jaws of starvation"[234.]

In 1835 and 1837, Ireland was toured by the French magistrate and prison reformer, Gustave de Beaumont. In the aftermath of his travels he wrote two volumes on Ireland entitled "A Tour of Ireland" in which he examined in great detail the Irish situation. Regarding the situation of the ordinary people of Ireland he wrote: "I have seen the Indian in his forests, and the Negro in his chains, and thought, as I contemplated their pitiable condition, that I saw the very extreme of human wretchedness; but I did not know then the condition of unfortunate Ireland."

"In all countries more or less, paupers may be discovered; but an entire nation of paupers is what never was seen until it was shown in Ireland...the misery of Ireland descends to degrees unknown elsewhere. The condition which in that country is deemed superior to poverty, would in any other be regarded as a state of frightful distress; the miserable classes of France, whose lot we justly deplore, would in Ireland form a privileged class. And these miseries of the Irish population are not rare accidents; nearly all are permanent, and those which are not permanent are periodic. Every year, nearly at the same season, the commencement of a famine is announced in Ireland, its progress, its ravages, its decline."[235.]

"Imagine four walls of dry mud, which the rain, as it falls, easily restores to its primitive condition; having for its roof a little straw or some sods, for its chimney a hole cut in the roof, or very frequently the door, through which the smoke finds an issue. One single apartment contains the father, mother, children, and sometimes a grandfather or grandmother; there is no furniture in this wretched hovel; a single bed of hay or straw serves for the entire family. Five or six half-naked children may be seen crouched near a miserable fire, the ashes of which cover a few potatoes, the sole nourishment of the family. In the midst of all lies a dirty pig, the only thriving inhabitant of the place, for he lives in filth. This dwelling is very miserable, still it is not that of the pauper, properly so called; I have just described the dwelling of the Irish farmer and agricultural labourer. All being poor the only food they use is the cheapest in the country – potatoes"[236]

Yet, in spite of their abject poverty, the Irish people were not depressed. In fact they displayed a greater Christian charity and hospitality than might be found in countries which were far better off, a fact which was noted upon by many visitors. Upon touring Ireland in the 1820's, Sir Walter Scott noted on the: "perpetual kindness in the Irish cabin; buttermilk, potatoes, a stool is offered or a stone is rolled that your honour may sit down...and those that beg everywhere else seem desirous to exercise hospitality in their own houses."[237.] The daughter of a British army officer stationed in Ballina wrote of the Irish that she: "would have fearlessly trusted the Irish peasantry in any circumstances...I never met a solitary peasant in my rambles but I addressed him and by this means got stores of legendary lore."[238] The contrast was complete on her return to England, when on her journey home: "we stopped opposite a cottage and asked for a glass of water. It was brought and the woman asked for payment. An Irish woman would have considered it an insult to be offered such. The (English) cottages were clean and neat and the country looked clean in comparison but the manners seemed far inferior."[239]

## The Devon Commission

As the conditions in Ireland were so dire, the government, fearing an exodus of Irish peasantry into England, set up a commission of enquiry into "Irish Poverty" in November 1843 led by the Earl of Devon, William Courtney. In his book "The

Land War in Ireland", the nineteenth century English historian, the Rev. James Godkin set forth the government's thinking:

"If the Irish people were not elevated, the English working classes must be brought down to their level. The facility of travelling afforded by railways and steam-boats caused such constant intercourse between England and Ireland, that Irish ignorance, beggary and disease, with all their contagion, physical and moral would be found intermingling with the English population. It would be impossible to prevent the half starved Irish peasantry from crossing the Channel, and seeking employment, even at low wages, and forming a pestiferous Irish quarter in every town and city."[240]

The Devon Commission consisted of English landlords. In spite of the fact that Daniel O'Connell described it as being "...perfectly one sided, all landlords and no tenants," the commission, which reported in February 1845 completed a factual report of what they found in Ireland. Their finding included the following;

- "It would be impossible adequately to describe the privations which they habitually and silently endure...In many districts their only food is the potato, their only beverage water...their cabins are seldom a protection against the weather...a bed or a blanket is a rare luxury...and nearly in all their pig and a manure heap constitute their only property"[241.]
- The commissioners could not "forbear expressing our strong sense of the patient endurance which the labouring classes have exhibited under sufferings greater, we believe, than the people of any other country in Europe have to sustain"[242.]
- The Commissioners found that: "A reference to the evidence of most of the witnesses will show that the agricultural labourer of Ireland continues to suffer the greatest privations and hardships; that he continues to

depend upon casual and precarious employment for subsistence; that he is still badly housed, badly fed, badly clothed, and badly paid for his labour. Our personal experience and observation during our enquiry have afforded us a melancholy confirmation of these statements; and we cannot forbear expressing our strong sense of the patient endurance which the labouring classes have generally exhibited under sufferings greater, we believe, than the people of any other country in Europe have to sustain"[243.]

The Duke of Newcastle who was a member of the Commission noted that: "In England and Scotland the landlords let farms, in Ireland they let only land"[244.]

When the report of the Devon Commission was presented to the government, it was rejected as it did not: "contain anything of striking novelty"[245] and that: "there was nothing in it that everyone did not know already"[246.]

The Commission also stated that the fact the situation in Ulster was much better was due to tenant rights. It found that outside Ulster, Irish tenants had no form of protection and could be summarily evicted. In spite of the fact that the report was rejected by the government, a bill allowing tenants in the other provinces limited compensation for improvements to their property in some cases, came before the House, but was rejected as being "a violation of the rights of property"[247.]

## The Coming of the Potato Blight

"The facts of the Irish destitution are ridiculously simple. They are almost too commonplace to be told. The people have not enough to eat. They are suffering a real though artificial famine. Nature does her duty. The land is fruitful enough. Nor can it be fairly said that man is wanting. The Irishman is disposed to work. In fact, man and nature together do produce abundantly. The land is full and overflowing with food. But something ever interposes between the hungry mouth and the ample banquet. The famished victim of a mysterious sentence stretches out his hands to the viands which his own industry has placed before his eyes, but no sooner are they touched than they fly."- The London Times – 28th June 1845

In mid August of 1845 potato blight was reported in the Isle of Wight. For those who had been watching its advance from the Americas in the early 1840's its arrival in the United Kingdom was not unexpected. One month later it arrived in Ireland, but it appeared that the blight did not extend to the whole country. In some parts of the country it had completely wiped out the crop, while in other parts, most of the crop had been untouched. However as the season continued, and the potato crop was harvested, the unthinkable happened. In those areas of the country that had seemed relatively blight free, potatoes began to rot after they were taken out of the ground. As Autumn grew more advanced, the hitherto minimalist reports on the situation which were being sent to London from British officials in Ireland grew more and more strident. Catastrophe beckoned unless the government took immediate steps to save the people from starvation.

## The Recollection of Jeremiah O'Donovan Rossa
As a teenager, Jeremiah O'Donovan Rossa witnessed the arrival of the blight:
"Coming on the harvest time of the year 1845, the crops looked splendid. But one fine morning in July there was a cry around that some blight had struck the potato stalks. The leaves had been blighted and from being green, parts of them were turned black and brown, and when these parts were felt between the fingers they'd crumble into ashes. The air was laden with a sickly odour of decay, as if the hand of death had stricken the

potato field, and that everything growing in it was rotting. This is the recollection that remains in my mind of what I felt in our marsh field that morning, when I went with my father and mother to see it.

The stalks withered away day by day. Yet the potatoes had grown to a fairly large size. But the seed of decay had been planted in them too. They were dug and put into a pit in the field. By and by an alarming rumour ran through the country that the potatoes were rotting in the pits. Our pit was opened and sure enough some of the biggest potatoes were half rotten…all hands were set to work to make another picking…but the potatoes rotted in the loft also and before many weeks the blight had eaten up the supply that was to last the family for the whole year.

Jeremiah O'Donovan Rossa

Then one of our fields had a crop of wheat, and when that wheat was reaped and stacked, the landlord put "keepers" on it, and on all that we had, and these keepers remained in the house till the wheat was threshed and bagged, and taken to the mill. I well remember one of the keepers going with my mother to Lloyd's Mill just across the road from the marsh field, and from the mill to the agent, who was in town at Cain Mahony's that day to receive rents.

When my mother came home she came without any money. The rent was £18 a year. The wheat was thirty shillings a bag; there were twelve bags and a few stone, that came in all to £18 5s and she gave all to the agent.

"There were four children of us there. The potato crop was gone; the wheat crop was gone."[248]

## Recommendations to the Government on Arresting the Starvation

In October 1845, during a meeting of Dublin City Corporation, the issue of measures to relieve the starvation was discussed and a plan to immediately address the situation was put forward by Daniel O'Connell. His plan included the following measures and was in the main adopted by the Corporation. The plan included the following measures;

- A prohibition on the exportation of cereals, dairy produce, beef and other foodstuffs from Ireland as had occurred during the famine of 1740.
- The importation without restriction of Indian rice.
- That all distilling and brewing should cease in order that the cereals devoted to this industry could be used to feed the starving population.
- In order to provide the people with work, schemes of land reclamation and railway construction should be organised and the people paid with foodstuffs.
- In order to provide capital to deal with the crisis, a loan should be raised whose security would be the £74,000 a year already coming from the sale of Irish timber abroad,[1] and furthermore absentee landlords should be taxed up to 50% of the earnings which they derive from their Irish estates.

Following the meeting, a deputation of around twenty people from the Corporation and other notable citizens (which included Daniel O'Connell, Lord Cloncurry who was Lord

---

[1] During the famine, the monies derived from the sale of Irish timber were used in the refurbishment of Trafalgar and Windsor Square in London.

Mayor, The Duke of Leinster and Henry Grattan Jnr.) visited the Lord Lieutenant, William á Court (Baron Heytesbury) where a presentation was made by Daniel O'Connell in which the measures proposed by the Corporation were put forward. Heytesbury was asked to consider them for adoption in order to "avert calamity" When O'Connell had concluded, Heytesbury read a prepared statement during which he pompously referred to Daniel O'Connell as "the gentleman who has just spoken".[249] He maintained that the situation was as yet unclear and that the proposals of the committee would be "maturely weighed"[250]. Meanwhile he assured them, two experts were over from England to compile a report on the situation. As soon as he had finished reading his statement, the deputation was shown out. O'Connell was furious at the apathetic attitude of the government and denounced their lacklustre response: "One single peck of oats, one bushel of wheat – aye, one boiled potato – would be better than all their reports."[251] The following day The Freeman's Journal carried a report on the meeting which concluded that the attitude of the Viceroy was: "They may starve! Such in spirit, if not in words, was the reply given yesterday by the English Viceroy to…the deputation which…prayed that the food of this kingdom be preserved, lest the people thereof perish"[252]

## The Exportation of Irish Food during the Great Starvation

"Weary men, what reap ye? – Golden corn for the stranger.
What sow ye? – Human corpses that wait for the avenger.
Fainting forms, hunger-stricken, what see you in the offing?
Stately ships to bear our food away,
amid the stranger's scoffing.
There's a proud array of soldiers –
what do they round your door?
They guard our masters' granaries
from the thin hands of the poor.
Pale mothers, wherefore weeping?
Would to God that we were dead-
Our children swoon before us,
and we cannot give them bread."
-"Speranza" (Jane Wilde)

"God sent the calamity to teach the Irish a lesson…and it must not be too mitigated" – Charles Trevelyan,[1] Permanent Secretary of the Treasury.

"Property ruled with savage and tyrannical sway. It exercised its rights with a hand of iron, and renounced its duties with a front of brass. The fat of the land, the flower of it's wheat, it's milk and honey flowed from its shores, in tribute to the ruthless absentee, or his less guilty cousin, the usurious lender. It was all drain and no return…England stupidly winked at this tyranny. Ready enough to vindicate political rights, it did not avenge the poor" – The London Times, Feb 25th 1847

---

[1] Charles Trevelyan was the front man of British "relief operations" for what Lord Deputy Heytesbury described as "The Potato Famine". Although he is reviled in Ireland, It must not be forgotten that he was a British civil servant carrying out the wishes of his masters.

"During those years in Ireland, '45, '46, and '47, the potato crops failed, but the other crops grew well, and, as in the case of my people in '45, the landlords came in on the people everywhere and seized the grain crops for the rent – not caring much what became of those whose labour and sweat produced those crops" – Jeremiah O'Donovan Rossa

England's Necessity
The arrival of the potato blight had also caused alarm in Britain, as since the industrial revolution the potato had come to occupy an important place in the English diet.
As we have seen in previous chapters, since the coming of the industrial revolution Ireland had become a granary to England, and more besides. Every agricultural commodity imaginable was exported to England in great quantity. If the English people were to be fed and remain unscathed by the failure of the potato, and the burgeoning English economy was to be untouched, Irish beef and agricultural produce would now be required more than ever. In effect it amounted to this; The British government now decided that Ireland would have to be sacrificed on the altar of English economic necessity. In the name of "political economy", market forces (export and import) could not be interfered with. Therefore other measures to "help" Ireland would have to be taken instead. At no stage, was even the partial closure of the Irish ports to the export of food considered by either Peel or Russell, the two Prime Ministers of the period and any suggestion that measures such as those put forward by the Dublin Commission should be adopted were dismissed out of hand.
Throughout the history of Ireland under English rule, we have seen how the Crown Forces have worked hand in hand with both planter and landlord in their various guises. As the landlords and their agents sought to "secure" the rent crops they were in turn assisted by Crown Forces (constabulary,

army units etc) as was the case whenever the landlords wished to impose their will upon their tenants (eviction etc.) This removal of food by the landlords was done in the name of private property, the vindication of political rights, the defence of the British economy and public order. The result was that entire families, communities and towns were wiped out by starvation.

An example clarifies the situation: On March 4th 1848, an inquest was held on the deaths of a husband, wife and children, all members of the Boland family who had died of starvation and disease in spite of the fact that Boland had a larger than average size farm of twenty acres on which he grew cereal crops to pay his rent along with an acre of potatoes to feed his family.

John Mitchel

Following the inquest John Mitchel, the editor of the "The United Irishman" wrote of the inquest and the killing of the Boland family; "Now what became of poor Boland's twenty acres of crops? Part of it went to Gibraltar, to victual the garrison; part to the South of Africa to provision the robber army; part went to Spain to pay for the landlord's wine; part to London, to pay the interest of his honour's mortgage to the Jews. The English ate some of it; the Chinese had their share; the Jews and the Gentiles divided it amongst them; and there was none for Boland"[253.]

Records of British Army troop deployments from the Kew records office show that as the potato blight arrived in Ireland, the already high number of regiments in Ireland was increased as it was feared that the failure of the potato would lead to food riots, and attacks on harvest convoys making for their ports of embarkation. Throughout the period of The Great Starvation, a total of 67 regiments of the British army along with the Irish Constabulary and diverse other Crown Forces units were engaged in providing assistance to the landlords and their agents in the removal of crops and the escorting of cartloads of grain and other produce to port[1] as it was felt that this was the only way of ensuring that rent crops which had been seized from the tenants reached their final destination – England. By mid 1847, when the will of the people to resist had been more or less broken Lord Deputy Clarendon was able to report to Prime Minister Russell that he received a report from the Commanding General, Sir Edward Blakeney who reported to him that; "…the country (Ireland) is tranquil and if it were not for the harassing duty of escorting provisions the troops would have little to do."[254]

An example of a harvest convoy bringing crops from the interior of the country to port was related by a government official located in Waterford in a report dated April 24th 1846; "…the barges leave Clonmel once a week for this place, with the export supplies under convoy which, last Tuesday consisted of 2 guns, 50 cavalry and 80 infantry escorting them on the banks of the Suir as far as Carrick"[255]

---

[1] "People starve in the midst of plenty, as literally as if dungeon bars separated them from a granary. When distress has been at its height, and our poor have dying of starvation in our streets, our corn has been going to a foreign market. It is, to our own poor, a forbidden fruit" – Journalist Dominic Corrigan, 1846.

## The Course of the Great Starvation
Autumn 1845 – Summer 1846

In the Autumn of 1845 the Conservative Prime Minister Sir Robert Peel, (who was already well aware that for a quarter of every year, almost a third of the Irish population was half starved) was initially reluctant to take measures which would compensate for the almost complete destruction of the potato crop stating that: "One must remember that the Irish have a terrible tendency to exaggerate"[256.] However, as those potatoes which had initially appeared sound rotted in storage pits, it became clear to Peel that some action would have to be taken. His initial measure was the appointment of a scientific commission to examine what, if anything, could be done with the remainder of the potato crop which had not yet rotted. Within a couple of days of arriving in Ireland, the scientists found that nothing could be done with the rotting potatoes. They then embarked on a lengthy process to see if starch could be removed from rotten potatoes that could perhaps be mixed with other substances to provide nourishment. However their lengthy research and reports were all of no avail.

Whilst the practical suggestions made to Lord Lieutenant Heytesbury by the Dublin Council delegation were ignored, other suggestions by those in government and parliamentary circles were considered including one from The Duke of Norfolk who suggested that curry powder should be imported from India and mixed with water as a suitable replacement for the potato.

As the price of food in Ireland began to rise, Prime Minister Peel ordered the secret[I] importation of quantities of cheap maize into Ireland, not for distribution to the starving but

---

[I] Peel feared that his action in the importation of maize would be contrary to the British Corn Laws.

rather for gradual releasing onto the market to prevent the price of corn from rising too high. By the time the first of this maize was made available to the market in March 1846, the purchase of such foodstuffs was beyond the buying power of most tenant families who nevertheless came to the depots in the hope of receiving something, but returned home with nothing. After having been open for a few weeks, the maize depots were closed as it was deemed that the price of corn on the market in general had been sufficiently reduced. Nevertheless, for those who could afford it, food remained plentiful. At this time relief committees were being formed across the country and Peel pledged to award grants to those who were raising money for the relief of the starving, which would match the amounts raised.

During the Winter of 1845, many people managed to eke out a survival by selling anything they had to obtain money and eating whatever was available including any hens they possessed and the family pig. Donkeys also became a source of food. More wealthy farmers who employed a farm hand or servant were forced to dismiss them and along with tradesmen they were the first to suffer destitution and hunger, being unable to pay their rents and their only source of food having failed. Such was the level of poverty and destitution that by February of 1846, typhus had appeared in the worst affected counties while dysentery became rampant. The rate of evictions multiplied. On one estate in Galway on the 13th March 1846, 76 families who were unable to pay their rents were evicted by police and troops and their homes destroyed so that they could not take shelter in the ruins. On March 23rd 1846, speaking in the House of Lords, Lord John Russell who was the leader of the Whigs stated that in the preceding year more than 50,000 families had been "…turned out of their dwellings without pity or refuge." He continued "…we have made Ireland, I speak it deliberately…we have made it the most degraded and most miserable country in the world...all the world is crying shame upon us; but we are equally callous to our ignominy and to the results of our misgovernment."[257]

If Lord Russell was serious in his concerns for the Irish people and his opinion that the situation was being mismanaged by the Conservative Prime Minister Robert Peel, then he would shortly have his chance to tackle the situation.

In late 1845, Peel had instructed the Board of Works to liaise with local committees regarding the provision of labour to the starving. However by June 1846 the scheme was only getting off the ground. By this time people were becoming more and desperate for food in order to feed their families as widespread starvation took hold. In London, parliament busied itself with the introduction of measures to maintain public order in Ireland, including a new coercion bill that allowed judges to sentence those who stole food to penal servitude of up to fifteen years. In spite of such measures there were attacks on flourmills and guarded convoys bringing produce to ports where they would be shipped to England. "The Freeman's Journal" reported: "There have been attacks on flour mills in Clonmel by people whose bones protruded through the skin which covered them – staring through hollow eyes as if they had just risen from their shrouds, crying out that they could no longer endure the extremity of their distress and that they must take that food which they could not procure...As we pass into Summer, we pass into suffering...Every week develops the growing intensity of the national calamity."[258]

In June 1846, the government reopened the depots of imported maize. However after only a number of weeks, the Secretary of the Treasury, Charles Trevelyan ordered them to be closed again his reason being that: "the indiscriminate sales have brought the whole country on the depots...without denying the existence of real and extensive distress the numbers are beyond the powers of the depots to cope with. They must therefore be closed down as soon as possible"[259.]

## The Repeal of the Corn Laws and the Change of Government

"The starving multitudes in England were to receive cheap corn but the starving multitudes in Ireland were to be left to their own resources" – Prof. Denis Gwynn.

"It is not the intention at all to import food for the use of the people of Ireland." – Sir Charles Wood, British Chancellor of the Exchequer, Summer 1846.

"If the rent devil *has* to be paid, it can surely be no advantage to his victim to withhold or decrease the means of making payment" – Davidson.

In England, as in Ireland, during the Summer of 1845 the potato crop had been heavily blighted. In spite of the transfer of food from Ireland to Britain, food was nevertheless scarce in England, so much so that by the Winter of 1845, the food situation among the workers in the large English industrial towns had become acute. English workers and their families did not have enough to eat.

For some time the large industrialists, had been lobbying the government to repeal the Corn Laws[I] that protected British landowners and landlords from the lower price of cereals grown overseas. The industrialists knew that cheaper cereal imports would allow them to continue to pay lower wages and also protect their profit margins. "Cheap food and low wages"[260] was their cry. However, the well-connected

---

[I] The "Corn Laws" encompassed all cereals including wheat, barley and oats.

Landowners, with their massive estates, were by far the more powerful lobbying group and neither the Whigs nor the Tories, who had many large landowners on their benches, had been prepared to undermine their position. Then, when the English food crisis struck in the Winter of 1845 – 46, Robert Peel felt compelled to resign but continued in his role as Prime Minister because of the failure of the Whig leader, Lord John Russell, to form an administration. Peel, who styled himself as being a champion for the working classes (as he came from a cotton spinning back-ground) now (as had been the case with Catholic Emancipation) felt compelled to act against his own wishes and repeal the Corn Laws so that English workers would have enough to eat. After the Christmas parliamentary recess of 1845, the Corn Laws were repealed in January of 1846. While Peel had used the case of Ireland as one of his reasons for their repealing, their repealing only served to completely undermine Irish tenants by lowering the prices of the commodities which they were forced to use to pay their rent, as when cheaper cereal products began to flow into England from abroad, the price of Irish cereals had to be lowered. When this happened, those who had thus far managed to pay their rents could not longer do so and now faced eviction. By this time the majority of Irish tenants could also not afford to buy corn at any price.

By repealing the Corn Laws, Pitt had divided his Tory party. A large section of the party known as "The Protectionists" under the leadership of Benjamin Disraeli were now determined to rid themselves of Peel's leadership one way or the other. In this they were to be assisted by Daniel O'Connell and his Repeal Party who once more threw in their lot with the Whigs in opposition to Peel.

In June of 1846, Russell saw his chance to unseat Peel and gain power for the Whigs. When Peel proposed another Irish coercion bill, Russell opposed it on the grounds that it contained nothing that would alleviate the situation in Ireland. With the help of the Irish Repeal Party and the Tory dissenters the Coercion Bill was defeated and Peel was forced to resign.

## Summer 1846 – Summer 1847

After Russell's public pronouncements on Ireland, there were high hopes that his administration would takes steps to at least improve the Irish situation, especially as they had ousted the Tories with the help of O'Connell's Repeal Party. However after the new Whig government took office in June of 1846, there was a change for the worse in the already limited government response to the situation in spite of the fact that the potato crop for 1846 was already showing signs of widespread blight.

The decision was taken to wind up the public works scheme and to cancel any further importation of maize, while shipments that had already been ordered were revoked. The policy of the new administration was that Ireland should be more or less left to its own devices, a policy encompassed in the neat French phrase; "Laissez faire" or "Leave alone".

In spite of his fine words only a few months earlier it was now apparent that Prime Minister Russell intended to do very little.

According to Charles Trevelyan, (who remained in post as Chief Secretary of the Treasury): "The only way to prevent the people from becoming habitually dependent on the government is to bring operations to a close. Uncertainty about the new (potato) crop only makes this more necessary. Whatever may be done hereafter, these things must be stopped now, or we run the risk of paralysing all private enterprise and having this country (Ireland) on you for an indefinite number of years."[261]

From Trevelyan's remarks it is clear that in his mind, Ireland was not an integral part of Her Majesty's United Kingdom but rather an English asset, only to be used for exploitation. That

Trevelyan's view was also the view of the establishment was the opinion of the editor of "The Cork Examiner" newspaper when he wrote in the Summer of 1846: "Talk of the power of England, her navy, her gold, her resources and her enlightened statesmen, while the broad fact is manifested that she cannot keep the children of her bosom from perishing with hunger. Perhaps, indeed Irishmen may not aspire to the high dignity of belonging to the great family of the Empire, they may be regarded as aliens, but when the Queen at her coronation swore to protect and defend her subjects, it is not recollected that in the words of the solemn covenant there was any exception made with regard to Ireland. How happens it then? While there is a shilling in the treasury or even a jewel in the crown that patient subjects are allowed to perish with hunger?"[262]

The government's policy was confirmed by Lord Russell in early August 1846 when he told the House of Commons: "We do not propose to interfere with the regular mode by which Indian corn and other kinds of grain may be brought into Ireland."[263] The new Chancellor of the Exchequer, Sir Charles Wood was more explicit: "It is not the intention at all to import food for the use of the people of Ireland."[264]

Lord John Russell

As Ireland descended deeper into the abyss, the editor of the United Irishman newspaper, John Mitchel watched: "…immense herds of cattle, sheep and hogs…floating off on every tide…bound for England; and the landlords were receiving their rents, and going to England to spend them; and many hundreds of poor people had lain down and died on the roadsides, for want of food"[265]

As the Summer of 1846 turned to Autumn, it was overwhelmingly clear that the failure of the potato crop was complete. The harvest of cereal crops remained unaffected. Evictions by bailiffs accompanied by police and military were now rife. Normally when a house was "tumbled" during an eviction, the walls remained standing, but now so many people were attempting to take shelter in the ruins of their former homes that their houses were knocked completely. The workhouses (which were forbidden to give any aid to persons not within their confines) were full. The Cork Examiner reported that in Listowel, Co. Kerry, a crowd of 5,000 people gathered outside the workhouse attempting to gain entry. As the English newspapers reported to the British public on the situation, there was growing disquiet among the population that within the borders of Her Majesty's United Kingdom tens of thousands of people were in the process of dying of starvation while hundreds of thousands more were without food. Russell's government had to be at least seen to be taking some measures to "alleviate the situation". Russell's first principle in alleviating the situation was that all monies used should be raised within Ireland and not by a grant from the Imperial Treasury. Furthermore the control of monies assigned to deal with the situation was to be in the hands of London appointed commissioners.

Having just closed the scheme of public works, Trevelyan now announced that it would be re-introduced, but that this time the cost of the scheme was to be paid for by the landlords out of public rates. The government would forward them the money but it would have to be repaid with interest. Trevelyan also stipulated that under the scheme there could be no cultivation of other crops to replace the potato at public expense, and that wages under the scheme had to be lower than those prevailing on the ordinary labour market. To this last stipulation there was widespread anger. In response The London Times commended Trevelyan and replied to the criticism: "Such are the thanks that a government gets for attempting to palliate great afflictions and satisfy corresponding demands by an inevitable but ruinous beneficence…It is the old thing, the old malady is breaking out. It is the national (Irish) character, the national thoughtlessness, the national indolence."[266]

Charles Trevelyan

As the previous scheme had been completely disbanded and a new one was being instituted it took many weeks for it to get off the ground. It was not to commence until the depths of winter. Meanwhile many thousands had died of starvation.

In some places where the depots still had a stock of maize, they were reopened after the closing of the public works scheme by local government officials, who sold maize at lower than market prices to those who could buy it. On Trevelyan's instructions the depots were ordered closed by the Commissary General, Sir Ralph Routh who wrote: "…the time has come to subject the people to a little pressure."[267]

In the Winter of 1846-47, due to the number of people dying of starvation, coffins were no longer available. Many were buried wrapped in straw, while others were dropped into mass graves by a coffin with a hinged bottom. In Bantry, Co. Cork a local Protestant clergyman described how: "…the bottom is supported by hinges at one side and a hook and eye at the other. In these coffins the poor are carried to the grave, rather to a large pit, which I saw at a little distance from the road, and the bodies are dropped into it...But I was told in this district the majority were taken to the grave without any coffin and buried in their rags; in some instances even the rags are taken from the corpse to cover some still living body."[268]

When the works finally started many were so starved that they could not work. Even when underway there were often long delays in the employees receiving payment and thousands of deaths from starvation occurred while families waited for their men-folk to receive payments due to them. According to one gentleman eyewitness the public works[I] consisted of "...the breaking up and rendering impassable at an enormous outlay of unexceptionably good public highways, the commencing of expensive and unnecessary new lines of road at a season of the year very unsuitable to such operations, many of them and most of them altogether unnecessary for any present or probable future wants of the county, appear to those who, like myself, are unskilled in the mysteries of government as an anomalous mode of meeting a calamity."[269]

Those who worked on the schemes were obliged to travel by foot for miles to the worksite and obliged to toil in all weathers in order to receive payment which was the equivalent of the price of a breakfast of Indian meal.[270]

They works were rightly felt by all the labourers to be useless, and starvation aside were not engaged in with any enthusiasm.

---

[I] On the issue of public works, Lord George Bentick proposed that a loan of sixteen million pounds should be raised, and the money used to construct a railway system in Ireland. The measure was defeated in the Commons as the government believed that such works should be left in the hands of private enterprise.

While much productive work could have been engaged in, such as the construction of railways or drainage, these "productive" works were reserved for private enterprise.

As Winter intensified, the thousands of deaths from starvation were accompanied by thousands of deaths from disease which was spreading rapidly. Called "Road fever" as it was brought from the countryside into the towns and cities by those seeking food and shelter, it was a mixture of typhus and fever brought on by the starvation and the weakness of the immune system.

By December 1846, 400,000 men were working on the scheme with many more desperate to avail of it but these were refused as the "quota" in the district in which they lived was full. The parish priest of Islandeady in Co. Mayo, Fr. Henry, recorded that on being told the scheme was full "the tears of agony and despair gushing from the eyes of hardy and aged men gave evidence of the intensity of their suffering"[271].

In December of 1846, Trevelyan ordered the maize depots reopened. The maize was to be sold at the market price plus 5%. When asked by Sir Randolph Routh if the prices should not be reduced, Trevelyan replied: "If the Irish once find out there are any circumstances in which they can get free government grants we shall have a system of mendicancy such as the world never knew"[272].

In March of 1847 there were 728,000 people on the Public Works Scheme. Many more wanted to join the scheme but were not allowed. Many of these attended the scheme for weeks before being finally officially admitted. A priest wrote how many of those who were finally admitted to the scheme, that they: "...had scarcely time to earn themselves the price of a coffin..."[273] before they died from starvation.

Due to the amount of money the scheme was costing, the government decided to abandon it in February 1847 and replace it with direct aid in the form of soup boilers which would distribute soup to those eligible. Anyone still renting land was barred from receiving aid.

While the scheme of public works was stopped with immediate effect, the new public aid scheme did not commence immediately, causing a rapid increase in deaths from starvation. From the countryside, starving people flocked to the nearest town in the hope of some help. From Macroom in Co. Cork a newspaper correspondent wrote how: "Every avenue leading to and in this plague-stricken town has a fever hospital having for its protection the blue vault of heaven. Persons of all ages are dropping dead in each corner of the town, who are interred with much difficulty after rats have festered on their frames."[274] In Cong, Co. Mayo the local Protestant minister reported that during the gap between the public works ceasing and the soup scheme starting deaths increased ten-fold.

## August 1847 - The "End of the Famine"
"Coroners juries would hold inquests on Irish people who were found dead in the ditches, and would return verdicts of "murder" against the English government, but England cared nothing for that" – Jeremiah O'Donovan Rossa.

The Soup Kitchen Act was the one effective measure that the British Government took throughout the entire period, with almost three million people receiving some form of bodily sustenance. It was to last for a few months. For its duration there were many areas in which insufficient rations were distributed. It is recorded that in one part of Mayo, during a period of eighteen days, food was given to the populace on only four.

As with all other relief measures, the British treasury under Charles Trevelyan hated the scheme due to the amount it was costing. In July of 1847 its end was signalled when the

Secretary of Dublin Relief Commissioners wrote that: "There is much reason to believe that the object of the Relief Act is greatly perverted and that it is frequently applied solely as a means of adding to the comforts of the lower classes...instead of...warding off absolute starvation."[275]

When it was found in the Summer of 1847 that the few seed potatoes that had been sown in late spring of 1847 appeared to be free of blight, the government decided that the "potato famine" was at an end and that any form of governmental assistance then in use would cease at the end of September. New Poor Law Legislation was announced. The already overwhelmed workhouses which had a maximum capacity to cater for 100,000 people would now be permitted to administer relief to people who did not reside in the workhouse with the stipulation that any person who was in possession of one quarter of an acre of land or above was not permitted to receive it. By October of 1847 the millions who had been in receipt of the government soup were looking to the Poor Law for help. The Cork Examiner described the workhouses as becoming "...the charnel houses of the whole rural population."[276]

Having announced the last measure which the government was to take during The Great Starvation, Charles Trevelyan wrote: "It is my opinion that too much has been done for the people. Under such treatment the people have grown worse instead of better, and we must now try to see what independent exertion can do."[277] Ireland was now to be left to what Trevelyan horrifically described as "...the operation of natural causes"[278.]

## "We are starving! – Give us something to eat"

The mass starvation[1] of the Irish people was by far the worst event of its kind ever recorded in the history of Europe in a time of peace.

### Report on the Starvation in Connacht by W.G Foster

"I have no doubt whatever, that in any other country the mortality would have been far greater; and that many lives have been prolonged, perhaps saved by the long apprenticeship to want which the Irish peasant has been trained, and by that lovely, touching charity which prompts him to share his scanty meal with his starving neighbour. But the springs of this charity must be rapidly dried up. Like a scourge of locusts, the hunger daily sweeps over fresh districts eating up all before it. One class after another is falling into the same abyss of ruin."[279]

"We entered a cabin. Stretched in one dark corner scarcely visible from the smoke and rags that covered them, were three children huddled together, lying there because they were too weak to rise, pale and ghastly; their little limbs, on removing a portion of the covering, perfectly emaciated; eyes sunk, voice gone, and evidently in the last stage of actual starvation. Crouched over the turf embers was another form, wild and all but naked, scarcely human in appearance. It stirred not nor noticed us. On some straw, saddened upon the ground, moaning piteously was a shrivelled old woman, imploring us to give her something, baring her limbs partly to show how the skin hung loose from her bones, as soon as she attracted our attention. Above her, on something like a ledge, was a young

---

[1] "The actual starving people lived upon the carcasses of diseased cattle, upon dogs, and dead horses, but principally on the herbs of the field, nettle tops, wild mustard and watercress and even in some places dead bodies were found with grass in their mouths." – Sessional Papers of the House of Commons, Vol 29, Ch. V, p256.

woman with sunken cheeks, a mother, I have no doubt, who scarcely raised her eyes in answer to our enquiries; but pressed her hand upon her forehead with a look of unutterable anguish and despair. Many cases were widows, whose husbands had been recently taken off by the fever, and thus their only pittance obtained from the public works was entirely cut off. In many the husbands or sons were prostrate under that horrid disease – the result of long continued famine and low living – in which first the limbs and then the body swell most frightfully, and finally burst. We entered upwards of fifty of these tenements. The scene was invariably the same, differing in little but the manner of the sufferers, or of the groups occupying the several corners within. The whole number was often not to be distinguished until the eye having adapted itself to the darkness, they were pointed out, or were heard, or some filthy bundle of rags or straw was seen to move. Perhaps the poor children presented the most piteous and heart-rending spectacle. Many were too weak to stand, their little limbs attenuated, except where the frightful swellings had taken the place of previous emaciation. Every infantile expression had entirely departed; and, in some, reason and intelligence had evidently flown. Many were remnants of families, crowded together in one cabin; orphaned little relatives taken in by the equally destitute and even strangers – for these people are kind to each other even to the end. In one cabin was a sister, just dying, lying beside her brother, just dead. I have worse than this to relate; but it is useless to multiply details, and they are, in fact, unfit."[280]

## The Testimony of Irish lawyer and Historian, A.M Sullivan

"My native district (Bantry, Co. Cork) figures largely in the gloomy record of that dreadful time. I saw the horrible phantasmagoria – would God it were but that! – pass before my eyes. Blank, stolid dismay, a sort of stupor, fell upon the people, contrasting remarkably with the fierce energy put forth a year before. It was no uncommon sight to see the cottier and his little family seated on the garden fence, gazing all day long in moody silence at the blighted plot that had been their last hope. Nothing could arouse them. You spoke; they answered not. You tried to cheer them; they shook their heads. I never saw so sudden and so terrible a transformation.

At first the establishment of public soup-kitchens, under local relief committees, subsidized by Government, was relied upon to arrest the famine. I doubt if ever the world saw so huge a demoralization, so great a degradation, visited upon a once high-spirited and sensitive people. All over the country large iron boilers were set up, in which what was called "soup" was concoted. Later on Indian meal stirrabout was boiled. Around these boilers on the roadside there daily moaned and shrieked and fought and scuffled crowds of gaunt, cadaverous creatures that once had been men and women, made in the image of God. The feeding of dogs in a kennel was far more decent and orderly. I once thought – aye, and bitterly said, in public and in private – that never, never would our people recover the shameful humiliation of that brutal public soup-boiler scheme. I frequently stood and watched the scene till tears blinded me, and I almost choked with grief and passion. It was heart-breaking, almost maddening to see; but help for it there was none."

"The first remarkable sign of the havoc which death was making was the decline and disappearance of funerals. Amongst the Irish people a funeral was always a great display, and participation in the procession was, for all neighbours and friends, a sacred duty. A "poor" funeral – that is, one thinly attended – was considered disrespectful to the deceased and reproachful to the living. The humblest peasant was borne to the grave by a parochial cortege. But one could observe in the summer of '46 that, as funerals became more frequent, there was a rapid decline in the number of attendants, until at length persons were stopped on the road and requested to assist in conveying the coffin a little way further. Soon, alas! Neither coffin nor shroud could be supplied. Daily in the street, and on the footway, some poor creature lay down as if to sleep, and presently was stiff and stark. In our district it was a common occurrence to find, on opening the front door, in early morning, leaning against it, the corpse of some victim who in the night time had "rested" in its shelter. We raised a public subscription, and employed two men with horse and cart to go around each day and gather up the dead. One by one they were taken to a pit at Ardnabrahair Abbey, and dropped through the hinged bottom of a "trap-coffin" into a common grave below. In the remoter rural districts even this rude sepulture was impossible. In the field and by the ditch-side, the victims lay as they fell, till some charitable hand was found to cover them with the adjacent soil."

"It was the fever, which supervened on the famine, that wrought the greatest slaughter and spread the greatest terror. For this destroyer, when it came, spared no class rich or poor. As long as it was "the hunger" alone that raged, it was no deadly peril to visit the sufferers; but not so now. To come within the reach of this contagion was certain death. Whole families perished unvisited and unassisted. By levelling' above their corpses the sheeling in which they died, the neighbours gave them a grave"[281]

## The Starvation Continues

"Ireland is like a half starved rat that crosses the path of an elephant. What must the elephant do? Squelch it – by heavens – squelch it!" – Thomas Carlyle.

In spite of Treveylan's assertion that the "famine" had ended in August of 1847, by the Summer of 1848 the starvation, and disease of the evicted wayfarers was at its height. In June of 1848 a roads inspector, making his rounds in Co. Galway found 140 dead on his route, due to famine and sickness forced to end their lives by the side of the road after being evicted. After the small blight free potato crop of 1847 there were high hopes for the crop of 1848 but the crop was a complete failure.

At the beginning of March 1848, the parish priest of Drung in Co. Cavan,, Fr. James Brady wrote the following regarding the situation in his district: "There are at present in this parish fifty farms vacant, the former occupants of which from time immemorial lived in comparative comfort but from the badness of the times, and unable to meet the demands of the landlords have been sent adrift, men, women and children to the amount of 200 beings in this inclement season of the year to beg or die and many have since died...I exhort all classes to discharge their duties in a Christian manner but when I see the landlords exterminating right and left, when I see the utter misery, deprivation and destitution of my poor people as I meet them on the highways – livid corpses raised from the grave can give but a faint idea of their wretched appearance, their eyes sunk in their sockets, their blue veins prominent in their fleshless foreheads and wishing for death as a happy release from their misery I cannot but exclaim that there is not a people on the face of God's earth who would sit down tamely and submit to such distress and deprivation as my unfortunate countrymen. They consider themselves happy if they can procure one meal of boiled turnips in the day. They cannot assemble for public worship on Sunday as their rags are in the pawn office and were a stranger to pass by when the bell tolls for prayers he would see those miserable being crawling from their wretched dwellings in view of the chapel and on their bare and bended knees imploring God and the heavens to look down with pity and compassion on them. Yes, I have seen the mother and child die for want of food. I have endeavoured with my whole heart and soul to administer the consolations of religion to the father of the family smitten by fever in a hovel, not habitation for a human being, and at the same time two of his children lay dead on one side of the fire for four days without coffins or the means of procuring them..."[282]

There were many ports in Ireland from which food was being exported to England. On November 14th 1848, from the Port of Cork, the following food was dispatched to England; "147 bales of bacon, 120 casks and 135 barrels of pork, 149 casks miscellaneous provisions, 1,996 sacks and 950 barrels of oats, 5 casks of ham, 300 bags of flour, 300 head of cattle, 239 sheep, 9,398 firkins of butter, 542 boxes of eggs."[283]

The scenes of early 1849 were if anything subdued. In most cases the will of the people to survive and fight for something to eat had evaporated. Skeletal forms moved around or lay dead in the fields. One eyewitness in Ballinrobe, Co. Galway wrote: "The streets are daily thronged with moving skeletons. The fields are strewn with dead...the curse of Russell, more terrible than the curse of Cromwell is upon us..."[284] Another eyewitness in Ballinrobe described how every hovel contained at least one dead body. The same eyewitness continued: "May God forgive our rulers for this cruel conduct."[285]

In May 1849 as thousands of people were dying every day, Lord John Russell said in the House of Commons "I do not think any effort of this House would in the present unfortunate state of Ireland, be capable of preventing the dreadful scenes of suffering and death that are now occurring in Ireland. I distinctly repeat that I do not believe it is in the power of this house to do so..."[286] It was now almost two years since the provisions of the "Soup Act" had been cancelled.

In a British revenue return which was dated January 5th 1849 and which calculated Irish taxes for the previous three years, Ireland, in the midst of manmade starvation had paid to the Crown £13,293,681.[287] In the year 1849 alone, there was exported to England from Ireland, among other commodities 12,187,990 kilograms of wheat flour, 46,469,858 kilograms of oat and meal, 595,926 head of cattle, 698,021 pigs, and 839,118 sheep.[288]

## Private Charity during the Starvation

All over the world, the story of Ireland's starvation was heard with incomprehension and pity. Incomprehension, that not in a colony of Her Majesty's Kingdom, but that in an integral part of it which was renowned for agricultural produce, people were starving and dying by the hundreds of thousands because of hunger.[1]

The hearts of many British people were initially stirred by the distress of the Irish. By 1847 they were 'weary' of the 'Irish famine' and no longer wanted to know about the suffering of Ireland.

In the previous chapter I have already recorded the reaction of Daniel O'Connell at their generosity that included in part almost £270,000 raised by the British Association and a collection in English churches that yielded almost £200,000. Yet the donations of many among the upper classes contradicted their willingness to dine upon Irish produce instead of protesting to the government that it should remain with those who had a right to it.

Queen Victoria appears not to have made any intervention with her Prime Ministers on Ireland's behalf but was instead content to donate £2,000 'for the relief of distress in Ireland'. Far away from Ireland's shores a wealthy Turkish Sultan, Abdul Majid, had heard of the starvation in Ireland and approached the British Minister in Turkey Lord Cowley,

---

[1] It is no exaggeration to say that the entire civilized world was shocked at the extermination of the Irish people. That such an event could occur under the governance of a nation which portrayed itself as an advanced world power affected the international perception of England for decades.

offering a donation of £10,000 to help the starving Irish. After being informed by Cowley that such a donation, being greater than the donation of Queen Victoria, could not be accepted without damaging Anglo-Turkish relations, the Sultan instead donated £1,000 after which he dispatched five shiploads of provisions from Thessoloniki to Ireland which arrived in Drogheda in May of 1847.

Help from the United States
Many nations of the world sought to assist Ireland in her man made plight. In this, the charity of the people of the United States of America was greater than all other charity put together. Many people prepared packages of foodstuffs on which the only word written was "Ireland". All such packages were carried for free by the rail companies and altogether around 10,000 tonnes of supplies was carried to Ireland aboard gun-less warships for distribution. Among the contributions from America, the best remembered is the donation of $170 (around $5,000 today) from the native Americans of the Chocktaw Nation.
As would be the case for decades to come vast sums of money were sent by the Irish in America and the Irish serving in the British Army to help their family and friends at home. Between 1848 and 1851 a total of £2,948,697 was sent. The vast majority of this money either found its way into the landlord's pocket to pay outstanding rents or was used to pay passage to the United States for those left behind in Ireland. In the decades following the famine, as evictions continued, emigration to Britain or the New World continued unabated. In 1852 alone 220,000 people left Ireland.
Some Protestants sought to take advantage of the desperate plight of the people by offering food in return for instruction and conversion to the Protestant religion. The most notable of these was the Rev. Edward Nangle who set up some thirty four

Protestant "schools" where food was given in return for Protestant instruction.

## Mass Eviction in the wake of Starvation

Rates and the Change in Agricultural Practice

In order to finance the new poor law system, local rates were increased. The rates paid by a landlord depended on the number of tenants he had. Due to the decline in rent payment and lower prices for cereals, a large number of landlords found themselves unable to pay and rushed to relieve themselves of unwanted tenants who could not pay their rents, while others went out of business.

Following the repeal of the Corn Laws, landlords in Ireland began to look at how they could continue to profit from their estates in a climate where corn prices had been undermined. Already under pressure to pay increased rates, many landlords now decided to abandon the growth of cereal crops completely and convert their acres into pasturage for the rearing of beef and dairy herds to satisfy the demands of the English market. In a climate where the Irish tenants (outside of Ulster) had no rights, the landlords, free to do as they pleased, proceeded to clear their estates of their tenants, and their squalid cabins.

As the mass exodus of Irish continued in the decades that followed, the London Saturday Review responded to an article by the Bishop of Tuam that lamented the exodus; "The Lion of St Jarlath's surveys with an envious eye the Irish exodus, and sighs over the departing demons of assassination and murder. So complete is the rush of departing marauders, whose lives were profitably occupied in shooting Protestants from behind a hedge, that silence reigns over the vast solitude of Ireland"[289.]

The Encumbered Estates Act

By the mid 1840's, the landlords of many Irish estates had, due to profligate spending and expensive living, already amassed huge debts that were serviced by the rents of their tenants. As rents dwindled in the years after 1845, coupled with higher rates and lower corn prices, many landlords became unable to adequately service their debts. Many landlords now undertook the mass eviction of their tenants but the disquiet among the bankers of the City of London at the situation reached such levels that the government decided to quickly intervene.

In 1849, an act was passed allowing banks and other financial institutions to seize these indebted or "encumbered" estates and resell them. Provision was also made for partially indebted landlords to sell up if they desired. In total around £23,000,000 worth of Irish land changed hands, becoming the property of an even more ruthless set of landlords who cared nothing for their tenants except to view them as their encumbrance. Determined to make a profit with their new venture, these landlords, upon taking possession of their estates demanded all back rent owed from the tenants, with failure to pay meaning immediate eviction and the "tumbling" of the dwelling. Many tenants did not even wait to be evicted but rather abandoned their homes, making for the nearest port of embarkation. Some landlords, in order to rid themselves of their tenants gave them enough money to pay their passage to England or America. According to police records for the period, during the years 1849-50 around 50,000 families were evicted from their homes while over two million people abandoned their homes for foreign shores between the years 1845 – 1855, their hearts burdened with malice, while in the twenty years between 1845 and 1865, the Clare historian Fr. Vaughan has calculated that 326,000 families comprising two million people were swept out of Ireland.

Evictions in Co. Clare - The Testimony of Captain Arthur Kennedy, Poor Law Inspector - May 7th 1849

"I (Captain Kennedy, Government Commissioner) find that my constant and untiring exertions make but little impression upon the mass of fearful suffering. As soon as one horde of houseless and all but naked paupers are dead, or provided for in the workhouse, another wholesale eviction doubles the number, who, in their turn, pass through the same ordeal of wandering from house to house, or burrowing in bogs or behind ditches, till, broken down by privation and exposure to the elements, they seek the workhouse or die by the roadside. The state of some districts of the Union, during the last fourteen days, baffles description. Sixteen houses containing twenty-one families, have been levelled in one small village in Killard Division, and a vast number in the rural parts of it. As cabins become fewer, lodgings however miserable, become more difficult to obtain; and the helpless and houseless creatures, thus turned out of the only home they ever knew, betake themselves to the nearest bog or ditch with their little all, and thus huddled together disease soon decimates them."

"Notwithstanding that fearful and I believe, unparalleled numbers have been un-housed in this Union (Kilrush) within the year (probably 15,000), it hardly seems credible that 1,200 more have had their dwellings levelled within a fortnight."

"I have a list of 760 completed, and above 400 in preparation. It appears to me almost impossible successfully to meet such a state of things; and the prevailing epidemic, or rather, dread of it, aggravates the evil. None of the houseless class can now find admittance, save into some over-crowded cabin, whose inmates seldom survive a month. I have shown Dr. Phelan some of the miserable nests of pestilence which I am at a loss to describe. Five families, numbering twenty souls, are not un-frequently found in a cabin consisting of one small apartment. At Doonbeg, a few days since, I found three families numbering sixteen persons, one of whom had cholera, and three in a hopeless state of dysentery. The cabin they occupied consisted of one wretched apartment about twelve feet square. It was one of the few refuges for the evicted and they were unable to reckon how many had been carried out of it from time to time to the grave.[290]

## Emigration and Coffin Ships

"The Irish are going, going with a vengeance. In a few years a Celtic Irishman will be as rare in Connemara as is the Red Indian on the shores of Manhattan" – The London Times.

In the three years 1846-49 over one and a half million people sought to escape the starvation and left Ireland either for North America or England. The number of departures rapidly increased after 1847 when many landlords paid the fares for their tenants as a means of getting rid of them, so that rates would not have to be paid for them. Due to the bad condition of many of the ships, some of which were not seaworthy and sank on their journey along with the disease and starvation that began on board, the ships became known as "coffin ships". Many of the ships especially on the transatlantic voyage set sail with only a fraction of the food and drinking water required for the voyage. On the "Elizabeth and Sarah" that set sail from Mayo in July 1846 no food was given to the passengers at all during the entire voyage. In 1847 alone 17,000 Irish people drowned while on their voyage to the new world. While most ships crossing the Atlantic made for New York, many also went to Canada, and it was especially on the Canadian crossings that the highest number of on-board fatalities occurred. On many journeys between one third and a half of the passengers perished while many more died from advanced starvation or disease after landing. In the Canadian port of Grosse Isle, which was the quarantine station for ships sailing up the St. Laurence River, at least thirty Irish emigrants died every day in 1847. In August of 1847, a report was compiled on the situation by the Montreal Board of Health that highlighted the hypocrisy of the English government. It included the passage: "Terrible as have been the tales of the slave trade, against which the British nation has so long protested...they (the slave ships) exceed not in horrors, nor perhaps equal the dreadful realities to which these unfortunate wanderers have been subjected"[291.]

## The Failure of the Act of Union

No one can be certain how many Irish people perished because of the Great Starvation. While around one and a quarter million people died as the direct result of starvation and malnutrition,[292] hundreds of thousands more died of disease and exposure. Of those that boarded the coffin ships, almost one fifth died without reaching the new world, while many thousands more perished after arriving. Those who were left behind in Ireland were generally the poorest, the weakest and the oldest as those who had the means, had fled the Irish charnel house. In the decades that followed untold numbers of people died from want, from the policy of forced emigration, and from the ruination of their health.

That the great starvation showed once and for all the failure of the Act of Union and the necessity for the Irish people to have their own government free from English interference may be gleaned from the concluding paragraph to the census of 1851 which showed that in the preceding six years the population of Ireland had been decreased by millions through famine, disease and emigration. The census concluded with the following words:

"In conclusion, we feel it will be gratifying to your Excellency to find that, although the population has diminished in so remarkable a manner, by famine disease and emigration, and has since been decreasing, the results of the Irish Census are, on the whole satisfactory."[293] [I]

---

[I] Before the great starvation, the population of Ireland was approaching half that of Britain. Following the rebellion of '98 and the forcing of the emancipation question England had regarded Ireland as a material danger which had once more reared its head at the height of the repeal movement. This smugness of English officialdom at the result of the census indicated, that with Ireland having been once more laid low, England viewed the "Irish threat" as having been successfully neutralized.

# Chapter 10

# The Irish Republican Brotherhood

## 1848 – The Young Ireland Rebellion
### A Different Path

After the July 1846 meeting during which the Repeal Movement and Young Ireland had parted company (see chapter 8), one of the Young Ireland leaders, William Smith O'Brien M.P wrote a letter to Daniel O'Connell in which he outlined his future path: "Ireland, instead of taking her place as an integral of the great empire which the valour of her sons has contributed to constitute, has been treated as a dependent tributary province; and at this moment, after forty three years of nominal union, the attachments of the two nations are so entirely alienated from each other, that England trusts, for the maintenance of the connection, not to the affection of the Irish people, but to bayonets which menace our bosoms, and to the cannon which she has placed in all our strongholds...slowly, reluctantly convinced that Ireland has nothing to hope from the sagacity, the justice or generosity of England, my reliance shall be henceforward placed upon our own country and her patriotism"[294] Apart from the last sentence, Daniel O'Connell would have agreed. Such was O'Connell's opposition to physical force that in spite of the fact that his repeal movement had ended in failure, he was determined to remain steadfast in seeing what parliamentary methods and mass movements could achieve. William Smith O'Brien and his comrades were now to try a different path, and although their small effort would end in failure, it would inevitably lead to the actions of other men in later decades of the nineteenth and in the first quarter of the twentieth century.

### Sedition and Treason Felony
In the late 1840's as the English government's connivance at The Great Starvation continued, the urge to act against the oppressor by Young Ireland grew ever stronger, a fervour that was only increased when they saw revolution erupt in several of the countries of Europe during 1848.

In April of 1848, O'Brien accompanied a delegation of the "Irish Confederation" to Paris. It was during this trip that Thomas "The Sword" Meagher was presented with a green, white, and orange tricolour flag by some French women who had made it after the French design, the white representing peace between the Gaelic / Republican nation (green) and those who adhered to the maintenance of the Act of Union (orange).

Upon O'Brien's return to Ireland, he was arrested along with half a dozen others,[1] but the proceedings against them fell through for lack of hard evidence and they were released. However John Mitchel, who in his own newspaper "The United Irishman" promoted active resistance against the removal and exportation of the country's corn and crops to England while the Irish people were starving to death was immediately re-arrested and charged with "Treason Felony" along with the newspapers publisher Charles Gavan Duffy. Both men were sentenced to transportation to a penal colony (Tasmania) for fourteen years.

---

[1] Thomas Francis Meagher , Michael Doheny, John Blake Dillon, James Stephens, John Mitchell and John O'Mahony

## The Rebellion

After the Young Ireland leaders (with the exception of Mitchell and Duffy) were released, they spread out throughout the south of the country in order to gauge public support for revolt as throughout this half of the country there was already widespread disturbances due in no small part to the removal of crops. In the early Summer of 1848 alone, almost 600 men were tried and sentenced to imprisonment, transportation or hanging at assizes in Limerick, Ennis and Clonmel.

William Smith O'Brien

By the end of July, following the suspension of habeas corpus by the government and the renewal of the Insurrection Act, O'Brien, now a wanted man following a recent altercation with the police, decided to act.[1] Re-united with his fellow leaders they travelled from Wexford, through Kilkenny into Tipperary gathering followers. On July 28th, at a village known as "The Commons" (Boulagh Common, now Ballingarry) the tricolour was raised and a large rally was held with the entrances to the village being blocked off to prevent O'Brien arrest. The following days, the village was still sealed off by the Young Irelanders when almost 50 policemen under the command of Sub-Inspector Trant arrived at the entrance to the village in order to execute the warrant for O'Brien's arrest. When Trant saw the barricades and the large crowd of Young

---

[1] In his book "Jail Journal" John Mitchell described the event as "A poor extemporized abortion of a rising..."

Ireland supporters who held the village, he decided to retreat. Trant and his men were now pursued and took refuge in a farmhouse, home to Mrs. Margaret Mc Cormack, (a widow), and her five children. When the police entered the house, they found the five children inside while Mrs. Mc Cormack was absent. When O'Brien and his men arrived, they surrounded the house and offered to let the police leave if they would surrender their weapons.   At this point Mrs. McCormack returned in a state of great agitation and asked that for her children to be released from the house. Trant refused both the proposal from O'Brien and the Widow's request. While the parley continued, a policeman opened fire.  While O'Brien dashed for safety a general firefight now ensued during which two Young Ireland leaders, Terence McManus and James Stephens were injured.

For the following few hours the intermittent fire-fight continued between both sides, the Young Irelanders crouched at the walls while the well armed police fired at anything that moved, resulting in a crush of locals and supporters who were at the garden walls of the house when firing broke out as they tried to stay as close to the walls as possible  By four o' clock in the afternoon, two people, Patrick McBride (a supporter of Young Ireland) and Thomas Walsh (a local man) had been killed and heavy police reinforcements were approaching the house. Those Young Ireland members that had taken a leading role in the shootout now managed to escape but before a week had passed many of them including O'Brien, Meagher and McManus were arrested. James Stephens managed to evade capture and escaped to Paris

The leaders of this small revolt against English rule were all sentenced to death for treason, but the government (not wanting to make Republican martyrs of them as they had of Robert Emmett less than half a century earlier) commuted their sentence to penal servitude in Tasmania.

While the Young Ireland movement now petered out, there remained the foundation stone which it had created for the building of the Irish Republican Brotherhood.

## The Irish Republican Brotherhood

"God on our side, we will triumph again
Pay them back woe for woe,
give them back blow for blow
Out and make way for the bold Fenian Men"
- Michael Scanlon

### The Founding of the Irish Republican Brotherhood and the The Fenians

In exile in Paris, James Stephens immersed himself in revolution ideology, studying the methods of various secret organisations while conversing with their members and leaders. During this period the idea and methods of a secret organisation for the winning of Irish freedom gradually formed in his mind. By 1856, (the same year that William Smith O'Brien was pardoned) Stephens was back in Ireland, and found himself somewhat disappointed at the lack of interest in political affairs among the ordinary people who were naturally more concerned with the extraordinary difficulties which they encountered in their day to day lives. Nevertheless, he wrote that the "...disaffection..."[295] of the people would "...not be hard to stir into insurrection".[296]

The task he now set himself was to found and establish a secret movement, which, through uprising and revolt would lead the Irish people to freedom from English rule and the establishment of an Irish Republic.

The first step towards the founding of what became the Irish Republican Brotherhood (I.R.B) took place in Dublin on St. Patrick's Day 1858 when Stephens and a few followers swore "...in the presence of God to renounce all allegiance to the

Queen and to take arms and fight at a moments warning to make Ireland an independent democratic republic..."[297]

The organisation was a secret oath bound movement and the creed of its members was that Ireland would never gain its independence from British rule except by the use of physical force.

Meanwhile in the United States of America the ranks of the Irish were swollen with those who had escaped from Ireland during The Great Starvation. They could not forget the trials they had endured because of English misrule, or those they had left behind, both dead and alive. While many of these people were prepared to finance an organisation that had Irish freedom as its aim, a few were determined to do what they could to strike a blow for Irish freedom. Among them was John O'Mahony, a friend of Stephens from '48 who was of like mind.

Stephens, convinced that the Irish in the United States would play a critical role not only in financing any Irish freedom movement but also in providing other key elements such as leadership and military know-how, now travelled to the United States and with O'Mahony founded the American branch of the I.R.B at the end of October 1858. The American branch was given a different name to the Irish one – it was called "The Fenian Brotherhood of America" and was named after the warrior band "Na Fianna" of the Irish hero of legend, Fionn Mac Cumhaill. Thereafter members of the I.R.B in Ireland were also commonly referred to as Fenians.

While in America, three men (among others) worked their way into Stephen's confidence in spite of the fact that he was warned against them. These were Pierce Nagle, J.J. Corydon and Godfrey Massey.

## The Funeral of Terence MacManus

One of the leaders of the 1848 rebellion who had made his way to America after escaping Van Diemen's Land was Terence MacManus from Fermanagh, who had arrived in the United States with fellow escapee Thomas Francis Meagher.[I] When MacManus died in 1861, the opportunity for promoting the aims of the I.R.B and enlisting new members in Ireland seemed too good to miss. His body was now returned to Dublin by the Fenians for an impressive funeral, the procession of which included thousands of members of the National Brotherhood of St. Patrick in uniform. Around 30,000 people attended MacManus's funeral and he was buried with great ceremony in Glasnevin cemetery by Fr. Patrick Lavelle.[II] Following the funeral, along with the associated publicity, membership in the I.R.B soared in both urban and rural areas with members pledging to free Ireland by force of arms, this in spite of the vocal opposition of the Catholic Church to the Fenians, as a secret society whose members were bound to take an oath: "binding (them) to obey the rules laid down by the heads of the association...without knowing the obligations that the oath involves"[298] In spite of this many individual clergy openly

---

[I] Meagher rose to the rank of Brigadier General in the Union Army during the American Civil War. Following the war he was appointed to the position of Secretary of State of Montana by President Andrew Johnson (whose grandparents had emigrated from Ballyeaston in north Antrim in the 1760s). Meagher also fulfilled the role of acting Governor of the territory. In 1867 he drowned in the Missouri River when he fell or was pushed from a steamboat at Fort Benton.

[II] Fr. Lavelle was known as "The Patriot Priest of Partry" (Mayo). This name was given him due to his tireless efforts to stop landlords from pressurising their tenants to convert to Protestantism.

sympathised with the Fenians such as the historian Fr. Jeremiah Vaughan from Co. Clare.[1]

## "The Irish People"

In 1863, Stephens, who had now returned to Ireland, established his own newspaper called "The Irish People". Careful to avoid the trap that John Mitchell had fallen into, Stephens and his editors disseminated the creed of the I.R.B. using words that just about stayed on the right side of the law. The Manager of the newspaper was the Cork Republican, Jeremiah O'Donovan Rossa, who, in the mid 1850s had founded his own organisation for Irish freedom called "The Phoenix National and Literary Society" which he soon merged with the I.R.B. The other members of the editorial staff included Charles Kickham, Thomas Luby, Denis Mulcahy with John O'Leary and James O'Connor as editors.

---

[1] Speaking to a gathering of Irish emigrants and descendants, along with supporters of Ireland's cause at The Cooper Institute, New York on November 21st 1866; Fr. Vaughan laid out the cause for Irish freedom. His speech ran in part: "The whole rule of England in Ireland, from the first invasion of robber-murderer Saxon to the present time, has been one of misrule. The ancient laws of Ireland, before the Saxon planted his foot upon her soil, were eminently just and wise. They enforced the practice of hospitality, the cultivation of music, poetry and literature, and exhibited a jealous regard for the security of property and the honour of women. To such a degree was the popular mind of Ireland dignified and elevated by the enforcement of these wise laws, that when St. Patrick came to Ireland and appeared before its senators, and presented to them the Gospel of Christ, they immediately recognised the truth of his teachings, and in an incredibly short space of time the whole island was converted. But since England has usurped domination over Ireland that unhappy country has been cursed with the vilest code of laws that ever disgraced a human government. There were three things which just laws would ever guard with jealous care – the security of life, of property, and of female honour. The English have never given laws securing either."

## 1867 – The Republic is declared
Dublin Castle moves against the I.R.B. Leadership.
When the southern states of the United States of America tried to break away from the northern states of the Union in 1861, the north's refusal to allow them go their own way heralded the onset of the American Civil War.

The war divided the Irish in America for its duration and there were many Irish fighting units formed on both sides. The organisation of The Fenian Brotherhood suffered as a result of the war but as the war neared its conclusion Stephens, who planned a return to Ireland of veterans (both Confederate and Union) to fight "at home" wrote in late 1864 to O'Mahony to remind him: "Let no man forget for an instant that we are bound to action next year"[299.]

James Stephens

In Ireland meanwhile, secret preparations and drilling for an armed uprising continued. Arms were in short supply but Stephens hoped for a shipment from the American Fenians following the end of the American Civil War in April 1865.

All the while, Dublin Castle was aware of everything that happened in the office of Stephen's newspaper and much more besides, thanks to an I.R.B. member named Pierce Nagle who was a Dublin Castle informer. The fate of the newspaper was sealed when the authorities intercepted plans for a rising along with money at Kingstown (Dún Laoghaire) railway station. On September 15th 1865, the office of the paper was raided and the police arrested the entire staff of the newspaper with the exception of Stephens and Kickham, both of whom were later apprehended.[1]

Stephens incarceration was only to be temporary however, as he escaped from Dublin's Richmond Jail shortly afterwards with the help of the warders (who were I.R.B. members) and the returned American emigrant, Colonel Thomas Kelly.

The other prisoners were not so lucky. In the trial that followed the raid before a "packed" jury the entire senior staff of The Irish People were given hefty prison sentences while O'Donovan Rossa was sentenced to life imprisonment due to a previous conviction.

After his escape, Stephens seems to have realised that the work that had been put into preparing a rising was completely insufficient and he now postponed the rising until an undetermined date the following year. In the aftermath of the newspaper raid, the government moved quickly to once more suspend "Habeas Corpus" in Ireland. On February 17th, the bill for suspension was both passed and signed into law by Queen Victoria, the haste of which did not escape the notice of one M.P. (a Mr. Bright) who stated in the House of Commons: "Never does the Government act with energy and promptness towards Ireland except upon a measure of repression or coercion...the conduct of every administration towards Ireland has been utterly devoid of statesmanship"[300.]

## The" Invasion" of Canada

With no rising imminent in Ireland and with a huge number of members of military experience at its disposal, the leadership of the Fenian Brotherhood of America now made plans for the invasion of British ruled Canada during the Spring of 1866, the prime mover for this project being Colonel William Roberts.

---

[1] Stephens managed to avoid arrest until mid November, when his hiding place in Sandymount, Dublin was betrayed.

The idea of such a venture was that if the Fenians could gain control of Canada, they could trade Canada for a free Ireland with the British government. Initially the U.S government paid little heed to the rumours of the Fenian attack from the U.S into Canada but when hundreds of armed Fenians were reported to be gathering along the border the government acted, sending troops to the frontier where Colonel Roberts and his officers were arrested. In spite of this, one contingent of Fenians under Col. John O'Neill reached Fort Erie and defeated an Anglo Canadian force commanded by Colonel Barker who with his men fled the field leaving their flags in the hands of the Fenians. It was all to no avail however as O'Neill was on his own and had no supplies. After his odyssey into Canada he returned to the border where he was forced to surrender to waiting U.S. forces.

## Colonel Kelly assumes leadership of the I.R.B.

By the Autumn of 1866, Stephens was proclaiming that his rising would take place "before the 1$^{st}$ day of January 1867". However as 1866 drew to a close, Stephens urged another postponement. Stephen's reluctance to act in spite of his many speeches and proclamations irked the I.R.B. leadership who now felt that he had become somewhat fearful of rebellion and had outgrown his usefulness. In late 1866 he was ousted from his position as "Acting Chief Executive of the Irish Republic" in favour of Colonel Thomas Kelly, who sailed from the U.S in January 1867 with the intention of launching a rebellion as soon as possible. Stephens now retired from any active role within the I.R.B. and withdrew from public life

## The 1867 Insurrection

After crossing the Atlantic, Kelly, knowing how damaging the failure to keep Stephen's promise was to the prestige of the I.R.B, not to mention the morale of its members, wasted no time in planning his revolt. After holding a secret council of delegates in Dublin, it was decided to fix February 12th 1867 as the day of action. Operations now moved to England where the initial phase of his plan would take place.

As the Irish members of the I.R.B. could not effectively rise without weapons, Kelly's plan was divided into two phases, the first phase being conceived by former U.S. army Captain John Mc Cafferty. After isolating Chester Castle in England by cutting all communications, it was to be attacked by a group of Fenians armed with revolvers under the command of a Frenchman named Cluseret, who was a Fenian sympathiser and also formerly of the U.S. Army. After neutralising the guard, the Fenian assault group would break open the armoury (which contained around 20,000 guns) and capture as many weapons as possible for immediate shipment to Ireland.

In Ireland, meanwhile, thousands of mobilised Fenians would, (unlike previous risings) not engage in open battle with Crown Forces but would rather harass them by means of guerrilla tactics and also the cutting of telegraph lines, rail links and anything that would immobilise the functioning of the English administration. Once armed, they were to hold the country in a state of siege until the arrival of help from the United States, when the task of freeing Ireland would be completed.

Thanks to the information passed to them by J.J. Corydon, who was a member of the circle of planners for the attack on the Castle, the police in Chester were fully aware of the Fenian plan. As members of the Castle assault group drifted into Chester on the morning of 11th February, they moved to their waiting positions for the attack the following day. However, after midday word reached them that the police were aware of their plans thanks to an unnamed informer. Immediately, the attack was called off, and the Fenians quickly dispersed throwing their revolvers into nearby canals before they departed the town. A message was sent to all units that the new date for the attack was March 5th. The news came too late for the Fenians in West Kerry who did not receive the countermand and engaged in brief action before realising that the rest of the country was not following suit. Without knowing who had betrayed them, the leadership revised their preparations for March 5th. In their midst was Corydon who once more relayed everything he knew to the authorities. Aside from the new date, the amended plan called for the seizure of Irish police stations and the removal of their weapons in lieu of the weapons that should have been provided from the Chester arsenal.

Colonel Thomas Kelly

Already in possession of a great deal of information, the Irish Constabulary were to find out everything they needed to know on the eve of the rising. As Godfrey Massey travelled to Limerick from Cork on the evening of March 4th, he was arrested on the platform of Limerick Junction, whereupon he immediately divulged to the police everything he knew. The rebellion, which never had much chance of success, was now doomed before it ever began. In spite of a few local successes such as the brief capture of a few police barracks in Dublin and Cork, the Crown Forces crushed the rebellion with little trouble. Nevertheless a Republic had been declared and a provisional government formed, both acts influencing a later generation of Irish freedom fighters. In the months that followed the limited March rebellion there were sporadic attacks upon infrastructure and Crown Forces as laid down in the plan but through suppression, force and the use of informers, the Fenians could gain no ground.

As a reward for putting down the rising, Queen Victoria bestowed the title "Royal" on the Irish Constabulary, which were known thereafter as the Royal Irish Constabulary (R.I.C.)

In spite of the informers, Colonel Thomas Kelly remained at large in Dublin and had not given up hope. In early September of 1867 he crossed over to Manchester along with Timothy Deasy to attend a meeting of the leaders of English cells so that the English Fenians could be reorganised and a "government in exile" formed. However, on September 11th both Kelly and Deasy were arrested for loitering in an Oak Street doorway as the police patrol suspected they were planning to burgle a business premises. As the two men were Irish, the police thought it worthwhile to carry out further investigations. Their descriptions were sent to Ireland and finally, their identities were confirmed by the informer; Corydon. Kelly and Deasy were now facing trial and death.

## "God save Ireland"

"Climbed they up the rugged stair, rang their voices out in prayer,
Then with England's fatal cord around them cast,
Close beside the gallows tree kissed like brothers lovingly,
True to home and faith and freedom to the last.
"God save Ireland!" prayed they loudly; "God save Ireland!" prayed they all
Whether on the scaffold high or the battlefield we die,
Oh! What matter, when for Erin dear we fall?"
– Timothy Daniel Sullivan

### The Rescue

After appearing in court on the charge of Treason on September 18th, Kelly and Deasy were being taken back to

Manchester's Belle Vue Gaol along with some other defendants (three women and a boy) when the prison van which was escorted by few policemen on foot, was held up by a man with a gun. When the van stopped, a group of around 30 Fenians, some armed with revolvers, who had been lying in wait behind a wall emerged and quickly surrounded the van.

While some pointed their guns at the policemen and made them lie on the ground, others armed with hammers, hatchets and crowbars attacked the door of the van while more climbed onto the roof. Unable to smash the door, the Fenians called to the policeman inside, Sergeant Brett, to pass out the keys. Brett refused. As Brett stooped to look through the keyhole, one of the group shouted; "Blow it open; put your pistol to the keyhole and blow it open!"[301] As the Fenians attempted to blow open the lock the courageous Brett was fatally shot in the head.

From the dead man's pocket, one of the female prisoners retrieved the door keys and passed them out through the air vent in the door. The door was then opened and the prisoners issued forth. Colonel Kelly and Captain Deasy would never be recaptured.

## The Trial

In the aftermath of the attack on the prison van, the Manchester police were enraged at the death of Sergeant Brett. They launched a veritable reign of terror upon the Irish in Manchester as a wave of anti-Irish hysteria swept the city. In the Irish districts, police raided and arrested at random while in other areas of the city anyone with an Irish accent was liable to arrest. In the media and among the "great and the good" there were widespread calls for the heaviest penalty – death – to be visited upon those responsible. Lines such as: "…if such an offence as this is allowed to go unpunished and unavenged, will any man's life be safe?"³⁰² were commonplace in the press.

By the end of October, the police had 28 men in custody who they suspected of being involved in the prison van raid. All 28 were brought before a grand jury, who found that all of them had a case to answer on the charge of murder. Although there was no evidence regarding who had fired the fatal shot, it was decided that five – Maguire, Larkin, Condon, O'Brien and Allen, should stand trial for murder by "common enterprise", as the police claimed that all five had been in the forefront of the attack. While none denied their adherence to the I.R.B., Larkin, O'Brien, Allen and Maguire denied that they were at the forefront of the attack or had anything to do with the death of Brett. Condon maintained he was not present at all.

As the trial got underway, the press proclaimed the guilt of the men and called for "justice" to be done. After five days of "evidence" much of which was later shown to be patently false,[1] the jury deliberated for one hour before finding all five guilty of Sergeant Brett's murder.

Before sentencing them to death, the Judge asked the men if they had anything to say. All five once more declared that they had nothing to do with Brett's death. Several decried the false testimony given by the witnesses and asked that God would forgive the witnesses for their perjury. Condon told the Judge "…it is all totally false…had I committed anything against the Crown of England, I would have scorned myself had I attempted to deny it…God save Ireland!"³⁰³ The cry of "God save Ireland!" was now taken up by all the defendants and repeated by each of them as one after one they were sentenced to be hanged.

---

[1] Most of the evidence had been fabricated by a detective and related to the court by his agent, a prostitute.

The most obvious miscarriage of justice was that of the off duty soldier Thomas Maguire. The "witnesses" who testified against him had so obviously perjured themselves that in the aftermath of the trial even the English press were forced to proclaim his innocence while witnesses came forward stating that he had been many miles away on the day in question. On the eve of execution Maguire was pardoned. The fact that it was shown that totally unreliable evidence had been used to convict him should have been enough for the Judge to order a retrial for the other men but such was the clamour for Irish blood that the Home Secretary ignored the many calls both at home and abroad for a retrial. At the last moment, Condon also managed to escape the hangman. As a citizen of the United States, he had his sentence commuted because of a telegram from the Secretary of State of the United States of America. He was now forced to spend many years behind bars in appalling conditions.[1]

The Executions
Guarded by around 1,500 police officers, O'Brien, Allen and Larkin were hanged on the morning of November 23rd in front of Salford Gaol. Fr. Gadd, who administered the last rites to the men wrote that the hanging was attended by a crowd of intoxicated "…inhuman ghouls from the purlieus of Deansgate and the slums of the City…No Irish mingled with the throng…they had obeyed the instructions of their clergy. Throughout Manchester…silent congregations with tear stained faces assembled for a celebration of early Mass for the eternal welfare of the young Irishmen doomed to die a dreadful death that morning." [304]

---

[1] Condon was made a Freeman of Dublin in 1909 and died in New York in 1918.

The executioner, William Calcraft, bungled the executions completely, miscalculating the men's weight and the length of rope to be used. While Larkin's neck was broken immediately, Allen and O'Brien lingered. Fr. Gadd wrote: "Calcraft then descended into the pit and there finished what he could not from above. He Killed Larkin"[305.] Fr. Gadd would not allow

From left to right – Allen, Larkin and O'Brien

Calcraft to repeat with Allen what he had done with Larkin. After stopping Calcraft, he held the hand of the doomed man while reciting the prayers for the dying until Allen breathed his last.

The example of the Manchester Martyrs who had faced their deaths with such equanimity had made certain that the I.R.B. would endure.

Following the hangings, in Dublin an estimated 150,000 people attended a commemorative funeral procession for "The Manchester Martyrs" in which three hearses with empty coffins were led by a massed band playing "The Dead March" in "Saul".

## "The Clerkenwell Outrage"

Three days before the Manchester Martyrs were hanged, An I.R.B. member, Ricard O'Sullivan Burke, who was heavily involved in the procurement of arms for the Fenians was arrested and charged with treason after he had bought a number of guns in Birmingham. Awaiting trial, he was detained in London's Clerkenwell Prison.

Determined to try and rescue him, it was decided by the local Fenian leadership to demolish by explosion a portion of the wall between the prison's exercise yard and the street outside during the prisoners exercise hour. On December 12th 1867, an attempt was made to detonate a device outside the prison wall without success. Undeterred, the Fenians determined to repeat the attempt the following day, this time with a much larger device. However, the prison authorities became aware that an attempted rescue was in the offing and moved the prisoners exercise time to the morning. When the Fenian group made their way up Corporation Lane with a large hand-cart in which a full barrel of gunpowder was concealed, the prison yard behind the wall on one side of the Lane was empty.

The amount of gunpowder contained in the Keg was extremely large (around 500lbs), far too large for the small task of creating a breach in a wall. When the barrel exploded, it destroyed not only sixty yards of the prison wall but also several tenement houses on the opposite side of the Lane Twelve people were instantly killed and 120 wounded. Of the wounded, 18 later died. Had Burke and the other prisoners been in the exercise Yard, they would most likely have been killed also. The following April, six men went on trial for murder at the Old Bailey, of whom one, Michael Barrett, from Co. Fermanagh was found guilty and hanged by the infamous Calcraft. It was to be England's last public hanging.

# Chapter 11

# The Land War

In the aftermath of the Great Starvation, the effect of the Encumbered Estates Act was to once more render the people of Ireland helpless and prostrate before the all-powerful landlords and the government that nurtured them. The drastic land clearances of Irish people from their land permitted under the act and carried out by the forces of the Crown, who always acted as the landlord's brutal enforcer, knew no bounds and continued unabated in the decades that followed.

For those who could pay their rent, it was increased year after year, for those who could not they were cast out onto the roadside, as the Act of the Ulster Plantation centuries earlier described: "to depart with their goods and chattels…into what other part of the realm they pleased."[306]

Even emigration did not mean escape, as those who laboured abroad, whether in England, the United States or Australia were desperate to assist those they had left behind and sent home vast amount of money to try and help them pay their rents. Between the years 1848 and 1864 an estimated £13,000,000 was sent home by the Irish in America, the majority of which found its way into the deep pockets of their landlords.

## The Felon

Among the leadership of the Young Ireland movement, there is one man whose writings were to play a prominent part in the formation of the ideology and actions of future leaders in the Irish battle for land justice and freedom from English rule.

With his penetrating intellect, James Fintan Lalor (1803-49) writing in his newspaper, "The Irish Felon" summarised both the issue at stake and the actions necessary for their remedy if the Irish tenant was to gain justice in his own land. In the issue of June 2 1848 he wrote: "...the entire ownership of Ireland, moral and material, up to the sun and down to the centre, is vested of right in the people of Ireland...this island is our own, and have it we will. There can be no property in eight thousand, against the property, security, independence and existence of eight millions, to take their food and give them famine, take their home and give them the workhouse. Such rights are the code of the brigand, and can be enforced only by the hangman."

In subsequent issues, Lalor set out his plans for a "Plan of Campaign" and a "No Rent Manifesto". The manifesto ran in part: "Refuse all rent except what remains after subsistence. Defy ejectment. The English Government must then either surrender the landlords, or support them with the armed power of the empire."

Following the failure of Smith O'Brien's attempt at insurrection in Ballingarry, Lalor determined that the cause of the Young Irelanders should not fall into abeyance and began planning for another rising in 1849, which had no better success than the first. Lalor was arrested during an attack on Cappoquin police station in Waterford. Always of fragile health, the rigours of police confinement did not help his constitution and he died of bronchitis at the end of December 1849.

## The Tenant Right League

In the early 1850s, the former Young Ireland activist, Charles Gavan Duffy now turned his attention to the plight of Irish tenants aided by an unlikely ally in the form of an English Protestant minister, the Rev. James Godkin. Godkin had travelled to Ireland with the aim of converting Catholics to Protestantism but upon his arrival had quickly abandoned this aim in favour of obtaining some measure of justice for the Irish people.

Following the introduction of The Encumbered Estates Act, disquiet had arisen among farmers in Ulster that their "Ulster Custom" of fair rent, free sale and fixity of tenure coupled with compensation for improvements made had not been guaranteed by the Act. Their cause was taken up by the Co. Down Landlord, William Sharman Crawford. Contacts between Crawford and Charles Gavan Duffy followed and this led to the forming of an all Ireland committee composed of both Catholics and Protestants known as the Tenant Right League (or the League of Tenant Farmers). However when only one candidate was returned to Parliament for the League in Ulster versus 49 in the rest of Ireland the all Ireland aspect of the League waned.[1]

Charles Gavan Duffy

---

[1] The Orange Order was opposed to the league and referred to it as "The Pope's Brass Band"

In the London Parliament, every effort made by the Tenant Right League to alleviate the situation of Irish tenant farmers through the introduction of legislation was always defeated. When Sharman Crawford introduced a bill into the Commons that allowed for the extension of the Ulster Custom to all tenants it was defeated by 167 votes to 57.

The League was now fatally weakened by a few of its number who betrayed their cause and instead looked to their own interests. Acquiescing with the governments desire to neutralise the group through bribery and corruption several of its M.P.s fell into the government's pocket in exchange for place and money. The most notable were John Sadlier who was made a Lord of the Treasury and William Keogh who was appointed Irish Solicitor General and later a Judge.

Throughout the 1850's and 1860's, the desperate plight of Ireland and her people continued unheeded by a government content to repel discontent with force while her agents ravaged both land and people.

## Ireland – "The Only Real Danger to the Noble Empire of the Queen"

The Effect of the Clerkenwell Explosion on British Opinion and Policy

Once the feelings of wounded national pride along with invaded order and authority had receded in the aftermath of the Clerkenwell explosion, the eminent citizens of London and their government wondered how such a thing could be prevented in the future? The many injustices endured by the Irish people at the hands of the English were now, perhaps for the first time, mentioned and seen as the real cause of Clerkenwell. If such terrible acts were to be prevented in the future, a measure of justice must be given to Ireland, not for Ireland's sake but rather in England's own interest.

William Gladstone, the British Prime Minister felt that if at least some attempt were made to release the strangle-hold with which England embraced Ireland, the will and desire of the ordinary people to support The I.R.B might be abated. He later said that the Clerkenwell Outrage: "first induced the British people to embrace in a manner foreign to their habits in other times, the vast importance of the Irish controversy"[307].

Gladstone now interested himself in Irish affairs and the danger that they posed to the tranquillity of the Empire. In a letter to Lord Granville he wrote: "To this great country (England) the state of Ireland after seven hundred years of our tutelage is in my opinion as long as it continues, an intolerable disgrace and a danger so absolutely transcending all others that I call it the only real danger of the noble empire of the Queen"[308].

After some deliberation, Gladstone finally decided on two policies that he felt would act as a tranquilliser to the Irish situation; the disestablishment of the Anglican Church in Ireland and a measure of land reform.

## The Disestablishment of the Church of Ireland

By 1870 the Anglican Church in Ireland had the allegiance of little over 10% of the population most of whom were English.[1] It had ever, by force, been supported by the Catholics of

---

[1] "In a country where human beings in droves perished annually of sheer starvation, the Anglican Archbishop of Armagh pocketed £75,000 a year, the Bishop of Derry £50,000 and so on down to their poorest Episcopal colleague who had to preach the gospel of poverty and self denial on a pittance of £12,000, with house free and various perquisites thrown in. This Church of an alien coterie took £2,500,000 yearly straight from the pockets of an impoverished people who rejected its tenets and loathed its practices...No wonder, either, that seven (Irish) Anglican bishops bequeathed nearly £10,000,000 in ready money to their relatives!" – "(Social and Economic Condition of Ireland", Clancy, 1872)

Ireland and was imposed on the Irish people as an English monument of Irish subjection and tyranny. It's establishment as the official church along with the forced monetary support of the Irish people was described by Lord Brougham as: "The foulest practical abuse that ever existed, opposed alike to justice, to policy, and to religious principles."[309]

In 1860 there were 199 parishes in Ireland without a single Anglican and in which a Protestant service had most likely never been held, yet the Catholic inhabitants of these parishes were still required by law to contribute to the support of the established church. Furthermore all Catholics entering government service had to take an oath that they would "…never weaken the Protestant religion or the Protestant Government in the United Kingdom."[310]

Historically opposed to disestablishment, in the aftermath of Manchester and Clerkenwell, Gladstone now changed course. He wrote: "When it came to this, that a great gaol in the heart of the metropolis was broken open under circumstances which drew the attention of English people to the state of Ireland, and when a Manchester policeman was murdered in the exercise of his duty, at once the whole country became alive to Irish questions and the question of the church revived."[311]

After triumphing in the election of 1868 during the campaign of which he had promised disestablishment, Gladstone introduced the measure for its disestablishment in March 1869[I]

---

[I] A Protestant Minister (the Rev. Myles) announced the diestablishment to his congregation from his pulpit in the following terms: "England had separated herself from God. We Irish Protestant have always been faithful to Her (England) and now She requites our fidelity with desertion. Caesar has cast us off. I will not preach disloyalty but I will say this – Let Caesar take care of himself for the future without our assistance."

that simultaneously abolished the so-called "Obnoxious Oaths".[1]

Under the measure, the Church of Ireland was now to be made self-governing and placed on the same legal footing as the Catholic Church. Although disestablished, the Church was to retain its vast stolen lands, "given" to it by the Crown. In 1880 the Church's property portfolio was worth £16,000,000.

The move was bitterly opposed by many in the Anglo Irish establishment who, concerned with the loss of prestige and money, delivered once more the speeches of old in opposition to the measure. Orangemen went further. Some Lodges pledged to "...kick her Majesty's crown into the Boyne"[312] if the proposal was passed. Surprisingly there were also opponents to its disestablishment among Presbyterians. One Presbyterian minister had hearkened back to the black days of Cromwell: "We will fight as men alone can fight who have the bible in one hand and the sword in the other... and this will be our dying cry, echoed and re-echoed from earth to heaven and from one end of Ulster to the other: "No Popery, no surrender!"

The break of the Anglican Church with the state was "cushioned" by the payment of £7,500,000 for the maintenance of the Protestant clergy along with a further £2,675,570 to be paid for the loss of private endowments, gratuities etc. A further surplus was allocated for the relief of "property obligations" most of which was pocketed by the Church.

Under the measure £770,000 was also paid to the Presbyterians as compensation for the ending of the annual payment of the so called "Regium Donum" (Royal Gift). £372,000 was also

---

[1] Oaths required of Catholics on entering government service. Although these oaths did not include any denial of a Catholic article of faith, they nevertheless required the taker to do all in their power to ensure that the Protestant faith was maintained as the religion of the realm.

given to the Catholic Church in lieu of the termination of the annual grant to the national Catholic seminary at Maynooth.

The 1870 Land Act
Whilst Gladstone's Disestablishment Act, was relatively clear cut, and could only be welcomed as an improvement by the majority of the Irish people, his first attempt at land reform, although well intentioned, was minimalist in the extreme and hardly improved the situation at all.

An eviction scene showing both RIC and Army in attendance

After studying various recommendations on improving the situation, which included the transformation of tenants into owners, he finally decided to adopt a limited version of the recommendations of his Chief Secretary, Chichester Parkinson-Fortescue. The Act which Gladstone hoped would: "close up and seal up for ever this great question"[313] failed to bring security to tenants other than those living in Ulster as The Ulster Custom where it existed, was now to be recognised by law. For the great majority the only measure in their favour was compensation for improvements if they surrendered their lease or were evicted for any reason other than non-payment of rent. However, even this measure only guaranteed the penniless tenant the right to a lawsuit to be funded by the tenant in the event that the landlord would not compensate.[1] Meanwhile, the landlord remained free to raise the rent as much as he liked, and one's years non-payment of an exorbitant rent still remained the most common reason for eviction following the Act.

In the decade following the Act, around 30 amendments bills were introduced whereby Irish M.P.s sought to improve upon the measures of the Act but every last one was either pigeon-holed or defeated.

## The Introduction of the Secret Ballot

The most important reform introduced by Gladstone during his first term as British Prime Minister was not one directed at Ireland specifically, but one which encompassed Ireland as part of the United Kingdom. This was the introduction of the secret ballot in parliamentary elections.

Those Irish tenants who were eligible to vote had ever done so before an agent of their landlord, who by his presence and the recording of names and how they voted exerted pressure upon them to vote either for the landlord or for the person the landlord desired to be elected as Member of Parliament for that constituency. If the tenant did not vote according to his landlord's wishes, he ran a significant risk of eviction or other punitive measures. In spite of this, tenants had often voted for their candidate of choice and faced the consequences. This measure of Parliamentary reform, went some way to free the tenants from the wrath of their landlord in so far as parliamentary elections were concerned.

---

[1] Of those tenants who did manage to bring a lawsuit, only 30% won their case, but were never awarded more than a pittance.

## The Home Government Association of Ireland.

The disestablishment of the Protestant Church of Ireland was something that Irish Protestants always feared would occur under an Irish home rule parliament. Never did they dream that such a measure could emanate from London especially since the Act of Union had promised that the maintenance of its establishment was both "fundamental and essential"[314]

### To Preserve the Link with England

With the disestablishment of the Church of Ireland, one of the obstacles for Irish protestant M.Ps to support domestic home rule for Dublin disappeared and there was renewed interest in the topic among middle and upper class protestants, an interest that was only increased when the Fenian, Jeremiah O'Donovan Rossa won the parliamentary seat for Tipperary in the election of 1869.

In order to bring an end to England's direct control over Irish domestic affairs and prevent the further growth of the Fenians, it was now felt essential by some upper class Protestants that those who wished to preserve the link with England through a measure of Irish home rule should act. They argued that if Ireland were to be exposed to a democratic and fair home rule government, the Fenians would lose their popular support and their project for complete separation from England must finally end. Furthermore the Tipperary election had served to show the Protestants that while the Catholic electorate would uphold church teaching in matters of faith and morals, they would not necessarily follow the advice of their priests in matters of politics.

### The Formation of The Home Rule Party

All of these considerations led to the organisation of a meeting on May 19th 1870 by the Dublin barrister, Mr. Isaac Butt, who had previously represented some of the Fenians at their court hearings.

At the meeting, Butt attempted to answer the objections of his fellow Protestants who feared that the Irish would be content only with complete separation from England. He told his audience: "It is we – it is our inaction, our desertion of the people and the country, the abdication of our position and duties that have cast these men into the eddys and whirlpools of rebellion. If you are but ready to lead them by constitutional courses to their legitimate national rights, they are ready to follow you. Trust me, we have all grievously wronged the Irish Catholics, priests and laymen. As for the men whom misgovernment has driven into revolt, I say for them that if they cannot aid you, they will not thwart your experiment. Arise! Be bold! Have faith, have confidence, and you will save Ireland – not Ireland alone, but England also!"[315]

Isaac Butt

Later, Butt moved the motion: "That in the opinion of this meeting the true remedy for the evils of Ireland is the establishment of an Irish parliament, with full control over our domestic affairs."[316] The motion was unanimously carried.

Following the formation of The Home Government Association – shortly to be known as The Home Rule Party, the group sought to establish a national organisation and by 1874 it was ready to contest that year's election. Its election results were indeed promising, with a total of 60 Westminster seats being won.

Despised at Westminster

Butt was a good natured and gentlemanly fellow who imagined that in Westminster the Home Rule Party should put forward its case on its merits and play by the book. However as the leader of a minority party despised for its cause by British M.P.s, he found parliament a thoroughly inhospitable place. Every measure put forward by his party during the parliament of 1874-80 was defeated. Butt was confounded.

Other M.P.s in his party, most notably John O'Connor Power and Joseph Gillies Biggar (a closet Fenian) decided that if they could not win at Westminster they could at least obstruct the business of the House of Commons especially when it came to the introduction of measures against the Irish people. They were to be joined in 1875 by the new member for Meath, Charles Stewart Parnell.

To Butt's displeasure, for endless hours the members of the house endured long rambling speeches interspersed with pages of quotations by some members of the Home Rule Party, all of which served to delay the passage of legislation. When Parliament was recalled immediately after Christmas of 1878 to deal with the war in Afghanistan, Butt urged the members of his party to desist from their obstructionism, which they refused to do. Butt's leadership was now fatally weakened, while Parnell was seen as a leader in waiting. In May of 1879 Butt fell ill with bronchitis and died from a stroke shortly afterwards. He was then temporarily replaced (until the end of the parliamentary term) as Party Chairman by the M.P.for Cork, William Shaw.

At the end of parliament's term the following year, Benjamin Disraeli (now Lord Beaconsfield) attempted to warn the Irish electorate against voting for The Home Rule Party in the forthcoming election by telling them: "A portion of its (Ireland's) population is attempting to sever the constitutional tie which unites it to Great Britain in that bond which has favoured the power and prosperity of both. It is to be hoped that all men of light and leading will resist this destructive doctrine."[317] However following the election the Home Rule Party returned to parliament with an extra 8 seats (68 in total) and a new leader, Charles Stewart Parnell.

## The Irish National Land League
### 1877-79 – The Return of the Potato Blight

The mid 1870's were what might be termed good years for the small tenant farmer. They had in the main been able to pay their rents and survive thanks to good market prices for their rent crops. However in the late 1870s, market prices for rent crops had fallen thanks to cheaper American cereal imports and then in 1877, the potato, which the tenant farmer depended on for his survival, was hit once again by blight which struck again in 1878 and 1879. Mass starvation was averted due to the work of charitable institutions but the tenants remained unable to pay their rents. In 1877 the number of families evicted from their homes was 1,323. By 1879 this figure had more than doubled to 2,667.

### The Formation of the Irish National Land League

In 1877 a man born in Straide, Co. Mayo but raised in Lancashire due to the eviction and emigration of his family, was released from prison. His name was Michael Davitt. A Fenian, in 1871, he had been sentenced to fifteen years on the evidence of the informer Corydon for distributing weapons for the purposes of rebellion.

After his release, he returned to his native Mayo where he determined to try and do what he could to organise resistance against the landlords in favour of tenant rights, as he was now convinced that the struggle for both nation and land must go hand in hand.

Even though he was not long released from prison, Davitt was already impressed by the public utterances of Charles Stewart Parnell, describing him as: "an Englishman of the strongest sort moulded for an Irish purpose."[318] Here, Davitt felt was a ready made leader for his cause. However, Parnell could not be seen to embrace the new neo-Fenian organisation that Davitt wished to form in favour of tenant rights unless the Fenians modified their tactics.

Parnell was approached and asked to meet with the American Fenian and leader of the Irish American organisation Clan na Gael (Irish Family) John Devoy. The secret meeting between the two men took place in Paris in March of 1879, where Devoy assured Parnell that the Fenians would no longer engage in armed action but would rather peacefully support the fight for home rule.

Michael Davitt

The following month, with the help of local Fenians, Davitt organised a demonstration against evictions in Irishtown, Mayo. In the aftermath of the meeting, a popular movement developed among the tenant farmers of the west of Ireland who were now determined to stand and fight to prevent their eviction and retain their holding. In the aftermath of the failed land act of 1870, the extension of the Ulster Custom to all tenants was now seen as the absolute minimum that must be conceded by the government. This was known as "the Three F's" – Fair rents, Fixity of Tenure and Free Sale. Davitt's fight was reinforced by the mass distribution of a newspaper of American origin called

"Irish World" which told the people of the development of land reforms in other nations by both peaceful and other methods.

Davitt organised another mass meeting of protest against eviction to be held in Westport for which he was eager to gain a prominent speaker. With confidence he approached Parnell, who, following his meeting with Devoy was eager to help.

At the meeting, Parnell, himself a landlord, had a clear message for those threatened by eviction: "...now, what must we do in order to induce the landlords to see the position? You must show them that you intend to hold a firm grip of your homesteads and lands. You must not allow yourselves to be dispossessed as your fathers were dispossessed in 1847..."[319]

In October of the same year, Michael Davitt (along with Parnell, Dillon, Brennan, Kettle and Sexton among others) officially founded the "The Irish National Land League" with Parnell as its president. The aims of the movement were to put a stop to rack-renting, evictions and to get a fair rent for the tenant. The final aim of the League was the transfer of land from the landlord to the tenant and the complete abolition of landlordism. Where exorbitant rents were demanded, the tenants were urged not to pay. In the face of this opposition, the landlords fought back: Gladstone noted that the notices of eviction issued by the landlords were now "falling like snowflakes"[320]

By involving himself in the land struggle, Parnell also hoped to further the cause of Home Rule, believing that victory over landlordism was an essential prerequisite for Irish legislative independence. Speaking in Galway he told his audience: "I would not have taken off my coat and gone to this work if I had not known that we were laying the foundation in this movement for the regeneration of our legislative independence."[321.]

## The Campaign against the Landlords

There now began an almost national movement of mass protest in which the tenant farmers took on not only the landlords but also those who tried to take advantage of the unrest by taking up the land of the dispossessed. Evictions were now the scene of popular demonstrations against landlords, with the protestors doing all they could to make things as difficult as possible for the bailiffs and police. As the police sought to enforce the landlord's wishes, violence often ensued. While the Land League did not ascribe to violence, this was not the case with more violent elements who adopted the Whiteboy methods of old. They targeted not only the property of the landlords and their agents but also the landlords themselves, a few of whom were assassinated.

### "A Sort of Moral Coventry"

Opposed to any violence and wishing to stop the ordinary members and supporters of the Land League from being sucked into such actions, Parnell recommended to them a different course in order that they might vent their anger and displeasure against landlords, their agents and those who sought to benefit from evictions. At a mass meeting of around 12,000 tenants and their families held in Ennis on September 19th 1880, Parnell outlined to his audience his plan for a new campaign of ostracization against their opponents: "What are you to do with a tenant who bids for a farm from which his neighbour has been evicted? Now, I think I heard somebody say "Shoot him!" – but I wish to point out a very much better way, a more Christian and more charitable way…you must show him what you think of him on the roadside when you meet him, you must show him in the streets of the town, you must show him at the shop counter…even in the house of worship, by leaving him severely alone, by putting him into a sort of moral Coventry, by isolating him from the rest of his kind as if he were a leper of old, you must show him your detestation of the crime he has committed."[322]

Parnell's plan rapidly spread throughout the country. Landlords and their agents and all those who took over land from which a family had been evicted were shunned and treated as social pariahs. No one would work for them and current employees were pressurised to quit. No tradesman, delivery-man or shopkeeper would serve them and the postman would not call. Speaking at a meeting in Knockaroo, Co. Mayo, Michael Davitt called to the attention of his audience a farm from which a family had just been evicted: "This farm I trust will not be tenanted by any man…if such a traitor to your cause enters this part of the country, why, keep your eyes fixed upon him – point him out – and if a pig of his falls into a boghole, let it lie there."[323]

### Captain Charles Boycott

The most famous campaign of ostracization, (and one that gave a new word to the English language) was that conducted against the Mayo land agent for Lord Erne, Captain Charles Boycott. Having issued eviction notices for numbers of his tenants he found that no one would work for him, while those in his employ left him. Furthermore those who endeavoured to buy supplies for his estate locally were not served at the merchants. In the Autumn of 1880, the crops on his estate in Co. Mayo remained in the ground while his corn although cut, remained un-threshed.

After his case had been highlighted in the press, large number of well to do Ulster loyalists and Orangemen were determined to help him but fearing trouble, the government restricted their number to 50 men from Cavan and Monaghan while also dispatching 1,000 soldiers to the district surrounding Boycott's House at Knocknamucklagh between Cong and Ballinrobe. After arriving at Claremorris train station, the Orangemen found that no one would convey them to Boycott's estate and were forced to walk there in torrential rain. For two weeks, the Orangemen laboured under police protection lifting vegetables and potatoes out of the ground and threshing 20 acres of corn. They resided in army tents and ate Boycott's potatoes for sustenance.[I] The weather was invariably atrocious and as the Orangemen's work neared completion, the worst storm in years hit the district. The cost of the operation including security for the Orangemen had been £10,000, while the value of the crops saved was around £1,000. While the Orangemen claimed victory for having saved Boycott's crops, the leaders of the Land League knew very well who had won. In the aftermath of the episode, the campaign of ostracization was thereafter referred to as "Boycotting".

## The 1881 Land Act

As the effects of Land League action took hold, Gladstone, who had lectured the Tories while they were in government that: "...force is not the remedy for Irish discontent..." now proceeded to (once more) suspend Habeas Corpus and introduce yet another Coercion Act for Ireland. Anyone could now be arrested and interned at the whim of the R.I.C. Furthermore army brigades equipped for mountain warfare were dispatched into Ireland to "quieten the populace". Their actions were encouraged by the Chief Secretary for Ireland William (Buckshot[II]) Forster who was determined to break the

---

[I] Underwhelmed by the outside help, Boycott did not even meet the Orangemen on their arrival. Furthemore he charged them for the potatoes and other foods from his estate which they ate.

[II] Forster was accused of authorising the use of buckshot to break up Land League protests.

Land League at all costs. However, for the boycotting campaign, neither Forster or Gladstone had any ready answer. Well aware of the many shortcomings of his 1870 Land Act and with the army and its commander Sir Garnet Wolseley tied up in Ireland when it was needed in Africa, Gladstone finally decided to act by setting up a commission during the Summer of 1880 to examine the shortcomings of the 1870 Land Act. Chaired by Lord Bessborough, the commission sat for five months until January of 1881, taking evidence from tenants and both landlords and their agents.

Returned once more as Prime Minister in the 1881 election, it now fell to Gladstone to deal with Bessborough's report, whose chief recommendation was that the "Ulster Custom" (of fair rent, free sale, and fixity of tenure along with compensation for improvements made) be granted nationally.

As the effects of widespread boycotting became apparent in the spring of 1881, Gladstone published his bill (which, in spite of being hacked and dismembered by the House of Lords) was the first real step forward for the Irish tenant farmer out of the evil land system which English governance had created. The main feature of the Act was that it granted the Ulster Custom nationally and placed it on a statutory footing. Furthermore, rack rented tenants could now appeal to the local land court where the judge had the power to fix what he deemed to be a fair rent for a period of fifteen years. Loans for land purchase were increased to 75%, but the landlord remained under no obligation to sell.

In spite of being an improvement, the Bill nevertheless fell far short of what was desired by the Land League or needed by the tenants. A high percentage of tenants were in arrears and the Bill did not allow those in arrears to access the land courts. Furthermore, tenants greatly feared that the land courts would side with the landlords. Other measures not included in the Bill was the need for rent adjustment in times of bad harvest or potato failure and the curtailment of the freedom of the landlords to evict at will tenants in arrears.

An often overlooked feature of the 1881 Land Act was the so called "Emigration Clause" which gave the government the power of mass deportation of "paupers" to the new world. At the beginning of 1883 this measure was put into effect allowing the government to forcibly send these "paupers" (who were in the main dispossessed and evicted tenants) to North America. Many shiploads of these tenants were gathered up and transported to Canada and the United States, where they were left penniless and just as destitute on the shores of the New World.

## Parnell Imprisoned

Parnell and the leaders of the Land League were sure that the 1881 Act, like the one before, would in reality change little on

Charles Stewart Parnell

the ground and decided not only that their campaign would not change course but that it would actually widen. During the summer of 1881, many harsh words were traded between Parnell and Gladstone while Parnell and Davitt spoke of the complete withholding of rent by the tenants as being the only fair rent. By October, Gladstone felt that he had heard enough from Parnell and the Land League. Using the terms of the Coercion Act, Parnell, Sexton and O'Kelly along with other Irish M.Ps were arrested on October 12th 1881 and committed to Kilmainham Jail for their public pronouncements against an

Act of the Realm and for "being reasonably suspected of treasonable practices." The Land League was also banned. At this time the Coercion Act then in force was used to imprison thousands of those suspected of being involved in actions against the landlords, their agents and those benefiting from the Land War. The banning of the Land League was quickly followed by the imprisonment of the editor of the Land League newspaper "The United Ireland", William O'Brien.

## The "No Rent" Manifesto

If Gladstone had intended that Parnell should rethink his strident criticisms of The Land Act while in prison, he was mistaken. Parnell decided that the withholding of rents should now become Land League policy. When William O'Brien arrived in prison, Parnell got him to draft a "No Rent Manifesto" which was made public on October 22$^{nd}$. The text was a call to arms to the tenants to engage in an all out struggle against the landlords by the complete withholding of rents: "…until Government relinquishes the existing system of terrorism and restores the constitutional rights of the people…It is as lawful to refuse to pay rents as it is to receive them. Against the passive power of the entire population military power has no weapon. Funds will be poured out unstintingly for the support of all who may endure eviction in the course of the struggle. Our exiled brothers in America may be relied upon to contribute…to starve out landlordism and bring English tyranny to its knees…"

Considering the amount of privation that the measure was likely to cause, the Manifesto was opposed by many, including the Nationalist newspapers, The Nation and The Freeman's Journal along with the Catholic Bishops. Tenants who had the means to pay were also unwilling to put their families and livelihoods in danger by risking eviction. Nevertheless, many did follow Parnell's instruction and in the Spring of 1882 numerous Whiteboy actions were committed by disparate groups against landlords and those who sought to benefit in the midst of the chaos.

## "The Kilmainham Treaty"

By mid spring of 1882, Gladstone could see that the imprisonment of Parnell had not had the desired effect. Furthermore 50,000 troops, many of whom were needed in other parts of the Empire were now engaged in Ireland in the maintenance of "public order". Realising that Parnell was the only man who could effectively restore order in Ireland, Gladstone desired to come to terms with him. Parnell was also anxious to bring the Land War to a conclusion on favourable terms. Contacts followed between the two sides which were facilitated by one of Parnell's M.Ps, Captain William O'Shea and an agreement was reached between Parnell and Gladstone around the end of April. For his part, Parnell agreed to bring an end to the "outrages" and to do what he could to restore order in Ireland if Gladstone would supplement his Land Act with a further act which would address the outstanding issues of the 1881 Act and give security to the thousands in arrears. A further request by Parnell was that Gladstone would replace the Chief Secretary for Ireland William Forster who was the current prime mover and face of coercion.

On May 2$^{nd}$ 1882, Gladstone informed the House of Commons that Parnell had been released and that a supplementary bill for the 1881 Land Act would shortly be introduced in parliament. This was to be accompanied by the renewal of the Coercion Act. Following Parnell's release, William Forster was forced to resign.

## The Irish National League

As the Land League was now banned, a new body to replace it was organised and officially promulgated at a national congress held in Dublin on October 17th 1882. At the conference the treasurer of the League gave a closing statement of finances after which the Land League was officially dissolved and the new organisation named "The Irish National League" officially came into being.

As the Land League had successfully achieved many of its aims, the new National League was not to be consumed by the land question but rather by other issues including the achievement of self-government and the improvement of living conditions for the Irish people. As the new League was national and not agrarian in its aims, it was dominated by the Irish Parliamentary Party and one month after the formation of the new League the Home Rule Party effectively amalgamated with it thus providing the country with a unified political voice at home and in England.

In spite of the best efforts of Dublin Castle, the new League through its newspapers continuously highlighted the distress of the tenant farmers of the West and North West. As the 1885 general election approached, the National League was an effective electoral machine in the garnering of support for the Irish Parliamentary Party.

## The Plan of Campaign

Despite the 1881 Land Act, the evictions continued. When agricultural prices dropped in the mid 1880s, tenants who had up to this point been able to pay their rents were no longer able to do so. Following a dramatic increase in evictions on many estates, Timothy Healy of the Irish National League came up with a new plan which was organised by other leaders in the League in particular John Dillon, William O'Brien and the League's secretary Timothy Harrington.

The plan's main emphasis was to forcibly obtain a reduction in rents for those affected by poor harvests or when rack-renting continued. A tenant unable to pay the full rent would offer the landlord a reduced rent which he was able to pay. If the landlord refused the proffered rent, the tenant was to withhold all payment and instead give the money to the Trustees of the Irish National League after which the money would be put into a central fund for the assistance of the evicted. If the landlord thought better of his refusal the monies in the fund were used to pay the reduced rent the tenant had sought.

On some estates the Plan of Campaign met with success while on others, especially those with absentee landlords there was a stubborn refusal to countenance any rent reduction. On these estates, evictions were met with boycotting and mass demonstrations often accompanied by "Whiteboy" actions which were not approved by the Campaign organisers. Unlike previous actions by the Land League, the Plan of Campaign was supported by many Catholic Bishops and priests, a move that was welcomed by the organisers.

As the beginning of the Campaign coincided with the first Home Rule Bill, Parnell found himself in a difficult position but was unable to influence the determination of the Irish National League executive to continue with the campaign. When the Conservative government under Salisbury took office, the Campaign was declared to be criminal and Salisbury's government now passed a Coercion or Crimes Act that did not require year on year renewal.

### The "Landlord League"

After Salisbury became Prime Minister, he determined to break the Plan of Campaign and appointed Arthur Balfour as Chief Secretary of Ireland with this as his primary task.

Now, both the R.I.C. and the Army were on the front line of the evictions from the beginning instead of waiting to be called upon by the landlords. Crown Forces opened fire on protestors and battering rams were used to smash down cottages that had been barricaded with the tenants inside. In

Mitchelstown, Co. Cork, violence erupted at a rally against evictions. After stones were thrown at the Crown Forces, they opened fire on the protestors resulting in the deaths of three men.

The Campaign continued despite a Papal Letter[1] condemning it, as many Irish Bishops and clergy felt that Rome did not understand the issues at stake and continued to give it their support. The government now responded with a type of "Landlord League" whereby those landlords with sufficient funds would buy out estates threatened by loss of rent due to the long running campaign. Mass evictions followed and the Irish National League organisers were unable to cope with the demands for assistance. Parnell continued to remain aloof from the campaign, refusing to either condemn it outright or support it directly.

## Selling the Land of Ireland to the Irish People

"England has done herself so well in the past out of Ireland that she can never get out of Ireland's debt." – General Frank Crozier

Over centuries the English Crown along with successive English parliamentary administrations had stolen the land of Ireland from its people, this process being finally concluded in the aftermath of The Treaty of Limerick in 1691. In 1870, when Gladstone introduced his first land act in Parliament, less than 3% of Irish land was in the possession of its rightful owners while 50% of the land, divided into vast estates was in the possession of 750 English families. While most of the land of Ireland was in the possession of the Crown sponsored

---

[1] After the London government prevailed upon Pope Leo XIII to intervene, the Pope sent over Monsignor Perisco to make a judgement on the situation. However the Irish Bishops felt that Perisco had not properly understood "the element of provocation"

landlords there was also a minority of Anglo Irish Protestant farmers in many parishes whose ancestors had been "gifted" land by Cromwell or the Crown in lieu of payment for "services rendered".

As the land war had progressed, tens of thousands of British soldiers which the government required elsewhere to fight in "Queen Victoria's little wars" had been tied down in Ireland. In 1881 Gladstone had passed his second land Act but still the Land War continued. Then as part of the "Kilmainham Treaty", Gladstone had agreed to supplement the Bill with further measures, a number of which were aimed at tenant land purchase that would allow some of the land of Ireland to be sold back to the descendants of those who had centuries earlier been dispossessed. As more land acts followed and their scope widened, more and more tenants availed of them. However in many parts of the country, especially in Ulster, the legislation would see the government sell the land not to the descendants of the dispossessed but rather to the descendants of the Planters.

## The Land Purchase Acts

### The Ashbourne Act

In 1885 the first substantial purchase scheme allowing tenant farmers to buy their holding from the Landlord was introduced. Called the Ashbourne Act after its chief architect Baron Ashbourne, this Act set up a government loan scheme worth £5,000,000 and allowed the Tenant to borrow 100% of the purchase price of his holding, as set by the landlord if he agreed to sell the holding. The terms of the government loan would see the tenant pay back the purchase price over almost 50 years at the rate of 4% interest. On average the purchase price of a small-holding at this time was the equivalent of almost twenty years rent so the scheme made good economic sense for the tenant if he was allowed to avail of it. As the flagship scheme for land purchase, the main thrust of the Ashbourne Act was repeated in a later supplementary Act which allowed for new loan funds for tenant land purchase.

## The Balfour Act

In 1887, after the Conservatives had taken office, Arthur Balfour who was then Chief Secretary for Ireland introduced his own deeply flawed land act. Among it's many faults, the Act saw the tenant pay the landlord for the cost of improvements to the property which he himself had made as part of the purchase price. Although setting aside a great deal of money for land purchase, the Act was not very popular and was condemned by Parnell.

In the early 1890's, the number of bankrupt estates in Ireland rose sharply, and it was in response to this banker's crisis that the government looked again at Balfour's Act which was finally amended in 1896. The new amended Act saw the government in the form of the land commission buy the bankrupt estates and then sell their constituent farms to the tenants. The dissolution of these bankrupt estates saw almost 50,000 families borrow the purchase price of their homestead from the government to be repaid with interest in the decades that followed.

## The Wyndham Act

Following the Balfour Act, the movement for tenant land purchase continued unabated. In 1902 a land conference was organised, chiefly by the Irish Parliamentary Party led by John Redmond. Under some pressure from the government, the Chief Secretary for Ireland, George Wyndham (after whom the subsequent land act was named), supported the conference.

During the conference discussions, the primary topic of interest was the issue of the difference in price between that which the tenant was willing to pay and that which the landlord demanded. Wyndham on behalf of the government finally agreed that the government would pay the difference. Whilst compulsory land sales by the landlord were not on the table, Wyndham agreed that absentee landlords should be compelled to sell those holdings that the tenants wanted to purchase. Following the conclusion of the conference, a new land act (1903) was introduced into parliament that saw the allocation of £12,000,000 to the scheme and the transfer of a further nine million acres into tenant ownership.

Further minor acts (Bryce) in 1906, (Birrell) 1909, and (Soldiers and Sailors) 1919 saw a further four million acres transferred into tenant and labourer ownership with the 1906 Act providing for the construction of small cottages for labourers.

"Double the Value"

At first glance the Wyndham Act and other subsequent Acts appeared to be 'generous'. This was not the case. Having sold the Irish their own land,[1] the Irish were to pay back the purchase price in instalments spread over sixty eight years before obtaining the legal right to it. As with all long term payments there was an element of usurious interest in the repayment which would in fact mean that the tenant would, according to the Acts, pay twice the actual value of the land over the term.

---

[1] To this day, vast amounts of Irish land still remains the property of the families of former British landlords.

# Chapter 12

# Home Rule for Ireland?

## "Coercion Plus"
### The Phoenix Park Murders

Following the resignation of William Forster as Chief Secretary for Ireland, Gladstone replaced him with his nephew by marriage, Lord Fredrick Cavendish, a man lacking Forster's ruthlessness. Four days after his appointment, on May 6th 1882, Cavendish arrived in Dublin where he took up residence in the Viceregal Lodge in the Phoenix Park, That very same evening he went walking in the Phoenix Park with the Permanent Secretary, Thomas Burke, the highest-ranking civil servant in the Dublin administration. As the two men walked in the Park they paused to watch from a distance a Polo match then in progress. As their attention was fixated on the game, they were approached from behind by a number of men armed with twelve-inch surgical knives who quickly stabbed both men to death before escaping in a waiting cab. When Burke had been spotted walking in the Park the assassins were not aware of the identity of the man that accompanied him.

The murders were carried out by a Fenian splinter group called: "The Irish Invincibles" and had links within both the Fenian movement and The Land League. Led by James Carey, their leadership had determined that the violent oppression of the Land League should be not only opposed but countered by the assassination of William Foster. Having failed to find a suitable opportunity to assassinate Foster, the group decided to target Thomas Burke instead. The fact that Parnell had just been released from prison had not altered their intentions as the country was on fire with anger against the heavy handedness of the government's opposition to the Land League and the government's hand in glove approach to the repression of the landlords. During the previous year there had been thousands of arbitrary arrests including many newspaper editors who had printed "seditious" articles. Even children had not escaped as those caught in the act of whistling anti English tunes (such as "The Peeler and the Goat") had been arrested. Martial law had been proclaimed in several counties. During the first four months of 1882, 519 families had been evicted, while the total for the previous year was almost 3,500.

The Repression Act of 1882

Since the Act of Union in 1801, Coercion Acts for Ireland had been passed at the rate of almost one a year. Ireland, although a de facto part of the United Kingdom was nothing more than a police state.

When news of the Phoenix Park murders reached London, there was universal outrage. After deliberating on its response, the usual answer of the government was forthcoming – more coercion, and the punishment of the Irish people as a whole. The Special Crimes Act followed and trial by jury was suspended for many important cases.

There followed numerous blatant miscarriages of justice, where in some cases people were hanged on the strength of evidence that was obviously perjured as the Lord Justices seemed quite content that "any Irishman would do". Among the most notorious of these, were the hanging of Myles Joyce in the case of the "Maamtrasna Murders" and the hangings of

Patrick Walsh and Francis Hynes for the murders of Martin and John Lydon in Galway.[I] Twenty counties were placed under martial law while meetings were dispersed at will by the police and the papers of the organisers seized.

When the practice of jury trial returned the government once more employed the tactic of Jury-packing even in counties with a nine to one Catholic majority in order to obtain the required outcome in Crown prosecutions.[II]

## Dublin Castle – Centre of English Rule in Ireland

The system of governance to which Ireland was then and afterwards exposed was nothing new, merely the repetition of the practice of coercion as used for centuries, The English unionist politician, Joseph Chamberlain (father of Neville Chamberlain) described it in the following terms: "I do not believe that the great majority of Englishmen have the slightest conception of the system under which this free nation attempts to rule the sister country (Ireland). It is a system which is founded on the bayonets of thirty thousand soldiers encamped permanently as in a hostile country…An Irishman at this moment cannot move a step; he cannot lift a finger in any parochial, municipal, or educational work, without being confronted with, interfered with, controlled by an English official appointed by a foreign government and without a shade or shadow of representative authority."[324]

---

[I] Attempting to prevent the hanging of these men through "The Freeman's Journal" which he edited, E. Dwyer Gray M.P was sentenced to three months imprisonment and a fine of £500.

[II] In a crown prosecution in Sligo in 1886 the jury was packed with Protestants despite the county being 90% Catholic. Furthermore liberal Protestants were discharged and replaced while the Catholic magistrate was ordered to stand aside to allow the case be heard by a Protestant.

Whilst the Lord Lieutenant (or Viceroy) was the representative of the British Monarch, the power of the English government in Ireland resided in the hands of the Chief Secretary for Ireland who was also a member of the Cabinet. His centre of operations in Ireland was Dublin Castle.

Since the thirteenth century, Dublin Castle had been the heart of English rule in Ireland. Here, campaigns of war, terror, subjugation and rule had been devised. In the late nineteenth century, while its methods of operation had changed, its role had not. From here the control of all government departments was directed, all appointments (police, judicial and local) approved and every facet of Irish life monitored and reacted to, invariably with coercion. No person even remotely associated with organisations or movements tainted with the smell of disaffection to Her Majesty could be approved for office, while many posts, especially most of the more important ones, were filled with Englishmen.

Dublin Castle was also the nerve centre of the Dublin Metropolitan Police (D.M.P.) and the Royal Irish Constabulary (R.I.C.) who were the local enforcers of English governance that reported to Dublin Castle from every corner of the country in response to demands for information on the situation locally. One such demand for information read:

"SECRET – 9th NOVEMBER 1886

Furnish without delay a list of persons in your sub-district now alive, who for the last five years have taken a prominent part in the Irish National movement either as Fenians or Nationalist. The list is to include;
- All Fenians or members of the I.R.B. to rank of county centre or whose influence is worth noting.
- Prominent secret society men of considerable local influence, who have taken, or are likely to take, a leading part in the commission of outrages.

- Active influential Fenians who travel about the country organising and promoting the interests of secret organisations.
- Roman Catholic clergymen, and other persons of note who take a leading part in the National Movement, and from their position and status have influence over the people.
- Persons of prominence who move about between Ireland and Great Britain, or who are in the habit of visiting Ireland from America; also persons of note, who have recently returned from America to settle in Ireland. In the list opposite each man's name, his antecedents, character, opinion (whether extreme or moderate); in fact everything known about him in connection with the Fenian or National movements should be given. The list to be in the following form..."[325.]

The Power of the Chief Secretary for Ireland was absolute. Even the Viceroy could not act without his advice, while the final say over appeals for clemency in the case of death sentences was in his hands. With direct control over the R.I.C he was responsible for the nomination of all officers while every man whose application for membership of the R.I.C had been locally approved, had then to present himself at Dublin Castle for further examination and final endorsement.

## The First Home Rule Bill

### The 1885 Election

Following the Phoenix Park murders, Parnell, with his overt links to the Land League and his covert links to Fenianism was now seen by many in England as the public face of Irish outrage and was accused of complicity with those who had perpetrated it. In spite of Parnell having vehemently denied all accusations levelled against him and publicly condemning the

Phoenix Park murders, Gladstone was forced by political and public opinion to cancel all plans of cooperation with Parnell, a move reinforced by Parnell's ambiguity over where Ireland's future lay – Home Rule or complete independence. In one such ambiguous speech in Cork, Parnell told his audience: "No man has a right to fix the boundary to the march of a nation. No man has a right to say to his country: thus far shalt thou go and no further. We have never attempted to fix the ne plus ultra to the progress of Ireland's nationhood and we never shall."[326]

William Gladstone

With Ireland in the grip of the Special Crimes Act, Parnell for his part could not be seen to support Gladstone in parliamentary votes and the Irish Parliamentary Party now sided with the Conservatives, a move which was designed to demonstrate to Gladstone that he would need the help of the Irish if he wanted to stay in power.

After helping to oust Gladstone from power, a minority Conservative administration under Salisbury took office with Parnell's support. An election was called in August 1885 after which Parnell and the Irish Parliamentary Party returned to Westminster holding the balance of power thanks to the 1884 United Kingdom Reform Bill which had massively increased the Irish electorate.

The result of the election saw the Liberals returned to power with 335 seats, the Conservatives with 249 seats and the Irish Parliamentary Party with 85 out of a possible 103 Irish seats along with one seat won in Liverpool by T.P. O'Connor. The election saw the Liberals lose all their Irish seats.

### The "Hawarden Kite"
By this time, Gladstone, having satisfied public and parliamentary opinion with his punishment of Ireland following the Phoenix Park murders once more felt he was in a position to court the support of Parnell in order that he would support the Liberals in power. Furthermore he had come to the realisation that a limited measure of Home Rule for Ireland that would grant to Dublin a parliament with limited domestic powers was a demand that he was no longer prepared to oppose. With Parnell at the helm of the Irish and keeping a lid on Fenian activity, home rule for Ireland would be in England's interest as it would ensure the demise of Fenianism and give security to England.

In December of 1885, Gladstone let it be known through the "kite flying" of his son Herbert who supplied the story to the London media, that his father's attitude towards home rule for Ireland had changed and that he was now prepared to introduce a bill that would grant Ireland a limited measure of home rule. Called the "Hawarden Kite" after Hawarden Castle, where Gladstone lived, the kite now allowed Parnell to once more change the allegiance of the I.P.P. to the Liberals. Gladstone was in earnest. His home rule bill was introduced almost as soon as he took office.

### The Introduction of the First Home Rule Bill
Having drafted the Bill himself without reference to his party or his advisors, Gladstone introduced the measure in the House of Commons in March 1886 which although extremely limited in scope did not have the support of all his M.P.s. Those who did not support the Bill (sixteen in total) were known as Liberal Unionists and they made it clear that on any

vote concerning the Union they would give their support to the Unionist Conservatives.

Parnell regarded the terms of the Bill as giving any future Dublin parliament too little in the way of power.[1] but nevertheless gave it the support of his party in spite of the opposition of the Irish Republican Brotherhood.

The Conservative Party which now looked forward to another term in opposition regarded the Home Rule Bill with some satisfaction as the instrument which they could use to rejuvenate and unite their party in opposition to a Bill intended to "break up the Union at the very heart of the British Empire." Realising that strong conservative opposition to such a move would be popular not only in England but also among some Liberals and Unionists in Ulster and beyond, Lord Randolph Churchill, who was leader of the Conservatives in the House of Commons told his party: "The Orange Card is the one to play."[327]

When news of the impending Home Rule Bill had been made public, Randolph Churchill had travelled to Belfast, then an industrial city to match any in the world. Aside from the desire of Ulster Protestants not to be drawn into an all Ireland parliament where Catholics would be in the majority, they felt that being attached to Dublin instead of Westminster would put a brake on their burgeoning industries and trade. In Belfast, Churchill's opposition to Home Rule had won him the support of Liberal Unionists in the city. On February 22nd Churchill addressed massive rallies in Belfast and later in Larne where he had advised his audience to organise and fight against the measure telling them: "Ulster will fight and Ulster will be right"[328] In preparation for the Bill's passage, a Unionist "Loyal and Patriotic Union" was carrying out manoeuvres so

---

[1] The Bill gave Ireland control over domestic affairs only with executive power remaining in the hands of the Viceroy. Under the Bill, England retained control over foreign trade along with a host of other measures.

that Home Rule could be resisted by a volunteer paramilitary force.

In spite of vociferous opposition from Unionists, Gladstone was not prepared to turn. During his speech introducing the Bill, Gladstone told the House: "I cannot allow it to be said that a Protestant minority in Ulster, or elsewhere is to rule the question at large for Ireland. I am aware of no constitutional doctrine tolerable on which such a conclusion could be adopted or justified..."[329]

Randolph Churchill

For his part Parnell attempted to win over Unionist support: "We cannot give up a single Irishman. We want the energy, the talents and the work of every Irishman to ensure that this great experiment shall be a successful one..."[330]

Following two months of debate, the Bill was defeated in the House of Commons by 341 votes to 311, the votes against including 93 Liberals. Following the vote, Gladstone, humiliated by the size of the rebellion within his Party resigned. In the election that followed the Conservatives returned to power with the support of the Liberal Unionists.

In most of Ireland the rejection of the Bill was not seen as a disaster but rather as a first step. The idea that a Home Rule Bill for Ireland would be introduced into the Commons by a British Prime Minister had been unthinkable even one year before. The rejection of the Bill was hopefully seen as the first nail in the coffin of the Act of Union.

In much of Ulster however the Bills rejection was greeted with celebrations, drunkenness and violence both in Belfast and further afield. In Belfast the rioters continually charged police lines hurling paving stones. In danger of being overwhelmed the police had opened fire killing seven. In Portadown, Co. Armagh, loyalist mobs had entered Catholic areas where they burned houses. All Summer long the "celebrations" continued. By the end of Summer over fifty people, rioters, Catholics and R.I.C men had been killed.

## The Piggott Forgeries

In 1887, the London newspaper The Times published two letters which they claimed were written by Parnell prior to the Phoenix Park murders. While the first letter to an unnamed person condoned the murder of Burke and apologised for the murder of Cavendish as an "accident" the second letter appeared to instigate the murders and was apparently written while Parnell was in prison. It ran in part: "What are these people waiting for? This action is inexcusable. Our best men are in prison and nothing is being done. Let there be an end to this hesitancy. Prompt action is called for. You promised to make it hot for old Forster and Co. Let us have evidence of your power to do so…"

There were spelling mistakes in the letters and they were not in Parnell's style. Furthermore, the signature was not one that Parnell had used since the early 1870's.

However, such was the clamour to discredit Parnell among Conservatives and Unionists that The Times did not make any attempt to verify the letters but published them as a sensational scoop.

In spite of Parnell's rejection of the letters and the idea that he had approved of the murders in any way, the governing Conservative Party decided to hold an inquiry. The inquiry sat 128 times and at times treated Parnell like "dirt" according to

William Gladstone's daughter Mary. In spite of this Parnell was cleared and the source of the forgeries was traced to one Richard Piggott who managed to escape Britain after which he went to Madrid where he committed suicide.[1]

During all this time the Special Crimes Act remained in force under the watchful eye of Arthur Balfour, the Chief Secretary for Ireland whose reputation for ruthlessness and severe action was by now infamous. During the previous three years 5,000 people had been charged under the Act many with trumped up charges of disaffection. While many were charged with singing "seditious songs" or with giving their name to the police in Irish, one boy was arrested and charged with looking at a policeman "with a humbugging sort of smile"[331].

Arthur Balfour

Following his clearance by Parliamentary enquiry, Parnell now became widely known by the title that had been given to others before him – "The Uncrowned King of Ireland". Parnell was now at the height of his power, but at Christmas 1889 he received an unwelcome letter. He was named as the co-respondent in a divorce case.

---

[1] The London Times were ordered to pay Parnell £5,000, and also the enquiry's costs which amounted to £25,000.

## The Adultery Scandal

Since 1881 Parnell had been engaged in an adulterous affair with Catherine "Kitty" O'Shea, the wife of Captain William O'Shea, who had been an M.P for the Irish Parliamentary Party. O'Shea was aware of the affair but does not appear to have made any significant moves to either bring an end to the affair or to officially separate himself from his wife. By the late 1880's he had come to the decision to divorce his wife once his wife's aged aunt was dead, waiting until then in order to benefit from her estate. After the aunt died he acted, hoping to benefit to the tune of £20,000. However, the deceased aunt's will was contested by other members of the family, and his wife was not in a position to pay up. The divorce case had then proceeded to a full hearing in open court, before a judge and jury. Both Parnell and Mrs. O'Shea had declined to appear in court, leaving the way clear for Captain O'Shea's testimony and those of his witnesses to go almost unchallenged.

Both in Ireland and England the news of the affair and the lengths to which Parnell went to lead a double life greatly damaged his reputation, which had been at an all time high following the forgeries debacle.

Gladstone asked Parnell for his temporary retirement from the leadership of the Irish Parliamentary Party as the many nonconformists in the Liberal party demanded. In an open letter to the I.P.P. Gladstone had written; "His (Parnell's) continuance at the present moment in the leadership...would render my retention of the leadership of the Liberal Party...almost a nullity."[332]

The Home Rule Party was split on the issue. A short time before, Parnell had been the hero of Ireland, but now having lost the support of Gladstone along with much of his support both in England and Ireland, he was fast becoming a liability. For his part Parnell refused to resign saying that Gladstone should not be allowed to decide who was the leader of the Irish

Parliamentary Party. Finally, at an extremely stormy series of meetings of the I.P.P. almost a year after he had been served with the divorce proceedings, Parnell was officially ousted by his party by 45 votes to 29.

## The Split within the Irish Parliamentary Party and the death of Parnell

The vote to unseat Parnell was not to be the end of the matter. In the aftermath of the vote, Parnell refused to relinquish the leadership even after the majority of his M.P.s had voted to remove him as their leader. The I.P.P. was now split into two factions; The Irish National League led by John Redmond (Parnellite) and The Irish National Confederation led by Justin McCarthy (Anti Parnellite).

Returning to Ireland to fight for his political survival in a number of by-elections in which he hoped to see the Parnellite candidate returned, Parnell remained determined to fight for his political survival.

Upon his return Parnell was greeted by large crowds in Dublin, but when he travelled outside the capital there was now much hostility towards him not only on account of his affair but also because people felt deceived by what amounted to his double standards. In each by-election that Parnell campaigned in, the Parnellite candidate failed to win a seat. As the Summer of 1891 continued into Autumn, Parnell's stubbornness to acknowledge defeat continued, but at the cost of his health. Already suffering from kidney disease and physically and mentally exhausted, he continued campaigning in Ireland throughout a wet September. At the end of the month, during an open-air meeting in Galway, he was drenched and without a change of clothes. Returning to England a few days later, he was very ill by the time he reached his home at Hove in Sussex. After taking to his bed he died from heart failure on the morning of October 6th 1890.

On October 11th his body was brought back to Dublin and interred in Glasnevin Cemetery. Remembered as a hero of the Irish people who was cut off in his prime by a scandal of his own making, Parnell's legacy was nevertheless to withstand the test of time despite the fact that his refusal to stand aside from the leadership of his Party would cause a split that would not be healed until 1900 when the two factions within the Party reformed under John Redmond.

## The Second Home Rule Bill

Despite the division within the Irish Parliamentary Party the general election of 1892 once more saw Irish M.Ps hold the balance of power at Westminster with The Irish National Confederation winning a total of 71 seats while the Parnellite faction won 9. Their votes were more than enough to help Gladstone unseat the Conservatives and return the Liberals to power. In spite of losing power in 1886 after the introduction of the First Home Rule Bill, Gladstone's priorities on re-entering government were to introduce a second home rule bill for Ireland and to dis-establish the Anglican Church in both Wales and Scotland.

Once more Gladstone chose to keep the drafting of the second Home Rule Bill to himself, excluding even his Chancellor. This resulted in numerous financial miscalculations in the Bill regarding Irish contributions and taxations. Even though the Irish were propping up his government not once did he engage in consultation with the Irish M.P.s on the Bill's terms.

The Bill was in many respects very similar to the 1886 Bill, with one key difference – Irish representation at Westminster would continue, although at a slightly reduced level. In many respects, what Gladstone proposed was very similar to the legislative assemblies now in operation in Northern Ireland,

Wales and Scotland with control of local issues being devolved with all other matters being decided in London.

If Gladstone had hoped that this change allowing Irish M.P.s to continue to hold their seats at Westminster would make the Unionists look more favourably upon the Bill he was wrong. The Unionist strongholds of Ulster once more resounded with marches and rallies in opposition to any measure that would introduce an Irish legislative assembly. In any event the Unionists knew, (as Gladstone must also have known) the Bill would fail to get through the Conservative dominated House of Lords, even if it passed through the House of Commons.

The Bill's passage was contested paragraph by paragraph throughout its passage by the Unionist Conservatives but finally passed its second reading in the House of Commons in early September 1893 after which it went to the House of Lords where the majority against the bill was over ten to one. There were only 41 votes in favour of the legislation with 419 against. In the wake of this drubbing, Gladstone, now nearing retirement, had not the stomach to do anything more. The following year, he retired and in 1895 the Conservative Party returned to power until 1905.

## Killing Home Rule?

Upon their return to power, successive conservative governments under Robert Cecil and Arthur Balfour sought to "pull the rug" from under the Home Rule Movement which had already been severely weakened. Between 1895 and 1905 a definite effort was made by the two Conservative administrations to improve various aspects of Irish life and to make the Irish people feel for the first time that the London government would act with a measure of consideration towards them. After centuries of exploitation, the English government now adopted an attitude, which although self-serving improved the lot of many especially in the poorest parts of rural Ireland. This series of ameliorative measures was known as the policy of "Killing Home Rule with Kindness".

## The Congested Districts Board

The most important of the measures undertaken by the government was the establishment of "The Congested Districts Board" by Sir Arthur Balfour which sought through the purchase of estates and the building of small houses to re-house labourers and cottiers who lived in large groups of overcrowded cabins especially in areas west of the Shannon and along the western seaboard. These people, in return for rent were re-housed in newly constructed stone and slate small houses and were also allocated small holdings which were to be used as micro-farms in order to improve their means of living and to raise income by the sale of butter, eggs and other agricultural produce.

At the outbreak of the Great War in 1914, the Board attempted to outlaw turf cutting in some areas under the guise of war economy, this in the knowledge that most people had no other way to heat their homes. Turf cutting continued however and despite obtaining injunctions against turf cutting tenants, the Board was unwilling to start a "turf war" and did not involve the Crown Forces or press the issue.

Other measures taken by the government included the construction of a nationwide light gauge railway system, the encouragement of cottage industries and grants for industry in rural areas.

## Agricultural Reform

One employee of the Congested Districts Board, Horace Plunkett, undertook a reformation of Irish agriculture which still reverberates today.

Plunkett founded the "Irish Agricultural Organisation Society, which through its credit unions advanced loans to farmers for the improvement of their holdings at very low interest rates. From this beginning, Plunkett began to advance the idea of cooperation among small farmers and, acting under his advice and tutelage, the agricultural Co-operative movement was established from which the large present day Irish dairy companies hail. The Co-op movement began with the foundation of local "creameries" in many districts. Up to this point farmers had manufactured butter on their own farms with the inherent differences in quality and skill that might be expected. However once farmers joined a local creamery by purchasing a number of shares in this mini company, butter was produced on a large scale and to a very high quality. As the quality improved so did the prices which gave the local farmers a better standard of living than that to which they had been accustomed. As the movement progressed with enviable results, the government saw the benefits of the new co-operative movement in the supply of agricultural produce to Britain and established the Irish Department of Agriculture and Technical Instruction to which Horace Plunkett was appointed as Vice-President.

The Local Government Act
One of the other significant measures taken was the passing of The Local Government Act in 1899 whereby the government, by giving a very limited measure of power to locally elected officials in areas such as road maintenance, sanitation and the establishment of Technical Schools, hoped to further smudge the issue of home rule for Ireland. However, when a report of the royal commission on Irish finances found that the Irish people were paying far too much taxation (to the tune of £3,000,000 per year) to the Crown, no remedial measures to

correct the situation (despite the recommendation of the Commission) were introduced.[I]

## The Visit of Queen Victoria

The activities of the Conservative and Unionist government were followed in 1900 by the visit of the eighty-one year old Queen Victoria to Ireland during which the government went to great lengths to show the Queen how loyal Ireland was to both Crown and Union. Nevertheless protests against the royal visit were organised and the Corporation of Dublin would not present the Queen with a so-called "loyal address" (which was expected of them) but rather a letter of welcome instead. Although her visit was proclaimed as an acknowledgement to the Irish for the huge numbers of men which they had been and were providing to the British Army, the visit was in fact nothing more than a veiled recruitment drive for the English fight against the Boer republics.[II]

Queen Victoria

---

[I] The report recommended that because of "the flagrant evil of wasteful and disproportional expenditure" Ireland "should for a period be exempted from contribution to the expenditure of the Empire."

[II] Following the outbreak of the Boer War, Michael Davitt resigned his seat in parliament.

# Part 4

# Freedom?

# Chapter 13

# Gaelic Awakening

"...not free merely, but Gaelic as well; not Gaelic merely, but free as well." – Patrick Pearse.

### The Steady Decline of Gaelic Culture
Towards the end of the nineteenth century when issues of dire poverty and need had faded a little into the background, many Irish people found that their attention was being sought by disparate groupings on the issue of national culture and national identity.

This in turn was to feed into the subsequent fight for freedom as where a love for Irish language, customs and folklore was to be found invariably the seeds of Irish nationalism had also been planted.

For centuries, the invader had sought to eradicate Gaelic culture and identity. However in spite of English labours in this regard, the Gaelic language, music, storytelling, had, like the Catholic faith remained intact, along with the harder-to-define aspects of Gaelic identity that had remained with the Irish people since Gaelic times, such as leaving the door of one's dwelling open as a sign of welcome to passers-by and the readiness of the Gaelic people to share what little they had with those who called for a visit or "céili".

However, since the Act of Union (1801) and especially in the aftermath of The Great Starvation (1845-52) there had been a haemorrhaging of the outward signs of Gaelic culture and identity, especially the loss of the national language.

Culturally, the loss to Ireland incurred by The Great Starvation was almost irretrievable. The effect of mass death and emigration on Irish cultural life cannot be over-estimated. In Kerry and Mayo where populations were reduced by 50% the richness of Gaelic life and folklore was lost forever with the generations who were buried in the mass graves.

By the late nineteenth century whole counties of Ireland ceased to be Irish-speaking.

The decline in the Gaelic language was not just due to the Great Starvation. Daniel O'Connell also had discouraged the speaking of Irish and recommended that the people learn English in order that they should be able to adequately fight for their rights. The loss was also due to the emergent English education system, (since the Act of Union) which sought to eradicate not only the Irish language but also Irish history. The intention of the new education system was that Irish children were to be converted into mirror-images of their English counterparts with a love and appreciation of all things English while all things Gaelic were condemned as a sort of remnant of barbarism.

Between 1851 and 1891 the number of people using Irish as their first language had reduced from 23% to 14.5%. The establishment portrayed Irish as a backward language, (the Daily Mail had described it as a "barbarous tongue") only suitable for peasants, and as such it had retreated largely to the Western seaboard, while English was the language of Industry, advancement and Empire. In schools all subjects were taught through English and the speaking of Irish by pupils was often harshly reprimanded, until the restrictions on teaching Irish were relaxed in 1878.

## "Shoneens"

The effects of Anglicisation seemed to amplify with the small improvements that occurred in living standards. As the nineteenth century progressed, as in many other respects the Irish had adopted English ways and customs often by necessity or force rather than choice. In many other aspects of Irish daily life, England's influence was also prevalent by the late nineteenth century. Most books were authored by English or Anglo Irish writers. English games (such as cricket) were popular, especially among Irish upper class Catholics while English customs, fashions and music had been widely adopted. While the Protestant ascendancy would for the most part always define themselves as British, among the Catholics there was a variation in opinion depending to a large extent on class and outlook with those who readily adopted English ways and affinity for the Crown being described by those who did not as "Shoneens" or "little John's" in reference to the English caricature "John Bull".

As the English garrison class virtually owned and controlled Irish cities and towns, one of the most important methods of Anglicisation was the naming of streets and even towns after British viceroys, landlords, royalty and popular heroes and the erection of statues and monuments to them. This had the effect of imposing on the Irish mind who their masters were. To this day the majority of these street names and monuments remain.

## The Gaelic League

This loss of Irish language, games and customs did not go unnoticed and in various quarters, concerned citizens both Irish and Anglo Irish determined to take action to prevent the loss of much of the Gaelic way of life.

The last period where there had been something of a Gaelic cultural revival was in the half century prior to the famine. This earlier work was to prove an important starting point in the re-awakening of Gaelic culture and sentiment in the late nineteenth century as without it many traditions might have been lost completely due to the effects of the Great Starvation.

Following on from a gathering of Gaelic harpers in Belfast in 1792 where he had been asked to write down the notes they played in order to collect their tunes, the Englishman, Edward Bunting had travelled throughout Ulster and Connacht collecting Irish airs, transcribing them and publishing them in order to preserve them. It was some of these airs that were used in famous songs by the poet Thomas Moore including "The Minstrel Boy" and "Let Erin Remember the days of Old". At this time too the translation of that unparalleled work of Irish history "The Annals of the Four Masters" was completed and published by John O'Donovan and other important works including "Manners and Customs of the Ancient Irish" and "Manuscript Materials of Ancient Irish History" were also collected and published.

The Gaelic League was founded in 1893 by the professor of Irish at St. Patrick's College, Maynooth, Fr. Eugene O'Growney, a civil servant from Belfast named Eoin MacNeill along with the son of a Church of Ireland clergyman Douglas Hyde.

The primary objective of the Gaelic League or "Conradh na Gaeilge" was the revival of the Irish language leading to the promotion of Irish culture through music, literature and tradition. By these methods it was hoped to awaken in Irish people a feeling that they were members of the Irish nation and not just residents of a province of England.

## Douglas Hyde

For Hyde (who was of English lineage) the decline in Irish language and customs, which as a young boy, he had grown to love, was a disaster. During a speech shortly after the League's foundation he told his audience: "…in fact I may venture to say that, up to the beginning of the present century, neither man, woman or child of the Gaelic race, either of high blood or low blood, existed in Ireland who did not either speak Irish or understand it. But within the last ninety years we have, with an unparalleled frivolity deliberately thrown away our birthright and Anglicised ourselves."[333]

As a cultural organisation Conradh na Gaeilge received widespread support from the Catholic Church, Irish politicians, and the general public alike with branches of the league being set up throughout the country, although mostly in urban areas. By 1906 the League had almost 900 branches with a membership of 100,000 and while it did not succeed in halting the reduction of the area where Irish was the daily spoken language, it did succeed in re-introducing Irish into the areas where it had died out, especially by organising the introduction of Irish into national schools. (By 1906, 3000 national schools were teaching Irish) The League organised "Feiseanna" or festivals where there were competitions in singing, dancing and storytelling and also created an awareness and pride in Irish national identity among its members while its activities were attended by thousands of members from all over the country.

Douglas Hyde

One of the most important achievements of the League is that they were successful in their campaign to make St. Patrick's Day a national holiday (with public houses closed!) The Gaelic League by stressing Irishness also had a political impact, as many of its members often strayed from the cultural into the political question of how independence could be achieved as they felt that a nation with a separate Irish tradition was justification for a separate Irish nation.

In 1915 at the League's General Meeting (Ard Fheis) that was held in Dundalk, the League's constitution was amended and thereafter included the aim of a "free Gaelic speaking Ireland".[I] After this change Douglas Hyde left the League, never to return.

## Patrick Pearse

The league also had its own magazine called "An Claidheamh Solais" (The Sword of Light). In this magazine its aims and ideas were disseminated along with traditional Irish poetry and prose. Any form of imitation of English ways was campaigned against with self-reliance encouraged for music, literature and even industry. The editor of An Claidheamh Solais was a young barrister and schoolteacher by the name of Patrick Pearse who was fluent in the Gaelic language. A fervent Catholic, he had as a boy knelt down and promised God that he would dedicate his life to Ireland's freedom.[II] A prolific writer and poet, he was disgusted by the English education system then being enforced in Ireland and had published an essay entitled "The Murder Machine" against it. After qualifying as a lawyer he had established a private school for educating boys called "St Enda's" at Rathfarnham in Dublin which endowed his boys with a great love of all things Gaelic. Following on from this he established a senior school

---

[I] The 1916 leader, Patrick Pearse described The Gaelic League as "the most revolutionary influence that had ever come into Ireland" and "the germ of all future Irish history".

[II] * At his court martial in the aftermath of the 1916 Easter Rebellion, he recalled this episode to the Crown prosecutors.

for girls named "St. Ita's". His love of Ireland led him to the realisation that education would not be enough to win Ireland's freedom – physical force would also be required.[1] This led to his joining the Irish Republican Brotherhood. The members of the Supreme Council of the I.R.B were quick to see in Pearse his absolute devotion to Ireland and her complete freedom from English rule. After becoming a member of the I.R.B it was not long before he was appointed to its Supreme Council.

## The Gaelic Athletic Association

Michael Cusack

While trying to revive sport in general among the Irish with his friend Pat Nally, it became obvious to Michael Cusack that, as far as the ancient Irish game of hurling was concerned, it was necessary to define the rules to be followed as many different forms of the game existed in different parts of the country. Along with a number of other like minded men who wished to see a more widespread revival of Gaelic games and culture a meeting was held in Hayes' Hotel, Thurles, Co. Tipperary at the start of November 1884 where the "Gaelic Athletic Association for the Preservation and Cultivation of National Pastimes of Ireland" was founded. The Association was to extend to parish, county and provincial

---

[1] In November 1913, Pearse wrote: "Whenever Dr. Hyde, at a meeting at which I have had a chance of speaking after him, has produced his dove of peace, I have always been careful to produce my sword and to tantalise him by saying that the Gaelic League has brought into Ireland "Not peace but a sword."

level with rules drafted by Maurice Davin for its sports and athletics. Pat Nally had been unable to attend the Association's founding meeting as he had been jailed for the so-called "Crossmolina Conspiracy", an alleged attempt to kill landlords' agents.[1] Nally was a member of the Fenians (IRB) as were four of the seven men who attended the meeting that day. Charles Stewart Parnell, Michael Davitt and Archbishop Croke of Cashel were invited to become patrons of the association. The call to native sports and athletics was a great success and by 1889 the GAA had a membership of over 50,000 people.

However when the IRB tried to secure control of the GAA for political ends, the Catholic Church withdrew its support from the organisation as it wanted it to remain outside politics. As a result, in 1892 the membership plummeted to 5,446 . It was not until 1895 when the I.R.B. influence over the Association declined that Archbishop Croke again gave the G.A.A his support and most of the former members returned.

The Gaelic nature of the Association was underlined by the exclusion of all other sports. Members were banned from engaging in "foreign" games. Furthermore members of the Royal Irish Constabulary, or any of the other "Crown Forces" were prohibited from joining, underlining the fact that the association saw in them agents of a foreign power.

## The Anglo Irish Literary Revival

William Butler Yeats was born in 1865 into a Protestant Anglo Irish family and grew up in Co. Sligo during the period of the Land War and the initial struggle for home rule. This period had a large impact on his outlook until finally he became a supporter of home rule.

---

[1] Pat Nally died in Mountjoy Jail in 1891.

As a poet his aim, along with that of like-minded members of the Anglo Irish community, was that they would through a national litreature cater for the scholarly needs of Ireland and so preserve a sense of Irish nationhood. Their impact, although important, would be limited largely to the upper classes.

Together, with the widow of a former British Governor of Ceylon, Lady Gregory, and her friend Edward Martyn, Yeats founded the Irish National Theatre later to be The Abbey Theatre. Lady Gregory in particular was interested in ancient Irish folklore and legend and through her efforts the ancient Irish warrior Cuchulainn and his warriors were resurrected and played their part in Gaelic and nationalist sentiment.

It was felt by many that the sword of the Anglo Irish Literary Revival was somewhat double edged, as it also had a negative influence. In October 1903 a play by J.M Synge called "In the Shadow of the Glen" played at The Molesworth Hall in Dublin during which Arthur Griffith and Maud Gonne walked out in protest at the denigration of traditional Irish values.

Yeats' most important contribution to the Gaelic revival was possibly his play "Caitlin ni Houlihan" about an old woman (who was really a young Irish Queen) calling the hero Michael to leave his love Delia to fight for Ireland in 1798. Caitlin Ni Houlihan was to be a popular symbol for Ireland calling her menfolk to arms in the following two decades.

# Chapter 14

# The Home Rule Crisis

"We cannot forget how England planted these people for the purpose of safeguarding the British position in Ireland and how faithful they have been to that trust" – The English Morning Post

## The Death of Queen Victoria

On January 22$^{nd}$ 1901 Queen Victoria died after a reign of almost sixty-four years. The years of her reign as Queen were more destructive for Ireland than the reign of any other English monarch during Ireland's Centuries of Trial.

The following stark statistics illustrate this fact. During her reign, almost 1.5 million people died of famine. 3.7 million people were evicted from their homes. Over four million people were forced to abandon their country for foreign shores. The number of people evicted from their homes amounted to 75% of the entire population, which rapidly declined during her reign because of starvation and emigration. From the time of her coronation until her death, Ireland's population had declined by over 50%.

# Sinn Fein

## Arthur Griffith

Born in Dublin on March 31st 1871, Arthur Griffith emigrated to South Africa after the fall of Parnell and the subsequent split of the Irish Parliamentary movement. After working in the mining industry in South Africa for a number of years, and as the centenary of great rebellion of 1798 approached, he accepted the advice and encouragement of his old school friend William Rooney, to return to his native land and to do what he could to help in the struggle for Ireland's parliamentary independence.

Arthur Griffith

A disciple of Parnell's strategy and thinking, Griffith was opposed to the use of physical force and was not a republican.

After returning to Ireland he re-established John Mitchel's newspaper "The United Irishman" in 1898, the centenary year of the "Rebellion of '98". In his editorials he advocated the proposal of "Dual Monarchy". The idea of Dual Monarchy was not a new one but dated back to Daniel O'Connell's time. It was in effect an advanced form of Grattan's parliament and meant that Ireland should be completely free of British interference except for the acceptance of the King of England as Irish head of state

In a series of articles, Griffith expanded the notion using the example of Hungary, which had gained autonomy from Austria by refusing to send her members of parliament to Vienna. He advocated that by following such a course Ireland might achieve the same. In The United Irishman he wrote:

"Let us renounce the disastrous policy of making the parliament house of England the arena of Irish struggle. Let us make the dissolution of the British Empire our immediate object"[334] and "Ireland has maintained a representation of 103 men in the English parliament for 108 years…The 103 Irishmen are faced with 567 foreigners."[335] He finally published the collected articles on Dual Monarchy in book form in 1904 entitled "The Resurrection of Hungary".

When the English invaded the Boer Republics in 1899, Griffith was heavily involved in the work of the Irish pro-Boer committee, and spoke regularly at their rallies and meetings along with James Connolly and Maud Gonne. These meetings attracted thousands of people and were constantly being proclaimed as illegal by Dublin Castle. They were frequently broken up by mounted police and baton charges.

In 1910 Griffith prophetically wrote: "Ten years hence the majority of Irishmen will marvel they once believed that the proper battle-ground for Ireland was one chosen and filled by Ireland's enemies."[336]

## The Founding of Sinn Fein

Describing the policies of the Irish Parliamentary Party as; "useless, degrading and demoralising"[337] Arthur Griffith took the step of offering the Irish electorate an alternative to the I.P.P. with the founding of his political movement "Sinn Fein" in 1905.

The position of The Home Rule Party was that self-governance could only be achieved with the permission of Westminster, even though they held as Griffith did that the Act of Union was illegal. By setting up a political party Arthur Griffith hoped to win the support of those who disagreed with the Home Rule Party but had no political home. Although as a political party, his movement professed peaceful means he won the support of a good number of I.R.B members and other protest groups that had formed to demonstrate against the visit to Ireland of King Edward VII in 1903.

Also drawn to Griffith's movement were notables such as Sir Roger Casement (who had earned international renown after publishing a report into Belgian atrocities in the Congo) and Countess Constance Markievicz (nee Gore-Booth) who was a member of a Protestant[1] landed Anglo Irish family (and had married a Polish Count). Those with influence in the Gaelic League were also drawn to the movement and as time progressed very many of them became involved with the I.R.B. Widespread public support for the new party however remained elusive. In the early years of the twentieth century Irish home rule did not seem to have the distant prospect that it once had, and so the Sinn Fein movement did not garner a lot of public support. When the Home Rule Party M.P for North Longford, Charles Dolan resigned his seat in 1908 because of the debacle over the Irish Council Bill (see below) and offered himself for re-election as a Sinn Fein M.P he was defeated by a large margin. This defeat, largely due to Griffith's policy of abstentionism from Westminster led many to think that the Sinn Fein party might fade away without making any significant political impact. However Griffith's pronouncements and articles on an Irish Ireland that promoted Ireland first, Irish self reliance and the Irish nation continued to have a national impact, in spite of the failure of Sinn Fein to achieve an electoral breakthrough.

---

[1] Countess Markievicz converted to Catholicism during the Easter Rebellion in 1916.

## The Reforming of the Irish Republican Brotherhood

Parallel with the foundation of Sinn Fein, the Irish Republican Brotherhood was also re-organising under the watchful eye of the Fenian veteran Thomas Clarke who had been released from prison in 1898 after a fifteen-year prison sentence for his Fenian activities in the early 1880's.[1] After spending a number of years in New York, Clarke had returned to Dublin where he had opened a tobacconist's ship on Amiens St. before moving to another premises on Great Britain St. (Parnell St.), both premises serving as meeting points and planning centres for I.R.B. activities.

Thomas Clarke

During the first decade of the 19th century the national membership of the I.R.B. was in the hundreds and slowly growing thanks to the steady stream of new members who came to it from the Gaelic League and Sinn Fein. As a veteran, Tom Clarke naturally assumed a leadership role, often more akin to guidance and mentoring for the younger leaders of the movement, Bulmer Hobson, Denis McCullough, P.S O'Hegarty and especially Sean McDermott. However as a former convict Clarke was careful that his name should not enter the public domain lest he should harm the cause in any way.

---

[1] During his time in prison, Clarke was subjected to repeated torture and the most atrocious conditions which resulted in his premature ageing. Although Clarke was released "only" physically damaged by the effects of his incarceration some of his Fenian comrades who were also subjected to similar conditions were bordering on insanity when released.

For the rank and file the leaders of the I.R.B were often not known, while the leadership did its utmost to collect information from all around the country. According to O'Hegarty: "We kept the whole of Ireland and every happening, and every possible happening, constantly under view, and we threw our weight wherever it seemed to us that we could best advantage the cause."[338]

Ever since the Irish Republic had been declared decades earlier, the membership of the Supreme Council considered itself a provisional Irish government in waiting, watching for the time when, as John Mitchel had written years earlier, the circumstances might be right for: "…a third way, how in the event of a European war, a strong national party in Ireland could grasp the occasion to do the work instantly."[339]

## Continued Sectarianism within Government

The year 1909 was the eightieth anniversary of the achievement of Catholic emancipation.

Following emancipation, all government posts, with a few notable exceptions were in theory not only open to Catholics, but in a country like Ireland where Catholics were over three quarters of the population they had a right to them. However in the corridors of power, Irish Catholics continued to be discriminated against.

While the lowly offices of the civil service were readily available to Catholics, the government, with some exceptions continued to appoint Protestants to all the higher posts. In 1908, the statistics for the higher positions in the Irish government show the inherent discrimination of the government against the appointment of Irish Catholics; 15 out of 18 High Court judges were Protestant, 30 out of 37 county police inspectors were protestant while only 4 out of 124 District Inspectors were Catholic. In the local courts, the number of Catholics was higher – here 19 out of 68 judges were Catholic.

This discrimination meant that a low ranking Catholic civil servant who wished to advance his career was forced to leave Ireland and look for a higher-ranking post in England.

## An "Instalment" of Home Rule rejected

After a decade in opposition, the Liberal Party under the leadership of Henry Campbell-Bannermann finally returned to power in 1906 with a large majority. As Bannermann had no need for the support of the Irish Parliamentary Party, he proposed a watered down version of home rule for Ireland called "The Irish Council Bill" that gave limited powers to an elected council over which the Lord Lieutenant would have control. John Redmond, the leader of the I.P.P. wanted to go along with the Bill but due to the level of opposition within his party he was forced to declare against it in public after which the Bill was dropped in 1907. Politically damaged by the affair, Redmond sought to claim credit for the Universities' Act of 1908 which established three national universities of Ireland in Dublin, Cork and Galway which would be Catholic in their ethos. However in 1909, his acquiescence in the Treasury Act (which reduced the effectiveness of the land purchase schemes) caused another split in his party. Seven M.P.s led by William O'Brien and T.M Healy now broke away forming the "All for Ireland Party".

John Redmond

In Ireland, the weakening of Redmond's position caused some within the United Irish League and among the public at large to come to the conclusion that he and many of his parliamentary colleagues had "gone native" – that they had been fatally weakened by their lives at Westminster and the corrosive atmosphere of compromise prevalent at Westminster in all affairs pertaining to Ireland. This premise was confirmed in 1911 with the passage of the Parliament Act with Redmond's support under which he and the members of his party agreed to accept monetary payment from the British Treasury for being M.P.s thereby repudiating the notion that Irish nationalists would not accept monies from the Crown.

## The Third Home Rule Bill
"This Act will be born with a rope around its neck"- William O'Brien M.P.

### Curbing the power of the House of Lords
Both in 1886 and in 1893 when Gladstone had introduced Home Rule bills in the House of Commons, Unionists had not only voiced their opposition but in Ulster they had rioted at the prospect and many people had been killed.

In spite of the introduction of the Acts and their outright opposition, Unionists always felt secure in the certain knowledge that even if a home rule bill got through the Commons, the overwhelmingly Conservative and Unionist House of Lords would always reject it. This was the Unionist back stop against any form of home rule for Ireland.

The Liberal party saw this all-effacing power of the Lords as a nuisance that they could not overcome. The final straw for the Liberal Party came in 1909 when the House of Lords rejected the so-called "People's Budget" of the Liberal Chancellor David Lloyd George.

After the general election of December 1910, the second of that year, neither the Conservatives nor the Liberals had a majority. Once more The Irish Parliamentary Party held the balance of power. The Liberal Party leader Herbert Asquith who had fought the election with a pledge to tackle the problem of the Lords veto now approached the leader of the I.P.P. John Redmond with a proposal. If the I.P.P. would enter a coalition with the Liberals and support a bill limiting the power of the Lords, Asquith for his part, would introduce another home rule bill for Ireland.

Herbert Asquith

When "The Parliament Act" passed in August 1911 the blocking power of the House of Lords was finally neutralised. By threatening to swamp the House of Lords with Liberal appointed Peers, Asquith had forced their Lordships to bow to the inevitable and accepted a reduction in their power. The Parliament Act meant that a bill that was passed in the House of Commons in 3 successive sessions and then subsequently rejected in the House of Lords, would become law provided that two years had elapsed between the second and third reading of the bill in the House of Commons. In effect a bill that the Lords rejected could only be delayed for two years before becoming law.

Unionist Opposition

Due to a wealthy Protestant upper class, a section of north east Ulster was the most industrialised part of the country and the only part of Ireland that had experienced the industrial revolution of the nineteenth century.

Here, unlike the rest of the country, the descendants of the Scottish and English Planters were firmly in the majority. The sizeable Catholic minority were viewed as a threat that was constantly countered by prejudice and sometimes by violence and pogrom.

Aside from their anti Catholic bias and inherent cleavage to the English Crown, unionists felt that the prosperity that they had achieved depended on the union and the trade that went with it. If the union was broken and Ireland became a semi-independent British colony, then trade with the United Kingdom and the empire would be subject to tariffs and a different trading relationship. The prosperity they had enjoyed would diminish.

The other important factor for the Unionists was their sense of belonging. The plantation of Ulster although not complete had by far been the most "successful" plantation in Ireland. The Ulster Unionists had only identified with the South of Ireland in so far as they felt empathy with the unionist minority that lived there. However Britain was their ancient homeland and they did not want the umbilical cord to their motherland to be cut. They were proud to be British and were in fact more British than the British themselves. Their forefathers had come to Ulster to dispossess, to colonise, to oppress and to "uphold the reformed faith". Now, to be forced into an all Ireland Parliament with a Catholic Irish majority was not only unconscionable, it was something to be feared.

## Sir Edward Carson

As far back as 1905, (thirteen years after the second Home Rule Bill) an Ulster Unionist Council had been formed to prepare for the threat of Home Rule. Since 1910 their leader was the famous Dublin Barrister and Member of both Parliament (for

Trinity College) and the Privy Council, Sir Edward Carson. A stubborn man of resolute purpose, he was not specifically "Ulster minded" and believed that Ireland's place and not just Ulster's was as an integral part of the United Kingdom. However Carson realised that the blocking of Home Rule for all of Ireland was not a practical option while Ulster, as a whole had a small Protestant majority thanks to the populous city of Belfast. This M.P and barrister was willing to lead a Protestant crusade against the will of parliament so that the colonists of Ulster could dismember not just Ireland, but the province of Ulster in order to stay within the United Kingdom. By debate or by force he was prepared to do his utmost to "persuade" London to allow the majority of the northern unionists remain outside any provision for Irish home rule. His second in command was the son of a Belfast Whiskey millionaire named Sir James Craig who was a brilliant organiser, a former member of the British Army who had soldiered against the Boers in 1899 and an M.P.

## Forming a Unionist "Sinn Fein"

Once the bill for the restriction of the power of the House of Lords was published, Unionist preparations for defence against Irish home rule went into overdrive. In order to convince the British population at large that Unionists were serious about their opposition and that they would not accept Home Rule even if passed by parliament, Craig organised huge demonstrations and rallies including on his own estate outside Belfast in September 1911. At this rally, Carson addressed a crowd of 50,000 people telling them: "We will yet defeat the most nefarious conspiracy that has ever been hatched against a free people" and "We must be prepared the morning Home Rule passes, ourselves to become responsible for the government of the Protestant province of Ulster".

As far as the "Protestant province" was concerned Carson was only partially correct for five of the nine counties of Ulster had, according to the census of 1911 a Catholic majority.[1] Carson, obviously not in any way acquainted with the Gaelic language gave his audience a new rallying cry that they readily adopted. He told them: "We must rely upon ourselves". In Gaelic this translates as "Sinn Fein".

Edward Carson

As with previous home rule bills, the Ulster Unionists had the solid support of the British Conservative Party whose leader, Andrew Bonar Law was the son of a Coleraine (Derry) Presbyterian Minister. On the eve of the introduction of the third home rule bill he addressed a monster rally of 100,000 people in Belfast telling them: "You hold the pass, the pass for the Empire…"[340]

## The Third Home Rule Bill

On April 11th 1912, as the Belfast built luxury liner "R.M.S Titanic" embarked from Queenstown (Cobh) on her doomed voyage to the New World, Prime Minister Herbert Asquith

---

[1] According to the census of 1911 the percentage of Catholics for the counties of Ulster was as follows; Cavan 81.5%, Monaghan 74.7%, Donegal 78.9%, Tyrone 55.4%, Fermanagh 56.2% Antrim 20.5%, Derry 45.8%, Down 31.6%, and Armagh 45.3%. (Some counties, especially Armagh would have had a great percentage of Catholics except for the pogroms of the late eighteenth century which had seen tens of thousands of Catholics driven from their homes and into the south.

introduced the Home Rule for Ireland Bill in the House of Commons.

Titled; "An Act for the Better Government of Ireland" the Home Rule Bill was like its predecessors a fairly tame affair that would give a Dublin parliament control of limited domestic affairs only.

With the King of England as head of state, the Bill allowed for an Irish parliament of one hundred and sixty four members with an upper house (senate) of forty members.

According to the Bill there was to be no provision for the appointment of an Irish Prime Minister. Power and leadership would remain with the Lord Lieutenant who would be head of the Irish Executive and also appoint ministers and nominate senators and judges. Even the introduction of new taxes would still be controlled by Westminster and control over the Irish police would remain with Westminster for a further six years. The return of an Irish Parliament would also see the return of Poynings Law as Westminster would have the final say on every piece of legislation introduced in the Dublin legislature and would be able to overrule any issue decided on by a Dublin parliament. Unionist concerns about "Rome Rule" or Catholic domination of the parliament were given special attention. The Bill forbade the passing of any legislation that gave preference to any creed. Furthermore the provisions of the Home Rule Bill allowed for the over-representation of Ulster and if there was a situation of deadlock, a combined sitting of Commons and Lords (which would have a unionist majority) was provided for.

While John Redmond and his party welcomed the Bill, the response of Edward Carson was that home rule for Ireland should also mean home rule for the Protestants of Ulster, a proposal rejected out of hand by Asquith who told Carson that a small minority could not veto the verdict of an entire country.

With the terms of the Bill clearly biased in their favour, one might be forgiven for thinking that the Unionists were getting worked up about very little.

## The Solemn League and Covenant
<u>Reaction in Ulster to the Home Rule Bill</u>

As with previous home rule bills, there was a great deal of rallying and speech making among unionists in response to the Bill's introduction, which reached fever pitch during the Orange Order marching season which extended from late Spring until the end of the Summer. There was also much rioting along with attacks upon the Catholic population, while in the Belfast shipyards around 2,000 Catholic workers were driven out along with the Protestant trade unionists who complained of their expulsion.

During July, the Conservative Party leader Bonar Law returned to Belfast where he encouraged the Unionists in a campaign of civil disobedience and violence. He told his audience: "There are things stronger than Parliamentary majorities. There will not be wanting help from across the Channel when the hour of battle comes."[341]

In England, at a great Unionist rally held at Blenheim, Bonar Law had told his audience: "I can imagine no length of resistance to which Ulster will go, in which I shall not be ready to support them, and in which they will not be supported by the overwhelming majority of the British people"[342].

This was treasonous talk and it certainly gave oxygen to those Unionists who were actively considering the organisation of a paramilitary force in order to keep Ulster within the Union.

"Ulster Day"

Deciding to enlist the Protestants of Ulster[1] in his "nefarious conspiracy" to defeat the Home Rule Bill, Edward Carson, Sir James Craig and Lord Londonderry devised a "Solemn League and Covenant" to be signed by men and women.

On "Ulster Day", Saturday September 28th 1912, almost 220,000 men signed the document (that hearkened back to the Scotch Covenanters) which pledged them to use "...all means which may be found necessary to defeat the present conspiracy to set up a Home Rule Parliament in Ireland. And in the event of such a Parliament being forced upon us, we further solemnly and mutually pledge ourselves to refuse to recognise its authority."[343]

The day of the Covenant's signing was almost akin to a Sabbath day. All factories were closed and the upper classes all attended Church services where they sang the hymn "O God Our Help in Ages Past".

In Belfast, the service attended by Carson was followed by a procession to City Hall led by a banner dating from The Battle of the Boyne. Edward Carson was the first to sign the document. There was a theatrical aspect to the whole affair as some of the signatories dispensed with ink and dipped the fountain pen in their own blood before signing. A separate document for ladies was signed by almost 230,000 women who pledged to support their menfolk. In Belfast City Hall there were enough desks so that 550 people could sign at the same time. The signing of the Covenant was not merely a paper exercise. In the weeks after its signing many Unionist clubs were formed and every able-bodied man who had signed the document was called upon to register for "military service"

---

[1] Since the "Home Rule Crisis" Unionists have been wont to prefix everything with "Ulster" creating the fiction of a Unionist province.

against home rule while others were called on to enlist for "political service."

Under the Coercion Act, only Crown Forces were permitted to train with weapons. Carson now applied to the Belfast Courts for an exception for his "Ulster Defenders" which was readily granted. However Carson's speeches (along with those of Bonar Law and countless others) were contrary to the 1887 Crimes Act that remained in force. Since its introduction thousands of nationalists had been imprisoned for "seditious" language or tendencies. Carson acted with impunity for he knew that no one had ever been arrested for acting against Ireland's interest. This M.P and Barrister openly told his followers that he did not "...care two pence whether it was treason or not."[344] I

## Prime Minister Asquith deceives the Irish Parliamentary Party

In January 1913 as the Home Rule Bill moved through its final stages in the House of Commons, Craig introduced an amendment to try and have the nine counties of Ulster excluded telling the Commons: "All we propose to do is to prevent Home Rule from becoming law in our own part of the country". The amendment was supported by Bonar Law who declared that the Ulster Unionist would: "prefer to accept the Government of a foreign country"[345] sooner than be ruled by Irish nationalists.[II]

---

[I] In later years Carson would boast: "The covenant was a challenge to the government, and they dared not take it up. It was signed by soldiers in uniform and policemen in uniform and men in the pay of the government and they dared not touch one of them."

[II] Some unionists had proposed the notion that Ulster should be ruled by the German Kaiser.

Carson, in remaining steadfast, was causing ripples in the government with regard to the "courageous" decision they had taken in voting to allow home rule for all Ireland.

Amidst disquiet in the Liberal ranks, King George VI whose sympathies lay with Carson and the Unionists arranged backroom negotiations between Bonar Law and Asquith during which Asquith confided to Bonar Law his opinion that Nationalists were powerless without the Liberal Party. They discussed the exclusion of six counties of Ulster (Antrim, Derry, Down, Armagh, Tyrone, and Fermanagh), from the Home Rule Bill which could only be repealed by plebiscite. All of this was very encouraging for Carson, for in demanding the exclusion of all of Ulster from home rule, his final position was the exclusion of those four counties with a Protestant majority (Antrim, Down, Armagh and Derry) along with the two counties (Fermanagh and Tyrone) that had a small Catholic majority. Redmond and the Irish were kept in the dark about the ongoing secret discussion. Asquith only informed him that Bonar Law had suggested the permanent exclusion of the nine counties of Ulster, which Asquith told him he had rejected.

In spite of these back-channel discussions Carson decided to prepare for all eventualities. On the 24th September 1913, he morphed the Ulster Unionist Council into the "Central Authority of the Provisional Government of Ulster" which determined that an Ulster Provisional Government would come into effect as soon as Home Rule became law. Speaking in Newry two weeks before Carson had told his audience: "I am told it will be illegal...the government dare not interfere...Don't be afraid of illegalities"[346.]

## The Ulster Volunteers

In 1910, even before the introduction of the Home Rule Bill, the far sighted Ulster Unionist Council were obtaining prices from Germany for a large shipment of arms and ammunition. By

March of 1911 the deep-pocketed businessmen of the council had voted for the allocation of funds for the buying of weapons. Once the Parliament Act was introduced in the Commons, groups of Unionists had begun paramilitary training all over Ulster but it was not until the Bill had completed its journey through the Commons in January 1913 that the Ulster Unionist Council decided to unite the various Unionist warrior bands under a common umbrella which would be called the Ulster Volunteer Force (U.V.F.).

The recruitment and organisation of the Force was to be done through the existing Orange Lodges and the Unionist Club network. One hundred thousand men between the ages of 17 and 65 were to be enlisted. Wooden rifles were, little by little being replaced by the actual thing as guns were being steadily purchased in England in small numbers. On June 4$^{th}$ 1913, the Unionist newspaper 'The Northern Whig' admitted that; "...a good many thousand of modern army rifles have been received and distributed...those engaged in the gun running have managed to get all their consignments through without arousing the suspicion of the customs or disturbing the tranquillity of the constabulary..."[347.]

By June of 1913 when the U.V.F. obtained the services of the retired General Sir George Richardson as Commander, recruitment was already at 50,000. Carson wrote to the Conservative Leader Bonar Law: "...everything here is going on splendidly..."

## Southern Volunteers

Events in Ulster had at the outset been watched with amused interest in the South and certainly not taken very seriously. The leader of the Home Rule Party John Redmond had naively assured anyone who would listen that there was no need to worry about the bluff[1] emanating from Ulster and that Home Rule was basically a done deal.

By the Autumn of 1913 the burgeoning strength of the U.V.F was becoming a general cause for concern among nationalists. However, when Redmond had been approached by one of his M.P.s with regard to the organisation of a southern volunteer movement he declined. In Dublin the leadership of the Irish Republican Brotherhood (Thomas Clarke, Sean Mac Diarmada and Bulmer Hobson) felt that a similar volunteer movement ought to be created in the South as a counterweight against the U.V.F and to ensure that the British government would keep it's word. However the I.R.B itself could not be seen to organise a southern volunteer movement as it would fail to gain mass support and would certainly attract the suspicion of the authorities.

At Hobson's behest, a history professor and leading member of the Gaelic League, Eoin Mac Neill, who had written an article in favour of a southern volunteer movement in the Gaelic League magazine was encouraged by the publisher of the magazine, Michael (The) O'Rahilly to start such an organisation after which Mac Neill set about forming an organising committee.

Even while the Irish Volunteers were being organised, a group called the "Midland Volunteer Force" came into being in Athlone and on October 22$^{nd}$ 1913 manoeuvres were held with about five thousand men taking part.

## The Dublin Lockout and the Irish Citizen Army

Running parallel to the organisation of The Irish Volunteers was the organisation of The Irish Citizen Army by the Trade Union Leader Jim Larkin who was assisted by James Connolly.

---

[1] Redmond referred to Carson as "King of the Bluffers".

The Irish Citizen Army was born as a result of the Lockout of 1913 when the Dublin businessman, William Martin Murphy locked out employees seeking employer recognition of the Irish Transport and General Workers Union. The situation quickly escalated and soon involved around 400 employers and 23,000 employees. At demonstrations in favour of Union recognition, the workers were subject to Police baton charges against which they were powerless to adequately defend themselves. The worst

James Larkin

incident occurred on August 31st 1913 when the attendees at a huge meeting addressed by Jim Larkin were baton charged. A woman, Alice Brady, along with two men, Nolan and Byrne, were killed.

It was at this time that James Connolly, who was the Ulster organiser for the Irish Transport and General Workers Union came to Dublin to help Jim Larkin in the organisation of the widespread strikes and the organisation of a defence unit for the workers called "The Irish Citizen Army." The inaugural meeting of the Citizen Army took place on November 23rd 1913 following the release of Jim Larkin (who did not possess the same immunity from prosecution as Edward Carson) from prison for sedition.

The following year, the Dublin strike ended in failure but the Irish Citizen Army remained. With the departure of Jim Larkin for the United States the movement was now firmly under the leadership of James Connolly who saw the cause of the worker and the cause of a free Ireland as two sides of the same coin. The small but highly motivated Citizen Army now evolved into a force for the achievement of a free Ireland.

### The Irish Volunteers

The inaugural meeting of the Irish Volunteers took place at The Rotunda Rink in Dublin on November 25th 1913 under the leadership of Eoin Mac Neill. Over one third of the thirty-member committee were members of the I.R.B. On that evening alone 4,000 men enrolled. As Unionist sabre rattling intensified in the Spring of 1914 the ranks of the Irish Volunteers swelled to over 100,000. The biggest problem of all was the lack of weapons, for no sooner had the Irish Volunteers been formed than the English government prohibited the importation of arms and ammunition into Ireland. By this time the U.V.F had already imported around 80,000 shotguns, rifles and revolvers. Nevertheless vigorous attempts were made under the leadership of The O'Rahilly to import some weapons while the organisation of a training program was undertaken by Liam Mellowes. Patrick Pearse who had enrolled that first evening wrote afterwards: "…we are about to attempt impossible things, for we know that it is only impossible things that are worth doing"[348]

Michael (The) O'Rahilly

At the outset Redmond was not involved with the movement but later felt that from it, could stem a new political movement that would be a threat to his Home Rule Party. As the Irish Volunteers rapidly grew, Redmond determined to take control. In the sure knowledge that the majority of volunteers were supporters of the Home Rule movement, Redmond sent the leaders of the Irish Volunteers an ultimatum in which he "proposed" to put an equal number of his own nominees on the committee. In order to prevent a split in the movement, Hobson argued for acceptance of Redmond's leadership while Tom Clarke along with Patrick Pearse, Eamonn Ceannt, Sean McDermott and Con Colbert were against it. After a vote the leadership of the volunteers reached the decision to allow Redmond to more or less take charge of the Irish Volunteers, Tom Clarke was outraged at Bulmer Hobson's support for Redmond, feeling that his speech in favour of going along with Redmond's plan had been crucial. After a furious row the pair never spoke again. Nevertheless, the unity of the Volunteers appeared to be preserved even if only for a few months.

## The Home Rule Bill Passes Unaltered

By the Spring of 1914, Prime Minister Asquith was bent on a compromise to his Home Rule Bill in order to satisfy the minimum demands of the Ulster Unionists. Having reached an understanding with the Conservative leader, Bonar Law, Asquith was not much concerned if he now was to lose the support of the Irish Parliamentary Party. Before the bill passed its third reading Asquith was talking about the exclusion of four of the Ulster counties. John Redmond the leader of the Irish Parliamentary Party was angry at the degeneration of the Home Rule Act into a botched job and spoke of the "...mutilation of the Irish nation..."

After much negotiation with Asquith, Redmond agreed to the notion of a plebiscite for any county that wished to be excluded from Home Rule. The exclusion was to be for a period of six years after which the county would, in the absence of any further measures join the parliament in Dublin. Afterwards, Asquith assured Redmond that Carson had rejected this proposal and that the Home Rule Bill would proceed in its original form. At the repeat second reading of the bill on March 9th 1914, the notion of a county by county exclusion was flatly rejected by Carson who called it a "sentence of death with a stay of execution" The Bill passed unaltered and Home Rule was due to come into effect from September 1914 with Asquith's caveat that an amending bill would also be introduced before the Bill came into effect.

## "The Curragh Incident"

While negotiations over the "Ulster Question" were supposed to continue following the Bill's entry onto the statute book, the question doing the rounds in both governmental and military circles was "Will Ulster be coerced"? Will the army move against the U.V.F if ordered?"

It was well known among the higher ranks of the British Army that the Director of Military Operations at the War Office, Sir Henry Wilson (an Anglo-Irishman) was vehemently opposed to Irish Home Rule and was actively conspiring with the leaders of the Ulster Unionists, the U.V.F and the Conservative Party. It was a certainty that he would not engage in any military activity against the U.V.F.

The Commander in Chief of the British Army in Ireland Sir Arthur Paget now asked his senior officers in the Curragh Camp "If you are ordered to move against the Ulster Volunteers, will you obey or be dismissed instead?"

In the certainty that no form of military discipline would follow, sixty Cavalry officers including the Commanding Officer of the Curragh Camp, Sir Hubert Gough replied that they would not obey orders to move against the U.V.F. When Sir Douglas Haig the Commanding Officer at Aldershot told Asquith that he supported Gough, Asquith assured Gough that neither he nor his officers would be called on to engage in any military action against the Ulster Unionists. All Carson's suppositions had been correct. The mutilation of Ireland was now assured.

## Gun Running

<u>The Larne Gun Running</u>

By the Spring of 1914, the leadership of the U.V.F. was in possession of over £1,000,000 in donations, raised for the purpose of further arming itself. By this time, its members already had over 10,000 guns imported from England but this source of weaponry had begun to dry up. Within weeks of the Home Rule Bill completing its passage through parliament, the decision was taken by the leadership to proceed with plans to import a much larger quantity of arms and ammunition from Germany, and a well-prepared operation was now put into effect.

Following the purchase of 24,000 guns and 3,000,000 rounds of ammunition in Hamburg, the shipment was brought by the arms dealer on a barge to the Danish island of Langeland in the Baltic Sea. Here, the arms and ammunition were transferred to the ship "S.S Fanny" under the command of Major Fred Crawford. On April 1st 1914, Crawford's ship left Langeland in something of a hurry as word had reached him that Danish customs officials suspected that the weapons might be bound for Icelandic nationalists and there was a danger that the entire shipment might be seized. After the Danish customs got wind of the arms shipment, the story got out and it was surmised in The Times that the shipment was probably bound for Northern Ireland. In order that the government could be seen to be taking action, the First Lord of the Admiralty, Winston Churchill now ordered a (small and ineffectual) cordon of warships to be placed around the Northern Irish coast.

So as not to attract undue attention Major Crawford had the consignment transferred to a coal ship from Glasgow called the Clyde Valley off the Wexford coast. For this special mission it was renamed the "Mountyjoy II" after the ship Mountjoy that broke the siege of Derry in 1689.

On the 25th April the ship successfully docked in the port of Larne whilst a decoy ship the SS Balmerino attracted attention to Belfast Lough where there was also decoy transport waiting. Within the north east of Ulster a substantial land operation had also been mounted by the U.V.F and Larne had been sealed off from police "interference". U.V.F members had been summoned from all over and trucks and cars spread the ships cargo far and wide while yachts received weapons from the Mountjoy II and brought them to Bangor and Donaghadee. How much the police knew about the operation can only be guessed, but they certainly turned a blind eye to the well-executed operation and made no effort whatsoever to intervene at any stage.

## The Howth Gun Running

News of "The Curragh Incident" and the large gun running operation in Ulster gave impetus to the recruitment and training of the Irish Volunteers but could do nothing to improve their weapons situation. A small group of mostly Anglo-Irish sympathisers who were in favour of Home Rule now decided to make some effort to remedy the situation. Of their number, only one, Sir Roger Casement (who was a British government diplomat) had anything to do with the Volunteers. The others were Mrs. Alice Stopford Green, Erskine and Mary Childers, Mary Spring Rice, her cousin, Conor O'Brien and the author Darrell Figgis.

Before the end of May 1914, using money mostly collected from among their group, Erskine Childers along with Darrell Figgis went to Hamburg and purchased 1,500 obsolete Mauser rifles along with 45,000 rounds of ammunition. Childers now returned to Ireland in order to finalise the Irish end of the operation, leaving Figgis to take charge of the Hamburg end.

The transportation of the cargo did not present any problem, as both Childers and O'Brien were accomplished sailors and owned yachts. Childers's yacht the "Asgard" was much bigger than O'Brien's "Kelpie" and would take the lion's share of the load.

At this stage Bulmer Hobson was taken into the group's confidence and was asked to organise the shore party for the reception of the Asgard's load at noon on the 26th July at Howth Harbour.

Both Yachts left Dublin for Hamburg around the end of June with neither having a wireless set. They were scheduled to meet with a Tug organised by Figgis at the Roetigen Lightship in the North Sea on July 12. Everything went according to plan, the only "casualty" being three boxes of ammunition that had to be dumped overboard as they could not be made to fit on either yacht. Both Yachts were literally packed with the cargo, making the return journey very uncomfortable for the sailors

While the Asgard was bound for Howth, Conor O'Brien was known to the authorities so his Yacht, the Kelpie was going to give its load to the yacht "The Chotah" off the coast which would then head for Bere Island and from there to Kilcoole in Wicklow a week later.

By this stage it had been necessary to let a few Volunteer commanders in on the secret of the weapons shipment.. For a number of Sundays leading up to the 26th these commanders had organised large numbers of volunteers to partake in long route marches to various parts of Dublin so as to put the police off guard as since the Larne gun running the police had been watching out for an arms shipment for the Irish Volunteers. On the 26th the Volunteer "route march" arrived in Howth just as the Asgard approached. A number of taxis were also waiting and these were loaded with the ammunition and some of the rifles. The Volunteers carried the remaining weapons towards the city but were met at Clontarf by Police supported by an army detachment. Dublin Castle had been informed, most likely by the coastguard. The weapons were passed back to the rear of the column and spirited away across fields or hidden in ditches. A group of the Irish Citizen Army who were training nearby also helped to disperse the weapons.

## Bachelor's Walk

In the afternoon, as the British Army (Kings Own Scottish Borderers) returned to Barracks in the city, following their failure to seize the weapons, they were followed along by a crowd who jeered at them and threw stones. The soldiers responded with rifle fire and bayonets on the crowd killing three people and wounding 38.

To those in the South the stark contrast between the northern and southern gun running could not have been clearer. While the Ulster operation had been carried off without incident, the other much smaller shipment destined for the Irish Volunteers had been responded to by the attempted seizure of the weapons and the killing and injuring of over 40 people.

When taken with the Conservative and establishment support for the illegal position the Unionists had adopted along with the Curragh incident which had been supported by the highest ranks of the British army and the lack of interference by Police in the Larne gun running, it seemed to many that Home Rule for Ireland was ebbing away to be replaced by a division of the country into two parts.

## Home Rule "...rendered a nullity"

As the year progressed the opposition of the Unionists to anything except exclusion remained implacable. Their final position was now the permanent exclusion of the four counties of Antrim, Tyrone, Derry and Down together with North Fermanagh and North and mid Armagh. Redmond conceded a county by county exclusion by plebiscite with no time limit.

Behind the scenes, the Ulster Unionists along with the Unionist Conservatives and House of Lords in London were actively conspiring to torpedo "Home Rule for Ireland".

Under the amending Act of the House of Lords, the Lords could not reject Asquith's Home Rule Bill, but they could counter the Bill with an amended Bill of their own.

On July 8th 1914, the Lords counteracting bill was published. It allowed for the permanent exclusion of all Ulster from the Home Rule Bill.

In the ensuing deadlock, a conference called by King George V was held at Buckingham Palace which was supposed to agree on an area of Ulster to be excluded from the Home Rule Bill. On July 24th 1914 the conference adjourned without agreement as on the previous day Austria had given her ultimatum to Serbia. The First World War was now days away.

Carson now boasted that Home Rule for Ireland had been "...rendered a nullity."[349]

Although the bill officially became law on September 18th 1914 Redmond had agreed that the bill be immediately suspended for at least 12 months or until war's end when an amendment would be brought which would "deal with Ulster". Both Redmond and Carson encouraged their respective volunteer organisations to enlist in the British Army and display their loyalty to the King.

# Chapter 15

# "For The Defence of Small Nations"

"The cry, 'Remember Belgium' is good for Belgians, the cry 'Remember Ireland' is sound sense for Irishmen" – Eamonn Ceannt.

### The Split in the Irish Volunteers

Following the outbreak of war between England and Germany, John Redmond's decision to encourage the Irish Volunteers to enlist in the British Army was regarded by the I.R.B. and Sinn Fein with disgust as they were determined that the Irish Volunteers should not be asked to fight in England's war at least until Irish home rule was an assured fact.

There now occured an effective split within the Volunteer movement. The pro-Redmond volunteers, consisting of around 90% of the volunteer membership transferred their allegiance to a new volunteer organisation called "The National Volunteers", (some of whom enlisted within the ranks of the British Army), while the other 10% believing that their duty was to stay on call for Ireland remained as The Irish Volunteers.

Following the split The Irish Volunteers were composed of Republicans and I.R.B members, all of whom viewed the home rule debacle as a sell-out, Other Irish volunteers were supporters of Sinn Fein and Griffith's "Dual Monarchy" proposal. All were of the opinion that the place of an Irishman was not in the ranks of the British army. A new newspaper which heralded the "Ireland first" doctrine of this reborn Volunteer movement was launched entitled "Nationality".

If Redmond (or anyone else) believed that his support and that of the National Volunteers was any sort of guarantee of Irish home rule as originally proposed by Asquith, they were very much mistaken. In parts of Ulster the U.V.F. were already joining "their" 36th Ulster Division (in which Catholics, with the blessing of the government, were "actively discouraged" from enlisting) in order to ensure that most of Ulster would be excluded from the Home Rule Bill. It would not take a prophet to predict the final outcome. On September 18th, in an address to the House of Commons, Asquith declared that the spirit of patriotism displayed by the U.V.F now made the coercion of Ulster "unthinkable".[350] No such "words of comfort" were addressed to the National Volunteers whose enlistment in the ranks of the British Army exceeded that of the U.V.F as a percentage of their membership.

## England's Difficulty - Ireland's Opportunity

In encouraging the founding of the Irish Volunteers, the I.R.B leadership had hoped that it would wield both authority within and leadership over that organisation. However John Redmond's interference had put paid to that.

With the smaller Irish Volunteers now reforming under the firm control of the I.R.B., Tom Clarke held a meeting not just with the senior leadership of the I.R.B but with others including Arthur Griffith in order to discuss future strategy.

Sean T. O'Kelly later recorded the momentous decisions taken at the meeting and recalled the qualities of the men who would be the driving force for the rebellion now being planned:

"They called into conference other leaders of progressive national thought in Ireland, and, three weeks after the war had commenced, a meeting was held in my office in the Gaelic League building, 25 Parnell Square Dublin, at which it was decided that Ireland should make use of the opportunity of the European War to rise in insurrection against England. There were eight or nine people at that meeting, including Tom Clarke, Pádraic Pearse, Seán MacDermott, Eamonn Kent, William O'Brien, Seán McGarry, a man named Tobin, and myself."

"At that meeting it was decided that a Rising should take place in Ireland – if the German Army invaded Ireland; secondly if England attempted to enforce conscription on Ireland; and thirdly, if the war were coming to an end and the Rising had not already taken place, we should rise in revolt, declare war on England and, when the conference was held to settle the terms of peace, we should claim to be represented as a belligerent nation. All present at that meeting, which was representative of all shades of advanced political thought in Ireland, pledged themselves and their organisations to do all in their power to carry out the agreement arrived at, and to prepare the public mind for the great event that was to come."

"If one man could be responsible for the inspiration of Easter Week, or for the carrying through successfully of the resolution to revolt – credit for that must be given to Tom Clarke. Clarke can truthfully be described as the man, above all others, who made the Easter Rising. He, it was, who inspired it originally, and he, it was, who, in broad outline, laid the plans. To Seán MacDermott must be given the credit for filling in these plans-for seeing to the successful carrying out of the details necessary for such an undertaking."

"James Connolly supplied the driving force. As well as being a man of brains and highly cultivated intelligence, he was in everything a man of action. If it were not for the insistence of Connolly the Rising might not have taken place just exactly at that time...He with his great yearning for freedom for his native land and for that liberty which would give a chance to Ireland to work out a worthy social system for the downtrodden, was restless and eager and insistent that the Rising should come off at the earliest possible moment."

"Pádraic Pearse, probably the ablest and most inspiring figure of that time, interpreted worthily the traditional aspirations and ideals of Irish nationalism, and symbolised in himself the unity of idea of the different races that go to make up the Irish nation. He was well fitted to be chosen by his colleagues as the most outstanding figure of his time and the one who probably could fill most suitably the position of first President of the Irish Republic."

"MacDonagh, Kent (Ceannt) and Plunkett were all of them men of high intellectual attainments. Kent and MacDonagh were certainly products of the Irish-Ireland movement. They developed their Irish Nationalism through their acquaintance with Gaelic culture. Joseph Plunkett, who was younger than all the others, was a student of wide international culture. Despite his delicate health, he took an active part in all the deliberations and preparations for the Rising, and even undertook dangerous and arduous journeys over the continent necessary for the working out of the plans."[351]

As the Supreme Council of the I.R.B undertook the planning of the insurrection against English rule, it was decided to form a Military Committee out of the membership of the Supreme Council as a means of providing greater secrecy. This committee consisted of Patrick Pearse, Joseph Plunkett and Eamonn Ceannt.

## Roger Casement in Germany

Sir Roger Casement was a most unlikely Irish Republican. Knighted for his services as a British consul, he was an Antrim Protestant who would have fitted in splendidly with Carson and Craig. However, (although not a member of the I.R.B) he had chosen the company of Irish republicans who were at first somewhat unsure what to make of his offer of service. After some deliberation, the I.R.B decided to send him to the United States to liaise with the Clan ná Gael organisation to see if some measure of assistance could be obtained from Germany for a military rising against English rule.

Roger Casement

After approaching the German ambassador in Washington, Casement determined to go to Germany and speak to the German government directly. By mid November 1914, he was in Germany and in talks with State Secretary von Zimmerman who agreed that Casement would be allowed to recruit Irishmen from German prisoners of war, to fight with an Irish brigade in Ireland, for Irish independence. All through 1915, Casement remained in Germany (where he was joined by Joseph Plunkett) the promising start to his mission now resulting in little success. His attempt to recruit pro-Redmond Irishmen from among German prisoners of war had been a failure with only fifty men enlisting while his negotiations with the German government regarding the sending of German officers and a German expeditionary force to Ireland had gotten nowhere. Unknown to him, the Germans were in direct contact with John Devoy of Clann na Gael in the United States. While Casement regarded a German Expeditionary Force as essential, Devoy was prepared to accept a shipment of arms to the Irish rebels as the only German help.

## The Funeral of Jeremiah O'Donovan Rossa

When the Fermanagh man Terence MacManus, (who had taken part in the 1848 rebellion) died in the United States in 1861, his body had been returned to Ireland so that a mass public demonstration of national fervour could be held. MacManus's funeral had greatly increased the profile and the membership of the Fenians, and, had re-awakened in many a feeling of Irish national identity that had been dulled by hardship and starvation.

When Jeremiah O'Donovan Rossa, who was one of the Fenian founding fathers, had died in New York on June 29th 1915, Tom Clarke received a telegram from John Devoy reporting his death. In reply Tom Clarke had sent the message to Devoy: "Send his body home at once".

As John Devoy prepared to return O'Donovan Rossa's mortal remains to his homeland for burial, Tom Clarke, assisted by Sean MacDermott organised a special group called "The Wolfe Tone Memorial Committee" which planned the funeral as a great demonstration in favour of full Irish independence. By far the best orator among the leadership of the I.R.B. was Patrick Pearse and Clarke decided that he should give the graveside oration.

As a rebellion was then in planning, the senior leadership were being extra careful about the tone of their public utterances in order not to draw attention to themselves. However, for this occasion Clarke instructed Pearse to make the oration as "…hot as hell"[352].

When O'Donovan Rossa's remains arrived in Dublin at the end of July they were taken to Dublin's Pro Cathedral where they remained for one night before the high-altar, guarded by a section of Irish Volunteers. Following this his remains were removed to Dublin's City Hall, where they again lay in state until the funeral on August 1st.

## "The Fools, the Fools, the Fools!"

Following the requiem mass, the cortège made its way to Dublin's Glasnevin cemetery escorted by an armed detachment of Irish volunteers. Tens of thousands of people lined the route while unarmed national volunteers joined in the procession.

At the graveside, Patrick Pearse delivered the oration: "…I propose to you then that, here by the grave of this unrepentant Fenian…we ask of God, each one for himself, such unshakeable purpose, such high and gallant courage, such unbreakable strength of soul as belonged to O'Donovan Rossa…Splendid and holy causes are served by men who are themselves splendid and holy…The clear true eyes of this man almost alone in his day visioned Ireland as we of to-day would surely have her: not free merely, but Gaelic as well: not Gaelic merely, but free as well…Life springs from death: and from the graves of patriot men and women spring living nations. The Defenders of the Realm have worked well in secret and in the open. They think that they have pacified Ireland. They think they have purchased half of us and intimidated the other half. They think they have foreseen everything, think they have provided against everything; but the fools, the fools, the fools! – they have left us our Fenian dead, and while Ireland holds these graves, Ireland unfree shall never be at Peace."[353]

Patrick Pearse

## Planning an Insurrection

With the split in the Irish Volunteer Movement at the outbreak of war, English efforts in Ireland were largely directed towards the recruitment of soldiers for the British Army and for once the focus and attention of Dublin Castle was not firmly fixed on anything that might constitute an internal threat to the security of the realm. Nevertheless there were prosecutions for the usual charge of sedition among the editors of Republican newspapers, but because of the war, magistrates were forbidden from imposing sentences of greater than six months for such offences.

With the onset of war, restrictions on the importation of arms and ammunition had also been relaxed and so, during the second half of 1915, the amount of weaponry available to the soldiers of the Irish volunteers increased due in no small part to monies collected from the Irish community in the United States. Those volunteers who could afford a rifle purchased their-own. Recruitment into the ranks of the Irish Volunteers increased, assisted by a steady stream of men who returned home from England in order to join up.[1]

While Dublin Castle was aware of much that was occurring within the I.R.B / Irish Volunteer movement, it was felt more prudent to adopt a non interventionist policy – the logic being that this small group had little public support with the vast majority of the Irish people continuing in their support for John Redmond. To move against the Volunteers and Citizen Army and disarm them might provoke trouble, public sympathy, and a decline in the number of Irish men joining the British army. In the country at large the R.I.C continued to act as the eyes and ears of Dublin Castle and were ordered to

---

[1] One of these was a London post office worker originally from Co. Cork. His name was Michael Collins.

report on the "disaffected" or "politically dangerous" in their districts.

## A Date Decided

At the beginning of January 1916, the Supreme Council of the I.R.B met and after much discussion set a date for the commencement of an insurrection against British Rule. Easter Sunday, April 23rd was chosen.

The fact that the Council decided to proceed at this time without any of their original pre-requisites for an insurrection having been met was due in large measure due to the extended stalemate on the western front and the danger that the government might proceed with the implementation of some sort of botched Home Rule. (This danger will be discussed later.) Following the decision, planning for the rising proceeded apace.

## The 'Kidnapping' of James Connolly

James Connolly was a member of the I.R.B, but he was not a member of its Supreme Council, nor was he privy to its decisions. While the Supreme Council of the I.R.B did all it could to maintain secrecy, Connolly's very small Citizen Army seemed determined to draw attention to themselves by undertaking mock attacks on government buildings and open reconnaissance missions. With the date for the Rising now set, the I.R.B. leaders felt Connolly's actions compromised their planning for a rising.

After Connolly confirmed to the Volunteer leadership in mid January 1916, that he was preparing to launch a rising on his own, he mysteriously disappeared from his headquarters at Liberty Hall in the company of two members of the I.R.B and was detained by the I.R.B leadership for three days. In direct conversation with Tom Clarke during his "disappearance", Connolly put forward his case for urgent action. After being sworn to secrecy, Connolly was informed of the Rising then in planning, and the expected German arms shipment. A meeting of minds was reached. Now basically co-opted onto the Supreme Council of the I.R.B, Connolly took part in the planning for the Rising. Although the insurrection would now be a joint venture between the Irish Republican Brotherhood, the Irish Volunteers and the Irish Citizen Army, it's undertaking and planning was strictly an I.R.B affair. While James Connolly was now included in the planning, many among the leadership of the Irish Volunteers who believed that the Volunteers should only take defensive action to prevent themselves from being disarmed by the government were not. This number included the Chief of Staff Eóin Mac Néill, the Secretary Bulmer Hobson and Michael "The" O'Rahilly who was Treasurer. In effect, the manpower of the Irish Volunteers was being harnessed by the I.R.B without the knowledge of many of their most senior leaders.

James Connolly

### The Plan

The final plan for the I.R.B insurrection called for the seizure of a number of strong points in Dublin by a force of around 3,000 men and the encirclement of military strong-points elsewhere in the country in order to prevent the transfer of reinforcements to Dublin by land. The strong-points in the capital were to be situated so as to hamper the movement of British troops towards the city centre and the General Post

Office (G.P.O) where the headquarters of the rebellion and the Provisional Government were to be located. Garrisons were to be situated at:

- The G.P.O. This garrison was to consist of a mixed force of Irish Volunteers and Irish Citizen Army under the command of James Connolly.
- The Four Courts. (First Battalion of the Irish Volunteers commanded by Edward Daly) This garrison was to disrupt troops coming from the Royal Barracks and Marlborough St. The approach to the Four Courts was to be covered by a detachment commanded by Sean Heuston in the Mendicity Institute near Usher's Island.
- South Dublin Union Workhouse. (Fourth Battalion of the Irish Volunteers commanded by Eamonn Ceannt with Cathal Brugha as second in command) This garrison was to disrupt troops coming from Kingsbridge Station and Richmond Barracks
- The Jacob's Biscuit Factory (Second Battalion commanded by Thomas McDonagh, who was to be accompanied by the Volunteers Quartermaster-General Michael O'Hanrahan. Brigade Headquarters was to be stationed here.
- St. Stephen's Green (commanded by Irish Citizen's Army Chief of Staff Michael Mallin, with Christopher "Kitt" Poole as second-in-command. These men were to disrupt troops coming from Harcourt St. Station and Portobello Barrack. After being occupied, St. Stephens Green was to be fortified and entrenched.
- Boland's Mill (Third Battalion Irish Volunteers commanded by Eamonn DeValera) This garrison was to hamper the arrival of troops into the city from Kingstown harbour and England and also the movement of troops from Lansdowne Road to Westland Row.

- Numerous other locations were to also to be occupied by Irish Volunteer detachments including Rowe's Distillery, Watkins Brewery and the Jameson Distillery.[I]
- In order to disrupt rail transport Westland Row Station, Harcourt St. Station and the North Dublin Union Workhouse (which commanded the approaches to Broadstone Station) were also to be occupied. At Fairview the northern rail line was to be cut.

Furthermore, many additional smaller buildings were to be occupied as outposts for the larger buildings while snipers were to be located at as many critical positions as possible. In so far as numbers would allow the soldiers of the Irish Volunteers and the Citizen Army were to be assisted by the women of the Irish Volunteers Auxiliary organisation, Cumann na mBan.[II]

Within the capital, the plan also called for an attack to be mounted against Dublin Castle.

In order to mobilise the Irish Volunteers for the uprising, on April 3rd 1916 Commandant Patrick Pearse issued an order that three days of training for the Volunteers were to be held nationwide commencing on Easter Sunday April 23rd. The order was issued without the knowledge of the Chief of Staff,

---

[I] Unlike the 1798 rebellion where alcohol had on many occasions destroyed the discipline of the rebels, little if any alcohol was consumed by the insurgents during the 1916 rebellion.

[II] After the formation of the Irish Volunteers, the "Cumann na mBan" (Women's Council) was formed in early April 1914 replacing and amalgamating with "Inghinidhe na hÉireann" (Daughters of Ireland). As a subsidiary of the Irish Volunteers, the Cumann na mBan leadership subordinated itself to the needs of the Volunteers carrying out duties such as preparation of provisions, secretarial work and nursing.

Eóin Mac Néill, who was both angry and suspicious when he found out. At a meeting with Pearse, he demanded an undertaking that no further orders, other than those of day-to-day business should be issued without his permission. Commandant Pearse acquiesced, but along with the other members of the I.R.B Supreme Council was now very fearful that Mac Néill might later issue an order countermanding the manoeuvres order that Pearse had just issued.

As Easter drew near, the Supreme Council also turned its attention to the political as well as the military aspects of the Rising with the drafting of a proclamation to the Irish People and the formation of a Provisional Government.

## The Imperative

Militarily, the plan did not stand up to scrutiny, for the Irish were lightly armed and small in number. Having once seized their objectives, their only plan was to stand their ground and fight against the superior firepower of the British that would soon bear down upon them.

Nevertheless the I.R.B leadership was determined to act. By 1916, the war in Europe was in complete stalemate with no sign of imminent victory for either side. The Home Rule Act was already on the Statute Book and the I.R.B leadership were fearful that the government might act upon it before the war in Europe ended. While the vast majority of the Irish People supported Home Rule and the Irish Parliamentary Party, they still believed that the partition of the country would not be the result of the Home Rule Bill, especially since thousands of Irishmen were paying for home rule for all Ireland with their blood on the Western Front. The I.R.B were convinced otherwise. They knew that when home rule with partition became a fact, the majority would accept it and the imperative for action would be lost. While home rule was not yet accomplished their hope was that a republican insurrection along with their declaration of an Irish Republic might yet change everything.

For Patrick Pearse especially, the need to act now coincided with the need for Ireland to reassert her nationality, her Christian heritage, and her will to prove that her men were willing to die in their bid to assert their claim to complete freedom from what might be her future place as an English dominion: "...bloodshed is a cleansing and sanctifying thing and the nation which regards it as a final horror has lost its manhood... "

## The Eve of Rebellion

### The "Aud" Departs Lubeck

At a meeting of Imperial German Naval High Command in Berlin in early March 1916, it was decided to assist the proposed Irish rebellion as a means of tying down British army units in Ireland. The minutes of the meeting record the German intentions; "...Even if the English succeed in suppressing the rebellion quickly we can still count on a strong moral effect" "(It is)...the urgent wish of the General Staff that a substantial (English) force will be tied up in Ireland, far from the European mainland."[354]

The instructions from the German High Command regarding the transfer of arms to Irealnd were transmitted to New York and from there to Ireland; "Between 20th and 23rd April...Irish pilot boat to await the trawler at dusk north of the Island of Inishtookert, at the entrance to Tralee Bay, and show two green lights close to each other at short intervals. Please wire whether the necessary arrangements in Ireland can be made secretly through Devoy."[355]

On April 9th, the steamer Aud[I] set sail from Lubeck, under the command of Captain Karl Spindler with a cargo of 20,000 rifles, some Maxim machine guns and explosives along with one million rounds of ammunition. Spindler's destination was the pier at Fenit, Co. Kerry. After travelling a circuitous route in order to avoid the Royal Navy the Aud slipped through the British blockade into the North Atlantic on April 16th thereafter travelling a gradual south-easterly course. Although well equipped, and disguised as a Norwegian steamer with a load of lumber, the Aud did not possess a wireless telegraph set, a fact that the I.R.B leadership were not aware of.

After the Aud had departed, Roger Casement (who was by now consumed with fear and doubt about the success of the impending insurrection) persuaded the German government that his presence in Ireland was indispensable to the success of the rising and that he should be brought to Tralee Bay to be there when the Aud arrived in order to take charge of the weapons. A U Boat, the "U19" commanded by Lieutenant Weisbach[II] departed Kiel on April 12th with Casement aboard. Accompanying Casement were Daniel Bailey who was one of the few Irish prisoners of war who had joined the Irish Brigade and Robert Monteith, an officer in the Irish Volunteers who had travelled to Germany to help arrange the procurement of arms the previous year.

---

[I] The Aud was previously an English cargo steamer called the "SS Castro". Captured by the Germans at the outbreak of the First World War, she was renamed "Libau" until designated to carry weapons to Ireland when she was given the name "Aud". By being designated "Aud" the ship was posing as the steamer "Aud" from the neutral country of Norway. The "real" Aud was sunk by the German U Boat "UB-18" of the coast of Portugal at the end of November 1916 after the commander of the U Boat determined that she was carrying an illegal cargo.

[II] Weisbach was the U boat Commander who sank the Lusitania.

## A Change of Plan

As plans for the insurrection firmed up, the I.R.B leadership decided to move the date for the uprising from Easter Sunday to Easter Monday as the annual Easter Monday race meeting at Fairyhouse Racecourse in Co. Meath was a favourite of British Army officers stationed in the Capital. By moving the rebellion to that day the capital's barracks would be without a great many officers, something that would be of great assistance to the rebels during the early stage of the rebellion.

Furthermore, a full moon was due around the time that the German weapons were supposed to arrive off the Kerry Coast (between Holy Thursday, April 20$^{th}$ and Holy Saturday, April 22$^{nd}$). It was felt by the leadership that the early arrival of the weapons coinciding with the full moon might lead to trouble either with the navy or the R.I.C and the possible loss of the weapons upon which the rebellion outside Dublin depended.

As there was no direct contact between the I.R.B and Berlin and no secret telegraph code existed between the I.R.B in Dublin and Devoy in New York, a message was taken personally to New York by Philomena Plunkett (sister of Joseph Plunkett) and transmitted from there to Berlin by Devoy. It read; "Arms must not be landed before the night of Easter Sunday, 23$^{rd}$. This is vital. Smuggling impossible."[356] When Devoy's message arrived in Berlin on April 15$^{th}$, the Aud had already set sail. There was no subsequent communication either directly or indirectly to the I.R.B leadership that Captain Spindler of the Aud was unable to receive the change in plan. Having heard nothing, as far as the I.R.B leadership were concerned, the shipment of weapons would not arrive at Fenit Pier until Easter Sunday night where it would be met by Irish Volunteers of the Kerry Brigade under the command of Austin Stack. No precautionary lookout was kept.

Plans Discovered

Since the early Spring of 1916, the British Secret Service had been monitoring all wireless communications between the United States and Germany. As these included those from Devoy and the German Embassy relating to the provision of arms for the rising, the British Government was aware that an insurrection was being planned in Dublin. Curiously, Dublin Castle was not informed of the impending rebellion until Tuesday April 18th when a message was sent from London that a German boat carrying a cargo of weapons was due; "to arrive on the 21st and that a Rising was timed for Easter Eve."[357]

Following receipt of this communiqué by Dublin Castle no arrests ensued, neither was there any action taken except for an instruction to the R.I.C. that they should be extra vigilant for any suspicious behaviour. The instruction to be vigilant for a German gun running ship, transporting weapons to Ireland was also passed on to the Royal Navy. Dublin Castle had decided to let matters develop and watch and wait a while longer.

As Holy Week of 1916 progressed, the Chief of Staff of the Irish Volunteers, Eóin Mac Néill became convinced that something more than manoeuvres were going to commence on Easter Sunday. Along with Bulmer Hobson and Commandant J.J O'Connell they confronted Pearse on Holy Thursday April 20th and demanded that he tell them everything. His hand finally forced, Pearse confirmed their suspicions at which MacNéill, horrified at the prospect of an imminent rebellion became very animated and assured Pearse that he was determined to disrupt the plan in whatever way he could, short of informing Dublin Castle. Thereafter MacNéill attempted to exert complete authority over the Irish Volunteers in Dublin, sending out the command that all orders not signed by him, Hobson or O'Connell were not to be followed.

## The Scuttling of the Aud

On April 20th Spindler arrived in Tralee Bay, the first day that his original schedule had specified for the delivery of the weapons. Having taken up a position near Innishtookert Island, Spindler observed the shore for any sign of the Irish who were to meet him. There was no-one. He later wrote: "No pilot boat came and there was no evidence on shore of any preparation to receive us...I decided to stop as long as possible, because I thought there was some misunderstanding as to the plans...the Irish would probably wait for darkness to come on board. When it became dark I gave the arranged night signals but made no connection with anyone at sea or shore. With morning came a wonderful spring day – Good Friday."[358] Spindler continued to wait. A Royal Navy patrol boat approached, but Spindler stood his ground. When the patrol boat drew up alongside, its officer came on board and departed shortly afterwards apparently convinced that the Aud was indeed the neutral ship that it pretended to be. However some hours later another patrol boat approached. Spindler knew the game was up. He immediately ordered the ship's anchors to be pulled in and departed. A chase now ensued with the Royal Navy patrol boat being joined by other Royal Navy boats in the area. By 7pm on Good Friday Spindler had been cornered by the Royal Navy and had now no option but to surrender.

After being signalled to follow the Royal Navy patrol boat "Bluebell", the Captain of the Bluebell ordered a shot to be fired across Spindler's bow as a warning. Early on the morning of Holy Saturday as the Aud neared Daunt Rock at the entrance to Cork Harbour Spindler and his crew set explosive charges on the Aud and raised the German Imperial flag on her mast. After the initial explosions, the crew immediately took to the lifeboat. As another warning round from the Bluebell hit the sea nearby, Spindler raised a white flag on the lifeboat as the Aud with her precious cargo began her descent beneath the waves.[1]

It would be some time before anyone in the Irish Volunteers or the I.R.B learned of the Aud's fate. The "imminent arrival" of the Aud and the weaponry she had contained would continue to figure in the plans for the rebellion a while longer.

## The Capture of Roger Casement

Early on Good Friday morning as Captain Spindler watched for any sign of communication from the shore, Roger Casement and his two companions were rowing ashore towards Banna Strand, (not far from Fenit) in a small boat after being dropped off by the U boat. Captain Weisbach had already spotted the Aud some distance away but had continued on towards Tralee Bay, not wishing to draw attention to the Aud.

When the three men came ashore, Casement was completely exhausted and was suffering from a recurrence of the Malaria that he contracted while in Africa. While Bailey and Monteith headed for Tralee where they hoped to make contact with Austin Stack, Casement stayed behind.

In Tralee, Monteith succeeded in getting a message sent to Dublin (to be delivered by hand) relating the quantity and type of weaponry aboard the Aud. Believing that Eóin Mac Néill was in charge of the planning of the Rising, Monteith addressed the message to him, but the messenger knew better. He took the message to James Connolly at Liberty Hall.

Meanwhile, Roger Casement remained near Banna Strand where he took shelter at an ancient ring fort called "McKenna's Fort." Some time later he was discovered by an R.I.C. patrol

---

[1] "About five minutes after the first explosion a dull, rumbling noise came from the Aud. The cargo and bunkers were shifting. The masts tottered. The blazing bow rose perpendicularly out of the water and the next moment the Aud, as if drawn down by an invisible hand, sank with a loud hissing noise. Our good old Libau was no more." – Karl Spindler.

and arrested although they had no idea who he was and why he was there. Later that day, Austin Stack heard of Casement's arrest and decided to take the dangerous step of going to the R.I.C station to see if he could talk to him. After arriving at the police station, Stack was himself arrested.

## "Danger Averted"

By the morning of Holy Saturday, the authorities in Dublin Castle were both jubilant and relieved. They had just received the news of the destruction of the German Arms shipment along with the incarceration of her crew and had also heard about the arrest of a man near Banna Strand along with the arrest of the Commander of the Kerry Volunteers, Austin Stack. A news blackout on the events in Kerry was immediately ordered, but the news of the arrest of a man at Banna Strand had already emerged and by Saturday evening was being carried in the newspapers. Nothing was mentioned in the newspapers regarding the destruction of a boat at the entrance to Cork harbour.

Relief in Dublin Castle now turned to complacency. With the weapons destroyed, any prospect of an imminent uprising appeared to be firmly quashed. It was the Easter holiday weekend. The Chief Secretary, Augustine Birrell was away, and it would take a few days to collate all available information into a list of people to arrest on the charge of "hostile association". Next week would be time enough to round up the "Sinn Fein trouble-makers" (for the government firmly believed that Sinn Fein were responsible for the planning of the insurrection). The following morning (Easter Sunday) the Under Secretary Sir Matthew Nathan met with the Viceroy Lord Wimborne. Both men concurred. The danger had passed. Nathan now sent a telegram to London to Chief Secretary Birrell advising him of the situation and requesting authorisation to conduct raids upon all premises associated with the Irish Volunteers and the Irish Citizen Army.

## Manoeuvre Orders – "Rescinded"

Early on Good Friday morning, Patrick Pearse along with Thomas MacDonagh and Sean MacDermott went to see Eóin Mac Néill in an attempt to persuade him to allow the insurrection to go ahead. They told MacNéill of the imminent arrival of the German arms shipment and of the plans already in train for the recovery[1] and distribution of the weapons. The Manoeuvre orders had been issued weeks ago - to cancel them now was unthinkable. The effect of cancellation on the morale of the Irish Volunteers would be disastrous. Now was the time to act! Finally, Eóin Mac Néill agreed to let events take their course.

When news reached the Military Council that the man arrested at Banna Strand was none other than Roger Casement, it only increased their determination to act before the expected Dublin Castle security operation against the Volunteers. When the news was relayed to Eóin Mac Néill he took the opposing view, remaining immovable to the entreaties of Thomas MacDonagh. While MacDonagh reported to the Military Council, Mac Néill immediately took action to ensure that Irish Volunteers all over the country would be informed that their ordered mobilisation was cancelled. Messengers were dispatched and a notice was placed in the newspapers that would be carried all over the country. The O'Rahilly was

---

[1] Early on Good Friday five men went from Dublin to Killarney to link up with Austin Stack. In Killarney they were met by two cars that were to bring them to the coast. The driver of the second car, Thomas MacInerney lost sight of the first car which he was following and took the wrong road. In the darkness he drove over the pier at Ballykissane into the Atlantic Ocean and was drowned along with his three passengers.

summoned to Mac Néill and ordered to go to Limerick at once to prevent the distribution of weapons to Volunteer units.

The following morning, Easter Sunday April 23rd, The Sunday Independent carried Eóin Mac Néill's notice:

"Owing to the very critical position, all orders given to the Irish Volunteers for tomorrow Easter Sunday are hereby rescinded and no parades, marches or other movements of Irish volunteers will take place. Each individual Volunteer will obey this order in every particular."

### "Orders from the Captain"

Their plans for a rebellion apparently in tatters, a meeting of the Military Council was held in Liberty Hall on Easter Sunday morning presided over by the Fenian veteran Thomas Clarke. An aura of gloom pervaded the room. Nevertheless, after an in depth discussion of all that had happened, they decided that the element of surprise was still with them. It was true that any remote chance of success of their rebellion had been lost but they could still succeed in launching a rebellion that by it's very failure might lead to greater things. All present were in agreement. An insurrection would be undertaken in Dublin to commence at 12 P.M on Easter Monday.

Early on the morning of Easter Monday, April 24th 1916 an order was sent out to the Irish Volunteers within Dublin signed by the Commandant of the Dublin Brigade Thomas MacDonagh and countersigned by Pádraic Pearse. It read:

"The four City Battalions will parade for inspection and route march at 10 a.m. today"

### A Parade for Irish Freedom

When the parade was held at Liberty Hall at 10 a.m. on the morning of Easter Monday, the number attending was far less than the Military Council had hoped for. While almost the entire Citizen Army had answered the summons, there were only 1,100 Irish Volunteers, a fact blamed on the countermanding order of Eóin Mac Néill. All were armed.

A holiday atmosphere pervaded the Capital. None of the passers by passed much attention on the by now familiar sight of parading Volunteers and Citizen Army. The men were divided up into contingents and after receiving ammunition, some rations and extra kit they marched off in different directions. One contingent headed for the General Post Office on Sackville St. (O'Connell St.) where they were ordered by James Connolly to seize the building and prepare it for immediate defence.

Once inside, the insurgents ordered all post office workers to vacate the building. One of the volunteers, Quartermaster Michael Staines (the son of a serving RIC officer) later recalled: "I got six men and made for the stairs – the staff were coming down, most of them appeared hostile, but one girl named O'Callaghan said to me "That's the stuff to give them Michael". When the stairs were free we ran up them. I heard the shout "Halt" and saw six soldiers pointing their rifles at us. We rushed up and I shout to my men to fire which they did. We were armed with revolvers. One man, a sergeant fell, I ran up with my men and seized the rifles. I demanded the ammunition but found they had none."[1359] Two flags were hoisted. One was the tricolour of the "Young Irelanders" of 1848 while the other was a green flag bearing the inscription "Irish Republic".

---

[i] Following the engagement, Staines arranged for the transfer of the wounded sergeant to Jervis St. Hospital.

# Chapter 16

# "In the Name of God and of the Dead Generations"

## The Proclamation of the Irish Republic

As the General Post Office was being occupied, all of the other city buildings outlined in the plan were seized without difficulty along with the numerous smaller premises that were to either provide cover to the larger buildings or to prevent their occupation by Crown Forces. As this was occurring a group of Fianna Éireann scouts attacked the Magazine Fort in the Phoenix Park. Despite being driven off by the garrison they nevertheless succeeded in destroying some ammunition. As with the other buildings, inside the G.P.O. the soldiers of the Irish Volunteers and Citizen Army set to work constructing barricades and clearing fields of fire. In the G.P.O. windows were broken and barricaded with heavy mailbags and furniture which came not just from the G.P.O but from buildings nearby. In many of the occupied buildings some level of siege preparations were made[1] and utensils were filled with water in case the mains should be turned off. While telegraph wires were cut, in many instances the telephone

---

[1] Soldiers from the G.P.O. garrison requisitioned large amounts of food from the nearby Findlater's Emporium.

connections were overlooked. As these activities took place, a small number of people looked on in shock or bewildered amusement while others carried on their daily business as normal.

At 12.45pm Commandant Patrick Pearse and Tom Clarke emerged from the main door of the building with an armed guard and Pearse standing "on the edge of the footpath at a point in front of the window where there is now a door, on the Prince's St. Side of the portico"[360] read in a loud voice the prepared proclamation which had been signed the previous day;

## Poblacht na h-Éireann.

----------

## The Provisional Government
## Of the
## Irish Republic
## To the people of Ireland

Irishmen and Irishwomen: In the name of God and of the dead generations from which she receives her old tradition of nationhood, Ireland, through us, summons her children to her flag and strikes for her freedom.

Having organized and trained her manhood through her secret revolutionary organization, the Irish Republican Brotherhood, and through her open military organizations, the Irish Volunteers and the Irish Citizen Army, having patiently perfected her discipline, having resolutely waited for the right moment to reveal itself, she now seizes that moment, and supported by her exiled children in America and gallant allies in Europe, but relying in the first on her own strength, she strikes in full confidence of victory.

We declare the right of the people of Ireland to the ownership of Ireland and to the unfettered control of Irish destinies, to be sovereign and indefeasible. The long usurpation of that right by a foreign people and government has not extinguished the right, nor can it ever be extinguished except by the destruction of the Irish people. In every generation the Irish people have asserted their right to national freedom and sovereignty: six times during the past three hundred years they have asserted it in arms. Standing on that fundamental right and asserting it in arms in the face of the world, we hereby proclaim the Irish Republic as a Sovereign Independent State, and we pledge our lives and the lives of our comrades in arms to the cause of its freedom, of its welfare and of its exaltation among the nations.

The Irish Republic is entitled to, and hereby claims, the allegiance of every Irishman and Irishwoman. The Republic guarantees religious and civil liberty, equal right and equal opportunities to all its citizens, and declares its resolve to pursue the happiness and prosperity of the whole nation and of all its parts, cherishing all the children of the nation equally, and obvious of the differences, carefully fostered by an alien government which has divided a minority from the majority in the past.

Until our arms have brought the opportune moment for the establishment of a permanent National Government, representative of the whole people of Ireland, and elected by the suffrages of all her men and women, the Provisional Government, hereby constituted, will administer the civil and military affairs of the Republic in trust for the people. We place the cause of the Irish Republic under the Most High God, Whose blessing we invoke upon our arms, and we pray that no one who serves that cause will dishonour it by cowardice, inhumanity or rapine. In this supreme hour the Irish nation must, by its valour and discipline, and by the readiness of its children to sacrifice themselves for the common good, prove itself worthy of the august destiny to which it is called.

Signed on behalf of the Provisional Government,<br>
Thomas J. Clarke<br>
Sean Mac Diarmada.    Thomas MacDonagh.<br>
P.H. Pearse.    Eamonn Ceannt.<br>
James Connolly.    Joseph Plunkett.

## The Rebellion in Dublin

<u>The First Military Casualties of the Rising</u>

After the reading of the Proclamation, there was a muted response mingled with a few cheers from the onlookers. After the public reading of the Proclamation, runners from the G.P.O. carried printed copies of the Proclamation to the buildings occupied by other units, or posted them in public places.

As the G.P.O. was being prepared for defence a message was received at the communications office in Marlborough Barracks regarding a disturbance on Sackville St., after which a patrol of lancers was dispatched from the Barracks to investigate. Less than an hour after Pearse had read the Proclamation the Lancers appeared at the northern end of Sackville St., their horses walking at a canter towards the G.P.O. Their progress down Sackville St. had been noted in the G.P.O. By the time they had advanced as far as Nelson's Column, the windows of the G.P.O. were bristling with rifles which now opened fire on the group killing three and fatally wounding a fourth.

Following the action, the men in the GPO were in high spirits. That evening Fr. O'Flanagan arrived from the Pro-Cathedral after receiving a message from Pearse that "some of the boys would like to go to confession".[361] Fr.O'Flanagan stayed with the men in the GPO for the rest of the week acting as their chaplain.

Elsewhere in Dublin, the Volunteers occupying the Jacob's Biscuit factory were jeered at by onlookers and told to go to France if they were looking for a fight. One bystander ignored the warnings of a Volunteer officer as he tried to take a rifle from a volunteer and was shot in the leg.

At Dublin Castle a small group of men under the command of Sean Connolly approached for an attack. When the unarmed policeman on duty attempted to stop them entering, he was shot dead. After a brief foray into the Castle Yard and the guardroom the Volunteers decided to retreat before they were outnumbered. They were not aware that the entire Castle garrison consisted of the armoury detail of a corporal and a section of soldiers. After retreating, Connolly's group then occupied local buildings including the City Hall. Here, as Sean Connolly hoisted the tricolour, he was shot dead.

On Easter Monday, a group of British army reservists were taking part in a route march. These were the soldiers of the Volunteer Training Corps who were locally referred to as the "Gorgeous Wrecks" due to the motto "Georgius Rex" (King George) on their belt buckles and armbands. In the morning they had embarked on a route march in the hills outside the city with rifles and kit but without ammunition. During a rest from their exertions a passer-by informed them of the commencement of the rising. Their commander, Major Harris decided that they should immediately return to their base at Beggars Bush barracks in order to be issued with ammunition so as to be ready to take part in the fighting. As they neared their H.Q. they came under fire from the outposts of Boland's Bakery that were under the command of Michael Malone. As the men scattered attempting to reach the safety of the nearby barracks five men were killed and eight injured.

## Crown Forces dispatched to Dublin

As the government became aware of the extent of the rebellion and the buildings occupied, immediate steps were taken to draft reinforcements and artillery into the city both from within Ireland and from England, while the unarmed Dublin Metropolitan Police were withdrawn from the streets, a fact not lost on the people of the slums and tenements of the inner city. Looting of many commercial premises followed, especially of the Clerys Department Store on Sackville St.

On Easter Bank Holiday Monday, the number of British troops within the city numbered less than 1,500. This figure was normally 2,500 but thanks to the bank holiday many officers and soldiers were on leave. Of the 1,500 only 400 were immediately ready for deployment and were hurriedly dispatched for the protection of the centre of the English government in Ireland – Dublin Castle. As the Castle was reinforced, the group occupying the buildings around City Hall came under severe pressure from a constant fusillade of machine gun and rifle fire. By Tuesday morning another three of Sean Connolly's men had been killed and the remainder were forced to withdraw. However Dublin Castle continued to come under fire from the Volunteers located in Bishop's St, the location of the Jacob's Biscuit Factory. When the soldiers at Dublin Castle finally realised where the firing was coming from, an attack was launched towards Bishop's St., but the attack was broken off after numbers of the soldiers were hit.

By Tuesday, the number of soldiers within the city had more than doubled following the dispatch of 1,600 soldiers from the Curragh along with artillery from Athlone. The plan of the British Army to dislodge the rebels was simple. As the buildings the rebels had occupied were all in and around the area of the city centre, the army intended to form an outer cordon on the district that would be gradually closed like a noose until all rebel positions were neutralised.

By Tuesday evening the British army had split the republican positions into two sections by establishing a line running from Trinity College to Dublin Castle and onto Kingsbridge (Heuston) Train Station.

### Mount Street Bridge

When news of the rebellion was received in London on Easter Monday, two infantry brigades of the North Midland Division were given their marching orders. They departed England on Tuesday arriving at Kingstown (Dún Laoghaire) Harbour at five o'clock on Wednesday morning. When the Division arrived in Kingstown (then a very English or anglophile area of the city suburbs), they were met by local women who provided them with breakfast. One of the soldiers later remarked: "...they were just like one of us...they seemed to be as pleased as could be that we'd arrived..."[362]

The North Midland Division then split into two columns. While the fifth and sixth battalions of the Sherwood Foresters marched unhindered through Stillorgan and onto Kilmainham, thereafter to join the noose being slowly drawn around the city centre, the other column which consisted of the seventh "Robin Hood" Battalion marched directly towards the city centre where they were destined to encounter the outposts of the 20 man garrison from Boland's Mill located near Mount St. Bridge.

The outposts which were under the command of Lieutenant Michael Malone[I] consisted of 11 Volunteers split between two buildings (7 Volunteers in Clanwilliam House and 4 in the Parochial Hall) while a further two men (one of whom was Michael Malone) were stationed at 25 Haddington Road. Volunteer snipers were also located atop nearby buildings.

---

[I] Michael Malone was brother in law of Theobald Wolfe Tone Fitzgerald who painted the "Irish Republic" flag which flew over the GPO.

As the columns of Sherwood Foresters under the command of Colonel Fane approached the junction between Haddington Road and Northumberland Road they came under fire from 25 Haddington Road. The firing was deadly accurate and as the soldiers at the head of the column were hit, the soldiers behind them threw themselves on the ground and attempted to "get a bead" on the location of the firing. Unable to determine exactly which house the firing was coming from, the officer at the top of the column commanded his men to charge at the general direction of the firing sooner than watch them getting picked off, but the charge was quickly brought to a halt by the constant and accurate firing coming from the outposts and snipers.

The Commander of the army General Lowe sent forward orders that the outposts were to be taken in frontal assaults, Fane disagreed, believing the positions should be outflanked. Time after time junior officers commanded their men to charge towards the danger. As the bodies piled up, the Sherwood Foresters imagined that the foe they faced was in the hundreds. For the whole day the handful of volunteers continued to hold the English soldiers at bay whilst inflicting enormous casualties on them.

Finally the English tactics reverted to concentrated sniping until finally intense firing engulfed the outposts. Around 8.p.m the final assault against the outposts took place. General Maxwell later wrote how; "…after careful arrangements, the whole column, accompanied by bombing parties, attacked the schools and houses where the chief opposition lay, the battalions charging in successive waves carried all before them."[363]

Fire now engulfed Clanwilliam House, the result of incendiary rounds. The building had already been cut to ribbons by the steady stream of bullets which had lacerated it since morning. Nevertheless the handful of Volunteers occupying the House kept firing at the enemy. As the enemy strength became overwhelming the Volunteers knew that the time to evacuate was drawing near. In the last chapter of the fire fight, Patrick Doyle was killed along with Richard Murphy who had been supposed to get married during Easter week. Although dead, Murphy remained at his post in the kneeling position - rifle at the ready.

As the remaining Volunteers prepared to depart, George Reynolds took one final shot, receiving a bullet in the hip in return. As he lay dying the other three volunteers knelt down and said a prayer for him before departing across the wall of the house next door and down an alley.

Following the evacuation of the Parochial Hall, four volunteers were captured. One of the Sherwoods attempted to murder Volunteer Joe Clarke with a bullet to the temple but Clarke moved his head at the critical moment. A second shot was prevented by a nearby doctor attending a wounded Sherwood Forester.

When the British army finally secured their passage across Mount St. Bridge, six officers had been killed or wounded along with two hundred and sixteen among the lower ranks. The Volunteers had suffered six casualties.

### The Destruction of the City Centre

In spite of the many street barricades erected by the rebels, by Thursday of Easter week the British infantry were slowly but surely working their way towards the city centre, raking the streets with machine gun fire and blasting any suspicious building with eighteen pounder artillery guns. Assisting with this task was the armed steam yacht "Helga" which had two twelve pounder naval guns. After sailing up the Liffey on Wednesday the Helga first opened fire on Liberty Hall before proceeding to assist the ground artillery in the destruction of the entire city centre where many buildings not occupied by the insurgents were sent crashing to the ground. High explosive shells were followed by incendiary shells and the city centre soon became a blazing inferno. In the G.P.O, the rebels were forced to retreat from the upper floors which were the target of heavy shelling. As the British troops advanced under cover of their barrage, they were continuously sniped at while the barricades thrown across the streets impeded their progress.

In London, it was decided to replace General Lowe with General Sir John Maxwell as Commander of the Army in Ireland and by Friday morning of Easter Week, Lowe had arrived in Dublin determined to bring the insurrection to a speedy conclusion telling the populace in his proclamation: "If necessary I shall not hesitate to destroy all buildings within any area occupied by the rebels."[364] With the areas under the control of the Provisional Government now effectively surrounded and cordoned off, the British Army set up screening stations so that anyone suspected of involvement in the insurrection would be detained while attempting to exit the area.

## The South Dublin Union and St. Stephen's Green

The South Dublin Union (Hospital and Poorhouse) was a huge complex of buildings. The initial plan for the Insurrection had called for the seizure of the entire complex but because of the greatly reduced number of Volunteers only a limited number of buildings could be taken and held by the men of the fourth company under the command of Eammon Ceannt.

Initial attacks by Crown Forces who came from Richmond Barracks were driven off, and it was during one of these attacks that one of the hospital's nurses; Margaret Keogh was killed.

In command of the Ardee St. outpost of the South Dublin Union was a Limerick man, Con Colbert. As his outpost was in danger of being overrun, Colbert was forced to withdraw from Ardee St. to Marrowbone Lane. As the week progressed British troops were gradually able to overrun all the streets surrounding the South Dublin Union. As one outpost was surrounded, the rebels attempted to move to another position finally occupying the Nurses Home.

At St. Stephens Green where a company of around 100 insurgents were located, trenches had been dug which finally came under fire from English soldiers located on the roof of the nearby Shelbourne Hotel which the rebels had not occupied. Due to the intense and accurate firing of the English, the rebels in this area which were under the command of Michael Mallin were forced to abandon both their outposts and the Green. Mallin then retreated into the nearby Royal College of Surgeons which had been taken over by some soldiers under the command of Countess Markievicz whom Mallin had invited to join the rebel position on Easter Monday. By the time the withdrawal was complete seven Irish soldiers had been

Éamonn Ceannt

Con Colbert

killed.

Around the Four Courts, Volunteers located in eight other buildings in the surrounding area supported this garrison. As British troops poured into the city these buildings were first isolated and the rebels within were forced to withdraw.

As the South Stafford regiment advanced through North King St. towards the city centre, twelve unarmed civilians were shot dead and many more treated with brutality.

### Twenty Six Against Five Hundred

Since the beginning of the rebellion, the Mendicity Institute had been held by a number of Irish Volunteers under the command of Séan Heuston. While also covering the Four Courts garrison, the Volunteers had taken Collins Barracks under fire. Initially it was thought that this post could hold out for a few hours, but by Wednesday morning, Heuston's men, by now almost totally surrounded, were still in position holding back hundreds of English soldiers from advancing towards the city centre.

One of Heuston's men Seamus Brennan, later gave an account of the final hours in the Mendicity Institute and the decision by Séan Heuston to surrender: "Our tiny garrison – now twenty six – had battled all morning against three or four hundred British troops. Machine-gun and rifle fire kept up a constant battering of our position. Séan visited each post in turn, encouraging us. But now we were faced with a new form of attack. The enemy, closing in, began to hurl grenades into the building. Our only answer was to try to catch these and throw them back before they exploded. Two of our men Liam Staines and Dick Balfe, both close friends of Séan's were badly wounded doing this.

We had almost run out of ammunition. Dog-tired, without food, trapped, hopelessly outnumbered, we had reached the limit of our endurance. After consultation with the rest of us,

Séan decided that the only hope for the wounded and, indeed, for the safety of all of us, was to surrender…One of our party went out into the yard behind the Institution waving a white flag and we followed. As we crossed the yard we were fired on by a British sniper and one of our men, Peter Wilson of Swords was shot dead.

The British were infuriated when they saw the pygmy force that had given them such a stiff battle and caused them so many casualties. They screamed at us, cursed us and manhandled us. An officer asked who was in charge and Seán stepped out in front without a word.

We were forced to march to the Royal (now Collins) Barracks with our hands up, held behind our heads. In the Barracks we were lined up on the parade ground. Here we were attacked by British soldiers, kicked, beaten, spat upon. This stands out very clearly in my memory."[365]

Séan Heuston

### Final Hours in the G.P.O.
By Easter Friday the G.P.O. garrison were under severe pressure, for following the heavy shelling on Thursday, the entire building had caught fire by Friday morning. On Easter Thursday James Connolly's leg had been shattered by bullets as he tried to determine the extent of enemy positions around the Post Office. Connolly was brought back to the GPO by a stretcher party where he was tended by the trainee doctor (and later Fianna Fail T.D and minister), Jim Ryan.

The General Post Office in the aftermath of the Rebellion

Yet, not all the rebel garrisons faced the same dilemma. The Boland's Mill Garrison under the command of Eamonn deValera which had caused so much trouble for the arriving English troops earlier in the week remained in a solid state of defence along with the Four Courts under Commandant Daly. The South Dublin Union under the command of Eamonn Ceannt continued to hold on with difficulty while the College of Surgeons garrison remained isolated but intact.

With the G.P.O. ablaze the rebel leaders now realised that their tenancy of the building was coming to an end. A plan was formulated to abandon the G.P.O, after which the soldiers of the Garrison would make the hazardous journey on foot across Henry St. into a lane before turning left into Moore St. from where they would turn into Parnell St. North to the Williams and Woods Jam Factory where a new H.Q. would be established. Unwilling to risk the lives of the three women who had helped the fighting men, Pearse told them that they could not accompany the garrison, assuring them that their courage had inspired the men of the garrison to continue the struggle. He told them "You all deserve a foremost place in the history of this nation." The Red Cross nurse Elizabeth

O'Farrell remained with the garrison in order to tend to the wounded.

From his G.P.O. Headquarters, the President of the Provisional Government, Patrick Pearse issued one final document before ordering the building's evacuation. He wrote in part: "If they (the Irish Volunteers and the Irish Citizen Army) do not win this fight, they will at least have deserved to win it. But win it they will, although they may win it in death. Already they have won a great thing. They have redeemed Dublin from many shames, and made her name splendid among the names of cities... If we accomplish no more than we have accomplished, I am satisfied. I am satisfied that we have saved Ireland's honour. I am satisfied that we would have accomplished more, that we should have accomplished the task of enthroning as well as proclaiming, the Irish Republic as a Sovereign State, had our arrangements for a simultaneous rising of the whole country, with a combined plan as sound as the Dublin plan has been proved to be, been allowed to go through on Easter Sunday. Of the fatal countermanding order which prevented those plans from being carried out, I shall not speak further. Both Eóin Mac Néill and we have acted in the best interests of Ireland...For my part, as to anything I have done in this, I am not afraid to face either the judgement of God or the judgement of posterity."[366]

## Number 16, Moore St.

The first group to leave the Post Office consisted of The O'Rahilly along with a small group of men who were to act as a reconnaissance party for the main group. After making their way to Parnell St., The O'Rahilly was to return to the G.P.O. and report on the situation. In his attempt to get back with his report, The O'Rahilly was shot dead as he tried to navigate his way through Moore Lane.

Nevertheless, the evacuation and the journey through the bullet swept streets had to proceed. During this time James Connolly was carried on a stretcher. By the time the corner of Moore St. and Moore Lane was reached, the group was forced to take refuge having already suffered 17 casualties. In an effort to advance to Parnell St., the Irish soldiers tunnelled through the houses but could not get past number 16 Moore St. After passing a restless night in which the centre of the city continued to be pulverised, morning came. Pearse watched as some local inhabitants attempted to evacuate a burning house while carrying a white flag. They were shot dead. Horrified by the indiscriminate killings perpetrated by the Forces of the Crown, Pearse reluctantly decided that surrender was now the only correct course. The issue was discussed by Pearse, Clarke, Plunkett and Mac Diarmada along with Connolly around whose bed they sat. After debating the matter, the majority decision in favour of surrender was taken at midday.

Surrender

Carrying a white flag, Nurse Elizabeth O'Farrell warily approached a British Army barricade on Parnell St. She returned to 16 Moore St. with the message that only unconditional surrender would be accepted. At half past three on Easter Saturday April 29th, Pearse accompanied by Nurse Farrell surrendered to General Lowe at the junction of Moore St. and Parnell St. After being taken into custody, Pearse wrote the surrender order that was then typed multiple times, signed by Pearse and dispatched to the rebel garrisons. It read; "In order to prevent further slaughter of Dublin citizens, and in the hope of saving the lives of our followers now surrounded and hopelessly outnumbered, the members of the Provisional Government present at Headquarters have agreed to an unconditional surrender, and the Commandants of the various districts in the City and Country will order the commands to lay down arms."

In spite of the order to surrender, the garrisons at the Four Courts and Boland's Mill were reluctant to obey. The Four Courts surrender only occurred after Thomas MacDonagh had visited Pearse at Richmond Barracks, while in the South Dublin Union, Eamonn Ceannt persuaded his soldiers by telling them: "If Tom Clarke who served fifteen years in British dungeons has surrendered, then I don't think it's any shame on us to surrender too."[367]

After the surrender, the G.P.O. garrison followed the instructions given them by Nurse Farrell: "Proceed down Moore St., into Moore Lane and Henry Place, out into Henry St. and around to the (Nelson's) Pillar to the right hand side of Sackville St., march up to within a hundred yards of the military drawn up at the Parnell Statue, halt, advance five paces and lay down your arms."[368]

After halting at the Gresham Hotel, the soldiers of the Garrison were marched to a small green area in front of the Rotunda Hospital after which they were searched and had their details taken. In this cage, surrounded by soldiers they spent the night after being warned to remain lying down as if they should rise even to their knees they would be shot. Describing the officer Captain Percival Lea Wilson in charge of the guard detail as a "demon in human form",[369] one of the Volunteers, Brian O'Higgins later wrote about the insults showered on the prisoners by Lea Wilson[I] and his men. One conversation he later recalled went as follows:

---

[I] During the War of Independence, (1919-21) Lea Wison was stationed in Wexford. He continued to be "particularly odious" in the discharge of his duty and because of this, came to the attention of the IRA and was identified as the officer who had mistreated the prisoners following their surrender in 1916. On June 15th 1920 he was shot dead as he returned home. There is a stained glass window dedicated to his memory in the Church of Ireland in Gorey, Co. Wexford.

"Which are the Sinn Feiners or the Germans the worse, boys?"
"The Sinn Feiners, Sir."
"What should we do with these swine?"
"Shoot them Sir."
"Aye and shoot them we will."370

Brian O'Higgins also recalled the return of the same officer; "Later on he came along with a group of brother officers and walked right round us while he kept up a running fire of insulting remarks, addressed to the others, but intended for our ears. Now and then he would strike a match, hold it close to the face of the prisoners nearest to him and say: "Does anybody want to see the animals? Now is the time. Aren't they beautiful specimens of Irish soldiers?" and other things that would not bear repetition."371

Any volunteer attempting to relieve himself was clubbed to the ground. This happened to Tom Clarke.[1] No water or food was issued. After arriving at Richmond Barracks on Sunday afternoon water was issued to the prisoners in a bin into which they had relieved themselves a couple of minutes before.

At Richmond Barracks, some prisoners including Tom Clarke were strip-searched. One Volunteer prisoner, Eamonn Dore later recalled: "Tom Clarke had been wounded at the elbow-joint and his arm was in a sling so that he could not get his coat off quickly. The officer pulled the arm straight, opening the wound and tore off his coat."372

## The Rebellion outside Dublin

The Volunteers outside the capital reluctantly obeyed the countermanding order of Eoin MacNeill as published in the newspapers on Easter Sunday. However as news of the

---

[1] Capt. Wilson was heard to say of Tom Clarke: "This old bastard's been out before – he's got a tobacconist shop across the way."

rebellion in the Capital spread throughout the county some hundreds of volunteers travelled to Dublin in order to assist their comrades. While most of those who arrived at the beginning of the week were able to reach one of the rebel positions, this proved impossible later in the week during to the cordon established by the Crown Forces around the rebel positions.

Outside the Capital there were a small number of Volunteers who on receiving news of the outbreak of the insurrection in Dublin determined to follow suit in their own area of operations. This determination was further reinforced when after the outbreak of hostilities Mac Néill issued a further order calling on the Irish Volunteers to rise up. For most it was too late for as soon as the Rebellion broke, Crown Forces in the country at large turned their attention to local Volunteer units ensuring that any action by them would be both wasteful in lives and fruitless in gain.

The following is a brief account of some of the events that occurred outside the capital during Easter week 1916.

## North Dublin / Meath

The fifth battalion of the Irish Volunteers consisted mainly of volunteers from north County Dublin and was under the command of Commandant Thomas Ashe. On Easter Sunday morning, Ashe's men were already mustering when Mac Néill's countermanding order was received, Ashe, regarding the order with disgust, ordered his men to stand down but admonished them to be ready to muster at a moment's notice. On Easter Monday a dispatch rider from the Capital brought Ashe an order from Pearse; "Strike today at one o'clock"

The early part of the week was spent attempting to disrupt communications and train lines in north Dublin while in Swords and Donabate, Ashe's men attacked the R.I.C. barracks, the Donabate barracks surrendering only after a prolonged battle. However Crown Forces at other smaller barracks abandoned them and moved into the larger towns. As the week progressed, some of Ashe's men, realising that a national effort had not taken place became disillusioned and were allowed to go home, leaving only a hard core of around 50 fighters who would now take part in a final victorious mission. On Thursday night, Ashe summoned the local priest Fr. Kelvehan to their camp at Baldwinstown where he heard confessions and blessed the men.

Ashe's plan for Friday 28th was to sever the Athlone – Dublin railway line at Batterstown. However the Volunteers found their path blocked at Ashbourne barracks which had lately been heavily reinforced. Second in Command, Richard Mulcahy advised Thomas Ashe that the Barracks should be captured. After a prolonged battle the barracks surrendered after Volunteer Blanchfield threw a homemade hand grenade which detonated just in front of the barracks. All appeared over when suddenly, a sentry posted at nearby Rath Cross began firing his weapon to warn Ashe of the approach of a Crown Forces convoy from Slane that had stopped on hearing the rifle fire.

Richard Mulcahy was quick to see the possibilities. Immediately volunteers were dispatched on bicycles to flank the convoy and approach it from the rear. Within a few minutes the vehicles were surrounded. Along the length of the convoy, almost sixty R.I.C. men were offering an ineffective resistance with their revolvers and carbines. In a battle lasting over five hours eight members of the Crown Forces including Chief Inspector Alexander Gray were killed while fifteen more were seriously wounded for the loss of two volunteers and two civilians before the remaining R.I.C men surrendered.

In the aftermath of the battle, Thomas Ashe summoned doctors to treat all the wounded while the cars of the convoy ferried them to Navan hospital. No prisoners were taken as all uninjured R.I.C men were disarmed and instructed to return to their homes. This was to be the last action of the fifth battalion before the order to surrender reached them.

Galway

Outside the Capital, one of the most active areas was Galway where up to 1,000 volunteers under the command of Liam Mellowes engaged in attacks on barracks, communications infrastructure and the rail network commencing on Tuesday of Easter Week. In an action reminiscent of the Young Irelanders, Mellowes and his men took control of the towns of Athenry and Moyvore in a plan to remain there until Crown Forces should try and dislodge them. By Thursday, many badly armed Volunteers were surrounded in Moyvore and although Mellowes was determined to stand his ground, the local priest feeling that Mellowes's men were worthy of a better fate persuaded them to disband just as the arrival of British troops aboard H.M.S. Gloucester was imminent.

Liam Mellowes

Although many of his men were captured, Mellowes along with some of his officers managed to avoid capture thanks to James Miggins, the Station Master at Athenry, who held up a train full of British Soldiers just long enough for Mellowes and his men to escape.

Wexford

On Easter Wednesday, Commandant Peter Paul Galligan cycled by a circuitous route from Dublin to Wexford where he informed Commandant Robert Brennan that his Wexford Volunteers were to cut the railway line from Rosslare to Dublin in order to prevent the passage of troops by rail along the east coast route into the capital.

After assembling his men, Brennan and Galligan occupied the town of Enniscorthy. The railway line was cut and checkpoints were set up on all approach roads. Within the town, the R.I.C withdrew to the safety of their barracks where they remained holed up until Brennan was forced to stand down following the surrender order.

Following the occupation of the town, Commandant Galligan left Enniscorthy in command of a large body of men on a security operation into north Wexford, where he occupied Ferns and conducted patrols into the surrounding area forcing the R.I.C. to withdraw from the countryside.

## Crown Forces Atrocities

North King St.

Whilst many civilians had been killed by the indiscriminate use of artillery and machine guns, there were numerous civilian casualties due to the murder by Crown Forces of local residents in areas through which they advanced or in areas which they operated.

The worst example of this occurred during the advance of soldiers of the $2^{nd}$ and $6^{th}$ South Staffordshire Regiments through North King St. After separating the men from the women and children the men were murdered in cold blood. One of the residents, Sarah Hughes later recalled: "…one of the soldiers said "give those Irish pigs an ounce of lead"…my poor husband was brought to the top of the house and instantly shot dead for no crime at all…"[373.]

In another house in North King St., a local woman, Anne Fennel went into her neighbours house where she found: "...George Ennis being led upstairs...(his wife)...clung to him and refused to be parted from him...(the soldier)...shouted "Keep quiet you bloody bitch"...After a long time, it must have been a couple of hours, we heard a noise at the parlour door, and to our horror, poor Mr. Ennis crawled in. I will never forget. He was dying, bleeding to death, and when the military left the house he had crept downstairs to see his wife..."[374]

Twelve innocent civilians in the area of North King St. were murdered in this way.

During the inquests the jury requested that the officers responsible for these men should appear at the inquest but no effort was made on the part of the government to produce them.

In response to these and other stories of atrocity, General Maxwell wrote in a letter to The Daily Mail that the soldiers could not have been expected to use "velvet glove methods"[375] whilst putting down a rebellion.

## "Guilty but Insane"

On Easter Tuesday, April 25th, the notable Dublin pacifist and advocate of Women's Suffrage, Francis Sheehy-Skeffington was arrested at Portobello Bridge by the commanding officer of the bridge guard drawn from the 11th East Surrey Regiment. He was afterwards brought to Portobello (now Cathal Brugha) Barracks on suspicion of being a "Sinn Feiner".

After being detained for a couple of hours, Skeffington was removed from his cell by another officer – Captain J.C. Bowen Colthurst who was planning a punitive raid against the tobacco shop of Dublin Councillor James Kelly, whom he had mistaken for Sinn Fein Councillor Tom Kelly. Colthurst intended to use Skeffington as a hostage who would be shot if his patrol of 40 men came under fire.

During the patrol Colthurst and his men encountered a young man named James Coade who was on his way home following a Sodality Meeting at the nearby Church of Mary Immaculate Refuge of Sinners. During the questioning that followed, one of the soldiers smashed his rifle butt into Coade's jaw after which Colthurst shot him and left him for dead. Coade died the following day. The patrol proceeded to Kelly's shop and home which Colthurst and his men destroyed with hand grenades after arresting two men whom he found inside the shop - Patrick McIntyre and Thomas Dickson - who were both pro-union newspapermen.

Francis Sheehy Skeffington

Colthurst then returned to the Barracks with his three prisoners, who remained in custody until 10am the following morning, when they were executed by a party of soldiers on Colthurst's orders and with Colthurst in command. Sgt. Aldridge commanded the firing squad.

Following the executions, the three men were buried in unmarked graves in the barracks grounds, while the wall against which the executions had taken place was repaired by bricklayers who were commandeered by a party of soldiers from a nearby building site and were repeatedly threatened not to breathe a word of the work they were to undertake.

Hours after the executions Colthurst, now on another patrol shot two more men, one of whom (Richard O'Carroll) died of his wounds.

As Skefffington was a man with an international reputation, questions as to his whereabouts were being made. Colthurst, realising the delicate situation in which he found himself, ordered a raid on Skeffington's home in which he hoped to find something which would associate Skeffington with the Sinn Fein Party. The raid was conducted with great brutality[1] Upon their arrival at Skeffington's house, the soldiers announced their presence with a fusillade of bullets through the front door. Skeffington's wife Hanna, and his son Owen were arrested and copious amounts of documents were removed in an attempt to find something to link Skeffington to Sinn Fein but nothing "incriminating" was found.

As the questions regarding Skeffington's whereabouts continued, the British Army in Ireland now closed ranks around Colthurst, except for Sir Francis Vane who ended up being relieved from his command for refusing to let the matter drop.

On May 3rd, the commander of British troops in Dublin, Major-General A.E. Sandbach concluded following an investigation that "...Captain Bowen-Colthurst seems to have carried out his duties with discretion."[376] Colthurst was now dispatched from Dublin to take up a new command in Newry.

Resolute in his determination, Vane went to England and approached Lord Kitchener directly through a back channel. Following the meeting Colthurst was arrested on Kitchener's orders and brought before a military court martial in spite of the fact that military court martials were not allowed to be used by the army for the killing of a civilian,

---

[1] Following the raid the housemaid was so traumatised, she left her employment.

Realising that the evidence against Colthurst was overwhelming, it was decided by the army in Dublin that he should adopt the defence of "guilty but insane". The first doctor to whom Colthurst was brought refused to certify him and ended up in Africa for his refusal.[I]

At the court martial, Colthurst was painted by his brother officers as an extremely "decent chap", mentally affected by his experiences in France. He was found "guilty but insane" for the execution of Sheehy-Skeffington and the two newspaper men. His other crimes including the murder of Coade were not brought forward during the court martial.

Sir Francis Fletcher Vane

After spending one year at the mental sanatorium located beside Broadmoor Prison he was released. He was awarded a large sum of money and a pension in order to make a new life for himself in Canada.

General Sir John Maxwell remained highly displeased with Sir Francis Vane for having broken ranks with his brother officers in Dublin. He succeeded in having him dishonourably discharged from the army after submitting a damning report on him.[II]

---

[I] The son of Lord Fitzgerald, the Lord of Appeal wrote "The ...transportation of the doctor to Africa because he would not certify his (Coluthurst's) insanity (has) impress(ed) the public.

[II] It is quite clear that if Skeffington had not been one of Colthurst's victims, Colthurst would have escaped any prosecution whatsoever. The case highlights the impunity with which Crown Forces were able to act.

# Chapter 17

# Dying For Ireland

<u>Seated left to right</u>; Patrick Pearse, John McBride, Tom Clarke, Eamonn Ceannt, James Connolly, Joseph Plunkett
<u>Standing left to right</u>; Willie Pearse, Thomas MacDonagh, Sean Heuston, Michael Mallin, Sean MacDermott, Michael O' Hanrahan, Edward Daly, Cornelius Colbert.
<u>Pictured on wall behind</u>; Left, Roger Casement. Right, Thomas Kent.

## The Court Martials

Following the Easter Rebellion, a total of 187 people were assigned by the English military authority to be tried by court martial. These court-martials were held at Richmond Barracks and commenced on May 2nd.

The president of the court was Brigadier General Charles Blackader who was assisted by Lieutenant-Colonel George German and Colonel William John Kent.

The court-martials contravened the military code in several respects. They were held in secret and the prisoners were forbidden to have defence counsel. Furthermore, those prosecuting the prisoners had also taken part in the suppression of the Rebellion which meant that from the outset they were automatically prejudiced against the defendants.

The Court martial charge levelled against the defendants was as follows; "Did take part in an armed rebellion and in the waging of war against His Majesty the King, such act being of such a nature as to be calculated to be prejudicial to the Defence of the Realm and being done with the intention of and for the purpose of assisting the enemy."[377] A small number of the defendants would also be charged with inciting disaffection against His Majesty the King.

This charge, with such a wide scope could have been levelled against any of those involved in the rebellion. General Maxwell assured the public that his intention was to punish the ringleaders, but in spite of this assurance, men like Willie Pearse, Michael O'Hanrahan and John McBride[I] who had no input into the planning of the rising and were not commanders were sentenced to death. In total ninety defendants were sentenced to death.

---

[I] In John McBride's case the motive for his execution may have been his role in Boer War, where he had held the rank of Major in the Irish Brigade of the Boer Army.

Following the executions of Theobald Wolfe Tone in 1798 and Robert Emmett in 1803 they had become national heroes and martyrs for Irish independence. In the aftermath of the Young Ireland Rebellion of 1848 and the Fenian Rebellion of 1867, the government had decided that the creation of further Irish martyrs would be an unwise political move. In the aftermath of the Easter Rebellion, in which the rebels had fought a clean fight, there was no great public outcry in England for executions. Nevertheless the authorities dismissed any political consequences that might follow and commenced a daily series of executions.

However, as day after day more executions were announced, the public mood in Ireland that had, up to this point, condemned the rebellion began to change to one of sympathy for the rebels and outrage against the government. This outrage spread rapidly – to Irish soldiers serving in British uniform on the continent, to the United States and to sections of the English media. From the United States the British Ambassador reported: "...it is most unfortunate that it has been found necessary to execute the rebels... the attitude towards England has been changed for the worse by recent events..."[378]

From the Western front, Lieutenant Thomas Kettle, who was a former Nationalist M.P wrote home: "These men (the rebels) will go down in history as heroes and martyrs; and if I go down – if I go down at all – as a bloody British officer."[379]

Due to pressure from the government, General Maxwell was forced to commute the remaining sentences after fourteen executions by firing squad had taken place in the capital and one in Cork.

Among the leaders and commanders, only two escaped the death sentence, Commandant Eamonn deValera and Thomas Ashe. Both of these men were sentenced to death on May 8th but their sentences were commuted. Constance Markievicz, was also sentenced to death by court martial but the sentence recommended mercy and clemency on account of her being a female and was immediately commuted.

While most[I] of the prisoners did not deny taking part in the rebellion, the charge of it being done for the purpose of assisting England's (German) enemy was repudiated.

The executions took place in the Stonebreakers Yard at Kilmainham Gaol.

All those executed at Kilmainham Jail received the last rites from the Capuchin friars of Church St.[II] or the prison chaplain Fr. Eugene McCarthy.

James Connolly, who had ceased to practice the Catholic faith some decades before, returned to the Church in the days before his death.[III] Fr. Augustine recalled that shortly before Pearse was executed: "I said (to Pearse) I am sure you will be glad to know that I gave Holy Communion to James Connolly this morning." I can't forget the fervour with which, looking up to heaven he said: "Thank God, it was the one thing I was most anxious about…"[380]

---

[I] Michael Mallin denied all the charges proffered by the court.

[II] Fr. Albert Bibby, Fr. Aloysius Travers, Fr. Sebastian O'Brien, Fr. Augustine Hayden and Fr. Columbus Murphy.

[III] Before his death, James Connolly asked his wife Lillie to receive instruction in the Catholic faith. She was received into the Catholic Church on August 15th 1916.

## Lessons in Dying

"Our deeds of the last week are the most splendid in Ireland's history. People will say hard things of us now but we shall be remembered by posterity and blessed by unborn generations."
– Patrick Pearse

### May 3rd - Patrick Pearse

Patrick Pearse was the first to be executed on May 3rd at 3.30am.

Shortly before he was executed he wrote one final letter to his mother from his cell in Kilmainham Gaol: "…I have just received Holy Communion. I am happy except for the great grief of parting from you. This is the death I should have asked for if God had given me the choice of all deaths, - to die a soldier's death for Ireland and for freedom. We have done right. People will say hard things of us now. Do not grieve for all this, but think of it as a sacrifice which God asked of me and of you."

### May 3rd -Thomas MacDonagh

Hours before his execution Thomas MacDonagh wrote a statement from his cell in which he bade farewell to his family and appealed for financial help for them. Of the rising he wrote: "I have been actuated by one motive only, the love of my country, the desire to make her a sovereign independent state. I still hope and pray that my acts may have for consummation her lasting freedom and happiness…I am ready to die, and I thank God that I die in so holy a cause."[381]

In July 1916 Fr. Aloysius who had ministered to him wrote: "He received the last rites of his Church with the utmost reverence from a priest who was his friend; he knelt for a long time in prayer on the bare floor of his cell in Kilmainham Jail with the Crucifix clasped in his hands…Thomas MacDonagh died as he had lived, with no rancour in his heart, with his courage high and unshaken, and with a firm faith in the Saviour by whose Precious Blood we are redeemed. May he rest in peace..."[382.]

## May 3rd – Tom Clarke

Tom Clarke's wife Kathleen (who was a sister of Ned Daly) was a prisoner in Dublin Castle. In the hours before her husband's death she was brought to see him. She later described how her husband told her he was relieved that he was to be executed instead of being sent back to prison. He gave her a message addressed to the Irish people:

"I and my fellow-signatories believe we have struck the first blow for freedom. The next blow, which we have no doubt Ireland will strike, will win through. In this belief we die happy."[383]

## May 4th – Edward (Ned) Daly

In the hours before his death Ned Daly was visited by three of his sisters, Kathleen (whose husband Tom had been executed the previous day) Madge and Laura. They found him lying on the floor of his cell. Madge later recalled: "He looked more like a brave young knight who had won some great victory...and so he had, of course, for he and his comrades had saved the soul of Ireland." "My first words were: Oh! Ned! Why are they giving you the highest honours? You must have done great work to earn a place with Tone and Emmett and all the others. He said "I did my best." Then he spoke of the great fight and, in glowing terms, of all the men, especially those in his own command. Such soldiers, such heroes, never lived, he said. They never lost heart until the order to surrender came. Then big, strong men cried like children and rebelled too, against the order. Speaking of himself, he said he was glad and proud to die for his country; that he knew that the week's fight would bring new life to Ireland; that he felt an absolute conviction, facing his God in a few hours, that the next effort would bring victory; that his only regret was that he would not be there to take part in it."[384]

One of the Capuchin priests recalled: "I remember well seeing him coming down from the prison cell where he had been to Confession and received Holy Communion. He was calm and brave as when he was with his men in the Church Street area…As I shook his hand for the last time I felt intensely all that was meant by marching out blindfolded to his death, such a gentle, noble, brave young Irishman."

### May 4th – Willie Pearse

Willie's sister Margaret recalled that when she and her mother visited him: "(We) found Willie standing, ready to receive us. There were three military officers with him, each holding a candle, the only available light. We talked quietly, calmly, and chiefly on personal matters – some letters and books about which Willie was anxious. We told him how proud we were of him and of Pat, and that we were satisfied they had done right."[385]

Fr. Augustine recalled: "He was beautifully calm, made his confession as if he were doing it on an ordinary occasion and received Holy Communion with great devotion. A few minutes later he stood before the firing squad and, with Our Lord in his heart, went to meet his noble brother in a better land."

### May 4th – Michael O'Hanrahan

After his execution his sister Eily recalled: "Micheál's cell – it was No.67 – was in absolute darkness and was empty except for a bucket and a sack on the floor in one corner. We rushed forward into Micheál's outstretched arms. (He)…was his usual calm self. He seemed to have no fear of death awaiting him. His chief concern was his mother and us his sisters...He...sent...to mother and to our sister, who had stayed behind with her, "his heart's love and his promise to remember them in God's home above." (I) managed to say quietly: "Ned Daly is going with you at dawn.""[386]

## May 4th – Joseph Mary Plunkett

Joseph Mary Plunkett was married to his fiancée Grace Gifford in the prison chapel Kilmainham, on the night of May 3rd by the prison chaplain Fr. Eugene McCarthy. Although parted immediately after the ceremony, Grace Plunkett was allowed to visit her husband in the presence of soldiers for ten minutes shortly before his execution. On his way to the Stonebreakers Yard he told Fr. Sebastian: "Father, I am very happy. I am dying for the glory of God and the honour of Ireland." Fr. Augustine later wrote: "He was there, his hands tied behind his back, waiting to face the firing squad...I noted his courteous "Thank you Father"; his face reminded me of St. Francis and "Welcome, Sister Death." He was absolutely calm, as cool and self-possessed as if he looked on what was passing and found it good. No fine talk. No heroics. A distinguished tranquillity- that came from his nobility of soul and his faith – nothing more."

## May 5th - John MacBride,

Fr. Augustine recalled: "On reaching the prison I was immediately shown to a cell and on its being opened I gripped the hand of Major MacBride. He was as quiet and natural as ever. His very first words expressed sorrow for the surrender, and then he went on quickly to say that on his asking for water to have a wash a soldier had brought him a cupful. "I suppose," he added with a smile, "they think I could wash with that much." He began his confession with the simplicity and humility of a child. After a few minutes I gave him Holy Communion and we spent some time in prayer. I told him I would be with him to the last and that I would anoint him when he fell."

When John MacBride was already blindfolded and had the piece of paper pinned on his heart as a target for the soldiers Fr. Augustine recalled: "...I whisper in his ear: "We are all sinners. Offer up your life for any faults or sins of the past." And this brave man, fearless of death, responds like a child, yet firmly: "I'm glad you told me that, Father. I will."[387]

## May 8th - Sean Heuston

To his sister May, who was a Dominican nun in Galway he wrote: "The priest was with me and I received Holy Communion this morning...I have no vain regrets...If you really love me teach the children in your class the history of their own land..."[388.]

Fr. Albert recalled: "He was perfectly calm and said with me for the last time: "My Jesus mercy." I scarcely had moved away a few yards when a volley went off, and this noble soldier of Irish Freedom fell dead. I rushed over to anoint him; his whole face seemed transformed and lit up with a grandeur and brightness that I had never before noticed...never did I realise that men could fight so bravely and die so beautifully and so fearlessly as did the heroes of Easter Week. On the morning of Séan Heuston's death I would have given the world to have been in his place, he died in such a noble and sacred cause, and went forth to meet his Divine Saviour with such grand Christian sentiments of trust, confidence and love."[389]

## May 8th - Eamonn Ceannt

Following his court martial Eamonn Ceannt wrote to his wife: "Trial closed. I expect the death sentence which better men have already suffered. I only regret that I have now no longer an opportunity of showing how I think of you now, that the chance of seeing you again is so remote. I shall die like a man for Ireland's sake."[390]

To those who he knew would follow the path which he had taken, he had the following advice: "...never to treat with the enemy, never to surrender at his mercy but to fight to a finish."[391]

In his final letter to his wife an hour before his execution he wrote: "...I am here without hope of this world and without fear, calmly awaiting the end. I have had Holy Communion and Fr. Augustine has been with me and will be back again...I remember all and I banish all that I may be strong and die bravely. I have one hour to live, then God's judgement and, through his infinite mercy, a place near your poor Grannie and my mother and father and Jem and all the fine old Irish Catholics who went through the scourge of similar misfortune from this Vale of Tears into the Promised Land."[392]

### May 8th - Michael Mallin

On May 7th Michael Mallin wrote a long farewell letter to his wife: "...I do not believe our blood has been shed in vain. I believe Ireland will come out greater and grander but she must not forget that she is Catholic, She must keep her faith. I find no fault with the soldiers or police. I forgive them from the bottom of my heart, pray for all the souls who fell in this fight Irish & English. God and his Blessed Mother take you and my dear ones under their care a husband's blessing on your dear head my loving wife a father's blessing on the heads of my children...."[393.]

Hours before his death, his wife and four small children visited him in his prison cell. His wife was five months pregnant with their fifth child, Maura Constance.

## May 8th - Con Colbert

To his sister Lila he wrote: "I did not like to call you to the Gaol to see me before I left this world because I felt it would grieve us both too much, so I am just dropping you a line to you to forgive me anything I do owe you and to say "Goodbye" to you and all my friends and to get you and them to say a prayer for my soul. Perhaps I'd never get the chance of knowing when I was to die again and so I'll try and die well. I received this morning & hope to do so again before I die. Pray for me, ask Fr. Devine & Fr. Healy & Fr. O'Brien to say a Mass for me also any priests you know. May God help us – me to die well – you to bear the sorrow. I am your loving brother, Conn."[394]

## May 12th – James Connolly

James Connolly's eldest daughter Nora recalled: "On Sunday afternoon a note was let in the letter-box addressed to Mama. It read: "If Mrs. Connolly will call at Dublin Castle Hospital on Monday or Tuesday at 11 o'clock she can see her husband." Mama was in terror that Papa's time had come but everyone had been telling her that the fact of his being wounded was a good thing for him; that as long as he was wounded he would not be executed; that by the time he was well again public feeling would be so strong that the authorities would hesitate to shoot him…They'll never execute a wounded man was the cry. …I said to Papa that there was great talk among the people that because he was wounded he wouldn't be executed but he said "No. No…I remember what happened to Scheepers[1] in South Africa. He was wounded and they

---

[1] Commandant Gideon Scheepers was a member of the Boer Commando that invaded Cape Colony at the beginning of the Second Boer War. He was captured by the British on October 12th 1901 in the Ladysmith District. Although suffering from appendicitis and enteric fiver the British executed him for war crimes whilst tied to a chair on January 18th 1902.

executed him. That will have no effect on what they decide to do and that's that."

At one' clock in the morning of May 12th a British army lorry arrived at the Connolly household. The officer conveyed the message that "James Connolly wishes to see his wife and eldest daughter."

Nora later recalled: "When we were shown in Papa said: "Well Lily, I suppose you know what this means?" She said: "Oh no, Jim. Oh no!"…Papa said: "I fell asleep for the first time tonight and they wakened me up at eleven and told me I was to die at dawn."…One thing he said to Mama I remember: "The Socialists will never understand why I am here. They will all forget I am an Irishman."[395]

James Connolly's shattered leg was encased in a cage. He was very weak. He was first transferred from Dublin Castle to Kilmainham and was carried to the Stonebreakers Yard on a stretcher with a British Army surgeon attending and then transferred to a chair. Due to his wounds he was unable to sit in the chair. He was tied to the chair for the execution, his body resting on it at an angle of around forty five degrees. The surgeon asked him if he would pray for him and those who were about to execute him. James Connolly replied: "Yes, Sir, I'll pray for all brave men who do their duty according to their lights."[396]

May 12th - Sean Mac Diarmada.

Shortly before his execution Seán Mac Diarmada penned a short statement: "I, Seán Mac Diarmada, before paying the penalty of death for my love of Ireland, and abhorrence of her slavery, desire to make known to all my fellow-countrymen that I die, as I have lived, bearing no malice to any man, and in perfect peace with almighty God. The principles for which I give my life are so sacred that I now walk to my death in the most calm and collected manner. I meet death for Ireland's cause as I have worked for the same cause all my life. I have asked the Rev. E McCarthy who has prepared me to meet my God and who has given me the courage to face the ordeal I am about to undergo, to convey this message to my fellow-countrymen. God save Ireland."[397]

## The Trial and Execution of Thomas Kent

### The Battle of Bawnard House

In the aftermath of the Rising, all over the country the R.I.C proceeded to round up many of those involved in the I.R.B, the Irish Volunteers and Sinn Fein.

In the early hours of the morning of Tuesday May 2nd, 1916, a party of R.I.C men under the command of Head Constable Rowe surrounded Bawnard House, at Castlelyons, Co. Cork which was the home of the Kent family. Inside the house were 84 year old Mrs Kent and her four sons William, Richard, David and Thomas who held in the house a number of volunteer weapons.

After refusing to surrender, a fire-fight ensued between the occupants of the house and the constables during which Mrs. Kent assisted her sons by reloading their guns. During the battle Rowe was killed while David Kent was seriously wounded.

As the battle continued, the R.I.C. summoned British army reinforcements from nearby Fermoy. After a standoff lasting four hours the Kents surrendered. While Mrs. Kent and her sons emerged from the house, Richard Kent attempted to escape but was shot and seriously wounded.

### The Execution of Thomas Kent

Following the battle, both David and Richard were escorted to a military hospital where Richard died two days later. While Mrs. Kent was released the same day, Thomas and William Kent were taken to Cork Detention Barracks where both men were tried by court-martial on May 4th for the murder of Head Constable Rowe. William was acquitted while Thomas was found guilty and sentenced to death, the sentence being carried out at the Barracks on May 9th.

Thomas Kent was attended by the Chaplain of Cork Military Hospital, Fr. John Sexton to whom he gave his Pioneer Temperance Badge asking him to give it to Fr. Ahearne of Castlelyons who had presented it to him. Just before his execution Thomas Kent was offered alcohol in order to preserve his courage. He replied: "I have been a total abstainer all my life and a total abstainer I'll die. I have done my duty as a soldier of Ireland and in a few moments I hope to see the face of my God."[398]

In 1925 the commander of the firing squad, Hereward T. Price recalled that Thomas Kent died "very bravely...not a feather out of him."[399]

## The Trial and Execution of Roger Casement

Following his arrest at McKenna's Fort, Roger Casement was taken from the local R.I.C. Barracks at Ardfert to Arbour Hill Barracks in Dublin. As a Knight of the Realm there would be no court-martial for him. He was transferred first to Brixton Prison and then to the Tower of London. In London a charge of High Treason awaited him at the High Court of Justice. This trial took place between the 26th and the 29th June 1916. The prosecuting counsel was the Attorney General, Sir F.E. "Galloper" Smith, a disciple of Carson's who had previously declared that he would not recognise any law that provided home rule for Ulster.

### "Hanged on a Comma"

As Roger Casement's "treason" had been committed in Germany, and the only provision in law which would allow him to be hanged for treason had to be for treason committed within the Empire, the prosecution were forced to resurrect a centuries old provision dating back to Norman times when the King of England also had French possessions. This Norman French document was unpunctuated and, as read, still would not allow Casement to be hanged. The prosecution put forward the case that a comma should be inserted into the centuries old document, altering its meaning to allow for treason committed whenever the acts were done. The prosecution's affirmation was granted by the Crown.

## Speech from the dock

Roger Casement was, as expected, found guilty of high treason on June 29th. Before the sentence of death was passed, the Judge, as required, asked Casement if he had anything to say. Casement then read a long speech from the dock that he had written while in custody. After asserting that the court did not have the jurisdiction to try him, Casement added "...But for the Attorney-General of England there is only "England" – there is no Ireland, there is only the law of England – no right of Ireland; the liberty of Ireland and of Irishmen is to be judged by the power of England. Yet for me, the Irish outlaw, there is a land of Ireland, a right of Ireland...Conquest my Lord, gives no title, and if it exists over the body, it fails over the mind. It can exert no empire over men's reason and judgement and affections; and it is from this law of conquest without title to the reason, judgement, and affection of my own countrymen that I appeal...That blessed word "Empire" that bear so paradoxical a resemblance to charity! For if charity begins at home, "Empire means in other men's homes and both may cover a multitude of sins. I for one was determined that Ireland was much more to me than "Empire," and that if charity begins at home so must loyalty...In Ireland alone in this twentieth century is loyalty held to be a crime..."[400.]

### His Conversion and death

After being sentenced to death, Roger Casement was taken to Pentonville Prison, as an appeal was still in prospect. Protestant by birth, he longed to spend his last days in the company of an Irishman. For this reason, on his arrival at Pentonville he declared his wish to become a Roman Catholic. When the Catholic Chaplain of Pentonville Prison, an Irishman, Fr. Thomas Carey, came to his cell, he explained to Casement that he could not be baptised a Catholic, unless he be convinced that the Catholic Church was the one true church of Christ and that his duty to God lay in his becoming a Catholic. For days Roger Casement and Fr. Carey talked, debated and argued. At length Roger Casement became convinced that the Catholic Church was the one true Church of Christ and was, just before his execution received into the Church and Her sacraments.

On the evening before his death he wrote: "If I die tomorrow, bury me in Ireland, and I shall die in the Catholic faith, for I accept it fully now. It tells me what my heart sought long – but I saw it in the faces of the Irish. Now I know what it was I loved in them – the chivalry of Christ speaking through human eyes. It is from that source all lovable things come, for Christ was the first Knight...God gave me into this captivity and death, and I kiss the Divine Hand that leads me to the grave...And now good-bye. I still write with hope – hope that God will be with me to the end...And if I die as I think is fated, tomorrow morning, I shall die with my sins forgiven and God's pardon on my soul and I shall be with many brave and good men...Surely it (Ireland's) is the most glorious cause in history....Ever defeated yet undefeated"[401].

On the morning of his execution Roger Casement thanked Fr. Carey for bringing him to the true faith and told him that he "wholly accepted, wholly believed and wholly trusted in the Divine Plan – Christ's Catholic Church"[402]. He told Fr. Carey that although it was the morning of his execution, he desired to live a few years longer if only to show that he was a loyal Catholic and that he had become a Catholic out of conviction.

Roger Casement's final words at the place of execution were: "Into Thy hands, O Lord, I commend my spirit. Lord Jesus, receive my soul."[403]

# Chapter 18

# After the Battle

## Mass Imprisonment

Following the Easter Rebellion the majority of internees were imprisoned in Kilmainham Gaol and Richmond Barracks, their accommodation consisting of bare cells with around 30 people to a room. The number of incarcerated included almost 3,500 men and around 80 women, many of whom had not taken part in the Rebellion but were rounded up afterwards. There was madness in the method of the government as the overcrowded prison cell in which the men were interned became, according to one internee "…the University in which the doctrines, methods and hopes of the men of Easter Week were folded into the life of men from every part of Ireland."[404]

Of the number arrested 1,706 were deported to Britain. The scene of the mass deportations was the first sign that the rebels had, that the mood of at least a section of the public had changed since the executions. Many people turned out to see them off, cheering them and attempting to put gifts of food and tobacco in their pockets, as their hands were manacled.

While the leaders were separated from the rank and file and imprisoned mostly in Dartmoor, (this number included Arthur Griffith, Thomas Ashe, Éamonn de Valéra, Eoin Mac Néill, and William Cosgrave) many of the rank and file were to end up in Frongoch, an internment camp in Wales. The I.R.B. men in Frongoch were led by Michael Collins, who quickly realised that this was an ideal opportunity to prepare the men for the future. Contacts were established and information gathered on people who would help the Volunteers such as policemen who were sympathetic to the cause of Irish freedom and would pass on useful information. Educational classes like the learning of spoken Irish were also organised being interspersed with military subjects such as guerrilla warfare.

## "A Nefarious Scheme"

As the attitude of the American public hardened against the British government in the aftermath of the Rebellion, the prospect of America joining the English in their war against Germany receded. To the British cabinet something needed to be done and done quickly to reverse this trend before that November's presidential election when the Minister for Munitions, David Lloyd George feared that "…the Irish-American vote will go over to the German side…unless something is done even provisionally, to satisfy America."[405]

David Lloyd George

Entrusted by the Cabinet with the resolution of the "Irish Question" Lloyd George returned to the pre-war proposal for the partitioning of Ireland determined to give the Unionists of Ulster, not just the four counties of Ulster in which they were in a majority but also the counties of Tyrone and Fermanagh in which the Catholics held a slender majority, as Unionists would be in a majority of the six county entity. The other three Ulster counties of Cavan, Monaghan and Donegal all contained large Catholic majorities, and would have to excluded, as this would tip the balance in favour of the Catholics.

From the outset Lloyd George worked hand-in-glove with the leader of the Ulster Unionists, Sir Edward Carson and his amending bill was couched in language full of ambiguity: "The Bill is to remain in force during the continuance of the war and a period of twelve months thereafter; but if Parliament has not by that time made further and permanent provision for the Government of Ireland, the period for which the Bill is to remain in force is to be extended by Order…"[406]

To Sir Edward Carson, Lloyd George confided: "My dear Carson…we must make it clear that at the end of the provisional period Ulster does not, whether she wills it or not, merge into the rest of Ireland."[407]

When Lloyd George and Carson had sorted out everything between them, the government informed John Redmond of the proposed terms of the future governance of Ireland legislation. John Redmond, aware that the public mood was changing away from his party and home rule, was desperate to get some form of home rule bill passed before the tide turned against him for good as only home rule as an accomplished fact could restore the political initiative to him.

At a meeting of the M.Ps of the Irish Parliamentary Party Redmond threatened to resign unless the members of his party supported Lloyd George's plan. However the forced approval of his party now backfired as when the legislation became public there was national outrage especially among the Catholics and nationalists of Ulster. Mass meetings followed and the members of the I.P.P were roundly condemned for their acquiescence in what Bishop McHugh of Derry termed a "nefarious scheme".[408]

When the proposed Bill came before the Commons in early July of 1916, the mask of short-lived exclusion for the six counties which Prime Minister Asquith had worn for

Redmond's benefit was finally dropped. In reply to a question by Edward Carson, Asquith informed the House that under the Bill, Home Rule for Ireland would not impact upon the six counties without a further bill being introduced into the House while Lord Landsdowne assured the House of Lords that the exclusion of the six counties from the provisions of the bill was both "permanent and enduring".[409]

With the electoral quicksand on which the Irish Parliamentary Party stood now threatening to swallow them up, Redmond once more turned the I.P.P. about-face in an effort to save face. Forced by national outrage to withdraw the support of the Irish Parliamentary Party from the proposed Bill, it appeared the Bill was now dead in the water as it could not proceed without Irish support.

Lloyd George's secret deal with Carson also had the effect of causing division within Irish Unionism as a whole. By advancing the cause of Unionism within six of Ulster's counties, Carson was cutting loose the Unionists in the rest of the country, leaving them to a future he wanted no part of, which was something most of them resented. The majority of southern Unionists felt that Unionism should remain united and participate within an Irish Home Rule parliament which would have a great many safeguards for the Unionist minority. Committed to the Ulster Unionists, Lloyd George was not for turning and bided his time. After taking over from Asquith as Prime Minister he promoted Sir Edward Carson to his war cabinet as Minister without Portfolio.

# Chapter 19

# A Changing Political Landscape

### The First Prisoners Are Released

Since the suppression of the Rebellion, events of the English Government's own making had conspired to arouse public feeling in favour of the Easter Rebellion. The executions, the influx of thousands of troops along with nationwide martial law, and now the formal admission by the Government that the ultimate sacrifice paid by so many Irishmen in British uniform was not to warrant the introduction of Home Rule as initially promulgated, all had a cumulative effect. With each passing week more and more people viewed the paltry freedoms which home rule might grant with disdain. New life stirred within the seeds sown by the rebels of Easter Week.

As the result of Lloyd George's machinations during the Summer of 1916, his determined effort to partition Ireland resulted in the formation of the "Irish Nation League" in August 1916 whose members consisted in the main of disaffected I.P.P supporters determined to fight partition. Like Sinn Fein, the League pledged that any of its members who were elected to Westminster would refuse to take their seats. However the new movement was too similar to the original incarnation of Sinn Fein and did not garner much public support. In the first by-election after the Rising which took place in west-Cork at the end of the year, the I.P.P candidate was successfully returned ahead of the Sinn Fein candidate who finished third.

When the first prisoners were released at Christmas of 1916, as a sop by the new British administration (led by Lloyd George) to American public opinion,[1] those released included Michael Collins who immediately became the secretary for the National Aid Association which had been formed in the aftermath of the Rebellion to help the families of the dead and imprisoned. As well as offering assistance, under Collins's leadership the Association was now used for political reorganisation.

On his return to Ireland, Collins found a national network organised as "Gaelic League Branches" already in place which existed solely for the purposes of advancing the cause of total freedom from English rule. Showing his penchant for organisation Collins seized upon this nucleus and began expanding it. By the Spring of 1917 the Irish Volunteers were re-forming in earnest along with the women's auxiliary corps; Cumann na mBan.

## Electoral Victories for a New Force in Irish Politics

Following the death of the Irish Parliamentary Party M.P for Roscommon, J.J. O'Kelly, a by-election was called for the beginning of February 1917. Seeing in this election the ideal opportunity for Irish nationalism to gain a foothold, a group of disaffected I.P.P supporters and Republicans led by Fr. O'Flanagan approached the father of Joseph Plunkett, who had been executed following the rebellion. A Papal Count, George Plunkett agreed to allow his name be put on the ballot paper. Those who had nominated him along with many I.R.B members in the parishes of Roscommon now began a large canvassing campaign.

---

[1] At this time Lloyd George was attempting to woo the United States government into the First World War on England's side.

On January 22nd 1917, President Woodrow Wilson of the United States had addressed Congress on the possibility of the U.S entering the war on the Allied side. He told his audience that American intervention and a subsequent Allied victory would bring "...government by the consent of the governed" to Europe. His words were now seized upon by the burgeoning Irish nationalist movement and in his pre-election speeches, Count Plunkett advocated that Ireland should receive the same treatment that Wilson promised for all Europe.

George Noble Plunkett

Plunkett's words struck a definite chord with the electorate and when the votes were counted following the election, Count Plunkett received 3,000 votes, while the I.P.P candidate received 1,700.

Following Plunkett's victory, Dublin Castle meticulously applied the Coercion Act then in force resulting in the incarceration or re-incarceration of many leading republicans along with hefty fines or imprisonment for anyone who distributed seditious materials, sang disloyal songs, refused to give their name in English or proclaimed their loyalty to the Republican cause.

Meanwhile in London, David Lloyd George told a meeting at the Guild Hall that "...to have a well-knit and powerful Empire, we must convert Ireland from a suspicious, surly and dangerous neighbour to a secure and friendly Ireland."[410]

When the first anniversary of the rebellion came around at Easter 1917, the Crown Forces were incapable of dealing with the demonstrations which marked the events of one year which threatened to change the Irish political landscape forever.

Among those who commemorated the first anniversary of the rebellion there remained many different views on the way forward. While all agreed that the day of the Irish Parliamentary Party was at an end, there were differences as to what direction the Irish people should now take. At a nationalist convention called by Arthur Griffith following Plunkett's victory, Griffith, a pacifist, remained implacable that the original Sinn Fein policy of Dual Monarchy was the correct path forward while Republicans urged that the country should fulfil the aims of the Easter patriots, especially now that the sword of partition hung over the country. A definitive turning point in this national debate was reached when, in the South-Longford by-election of May 9th 1917 the avowed republican Joseph McGuinness, then a prisoner in Lewes Jail, was elected. All over the country his victory was celebrated with bonfires and parades. The people of Longford appeared to have spoken for the people of Ireland – the Republican path was the way forward. The transition of Sinn Féin from the policies devised by Griffith to one which embraced the politics and aspirations of the Easter Rebellion, was underway.

## Lloyd George Announces a National Convention

Seeing public opinion in Ireland turning against home rule, Lloyd George attempted to upset the consensus by announcing an Irish National Convention to decide the question of Ireland's future within the Empire. Once more, Lloyd George was undertaking a measure for American consumption[1], and

---

[1] On January 14th, 1917, an interview with the prominent Conservative Unionist F.E (Galloper) Smith appeared in The Boston Globe. Smith, who was the Attorney General for England and Wales inadvertently divulged how the

by declaring that the Unionists of Ulster would have the same number of "hand-picked" candidates as the rest of the country and that they should not be bound by its decisions, he had also decided its outcome – stalemate - after which he should have to intervene to impose a "settlement" of what was commonly referred to in Westminster as "The Irish Question".

While Redmond agreed that his Party would participate in the Convention, Arthur Griffith, whose Sinn Fein Party had been allotted five out of the one hundred and one Convention seats, announced he was boycotting it, telling the Irish people that: "He (Lloyd George) is armed to assure the world that England left the Irish to settle the question of government for themselves and they could not agree."[411] Griffith's opinion was shared by many others who also decided to boycott the Convention. By the time the Convention (which was chaired by the agricultural reformer Horace Plunkett) held its first meeting in Trinity College at the end of July 1917, ninety percent of those attending were in favour of partition.[I]

## DeValera is elected to the British Parliament

As part of the preparatory measures leading up to the Convention, Lloyd George agreed to release the remainder of the mostly high ranking republican prisoners, whose continued incarceration were seen as conflicting with the apparent chief aim of his Convention; that the future of Ireland should be decided by Irishmen.[II] Already one of the prisoners

---

members of the Convention had been basically employed by Lloyd George for one guinea a day to keep talking until the United States should enter the war.
[I] Members of the Convention were entitled to post letters for free at a special Convention post office established at Trinity College. General Crozier afterwards revealed that Dublin Castle made copies of all letters sent by Nationalist members before sending on the letters to the recipients.
[II] This move was insisted on by Horace Plunkett as a condition for his assuming the role of Chair of the Convention.

(Joe McGuinness) had been elected as an M.P, while another, Éamonn deValera, the last surviving Dublin Commandant of theEaster Rebellion, had been nominated to fight a by-election in East-Clare as a Sinn Féin candidate following the death in action on the Western Front of Major Willie Redmond M.P, (the brother of John Redmond) who was killed at Messines Ridge during the Third Battle of Ypres.

On June 16th, the newly released prisoners returned to Dublin where they received a tumultuous welcome, many of them finding it difficult to believe how the mood of the country had changed since they had departed for England.

Eamonn deValera

In East-Clare, DeValera's opponent was a lawyer and Crown Prosecutor, Patrick Lynch, who was the candidate for the Irish Parliamentary Party. From the area and well respected in the constituency, a sympathy vote could be expected for him on account of the death in action of Major Redmond. There was also a distinct element among Lynch's supporters who resented De Valera's being parachuted into the constituency and these men did not hesitate to stir up trouble at De Valera's campaign rallies.

The only topic during the campaign was the national way forward; Home Rule for a partitioned Ireland or the continuation of the struggle for an independent country. Assisted by the forces who had helped McGuinness to victory in the Longford by-election, DeValera left the people of East Clare in no doubt as to where he stood; for an independent 32 county nation, totally free from English interference. He told the people of Clare: "We want an Irish Republic because if

Ireland had her freedom, it is I believe the most likely form of government. But if the Irish people wanted another form of government, so long as it was an Irish government, I would not put in a word against it...Give Unionists a just and full share of representation but no more than their just share." DeValera also did not shy away from the prospect of future conflict: "You have no enemy but England...Although we fought once and lost, it is only a lesson for the second time...Every vote you give now is as good as the crack of a rifle in proclaiming your desire for freedom."[412]

In vain Lynch attempted to hold back the changing tide, even resorting to the threat of what England would do if this national trend continued. Polling day on July 10th saw a huge turn-out which saw deValera sweep to victory by 5,010 votes to 2,035 for Lynch.

Up and down the country, deValera, as the only surviving Commandant of the Easter Rebellion in Dublin, was now looked upon as the natural successor to Patrick Pearse. His victory in East-Clare coupled with the return of the prisoners saw a large increase in the drilling and parading of the Irish Volunteers whose ranks grew ever larger. As the Volunteers were without weapons, the men paraded and drilled in uniform with hurley sticks instead of rifles.

In August of 1917 there was another Sinn Féin by-election victory in Kilkenny city when William T. Cosgrave (who had his death sentence commuted following the Easter Rebellion) was elected following the death of yet another IPP member of parliament.

# Chapter 20

# The Emergence of a Republican Political Movement

## The Killing of Thomas Ashe

Following DeValera's election victory there was a marked increase in Government activity against the burgeoning national movement. Invoking the Defence of The Realm Act (DORA) all persons who were not members of the Crown Forces were banned from drilling, carrying offensive weapons or from wearing uniforms. Newspapers were suppressed and raids for both weapons and seditious materials ordered. The arrests encompassed many of the recently released. Following a speech at Ballinalee in Co. Longford, an arrest warrant was issued for Commandant Thomas Ashe, who had commanded the Volunteers during the Easter Rebellion at the successful Battle of Ashbourne. Only released on June 16th, he was now a wanted man on a charge of sedition. After a short time on the run, Ashe, who was now President of the I.R.B Supreme Council was arrested, found guilty and sentenced to two years hard labour among the common criminals in Mountjoy Jail. Along with his fellow Republican prisoners, Ashe demanded to be granted prisoner of war status on September 18th 1917. Following their refusal to grant this, the prison authorities retaliated against this "trouble making" by removing the beds, bedclothes and furniture from the cells of the Republican prisoners and also denying them their boots. Using the only weapon at their disposal, Ashe and his comrades immediately went on hunger strike upon which the prison authorities ordered that they be force-fed. Fearing that his men would suffer internal damage, the leader of the Republican prisoners, Austin Stack, told his men not to offer resistance during the force-feeding.

The procedure was more akin to torture than feeding and resulted in bleeding from the nose and throat, followed by swelling of the larynx and windpipe. The feeding tubes were not sterilised prior to use. According to Stack, the doctor used: "...more force than skill, gritting his teeth practically"[413] while after his force feeding on Sunday 23rd, Ashe remarked to the doctor that he was "sorry to see him reduce a noble profession to the level of an executioner"[414]

Thomas Ashe

In spite of the state of Ashe's health, the prison medical orderly declared him as; "fit for close confinement, fit for scale punishment no. 1 and 2. Also deprivation of mattress, fit for restraint in handcuffs, waist belt, muffs, restraint jacket or jacket in splints."[415]

Despite his swollen throat, Ashe was again subjected to force-feeding on Tuesday 25th during which the feeding liquid was forced into his lungs. After collapsing in the doctor's chair, he was transferred from Mountjoy Jail across the road to the Mater Hospital where he died a few hours later.

At the inquest which followed, the Prison Board refused to give evidence and a verdict of death due to the treatment he had received was returned. The jury also condemned the policy of force-feeding. Four days after Ashe's death, prisoners who were incarcerated because of breaching the Defence of the Realm Act were granted special status akin to prisoner of war status. However, a few weeks later this measure was reversed and by the beginning of 1918, Republican prisoners were once more on hunger-strike for special status.

Ashe's funeral, which was organised by The Wolfe Tone Memorial Committee, was in the tradition of the great Fenian funerals of Jeremiah O'Donovan Rossa and Terence MacManus but much larger, being the largest demonstration of Irish nationality since Daniel O'Connell's monster meeting at the Hill of Tara. However on this occasion there was outrage and anger because of the treatment Ashe had received while in custody. After the lying in state in City Hall where thousands had filed past the coffin which was surrounded by a guard of honour of Irish Volunteers, tens of thousands followed two hundred priests, Irish Volunteers, members of the Citizen Army along with members of all the Gaelic associations and clubs to Glasnevin Cemetery where Ashe was interred with full military honours. Of all that had occurred since the Easter Rebellion, the death of Thomas Ashe was a defining moment. Following his funeral The London Daily Express wrote that; "The Circumstances of his death and funeral have made 100,000 Sinn Feiners out of 100,000 constitutional nationalists"[416] while The Daily Mail commented that "Sinn Fein is pretty nearly another name for the vast bulk of the youth of Erin."[417]

## A New Sinn Fein and A New National Leader

In the aftermath of the Easter Rebellion, those who had been imprisoned and their supporters had no real political organisation of their own except for the secretive Irish Republican Brotherhood which could never be used to garner the widespread support needed to unseat the Irish Parliamentary Party as the voice of the Irish electorate.

The Easter Rebellion had been erroneously labelled by both Government and press as "The Sinn Fein Rebellion". In fact the political party which Arthur Griffith had founded, (which did not espouse a complete break with England, but rather a policy of "Dual Monarchy") was quite by accident becoming the political party of Irish nationalism in spite of the fact that it had nothing to do with the Rebellion. Many supporters of the Republic, especially among the Irish Volunteers, were unhappy with this situation and felt a clean break ought to be made with Sinn Fein, most of whose original policies were now seen as totally redundant. A split in the national movement beckoned, which DeValera wanted to avoid at all costs in order to achieve the greatest level of national unity possible and to keep both the military and political arms of the movement united, with the Volunteers under the control of the political leaders.

Prior to the annual Sinn Fein Convention (Árd-fheis) which was due to take place at the end of October, an agreement, along with a form of words was arrived at between the disparate elements among the national movement which would see the name Sinn Fein maintained, along with some good and useful Sinn Fein policies such as "Ireland First". The aim of an independent Irish Republic was formally adopted.[1]

---

[1] The agreement stated: (1) Sinn Féin aims at securing the international recognition of Ireland as an independent Irish Republic. (2) Having achieved that status the Irish people may by referendum freely choose their own form of government."

When the Sinn Féin Árd-fheis convened on October 25th, 1917, there were 1,700 delegates in attendance representing over 1,000 Sinn Fein local clubs (Cumann) scattered throughout the country. Prominent among the attendees was a good number of young priests "with the dust of Maynooth still on their boots"[418] Unlike many older priests and bishops who still supported the IPP, many of the younger generation had embraced the National Movement. It was a palpably momentous occasion as the delegates knew that the majority of the people of Ireland were behind them when they voted to; "Deny the right and oppose the will of the British Parliament and British Crown or any other foreign government to legislate for Ireland"[419] and to "Make use of any and every means available to render impotent the power of England to hold Ireland in subjection by military force or otherwise."[420]

When it came to the question of who would be the leader of the new Sinn Fein, Arthur Griffith, realising that he did not command the loyalty of the Volunteers, did not bring the issue to a vote, but instead withdrew[I] in favour of DeValera who in his acceptance speech quoted Grattan who almost 150 years earlier had attempted to establish an Irish nation governed by English and Anglo-Irish colonists: "We have nailed that flag to the mast; we shall never lower it...Esto perpetua!"[II]

Following the successful Sinn Fein Convention, a Convention of The Irish Volunteers was held at Croke Park on November 19th. Here also, deValera was returned as President while other appointments included Cathal Brugha as Chief of Staff, Michael Collins as Adjutant- General and Director of Organisation while Richard Mulcahy was appointed as Director of Training and Chief of Staff.

---

[I] Count Plunkett also withdrew in favour of DeValera.

[II] The Vice-Presidents were Fr. O'Flanagan and Arthur Griffith, Treasurers were Larry Ginnell and Liam Cosgrave, Secretaries were Darrell Figgis and Austin Stack

## Making a Start on the Undermining of British Rule

On October 23rd a debate on Ireland took place in the London House of Commons where the intentions of the government in continuing with its policies of suppression and repression were made abundantly clear. During the debate Henry Duke, the Chief Secretary for Ireland presented a: "blood-curdling picture of Irish rebellion and conspiracy"[421] while Lloyd George reinforced his recent rhetoric on "converting" Ireland by telling the members of the House that his government would continue to "suppress all attempts at incitement"[422] and that "...there is a great deal of talk among Sinn Feiners which does not mean Home Rule. It does not mean self-government. It means complete separation, it means secession. The words which are used are "sovereign independence." This country could not possibly accept that under any conditions."[423]

Before the Winter of 1917-18 had ended, Sinn Fein, through its national network of clubs was attempting to "render impotent the power of England" by intervening in landlord / tenant disputes and the ongoing food crisis which threatened to turn into yet another artificial famine. The food crisis was due to the demand for Irish foodstuffs in Britain and the enforcements of the government in this regard. Sinn Féin appointed its own National Food Controller, Diarmuid Lynch, and under his guidance, Sinn Féin Clubs took action. In the west of Ireland some Landlords were informed that sections of their land were being cleared of livestock so that small labourers could be provided with a small holding (conacre) for a reasonable rent which was given to the landlord. Other measures carried out by Sinn Fein were rationing schemes and the removal of livestock on transit to port, bound for England, in order that they be slaughtered to feed the local populace. The Volunteers also acted as an effective local police force in their areas and in some cases prevented locals from carrying out activities which threatened to descend into the "Whiteboy" actions of previous times.

As the weeks passed, the response of the Crown Forces to Sinn Féin activities grew more and more heavy handed with meetings being frequently broken up with the assistance of bayonet wielding soldiers resulting in both injury and death to some of those attending. Raids by the police were commonplace while heavy censorship was imposed on local newspapers and on some international mail. Some editors who defied the instructions of the Press Censor that the publishing of "comments of a nature likely to cause disaffection" would result in "grave risk to those responsible" had their offices raided, their printing apparatus smashed and their newspaper suppressed. Other editors attempted to keep within "the letter of the law" but twenty eight of these were forbidden from sending copies of their newspapers out of the country in an attempt to keep the true nature of the situation in Ireland out of the international press. At the end of February 1918, County Clare was declared a special military area resulting in an influx of British soldiers.

## The End of Lloyd George's Convention.

Meanwhile, Lloyd George's Convention on the future of Ireland was deadlocked. The Ulster Unionists were applying their "not an inch" motto in spite of the fact that both the Southern Unionist delegation and the I.P.P admitted concession after concession to the Ulster Unionists. As the deliberations continued, the Government, with an eye on the next general election, announced that it was redrawing the boundaries of Irish constituencies, which in effect was aimed at giving the Unionists a number of additional seats. The I.P.P were outraged but in spite of their protests the measure proceeded and only served to show once more how powerless the I.P.P were in Westminster.

At the Convention, the I.P.P had given into all the Unionist demands except one. The Ulster Unionists wanted the powers of Customs and Excise to remain with Westminster while the I.P.P insisted that they should be transferred to Dublin. Finally, to the dismay of his colleagues, Redmond gave in on this also but was forced to withdraw from the Convention due to ill-health. On February 25$^{th}$, Lloyd George dissolved the Convention, communicating to the members that all remaining issues including Customs must be deferred to the end of the war. The Convention had served Lloyd George's purpose and was now dissolved.

On March 6$^{th}$, John Redmond died and was replaced as leader of the I.P.P by a totally disillusioned John Dillon. When the by-election for John Redmond's seat was held a few weeks later, his son Captain Willie Redmond defeated the Sinn Fein candidate by 500 votes.

## Fighting Conscription

Since the outbreak of the Great War, all emigration to the United States from both Britain and Ireland had been halted, while many Irishmen in England who did not want to fight in the ranks of the British army had returned to Ireland to escape conscription. More young Irishmen were now living and working in Ireland than at any time since The Great Starvation. Ever since the Easter Rebellion,, the conscription of Irishmen into the British Army had been advocated in many quarters in England as a method of "solving" the rebellious atmosphere which had seized the country. Following the Sinn Féin Convention and the emergence of a united national front for a free and independent Ireland, these calls grew ever more frequent especially from the army, who according to John Dillon, saw conscription as a good way of killing Irishmen who would otherwise be in danger of fighting for Irish independence. Speaking at the beginning of December 1917,

Dillon told his audience how: "the military men have pressed on the government the policy of seizing these young fellows, scattering them among the English regiments and getting them to France, and if they did not fight there, shooting them."[424]

In mid-March of 1918, the German army launched a massive new military offensive on the Western Front. Called "Operation Michael", it was an effort to bring final victory for Germany before the United States Army arrived in France in overwhelming strength. Having introduced conscription in England in 1916, the government was desperate for more cannon-fodder to fill the ranks of the slaughtered, and now decided to take the risky step of introducing conscription in Ireland despite being warned by the Irish Secretary H.E Duke that they "might as well recruit Germans."[425] When Lloyd George announced the measure in Parliament at the beginning of April, he proclaimed that once the measure was introduced, the Government would (as a reward to the Irish people) make immediate preparations for the implementation of Home Rule in Ireland.

While conscription was (with the exception of the Unionists) universally opposed in Ireland, the very suggestion that Home Rule should be granted after conscription was introduced. was met with outrage by the I.P.P members in parliament who voted against the measure which passed on April 16th. The measure now only required the go-ahead from the government in order to be put into effect. Following the vote the I.P.P left the Commons in protest, returning to Ireland to assist with the organisation of the anti-conscription movement.

In Ireland, the idea that Home Rule would be offered in return for the introduction of conscription was greeted with derision. For those who wanted Ireland to be independent and free, the very idea of forced recruitment was anathema. Furthermore, in order to avert the introduction of a limited form of Irish

Home Rule, Republicans considered that conscription needed to be fought against by every means possible.

In Dublin, a broad based "National Cabinet"[1] against conscription quickly formed under DeValera's leadership, with both Sinn Fein and the I.P.P prominent among the leaders. An anti-conscription pledge drafted by DeValera was signed outside church doors on Sunday April 21st. In the pledge the authority of the British government to enforce conscription was denied, with the signatories vowing to "resist conscription by the most effective means at our disposal" because of "...Ireland's separate and distinct nationhood." On that Sunday all Masses offered throughout the country were for the intention that Ireland would be preserved from conscription. The Bishops also issued a joint statement describing the measure as an "oppressive and inhuman law which the Irish people have a right to resist by every means consonant with the law of God", while in Dublin the Trade Union Congress called a national strike for April 23rd. During this time the membership of the Irish Volunteers dramatically increased. Parades and training were held openly in an attempt to show the British the strength and solidarity of the opposition to conscription.

The Anti-Conscription Pledge

In the face of such opposition, the government, although still determined to enforce conscription hesitated and then decided

---

[1] This was the term used by DeValera to describe the alliance.

to replace the Viceroy, Lord Wimborne, with Field Marshal Lord French, who following his appointment, told his friend Lord Riddell: "If they leave me alone I can do what is necessary...If they (the conscripts) do not come we will fetch them."

Lord French also advised the government to send armoured cars and aeroplanes to Ireland to assist him in the enforcement of conscription. On April 25th DORA was amended. The definition of "persons of hostile origin" was altered to include persons of Irish birth.

## "The German Plot"

In Early April of 1917, a German U boat dropped a man named Joseph Dowling, off the Galway coast. Dowling, a former Connacht Ranger was a soldier in Roger Casement's now defunct Irish Brigade and had been sent to Ireland by the Germans in order to make contact with Sinn Féin, without the prior knowledge of any of the leaders of either Sinn Féin or the Irish Volunteers. While coming ashore Dowling had landed his dinghy on an island off-shore and had remained there until discovered by the RIC, who had held him in custody until they found out who he was. After determining that Dowling was a member of Casement's Irish Brigade he was then court-martialled and sentenced to penal servitude for life.

Despite the fact that there was no mention of a German / Irish conspiracy during Dowling's court-martial (during which he refused to offer any defence) the government decided to use this incident as a pretext to round up the leadership of Sinn Féin.

Following his arrival in Ireland in early May, Sir John French announced that the government had evidence of a "German Plot" within the Sinn Fein movement. On the night of May 17th a round-up of prominent members of Sinn Féin and the Volunteers commenced which continued into the following day. Michael Collins had fore-knowledge of the round-up from a Dublin Castle informant, and avoided arrest. Collins warned numbers of those who were detained including Éamon deValera of their imminent arrest but they recognised in this move another British government "own goal". Most made no attempt to go into hiding. They allowed themselves to be arrested and imprisoned knowing that the so-called "German Plot" was in fact a British Government plot. A total of 73 arrests of prominent Sinn Fein members took place after which Lord French issued a proclamation calling on all Irish people to "aid in crushing the said conspiracy". Ironically the English arrested those who were at the political end of Sinn Fein, while leaving those like Collins, Boland and Mulcahy who advocated force in ridding Ireland of the English.

Following the arrests, the government made no attempt to begin trial proceedings or to prove to the public the actual existence of "The German Plot" despite repeated calls for it to do so. The Irish leaders were now subject to internment with no definite release date.

## "Crush the National Movement"

If the government had hoped that Sinn Féin, bereft of its leadership, might now wither on the vine, it received a definite answer in mid June when Arthur Griffith (who was being interned in England) was returned as the MP for East Cavan with a majority of 1,500 votes over O'Hanlon, his IPP opponent.

Griffith's victory in Cavan coincided with an upsurge in Crown Forces activity which was ordered by Dublin Castle on May 28th. A secret order was issued to the RIC which read; "It is the desire of the government that vigorous measures be taken to deal effectively with the present activities of disloyally affected persons. It is expected that the police will be particularly vigilant in obtaining information, and that prompt action will follow."[426]

In early June, RIC and army patrols were dramatically increased in an effort to prevent drilling by the Volunteers. Parish halls in many areas were ordered shut. Spying was encouraged with informers being paid out of secret service funds while public rewards were offered for any information regarding the landing of weapons or their whereabouts. On June 15th twelve further counties[1] along with the cities of Limerick and Cork were declared as special military areas with all people arrested for disaffection in these areas being removed to Dublin for "special jury" trials. On June 18th agricultural fairs were banned along with political rallies.

On July 4th 1918 Dublin Castle declared that Sinn Féin, The Gaelic League, The Irish Volunteers and Cumann na mBan were dangerous associations. Their meetings were declared illegal. Furthermore anyone arrested at an illegal meeting was liable to receive a substantial prison sentence. Before the public had even heard of or digested the proclamations of July 4th, further measure were issued by Dublin Castle on July 5th banning; "the holding of or taking part in any meetings, assemblies, or processions in public places." In the explanatory note accompanying the order which was sent to all RIC districts for distribution, the police were ordered to break-up in particular all sports and cultural gatherings which resulted in many baton charges, injuries and arrests during the Summer of 1918. In mass-defiance of the order 1,500 hurling matches were played nationally on August 4th. Despite the fact that the country remained relatively peaceful and crime free, this government, like countless English governments and

---

[1] Westmeath, Tipperary, Sligo, Tyrone, Longford, Kerry, Cork, Limerick, Mayo, Galway, Queen's County (Laois) and King's County (Offaly).

monarchs before it, seemed determined to goad the people of Ireland into rebellion for their own ends.

## The End of The Great War

Such was the level of government induced anti-government sentiment during the Summer of 1918 that the authorities made no attempt to enforce conscription despite the entreaty of General Sir Henry Wilson that its implementation would be "both a war measure and a peace measure." Another Irish recruitment campaign was launched instead with its posters telling the Irish public that "…America will see Her (Ireland's) rights are secured" or "Ireland at the Front Looks to Ireland at Home to Answer the Call". The campaign was a dismal failure.

In France the arrival of tens of thousands of soldiers of the United States Army (a great number of whom were of Irish lineage) during the Summer of 1918 was finally turning the war in favour of the Allies. When the Americans achieved a decisive breakthrough in the Meuse-Argonne sector in the Autumn of 1918, the entire German front came under sustained pressure. Kaiser Wilhelm II now found the rug on which he was standing being pulled from under him by those behind him. Despite the fact that the German army remained deep in French territory, the German Home Front was collapsing and mutinies were breaking out in some units especially among the navy. By early November of 1918, the Kaiser was being forced to consider abdication. As Wilhelm departed into Dutch exile an armistice was being agreed between the warring parties for November 11th. At 11.11 am the war ended. Forty nine thousand men of Irish birth who had enlisted in the ranks of the British army had been killed along with thousands more in the ranks of the Allied armies. Many thousands more had suffered life changing injuries in "the war to end all wars."

# Chapter 21

## "Citizens of A Free and Gaelic Ireland"

"If you asked the people of Ireland what plan they would accept, by an emphatic majority they would say 'We want independence and an Irish Republic'." – David Lloyd George.

### The Establishment of Dáil Eireann
A National Plebiscite on the Way Forward
With the ending of hostilities on November 11th a general election beckoned. Determined to return as Prime-Minister of his coalition government, Lloyd George had once more assured the Unionists and the Conservative leader Andrew Bonar-Law of his de-facto commitment to partition Ireland, declaring that since his Convention had "failed" he had a right to introduce a settlement – Home Rule for Ireland with the exclusion of six of Ulster's counties. In a letter to Bonar Law, Lloyd George wrote: "I can support no settlement that would involve the forcible coercion of Ulster."[427] Regarding the immediate introduction of Home Rule, he demurred: "I recognize however that in the present condition of Ireland such an attempt could not succeed, and that it must be postponed until the condition of Ireland makes it possible. As to this last point, the Government will be chiefly guided by the advice it may receive from the Lord Lieutenant and the Irish Government."[428] Since the previous general election almost a decade before, the number of those entitled to vote had greatly increased because of the 1911 Electoral Reform Bill. For the first time the

electorate now included all males over twenty one, and all females of fixed dwelling over the age of thirty, while women were now allowed to stand as candidates for Parliament. In Ireland the effect of these changes was to see the electorate increased by two thirds.

On November 25th 1918 the House of Commons was dissolved pending the election which was fixed for December 14th. Sinn Féin was ready to contest the so-called "Khaki Election" despite the fact that many of its leaders remained in prison, its newspapers were banned and it was forbidden to hold election rallies. Of its seventy three election candidates, forty-seven were incarcerated, with some of the more prominent prisoners standing as the Sinn Fein candidate in more than one constituency.

The IPP, realising that it was in a fight for its very survival did not field a candidate in twenty-six constituencies in which it felt it had no chance of success while the Southern Unionists, who also wanted home rule for Ireland without partition also did not field a candidate in many constituencies.

With the depleted ranks of those with experience being filled by novices due to the mass incarceration, Sinn Féin nevertheless began its campaign with Robert Brennan as its Director of Elections. Almost immediately after the election was called, Brennan was arrested and his place was taken by James O'Mara.

In its election manifesto Sinn Fein set out the path it would take following the election;

"Sinn Féin aims at securing the establishment of (the) Republic;
1. By withdrawing the Irish Representation from the British Parliament, and by denying the right and opposing the will of the British Government or any other foreign government to legislate for Ireland.

2. By making use of any and every means available to render impotent the power of England to hold Ireland in subjection by military force or otherwise."

In the weeks leading up to the poll, Sinn Féin campaigning was clamped down on by the Crown Forces at every opportunity by further arrests and raids resulting in the seizure of election material and the destruction of printing and other equipment. When polling day arrived an effort was made by the Volunteers in some urban areas to "correct" the disadvantage given them by voting for those Irishmen whose names were on the register but were either dead or ill.

When the votes were counted after polling day, the margin of the Sinn Féin victory exceeded everybody's expectations, while the IPP vote had all but collapsed. Sinn Fein had garnered 70 percent of the national vote, winning 73 seats while the Unionists having the advantage of many constituencies being redrawn in their favour won 26. The IPP saw its eighty seats reduced to seven (six in Ireland along with a seat won in Liverpool). Its tally would have been even smaller but for an Ulster electoral pact, which saw Ulster's constituencies divided between the two parties so as not to split the nationalist vote Here, nationalists won a majority of the votes in five of Ulster's nine counties including Fermanagh and Tyrone, two of the six counties which Lloyd George was determined to place under the control of the Unionists.

### The First Dáil Convenes

Having received an overwhelming mandate from the electorate, the Sinn Féin MPs appointed a committee led by one of their number, Sean T.O'Kelly, to make preparations for the opening of an Irish parliament. The committee's chairman was the newly released Count Plunkett, who dispatched a letter to every MP in the country inviting them to attend the first session of an independent Irish parliament to be called "Dáil Eireann".[I]

On the afternoon of January 21st, 1919 the Dáil convened in the round room of the Mansion House. The event was common knowledge and a large crowd had gathered outside the building under the gaze of policemen. There were also many Irish Volunteers and international reporters present.

Contrary to everyone's expectations, and in light of all the actions it had taken against the national movement since the Easter Rebellion, Dublin Castle made no attempt to interfere despite the fact that they had carried out a raid on Sinn Féin headquarters on January 11th, where they had seized many documents. At this time world leaders were assembling in Paris for the Peace Conference following the November armistice and there were both French and other international reporters in Dublin for the commencement of the Dáil.

At this time England could not be seen internationally to crush self-determination in Ireland while apparently upholding it in Paris[II], and also began releasing a number of Sinn Féin prisoners who had gone on hunger strike. These prisoners were released under legislation known as the "Cat and Mouse Act" which meant that those released could be re-arrested at any time to complete their sentence.

As many of Sinn Fein's newly elected MPs remained in prison, only 27 Sinn Fein MPs attended with no attendance from either the IPP or the Unionists. Following opening prayers for the guidance of the Holy Ghost, a roll call of the elected members, who were now each to be referred to as "Teachta Dála"[III] (TD) took place. When the name of an imprisoned TD was called out, the clerk of the Dáil received the answer: "Fé ghlas as

---

[I] Dáil Eireann – Assembly or Parliament of Ireland
[II] The Dublin Castle Government Council debated whether or not to prevent the meeting of Dáil Eireann but decided against it by one vote.
[III] Teachta Dála – Deputy of the Assembly

Gallaibh" or "Imprisoned by the Foreign Enemy." When the names of Michael Collins and Harry Boland were called other T.Ds indicated that they were present. In fact they had departed for England on a mission to rescue Éamon deValera from Lincoln Prison. Before the business of the Dáil began in earnest, Cathal Brugha was elected as Speaker or "Ceann Comhairle". All the proceedings and speeches were conducted "as Gaeilge" (in Irish) while applause from the public isles was forbidden.

### "We are now done with England"

Following the passage by vote of a provisional Dáil constitution which laid down the mechanisms of government and the procedures to be followed by the Irish parliament, all present stood for the reading of the Declaration of Irish Independence by the Speaker, Cathal Brugha;

The Declaration of Irish Independence
Whereas the Irish people is by right a free people:
And whereas for seven hundred years the Irish people has never ceased to repudiate and has repeatedly protested in arms against foreign usurpation:
And whereas English rule in this country is, and always has been, based upon force and fraud and maintained by military occupation against the declared will of the people:
And whereas the Irish Republic was proclaimed in Dublin on Easter Monday 1916 by the Irish Republican Army acting on behalf of the Irish people:
And whereas the Irish people is resolved to secure and maintain its complete independence in order to promote the common weal, to re-establish justice, to provide for future defence, to insure peace at home and good will with all nations and to constitute a national polity based upon the people's will with equal right and equal opportunity for every citizen:

And whereas at the threshold of a new era in history, the Irish electorate has in the general election of December of 1918 seized the first occasion to declare by an overwhelming majority its firm allegiance to the Irish Republic:

Cathal Brugha

Now therefore, we, the elected representatives of the ancient Irish people in national parliament assembled, do in the name of the Irish nation, ratify the establishment of the Irish Republic and pledge ourselves and our people to make this declaration effective by every means at our command:

We ordain that the elected representatives of the Irish people alone have power to make laws binding on the people of Ireland, and that the Irish parliament is the only parliament to which that people will give its allegiance:

We solemnly declare foreign government in Ireland to be an invasion of our national right which we will never tolerate, and we demand the evacuation of our country by the English garrison:

We claim for our national independence the recognition and support of every free nation in the world, and we proclaim that independence to be a condition precedent to international peace hereafter:

In the name of the Irish people we humbly commit our destiny to Almighty God, Who gave our fathers the courage and determination to persevere through long centuries of a ruthless tyranny, and strong in the justice of the cause which they have handed down to us, we ask His Divine blessing on this the last stage of the struggle we have pledged to carry through to freedom.[429]

Following the reading of the Declaration of Independence, Cathal Brugha addressed the Assembly: "You understand from what is asserted in this Declaration that we are now done with England. Let the world know it and those who are concerned bear it in mind."

All the Deputies now stood and together said:"We adopt this Declaration of Independence and we pledge ourselves to put it into effect by every means in our power."

## The Paris Peace Conference

It was the hope of the TDs that following the many lofty speeches of President Wilson of the United States with regard to the reasons that the United States had entered the Great War, some progress would be made on achieving international recognition for Ireland's vote for independence at the Paris Peace Conference. With this aim in mind delegates to the Conference[1] were nominated and a resolution was passed calling upon "every free nation to support the Irish Republic...at the Peace Congress" as Ireland was "resolutely and irrevocably determined, at the dawn of the promised era of self-determination and liberty, that she will suffer foreign domination no longer."

This was a vain hope, for President Woodrow Wilson (who was of "Ulster Scots" lineage) had no interest in Ireland or in Irish-America except to try and satisfy Irish-American opinion with a few well placed words so that they might still vote for him. In spite of the fact that both the House of Congress and the Senate passed motions in favour of the "aspirations of the Irish people for a government of their own choice" Wilson had

---

[1] The Dáil appointed Count Plunkett, Éamon deValera and Arthur Griffith as delegates. Sean T. O'Kelly was dispatched to Paris as Envoy in order to try and secure their admittance to the Conference. Despite remaining in the city for a number of months he failed to make any headway. President Woodrow Wilson absolutely refused to meet him while Clémenceau of France ignored him.

no intention of causing any unnecessary strain to Anglo-American relations. Nevertheless one of Wilson's "Fourteen Points" which he expounded on at the Conference (much to the discomfort of the English delegation) advocated the "adjustment of colonial claims (so that) the interests of the populations concerned...have equal weight."[430]

## "For the Benefit of the Irish People"

The concluding business of the first meeting of Dáil Eireann was the reading and subsequent adoption of what was entitled "The Democratic Program of Dail Éireann". This significant document aimed to put the moral and material well-being of the Irish people at the centre of government as Gaelic (or Brehon) law had before it. In its scope, the desire to root out the many cancers inherent in English rule which had caused so much suffering in Ireland was apparent;

The Democratic Program of Dáil Éireann
"We declare in the words of the Irish Republican proclamation the right of the people of Ireland to the ownership of Ireland and to the unfettered control of Irish destinies to be indefeasible, and in the language of our first President, Pádraic Pearse, we declare that the nation's sovereignty extends not only to all men and women of the nation, but to all its material possessions; the nation's soil and all its resources, all the wealth and all the wealth producing processes within the nation and with him we re-affirm that all rights to private property must be subordinated to the public right and welfare. We declare that we desire our country to be ruled in accordance with the principles of liberty, equality and justice

Dail Éireann in session in the Round Room of the Mansion House

for all, which alone can secure permanence of government in the willing adhesion of the people.

We affirm the duty of every man and woman to give allegiance and service to the commonwealth, and declare it is the duty of the nation to assure that every citizen shall have opportunity to spend his or her strength and faculties in the service of the people. In return for willing service, we, in the name of the Republic, declare the right of every citizen to an adequate share of the produce of the nation's labour.

It shall be the first duty of the government of the Republic to make provision for the physical, mental and spiritual well-being of the children, to secure that no child shall suffer hunger or cold from lack of food or clothing or shelter, but that all shall be provided with the means and facilities requisite for their proper education and training as citizens of a free and Gaelic Ireland.

The Irish Republic fully realises the necessity of abolishing the present odious, degrading and foreign poor-law system, substituting therefore a sympathetic native scheme for the care of the nation's aged and infirm, who shall no longer be regarded as a burden, but rather entitled to the nation's gratitude and consideration. Likewise it shall be the duty of the Republic to take measures that will safeguard the health of the people and ensure the physical as well as the moral well-being of the nation.

It shall be the duty of the government of the Republic to promote the development of the nation's resources, to increase the productivity of the soil, to exploit its mineral deposits, peat bogs, and fisheries, its waterways and harbours, in the interest and for the benefit of the Irish people.

It shall be the duty of the Republic to adopt all measures necessary for the re-creation and invigoration of our industries, and to ensure their being developed on the most beneficial and progressive co-operative industrial lines. With the adoption of an extensive Irish consular service trade with foreign nations shall be revived on terms of mutual advantage and good will; while undertaking the organisation of the nation's trade, import and export, it shall be the duty of the Republic to prevent the shipment from Ireland of food and other necessaries until the wants of the Irish people are fully satisfied and the future provided for.

It shall devolve upon the national government to seek the co-operation of the governments of other countries in determining a standard of social and industrial legislation with a view to general and lasting improvements in the conditions under which the working classes live and labour."[431]

That evening an order was issued from Dublin Castle. It ran; "Press Censor to all Irish newspapers: The Press are informed with reference to the Dáil Éireann Assembly, which was held in Mansion House Dublin, on January 21, that the following are not for publication: 1. The Democratic Program. 2. The Declaration of Independence. 3. Speeches of the Proposer and Seconder of the Declaration of Independence."[432]

In spite of this, copies of the day's proceedings in Dáil Éireann were widely disseminated.

## The Government of the Republic

"Our attitude towards the powers that maintain themselves here against the expressed will of the people shall then, in a word, be this: We shall conduct ourselves towards them in such a way as will make it clear to the world that we acknowledge no right of theirs. Such use of their laws as we shall make, will be dictated solely by necessity, and only in so far as we deem them for the public good" – Éamon deValera.

<u>Escapes and Releases</u>
The following day the Dáil met again, this time in closed session in order to choose a caretaker "Príomh Aire" or Prime Minister (combining the roles of head of state and prime minister) of the Republic until Éamon deValera, who was then in Lincoln Jail should be in a position to take up the role. Cathal Brugha was elected and chose four ministers for his cabinet; Foreign Affairs was assigned to Count Plunkett, Finance to Eoin MacNeill, Home Affairs to Michael Collins and National Defence to Richard Mulcahy.

On February 3rd, deValera, who had managed to copy the master key of Lincoln Prison escaped from his incarceration along with two fellow prisoners Séan McGarry and Séan Milroy, assisted by Harry Boland and Michael Collins from outside. A wanted man, deValera[1] was in no position to take up his role as Príomh Aire and Brugha's caretaker administration continued in operation. However by the end of February the great plague of influenza or "Spanish Flu" was ravaging England's prisons and the previous December of 1918 Volunteer Captain Richard Coleman had died of the disease in the damp conditions of Usk Prison. On March 6th Pierce

---

[1] Thanks to Monsignor Curran (who was secretary to the Archbishop of Dublin) DeValera was given refuge in the Drumcondra Road gatehouse of the residence of Archbishop Walsh of Dublin

McCann T.D died in similar conditions in Gloucester Prison. With the Paris Peace Conference then in progress, Lloyd George was greatly afraid of the view internationally, if more of Ireland's elected representatives were to die in prison while being incarcerated without trial for their supposed involvement in a government contrived plot. Following McCann's death the decision was taken to release the remaining Sinn Féin prisoners who had been interned in England following the "German Plot" roundup. However there were still many Sinn Féin prisoners held in jails in Ireland. One of these, Robert Barton T.D (who had been jailed for a seditious speech) managed to escape from Mountjoy Jail on March 16th using a file smuggled into the prison by Richard Mulcahy. Barton left a note behind for the prison governor which stated that "owing to the discomfort (I) feel compelled to leave...will send for my luggage later."[433] Barton's escape was followed two weeks later by that of 20 Irish Volunteers who escaped from Mountjoy with the aid of a rope ladder. The incident was a major source of embarrassment to Dublin Castle.

### DeValera's Cabinet

After the "German Plot" prisoners returned to Ireland, DeValera appeared more frequently in public and on April 1st took up his duties as Príomh Aire after which he appointed a new and wider ranging cabinet.

DeValera's cabinet included Countess Markievicz (the first woman to be elected to Westminster following the Electoral Reform Bill) as Minister for Labour. The other ministers were Cathal Brugha as Minister for Defence, Michael Collins as Minister for Finance, Count Plunkett as Minister for Foreign Affairs, Eoin Mac Neill as Minister for Industry, Arthur Griffith as Minister for Home Affairs, Robert Barton as Minister for Agriculture and Laurence Ginnell as Minister for Information.

Richard Mulcahy was appointed as Chief of Staff of the Army of the Republic which would thereafter be referred to as the National Army or the Irish Republican Army (I.R.A). Sean T. O'Kelly was appointed as Ceann Comhairle.

Constance Marckievicz

## Fund Raising

Even before his escape from prison, deValera was determined to visit the United States, in order to arouse widespread American support for the cause of the Irish Republic and to raise money, as The Dáil could not hope to successfully supplant English rule and attempt to conduct an independent system of government without funds. Initially deValera delayed his visit to America in case an opportunity to meet President Wilson in Paris should arise, but this never occurred, and by mid June of 1919 deValera was in New York, the city of his birth.

As the English remained in firm control of Irish taxes, the Dáil also decided to raise its own funds through independent means, by issuing Government bonds to the value of £250,000, an amount that was later increased.

The Minister for Finance, Michael Collins took out advertisements in the provincial papers, informing people about the bonds, and the purposes for which they would be used. These included the establishment of Republican courts, a new civil service, a mortgage bank and the establishment of a

Commission on Industrial Resources. The newspapers in question were temporarily suppressed.[1]

The loans were a success and were heavily subscribed both at home and abroad, raising over five million pounds sterling (in modern terms) for the Republican government.

## Republican Courts

In June of 1919, the Dail passed a decree establishing a system of arbitration courts which would replace local British courts. As the months progressed these courts along with a system of Republican policing would successfully supplant the legal control held by the Crown in many counties especially in the west of the country. As this occurred, even landlords were forced to resort to these courts in the case of land disputes. The courts had the support of the local community and their rulings were generally obeyed. One of the leading Barristers who provided his services to the Republican courts (Kevin O'Shiel) later wrote that their aim was: "to eliminate all prejudice and do plain and simple justice to every man."[434]

By the Summer of 1920 a large number of Crown assizes were unattended, with Crown judges sitting before empty courts. At this stage a clamp down on Republican courts by Dublin Castle commenced. The RIC were instructed to arrest any person taking on the duties of a policeman. On June 17th 1920 the RIC targeted Republic courts in Charleville and Kilmallock where they shot dead Republican police and released the prisoners who were in their custody.

---

[1] The bond-drive officially got underway at the school which Patrick Pearse had founded; St. Enda's in Rathfarnham, the event being recorded on film. In the film Michael Collins is seated at the "butchers block" on which Robert Emmett's head was cut off in 1803 and is seen issuing bonds to T.Ds and the widows and mothers of the leaders of the Easter Rebellion.

# Chapter 22

## An Approaching State of War

"The principal cause of the trouble is that for five years emigration has practically stopped. In this country there are from one hundred thousand to two hundred thousand young men from eighteen to twenty-five years of age who in normal times would have emigrated." – Viceroy Lord John French.

### The Irish Republican Army

Following the meeting of Dáil Eireann and the subsequent Declaration of Independence the reformed Irish Volunteers were seen as the army of the Republic and increasingly adopted the name and initials first seen upon the flags of the Fenians during their 'invasion' of Canada in the Spring of 1866 – "I.R.A" or Irish Republican Army.

However at this time, the IRA were not officially answerable to the government of the Republic but to their own leadership which included high ranking IRB men.[1] To the Minister for

---

[1] One former IRB member, Commandant John Macken later recalled; "(IRB) meetings were held monthly. At these meetings we discussed current events, but nothing concrete in the way of hostilities against the British was ever done. I am at a loss still to understand what real purpose the organization served at this stage when we had an oath bound volunteer force. To my mind it only led to dissension, as the ordinary volunteers must have wondered what was going on behind their backs by what appeared to be a chosen few. When the Treaty was signed, the IRB executive failed hopelessly to give any definite lead to its members."

Defence, Cathal Brugha, (who had been an IRB member and now believed the IRB unnecessary) it was essential that the IRA take an oath of allegiance to the Government of the Republic so that any clandestine body or group of persons with an agenda of their own could not exercise undue influence over it. On August 20th 1919, Brugha introduced and Terence MacSwiney seconded the measure in the Dáil, proposing that all Volunteers, TDs and any person holding office or working for the Irish government should take the following oath:

"I, A.B., do solemnly swear that I do not and shall not yield a voluntary support to any pretended Government, authority or power within Ireland hostile and inimical thereto, and I do further swear that to the best of my knowledge and ability I will support and defend the Irish Republic and the Government of the Irish Republic, which is Dáil Eireann, against all enemies, foreign and domestic, and I will bear true faith and allegiance to the same, and that I take this obligation freely without any mental reservation or purpose of evasion, so help me God."

The measure was successfully adopted, although with some opposition. Michael Collins who was very powerful within the IRB and held the posts of both Director of Organisation and Director of Intelligence on the IRA Executive put forward the argument that if someday the Dáil betrayed the Republican cause the IRA would be placed in a difficult situation.

## Arming the IRA

As the Volunteers re-formed and recruited after the Easter Rebellion the ever-present question among its members was how to get weapons as there was little hope that a substantial arms shipment from abroad could be landed in Ireland. Certainly there were plenty of weapons in the country but the majority of these were in the hands of the Crown Forces. If the IRA were to get weapons or explosives, they would have to launch raids on some of the many barracks of the RIC scattered throughout the country, against army patrols and outposts, or on the homes of those Unionists who possessed shotguns and rifles. Hardware shops which sold shotguns could also be targeted along with those weapons still in the hands of John Redmond's "National Volunteers".

Even before the 1918 election a number of raids had been conducted by some units of the Irish Volunteers in an attempt to get weapons. The first such raid took place on St. Patrick's Day of 1918 when a Volunteer unit on the Beara peninsula in Co. Cork raided the RIC barracks in the village of Eyeries and captured five police carbines. A similar raid also in Cork, took place against the Gortatlea RIC barracks on April 13th and resulted in the deaths of two volunteers; Richard Laide and John Browne, when a returning RIC patrol surprised them and shot them down in the barracks. The other Volunteers taking part in the raid managed to escape taking with them a quantity of gelignite. The deaths of Laide and Browne did not deter other Cork volunteers from undertaking similar action. On July 7th, two RIC constables travelling between Ballingeary and Ballyvourney were ambushed and following a brief scuffle their weapons were captured.

In the aftermath of the Easter Rebellion and the subsequent change in public outlook, there were always a number of British soldiers of Irish extraction who were sympathetic to the Republican cause and would arrange for the secret "transfer" of British Army property into the hands of the Republicans. On one occasion early in 1918 a British army Captain escorted IRA Vice-Brigadier Peadar Clancy and Nicholas Laffan into Islandbridge Barracks where the men filled the boot of their car with handguns and ammunition before the Captain brought them out again. In this time of war the British army was somewhat careless about the issuing and return of weapons meaning that a feckless soldier who wanted to make a few pounds could do so by selling his weapon. In one "scheme" of this kind, a British army deserter in Dublin known as "Mouse" organized for his "ex-comrades" to sell Lee Enfield rifles to the Volunteers for £3 each.

In Britain too, sympathizers of Irish lineage could also be found. While many contributed money to the cause others did what they could to procure small amounts of weapons and ammunition and organize for their shipment to Ireland. On one occasion the Dublin Quartermaster Michael Staines received word that a large shipment of ammunition was in small bags hidden inside sacks of oats that had been imported from Britain by Dodd's Grain Merchants in Smithfield. Volunteer George Fitzgerald later recalled that such was the volume of sacks…"though we worked late into the night we weren't able to empty all the sacks and only a portion of the ammunition was cleared".[435] The following day Dodd's was raided by Crown Forces.

Following the general election and the meeting of the Dáil, where the 1916 declaration of the Irish Republic had been ratified, the number of weapons raids by the new I.R.A greatly increased as the units of the IRA sought to arm themselves for the fight for independence that was coming. During the Spring of 1919 the greatest success in this regard was achieved on the 19th March by an IRA raid against an airfield of the Royal Flying Corps at Collinstown, Co. Dublin.[1] In order to gain access to the base the volunteers poisoned the guard dogs and then managed to overpower the magazine detail before escaping with 75 Lee Enfield rifles. The following month in Araglen, Co. Cork the RIC barracks was raided and its armoury cleaned out, while in Co.Donegal the British Army

---

[1] Now the location of Dublin Airport.

post at Ned's Point was raided and cleared while almost all the British soldiers were at a local dance.

By the end of 1918, the IRA had its own grenade and bomb manufacturing facility in the basement of the Heron & Lawless engineering works on Parnell St. Originally the grenades manufactured were of a crude pipe-bomb variety but following the acquisition of an industrial lathe, the "Shop" began to manufacture Mills type grenade cases on an industrial scale with all those involved in this and other similar operations being instructed to stay away from Sinn Féin rallies and meetings and under no circumstances to voice their support in public for the cause. Similar workshops were organized in many other areas of the country. While some concentrated on grenade production (such as the workshop in Bailieboro, Co. Cavan) others specialized in the construction of mines and large bombs.[1] Gelignite was the explosive most widely used in these devices and was captured in large quantities along with the required "No. 6 detonator" until British security improved and gelignite became harder to obtain. This necessitated the manufacture by the IRA of "home-made" explosives known as "Irish War Flour" or "Irish Cheddar".

## Soloheadbeg and Knocklong

Although content with the progress that the national movement had made since 1916, Commandant Séan Treacy of the Third Tipperary Brigade was afraid that the fighting spirit of the men of 1916 was being eroded. Determined that the shooting war of Easter Week 1916 should be resumed even without the official sanction of higher authority, he talked over the matter with his Quartermaster, Dan Breen. The pair came

---

[1] These devices were what would be known today as IEDs or Improvised Explosive Devices.

to the decision to ambush the RIC guarded cart which frequently brought explosives to the Quarry at Soloheadbeg (near where Treacy was born) and unlike previous raids for weapons, of shooting down the RIC men at the first sign of resistance. Dan Breen later recalled ""Treacy and I had discussed the situation and had agreed that some positive military action was necessary. So about this time we were discussing the feasibility of attacking the R.I.C. escort which accompanied explosives to Soloheadbeg Quarry…We expected there would be an escort of around six armed police and we had the full intention not alone of taking the gelignite they were escorting but also of shooting down the escort, as an assertion of the national right to deny the free passage of an armed enemy. We had to wait in readiness for weeks while we expected this gelignite to come along…Treacy and I had decided that we were going to shoot whatever number of police came along as an escort with this gelignite. Treacy had stated to me that the only way of starting a war was to kill someone and we wanted to start a war, so we intended to kill some of the police whom we looked upon as the foremost and most important branch of the enemy forces which were holding our country in subjection. We felt we were merely continuing the active war for the establishment of an Irish Republic that had begun on Easter Monday 1916."[436]

Séan Treacy

When Treacy's commanding officer Seamus Robinson returned to Tipperary after being released from Prison, Treacy informed him of the raid but did not tell him that he intended to resume the shooting war. Robinson agreed that the raid should take place and together with Séan Hogan[I] and a few other men they stood in readiness until Patrick O'Dwyer arrived on his bicycle on the morning of January 21st (the first day of the Dail session) to tell them that the explosives-laden cart with police escort had departed Tipperary town. The IRA men dispersed to their pre-arranged locations. Patrick O'Dwyer recalled what happened when the cart arrived: "I heard Dan Breen and Séan Treacy shout, "Halt, put your hands up". Robinson and I immediately started to get out onto the road, and almost simultaneously either one or two shots rang out. I distinctly remember one of the RIC men bringing his carbine to the aiming position and working the bolt, and the impression I got was that he was aiming at either Robinson or myself. Then a volley rang out and the constable fell dead at the roadside."[437]

The horse and cart loaded with 76 kg of gelignite along with 38 detonators and the weapons of the two RIC men were captured. The cart driver, Edward Godfrey, and the accompanying council employee Patrick Flynn were uninjured. Everyone in the IRA detail knew of the "Hue and Cry"[II] that must surely follow the attack and quickly dispersed, the most in danger being Dan Breen whose mask had slipped from his face as he jumped across a gate onto the roadway, something which enabled the Crown Forces to identify him and issue a wanted poster with a reward of £1,000 for information leading to his capture.

The incident came as something of a shock to the country and was almost universally condemned as murder as were the killings of other RIC men during 1919. The two RIC men,

---

[I] Hogan, Robinson, Treacy and Breen were known in IRA circles as "The Big Four"
[II] "Hue and Cry" was the title of the RIC "Gazette" or bi-weekly newspaper which was circulated to all RIC stations. Providing a list of "most wanted" on its front page, it then proceeded to arrests sought on a county by county basis.

Constables O'Connell and Mac Donnell were both family men stationed in Tipperary town. The most notable response not condemning the incident came from the Catholic Bishop Fogarty of Killaloe who said two days after the incident: ""The fight for Irish freedom has passed into the hands of the young men of Ireland and when the young men of Ireland hit back at their oppressors it is not for an old man like me to cry 'Foul.'"438 [I]

In the aftermath of the shooting the heavy-handed methods of the Crown Forces in their search for the perpetrators would contribute to a change in public attitude. Already the lower echelons of the RIC, composed as they were of Irishmen in the pay of the Crown were widely regarded with fear and disdain. In the months that followed as they worked hand-in-hand with other elements of the Crown's security apparatus in what was to become a reign of terror they came to be regarded as traitors to their country and an impediment to freedom.

After the killing of the two policemen, martial law was proclaimed in South Tipperary. The area bristled with Crown Forces, 3,000 soldiers on top of the RIC. That Spring, other parts of the country also had full-scale martial law introduced including Westport following the killing of a magistrate at the end of March. During an attempt to rescue the injured Robert Byrne of the 2nd Limerick City Battalion from hospital on April 6th Constable Martin O'Brien had been killed and the city was placed under martial law[II] Martial law played no small part in increasing the level of public animosity towards the RIC who conducted checkpoints with the British army, checking passes,

---

[I] For his unwillingness to condemn the actions of the IRA and his overt support of the fight for freedom, Bishop Fogarty would later become the object of a Dublin Castle murder plot.

[II] Byrne later died from his wounds. The declaration of martial law in the city led to the forming of a "workers cooperative" known as "The Limerick Soviet".

conducting body searches and generally making life as difficult as possible for the population.

In early May Sean Hogan was arrested at Annfield and after being taken to Thurles was being transferred to Cork. Knowing that he might well face a firing squad, his comrades were determined to rescue him and contacted the local (Galbally, Co. Limerick) IRA unit for assistance.

The rescue of Sean Hogan was planned to take place on May 13th when the Cork train halted at the Knocklong Station in Co. Limerick. Four[I] of the rescue party had already boarded the train at Emly station in order to determine the carriage in which Hogan was interned while four more waited at Knocklong.[II]

When the train stopped at Knocklong Sean Treacy and Ned O'Brien boarded the carriage in which Hogan was interned and quickly made for his compartment. They were immediately involved in a gunfight during which two RIC men; Wallace and Enright were killed. When the pair entered the carriage Wallace had his gun pointed at Hogan's head and was about to kill him, sooner than see him rescued. He was shot dead before he could accomplish this. Treacy and Enright then became involved in a life or death struggle during which Treacy dropped his gun while Enright attempted to bring his revolver to bear before Treacy managed to wrest it from his hands and shoot him. The fight over, Hogan was rescued and brought to a nearby butcher's shop where his handcuffs were severed with the aid of a meat cleaver. Once out of danger the men took refuge in safe-houses where local doctors were summoned. In spite of the massive search which followed "The Big Four" remained at liberty until their escape from the district but two local men, Maher and Foley were arrested.

---

[I] Edward Foley, James Scanlon, Sean Lynch and JJ O'Brien.
[II] Seamus Robinson, Dan Breen, Sean Treacy and Ned O'Brien.

While Foley had taken part in the rescue, Maher had not. Both men were sentenced to death and were executed on June 7th 1921. Their final message on the night before their execution was "Our souls go to God at 7.00 in the morning and our bodies when Ireland is free shall go to Galbally."

## The Choice

"England must be given the choice of evacuating the country or holding it by foreign garrison with a perpetual state of war in existence." – Editorial, IRA newspaper "An t-Óglách"

The IRA Executive had been taken unawares by Soloheadbeg. The Tipperary men had signalled an escalation in hostilities which the Executive had not intended.[1] Nevertheless the IRA Executive was not going to disown the action. The incident now made the issuing of guidance to the IRA regarding the undertaking of weapons seizures paramount. Around a week after Solohedbeag the IRA Executive met after which they issued directions to the membership in the IRA news-sheet "An t-Óglach" (The Volunteer) at the end of January. When the newssheet appeared it informed the membership that they were justified "in treating the armed forces of the enemy – whether soldiers or policemen – exactly as a national Army would treat the members of an invading army; that a volunteer was now not only entitled but bound to resist all attempts to disarm him. In this position he has the authority of the nation behind him..."[439] This guidance could have been loosely interpreted as a notice to commence general hostilities for which the IRA was not ready, so a general order was also issued to the IRA to avoid taking life where possible when acquiring arms and explosives.

---

[1] While Michael Collins welcomed the development others such as Richard Mulcahy and Cathal Brugha did not.

As the year progressed, IRA commanders were encouraged (by Michael Collins in particular) to seize weapons for their units and the number of police casualties increased throughout the year. By the end of the year 15 RIC men and one soldier had been killed.

The attitude of treating the RIC as an invader as recommended by An t-Óglach was reinforced on April 10th when the Dáil announced that all RIC members were to be ostracized or boycotted. By this act it was hoped by the Dáil that many of the RIC rank and file would be persuaded to make "the choice" and resign their posts.[1]

## An Escalating Situation

### The Formation of "The Squad"

In the months that followed Soloheadbeg, the primary emphasis of IRA action was to acquire weapons but this was not the only emphasis. As IRA Director of Intelligence, Michael Collins was determined to try and eliminate the secret eyes and ears on which British control of Ireland depended – their intelligence network, which not only consisted of police officers but also of those who supplied information. Planning in this regard was now undertaken, and in the early Summer of 1919, Quartermaster Dick Mc Kee set in motion the formation of what later became known as "The Squad". The first victims were two members of G Division of the Dublin Metropolitan Police (known as "G men") who were involved in operations against the Republican movement.

---

[1] One RIC constable who decided to resign was Daniel Crowley who was stationed in Clogheen in Co. Tipperary. He later recalled that the RIC were required to go on military patrols: "They (the RIC) were required to go on an armoured car with a machine gun and every man who took a prominent part in the Sinn Fein movement,, they were to stand in front of his house and turn the machine gun on it. In this armoured car there were put one hundred and twenty cans of petrol and also one hundred and twenty mills bombs and the reason for this is that they were for burning houses."

Despite being warned on a number of occasions to cease his intelligence work, Detective Sergeant Smyth persisted. On July 30th as he was returning to his home in Drumcondra he was shot and wounded, dying a few weeks later. The second victim of the Squad had come to the attention of Michael Collins at the end of the Easter Rebellion. Detective Daniel Hoey had been responsible for pulling Sean Mac Diarmada from the ranks of the prisoners bound for England following the surrender at the end of the Easter Rebellion, thus ensuring MacDiarmada's execution. On September 12th Detective Daniel Hoey was assassinated in Townsend St. Dublin.

Following the killing of these two high-ranking intelligence officers, "G" Division was in turmoil. In an effort to restore morale and regain the initiative in the intelligence war, Detective Inspector William Forbes Redmond was dispatched from Belfast to Dublin to take command of "G" Division, a fact relayed to Michael Collins who now set in train an operation by The Squad to eliminate him.

### A Modern Version of an Old Policy

As raids for weapons by the IRA continued numbers of RIC men were killed. However on Sunday 7th September, the first British soldier to be killed in Ireland since the Easter Rebellion met his end during a weapons raid in Fermoy, Co. Cork when the Commandant of the Cork No.2 Brigade, Liam Lynch led a meticulously planned hold up involving twenty five volunteers and three cars against a party of British soldiers on their way from the Fermoy Barracks to a church service in the Methodist Church at the far end of town. Following the hold up a scuffle ensued and as one of the soldiers lunged at Lynch with the butt of his rifle, he was shot dead. Three other British soldiers were wounded in the incident before the IRA made good their escape with fifteen Lee Enfield rifles.

In the aftermath of the incident, a large Crown Forces Operation was launched throughout the Fermoy area with troops and police being dispatched far and wide. What ensued was but a foretaste of things to come. The search for the IRA men was a brutal affair resulting in the injury of many innocent locals who were struck with the butts of the soldier's rifles. At Ballynoe, a match-making party was raided and those attending it were brutally treated. On the evening of Monday September 8th, the soldiers of the East Kent Regiment who were stationed in Fermoy Barracks, came out in great numbers into the town of Fermoy, seeking revenge for the killing of their comrade and the loss of the rifles. Their revenge had the appearances of a military operation with a whistle blowing officer appearing to direct operations. Windows were smashed, shops were looted and the town generally wrecked from end to end. No action was taken against the perpetrators and the price tag of their orgy of destruction was around £120,000 (in modern terms). Two days later the whole area was placed under martial law. The sack of Fermoy was a warning. If the IRA continued their operations then the Crown Forces with the support of the English government would resort to a modern version of the scorched earth methods of

Commandant Liam Lynch

former times[1] and target both civilians and the civilian economy.

In the aftermath of Fermoy, the East Kent Regiment was redeployed to Cork City. That no action had been taken against them for the Sack of Fermoy became obvious on November 10th when they once more went on a spree of destruction and looting in Cork city centre. This was in line with a marked increase in "punitive measures" being undertaken by Crown Forces in the last quarter of 1919 which saw similar actions by other Regiments taking place in Athlone and Kinsale.

## The Suppression of Dáil Eireann

On the same day that the sack of Fermoy took place, Dublin Castle announced the suppression of Dáil Eireann, declaring it to be a "dangerous association". All public meetings of the Dáil were now prohibited, and the freely-elected Parliament of the Irish people went underground, now forced to conduct its business in out of the way places or in the hours of darkness.[II]

The suppression of the Dail was later followed by the searching of the Mansion House and a raid against Sinn Féin headquarters. Some TDs were arrested and interned without any news of the location of their internment being given to their families.

When news of the suppression of the Dáil reached the United States it had the effect of increasing the profile deValera's visit in the press. Huge crowds attended the rallies at which

---

[1] In former times when "scorched earth" had been employed by Crown Forces, they had removed the ability of the people to support the fighting men by the wholesale destruction of crops and animals and the laying waste of homes. They had also removed the willingness of the men to fight by the murder of their families and the population at large.

[II] In mid October the Árd-fheis of the Sinn Fein party took place between midnight and three in the morning.

deValera spoke where he explained to the citizens of the U.S how the freely elected government of the Irish was being suppressed.

Having moved against Dáil Eireann, the British government feared more than ever that Sinn Féin would sweep the board in the municipal elections due to take place in mid-January and the local elections in June of 1920. Whilst the elections were due to take place in both Britain and Ireland, the London government proceeded with the introduction of a new system of voting called proportional representation which had been part of the Local Government of Ireland Act (1919) The measure was introduced for Ireland only in an effort to increase the number of seats of non Sinn Féin candidates. The new system was quite different to the "first past the post" system used in previous elections but Dublin Castle decided not to explain the new system to the electorate in the hope that the "mere Irish" who supported Sinn Féin would spoil their ballots.

## A Failed Assassination Attempt

On December 18th Winston Churchill informed the House of Commons that the number of British troops stationed in Ireland had reached 43,000. These troops were accompanied by scores of tanks whose previous deployment had been the trenches of the Western Front.[1] The primary purpose of the troops was the assistance of the RIC in their attempt to smother the national revolt by the suppression of almost every aspect of

---

[1] Ireland is "like a country invaded in time of war" was the opinion of the Westminster Gazette. The newspaper accused Lord French of being in charge of "a system of coercion such as there has not been in living memory. Former cabinet minister Sir Herbert Samuel concluded "If what is now going on in Ireland had been going on in the Austrian Empire, all England would be ringing with denunciation of the tyranny of the Hapsburgs and of denying people the right to rule themselves."

day to day life which by the end of 1919 included all public meetings, fairs, Gaelic cultural and sporting events and much of the popular press. In all areas where martial law had been declared (which by mid January of 1920 included Kilkenny, Wexford and Waterford) hundreds of household raids were taking place on a daily basis.

December 19th saw the execution by the IRA of a long planned attempt on the life of Lord French while he was returning to the Viceroy's residence in Dublin's Phoenix Park after a sojourn at his country residence outside the town of Frenchpark in Co. Roscommon. Upon his arrival at the nearby Ashtown Railway station, French had elected to travel in the first car of the convoy while his luggage followed in the second. The IRA had expected the opposite and concentrated their fire on the second car. Nevertheless Lord French had a narrow escape with a bullet passing through the back of the car just inches from him. One IRA soldier, Martin Savage was killed in the engagement while the driver of the second car, Corporal Appleby was detained by the IRA, and then released unharmed. In the aftermath of the incident, the RIC who had already been issued with an array of revolvers and shotguns to augment their carbines, were issued with Mills Bombs (hand grenades).

## Lloyd George Introduces a Partitionist Home Rule Bill

On December 22nd Lloyd George formally abandoned his pretence of working towards an all Ireland home rule. Taking full advantage of the absence of Irish M.Ps, he introduced his "Better Government of Ireland Bill" in the House of Commons. In a speech aimed at American public opinion, Lloyd George erroneously compared Ireland to the Southern States of America which had attempted to break away from the United States in 1861 telling the House that "Any attempt at secession will be fought with the same resources, with the same resolve as the Northern States of America put into their fight against the Southern States".

The terms of the Bill were drafted by a cabinet committee chaired by the former Unionist leader Walter Long and proposed to create two parliaments on the island of Ireland.

In spite of their earlier avowed opposition to home rule, the unionists of Ulster were apparently prepared to accept their own home rule parliament by which they would have "restricted governance" over six counties of Ulster.[1] The designs of the government and the actual opinion of the Unionists regarding Home Rule for Ulster were disseminated by Captain William Craig in the House of Commons in March 1920: "We believe that so long as we were without a Parliament of our own, constant attacks would be made upon us, and constant attempts would be made to draw us into a Dublin Parliament, and that is the last thing in the world we desire to happen…We see our safety in having a parliament of our own, for we believe that once a parliament is set up and working well, as I have no doubt it would in Ulster, we should fear no one."[440]

Just as the design of the Government in 1800 was that the Irish should never have governance over their own country, in 1920 the design had altered so that six counties of Ulster should remain forever separated from the rest of the Country in a

---

[1] As Lloyd George's partition bill proceeded into its second reading beginning on March 29th of 1920 Sir Edward Carson explained to the Commons why the Unionists did not want the three counties of Donegal. Monaghan and Cavan included in Home Rule for Ulster; "We should like to have the very largest area possible, naturally. That is a system of land grabbing that prevails in all countries for widening the jurisdiction of the various Governments that are set up; but there is no use in our undertaking a Government which we know would be a failure if we were saddled with these three counties."

Protestant fiefdom ruled by the descendants of the original planters.[I]

The Bill coincided with the announcement of a new recruitment drive in Britain for the RIC, by which it was planned to greatly expand the force with demobilized British Soldiers and to replace those RIC who had made the choice to leave with battle hardened veterans of the Great War. The plan had been condemned by the commander of the force, Brigadier General Sir Joseph Byrne as one which would only increase strife in Ireland.[II] Following his opposition to the move, and to the increasing militarization of the RIC, Byrne was replaced by the Ulster Orangeman TJ Smith after which almost all senior appointments in the RIC were given to Ulster Unionists in what was called the "Ulsterisation" of the RIC.

By the end of the year the RIC had abandoned many of their smaller county outposts and barracks because of their vulnerability-to-attack in weapons raids. Those in the larger towns were quickly reinforced and upgraded to the equivalent of mini fortresses.

---

[I] Lloyd George gave the Unionists everything they demanded. However to avoid any criticism that he intended to partition Ireland "forever" Lloyd George's Bill included "provision for an all Ireland council" as a sop to nationalists that some day, this Irish council might agree on the establishment of an all-Ireland parliament.

[II] In the Autumn of 1919 Byrne was sent on paid leave and officially removed at the beginning of April 1920. Regarding his removal The Daily Mail wrote that it was due: "to the fact that he has firmly stood out against a policy which could only result in infecting the whole of Ireland with the brutal madness of its rulers."

# Chapter 23

# A Fight for Irish Freedom

"Mr. Lloyd George says to Ireland, 'I will make the price of your freedom so terrible that you will not pay it.' – London Daily News

"Sworn to be free, no more our ancient sireland
Shall harbour the despot or the slave" –
Excerpt from "The Soldier's Song" by Peadar Kearney

## The British Government's Irish Policy

By the beginning of 1920, all the main elements of London's policy for tackling the "Irish Question" were in place.

The chief aim of the British government was the partitioning of Ireland and the successful formation of a Unionist administration within six of Ulster's counties, which would become a new "region" of the United Kingdom. In spite of international and domestic opinion and his inability to defeat the IRA, no peace with the Irish would be seriously entertained by Lloyd George until the establishment of the 'Ulster Parliament" was an accomplished fact as he feared that if peace came prematurely the 'southern Irish' would be in a position to upset his plans.

## War and Politics

During late 1919, Lloyd George and his government had readied as best they could their plan of campaign for the struggle with Irish Republicanism; Dublin Castle officials which the Viceroy, Lord French found "troublesome" had been replaced, culminating in the replacement of Ian MacPherson with Hamar Greenwood in the Spring of 1920. French had been given a free hand by Lloyd George to conduct the fight without inquiry or interference and with all the resources he asked for.

Sir Hamar Greenwood

As a campaign by the British army against the Irish would not go down well either internationally or at home, it had been decided to instead "militarize" the Royal Irish Constabulary with army weapons and new recruits in the form of unemployed veterans from the Great War. In this way most Crown Forces operations in Ireland could be referred to as police actions to restore law and order, while this militarized police could patrol the countryside at will and bring the war to the Irish.[1] A huge army was also in place to act as "back-up" and to provide assistance to the police in the establishment of cordons, the conducting of searches and a backup with heavy firepower whenever the RIC requested it.

---

[1] General Frank Crozier later wrote that General Hugh Tudor had told him that Crown Forces Operation in Ireland were being camouflaged as police operations because funds for police operations were easier to obtain than funds for military operations.

Within the political sphere, Lloyd George was determined that once partition was accomplished,, the Irish should abandon the Republic and accept the partition of their country. With these ends in mind, he had introduced his "Bill for the Better Government of Ireland" into Parliament by which he intended to partition Ireland and provide the "No Home Rule" Ulster Unionists with their own Home Rule Parliament[1]. In this way, whenever the Crown Forces succeeded in defeating the IRA or when Lloyd George decided on peace negotiations, the partition of Ireland would already be an accomplished fact.

For the other 26 counties, it was abundantly clear to the British government that a limited form of Home Rule as originally anticipated by the 1912 Act did not interest Sinn Fein and would no longer suffice. It was here that the political and military lines became entwined. As the Republican Government had sworn to uphold the Republic, it must be forced by repression, murder and "scorched earth" reprisals to a "change of mind", whereby the Republican leadership would accept the already established partition of their country and by way of self-government, some form of home-rule that would not act as a beacon or example to the other countries of the Empire who desired freedom and looked to Ireland to set the example.

## The Municipal Elections

As with the general election just over a year previously, the weeks leading up to the municipal elections on January 15th 1920 saw Dublin Castle and the Crown Forces engaged in intense action against Sinn Féin. Those caught distributing election literature or putting up posters were arrested and

---

[1] In the event of continued resistance to English rule Sir Edward Carson told the House of Commons that Ulster could be "a jumping-off place from which you can carry on all the necessary operations."

usually given a three month prison sentence for the possession of seditious materials.

When the votes were counted after election-day it appeared that the British government's exercise in trying to reduce support for Sinn Féin (and increase support for the Unionists) by the introduction of proportional representation had backfired. In spite of the failure of the British government to spend "a single penny"[441] explaining the intricacies of proportional representation to the public at large, less than 3% of votes cast in the January 15th election were deemed ineligible during the count.

As in the 1918 election Sinn Féin had the largest share of the vote winning a majority of seats on 172 out of 206 town councils and 11 out of 12 city and borough councils with Belfast being the only city council in Ireland remaining under Unionist control.

## Ulster

In the six counties of Ulster which England were determined to partition from the rest of the country, Sinn Féin had, contrary to London's intentions outperformed the Unionists, securing 23 town councils to the Unionists 22.[1] This slight victory of the Nationalists over the Unionists within the six counties which the Unionists were determined to sever from the rest of the country was difficult for the Unionists to stomach. Especially hard to take was the loss of "Londonderry" city council which was now controlled by Sinn Fein with Hugh O'Doherty as Mayor. Loyalists responded to the Sinn Fein victory by reforming the UVF within the city, and attacking the Catholic Bogside area (which was outside the city proper) from the city walls, killing four people. When rifle fire was returned from

---

[1] When the next elections took place in Northern Ireland (following partition) in 1924, the Unionist government had redrawn all constituencies in their favour (gerrymandering) and reverted to the "first past the post electoral system".

the Bogside by the IRA, Crown Forces fired into the Bogside killing a further six people.

In the aftermath of the election the first action of the town and city councils controlled by Sinn Féin was to pass a motion acknowledging "the authority of Dáil Éireann as the duly elected Government of the Irish people, and (undertaking) to give effect to all decrees promulgated by the said Dáil Éireann"[442] while in the cities of Derry, Cork, Waterford, Limerick and Dublin motions were passed denying "the right of the English Lord Lieutenant to appoint a High Sheriff for the city."[443]

## Sinn Féin Victorious

The London government had felt that it could safely suppress Dáil Éireann as an illegal and dangerous assembly as it was not an assembly of the people's representatives founded on United Kingdom law. According to London the members of Dáil Éireann had been elected to a legally constituted parliament in London which they refused to attend.

However the newly elected Sinn Féin members of local authorities were not refusing to take their seats on" legally constituted" local authorities. They would take their seats on the local councils, but refuse to recognize that England had any right to be involved in the running of local government in Ireland.[1] This was open revolt by legal means and this revolt could be expected to not only continue, but to intensify when Sinn Féin would most likely win control of a great number of county councils in the Summer of 1920. Furthermore, for the moment at least, all local revenues would now be in the hands of the Republican local authorities.

---

[1] At the installation of Vincent White as Sinn Fein Mayor of Waterford, White ordered the trappings of British rule be removed from the council chamber.

## A Dramatic Increase in Repression

As Sinn Féin began to take control of local government in Ireland, the scale of Crown Forces repression increased dramatically. During the month of January 1920, the number of Crown Forces raids was in the region of 1,000. In the shorter month of February this number had reached over 4,000. During each month hundreds of arrests occurred, usually on the charge of sedition.[I] Internment without trial was the order of the day.[II] Due to the demand on prison space some internees were placed in the asphyxiating hold of cargo ships while those who according to General Macready; "no evidence could be produced"[444] were transferred to prisons in England.

Any IRA attack, especially one which involved the death of a member of the Crown Forces was met with heavy punitive measures against the locality in which the attack took place. These were conducted with ever increasing brutality. When, on January 22$^{nd}$ Constable Michael Finnegan was shot dead in Thurles, the RIC responded with a rampage through the town, which targeted in particular the homes of the newly elected Sinn Fein councillors. The rampage concluded with the destruction by hand grenades of the offices of the "Tipperary Star" newspaper.

Following the assassination in Dublin on January 21$^{st}$ of Assistant Police Commissioner William Forbes Redmond by The Squad and the killing of another policeman in the city on February 20$^{th}$,[III] a night-time curfew was introduced in the

---

[I] While animal fairs were banned, farmers still tried to sell their animals at "illegal" gatherings. They faced one month in prison for a breach of DORA if caught.

[II] Among those incarcerated was Alderman Thomas Kelly, who was elected as Lord Mayor of Dublin while in prison.

[III] In May of 1920 the Dublin Metropolitan Police requested the British government that they should be allowed to no longer carry lethal firearms. The government acquiesced which was in fact an admission by London that although they continued to label the IRA as "murderers" they knew that they would not

capital in order to facilitate nightly raids by the Crown Forces. Of these raids Erskine Childers wrote: "As the citizens go to bed, the barracks spring to life. Lorries, tanks, and armoured searchlight cars, muster in fleets, lists of 'objectives' are distributed...the objectives are held for the most part by women and terrified children. A thunder of knocks: no time to dress, even for a woman alone, or the door will crash in. On opening, in charge the soldiers – literally charge – with fixed bayonets and in full war kit. No warrant shown on entering, no apology on leaving, if, as in nine cases out of ten, suspicions prove to be groundless and the raid a mistake. In many recent instances even women occupants have been locked up under guard while their own property is ransacked...Is it any wonder that gross abuses occur: looting, wanton destruction, brutal severity to women?"[445]

These raids varied greatly. If conducted in the aftermath of an IRA attack, they were generally conducted with more brutality than usual, resulting in the discharging of rounds into the ceiling or crockery, the ripping up of floorboards and the destruction of soft furnishings in the search for incriminating evidence. If a man was on the premises he was in great danger. If not shot out of hand, he was arrested, and sometimes shot "while trying to escape".

## The Assassination of the Lord Mayor of Cork

When the RIC had run riot in Thurles on January 20th 1920, they had attacked the home of the Chairman of Thurles District Council, Denis Morgan.[1] Some days later Morgan was arrested

---

target and murder unarmed policemen. Although the IRA continued to target armed detectives, especially those of "G" division, the rank and file of the DMP were by virtue of their action now immune from armed attack.

[1] The attack took place at night during which the RIC fired volley after volley through his bedroom window. Afterwards his family slept in the cold cellar of the house. His wife had a nervous breakdown and his son became ill with a

and interned with many others in the hold of a ship in Cobh, after which he was transferred to Wormwood Scrubs in London. While incarcerated, Morgan received word that both he and the Lord Mayor of Cork, Tomás Mac Curtain were on an RIC assassination list. While Morgan had been saved from assassination by his imprisonment, the RIC now proceeded against Tomás Mac Curtain who was also the Commanding Officer of the IRA Cork No. 1 Brigade.

On the night of March 19th/ 20th the streets around Mac Curtain's house at No.40 Thomas Davis Street were sealed off by police and military with no passers-by being allowed to enter the area. In the early hours of the morning of March 20th[l] men with blackened faces banged on the door. As Tomás Mac Curtain's wife, Eibhlís, looked out the window, the men burst into the house and rushed upstairs where they shot Tomas Mac Curtáin at his bedroom door.

Tomás Mac Curtain

Mortally wounded, Mac Curtáin died after a quarter of an hour. Shortly after his death the British Army raided the house and conducted a search of the property.

On the same day that Mac Curtain was assassinated, the post of Lord Mayor of Cork was assumed in a caretaker capacity by his deputy, Terence Mac Swiney. When the funeral of Tomás

---

heart condition from which he died while his father was in prison. Denis Morgan applied for a compassionate release which was refused.

[l] Tómas Mac Curtain's 36th birthday.

Mac Curtain took place the following day, it was the largest ever seen in Cork.[1]

Following the assassination of Tomás Mac Curtain a hearing was held in the Cork Coroner's court. In spite of the fact that the jury were selected by the police, the jury found that Mac Curtain; "was willfully murdered under circumstances of most callous brutality; that the murder was organized and carried out by the Royal Constabulary, officially directed by the British Government". A verdict of "willful murder" against three inspectors of the RIC along with some unknown members of that force and Lloyd George, Lord French and the Chief Secretary of Ireland Ian Mc Pherson was returned.

Replying to the verdict, Lloyd George said that he believed that the Lord Mayor had been assassinated by his own men of the Cork IRA because of his reluctance for armed action against the Crown Forces. However actions spoke louder than words. Following the verdict, one of the chief inspectors indicted, Oswald Swanzy was immediately transferred from Cork city to the Unionist town of Lisburn in Co. Antrim.

## The War from Spring to Autumn of 1920

"Many of the things done by the English police in Ireland in 1920 and 1921 and unjustly placed on Irish shoulders were really done by British authorities." – General Frank Crozier

### The Assassination of Judge Alan Bell

As the IRA attempted to disable Dublin Castle's intelligence apparatus, Lord French attempted to rejuvenate it. In November of 1919, French assembled a Dublin Castle secret

---

[1] The inscription on Tomás Mac Curtáin's coffin was in Gaelic. It read "Tomás Mac Curtáin, Commandant, 1st Brigade, Cork, Army of the Irish Republic and Lord Mayor of Cork, who was foully done to death by the servants of the foreigner on March 20 1920, in the fourth year of the Irish Republic, at the age of 37 years. May God have mercy on his soul."

committee with the intention of breathing new life into an RIC intelligence system designed for peace time operations. One of the key men on French's committee was Alan Bell, a former RIC District Inspector and now a Judge. As well as being in command of high ranking RIC men (like the assassinated William Redmond) who were involved in the intelligence war, Bell was tasked with tracking down those bank accounts in which Sinn Fein and Republican government funds were held and of confiscating the monies therein. Bell had launched a secret enquiry in which bank managers were required to testify and produce documentation for bank accounts which Bell was suspicious of. He had also ordered the Sinn Fein bank to be raided and seized the contents of the bank's safe which contained over £35,000 (in modern terms).

Despite being an important member of Dublin Castle's intelligence apparatus and a prime target for The Squad, Bell travelled daily by tram from his home in Monkstown (Dún Laoghaire) to his office in Dublin Castle, often without a guard. On March 26th, as Bell was on his way to Dublin Castle he was pulled off the tram at Ballsbridge by four members of The Squad after one of them, (Mick Mac Donnell) had placed his hand on Bell's shoulder and told him: "Come on Mr. Bell, your time has come."[446] After being pulled from the tram, Bell was shot dead on the roadway.

## "I Loathe the country...and its people"

The Spring of 1920 saw further high-level appointments by London to both the Crown Forces and Dublin Castle administration. In April of 1920, General Neville Macready (who had served as London Police Commissioner since the end of the Great War) was appointed to the role of General Officer Commanding in Chief (GOCinC) of British Forces in Ireland replacing General Shaw.

The appointment did not bode well for Ireland, as when in January of 1919, Macready's friend Sir Ian Macpherson had been appointed as Chief Secretary for Ireland, Macready had written to him to sympathize: "I cannot say I envy you for I loathe the country you are going to and its people, with a depth deeper than the sea and more violent than that which I feel against the Boche."[447]

Reluctantly accepting his posting out of a sense of duty to his friend, General French, Macready received instructions from the Chief of the General Staff, Sir Henry Wilson who according to Macready recommended "stamping out rebellion with a strong hand."[448] After taking up his role, Macready returned to London a few weeks later where he attended a cabinet meeting on May 11th and demanded the deployment of thousands more troops, and hundreds of armoured motor vehicles to Ireland, a request which the Prime Minister assured Macready would receive immediate attention. London asked Macready to also take control of the RIC which he refused, after which General Sir Hugh Tudor was appointed to the role of "Police Adviser".

General Neville Macready

Coinciding with Macready's appointment was the appointment of a new Chief Secretary, the Canadian Sir Hamar Greenwood whom London knew could be depended upon to "toe the party line" at all times. As 1920 progressed, Greenwood was to tell so many obvious lies about the Irish situation in the House of Commons that the term "telling a

Hamar" became double-speak for "telling a lie" among its members.

Having assumed their new roles, French, Macready and Tudor knew that they could depend on London to grant them most of the resources they requested. What they could not depend upon was politics. When Lord French requested Lloyd George to introduce general martial law within the island of Ireland in the early Summer of 1920, Lloyd George was forced to refuse as it would make a lie of his policy to present Ireland internationally as a country whose "murder gang" could be brought under control by the police. After this decision, both Macready and Tudor complained of the constraints being imposed upon them but Lloyd George could offer them no solace. Martial law could only be introduced on a limited county by county basis.

## Hunger and Other Strikes

On Easter Sunday, April 4th of 1920, members of the IRA carried out the order issued by their executive that every RIC barracks from which the Crown Forces had retreated were to be set ablaze and destroyed. On that evening hundreds of rural barracks were packed with straw and set alight as a "fitting commemoration of the Easter Rebellion". A number of Crown Revenue offices were also targeted.

The following day, Easter Monday, a hunger strike of republican prisoners demanding prisoner of war status began at Mountjoy prison in Dublin. For ten days large crowds of people gathered outside the prison in support of the prisoners.[1]

---

[1] A similar hunger-strike of Republican prisoners began at Wormwood Scrubs on April 21st. People who gathered in support of the prisoners were attacked by a mob. In the Commons, the Home Secretary excused the mob: "These young London men naturally showed their resentment at hearing people extol those whom they believed to be murderers.". Two nights later a crowd of mostly

The crowds were kept at bay by soldiers supported by tanks while aeroplanes buzzed the crowd in a vain attempt to disperse them. After one week of the hunger strike, the Irish Trades Union Congress called a general strike in support of the prisoners and following a national strike lasting three days the Republican prisoners were released. Following the release of the internees, the prison authorities had to report to Dublin Castle that they had also accidently released a number of convicted prisoners.

Not unlike many other parts of the country, at Miltown-Malbay in Co. Clare, bonfires were lit to celebrate the release of the hunger strikers. In contravention of DORA, people had gathered to celebrate when Crown Forces came on the scene and without warning opened fire on the crowd, killing three and injuring nine. No action was taken against the perpetrators and incidents involving the shooting dead of civilians continued. These shootings were often falsely dismissed by Dublin Castle as internal feuding among the IRA, or the shooting by the IRA of an alleged informer. Nevertheless, in an attempt to stop the press reporting on the shooting of civilians by the army or police, General Macready informed all editors of daily newspapers both in Ireland and Britain, that from the beginning of May, daily press bulletins would be issued outlining army operations, so that the press need not erroneously report on shootings in which the Crown Forces had no involvement.

As the build-up of Crown Forces continued in the Spring of 1920, in mid-May Dublin dock-men decided that they would no longer assist the Crown in the importation of weapons of war which were for the suppression of the fight for Independence. Following this 'wildcat' action by the dockers,

---

women praying outside the prison were again attacked and around 70 of them were injured.

the Irish Transport and General Workers Union backed them and instructed all its members to follow suit. In what was known as "The Munitions Crisis" for the remainder of 1920 both dockers and railway workers refused to operate trains or lifting equipment for loads which were destined for the forces of the Crown. Without pay, the strike pay of these men was collected from the ordinary people of Ireland who contributed to a voluntarily subscribed fund which eventually amounted to hundreds of thousands of pounds. Company managers reacted by mass suspensions or the sacking of workers.

While the British made some attempts to operate equipment with Royal Engineers, the transport network was effectively brought to a standstill. In order to transport personnel, weapons and equipment, the Crown Forces were now forced to use the road network leaving them susceptible to attack by the IRA which occurred with ever increasing frequency. This meant that many of the lightly armoured or soft-skinned vehicles then in use by the Crown Forces were unsuitable. To combat this army lorries were modified to give them high-sided armour and sometimes caged tops to repel hand grenades. One of the most frequently used of these modified lorries was the "Crossley Tender" which was used to transport both Crown Forces personnel and equipment throughout the country.

### "Tans" and "Auxies"

"The sins of ignorant youths without experience or training are to be judged differently from those of an organized administration preaching law and order in the King's name and with talk about 'German atrocities' on their lips" – Timothy Healy

"Those blackguards should never have been let loose in the country" – Major General Sir Oliver Nugent.

By early 1920 the first batch of English ex-soldiers for the RIC were arriving in Ireland to undergo training at the Phoenix Park Depot. As the struggle for freedom continued, recruitment for the RIC in England quickened and rapidly rose into the thousands.[I] As their numbers increased, training for most RIC recruits now took place at Gormanston in Co. Meath instead of the Phoenix Park.

With the influx of new recruits, complete RIC uniforms rapidly ran out. The new RIC men were initially issued a hybrid uniform and were generally clad in khaki tunics with RIC trousers and caps, an immediate distinguishing feature for the new force which resulted in them being labelled "The Black and Tans" or simply "Tans" by the Irish.[II] Within a number of months, the new recruits would be clad in the proper RIC uniform and the term "Tans" would then be applied to the RIC as a whole.

On July 28th recruitment commenced for an additional force whose foundation has been attributed to both Macready's predecessor General Shaw and the Secretary of State for Air, Sir Winston Churchill. Called the "Special Emergency Gendarmerie" or "Auxiliary Cadets" of the RIC, the Auxiliaries were to be composed of former army officers who had served with distinction in the Great War. Initially Lloyd George was reluctant to adopt Churchill's recommendation, as it promised to exacerbate the situation, by letting loose an even more battle hardened group of war veterans on the Irish people. However after Churchill received the support of General Sir Hugh Tudor, Lloyd George acquiesced.

---

[I] The number of new recruits for the militarized RIC eventually numbered around 10,000 excluding "Auxiliaries"

[II] It is traditionally recorded that the name "Black and Tans" originated with a pack of hounds of the same name that belonged to the Scarteen Hunt in Co. Limerick. The Irish War of Independence was commonly referred to by veterans as "The Tan War".

Whilst the Black and Tans, were supposed to bring a ruthless fighting backbone to the RIC[I], the Auxiliary Cadets were a force designed from their very inception to operate: "at the limit of law and order"[449] – a euphemism for committing crimes which the British government could excuse, smudge or confuse for the benefit of the press.

General Sir Hugh Tudor

Receiving payment of one pound a day (which was twice what an RIC constable was paid) the "Auxies" as they were referred to by the Irish, were not to be subject to military discipline or trial by any civil court. Indeed by their very constitution – a division of army officers of all ranks used to giving orders rather than taking them, coupled with their loose discipline spelt trouble.[II] They would not merge into the RIC proper but would form their own independent division, referred to as ADRIC (Auxiliary Division RIC) under the command of Brigadier General Frank Crozier[III]. The different companies of ADRIC

---

[I] RIC Constable Daniel Crowley recalled of the Tans: "I have seen them stop two girls of the town (Clogheen, Co. Tipperary) coming to the rosary at half past six in the evening, and they said to the girls 'Hands Up' and knocked them down...(they were)...trying to stir the people up."

[II] Following the burning of Cork City, General Hutchinson, attempted to remonstrate with "K" company of the Auxiliaries who were responsible, but their attitude to "a telling off" was so hostile he did not even attempt it.

[III] Before the outbreak of the Great War, Crozier (then on the British army retired list) had served as an officer training instructor for the Ulster Volunteer Force and at times a bodyguard commander for Capt. Craig.

were not evenly spread throughout the country but were concentrated on those areas where the IRA was strongest. As the numbers of this 'elite' unit were small (eventually amounting to less than 2,500) they initially used the RIC depot in the Phoenix Park as a base before moving to Beggars Bush Army Barracks in Dublin which then became their headquarters.

For one year from the Summer of 1920, both Auxiliaries and Tans would earn for themselves a fearful reputation for murder, brutality, looting, arson and reprisal attacks on both civilians and their property. Their actions in Ireland in 1920 and 1921 were to be so ruthless and devoid of humanity that they would leave a lasting psychological mark on the country.

By mid August, the first Auxiliary units were beginning to form up. Initially clad in similar attire to the Tans, they were sometimes mistaken for them. To the trained eye they might be distinguished by their footwear as being "officers and gentlemen" they generally wore knee length officer boots.

When their proper uniform was issued, it was dark navy, appearing black on first sight, along with a distinguishing bonnet bearing a yellow diamond crest with a harp surmounted by a crown.

As both Tans and Auxiliaries became active within the ranks of the RIC, the number of civilian deaths rapidly increased. These soldiers in police clothing always carried their weapons at the ready. As their lorries hurtled through towns, villages and the countryside at great speed, they held their weapons at the ready as if in a combat zone and would often open fire on the slightest pretext, resulting in the wounding or killing[1] of

---

[1] During July of 1920 four innocent civilians (Tom O'Donnell, Richard Lumley, Michael Small and Dan McGrath) are recorded as having been killed by bullets fired from the back of police lorries. Between January and June of 1920 thirteen people were killed by indiscriminate firing by the Crown Forces. One hundred

civilians or the destruction of property. There were also incidents of children who failed to get out of the way in time being driven over and killed.[1] If their convoy stopped in a village, all the inhabitants of the village without exception for the old, sick or infirm had to line up outside their houses where they were questioned and brutalized. Some common practices recorded by the Report of the British Labour Party included forcing inhabitants to drag the Irish flag in the mud, spitting on photographs of Republican leaders and the enforced singing of "God Save the King." Upon their departure, the Auxiliaries would invariably leave behind a trail of destruction and civilians wounded by 'pistol whipping' or worse.

## Council Elections and Pogroms

In June of 1920, the Irish people had another chance to decide whether or not they supported the fight for freedom. At the beginning of the month, the local elections commenced, once more being conducted under the system of proportional representation which gave the Unionists a better chance of winning seats on any of the county councils or rural district councils outside their enclave in the north-east of Ulster. When the votes were counted and released in mid June, Unionists had secured a majority of council seats in only the four north-eastern counties of Antrim, Armagh, Derry and Down while in all other counties Sinn Fein were the predominant party.

Following the municipal elections of the Spring, these elections added to the concern of Ulster Unionists that the national

---

and seventy two people were injured. Fifteen towns and villages were targeted in reprisal attacks.

[1] On June 6th 1920 a boy was driven over and killed by a Crown Forces lorry in Cappoquin, co. Waterford.

revolution might yet somehow encompass them through the ballot box.

As the anniversary of the Battle of the Boyne (July 12th) approached, Ulster Unionist tensions reached fever pitch. On July 12th Edward Carson in an uncompromising speech to a Unionist rally said: "...I am sick of words without action...we in Ulster will tolerate no Sinn Féin...we will take the matter into our own hands"[450] On July 16th a number of letters calling the Unionists to "action" were published in the Belfast Newsletter, in which one letter-writer declared that if words were not immediately replaced by deeds, then "Protestant Ulster" was doomed.

On the evening of July 19th Unionist mobs attacked Catholic areas of Belfast, burning Catholic homes and businesses. In the days that followed the pogrom not only continued in Belfast but spread to other areas. Night after night, Catholic areas of towns with a Protestant majority were attacked. When IRA men attempted to defend Catholic areas the Crown Forces appeared, but only to attack and disperse the IRA. In some towns (such as Dromore and Banbridge) the entire Catholic population was burnt out and forced to leave.

On the day that the men of Belfast returned to work after the "12th fortnight" (July 21st) a plan to drive out the Catholic workers was put into effect. In the Harland & Wolff shipyard Catholic workers were attacked, beaten and chased out of their place of employment. Men had their clothes ripped open in order to see if they were wearing a brown scapular or a miraculous medal as a means of determining if they were Catholic. The anti-Catholic orgy at Harland & Wolff quickly spread to other engineering businesses in Belfast and from there to the city's workshops, shops and offices. By the end of July around 11,000 Catholics (10,000 men and 1,000 women) had been driven out from their place of employment[I]. Tens of Catholics had been killed and hundreds injured. Any Catholic who dared return to their place of employment was threatened with immediate death.

## "The more you shoot, the better I will like it!"

By mid-Summer of 1920 there was almost a total lack of recruits for the RIC within Ireland while resignations from the force occurred on a daily basis.[II] While there were still RIC veterans who were willing to fall in with the wishes of their masters that they should run amok in the towns and villages of Ireland[III] there were those who had made the decision to no longer act against their fellow countrymen as the Government desired.

On June 17th 1920, the RIC barracks at Listowel, Co. Kerry was visited by General Sir Hugh Tudor and the Divisional Police Commissioner for Munster, Lieutenant Colonel Gerald Bryce Smyth, who addressed the men. His address was afterwards recorded by Constable Jeremiah Mee who was one of the men present. Before the visit, the other constables had appointed Constable Mee as their spokesman.

According to Mee's testimony, Colonel Smyth's address to the Listowel constables ran (in part) as follows: "Well, men, I have something of interest to tell you: something that I am sure you would not wish your wives to hear...If a police barracks is burned or if the barracks already occupied is not suitable, then the best house in the locality is to be commandeered, the

---

[I] This number was arrived at by a committee headed by Bishop Joseph MacRory.
[II] In August of 1920, Chief Secretary Hamar Greenwood informed the Commons that 556 constables had resigned within a two month period.
[III] Between the 23rd and 28th of June RIC reprisals against the civilian population were carried out in Newcastlewest, Limerick, Bantry and Kilcommon. During July the RIC carried out reprisal actions in Tralee, Ballagh, Enniscorthy, Tuam, Leap, Galbally, Arklow, Limerick City, Cork City and Tuam.

occupants thrown out into the gutter. Let them die there – the more the merrier. Police and military will patrol the country at least five nights a week. They are not to confine themselves to the main roads, but make across the country, lie in ambush and when civilians are seen approaching, shout 'Hands up!' Should the order be not immediately obeyed, shoot and shoot with effect. If the persons approaching carry their hands in their pockets, or are in any way suspicious looking, shoot them down. You may make mistakes occasionally and innocent persons may be shot but that cannot be helped, and you are bound to get the right parties some time. The more you shoot, the better I will like you, and I assure you no policeman will get into trouble for shooting any man.

Lt. Col. Gerald Smyth

Hunger-strikers will be allowed to die in jail – the more the merrier. Some have died there already and a damn bad job they were not all allowed to die. As a matter of fact some of them have already been dealt with in a manner their friends will never hear about.

An emigrant ship left an Irish port for a foreign port lately with lots of Sinn Féiners on board. I assure you men it will never land.

That is nearly all I have to say to you. We want your assistance in carrying out this scheme and wiping out Sinn Féin. Any man who is not prepared to do the job and is going to be a hindrance rather than help us had better leave his job at once."[451]

At this point Colonel Smyth addressed the first constable in line: "Are you prepared to cooperate?"[452] The constable in question referred Smyth to Mee who now took a step forward and answered for all the RIC men present: "By your accent I take it you are an Englishman and in your ignorance forget that you are addressing Irishmen."[453] After saying this Mee removed his cap, belt and bayonet and placed them on the table while saying: "These too are English. Take them as a present from me and to hell with you – you are a murderer!"[454] Enraged by Mee's words, Smyth ordered his immediate arrest by the constables present. The other constables refused and told Smyth that if anyone laid a hand on Mee the room would "run red with blood."[455] At this General Tudor, Colonel Smyth and their aides left the room.

Following Smyth's visit, Mee and his colleagues resigned from the RIC. Mee left Listowel for Dublin where he sought out Arthur Griffith and presented him with a written account of what became known as "The Listowel Mutiny". Mee now agreed to work under the direction of Countess Markievicz where he helped organize both aid and jobs for those RIC men who had resigned their posts with the assistance of a special fund established by the Republican Government.

As news of Smyth's address and the resignation of the Listowel RIC men became common knowledge, Smyth's assassination became a priority for the IRA. A resident of the gentleman's "County Club" on Cork's south Mall, he was shot dead while drinking in the bar on July 17th.

As his mother was from Banbridge,[1] it was decided to bury Smyth's remains there. On the day of his burial, Loyalist mobs once more attacked Catholic areas of both Belfast and Banbridge where they burnt out Catholic homes and

---

[1] Bryce-Smyth had been born in India, where his English father was "Punjab High-Commissioner"

businesses and killed Catholics. Crown Forces also became involved, in one incident randomly opening fire on Clonard Monastery with a machine gun, killing twenty-eight year old Brother Michael Morgan from Drumavaddy in the Parish of Denn in Co. Cavan.

Following Colonel Smyth's death, his younger brother, Major George Osbert Smyth, who was soldiering for the Crown in Egypt, requested a transfer to Ireland in order to avenge his brother's death. In Ireland he became involved in intelligence work, and on October 12th 1920, accompanied an attack against an IRA safe-house in Drumcondra where Séan Treacy and Dan Breen were staying.

During the early morning raid Osbert Smyth and Captain A.P White of the Surrey Yeomanry were killed. Treacy and Breen dove through an open upstairs window and broke through the glass of the conservatory below in order to escape. Severely wounded, Breen was afterwards brought to the Mater Hospital where he was hidden and nursed by the nuns. Treacy had not been severely wounded.[I] In the aftermath of the raid, the owner of the safe-house, Professor John Carolan was lined up and shot in the neck by a member of the raiding party. He died a few weeks later.

## "A Race of Treacherous Murderers"

In the aftermath of the Listowel Mutiny, Dublin Castle greatly feared that the resignation of the RIC constables of Listowel might be repeated by RIC veterans in other barracks or that the new members of the RIC (Tans and Auxiliaries) might have doubts about undertaking the sort of repression which the British government desired of them as "The Levellers" had in Cromwell's time.[II]

---

[I] Treacy was later killed on October 14th outside 94 Talbot St. Dublin in a shoot out with the British Secret Service.
[II] See Volume I, chapter 24 of "Centuries of Trial"

Dublin Castle now undertook a propaganda campaign to keep the RIC "on-side" or as Hamar Greenwood put it, to: "revive the morale."[456] Commencing in August of 1920, Dublin Castle began issuing to its constabulary a newsletter called "The Weekly Summary" which was produced by the two Dublin Castle press officers, Captains Darling and Pollard. In the newsletter, which was also distributed to the international media,[I] the IRA were consistently portrayed as murderers and gangsters with the language used being designed to instil and reinforce within the RIC a mentality of ruthlessness. Every action of the IRA was both magnified and exaggerated and described in such terms as could only increase the anger and hatred of the RIC against the members of the IRA, Sinn Fein and the people who supported them. In the third issue of The Weekly Summary, the members of the RIC were encouraged to make the country "an appropriate hell" for rebels. As the weeks went past and the war intensified, so did the rhetoric of The Weekly Summary. By the beginning of 1921, members of Sinn Féin were being described as people for whom: "the rope and the bullet are all too good"[457] while deValera was described as being a member of "a race of treacherous murderers."[458]

This propaganda translated into deeds. One of the more reprehensible acts not altogether uncommon among the Crown Forces was the substitution of a family member for the intended target, when the Tans or Auxies raided a home in search of one of more sons of the house who were members of the IRA and were 'on the run'. When the person in question could not be found, either a parent or sibling of the wanted man was sometimes taken out and shot in lieu.[II] If the wanted

---

[I] "The Weekly Summary" was soon discounted by the international media as its stories regarding IRA actions were so unbelievable.

[II] In one recorded case, the RIC executed a young sibling (who was suffering from tuberculosis) when his older brothers (who were all members of the IRA)

man was found to be at home he was arrested but generally did not arrive at the RIC station alive as he had been shot "while trying to escape."[1]

## Mass Resignations among the Judiciary

By the Summer of 1920, local Crown appointed magistrates were resigning on a daily basis. On July 22nd Cork magistrates resigned en-masse while in August alone, 148 magistrates tendered their resignation.

In his resignation letter, the Chief Magistrate for Galway, Sir Henry Grattan Bellew, who resigned on August 11th, outlined his reason for resigning which was typical of all those who decided to no longer work for the Crown: "His Majesty's Government has determined on the substitution of military for civil law in Ireland. I can act so far in harmony with the new policy that I beg herewith to resign the offices I hold as Magistrate and Deputy Lieutenant for His Majesty in the county of Galway. I hope my colleagues will follow my example so that the wrecking of Irish towns and the ruin of Irish industry may be proceeded with, without any camouflage

---

could not be found at their home address. During the month of August 1920 a disabled boy was shot in lieu of his brother at Bantry in Co. Cork. A similar incident almost occurred to the great grandfather of the author. When the RIC arrived at his house in search of the author's grandfather and his brother, both of whom were "on the run", their father was taken outside and put up against a wall to be shot. However due to the entreaties of his wife, the RIC relented and left the property without carrying out the execution.

[1] On August 14th 1920, Patrick Lynch of Hospital, Co. Limerick was arrested at his home by the RIC and later found shot dead on the Fair Green. It later transpired that the case was one of mistaken identity as Lynch was not an IRA member. On August 27th, two brothers, Sean and Batt Buckley was captured at their home outside Cork City by the Cameron Highlanders. Both men were handcuffed and thrown into the army lorry. Both were shot. Batt survived and lived to testify that they were not "shot while trying to escape" as was the common reason for such deaths.

or appearance of approval by Irishmen of the sabotage of their country."[459]

These mass resignations from the Crown judiciary coincided with the official establishment by the Dáil of countrywide Republican courts of justice on June 29th. The Dáil decree allowed for the acceptance of the mass of English law until amendments could take place. However, from the outset there were exceptions. Laws motivated by religious (anti-Catholic) or political animosity were excluded while commentaries upon Gaelic (Brehon) law were to be admitted and their application to current conditions considered. In spite of the attempts by Crown Forces to disrupt Republican courts, by the end of 1920 these courts were sitting in 27 counties, including five of the nine counties of Ulster.

The mass resignations by the judiciary were unexpected in London. On June 28th the Chief of the General Staff, Field Marshal Sir Henry Wilson[1] wrote in his diary: "I really believe we will be kicked out (of Ireland)." This sense of desperation in London also encompassed the Crown Forces in Ireland who began to torture Republican prisoners in an effort to extract information. In Bandon, following the severe torture of two Republican prisoners for information at the end of June 1920, one of them, Patrick Harte became mentally deranged, never to recover.

Attempted resignations from English service in Ireland's cause also occurred thousands of miles from Ireland. On June 28th 1920, 350 soldiers of the Connaught Rangers who were stationed at Jullundur, in the Indian Punjab region laid down their arms in protest at the crimes of the Crown Forces in Ireland. Of this number 61 men were court-martialled and

---

[1] Field Marshal Sir Henry Wilson thought the Crown Forces reprisals of "torch and burn" counterproductive. According to his diary entry for July 12th 1920, he preferred the identification and assassination of key Republicans.

sentenced to penal servitude, while one, James Daly from Tyrrellspass in Co. Westmeath was executed.

## The IRA At War

"...one of our first governmental acts was to take over control of the voluntary armed forces of the nation. From the Irish Volunteers we fashioned the Irish Republican Army to be the military arm of the government." – President Eamonn deValéra (March 1921)

While the British had unending resources in their fight against Irish independence, the IRA had very little in comparison. They relied mainly on their enemy to supply them with weaponry. However while the Crown Forces had the advantage of resources, the IRA had two more important and decisive advantages - they had the support of the majority of the people and they also possessed local knowledge of the areas in which they operated.[1]

Having forced the RIC from most of their smaller Barracks, the IRA now looked to engage with the enemy in the field. With neither the strength nor the resources to engage the enemy in open set-piece battles, the IRA had of necessity resorted to guerilla tactics which also showed the enemy that they were occupiers of a country which was not their own. Organizing themselves into mobile "hit and run" groups of between 15 and 30 men which were known as "Flying Columns" they relied on the support of the people in their operational area to feed and shelter them as they attempted to attack the enemy

---

[1] Within Ulster, where there was a large Protestant minority in some counties or majority in others, the IRA often struggled in the procurement of weapons or the prosecution of successful ambushes.

Flying column No.2, Third Tipperary Brigade

and disrupt his movements and communications[I] This method of operation infuriated the enemy, with reprisals for column actions by the Crown Forces falling very heavily on the communities which supported them.[II]

Without the women's paramilitary association "Cumann na Mban", the IRA could never have successfully prosecuted the war. From the delivery of dispatches to the carrying out of intelligence work, the nursing of the wounded, clerical duties, and the care of those dependents of Republican prisoners in Crown jails, the women of Cumann na Mban were essential to the Republican war effort.

---

[I] This was achieved by the blocking of roads by felled trees, the digging of trenches or masked traps on roads, the blowing of bridges or railway lines and the cutting of telegraph wires.

[II] The latter half of September of 1920 saw sustained acts of reprisal by the Crown Forces. On September 20th, the Crown forces destroyed houses in Tuam and Carrick-on-Shannon and sacked Balbriggan. The following day more properties were destroyed in Tuam, Drumshanbo and Galway City. On September 23rd, Co. Clare suffered greatly with reprisals taking place in Miltown-Malbay, Lahinch and Ennistymon. Three men were murdered. Towards the end of the month Ashbourne was targeted by the Auxiliaries with hundreds of thousands of pounds (in modern terms) being caused. Mallow was also targeted with the town hall being destroyed.

For the IRA, rules of military conduct composed by the Minister for Defence were issued to the soldiers through the IRA newspaper "An t-Óglach. Prisoners were to be properly treated and their personal effects were not to be retained. Any monies captured in intercepted mail bags were to be forwarded to the recipient. Looting of any sort, or the excessive consumption of alcohol was absolutely forbidden. When, out of necessity, provisions had to be requisitioned, receipts were to be issued in the name of the Republican Government to be redeemed at a later date.

Catholic or Protestant, Unionist or Nationalist, the IRA, as the army of the Government of the Irish Republic did not necessarily demand the loyalty of the Irish people. However they did demand that no citizen of Ireland should act against them. Any informer[1] who caused the death of an IRA soldier or compromised an attack and was caught could expect to be executed. Informers who were caught for less serious offences could expect to be banished from the country.

## The Restoration of Order in Ireland Act

"A lot of order has been restored in Ireland since the coming of Strongbow." – Brigadier General Frank Crozier

By the Summer of 1920, the British system of law and order in Ireland was collapsing. In previous centuries, English control of the country would have been rapidly and brutally restored as may be evidenced by previous chapters of Irish revolt. In 1920, repression on the scale of previous centuries was no longer possible. Well aware that the eyes of the world were on

---

[1] On September 3rd 1920, notices were posted on walls and hoardings in Dublin offering a reward for information against the IRA. "Be careful to give neither your name or address and to post by indirect means to 'D.W Ross, Poste Restante, GPO, London" the notice ran. During the war around 200 people are believed to have been executed by the IRA as spies.

Ireland, and that the situation in the country was being closely watched in the New World, every action of the British government had to be calibrated to give the correct impression internationally.

Unwilling to introduce full martial law on a widespread basis and finding DORA inadequate, the British government decided upon an additional measure, which although not martial law by name, replicated it in many respects. The Bill which became law on August 9th most likely originated in a cabinet meeting on May 31st during which the Irish situation was discussed at length.

During the meeting, Hamar Greenwood (somewhat ironically) told the British Cabinet that: "The great task (of the Crown forces) is to crush out murder and arson".[460] Greenwood informed the cabinet that: "throughout the great part of Ireland criminal justice can no longer be administered by the ordinary constitutional process..."[461] a state of affairs necessitating in his opinion, that a system of quasi military justice be imposed upon the country. Reinforcing Greenwood, Winston Churchill lamented that no-one was being hanged, while Lloyd George commented that if there was not a system of military justice it would be very difficult to "get convictions from Catholics."[462]

Following further discussion in Dublin, both Tudor and Macready were in favour of the additional measure. Although happy that the army and RIC (including Auxiliaries and Tans) were "getting into their stride"[463] as Macready put it, he favoured extreme measures by the government which would reinforce the actions of the fighting men. The new Bill was complete by July 30th and following the guillotining of the Commons debate, it received the King's assent on August 9th coming into force twelve days later.

Allowing for mass internment without trial, the Bill also allowed any prisoner to be tried by secret court-martial. Only when the death sentence was the prescribed punishment was a non-military lawyer allowed to be present. Any person believed to possess knowledge likely to be of use to His Majesty's forces could be arrested and sentenced to six months imprisonment, unless they co-operated. All local authorities controlled by Sinn Fein were to be denied funding while coroner's inquests were to be replaced at the request of the Lord Lieutenant by secret military inquiry.

With this armour of immunity from prosecution the Crown Forces now had carte blanche to engage in acts of terror. The Act gave truth to the words spoken in Listowel by Colonel Smyth that no policeman would get in trouble for shooting civilians or for any other punitive measures in which he was involved.

Dublin Castle moved quickly to avail itself of its new powers. At the beginning of September 1920, all coroner's inquests were abolished in ten of those counties in which the IRA were most active. In the first three weeks of September, the deaths of 18 unarmed people were believed to have been committed by the Crown Forces.[1]

The first hanging to take place under the new legislation was that of IRA volunteer, eighteen year old Kevin Barry, who took part in the ambush of a British Army lorry in Church St. Dublin on September 20th. The IRA had intended to hold up the soldiers who were collecting bread from Monk's Bakery, and capture their weapons. A gun battle followed during which Barry's weapon had jammed. Having taken cover under a British army lorry, the rest of the IRA unit were forced to retreat leaving three soldiers dead. Barry was then captured after his presence was innocently betrayed by a local woman. In army custody Barry was tortured during which his arm was

---

[1] During September, General Macready gave an interview to the French newspaper "La Libertié". He told the newspaper "...we have most of the names and the day may come when we shall be able to make a definite clearance of them."

dislocated. An account of his torture was written by Barry and smuggled out of the jail by his sister.[1]

Kevin Barry

In spite of the fact that Barry had not killed any of the three soldiers he was sentenced to death and hanged on All Saints Day (November 1st) 1920.

On the same day that Barry was hanged, Ellen Quinn who was seven months pregnant was shot dead by the RIC in Gort, Co. Galway. The RIC had opened fire from the back of a lorry while passing the house. An RIC inquiry afterwards found the murder to have been "a precautionary measure". During the first two weeks of November, 14 civilians were murdered by Crown Forces, the final victim being eight year old Annie O'Neill who was killed after an RIC patrol opened fire from the back of a lorry at a group standing in a gateway on November 13th.

## "There can be no Truce with the Powers of Hell"

In the aftermath of the assassination of the Lord Mayor of Cork and Commandant of the First Cork Brigade, Tomás Mac Curtáin, his deputy Terence Mac Swiney had been elected to both posts unopposed. Already a TD for the constituency of

---

[1] "The...officer...ordered the sergeant to put me face down on the floor and twist my arms...the sergeant knelt on the small of my back, the other two placed one foot each on my back and left shoulder, and the man who knelt on me twisted my right arm, held it by the wrist with one hand, while he held my hair with the other to pull back my head. My arm was twisted from my elbow joint. This continued to the best of my judgement for five minutes..."

Mid-Cork, Mac Swiney was a widely acclaimed Gaelic scholar, teacher and the author of many poems and plays.

Immediately following his election as Mayor of Cork, Mac Swiney had addressed his fellow councillors: "We see in the manner in which the late Lord Mayor was murdered an attempt to terrify us all. Our first duty is to answer that threat in the only fitting manner: to show ourselves unterrified, cool, and inflexible for the fullfilment of our chief purpose – the establishment of the independence and the integrity of our country and the peace and happiness of the Irish Republic. To that end I am here. This contest on our side is not one of rivalry or vengeance, but of endurance.

Terence Mac Swiney

It is not those who can inflict the most but those that can suffer the most who will conquer, though we do not abrogate our function to demand that murderers and evil-doers be punished for their crimes. It is conceivable that the army of occupation could stop our functioning for a time. Then it becomes simply a question of endurance. Those whose faith is strong will endure to the end in triumph.

It is not we who take innocent blood, but we offer it, sustained by the example of our immortal dead and that divine example which inspires us all for the redemption of our country. Facing our enemy we must declare our attitude simply. We see in their regime a thing of evil incarnate. With it there can be no parley any more than there can be truce with the powers of hell. We ask no mercy and we will accept no compromise."[464]

On August 12th, MacSwiney was arrested at City Hall and court-martialled on the charge of "being in possession of documents the publication of which would be likely to cause disaffection to His Majesty." Refusing to recognize that the court had any jurisdiction or authority, Mac Swiney would not enter a plea and went on immediate hunger strike in protest at his incarceration. In this he was not alone as the day before his arrest a hunger-strike had begun among the Republicans at Cork jail. After three days MacSwiney was transferred to Brixton Prison in England where he continued to refuse food and made it known to the British government that he would not relent from his protest.[I] His case quickly drew international attention and pleas for his release came not only from abroad but from influential persons in Britain. Among the prominent people to visit Mac Swiney in prison was Archbishop Mannix of Melbourne who had the previous month condemned English rule in Ireland at a rally in New York. Mannix had arrived in England by force on August 9th after his Irish bound liner was intercepted by a Royal Navy destroyer in the Atlantic and Mannix was removed onto the destroyer as London had decided to bar him from entering Ireland.[II]

In spite of international pressure Lloyd George was determined not to appear weak and refused to release MacSwiney as he feared a mutiny among the British garrison in Ireland. MacSwiney died after 74 days on hunger strike in Brixton Prison. The government, fearing a funeral and mass demonstration in the tradition of the great "Fenian funerals" refused to allow the coffin with his remains to enter Dublin[III]

---

[I] He wrote "...then the British Government can boast of having killed two Lord Mayors of Cork in six months."

[II] Archbishop Mannix was going to Ireland to visit his aged mother. Having over-reacted the affair left Lloyd George looking very foolish.

[III] Terence MacSwiney's family refused the request of the British government for his body to be shipped directly to Cork. At the Holyhead train which would have brought MacSwiney's remains and the mourners to the Dublin ferry, the coffin

and he was brought by ship directly to Cork, his coffin escorted into the harbour by a motor tug full of Auxiliaries. On October 31st, following requiem Mass at the North Chapel on Shandon St., Mac Swiney was interred in St. Finbarr's Cemetery, close to the grave of Tomás Mac Curtáin.

## The Pogroms Continue

Transferred to Lisburn, Co. Antrim in the aftermath of the Coroner's Verdict which found him guilty of the willful murder of Tomás Mac Curtain, District Inspector Oswald Swanzy had become a target for assassination by the IRA. On Sunday August 22nd, Swanzy was assassinated with Mac Curtain's own pistol (among other weapons) by four IRA men who waited for Swanzy outside the Protestant Church.

With their simmering passion of hatred against the Catholics of the town now ablaze in the aftermath of the shooting, many Unionists embarked on a pogrom in the town which did not cease until almost every Catholic[1] was driven out, and their homes set ablaze. The Pogrom quickly spread to Bangor and Banbridge and from there to Belfast where for ten days the Catholic communities were targeted and 31 Catholics were killed. The London Daily News correspondent in Belfast reported that: "…this was a deliberate and organized attempt, not by any means the first in history, to drive out the Catholic Irish out of North-East Ulster, and the machinery that was being used was very largely the machinery of the Carsonite army of 1914."[465]

The anti-Catholic pogrom in Belfast finally subsided on September 3rd only to erupt again on September 26th following the shooting of a constable. Ten Catholics were murdered in

---

was removed from the care of the family by Crown Forces and the family forcibly removed from the train.

[1] A group of Protestants prevented the mob from torching the Catholic Convent in the town. The Catholic presbytery was burnt to the ground.

Belfast in the following three weeks while arson attacks and beatings continued unabated.

In the aftermath of the Pogroms, Sir James Craig visited the Belfast shipyard where the first pogrom of the year had been initiated and from where all Catholic workers[I] had been expelled. As he unfurled the union flag he said: "Do I approve of the action you boys have taken in the past? I say yes..."[466]

## The Ulster Special Constabulary

In the Summer of 1920, it was proposed in London by James Craig that recruitment for an Ulster Special Constabulary, from among those who were well disposed to the Union take place within the six counties which the British government intended to partition, as a preparatory measure for the implementation of "Home Rule" for Northern Ireland. Lloyd George agreed. The formation of the new Government of Northern Ireland would be much smoother if a sizeable Unionist police force were already in place to reinforce and augment the RIC. The cost of the new force would be paid for by London.

Captain James Craig

When the formation of the Special Constabulary was promulgated The Belfast reporter for the London Daily Mail wrote: "It seems to me the most outrageous thing which they

---

[I] From the Autumn of 1920, most Protestant employers in the six counties required all workers to sign an oath of allegiance to the monarchy in order to obtain or retain employment.

have ever done in Ireland...A citizen of Belfast who is 'well disposed' to the British Government is almost, from the nature of the case, an Orangeman, or at any rate a vehement anti Sinn Féiner. These are the very people who have been looting Catholic shops and driving thousands of Catholic women and children from their homes.[1] We hope it may still be possible to stay the horrors which the execution of this incredible order will almost certainly entail. If it is not, and if the expected results follow, there can be no hope left of rehabilitating the shaken credit of the British Government in Ireland."[467]

On November 1st 1920, the Ulster Special Constabulary was brought into existence. As with the formation of 16th Ulster Division at the outbreak of the Great War, Catholics were not encouraged to join. Viewed by the Protestants as a force not for the impartial maintenance of the peace but rather a force for the protection of the new Protestant state, around thirty two thousand Protestants enlisted. Whole UVF units joined en-masse.

The "Specials" consisted of three categories. The "A" Specials were designated to serve on a permanent basis beside the RIC for as long as the 'emergency' continued. The "C" Specials consisted of older men who performed ancillary tasks such as clerks, cooks, medics and drivers. However it was the part-time "B" Specials, which consisted of around 20,000 men, (chiefly former members of the UVF) who were to become notorious for crimes against Catholics up until their disbandment in 1970.[II]

---

[I] With the introduction of this measure history was being repeated.In the late eighteenth century those mobs who had been involved in attacking and burning out Catholics in Ulster (Armagh Outrages) had been recruited into both the yeomanry and militia after which they continued to conduct atrocities against the Catholics in uniform.

[II] The "expected results" of the Daily Mail reporter did indeed materialise. In the aftermath of the 1921 election and the first meeting of the 'Ulster Parliament' officers of the Ulster Special Constabulary raided the Magee home at Corrogs,

The Destruction of Irish Industry
In their punitive measures against the Irish people for the support of the Republic, one of the prime targets was Irish agriculture and the widespread industry that had been spawned by Horace Plunkett and the Cooperative movement since the beginning of the century.

Since April of 1920, Crown Forces had begun targeting local creameries in areas where punitive measures had been undertaken. Whilst the destruction of a local creamery and its adjacent agricultural store greatly affected the community in which the creamery was located, agricultural manufacturing at a higher level was not affected. Beginning in August of 1920, the Crown Forces began targeting factories and mills, burning down four sites between August 6th and 17th. On August 22nd the manufacturing creamery at Knocklong in Co. Limerick, which was owned by the Unionist Sir Thomas Cleeves was destroyed. As it serviced the farms of a huge area the effect of the creameries' destruction was catastrophic. Sir Horace Plunkett demanded that these destructive acts (which would eventually encompass over 100 agricultural creameries and industrial sites) be investigated but his plea fell on deaf ears. In its press releases to the media Dublin Castle ignored the destruction wrought by the Crown Forces on the economic life of Ireland.

---

Co. Down where they murdered the father and son, leaving the second son badly wounded. They also beat up the daughter.
Following the killing of two members of the "A" Specials on March 23rd 1922, suspected members of the "B" specials entered the Mac Mahon home on Kinnaird Road the following day. They forced Owen Mac Mahon and his six sons along with two other men into one room and opened fire on them for five minutes. All were killed except the youngest son, twelve year old Michael Mac Mahon who was partly protected by furniture and played dead. No one was ever charged. At the end of the month an RIC man was shot dead in Belfast. On April 1st, ten constables went on the rampage in a Catholic area near the centre of the city shooting dead five Catholic men and a six month old baby.

IRA Prisoners in Ballykinlar Internment Camp

The Internment Camps

Following the assassinations of British officers on the morning of Bloody Sunday, a mass roundup of Republican suspects was initiated by Dublin Castle. All over the country, known Republicans whom the RIC suspected of being members of the IRA or leading members of Sinn Fein were detained, along with those Republicans who had previously been detained and released. By the end of November over 500 additional "persons of interest" had been arrested and interned, with the available prison spaces quickly being filled. As the arrests continued, a new internment camp was opened beside the army base at Ballykinler in Co. Down. By year's end the camp at Ballykinler, had reached its capacity and additional camps were opened on Spike Island, Bere Island and the Curragh.

The Ballykinler Camp was by far the largest of the internment camps. Holding around 1,000 prisoners in forty wooden huts, the Republican prisoners interned there led a regimented existence which they made the most of by internally organized education, (Irish history, language and poetry) drama and sports, with many prisoners who possessed a trade (tailor, barber, teacher) making use of it for the good of their fellow prisoners. Thanks to the Society of Friends, a library was also established within the camp. Although not now involved in the fight for freedom, imprisonment was not without it dangers. On January 17th, 1921 two prisoners were shot dead by a sentry without warning while on September 21st, a prisoner, Tadhg Barry whose release was imminent was shot dead whilst saying goodbye to the prisoners in the adjacent camp. In November a further prisoner (named Tormey) was shot dead for being in close proximity to the barbed wire fence separating the adjacent camp.

## "In the Highest Traditions of the Service"

"I have yet to find one authenticated case of a member of this Auxiliary Division being accused of anything but the highest conduct characteristic of them." – Sir Hamar Greenwood

In every location in which they were stationed, the Auxiliaries were guilty of criminal activity. At the lower range of this activity was the stealing of provisions, the demand for free alcohol in public houses along with the 'insistence' that the proprietor of the premises cash false bank cheques. At the higher end of the scale were crimes sometimes too horrific to contemplate.

Already guilty of murders and atrocities in the locality, in the second half of November of 1920, a horrendous series of murders were perpetrated by members of "D Company" of the RIC Auxiliary Division, who were based at Lenaboy Castle on the Taylor's Hill Road in Galway.[I]

The first murder was that of the Galway priest, twenty eight year old Fr. Michael Griffin, who was curate at the Church of St. Joseph, at Rahoon in Galway City. Like many younger priests of the period, Fr. Griffin had sympathy for those engaged in the fight for freedom, and was outspoken in his condemnation of the atrocities being perpetrated by the Crown Forces, especially the Lenaboy Auxiliaries,[II] and of the government which was ultimately responsible for their actions.

Fr. Michael Griffin

Already a marked man due to his condemnations, following the execution by the local IRA of a traitor in their ranks, Patrick Joyce, who had been feeding information on IRA members to the RIC and Dublin Castle, Fr. Griffin along with a number of other local priests had been threatened with death by the Auxiliaries when it emerged that Joyce had received the last rites before his execution.[III]

In the aftermath of Joyce's execution, the Crown Forces abducted and murdered a Sinn Féin councillor, Michael Walsh

---

[I] D Company was under the command of Major Arthur Nicol MC.
[II] Following his murder, Sir Hamar Greenwood, while giving a statement in the House of Commons would describe Fr. Griffin as "a notorious Sinn Feiner".
[III] In their opinion this was a sign that the priests were working in cooperation with the IRA. They failed or did not wish to realize that for the priests, the salvation of souls was their priority and that once contacted by the IRA they would not refuse to administer the last rites before an execution.

who had been implicated as giving support to the IRA, in the information which Joyce had given Dublin Castle. After Walsh's body was recovered from the sea at The Long Walk, Fr. Griffin had administered the last rites. During Walsh's funeral procession, the Auxiliaries had repeatedly charged the cortege in an attempt to disperse the mourners.

On the night of November 14th, Fr. Griffin was lured on some pretext from his home, arrested and brought to Lenaboy. A mock trial ensued and Fr. Griffin was murdered. On the 20th his body was discovered in a bog at Cloghscoltia, Barna[I] with a single gunshot to the head, after drunken Auxiliaries had boasted in a pub that they had killed "the bloody parson".[II]

Although Hamar Greenwood denied that the Auxiliaries were responsible[III], following his resignation as commanding officer of the Auxiliaries, General Crozier confirmed that the Auxiliaries stationed at Lenaboy had indeed been responsible for Fr. Griffin's murder.[IV] Enraged at the loss of their spy,

---

[I] On the night Fr. Griffin disappeared, seven houses were torched at Barna. It was afterwards realized that this had been a warning by the Auxiliaries to the locals not to report anything they may have seen.

[II] After his body was found, Fr. Griffin's colleague, Fr. O'Meehan said: "I have never met or associated with a nobler character, a truer sagart (priest) or a kindlier friend. His death under such circumstances will have a greater effect upon the conscience of the civilised world than even the martyrdom of the late Lord Mayor of Cork. May God have mercy on the murderers of the most innocent and childlike man I have ever known."

[III] When Fr. Griffin's murder was raised in the House of Commons by Joseph Devlin, Sir Hamar Greenwood replied that it was something that "no forces of the Crown would do" to which Devlin replied: "It is exactly what they would do".

[IV] General Crozier recalled: "I found out that the military inquiry into the murder of Fr. Griffin (held in lieu of an inquest) was faced with a 'frame-up' and that a verdict of murder against somebody 'unknown' would result. I told the military commander this and the name of the real murderer, but was informed that a senior official of Dublin Castle had been to Galway in front of me to give instructions as to 'procedure' in this murder investigation." Around two weeks following Fr. Griffin's murder, Crozier had his attaché case with the evidence of

Patrick Joyce, there is also strong evidence that the British Intelligence Service in Dublin Castle had a hand in either organizing or directing his murder.[1]

Six days after Fr. Griffin's body was discovered, the Galway Auxiliaries were engaged in the nationwide round-up which followed the assassinations on the morning of Bloody Sunday. At a farm at Shanglish in the south of the county, they arrested two brothers, Patrick and Harry Loughnane whom they immediately proceeded to torture. Then, after tying the brothers hands, the ropes were affixed to the rear of the RIC lorry which proceeded at increasing speed until the brothers collapsed on the road after which the lorries continued. It was not until December 5th that the remains of their bodies were found in a pool near Ardrahan. Both bodies were horrifically mutilated beyond recognition and burnt. Except for the chin, Harry's face and much of his head were absent. Patrick's face was not much better. This was because grenades had been detonated in their mouths. Patrick's legs, arms and wrists were broken. His torso had been carved with a knife or bayonet. Harry's right arm was dislocated and broken. Two fingers were missing.

Following the discovery of the bodies, the British authorities maintained that both men had successfully escaped from police custody following their arrest and that the Auxiliaries had nothing whatsoever to do with their deaths.

---

who was responsible for Fr. Griffin's murder stolen just as he was preparing to to travel to London to raise the matter there.

[1] Following Fr. Griffin's murder, the Lenaboy Auxiliaries received instructions (most likely from Dublin Castle) that the Bishop of Killaloe, Dr. Fogarty was to be murdered, tied in a sack and dropped from a bridge into the River Shannon. On the night Dr. Fogarty's house was raided, he was in Dublin meeting Archbishop Clune and so escaped.

# Chapter 24

## Ambush and Atrocity

"Law and order have given place to a bloody and brutal anarchy in which the armed agents of the Crown violate every law in aimless and vindictive and insolent savagery." – General Sir Hubert Gough.

As a member of Her Majesty's Opposition during the Boer War,[1] David Lloyd George had condemned the Conservative government for their policy of targeting civilians in reprisal for the attacks of the Boer Army. However twenty years later, as British Prime Minister, Lloyd George both organized and condoned in Ireland what he had previously condemned in South Africa.

As the ambushes and attacks conducted by the IRA against Crown Forces became more frequent, the reprisals of the Crown Forces became systematic. For almost every IRA action there was either a planned or an impromptu Crown Forces reprisal. These reprisals generally consisted in arrests, beatings and the destruction of property. Many resulted in murder, in some cases mass murder. Some of the incidents of IRA attack followed by Crown Forces atrocity are outlined below;

---

[1] In order to deprive the fighting men of the Boer army of the support of their people, the British removed them from the land and interned them in 'Concentration Camps'.

## Bantry, Co. Cork

On June 12th 1920 the IRA shot dead Constable Thomas King near Snave Bridge, Bantry. Nine days later an RIC patrol was ambushed at Cloonee Wood outside the town resulting in the death of Constable James Brett, while the other constables were injured.

The reprisal came two days later on June 23rd, when masked RIC men ran amok in the town smashing windows and tossing petrol bombs into a number of business premises and houses. Two days later the most reprehensible part of the RIC retribution occurred, when in the early hours of June 25th, the RIC raided the home of the Crowley family who lived on the Old Barrack Road, shooting dead Con Crowley, the severely disabled son of Jeremiah and Kate Crowley. Their intended targets had been two other sons of the house, Michael who was a member of Sinn Féin and Charles who was in the IRA and on the run. The following month the RIC sacked the nearby village of Leap.

## The Capture of General Lucas

In IRA attacks against the Crown Forces, prisoners were often taken and then searched, disarmed and released. However one prisoner was retained. On June 26th Commandant Liam Lynch led a group of IRA men to a cottage beside the River Blackwater where General Lucas and two army colonels (Danford and Tyrell) were on a fishing trip and captured them. During the capture Colonel Danford was injured. Tyrell was released in order to help Danford and to ensure that he received medical attention.

Lucas was held prisoner for one month during which he was, by all accounts well treated. During his internment by the IRA, British soldiers of the 17th Infantry Brigade carried out a series of reprisal attacks against towns and villages, especially Fermoy where even more businesses and properties were destroyed than had been the case the previous September. Also targeted in reprisals for General Lucas's capture were Limerick City, Kilcommon and Lismore.

When the capture of Lucas was reported in the British media, news of the reprisals also came to the fore, forcing commanding officers to issue reprimands to the junior officers who had led their men in the acts of atrocity.

In the aftermath of these attacks the British Attorney General for Ireland told the Commons: "British troops in Ireland have been instructed to behave as if they are on a battlefield."[468]

## Templemore, Co. Tipperary

On the evening of August 16th 1920, District Inspector William Wilson was assassinated by the IRA outside the Post Office in Templemore after which the IRA unit escaped from the area by car.

The reprisals began almost immediately. After commandeering all available petrol from the local garage, the RIC wrecked the establishment and proceeded towards the middle of the town shooting and tossing hand-grenades as they went. In the town centre they were joined by members of the locally garrisoned Northamptonshire Regiment. Several premises were looted, and the Town Hall, seat of the local Sinn Féin administration was torched while the Crown Forces responsible gave a rendition of "Sinn Feiners Lie Down" (which hearkened back to "Croppies Lie Down" in the aftermath of the 1798 rebellion).[469] While setting fire to the building, two soldiers of the Northamptonshire Regiment, (Lt. Col Beattie and L/Cpl Fuggle) were severely burnt and later died from their wounds.

## Galway City

On the evening of September 8th, 1920 as the evening train pulled into Galway station, a scuffle broke out on the platform between a Tan, Edward Krumm and an IRA man, Séan Turke. Krumm had just produced his pistol and discharged a couple of shots, causing panic among the people on the platform. Turke, fearing he was about to kill someone, jumped on him and tried to disarm him. Randomly firing his pistol, Krumm shot dead another Volunteer, 17 year old Séan Mulvoy before he was himself shot. Krumm died later from his wounds.

Within a very short time, the station was full of both RIC and Auxiliaries from Lenaboy Castle who immediately went on a rampage of destruction, beatings, looting and murder in the area.

Later that night they visited the home of IRA Volunteer Seamus Quirke, who had not been at Galway station that evening. After dragging him from the house he was shot a number of times and died that evening after receiving the last rite from Fr. Michael Griffin, after which rumours abounded that Quirke had told Fr. Griffin the name of the man who had shot him. Elsewhere another man, Seamus Broderick was also shot and left for dead after his family home was torched.

## Balbriggan, Co. Dublin

On the night of September 20th, following the killing[I] of a RIC District Inspector in Smyth's pub in Balbriggan, around 150 Auxiliaries who were based at the nearby Gormanston Army Camp arrived in the small town hell-bent on revenge. They immediately set about burning a row of 20 labourer's houses on Clonard St. after which they torched many other houses[II]

---

[I] District Inspector Burke along with a number of Tans were terrorizing a number of local people in Smyth's public house. When a few IRA men entered the premises with hand-guns and ordered the police to leave. Instead the police rushed them and one of the IRA men, Michael Rock, opened fire killing Inspector Burke.

[II] One of the houses belonged to the shopkeeper and town councillor, John Derham, who afterwards recorded what had happened. After the RIC cadets broke into his shop and from there into his house, he was dragged out into the

and the town's main employer, the Deeds & Templar Hosiery factory which employed 120 people. The factory was utterly destroyed. A number of men were arrested and taken back to the town barracks where they were beaten, two of these, John Gibbons who was a farmer and the town barber, James Lawless, were both tortured, shot, bayoneted and their bodies terribly mutilated. After over five hours of destruction the Tans left the town and went to nearby Balbriggan where two more men were murdered.

The ruins of the Deeds and Templar Hosiery Factory

In the aftermath of Balbriggan, General Macready told the American Press that the reaction of the Auxiliaries was "only human".[470] He continued: "Punishment for such acts is a delicate matter inasmuch as it might be interpreted as setting at naught the hoped-for effect of the training the officers have given their men."[471]

The events at Balbriggan were widely reported in the international media. London was forced to set in train an enquiry into the events there. By mid October the report had been published and on the 20th was raised in the House of

---

street while his wife was restrained. After being thrown on the street he was repeatedly stuck with rifle butts and removed to the town barracks.

Commons in London. Sir Hamar Greenwood told the House: "I myself have had the fullest investigation made into the case. I will tell the House what I found. I found that from 100 to 150 men went to Balbriggan and were determined to avenge the death of their popular comrade, shot at and murdered in cold blood. I find it is impossible out of that 150 to find the men who did the deed, who did the burning…I have yet to find one authenticated case of a member of this Auxiliary Division being accused of anything but the highest conduct characteristic of them."[472]

These repeated "unofficial" acts of reprisal were opposed by the Chief of the General Staff, Sir Henry Wilson who advised Lloyd George that reprisals should instead be "official" and should focus upon the leadership and members of the IRA: "If these men ought to be murdered then the Government ought to murder them"[473] he told him. Lloyd George was instead content to let the unofficial reprisals continue telling Wilson that the Government could not "possibly take the responsibility"[474] for a policy of official murder.

## Rineen, Co.Clare

On the afternoon of September 22nd 1920, the Mid-Clare IRA Brigade conducted a successful ambush at Drummin Hill, Rineen on a mobile RIC patrol travelling along the coastal road between Miltown-Malbay and Ennistymon. After throwing two grenades at the Crossley Tender, sustained rifle fire was directed at its occupants. Six RIC men (one of which was a Tan) were killed in the engagement. As the IRA retrieved the weapons and set fire to the lorry, ten lorries of British army regulars (who were conducting a search for a missing magistrate, Alan Lendrum) came on the scene and the IRA unit retreated under the covering fire of four of their comrades while the army opened fire on them with machine guns. Three

British soldiers were killed in that engagement and two IRA men injured.

The IRA column successfully escaped. Incensed by their losses and the escape of the IRA, the reprisals began immediately. The army torched the home and farm buildings of the local O'Gorman family and shot Sean Keane, a local farmer, who died some time later from his wounds.

That night the reprisals continued. In Ennistymon homes and businesses were torched by the RIC and the home of Thomas Connolly, the local secretary of the ITGWU was targeted and destroyed. Connolly was shot and his body thrown into the inferno. Also in Ennistymon, a fifteen year old boy, P.J Linnane was shot dead. In Lahinch, a mixed force of RIC and soldiers targeted the home of Daniel Lehane, whose two sons were members of the IRA column. After shooting Lehane dead, they torched his home killing another son Patrick who was hiding in the attic. Several other houses were destroyed in Lahinch while in Miltown Malbay eight houses were torched.

Further local murders took place in November and December, which may also have been in reprisal for the Rineen ambush. On November 16th four IRA men were picked up by the police in Killaloe and were tortured and shot dead. On December 22nd the same fate befell two more IRA men in Kilkee. However by this stage of the war the extra-judicial torture and murder of IRA men was not out of the ordinary.

When these atrocities became public knowledge, they were raised by the Labour Party in the House of Commons. As ever, Hamar Greenwood defended the atrocities, telling the House that the people of Miltown-Malbay and Ennistymon had colluded in the ambush while the houses which were destroyed were those of "notorious Sinn Féiners".[475]

## Mallow, Co.Cork

Having received intelligence from two IRA sympathizers on the civilian staff of the army barracks in Mallow that the majority of the garrison of the 17th Lancers were frequently absent from the barracks in order to exercise their horses, the soldiers of the IRA Cork No. 2 Brigade led by Liam Lynch and Ernie O'Malley, determined to raid the barracks and capture weapons. On September 28th, during the horse exercise, the IRA men gained entry after O'Malley had approached the civilian gate with a letter. In the Magazine, the IRA overpowered the soldiers. A sergeant was fatally wounded in the struggle. After capturing two machine guns and twenty-seven Lee-Enfield rifles, the IRA made good their escape.

On the night of September 29th, army lorries came to Mallow from the army barracks at Fermoy and Buttevant. Having formed up with the Lancers the British soldiers began their reprisal.

First to go up in flames was Mallow Town Hall which was doused in petrol. Other premises followed including the Town Hotel and garage. Most destructive to the town and to the local economy was the utter destruction of the Town's main employer, the Cleeves Condensed Milk Factory which employed 300 people.

## Tralee, Co. Kerry

Following the death on hunger strike of the Lord Mayor of Cork, Terence MacSwiney, the Commandant of the Kerry No. 1 Brigade, Patrick Cahill, ordered the Tralee Battalion to engage in a reprisal action against Crown Forces. On October 31st, this Unit kidnapped two Black and Tan Constables (Ernest Bright and Patrick Waters) who were afterwards executed and secretly buried.

Enraged at the abduction of their colleagues, along with the recent killing of RIC Constables in Killorglin and Ballyduff, the

Black and Tans now imposed a curfew on the town of Tralee, and ordered all businesses in the town to close. They also prevented provisions from entering the town and engaged in a number of "shoot and burn" actions, in which two innocent civilians were murdered and the County Hall burnt along with a number of businesses in the town.

Murders by the Black and Tans also took place outside the town. In Kilflynn a farm labourer was shot dead while working in a field while another civilian was murdered in Ardfert.

By the end of the first week of November, the 'Siege of Tralee was being reported in the international media, causing Sir Hamar Greenwood to order the RIC to call off the siege on November 10$^{th}$. However on the evening of the tenth, the Black and Tans captured Frank Hoffman, who was in the IRA. After bayoneting him, he was shot dead.

### Granard, Co. Longford

Commandant Sean Mac Eoin

Having declared that he was "sent to Longford to spill blood", on the evening of October 31$^{st}$ 1920, RIC District Inspector Phillip Howlett Kelleher, was assassinated in the bar of the Greville Arms Hotel, in Granard, Co. Longford. The following day an undercover RIC man, Peter Cooney was shot dead at Clonbroney.

On November 3$^{rd}$, a planned reprisal took place during which ten lorries of Crown

Forces entered the town of Granard. After burning and looting twelve properties[I] on the Main St, indicated to them by the local RIC, they then headed out of the town towards the village of Ballinalee, (home of Séan Mac Eoin, the local IRA Commandant) intent on continuing their reprisals there.[II] Ever since the assassination of Phillip Kelleher, Mac Eoin had been expecting a reprisal in Ballinalee and on that night his men were lying in wait on the approach roads to the village. The lorries approached from the Aughnacliffe direction and halted before the Catholic Church where Mac Eoin and three other men were waiting. After hearing the shout "Get the petrol cans" Mac Eoin called on the Crown Forces to surrender after which a protracted gun-fight quickly ensued. As fire was engaged the IRA successfully knocked out the enemy machine-gun with a hand grenade. After almost two hours the Tans and Lancers were forced to retreat back towards Granard, abandoning looted items along with much ammunition at the ambush site.

## Dublin City, November 21st 1920
The IRA Strike Against British Intelligence

By the Autumn of 1920, the Dublin Castle intelligence apparatus had become little more than a government organized assassination squad[III] whose chief aim was, the neutralizing of high ranking members of the Republican movement. In October alone seventeen Irishmen had been murdered while in early November, more prominent Republicans had escaped capture or worse. In one raid a large

---

[I] The properties included the Market House and the Greville Arms Hotel which belonged to the family of Michael Collins's girlfriend, Kitty Kiernan.
[II] Mac Eoin had also placed a group of IRA men in Granard but they were unable to prevent the torching of the town.
[III] General Frank Crozier later described them as "no secret service but a mere gang of 'agents provocateurs' and the like".

amount of information, including names and addresses of IRA members in the capital had been captured. The IRA leadership in the city came to the conclusion that if they did not act quickly their own destruction might easily follow.[I]

Following the ordering of an operation against British intelligence by Michael Collins, Dick McKee began the task of gathering and collating all available information on British agents who resided in boarding houses around Dublin. The information included addresses proffered by sympathetic domestic servants and information from IRA spies in the service of the Crown.

A list of fifty names and addresses was arrived at, but for lack of hard evidence the Minister for Defence, Cathal Brugha would only sanction the assassination of twenty British agents who lived incognito at different addresses within the precincts of the city centre.

On the morning of Sunday November 21st, fourteen men were shot dead by the IRA, while another died later of his wounds. Of these fifteen, two were cases of mistaken identity.[II]

## Bloody Sunday at Croke Park

On the same afternoon a Gaelic football challenge match was taking place at Croke Park between Dublin and Tipperary. Around 5,000 people were attending the match which was a fundraiser for the dependents of Republican prisoners. As the match got underway after three o'clock, the army arrived outside the grounds on Clonliffe Road apparently preparing to search those attending the match for weapons as they were leaving. Shortly afterwards the 'three-faces' of the RIC arrived

---

[I] General Crozier later wrote: (This)...resulted in the murder of Captain A. and others on Bloody Sunday, when Collins put them on the spot in the nick of time in order to forestall a similar action by the British authorities".

[II] The two cases of mistaken identity were Thomas Smith (Landlord) and Patrick McCormack a former British army captain (in the Great War)

- Regulars, Tans and Auxiliaries. They quickly surrounded the ground and guarded the exits. At around 3.25 pm, without any provocation, Crown Forces opened fire on the crowd from inside the Canal End Turnstiles through which they had just passed, causing panic and chaos among the crowd. Once the firing started, Crown Forces at other vantage points joined in, and for almost two minutes rapid fire was maintained upon the hapless crowd who were met by machine gun fire from an armoured car as they tried to escape through the exits.

When the firing stopped,[1] seven people were dead and seven more mortally wounded, two of these from crush wounds. Hundreds more had been injured. Among those murdered were a woman and two young boys. One of the Tipperary players, Michael Hogan was also murdered as was Thomas Ryan who was shot dead as he whispered an act of contrition into Michael Hogan's ear.

---

[1] The shooting at Croke Park was finally halted by Major E.L Mills of the Middlesex Regiment. Mills forwarded an accurate report to Dublin Castle on what had occurred at Croke Park after which he was discriminated against and finally forced from the service. His report was ignored. Following the submission of his report Mills was quickly blacklisted after inquiring into the murder of a Dublin civilian who had been shot dead by one of the Auxiliaries under his command.

## Murder in the Guardroom

On the evening before, two Dublin IRA officers, Dick McKee and Peadar Clancy, who had been involved in the planning of Sunday morning's assassinations were captured during a raid on their safe-house at Gloucester St. In a separate raid on Vaughan's Hotel on Saturday evening the RIC had taken into custody Conor Clune, who was a Gaelic League scholar and had nothing whatsoever to do with the IRA.[1] That Sunday evening, in an interrogation led by Captain William Lorraine King, the commander of "F" company of the Auxiliaries who were based in Dublin Castle, the three men were beaten and killed in a guardroom attached to Dublin Castle, which was located at Exchange Court. When Dick McKee's body was released it was, according to his IRA colleague Michael Lynch: "almost unrecognizable"[476] from torture wounds. On December 3rd, the military enquiry found that the three men were shot dead while trying to escape.

Peadar Clancy

## "Kill him! Kill him!"

On November 22nd, Sir Hamar Greenwood made a statement to the House of Commons regarding the deaths of the British officers in Dublin the previous morning. Despite

---

[1] Before the Great War, Clune had been a member of John Redmond's "National Volunteers".

his known penchant for "telling Hamars", Greenwood successfully succeeded in bringing the House into a state of excitement describing the killings in terms such as: "possibly a hammer was used as well as shots to finish off this gallant officer."[477] Following his statement, the Home Rule Party MP, Joseph Devlin stood up and addressing his question to both Greenwood and Lloyd George, asked why no mention had been made of those killed in Croke Park. Almost the entire House started shouting "Sit down! Sit down! As this occurred, Greenwood whispered something to his fellow MP, Major John Molson, who then grabbed Devlin and attempted to pull him across the bench. As he did so, the other MPs shouted at Molson: "Kill him! Kill him!" As Devlin attempted to extricate himself from Molson's grasp, the Speaker of the Commons suspended the House.

## Camlough, Co. Armagh – Dec 12th 1920

On December 12th 1920, one of the largest IRA actions of the war took place in Co. Armagh when Commandant Frank Aiken led 200 IRA soldiers in an attack against Camlough RIC Barracks. As firing erupted the RIC within the Barracks returned fire and quickly summoned Crown Forces from the nearby town of Newry to reinforce them. By the time reinforcements arrived, the Barracks was already ablaze and the IRA were awaiting the reinforcements whom they ambushed by flinging grenades on top of them from an overhead bridge forcing their retreat.

The following day, the Crown Forces returned bent on reprisal where they set fire to numerous homes and businesses in the small Catholic village.

# Co. Cork; Nov 28th – Dec 15th 1920

Kilmichael.

On November 28th 1920, a large IRA Flying Column consisting of around 40 men under the command of Commandant Tom Barry lay in wait at Kilmichael for the weekly patrol by cadets of "C" Company ADRIC, which brought them on a triangular route from their base in Macroom to Bandon via Dunmanway and then directly back to Macroom.

Commandant Tom Barry

Around five o'clock in the afternoon, as the patrol of 18 Auxiliaries in two Crossley Tenders approached the ambush area, the progress of the first lorry was slowed near a bend by Barry who stood in the middle of the road wearing a Volunteer's tunic. After throwing a grenade into the first lorry, which then exploded killing both the driver and the senior officer, Colonel Crake, Barry's men opened fire on the patrol and a lengthy battle which included hand to hand combat followed.

With the battle going against them, the remaining Auxiliaries who were the occupants of the second lorry called out their surrender. When some of the IRA men stood up to accept the surrender, the Auxiliaries recommenced firing, killing two men. From this point on, fire was maintained by the IRA on the enemy in spite of a further cry of surrender. Seventeen Auxiliaries[1] and three IRA men were killed in the engagement.

---

[1] One Auxiliary, H.F Forde, presumed dead by the IRA survived. He did not contradict Commandant Barry's version of events. Another Auxiliary, Cecil

Up to this time, the Auxiliaries were considered not only by themselves, but by the British authorities to be an elite force with the 'dash and elan' required to shrug off any IRA attack without significant loss. The Kilmichael ambush shattered this notion and now contributed to the introduction of martial law in much of Munster in December.

When the bodies of the Auxiiliaries were discovered by their comrades the following day, targets for reprisal were immediately sought. As the area was very rural only two farmhouses could be immediately located, both of which were burnt to the ground. At the beginning of December a number of reprisals took place in Fermoy. In one of these, the owner of the Blackwater Hotel, Nicholas Prendergast (who had served as a British army captain during the Great War) was abducted and murdered, in another a shopkeeper named Dooley was left for dead and his business along with two other premises torched.[1] However the rage of the Auxiliaries at the Kilmichael Ambush was not yet spent and would feed into the largest reprisal of the war on civilian infrastructure some days later.

In the aftermath of Kilmichael, post mortems were conducted on the bodies of the dead Auxiliaries by Dr. Jeremiah Kelleher whose son, District Inspector Phillip Kelleher had been assassinated in Granard. Dr. Kelleher alleged that the IRA had inflicted blunt force trauma wounds to some of the Auxilaries after death, a false allegation referred to in the proclamation of martial law by General French on December 10th, along with a claim that the men of Barry's column had worn British uniforms and helmets during the attack.

---

Guthrie escaped but was recaptured and executed by the IRA as he had murdered and boasted of murdering a civilian (Jim Lehane) in Ballyvourney.

[1] When the fires began, the English garrison in the town turned out and began to fight the numerous blazes. Immediately before departing the town in their lorries, the Auxiliaries slashed the fire hoses.

## The Destruction of Cork City Centre

Within the city of Cork, "K" Company of the Auxiliaries were behaving as befitted the best 'traditions' of their newly formed division, making life hell for the citizens of Cork by means of random raids, beatings, looting and general destruction.

On the evening of December 11th, 1920, two Crossley Tenders carrying an Auxiliary patrol from K Company, left the City's Victoria Barracks at 8pm and were almost immediately ambushed by the IRA who tossed grenades at the lorries resulting in the death of one cadet, Spenser Chapman and the injuring of around ten others.

As the barracks was close by, a huge manhunt for the IRA was immediately launched with the use of tracker dogs and searchlights. Houses within the vicinity of the attack were immediately set alight. As the Auxiliaries fanned out, they halted a tram at Summerhill and ordered the passengers off, where they treated them in their usual fashion. When a priest was noticed among the passengers, he was singled out for special treatment. After stripping his upper body of clothing, he was knocked to the ground and ordered to curse the Pope. When the priest refused, the Auxiliaries prepared to shoot him. However after one or more auxiliaries intervened, he was ordered to run and was shot at as he did so.

At Victoria Barracks, the Auxiliaries made preparations for an orgy of destruction.[1] Lorries were filled with cans holding

---

[1] The "Report of the American Commission" was of the "...opinion that the incendiarism in Cork during the night of December 11th-12th was not a reprisal for the ambush which took place at the same date at Dillon's Cross. The fires appear to have been an organized attempt to destroy the most valuable premises in the city, and we do not think that the arrangements could have been carried out if they had been hastily made after the unfortunate occurrence at Dillon's Cross." The Report of the British Labour Commission concurred: "The Commission was impressed by the sense of impending disaster which overhung the city of Cork during the time it was staying there. This uncertainty was ended

around 300 gallons of petrol along with grenades and then driven towards the city centre where the Auxiliaries who were already on the streets along with Tans from other barracks congregated. At first the police ordered all civilians to return to their homes at gunpoint. Once the streets were deserted the burnings began in an organized manner, conducted under military commands.[1] However, very quickly an uncontrolled orgy of bombing and burning began first in St. Patrick St and then across the River Lee. None of the larger businesses on St. Patrick St. escaped. The looting, especially of jeweller's shops was systematic. In many of the larger premises, shop assistants resided over the businesses nevertheless the windows were smashed on the lower floors before grenades were thrown in.

As the City's fire brigade came on the scene, their appearance infuriated the police mob who did everything in their power to prevent their work, including the repeated turning off of hydrants, the slashing of hoses, the stopping of water flow by lorries parked on hoses and the firing of shots at members of the fire brigade. When an ambulance attempted to transfer a wounded fireman to hospital it was fired at by the Auxiliaries.

At City Hall across the river, the destruction was complete. Here, Auxiliaries had entered the building and spread petrol and explosives throughout before retreating and detonating. The adjacent Carnegie Library, repository of many rare books received the same treatment. Hundreds of buildings were laid waste on both sides of the river, the cost of the destruction being over £105,000,000 in modern terms which was

---

by the tragic occurrences of Saturday, December 11th when the Regent Street of Cork was destroyed by incendiaries."

[1] The commander of "K" company, Lt. Col. Owen Latimer was instrumental in this regard and played a leading role in the looting which followed. According to a K company veteran, Latimer was the leader of the "hard core element" within K Company.

Cork City Centre – The Aftermath

comparable to the destruction of Dublin City Centre by the British during the Easter Rebellion. Thousands of people were out of work as a result of the destruction, which continued until dawn.

Elsewhere in the City, the Auxiliary Cadets were also at work. Around 2am, they broke into a house on Dublin Hill and took the brothers, Jeremiah and Con Delaney, who were both in the IRA, from their beds and executed them.

Following the destruction of Cork City Centre, "K" Company were transferred from Cork to Dunmanway with immediate effect.

Chief Secretary Greenwood first blamed the destruction on the IRA and then on the people of Cork, a lie not contradicted by the British Press[1] which resulted in the refusal of insurance companies to pay property owners for the damage.

---

[1] In the illustrated maps printed in some British papers the City Hall, although on the far side of the River Lee was placed on St. Patrick's St.

In their new base at Dunmanway, many Auxilary Cadets now wore pieces of burnt cork in their Glengarry bonnets, in celebration of their 'victory' over the people of Cork.

## Murders in Dunmanway

Following their arrival in Dunmanway, two lorries of Auxiliaries were leaving the village on the morning of December 15th to attend the funeral of Cadet Spenser Chapman in Cork. Before leaving Dunmanway, one of their number Vernon Hart, shot dead the local parish priest Canon Thomas Magner[1] (aged 73) after forcing him to kneel in front of him. He also murdered another man, Timothy Crowley, who was standing beside him. Timothy Healy KC who represented
some families of those murdered by the Auxiliaries recorded what happened: "A Government magistrate (Mr. Brady, RM) was driving a motor which broke down near Bandon. Canon Magner was on the road reading his office, and the RM asked him to get a lad who was passing on a bicycle to push the car. The priest complied, and as the boy began to shove it, a lorry of black and tans drove up. They jumped out and ordered the priest to his knees, then shot him and killed the boy who was helping Mr. Brady to start the motor. Brady ran to a cottage pursued by the murderers and found a hiding place."
Following the murders the Auxiliaries rifled the pockets of the dead men in search of valuables before throwing their bodies over a wall. That evening the Auxiliaries celebrated the murder of the priest.
As Brady, who had narrowly escaped with his life, was in a position to demand an enquiry, one was held.
However, as was the common practice with all such cases which came to an official enquiry Harte was found "guilty but

---

[1] On November 10th, Canon Magner received a letter ordering him to toll the bell of his church on Armistice Day. The letter was signed "Black and Tans". Canon Magner ignored the letter.

Auxiliaries

insane". Although ordered to be detained at His Majesty's pleasure in Broadmoor Criminal Lunatic Asylum, he served only a few months before being released. The other Auxiliaries were not prosecuted either for their part in the murders or the razing of Cork City centre.

"We took a Sweet Revenge"
The day after the murders, (December 16$^{th}$) one Auxiliary of "K" Company, Charles Schulze wrote to his mother; "I have never experienced such orgies of murder, arson and looting as I have witnessed during the past 16 days with the RIC Auxiliaries. On our arrival here (Dunmanway) one of our heroes held up a car with a priest and civilian in it and shot then both without cause or provocation…The burning and sacking of Cork followed immediately on the ambush of our men…Many who witnessed similar scenes in France say that nothing they experienced was comparable to the punishment meted out in Cork…General Higginson (the Commander of the Cork Garrison) arrived this morning to have a 'straight talk' with us about discipline etc. as he put it. I am afraid we struck terror into him for the 'straight talk' never materialized. He

was most amiable. I could tell you much more but sufficient for the day"[478]

However, in another letter to a girlfriend, Schulze exhibited his true feelings regarding the burning of Cork: "We are having a hell of a time here...You will have read all about Cork. Suffice to say I was there and very actively employed to boot until the dawn on Sunday...we took a sweet revenge..."[479]

Following the Burning of Cork, an enquiry, chaired by the British Army commander for Cork, General Strickland, began on December 18th. Both lawyers and the media were excluded and summoned witnesses appeared one at a time. Some witnesses who wished to appear to give their testimony were refused entry. Following the conclusion of his enquiry, General Strickland submitted a report to the British Cabinet. As General Strickland's enquiry was in progress, Lloyd George promised that the General's report would be made public, but later refused to keep his word. This meant that no Auxiliary was ever prosecuted.

## Bishop Cohalan's Intervention

In the aftermath of the burning of Cork the Bishop of Cork, Daniel Cohalan issued a decree on December 12th effective for his own diocese only. The decree stated that: "...anyone within the Diocese of Cork who organises or takes part in ambushes or attempted murder shall be excommunicated", which in effect excluded any active IRA soldier in his Diocese from the reception of the sacraments of confession and communion.

Arguably the Decree was aimed at not only the IRA but the Crown Forces also, but as the vast majority of the Crown Forces were not Catholic it was obvious that Bishop Cohalan blamed the IRA for the reactions of the Crown Forces and that the decree was in effect, for them only.

In the aftermath of the decree's publication it was the subject of much discussion among the officers and men of the IRA, the majority of whom were devout Catholics. To a man they ignored the edict as being unjust. The priests of the diocese who had up to this time administered the sacraments to the IRA soldiers continued to do so as before, and like the IRA viewed Dr. Cohalan's intervention not only as an overstepping of the mark but as a grave error.

This judgement was reinforced when, the ink being barely dry on the Bishop's decree, Canon Thomas Magner and Timothy Crowley were murdered without provocation and in cold blood by Auxiliary Cadet Vernon Hart and his comrades in Dunmanway.

# Chapter 25

# The War in 1921

"So long as Sinn Fein demands a Republic the present evils must go on" – David Lloyd George

In the light of the growing number of outrages being perpetrated in Ireland by the Crown Forces, both international and domestic criticism of the British government was growing. Unlike the Irish wars of previous centuries where the Crown Forces were able to perpetrate the most horrendous crimes with impunity until victory was achieved, the media was now playing its part, and many English people were growing uneasy at the seemingly never ending outrages being perpetrated against Irish civilians by their men at arms.

## Martial Law and Official Reprisals

"We can spread ruin; that we are doing…we can spread death; that we are doing" – 'Nation and Athenaeum' (London)

On December 10th, full scale military (or martial) law was declared in the counties of Cork, Kerry, Tipperary and Limerick in a proclamation by Lord French. This meant the appointment of British army commanders as "de-facto" governors of each county. The area under martial law was quickly extended with Wexford, Kilkenny, Clare and Waterford being added on January 5th 1921.

Crimes such as the possession of arms, the wearing of a volunteer uniform or the "harbouring, aiding or abetting" of rebels were all offences listed as liable for the death penalty as the British refused to apply the Hague Convention to Ireland and to recognize that IRA prisoners had any rights as belligerents.

In each county, the military governor was at liberty to enact any measure he saw fit. General Higginson issued a declaration on December 18th that in future all Crown Forces convoys would carry Republican prisoners as hostages,[I] while on January 3rd, General Strickland issued a declaration to the people of Co. Cork, that any citizen who gave sustenance to the IRA or failed to report the location of weapons would be either court martialled or "dealt with summarily."[480] His declaration continued: "…an attitude of neutrality is inconsistent with loyalty and will render the person liable under the order."

By law "official reprisals" or the destruction of civilian property could now legally take place in a district where an attack had been carried out against the Crown Forces, a measure which resulted in the destruction of many homes and properties.[II] Families whose homes were destroyed as a result of martial law were forced to rely on the charity of neighbours.

---

[I] These hostages (or "mascots" as they were referred to by the British) were plucked from their homes and interned at an army or police barracks. One of the hostages, Willie Long from Limerick would recall that while the RIC lorry in which he was a hostage was stationary, one of the Black and Tans took aim and shot a man emerging from a farmhouse some distance away. The Tan then jumped off the lorry and stepped the distance to the dead man. After returning to the lorry his boasted to his comrades: "Clean through the forehead at 220 paces. Not bad!" Around 600 civilians were shot dead by Crown Forces between January and June of 1921.

[II] The first official reprisals took place on January 1st in Midleton, Co. Cork when seven homes were destroyed. One hours warning was given to the inhabitants who were not allowed to remove furniture from the property before it was destroyed.

No compensation could be claimed in courts run by the Crown, for the destruction of their properties.

Following the declaration, General Macready issued a weapons amnesty on the 12$^{th}$ December declaring that weapons could be surrendered until December 27$^{th}$ after which the death penalty would be rigorously imposed for their possession. Following the first execution for possession of weapon on February 1$^{st1}$, the number of executions conducted by the Crown rapidly increased even in areas where martial law was not officially in force. By mid June, thirteen men had been killed by firing squad in Cork alone. Curfews were imposed as early as 8pm after which military cordons were drawn around entire districts which were then 'combed out' in the search for the IRA and for weapons. The number of "summary executions" or murders of IRA prisoners and high ranking Sinn Féin members by Crown Forces, also greatly increased. On March 6$^{th}$, 1921 during the hours of curfew, the Auxiliaries in Limerick murdered the Lord Mayor, George Clancy, the former Lord Mayor Michael O'Callaghan, and Joseph O'Donoghue.

Shoot on sight or after torture was now the order of the day for the Crown Forces within the martial law area. The worst incident of this kind was the murder of seven IRA prisoners on February 20$^{th}$ 1921 at Clonmult in Co. Cork after they had surrendered following the surrounding of their base by a party of soldiers of the Hampshire Regiment, who were afterwards reinforced by Tans and Auxiliaries. After an intense fire-fight lasting around an hour and a half the IRA were forced out of their base after the Crown Forces doused the building in petrol and set it ablaze. One of the IRA men who survived, Patrick Higgins, later recalled: "We were lined up alongside an outhouse with our hands up. The Tans came along and shot

---

[1] Cornelius Murphy was shot for being in possession of a revolver at Cork Detention Barracks.

every man. A Tan put his revolver to my mouth and fired. I felt as if I was falling through a bottomless pit."[481]

## Torching the "Big Houses"

Thus far during the fight for independence the majority of the big houses of the landlord and Garrison class had remained untouched by the IRA. Their owners had remained free to entertain the officers of Crown Forces although some large houses had been burned by the IRA to deny their use to the Crown Forces as billets.

In January of 1921, the actions of a wealthy member of the Garrison class were to significantly change matters and for the remainder of the conflict the 'Big Houses' of the Landlords would often be seen by the IRA as legitimate targets as these were locations where information was exchanged and attacks planned.

During the month of January the First Cork Brigade of the IRA meticulously planned and trained for an ambush of the large Crown Forces convoy which travelled every day between Macroom and Cork. The attack on the convoy was planned to take place on January 28th at Dripsey.

On the morning of the 28th the Crown Forces were informed of the imminent attack by a wealthy loyalist from the area, 70 year old Mrs. Maria Lindsay along with her chauffeur, James Clarke who were from Leemount House in Coachford.

As the IRA waited for the convoy of seven Crossley Tenders they were instead surrounded by soldiers of the Manchester Regiment who were supported by armoured cars. Almost totally cut-off except for a narrow laneway, the soldiers of the IRA successfully fought their way to safety. However many of them were wounded and five of their number had fallen into enemy hands.

In the aftermath of the foiled attack, the IRA learned who had informed on them and arrested both Mrs Lindsay and her chauffeur on February 20th. A letter was then sent to General Strickland which told him that if the five captured IRA men were executed, Mrs Lindsay and James Clarke would suffer the same fate. On February 28th 1921, the five IRA men; John Lyons, Thomas O'Brien, Patrick Mahoney, Timothy MacCarthy and Daniel O'Callaghan along with another IRA soldier Séan Allen were executed in Cork. On the same day six British soldiers were shot dead in Cork city while two weeks later Mrs Lindsay and James Clarke were executed as informers. Leemount Mansion was also burnt to the ground. For the remainder of the conflict, the burning of property spiralled. Already heavily engaged in the burning of Irish homes as a reprisal measure, the Crown Forces increased this measure significantly in reprisal for the burning of a big house. In reprisal the IRA stepped up its campaign of burning. following the issuing of a warning to the Crown Forces that for every Irish homestead burnt, two houses of active supporters of the British government would be targeted.

## The Resignation of Brigadier General Frank Crozier
### "A Heavy and Hidden Hand"

The officer in command of ADRIC, General Frank Crozier, had since the Division's formation in the Summer of 1920, attempted to apply some norms of military discipline to his men, companies of whom were scattered in strongholds all over the country. As his men were "officers and gentlemen", they should by right have required the minimum of discipline but this was not the case. The Auxiliaries had quickly become notorious not only for their atrocities but also for their law breaking.

Such discipline as General Crozier tried to enforce was effectively cancelled in the Autumn of 1920. Crozier afterwards recalled: "Up to November 1st 1920, I had 'dismissed' or 'dispensed' with the services of over fifty Auxiliary policemen (ex-officers) for various acts of indiscipline, but shortly after that date, a heavy and hidden hand came down. My powers of dismissal and dispensal were taken away from me."[482] It later transpired that both Dublin Castle and the London government were not concerned with the crimes of ADRIC but rather that dismissed officers should not reveal to the British press what they or their comrades had done and were doing in Ireland. The view of the British Government was that no matter what their crimes, all officers of ADRIC should remain in the service.

General Frank Crozier

Infuriated at interventions from the highest level, the tipping point[i] for General Crozier came in February of 1921 following looting in Trim and murders in Dublin both perpetrated by the Auxiliaries.

---

[i] During October of 1920 a group of Auxiliaries with blackened faces had attempted to impersonate the IRA and had held up Kilkenny post office. They had taken thousands of pounds. After Crozier had learned of this incident he had attempted to mete out justice to the men involved but was prevented at every turn.

## Trim and Drumcondra

On the night of February 9th, a number of lorries filled with Auxiliary cadets from "N" company who were stationed at the Trim Industrial School in Co. Meath, raided the shop of a Unionist grocer, Richard Chandler at Balbradagh, Trim, apparently searching for an IRA ammunition dump. During their search the Auxiliaries looted the premises of alcohol, groceries, suits of clothing and jewellery, downing bottles of alcohol as they did so. Clothing and soft furnishings were gathered in the shop's rear yard and set ablaze.[1]

On the same night as the Trim looting, in Drumcondra, Dublin, two men, James Murphy and Patrick Kennedy were arrested and taken to Dublin Castle. They were afterwards removed from the Castle by Captain William Lorraine King (Commander of "F" Company ADRIC) and two other Cadets and taken away in a car. The following morning the two men were found in a field in Drumcondra. James Murphy was dead while Patrick Kennedy was dying. Patrick Kennedy related how buckets were placed over their heads after which they were shot. In the aftermath of the shooting, a military court of inquiry was held during which the evidence of the dying Patrick Kennedy was deemed inadmissible, while two officers came forward with perjured alibis for King, who was cleared of all responsibility.

## "You can have a K.B.E in June"

Disgusted with the Dublin court of inquiry, Crozier had nevertheless decided that the Cadets involved in the Trim looting could not remain in the service and dismissed them.

---

[1] Richard Chandler later recalled that the Auxiliaries: "consumed up to £100 of drink in the shop...They ill treated my sister who is an invalid." The shop assistant recalled: "They smashed and burned all before them...(They were) like a lot of hungry animals. They would take a bite out of a cake and trample on the remainder."

However one of the dismissed men went to Dublin Castle and threatened that the dismissed men would make public the crimes of the Auxiliaries. Under pressure from the Castle Authorities to take the men back, Crozier refused to relent and the disgraced men left for England. Crozier was then contacted by an unnamed figure in the British government who told him: "Don't be a fool! If you continue to stick your toes in you'll miss the Honours list at the end of this show…you can have a K.B.E (Knighthood) in June. These men, if they are not reinstated will play hell in London and upset the Cabinet altogether."[483] Crozier still refused to bow to British Government pressure, after which he departed Dublin for Wales in order to unveil a memorial to those killed in the Great War. In his absence, his deputy General Wood, came under pressure from Dublin Castle and General Tudor in particular. Wood allowed the Trim miscreants to return despite having promised Crozier that he would not do so. Upon learning of this General Crozier felt that he had no other course open to him, than to resign his position at which General Wood was appointed to succeed him.[1]

## Death of a General

At the beginning of March 1921, the IRA in both Cork and Kerry (all members of the newly formed IRA First Southern Division under the command of Liam Lynch) finalized the planning of an ambush which was to see the death in action of

---

[1] Following Crozier's resignation another group of Auxiliaries whom he had suspended for holding up a Dublin Fire Station while their colleagues engaged in reprisal burnings were also returned to duty. The two Auxiliary officers who had informed Crozier about the Trim lootings were afterwards dismissed from the service while their colleagues who had committed the crimes remained. If General Wood had fallen in with the wishes of the Government in the hope of being awarded a KBE, he was to be disappointed.

a British General, the highest ranking casualty among the British forces in Ireland during the fight for independence.

On March 5th, General Hanway Robert Cumming had completed a tour of inspection of his operational area and was travelling by road from Killarney, Co. Kerry back to his HQ at Buttevant, Co. Cork. The convoy consisted of three lorries carrying around 40 soldiers of the Lancashire Regiment, an armoured car and a touring car in which Cumming was a passenger.

At Clonbanin, Co. Cork, a large IRA force of over 100 soldiers under the command of Commandant Sean Moylan lay in wait, his men being armed with rifles and one Lewis machine gun. Once Cumming's convoy entered the ambush area, fire was immediately opened on both the lorries and the car from elevated positions on both sides of the road, while the machine gun crew concentrated their fire on the armoured car. When a bullet entered the driver's viewing slit of the armoured car, the driver was wounded and the armoured car struck the ditch.

While attempting to exit his car and get to cover, General Cumming was struck in the head by a bullet and instantly killed.

Following his death, the protracted battle, lasting almost an hour, continued before the IRA broke off the attack. Cumming and at least three British soldiers had been killed, while no casualties had been suffered by the IRA

## Crossbarry- The Largest Battle

In the Spring of 1921 the IRA's 3rd Cork Brigade came under sustained pressure from Crown Forces who in the aftermath of Kilmichael were determined to neutralize the unit. Raids, arrests and interrogations increased and following an IRA ambush on an army train at Upton which went badly wrong, three IRA men were killed and a further three arrested. Eight civilians were killed in the deadly exchange of fire. Of the three men who were arrested, one, Pat O'Sullivan, was beaten to death with revolver butts while in hospital while another IRA Captain Patrick Coakley, became an informer.

Coakley told the British that the 3rd Brigade was based in the Ballymurphy area after which they discovered that a return to the area was planned. The staff officers of the Essex Regiment which was commanded by General Arthur Percival[I] immediately began planning an operation whereby the Essex Regiment and the Auxiliaries would completely encircle the area, search every house and detain or kill every male capable of bearing arms, thus annihilating the IRA unit. Within the area of operations were around 100 IRA soldiers, who were spread out among the houses and barns of the local population.

In the night-time hours of the morning of March 19th, the British operation began which would eventually involve well over 600 British soldiers[II] and around 100 Auxiliaries from

---

[I] The Essex Regiment, commanded by Sir Arthur Percival was to earn for itself a similar level of notoriety as the Auxiliaries during its deployment in Munster. To the British government, Percival was an efficient officer who would stop at nothing to achieve the task assigned him. To the Irish and the IRA in particular he was akin to a devil incarnate. According to Tom Barry, Percival was "easily the most vicious anti-Irish of all serving British officers." He was renowned for torture during the interrogation of IRA prisoners such as the pulling off of finger nails, the use of cigarette burns and also for riding around south Cork in an open saloon car with a weapon at the ready looking for targets. In July of 1920, Percival was awarded the Order of the British Empire for the capture of the Commander of the Third Cork Brigade, Tom Hales and also Patrick Harte who was the Brigade Quartermaster. Both men were tortured during which Hales's fingernails were pulled out and Harte suffered brain damage. Harte never recovered from his torture and died in a mental hospital in 1925. Percival would later go down in history as the General who surrendered Singapore in 1942 to a much smaller Japanese force – "the greatest military defeat in the history of the British Empire."

[II] According to IRA soldier Tom Kelleher, who was present at the battle three hundred British soldiers came from Kinsale, six hundred from Ballincollig and Cork along with twenty-four lorries of soldiers from Bandon.

Macroom who were desperate to come to close quarters with the IRA. As the cordon was formed, many of the Crown Forces dismounted from their lorries and proceeded on foot. They soon came across a farmhouse in which Charlie Hurley, the Commander of the No. 3 Brigade lay wounded following the failed Upton Ambush. Although Commandant Tom Barry heard the shots which killed Hurley, the alarm had already been raised. As the IRA formed up into sections of fourteen men each, Commandant Tom Barry was determined that the IRA would fight its way out of the encirclement and decided to withdraw his men within the cordon to Crossbarry, where he would engage the enemy on more favourable terrain and achieve more time to prepare for action before the encircling troops closed in.

At Crossbarry, the area was rapidly cleared of civilians and positions or fields of fire were allocated to the IRA sections. This battle was to be like no other for the IRA, for accompanying the men was the Assistant Brigade Adjutant, Florence Begley who had brought his Uileann pipes along and would play his pipes to the men during the action which followed.

Although the operation had begun some hours earlier, it was not until around 8am that the British lorries reached Crossbarry. Under observation from the right flank of the IRA positions the soldiers began to dismount and very quickly came under sustained fire from the IRA which knocked out a machine gun mounted atop one of the lorries. On this side the Crown Forces were forced to retreat enabling the IRA to recover weapons and ammunition from two destroyed lorries. Soon afterwards the left flank (southeast) of the IRA positions were forced to engage as were the sections facing the Bandon direction (southwest) as the enemy approached from both these directions. With the British forced to withdraw, the IRA prepared to retreat towards Gurranereigh, the only direction from which an attack had not come, but here too, a ragged line of British soldiers were spotted and quickly cleared by devastating fire from around one hundred rifles before the IRA successfully executed their retreat having suffered three fatalities. During a battle which had lasted for around one hour they had inflicted over twenty fatalities on the enemy.

In the aftermath of the battle, an infuriated General Percival blamed the Auxiliaries who had mustered at the wrong rendezvous area and had thus left a gap in the encirclement, enabling the IRA to escape. For the IRA, under the leadership of Tom Barry, they had achieved victory from the jaws of defeat. Had they even reached the point of being captured they would all have faced the death penalty as had the men who had escaped being murdered at Clonmult.

At the beginning of May 1921, a similar scenario also played out at Tourmakeady Co. Mayo following a successful ambush by the South Mayo IRA Brigade on an RIC convoy. A few hours after the ambush the IRA unit was surrounded by some hundreds of British soldiers but the IRA managed to hold them at bay until nightfall when they successfully broke through the cordon and escaped. In the days following the action, the Crown Forces conducted search and reprisal actions all over the district, burning shops and houses.

## The Burning of The Custom House

Following the return of President deValera to Ireland from the United States at Christmas of 1920, a full Cabinet meeting was held at which deValera put forth his opinion that a 'high-level' IRA attack was needed in order to bring Ireland's plight before the international media.

Although some members of the Cabinet had their reservations, it was decided that an attack should be launched by the Dublin IRA on The Dublin Custom House, a huge 18th century building, the destruction of whose files would cripple the English taxation system in Ireland.

After much planning, the attack took place just before 1pm on May 25$^{th}$ involving over 250 soldiers of the IRA.

When members of the Second Battalion entered the building they set it ablaze after dousing it in paraffin while their comrades held guard positions outside or prevented the Dublin Fire Brigade from mobilising.

Some of the IRA started to leave the building without completing the mission after believing the 'retire' signal had been sounded and were ordered to return. The mission now ran over-time, allowing the Crown Forces to arrive and encircle the building. Following a fire-fight lasting around half an hour during which three IRA soldiers were killed, the IRA dropped their weapons and tried to escape by mingling with Custom House Staff. However by this time, Crown Forces had set up numerous cordons around the building and managed to detain over 100 IRA men. Some who tried to break the cordon and escape were shot dead, while the Dublin Fire Brigade, who by now had arrived on the scene, managed to smuggle a number of IRA soldiers out of the building.

Although their mission was accomplished, the attack was a disaster for the Dublin IRA, who saw their ranks decimated and much of their weaponry lost.

# Chapter 26

## Treating With the Enemy

"I leave for the guidance of other Irish Revolutionaries who may tread the path which I have trod this advice; never to treat with the enemy, never to surrender at his mercy, but to fight to a finish." – Éamonn Ceannt. (on the eve of his execution)

On November 11th 1920, the British Government's Bill which partitioned Ireland (Better Government of Ireland Act) passed all its Parliamentary stages, becoming law on December 23rd. Having agreed not to oppose the Bill, but still maintaining that they did not want it, the Ulster Unionist M.Ps left the House of Commons before the vote, thereby ensuring that the partitioning of Ireland was a wholly British affair. The Bill although now officially law would not take force until the beginning of May 1921 when elections, as provisioned by the Act were due to take place on the island of Ireland followed by a meeting of two separate parliaments, one in Belfast and one in Dublin.

### Peace Moves

During the Winter of 1920 / 21, a number of exploratory meetings had taken place between Irish individuals acting independently and representatives from the British government with the aim of bringing about a truce in hostilities. The most promising of these peace moves was that of the Irish born Archbishop Clune of Perth, who at the end of

1920 was visiting ANZAC[I] troops stationed in Europe. Archbishop Clune[II] was the uncle of Conor Clune, who had been murdered in cold blood by Auxiliaries under the command of Captain William Lorraine King in the guardroom of Dublin Castle on the evening of Bloody Sunday.

Following initial contacts, Clune met with Lloyd George on December 1st and apparently found him amenable to a truce without preconditions. Clune travelled to Ireland as an unofficial representative of Lloyd George where he contacted Arthur Griffith and Michael Collins who told him that they would recommend a ceasefire to the Dail provided that there would be no English precondition demanding the surrender of IRA weapons. On Clune's return to London, Lloyd George's stance had hardened. Preconditions, which Lloyd George had not previously mentioned to Archbishop Clune now barred the way. These preconditions were outlined by Lloyd George in the Commons on December 10th, all of which[III] were repugnant to Irish Republicans. When Lloyd George later added the precondition of an IRA weapons surrender before the end of December, Dr. Clune returned to Australia, confiding in his friend Bishop Fogarty of Killaloe (who had recently avoided death at the hands of the Lenaboy Auxiliaries) that given such intransigence on the British side, passive resistance to British rule seemed to no longer be a viable alternative to that which the IRA offered.[484]

Following the failure of Dr. Clune's initiative, during the Spring of 1921, a good number of English newspapers, already weary of the blatant propaganda emanating from Whitehall

---

[I] Austrailia and New Zealand Armoured Corps.
[II] Archbishop Clune was not a supporter of Sinn Féin but was a supporter of the defunct IPP and a supporter of the British Empire.
[III] The preconditions were: 1. 'separate treatment for the six counties. 2. No part of Ireland would be allowed to leave the union. 3. No lessening in the military security of the Union in time of peace or war.

and Dublin Castle were attempting to provide their readers with a more accurate account of events in Ireland. In the political sphere, the burgeoning Labour Party, since publishing their own damning report on the British conduct of the war at the end of 1920 were continually pushing for official enquiries into Crown Forces atrocities. Within the Liberal Party, the former Prime Minister, Herbert Asquith condemned the Government's "…hellish policy of reprisals". In other quarters, the leaders of the English Protestant Churches had sent written protests to the Government over its actions in Ireland , while the leader of the Catholic Church in England, Cardinal Bourne, appealed to the Government for the Auxiliaries to be immediately withdrawn.[I] Elsewhere the English Peer, Lord Bentick had established his "Peace with Ireland Council" which was composed of eminent persons and scholars who sought to pressurize the government into calling a truce to hostilities.

Following the departure of Dr. Clune, the Under-Secretary for Ireland, A. W Cope was tasked with projecting feelers towards Irish Republicans.[II] Following these feelers, Cope informed London of his conclusion. If Ireland was not partitioned as London desired, and the Government of Ireland Act of 1920 cancelled, then he felt that Irish Republicans would be prepared to countenance that Ireland could remain within the Empire. Determined that the partitioning of Ireland should proceed as planned, Lloyd George did not act.

---

[I] On April 27th, Pope Benedict XV, donated £5,000 to the Irish people who were subject to "devastation and slaughter."

[II] DeValera was not contacted by Cope and discouraged members of the Dáil from engaging in these peace feelers saying that if the British were ready to make a peace offer they would do it 'in plain sight'.

## Partition Accomplished and Peace Offered
### The Second Dail

The beginning of May 1921 saw the coming into force of Lloyd George's Partitioning of Ireland Act and the 'summoning' of two parliaments on the island of Ireland by the new Viceroy, Lord Fitzalan[I] (James Talbot) to meet in June. Deciding to contest the election, Sinn Féin, announced to its followers that it would be used to elect members to The Second Dáil Eireann and to display to the British the desire of the Irish electorate for an independent Irish Republic.

Within the electoral area of the 'southern parliament' the election took place on May 19th. As expected Sinn Féin candidates swept the board and were returned unopposed in every constituency (with the exception of the Unionist stronghold of Trinity College) with a mandate for complete freedom from British rule.[II]

Within the six counties, Sinn Fein and IPP candidates won a quarter of the seats and had large majorities in the constituencies of Fermanagh and Tyrone in spite of significant repression and intimidation of both Catholic candidates and voters, many of whom stayed away from the polling stations as the result of intimidation.[III] Unhappy with their victory and the amount of votes cast for Sinn Féin, in the aftermath of the election Ulster Unionists MPs incited their followers to

---

[I] As a concession Fitzalan was the first Catholic Viceroy to be appointed to Ireland since the sixteenth century. London hoped that his appointment would be viewed as a goodwill gesture but Republicans were not deceived and viewed him as "a Catholic hangman".

[II] The Inner Cabinet of the Second Dáil under President deValera were; Arthur Griffith (Foreign Affairs), Austin Stack (Home Affairs), Cathal Brugha (Defence), Michael Collins (Finance), W.T Cosgrave (Local Government), and Robert Barton (Economic Affairs).

[III] On polling day a number of Catholics were assaulted either before or after voting. Numerous Sinn Féin or nationalist agents were who attended polling station in order to check registers and monitor voting were assaulted.

violence[1] which resulted in a further anti-Catholic pogrom in Belfast during which 18 Catholics were killed both by the mob and by "B" Specials. One hundred and fifty families were burnt out of their homes.

Options
With the partitioning of Ireland now in train, Lloyd George's cabinet debated their options as to what further measures could be employed in the twenty-six counties in order to bring the country to heel. 'Ulster' was nearly 'secure' but not quite - the Partition Bill also depended on the formation of a 'Southern Parliament' but this was not in prospect. The defeat of the IRA was as far away as ever and the people of Ireland had given a firm rebuttal to the Partition Bill and showed their support for an Irish Republic in the May election. Increased coercion, if such a thing were possible, seemed unwise given the growing hostility of the Press and international and English opinion to such a move. Yet there were those in the cabinet who proposed exactly that, especially the Colonies Minister, Winston Churchill who advised "a tremendous onslaught" in order to defeat the IRA and force the establishment of the 'Southern Parliament'. This was the policy which the cabinet decided upon.

During the latter end of May and for the entire month of June, thanks to longer days and dry weather, the Crown Forces did their utmost to bring the fight to the IRA. Night and day, lorries full of troops and police traversed mountain roads in search of their quarry. The IRA was now under severe pressure. Thanks to improved security by the Crown Forces, the capture of arms and ammunition by the IRA became more difficult but yet any sort of breakthrough against the IRA

---

[1] William Grant MP told his followers: "We must take steps to expel Sinn Féin from the six counties". Samuel Mc Guffin MP announced that the Unionists must: "...drive Sinn Féin bag and baggage out of the six counties."

continued to elude the forces of the Crown who continued to suffer significant losses.

In some parts of the country, especially in Connacht, the columns of the IRA were increasing in strength, with the province threatening to become as active as Munster in terms of IRA activity, while in Munster the (nationwide) divisional reorganization had greatly improved the IRA's operational ability.

## The King in Belfast

With the official establishment of the Ulster six county entity which Winston Churchill declared to be "unassailable", official preparations got underway for the opening of the 'Ulster' parliament by King George.

South of the border, in spite of intense action the Crown Forces had failed in their 'big push' against the IRA. There would be no meaningful 'southern parliament' on June 28th. However if a truce was offered by the British and accepted by the Irish the British Government hoped that the full introduction of the Better Government of Ireland Act could be achieved through negotiation, pressure and enforced compromise.

Following discussions between King George and his Prime Minister and then within the cabinet, a plan was arrived at – an initiative 'for peace in Ireland' which would come from the King directly.[1]

On June 22nd, King George V and Queen Mary arrived in Belfast to open the parliament which the Ulster Unionists maintained they did not want but were only too glad to accept.

---

[1] The British design of 'victory or negotiation once the Belfast Parliament is established' may have been in force from the beginning of the year. We must remember the words recorded by General Crozier and spoken by someone in high office before his resignation following the Trim looting: "Don't be a fool! If you continue to stick your toes in you'll miss the honours list at the end of this show...you can have a K.B.E (Knighthood) in June."

The Monarch and His Consort were received by the Protestant population with jubilation. The new Prime Minister of the six counties was to be James Craig as Edward Carson, who was suffering from ill health and was (unlike the other Unionists) against a six-county parliament agreed to bow out.

Craig invited his personal military adviser, the Chief of the General Staff, Sir Henry Wilson to attend but Wilson was forced to reluctantly decline in view of his role as Chief of the General Staff of the British armed forces.[1] He informed Craig that his time was taken up with the crushing of the Irish rebellion.

At the opening of Parliament the King read his speech which paved the way for the British to offer the Irish an unconditional truce;

"I speak from a full heart when I pray that my coming to Ireland today may prove to be the first step towards the end of strife among her people whatever their race or creed. In that hope I appeal to all Irishmen to pause, to stretch out the hand of forbearance and conciliation, to forgive and forget, and to join in making for the land they love a new era of peace, contentment and goodwill. It is my earnest desire that in Southern Ireland too, there may, ere long, take place a parallel to what is now passing in this hall; that there a similar occasion may present itself, and a similar ceremony be performed. For this the Parliament of the United Kingdom has in the fullest measure provided the powers. For this the Parliament of Ulster is pointing the way. The future lies in the hands of my Irish people themselves. May this historic gathering be the prelude of the day in which the Irish people, north and south, under one Parliament or two, as those Parliaments may themselves decide, shall work together in common love for

---

[1] General Crozier wrote of Wilson that he was: "...the greatest mischief maker and political claptrapper the British army has ever possessed..."

Ireland upon the sure foundation of mutual justice and respect."[485]

### A Letter from Lloyd George

Three days following the opening of the northern parliament, President deValera received a letter from Lloyd George offering peace. The letter began: "The British Government are deeply anxious that, so far as they can assure it, the King's appeal for reconciliation in Ireland shall not have been made in vain."[486]

There followed two weeks of consultation between the sides. Initially Lloyd George appeared unwilling to offer a truce but was apparently persuaded to accept one by Lord Midleton who acted as an intermediary between the sides. Finally the terms of the truce which would come into force at midday on July 11th were agreed in Dublin.

In the event of the failure of peace negotiations, London agreed that hostilities would only resume following a reasonable notice period. This was confirmed in the House of Commons on August 2nd. On July 8th DeValera sent a message to Lloyd George indicating his preparedness to meet him in London on July 14th, in order to discuss the basis for a peace conference.

## The Truce

As news of the impending truce between the Irish Republic and the Crown reached the streets of Belfast on July 10th, the anti-Catholic pogrom reignited. On the evening and night of July 10th, Unionist mobs in Belfast burnt out the homes of 161 Catholic families, killing sixty-one people.

When the truce came into effect on July 11th, many in Ireland breathed a sigh of relief. However, there were those especially among the fighting men of the IRA who greeted the news with an element of disbelief.[I] Since the war had begun they had fought and gained the measure of their enemy. The IRA in Munster were already preparing for a Winter offensive against the Crown Forces and felt confident of ultimate victory.[II]

Among the IRA, many believed that the truce would be of short duration as they distrusted English motives. Their firm belief was that the English would, by their well practiced art of 'Divide and Conquer' attempt to divide the IRA and the nation and also shatter its unity of purpose which had been unbroken until now. What they did not believe was that the English would ever agree to recognize an independent Irish Republic except by the continuance of the war until the British were finally forced to admit that they could neither win nor crush the resistance of the nation. For many of those who had fought the hardest and endured the most, the truce had come too early.

In its bid for independence, Ireland had paid a heavy price. What Ireland's political leaders could achieve through negotiation with "The Welsh Wizard" and his delegation remained to be seen, but their task was certainly fraught with difficulty. Aside from English expertise in the art of negotiation, the greatest obstacle seemed to lie with the establishment of the northern parliament, a bulwark constructed by the British and Ulster Unionists against the establishment of an independent 32 county Irish Republic, but even here, some doubted the seemingly unshakeable resolve of the London government in the establishment of 'Northern Ireland' as a political entity.

---

[I] Liam Deasy (Adjutant of the 3rd Cork Brigade) would later recall that when the news of a ceasefire broke during a meeting of officers from the First Southern Division, there was a stunned silence and an air of disbelief.

[II] According to Liam Deasy, The First Southern Division had around 30,000 rounds of .303 ammunition stockpiled for their Winter offensive.

Within the six counties, when the truce was declared, the native Irish were now even in greater danger as the desire of the Unionists to "drive them out" increased.[1] Following the truce deValera received numerous Nationalist delegations who begged that the Catholics and nationalists of Ulster would not be "bartered and sold".[487]

## Dublin and London, July to October 1921
### DeValera in London
After travelling from Dublin to London on July 12th with a five man delegation which included the Minister for Home Affairs, Austin Stack, deValera first met with Lloyd George on July 14th. Stack afterwards recalled: "We remained in London for about eleven days. During that time the President and Lloyd George met on three occasions, I think…after the second interview we had reason to believe they (the British) were not going beyond Dominion Home Rule."[488]

While Lloyd George was engaged in meetings with deValera, he also met with Sir James Craig, who told the press following his meeting with Lloyd George: "It now merely remains for Mr.deValera and the British people to come to terms regarding that area outside of which I am Prime Minister." Following this remark deValera was forced to protest, both in letter to the Prime Minister and in the public press in order to quash the rumours that he had in any way accepted the notion of the partition of Ireland. In his press statement, deValera maintained that he had: "no demand but one – the only one that I am entitle to make – that the self determination of the Irish nation be recognized."[489]

At their final meeting on Wednesday July 20th, Lloyd George presented his Government's proposals for a treaty between the

---

[1] Following the truce, the Catholic Bishop of Down and Connor commented that "Things (for Catholics) seem to be going from bad to worse."

two sides. The proposals completely ignored the notion of an independent Irish Republic, and instead offered that Ireland: "take her place in the great association of free nations over which His Majesty reigns."[490] The British offer was that of dominion status for Ireland, which would require elected representatives to take an oath of allegiance to the British Monarch. There were also exceptions to full dominion status such as the retention of control of the seas around Ireland and bases for the Royal Navy along with other defence requirements. Further demands were that Ireland should shoulder part of Britain's war debt from the Great War and free trade without tariffs between the two countries. Regarding the six counties which Lloyd George had just partitioned from the rest of the country, it was stipulated that: "The British government will therefore leave Irishmen themselves to determine by negotiations between themselves whether the new powers which the Pact defines shall be taken over by Ireland as a whole and administered by a single Irish body, or be taken over separately by Southern and Northern Ireland, with or without a joint authority to harmonise their common interests."[491] This proviso was dead in the water from the outset as it was obvious that Craig and that the Ulster Unionists wanted nothing whatsoever to do with a Dublin parliament.

After studying the British proposals, deValera advised Lloyd George that he could not accept them at which the British Prime Minister immediately threatened the resumption of the war. When this threat failed to change deValera's opinion, Lloyd George said that he would make his offer public and asked for a full written reply to the British offer. DeValera agreed provided that both were published together.

## Irish Rejection of the British Offer

Following deValera's return to Dublin, the British document was discussed at a full cabinet meeting of the Republican Government which took place in Blackrock. The proposals were rejected. However Austin Stack recalled: "I got the impression strongly forced upon me that Griffith and Collins and Mulcahy were inclined to view the proposals favourably."[492]

On August 10th, deValera sent his reply[I] to Lloyd George outlining the objections of the Republican Government to the British proposals.

Whilst the IRA had expected the truce to be of short duration, the British knew that the longer peace remained the harder it would be for the Irish to go back to war and once more endure what had gone before. Threats abounded of how Britain would make Ireland suffer if the war was renewed. On August 19th, Lord Birkenhead (F.E "Galloper" Smith) informed parliament that if the Irish would not come to terms with His Majesty's Government then England would undertake: "…hostilities on a scale never hitherto undertaken by this country against Ireland."[493] [II] Birkenhead's sentiments were echoed by Lord Curzon. If negotiations failed, unprecedented military action would be taken against Ireland.

---

[I] The reply informed Lloyd George that "Ireland's right to choose for herself the path she shall take to realize her own destiny must be accepted as indefeasible. It is a right that has been maintained through centuries of oppression and at the cost of unparalleled sacrifice and untold suffering, and it will not be surrendered. We cannot propose to abrogate or impair it, nor can Britain or any other foreign state or group of states claim to interfere with its exercise in order to serve their own special interests."

[II] When one considers what Ireland had previously suffered at the hands of the British, then this was indeed a horrific threat.

Letters

Lloyd George's proposals were submitted to Dáil Éireann on August 23rd where they were overwhelmingly rejected in spite of the sword of renewed war hanging over the country.

Following the Dáil session, President deValera wrote to Lloyd George to inform him of the rejection of his proposals by Dáil Eireann and to remind him that: "In Ireland's case, to speak of Her seceding from a partnership she has not accepted, or from an allegiance she has not undertaken to render, is fundamentally false, just as the claim to subordinate her independence to British strategy is fundamentally unjust."[494] Regarding further negotiations DeValera offered the appointment of representatives invested with plenary powers. Lloyd George reply was received on August 26th: "His letter iterated that the British offer gave Ireland all that Daniel O' Connell had asked for a century before. (Lloyd George did not allow for all that had passed since including the Great Starvation and the de-facto partitioning of Ireland): "We can discuss no settlement which involves a refusal on the part of Ireland to accept our invitation to free, equal and loyal partnership under one Sovereign."[495] To this deValera replied that his Government's rejection of July 20th was: "irrevocable" to which Lloyd George countered that: "…we can only resist (the Irish bid for freedom) as the generations before us have resisted."[496]

Growing impatient with his correspondence with deValera, Lloyd George offered a conference for September 20th, to be held in Inverness, Scotland. De Valera's reply agreeing with a conference to be held with the representatives of Ireland: "which recognizes itself as a sovereign State" unsettled Lloyd George in no small measure. Denouncing deValera's unwillingness to back down from his "original claims", Lloyd George cancelled the conference. On September 29th, whilst in Dundee, Minister Winston Churchill threatened that when hostilities with Ireland resumed it would be "…real war – not mere bushranging." He also divulged one of the major factors in the British reluctance to renew hostilities; the opinion of the American government and the hope of a permanent British alliance with the New World.

## An Invitation

On the same day as Winston Churchill's speech, Lloyd George sent a letter to deValera issuing a new invitation for negotiations and a clean-slate regarding all previous correspondence. The talks he proposed would begin again from scratch in London on October 11th. President deValera agreed to negotiations which would ascertain: "…how the association of Ireland with the community of nations known as the British Empire may best be reconciled with Irish national aspirations."[497] DeValera hoped that this could be achieved through a proposal which he had devised with the help of Erskine Childers known as "external association with the British empire."

Of the cabinet meeting which followed Austin Stack recalled: "It was suggested that the President should go himself, but he (deValera) had his objections. He pointed out that he was in the position of head of state as well as head of government, and that, in his absence, it would always be said that they (the Irish delegation) had to consult the President and their other colleagues in Dublin." In his reasoning, DeValera also maintained that as he had already rejected the first British offer, he should now remain in the background so as to be able to restart negotiations if they should fail and that if a treaty acceptable to the cabinet which involved compromise were reached, then he as President who was not on the front line of the negotiations would be able to 'sell' the agreement to Sinn Fein and the IRA. After deValera expounded his objections, a

Cabinet vote was taken. The cabinet approved of his position with the exception of Michael Collins and W.T Cosgrave.

The cabinet meeting now decided upon five negotiators or "plenipotentiaries" who would have the power to make an agreement between the English government and the government of the Republic despite London's misgivings over their designation as such. The men chosen to depart Dublin for London at the beginning of the second week of October 1921 were those whose ministerial remit was most relevant to the negotiations: Arthur Griffith (Minister for Foreign Affairs) who would lead the delegation, Michael Collins (Minister for Finance), Robert Barton (Economic Affairs), along with (George) Gavan Duffy TD and Eamonn Duggan TD. The secretaries were Erskine Childers, Finian Lynch, Diarmuid O'Hegarty and John Chartres.

Strict instructions accompanied the Plenipotentiaries on the powers entrusted to them including: "...before decisions are reached on a main question, that a dispatch notifying the intention to make these decisions will be sent to members of the cabinet in Dublin, and that a reply will be awaited by the Plenipotentiaries before the final decision is made"[498], and that: "It is also understood that the complete text of the draft treaty about to be signed will be similarly submitted to Dublin, and reply awaited."[499] Furthermore, Dublin was to be "...kept regularly informed of the progress of the negotiations."[500]

Following deValera's meetings with Lloyd George, the Irish delegation knew how far the British were prepared to go (dominion status) without conceding ground. As the delegates departed, the rest of the Republican cabinet were working on the Irish proposals which would be forwarded to London and submitted to the British delegation at the conference. The document was known internally as "Draft Treaty A"

# The Treaty Negotiations
## The London Conference
On October 11th, the first meeting between the two delegations took place at 10 Downing St. After taking their seats at the Cabinet Room table, Lloyd George introduced the Irish delegates to his delegation which included Sir Hamar Greenwood, Winston Churchill, Austin Chamberlain, Lord Birkenhead (F.E Smith) and Sir Laming Worthington Evans.

During this first meeting Lloyd George immediately sought to divide the members of the Irish delegation from their colleagues in Dublin telling them that if the negotiations failed, then "…the responsibility for failure will rest, not with those at the council table but with others." He then went over his previous offer again, laying out his Government's position while assuring the Irish delegates that England sought neither to control Ireland militarily or economically as a dominion.

Over the following days various strands of the previous offer were at British insistence discussed[1] while the question of loyalty to the Crown and dominion status were sidelined as Lloyd George and his cabinet seemed determined to stay away from the main issues for the moment at least.

On the question of Irish partition, with his victory on the question seemingly achieved, Lloyd George was quick to assure the Irish delegation that the British government would now stand aside and 'leave the question to Irishmen', claiming that London would maintain a "benevolent neutrality" towards the question of a united Ireland.

## A Defining Day
On October 24th, the Irish delegation presented the British delegation with a Memorandum outlining the Irish position which was based upon "Draft Treaty A".

---
[1] This included financial relations, war debt, and defence.

On the question of the six counties, the Memo contained proposals for a northern local government parliament under Dublin's control, for all the parliamentary constituencies of the six counties which voted not to send representatives to Dáil Eireann. Regarding dominion status, the Draft Treaty allowed that Ireland would cooperate with the British Commonwealth on all matters of mutual importance (external association) without any oath of allegiance to the British Monarch.

The Irish proposals were very far removed from British aims and the British delegation immediately sought to tear holes in them by insisting on the 'necessity' of allegiance to the Crown from which would automatically follow dominion status and Crown defence facilities in Ireland.

Lloyd George now proposed that in order for the conference to make progress, the leader of the Irish delegation, Arthur Griffith along with Michael Collins should engage in private conference with himself and Churchill. Griffith and Collins agreed and on this premise so did the remainder of the Irish delegation. However, developments were to show that once part of the Irish delegation was excluded, Lloyd George had the advantage. After October 24th, the Irish delegation as a unit would not sit in the Cabinet Room again and thus weakened, were constantly on the defensive, attempting to parry English demands and inevitably granting concessions. Lloyd George had successfully picked the Irish delegation apart[I] by separating those whom he deemed to be more amenable and pliable to his suggestions from those whom he deemed not to be.[II]

---

[I] According to the diary of the secretary of the British delegation, Thomas Jones, the suggestion for sub-conferences came originally from Griffith and Collins, this, prior to their suggestion in conference by Lloyd George. If this is the case, then Griffith and Collins were completely ignoring their instructions from Dublin and following their own agenda.

[II] Austin Stack would later recall: "For some time – perhaps a fortnight – we used to receive detailed accounts of the discussions and we followed them closely.

That evening Griffith wrote to deValera, to tell him how insistent the British were regarding acceptance of the Crown. DeValera replied: "We are all here at one that there can be no question of asking the Irish people to enter an agreement which would make them subject to the British King. If war is the alternative, we can only face it, and I think the sooner the other side is made to realize it the better."[501]

### Concern Among Members of the Irish Delegation
By the end of October, the weakness now inherent in the Irish delegation had become apparent to Robert Barton and Gavan Duffy along with Erskine Childers.

According to Barton: "...from the very moment Griffith and Collins met Lloyd George and Chamberlain alone, their power to resist weakened. They became almost pro-British in their arguments with us and Duffy and I often felt that we had to fight them first and the English afterwards."[502]

Then, following on from the 'sub-conference' meetings between Lloyd George and Griffith and Collins and Birkenhead who was accompanied by Churchill, there followed the submission of a letter to Lloyd George by Arthur Griffith which traded "recognition of the Crown" in return for "the essential unity of Ireland". The letter continued: "As to the North-East of Ireland, while reserving for further discussion on the question of area, I would agree to …the maintenance of existing parliamentary powers."

Lloyd George had requested this letter from Griffith on the pretext that he would use it to try and get James Craig to give way on Irish unity, or that he (Lloyd George) would resign if he failed.

---

There was nothing alarming to us in any of the reports (from London) up to about October 25th.

Unhappy with Griffith's compromising,[1] and the sure feeling that Collins was his partner in all compromises, Barton and Duffy were now tempted to consider their position as delegates (as was Childers as secretary) but they decided to remain in place in the sure knowledge that any final deal would be submitted to Dublin. Robert Barton would later recall: "In my opinion these conferences between the English and Griffith and Collins...sealed the doom of the Republic...It was not until later that Gavan Duffy, Childers and I realized that Griffith and Collins were prepared to settle for less than we thought possible to obtain. We had trusted them fully. We had complete confidence in them up to that time. Griffith had fought magnificent actions during the full conference. We had no reason to suppose at the time that he would agree in private to anything which he had not been agreeing to with five of us present...It was decided that one of us must go to Dublin to acquaint the Cabinet and deValera, that we were not at all sure that the reports given us of what transpired at private conferences were comprehensive."

After travelling to Dublin, Gavan Duffy expressed his fears to deValera. The President indicated that he was content to let matters develop so long as the delegation acted in concert on all major decisions. However he did send a letter to Griffith expressing the opinion that the Irish delegation were conceding too much ground.[II]

---

[1] Austin Stack: "I mentioned (to Griffith) the absolute necessity of procuring the services of some constitutional lawyer from America or Europe, if necessary to look after our interests. Mr. Griffith promised to look after this; I had a private conversation with him afterwards – it may have been some days later – and he repeated his promise...but it turned out the plenipotentiaries got no constitutional lawyer to act with them in London."

[II] Austin Stack: "The President then and there...dictated a letter to Mr. Griffith, informing him that our (the delegation's) views were giving in too much to the English in important matters..."

One of the matters on which they had already given way without consultation with Dublin was that the Republican Government would not import any more weapons into the country, thus giving a sure advantage to the British in the event of a return to hostilities.[1]

### Griffith Agrees to Lloyd George's "Technical Manoeuvre"

In the days following Griffith's letter, Lloyd George engaged in negotiations with James Craig where his apparent proposal to Craig of a 'northern parliament' subordinate to an all Ireland parliament was rejected outright. As far as Craig was concerned, he had his six counties and in the best traditions of Ulster Unionism, was content to hold what he had.

Following his talks with Craig and before the Unionist Party Conference at Liverpool, scheduled for November 17th,, a "Boundary Commission" was put forward by Lloyd George through Thomas Jones to Griffith and Collins as a 'clever' way to out-manoeuvre Craig's stubbornness. It was sold by Lloyd George to them as a negotiation tactic, a method of limiting the area of Unionist control if they (the Unionists) would not accept a local government parliament subordinate to Dublin. Lloyd George gave Griffith the impression that areas of nationalist majority in the six counties would, following the commission, come under the control of Dublin while Craig would be left with an area which in the long term would be unviable.

In response to Lloyd George, Griffith told him that if the English used the proposal of a boundary commission as a "technical manoeuvre" in their talks with the Unionists then the Irish delegation would not question this.

---

[1] Austin Stack: "Our people in London without consulting the Minister for Defence, agreed that there would be no more arms imported into Ireland.

Critically, Arthur Griffith, as the head of the Irish delegation, had now let Lloyd George 'off the hook'. Whereas previously Lloyd George had committed to resign if he did not prevail over the Unionists, now he only had to get them to agree to the principle of a boundary commission if they would not give way over a northern parliament subordinate to Dublin.

This Craig would never do, but Griffith or Collins would never manage to hold Lloyd George to account for it. They would instead be left with empty assurances while Lloyd George's government took positive action to reinforce the Ulster Constabulary by enlisting the loyalist paramilitaries to service within the Ulster Special Constabulary, this in direct contravention to the terms of the truce. Furthermore, as the RIC within the six counties was deemed to contain 'too many Catholics', the British Government would also connive with the setting up of a new police force; The Royal Ulster Constabulary.

Before entering further negotiations with James Craig, Lloyd George now pressed home his advantage with Griffith without Collins's knowledge. On a sheet, he detailed compromises on the Crown and partition and through his secretary Thomas Jones, asked Griffith not to repudiate them while he engaged in further talks with Craig. Griffith agreed (possibly signing the document) but said that he could not guarantee their acceptance by the Irish delegation as a whole.[1]

---

[1] Since Home Rule for Ireland was first put forward some fifty years previously, the mottos of the Ulster Unionists had always been "No Surrender", "What we have we hold!" and "Not an Inch". How Arthur Griffith and Michael Collins ever thought that the Unionists would take part in a meaningful boundary commission (where they would surrender Fermanagh, Tyrone, South Armagh and parts of Derry and Down to the Dublin government) remains unexplained. Furthermore, the English government, whose loyalty had ever been to the Unionists could never be an impartial broker in such a commission and any idea that they would undermine the Unionist position was unrealistic.

The document to which Griffith gave his assent enumerated how, if the Ulster Unionists did not accept that the northern parliament should be subordinate to Dublin, a boundary commission would follow. Following the boundary commission, the part of Ulster which remained outside Dublin's control would be under the control of the northern parliament which would then be subordinate to Westminster and not Dublin.

Lloyd George had achieved a major victory. He had got Arthur Griffith to accept the principle of a boundary commission, and that part of Ireland would remain under British control. Lloyd George would introduce this letter to the Irish delegation at the critical moment.

At the Liverpool Unionist Party Conference, Lloyd George prevailed. How? Beforehand, Birkenhead had a secret meeting with Salvidge, the Liverpool Unionist leader, where he informed him that a settlement was in sight which would keep Ireland in the Empire, guarantee England's naval interests in Ireland and not involve any coercion of Ulster under any circumstances. Salvidge then agreed to support the government in opposition to the proposed motion of censure.

## Irish Proposals Resubmitted

On November 16th, the British government submitted draft proposals to the Irish delegation. Whilst the majority of the document laid out the proposals submitted in July in offering Dominion Status and all which that entailed, this document proposed a boundary commission "in accordance with the wishes of the inhabitants", if the Unionist parliament preferred to remain outside Dublin's control. The length of time for the Unionist Parliament to opt out from the control of the Dublin parliament and opt in to a boundary commission was six months.

The British proposals were forwarded to Dublin and were on deValera's orders countered by modified Irish proposals on November 22nd, which insisted upon Irish sovereignty but offered to recognize the King as head of an association of states (of which Ireland would be a member) which would co-operate with the Empire.  Furthermore the Irish proposals offered concessions regarding Royal Navy facilities for a limited time and numerous economic concessions.  Regarding the north east of Ulster, the Irish proposals offered a local government northern parliament (which would be under Dublin's control) numerous safeguards.  What the proposals did not agree to was inclusion in the British Empire and the partitioning of Ireland.

As the British considered the Irish proposals, the Belfast pogrom once more erupted, this time lasting for four days during which twenty six Catholics were killed and almost one hundred wounded.

Following the re-submission of the Irish proposals, deValera went to the west and south-west where he engaged in a tour of inspection of IRA units.  In Clare on November 30th, he addressed the Mid Clare Brigade of the IRA and told them: "We are going to stand on the rock of truth and principle.  We will face the future with exactly the same confidence and knowledge we faced our work four weeks ago.  We know what can be done by the same powerful nation against us.  We know the terrorism, we know the savagery that can be used against us and we defy it!"[503]

In London, although unhappy with the Irish memorandum, at deValera's insistence Griffith did not go beyond its terms despite being personally told by Lloyd George's secretary Thomas Jones, that Lloyd George now despaired of an agreement.  At this point the British offered a number of concessions on trade and defence, and on Tuesday November

29th, Griffith was informed that the final British offer would be submitted to the Irish delegation on Thursday December 1st.

After receiving the British proposals, the Irish delegation returned to Dublin where a Cabinet meeting had been summoned for the morning of Saturday December 3rd.

In Belfast, following a communication from Lloyd George, Captain Craig announced: "Sinn Féin, fully alive as it is now to our unflinching determination not to go into an All-Ireland Parliament has to say by Tuesday (December 6th) next if she will still work for a settlement or else all negotiations are broken off...By Thursday next either negotiations will have broken down or the Prime Minister will send me new proposals for consideration by the Cabinet. In the meantime the rights of Ulster are in no way sacrificed or compromised."

## "You will split Ireland from top to bottom!"

At 11am, on the morning of Saturday December 3rd, the Republican Cabinet met to discuss what the British had termed "their final offer" which in almost all respects was identical to their offer of November 16th. However there was one important change which would completely transform any proposed boundary Commission. Instead of the boundary commission being (according to article 14) "in accordance with the wishes of the inhabitants"[504] this sentence was changed to "in accordance with the wishes of the inhabitants so far as may be compatible with economic and geographic conditions..."[505] This reduced any boundary commission to an undefined entity, subject to the instructions of the Crown-appointed President of the Commission.

Of the Cabinet meeting, Austin Stack recalled: "The discussion throughout was on the main questions – allegiance to the British Crown and partition."[506]

The meeting was a fractious affair and continued until evening. Stack later recalled:"Griffith argued all day in favour of acceptance" telling the other members of the Cabinet that he did not believe the Irish delegation should "break" on the question of allegiance to the Crown as in his view, this would cause division in Ireland. He argued that once as many concessions as possible were achieved and Craig had agreed to the articles on subordination of the northern parliament to Dublin, or a boundary commission, the Irish delegation should sign. In his turn Eamonn Duggan supported Griffith's position. Collin's opinion was that once more concessions were obtained on defence and trade the document should be signed and then put to the people, at which point the Republican government should recommend acceptance of the terms of the Treaty excluding the oath.

DeValera and other members of the Cabinet were unequivocal in their rejection of the British document unless alterations were made. When the matter was put to a vote, the majority of the Cabinet voted against acceptance of the Treaty, in particular dominion status, the oath of allegiance and the boundary commission which would enforce the partition of Ireland.

When the question of the progress of the Treaty talks was raised, Cathal Brugha raised the matter of the one on one sessions between Griffith, Collins, Lloyd George and other members of the British delegation, remarking that the other Irish delegates had been left in the dark. At this point when Brugha was informed that the sub-conferences were (apparently) a British suggestion, he remarked: "They chose their men well."[507] This remark provoked a furious outburst from Griffith.

As the crisis in the London negotiations had come, the discussion inevitably turned to whether or not deValera should accompany the delegates to London, to which deValera agreed. At this point Brugha asked Griffith: "Don't you realize if you sign this thing, you will split Ireland from top to bottom?"[508]

Griffith paused, reflected and then replied: "I suppose that's so. I'll tell you what I'll do. I'll go back to London. I'll not sign the document but I'll bring it back and submit it to the Dáil and if necessary to the people."[509]

Following this unequivocal assurance, the Cabinet voted that deValera should remain in Dublin.

At the final summing up of the Cabinet meeting, it was decided that the delegation should inform Lloyd George that they were not empowered to sign the Treaty on account of the articles relating to the oath of allegiance and partition. . It was decided as a negotiating tactic that partition should be the chief breaking point and the delegates should return to Dublin for a debate and vote on the Treaty in Dáil Eireann

## The Treaty is Signed

<u>New Irish Proposals</u>

On Sunday December 4th, following the return of the Irish delegates to London, Duffy, Barton and Childers drafted new proposals to be submitted to the British delegation embodying the agreed position of the Cabinet at the previous Saturday's meeting and putting forward the wording of an oath acceptable to the Republican Cabinet: "I do swear true faith and allegiance to the Constitution of Ireland and to the Treaty of Association of Ireland with the British Commonwealth of Nations and to recognize the King of Great Britain as Head of the Association."[510] They then found that neither Griffith or Collins were in favour of the submission of counter-proposals. Furthermore Collins, Duggan and Griffith refused to accompany them to Downing St. that afternoon to present the proposals. Finally Griffith acquiesced and accompanied them ostensibly to prevent a break with the British delegation. Without Collins's presence, the proposals were dead in the water. By his absence, Collins was showing the disunity of the Irish delegation. The British rejected the proposals, rounding on Gavan Duffy for rejecting Ireland's inclusion in the Empire, and telling the Irish delegation that they would send word to James Craig that the negotiations were at an end.

However, taking note of Collins's absence from the meeting, the British delegation felt that they had another roll of the dice in order to achieve their objectives. On Monday evening, Lloyd George's personal secretary, Thomas Jones contacted Griffith who is said to have told him that both he and Collins would accept the Treaty provided that a 'sweetner' were offered to the Dáil, consisting of a "conditional recognition of Irish unity, however shadowy, in return for the acceptance of Empire by Sinn Fein."[511] Following the meeting, Griffith contacted Collins and persuaded him to return to Downing St. the following morning. Griffith then asked Jones to organize a meeting between Collins and Lloyd George for the following morning.

On Monday morning December 5th, Collins met Lloyd George at Downing St. where Collins asked Lloyd George for a definite reply from Captain Craig in relation to his co-operation and agreement with a Boundary commission. Having not received Craig's co-operation, and unlikely to do so, Lloyd George assured Collins that with or without Craig the Boundary Commission would take place and would indeed save Ireland from long-term partition. Collins then agreed to a further meeting that afternoon with (part of) the Irish delegation.

## Griffith Breaks his Word to the Republican Cabinet

Just before 3pm that same day, Griffith , Collins and Barton returned to Downing St. for the final conference of the negotiations. That Collins and Griffith had brought Barton, a staunch Republican, was no mere coincidence.

Opening the conference, Lloyd George immediately launched a well planned attack which was designed to set Griffith at odds with his colleagues. Playing the opening gambit of his 'ace in the hole', Lloyd George raised the question of the boundary commission and partition remarking that Griffith had, (by agreeing to Lloyd George's proposals of November 12th) already given the British delegation his full support. Griffith did not disagree with Lloyd George, but replied that he needed to know if Craig would also agree to a Boundary Commission. Lloyd George replied that Craig's assent was immaterial and should not prove grounds for a disagreement between the delegations. The British would proceed with their proposal for a Boundary Commission with or without Craig while Griffith as head of the Irish delegation had given his assent to it. At this point the full nature of Griffith's agreement with Lloyd George was not revealed.

A break in the conference followed during which Griffith, Collins and Barton agreed that they must have Craig's written assent to his full cooperation with a boundary commission. The question of returning article 14 to its original form was not mentioned.

When the conference resumed following the intermission, Lloyd George was not present. Some minutes later he entered proffering an envelope with a protruding document containing the details of his "technical manoeuvre". He charged Griffith, that by pursuing the question of the Boundary Commission and partition he was reneging on his word given in the document which the Prime Minister held. Griffith replied that he would keep his word to the Prime Minister. While Collins was most likely aware of the document, Barton was not. Both men questioned its contents. Looking at Collins, Lloyd George said: "Do you mean to tell me, Mr. Collins, that you have never heard of this document from Mr. Griffith?"[512]

As the letter was passed for their examination, Lloyd George explained its meaning.

In saying that he would keep his word to Lloyd George, Griffith was not only breaking his word to the Republican cabinet but also breaking the terms set down by DeValera, which he had agreed to at the beginning of the negotiations. Griffith now formally separated himself from his delegation telling Lloyd George that while he had given his assent to the document, his colleagues had not. He agreed to sign the Treaty and would give the answer of his colleagues that evening. Winston Churchill would recall the conversation which followed: ""I will give the answer of the Irish Delegates at nine tonight; but Mr. Prime Minister, I personally will sign this agreement and will recommend it to my countrymen." "Do I understand, Mr. Griffith," said Mr. Lloyd George, that though everyone else refuses you will nevertheless agree to sign?" "Yes, that is so, Mr. Prime Minister," replied this quiet little man of great heart and of great purpose."[513]

With Griffith in the bag, and fully aware that Collins would follow suit, Lloyd George now turned his attention to Barton, telling him that he had understood that Griffith had agreed to the document on behalf of the delegation.

He attempted to brow-beat[i] and coerce Barton to submission while Collins and Griffith, who were both ready to sign made no attempt to call him to order.

Robert Barton later recalled: "Speaking for himself and his colleagues, the English Prime Minister, with all the solemnity and the power of conviction that he alone, of all men I met, can impart by word and gesture – the vehicles by which the mind of one man oppresses and impresses the mind of another –

---

[i] Gavan Duffy would recall: "The monstrous iniquity was perpetrated by the man who had invited us under his roof in order to make a friendly settlement. The position was this; that if we, every one of us did not sign and undertake to recommend, fresh hordes of savages would be let loose upon this country to trample and torture and terrify it." Lloyd George's tactics in Downing St. would be emulated in the following decade by Adolf Hitler in his meetings with the leaders of Austria and Czechoslovakia when he desired to gain control of their countries. (In the 1930's Lloyd George would meet Hitler twice and declare him to be "One of the greatest of the many men I have ever met".)

declared that the signature and recommendation of every member of our delegation was necessary or war would follow immediately."[514]

Lloyd George's concluding remarks were: "I have to communicate with Sir James Craig tonight; here are the alternative letters I have prepared, one enclosing the Articles of Agreement reached by His Majesty's Government and yourselves, the other saying that the Sinn Féin representatives refuse the oath of allegiance and refuse to come within the Empire. If I send this letter it is war – and war in three days! Which letter am I to send?"[515]

Michael Collins would recall that Lloyd George promised "immediate and terrible war in three days" if the signature of the other members of the Irish delegation did not follow.

## Hans Place

At their house at Hans Place, the entire Irish delegation met. His own compromised position having been revealed, Griffith now urged the others to sign telling them that no better terms could be achieved. Collins and Duggan agreed to sign. Throughout the negotiations, Michael Collins had been keeping the Supreme Council of the IRB informed of all that happened in London and they had agreed to go along with whatever Collins thought was best. ('What is good enough for you is good enough for us')

Two of the Irish delegates, weakened and confused by Collins's acceptance now stood alone; Gavan Duffy and Robert Barton. Both of these men now came under pressure from the other delegates that they would bear responsibility for the "terrible war" which would follow. Under pressure, both men agreed to sign. No attempt was made to contact Dublin by telephone. Doubtless, Griffith knew the answer he would receive if he did. His action and that of Collins especially (with his personal following among some IRA leaders and his role as

President of the IRB) was designed to hem the Dublin cabinet and the Dáil in a corner and deny them the full freedom they had previously possessed to choose Ireland's path. As Griffith had acknowledged the previous Saturday, his action in signing the Treaty would "split Ireland from top to bottom".
Duffy and Barton refused to accompany the others to Downing St, telling them that they would sign the document at Hans Place.

### The Treaty is Signed
"If they think they can rely on the word of Mr. Lloyd George and his friends they are not the sensible men I took them to be" – Cathal Brugha

Lloyd George later recalled: "He (Griffith) asked for a few hours to consider, promising a reply by nine o'clock. Nine passed, but the Irish leaders did not return. Ten, eleven, and they were not back yet. We had doubts as to whether we should see them again."[516I]
Having received the agreement of Duffy and Barton, Griffith, Collins and Duggan returned to Downing St. where they, along with the British delegation signed the Treaty[II] in the early hours of December 6th. The Irish delegation signed not only in contravention of their undertaking to the Republican Cabinet but also in contravention of the will of the Irish people as expressed during the recent election.

---

[I] In spite of Lloyd George's doubts it appears that while waiting for the Irish delegation to return he sent a copy of the final treaty to James Craig as the copy of the Treaty which Craig received was dated December 5th, while the actual Treaty was not signed until the early hours of the morning of December 6th.
[II] The terms of the Treaty can be read at : www.difp.ie

Michael Collins and Arthur Griffith

Compared to the document which they had presented at the meeting of the Republican Cabinet the previous Saturday, further amendments had taken place. On Collins's suggestion, the Ulster Unionists could now exclude themselves from Dublin's control within the first month following the ratification of the Treaty in the House of Commons instead of after six months.[I]

Regarding the Boundary Commission, Lloyd George had successfully 'sold a pup' to Griffith and Collins. The Boundary Commission would be a sham. Not one acre of the six counties would ever come under Dublin's control[II], while the Catholics within the six counties would be given over to the tender mercies of the Unionist and sectarian Government of Northern Ireland who refused to recognize the rights of the native inhabitants whose ancestral lands they now controlled.

---

[I] Collins insisted on this as he felt that the anti-Catholic pogroms would reach an unbearable level if the six month proviso were maintained. (By the Summer of 1922, 23,000 Catholics had been burnt out and around 500 people killed)
[II] Unable to make any progress in the Boundary Commission, the government of the Irish Free State would finally abandon it at the end of 1925, after being bribed by the British Government to accept a reduction in their part of servicing the British national debt.

As the Irish delegation departed Downing St., Lord Birkenhead remarked to Collins: "I may have signed my political death warrant tonight." The Treaty had apparently brought peace with England. Collins was unsure that it had brought peace within Ireland. Fully alive to the seeds of division which he had just sown, Collins replied to Birkenhead: "I may have signed my actual death warrant".

## Jubilation in England
In the days that followed, Lloyd George and his delegation assured the House of Commons and the British people of the great victory they had won. In the Commons, Winston Churchill said: "Sinn Féin demanded an independent Sovereign Republic for the whole of Ireland, including Ulster. We insisted upon allegiance to the Crown, partnership in the Empire, facilities and securities for the Navy, and complete option for Ulster. Every one of these conditions is embodied in the Treaty."[517] Regarding the Oath, Churchill described it as "far more precise and searching than the ordinary oath which is taken elsewhere – it mentions specifically membership of the Empire, common citizenship and faithfulness to the Crown, whereas only one of these matters is dealt with in the Dominion Oath."[518]

The failure of the Irish delegation to nail down the terms of the Boundary Commision allowed Lloyd George to proclaim: "We have recommended a Boundary Commission. It is not for me to say whether it will mean that the area of Ulster will be increased or diminished..."

Lloyd George was sure that he had chosen the right moment to offer the truce, after the establishment of the Northern Parliament, telling the Commons: "That accomplished fact – by legislation, by the setting up of the government – it was there to deal not in the abstract, not in an agreement, not in contention across tables, but in actual living government..."[519]

In the House of Lords, Lord Curzon echoed the Prime Minister's sentiment: "You would never have got this settlement had it not bee that Ulster, by legislation which we passed here in 1920, attained a separate being of her own."[520]

## The Bloody Aftermath
"If it's good enough for Mick Collins, it's good enough for me!"
When news of the Treaty's signing broke in Dublin, plans were formulated to dismiss Griffith, Collins and Barton from the Cabinet and arrest the members of the Irish delegation for high treason on their return. However it was realized that this would cause further division and the plans were revoked.

At the Cabinet meeting which followed the delegate's return, Griffith and Collins made the case for their actions having been correct, while Robert Barton was critical of deValera for not going to London himself. Much was said about the threat of "immediate and terrible war". Three members of the the Cabinet (Griffith, Collins and Barton) had already signed the Treaty. A fourth, W.T Cosgrave, joined them. When the vote was taken, it was four to three in favour of the Treaty.

The Dáil was summoned for December 14th. DeValera now issued a press statement that he could not accept the Treaty.

The sometimes acrimonious Treaty debate began on December 14th and concluded on January 7th. The question of the oath, the partitioning of Ireland and the abandonment of Ulster along with the threat of an even more terrible war featured in many speeches. Those in favour of the Treaty spoke of it being the best deal available. Above all their strongest argument in favour was that the Treaty had already been signed. It was presented as a 'fait accompli'. Facts which may well have secured the voting down of the Treaty such as the 'sub conferences and Griffith's letter were not revealed. Griffith also pointed out that if the Dáil rejected the Treaty and fighting resumed: "Ireland would be fighting with the sympathy of the world against her."⁵²¹

Whilst the Treaty was presented by those in favour as a 'fait accompli", Frank Fahy TD sought to turn this logic on its head: "Is not the declaration of the Republic also a fait accompli or have we been playing at Republicanism...Honour cannot be based upon dishonour...Let at least our word be our bond."

Nevertheless, the Treaty's signing had been as a gun to the head of the Dáil.

With every passing day and with every speech, tthe division deepended. To a woman, all the women TDs including Mrs Tom Clarke and Mrs Pearse spoke against the Treaty, with Mrs. Pearse declaring that she would uphold what her sons upheld. Mary MacSwiney (sister of Terence MacSwiney) addressed the pro-treaty TDs: "What chance would you have if on the twenty fourth of last May you came out for Dominion Home Rule?" She asserted that Griffith had never believed in the Republic and had now reverted to his old Sinn Féin policies which should have been consigned to history in 1918.[1]

Outside of the Dáil a significant number of TDs who were members of the IRB were urged by individuals on the Supreme Council to support the Treaty, and their leader Michael Collins.

Aside from the fact that the Treaty had already actually been signed, other pressures were brought to bear on the TDs, especially during the Christmas recess. In the country at large, businessmen and the wealthy (many southern unionists among them) were in favour. As a result the Irish media which they controlled was in favour. Many bishops hailing the security of peace also came out in favour. In the country at large: "If it's good enough for Mick Collins it's good enough for me"

---

[1] During the Treaty debate, Griffith affirmed Mary MacSwiney's assertion when he declared that he had always been and continued to be a disciple of Thomas Davis, who, in the middle of the nineteenth century sought home rule under the Crown.

became the slogan of those in favour while those who were initially reluctant to accept the Treaty now exaggerated its benefits.

Following the Christmas recess, in an attempt to salvage the Republic and proceed on a united front, deValera proposed in Cabinet certain alterations to the Treaty which were quickly undone after Griffith leaked the document to the press.

When the vote was taken on January 7th 1922, the result was 64 to 57 in favour of the Treaty's ratification. The resignation of deValera followed and it was proposed that Griffith succeed him. Griffith now came under pressure from those opposed to the Treaty, when they protested that he could not circumvent the Republican Constitution and that the Republic must remain in place until the people formally voted to dissolve it in a referendum. Although the Dáil had accepted the Treaty, it could not vote the Republic out of existence.

When Griffith replied that he would remain as President of the Republic until the Free State formally came into existence (twelve months later), his compromised credentials were questioned and deValera advised him for the unity of the country not to accept the role. However, the advice was ignored and Griffith was duly elected as President of the Republic, claiming that he would uphold it until the people voted. Nevertheless he would immediately proceed to dismantle it and the people would never formally vote for its revocation.

## "The Provisional Government of Southern Ireland"

Under the Treaty the Dáil had no power. The Treaty itself stipulated the summoning of a "House of Commons of Southern Ireland" under the Government of Ireland Act. What Lloyd George required (under Article 17) was that the House of Commons of Southern Ireland be summoned and a provisional government of southern Ireland formed. Once its members had signed the Articles of Agreement and sworn fealty to the King, the powers outlined in the treaty would be transferred to the provisional government of southern Ireland. It now fell to Arthur Griffith "to do the dirty work" as Michael Collins termed it. On January 11$^{th}$ 1922, Arthur Griffith summoned the "Parliament of Southern Ireland" to assemble at the Mansion House on Saturday, January 14$^{th}$. Sixty pro – Treaty TDs along with four Unionists elected for Trinity College.attended. After approving the Treaty, they elected a provisional government for the twenty six counties of Southern Ireland. Following the election of the Provisional Government of Southern Ireland, the transfer of power by the British began on January 16$^{th}$ at Dublin Castle. Following January 16$^{th}$, the withdrawal of British troops from the 26 counties commenced with some units transferring to the six counties, in order to reinforce the constabulary there. However British troops remained in barracks in the Curragh, Cork and Dublin as General Macready recalled: "due to the Republican attitude."

## No Other Law

"We have declared for an Irish Republic and will not live under any other law" – General Liam Lynch, IRA Chief of Staff.

"Take it down from the mast, Irish traitors,
The flag we Republicans claim,
It can never belong to Free Staters
You've brought on it nothing but shame."
-Eugene Mc Eldowney

Following the passage of The Treaty through the Dáil, it seemed to the majority of the fighting men of the IRA that many members of that parliament had not taken their oath to uphold the Republic seriously.

For the majority of the fighting men of the IRA, the Republic was a reality. They had endured much for the Republic and were not prepared to see it betrayed.

Their leaders were divided. Six of the Dublin Headquarters Staff were in favour of the Treaty and seven against. This division amongst the highest ranking IRA officers was replicated, in some areas, while in the south, where the heaviest of the fighting had been, the IRA officers were almost unanimous in their rejection of the Treaty.[I] They struggled to understand how Michael Collins had accepted the partitioning of Ireland and allegiance to the King of England.

With the establishment of the Provisional Government of Southern Ireland, a determined attempt was made to transform the IRA into the semblance of a regular or 'National Army'. Officers against the Treaty were passed over and in any event would have refused to serve. To the men, General Mulcahy proclaimed: "Our army remains the Army of the Irish Republic." However when many of the men realized that their leaders were working towards the dissolution of the Republic, they returned to the ranks of the IRA taking their weapons with them.[II] In effect two armies were now in existence.

Forced out of many barracks by numbers of their former comrades who belonged to the 'National Army', the IRA set up their local headquarters in hotels and other premises and continued to function as a separate entity from the army of the Free State. Meanwhile the Provisional Government proceeded with speed in the formation of a new 'National Army' recruiting many men who a year previously had been their

---

[I] Following the signing of the Treaty, only the IRA leadership in Longford, Donegal, Clare and Sligo were initially in favour

[II] The author is aware of one IRA soldier who after his release from British custody was issued the uniform of the Free State army and took part in the handover ceremony of Beggars Bush Barracks to the National Army. After realizing 'how things stood', he promptly deserted the ranks of the Free State army and rejoined his IRA comrades.

enemies and receiving new weapons from the British. Despite attempts to unite the army, before many months had passed a brutal and bloody civil war[1] would erupt, which would see former comrades in battle against each other.

Once more the British had divided – and conquered.

---

[1] On the night of April 14th 1922, the IRA seized and occupied the Four Courts in the capital as their Dublin HQ. Following the assassination on June 22nd of Field Marshal Sir Henry Wilson (who was both Chief of the Imperial General Staff and Security Advisor to James Craig) by men acting under previous instructions of Michael Collins which had not been rescinded, the Free State Provisional Government came under pressure from London to expel the IRA from the Four Courts.

At 4am on the morning of June 28th, the Free State army commenced a bombardment of The Four courts using British supplied artillery. The British had countenanced intervening themselves, but had decided against it, out of fear that their action would re-unite the Irish factions.

The Irish Civil War had begun. Before two months had passed both Arthur Griffith and Michael Collins would be dead,

# Afterword

## The Unfinished Revolution

"Not merely free – but Gaelic as well" – Patrick Pearse

"We do not seek to make this country a materially great country at the expense of its honour in any way whatsoever. We would rather have this country poor and indigent, we would rather have the people of Ireland eking out a poor existence on the soil; as long as they possessed their souls, their minds and their honour. This fight has been for something more than the fleshpots of Empire." – Liam Mellowes

At the signing of The Anglo-Irish Treaty in London on December 6th 1921, the Irish delegates, at the behest of Griffith and Collins had effectively taken away the freedom of action which the Dáil possessed and reserved it to themselves, thereafter presenting the Dáil with a 'fait accompli'.
If the delegates had returned with the proposed treaty as Griffith had promised, it is extremely unlikely (despite Lloyd George's bullying) that the British Government, already under pressure due to the manifold crimes their forces had committed, would have immediately relaunched their war while the Treaty was being considered by the Dáil.
What was undoubtedly achieved in London was the severing of Irish national unity. If all else had failed, the continuation of

the war would have been a terrible but worthy price to pay for its preservation.

What followed the signing of the Treaty was the splitting "of Ireland from top to bottom" and the asphyxiation of the Irish National Revolution, for with the signing of the treaty and the impending split in the national movement, the National Revolution ended.

Whilst the maintenance of national unity would have seen the continuance of the National Revolution, Ireland instead became a fully fledged dominion, which swore allegiance to the British Monarch. Whilst the flag and government changed and most British troops left the country, much else remained unchanged.

Much that was British was formally adopted by the government of the Free State while the outward signs of dominion remained.

Towns, streets, statues, post boxes and monuments named in honour of British monarchs, heroes, and landlords, and those responsible for our centuries of trial still stand and in every county of Ireland the detritus of English rule still remains to this day.[1]

---

[1] During the 1916 Easter Rebellion, Irish forces located in the General Post Office had sniped at the statue of the British hero, Admiral Nelson, who stood atop a huge tower a short distance away. Fifty years later, this monument, located on the Capital's main thoroughfare was still standing, until a bomb planted by the IRA demolished it.

In the author's own area (Cavan / Monaghan) there remain many monuments erected during British rule. In Monaghan, the royal coat of arms bearing the inscription "Dieu et mon Droit" remains over the courthouse which overlooks a huge monument to a landlord killed during the Crimean War. In Cavan, the statue of the 'Famine Landlord', Lord Farnham stands in a place of honour outside the town library. In both counties, countless street names along with other monuments and postboxes (bearing the royal coat of arms and the incscription 'VR' (Victoria Regina) and 'GR' (Georgius Rex) still bear testament to the unfinished revolution.

Irish place-names which had been anglicised by the English from their original Gaelic into nonsensical English words were not changed whilst the national language continued to exist at the peripheries.

Such was the demise of the National Revolution that even the history of our country as taught in our schools was sanitized in order not to reveal the horrors of our Centuries of Trial and offend the dominion's master, England.

When the Republic was finally declared again in 1949, there was little appetite among our leaders to return to and complete the Gaelic revolution of the first quarter century.

The Gaelic Ireland dreamed of by our revolutionary leaders, of a country, Christian, Gaelic and Republican has never come to fruition.

Fifty years following the ratification of the Anglo Irish Treaty, the government of the Irish Republic embarked on a process which would end with the effective handing over of Irish sovereignty into the hands of a European power whose dictates we cravenly obey in order to be seen as 'good Europeans'. Our sovereignty is now joined or 'pooled' with that of the European Union. Prostrate before its dictates, we are no longer masters of our own house and do not possess the key to our own door.

As of writing, it is difficult to name any significant way in which Gaelic Ireland lives today because of the independence of (part of) Ireland from England.

The aim of the first Dáil, "Citizens of a free and Gaelic Ireland" still remains to be realized.

# References

1. Journal of the Irish House of Lords – Vol 1, p465.
2. Martin Haverty – The History of Ireland, Ancient and Modern, p625.
3. John Davidson - Ireland's story told to the new democracy, p174.
4. John Davidson - Ireland's story told to the new democracy, p174.
5. John Davidson - Ireland's story told to the new democracy, p174.
6. John Davidson - Ireland's story told to the new democracy, p174.
7. Martin Haverty – The History of Ireland, Ancient and Modern, p628
8. John Davidson - Ireland's story told to the new democracy, p175
9. John Davidson - Ireland's story told to the new democracy, p175
10. John Davidson - Ireland's story told to the new democracy, p175.
11. Edmund Curtis – A History of Ireland From Earliest Times to 1922, p247.
12. Patrick Moran – The Catholics of Ireland Under the Penal Laws in the Eighteenth Century, p11.
13. Patrick Moran – The Catholics of Ireland Under the Penal Laws in the Eighteenth Century, p17
14. Patrick Moran – The Catholics of Ireland Under the Penal Laws in the Eighteenth Century, p17
15. Patrick Moran – The Catholics of Ireland Under the Penal Laws in the Eighteenth Century, p17.
16. Patrick Moran – The Catholics of Ireland Under the Penal Laws in the Eighteenth Century, p17
17. Irish Records Office, Presentments of Grand Juries for 1750
18. Henry A Jeffries - History Ireland Magazine – The Penal Days in Clogher.
19. Patrick Moran – The Catholics of Ireland Under the Penal Laws in the Eighteenth Century, p15.
20. Jonathan Bardon – A History of Ireland in 250 Episodes, p242.
21. Patrick Moran – The Catholics of Ireland Under the Penal Laws in the Eighteenth Century, p65.
22. William Young – Tour of Ireland, Volume II, p18.
23. Patrick Moran – The Catholics of Ireland Under the Penal Laws in the Eighteenth Century, p65.
24. Patrick Moran – The Catholics of Ireland Under the Penal Laws in the Eighteenth Century, p67.
25. Patrick Moran – The Catholics of Ireland Under the Penal Laws in the Eighteenth Century, p7.
26. Patrick Moran – The Catholics of Ireland Under the Penal Laws in the Eighteenth Century, p8.
27. Patrick Moran – The Catholics of Ireland Under the Penal Laws in the Eighteenth Century, p8.
28. Patrick Moran – The Catholics of Ireland Under the Penal Laws in the Eighteenth Century, p173.
29. Patrick Moran – The Catholics of Ireland Under the Penal Laws in the Eighteenth Century, p174.
30. Patrick Moran – The Catholics of Ireland Under the Penal Laws in the Eighteenth Century, p174.
31. Patrick Moran – The Catholics of Ireland Under the Penal Laws in the Eighteenth Century, p174.
32. Patrick Moran – The Catholics of Ireland Under the Penal Laws in the Eighteenth Century, p174.
33. Fr. Augustine O.M Cap. – Ireland's Loyalty to the Mass, p163
34. Fr. Augustine O.M Cap. – Ireland's Loyalty to the Mass, p163.
35. Edmund Curtis and R.B McDowell (Editors) – Irish Historical Documents 1172-1922
36. Fr. Augustine O.M Cap. – Ireland's Loyalty to the Mass, p169
37. Fr. Augustine O.M Cap. – Ireland's Loyalty to the Mass, p170
38. Patrick Moran – The Catholics of Ireland Under the Penal Laws in the Eighteenth Century, p156.
39. Henry A Jeffries -History Ireland Magazine – The Penal Days in Clogher.

[40] Fr. Augustine O.M Cap. – Ireland's Loyalty to the Mass, p163
[41] Henry A Jeffries - History Ireland Magazine – The Penal Days in Clogher.
[42] Henry A Jeffries - History Ireland Magazine – The Penal Days in Clogher.
[43] Tony Nugent – Were you at the Rock?, p40.
[44] Tony Nugent – Were you at the Rock?, p40.
[45] Fr. Augustine O.M Cap. – Ireland's Loyalty to the Mass, p175.
[46] Fr. Augustine O.M Cap. – Ireland's Loyalty to the Mass, p180.
[47] Fr. Augustine O.M Cap. – Ireland's Loyalty to the Mass, p174.
[48] Fr. Augustine O.M Cap. – Ireland's Loyalty to the Mass, p186.
[49] Fr. Augustine O.M Cap. – Ireland's Loyalty to the Mass, p186.
[50] Patrick Moran – The Catholics of Ireland Under the Penal Laws in the Eighteenth Century, p186.
[51] Patrick Moran – The Catholics of Ireland Under the Penal Laws in the Eighteenth Century, p176
[52] Patrick Moran – The Catholics of Ireland Under the Penal Laws in the Eighteenth Century, p177.
[53] Patrick Moran – The Catholics of Ireland Under the Penal Laws in the Eighteenth Century, p177.
[54] John Davidson – Ireland's Story told to the New Democracy, p188.
[55] Jonathan Bardon – A History of Ireland in 250 Episode, p274.
[56] Jonathan Bardon – A History of Ireland in 250 Episode, p275.
[57] Patrick Moran – The Catholics of Ireland Under the Penal Laws in the Eighteenth Century, p122.
[58] Patrick Moran – The Catholics of Ireland Under the Penal Laws in the Eighteenth Century, p13.
[59] Patrick Moran – The Catholics of Ireland Under the Penal Laws in the Eighteenth Century, p9.
[60] Jonathan Bardon – A History of Ireland in 250 Episode, p256.
[61] Elizabeth Hughes – The Hampshire Hearth Tax
[62] Patrick Moran – The Catholics of Ireland Under the Penal Laws in the Eighteenth Century, p158.
[63] Patrick Moran – The Catholics of Ireland Under the Penal Laws in the Eighteenth Century, p11.
[64] John Davidson – Ireland's Story told to the New Democracy, p182,183.
[65] Jonathan Bardon – A History of Ireland in 250 Episode, p251.
[66] Patrick Moran – The Catholics of Ireland Under the Penal Laws in the Eighteenth Century, p106
[67] Patrick Moran – The Catholics of Ireland Under the Penal Laws in the Eighteenth Century, p106
[68] Patrick Moran – The Catholics of Ireland Under the Penal Laws in the Eighteenth Century, p107
[69] Patrick Moran – The Catholics of Ireland Under the Penal Laws in the Eighteenth Century, p107,108.
[70] Patrick Moran – The Catholics of Ireland Under the Penal Laws in the Eighteenth Century, p123.
[71] Patrick Moran – The Catholics of Ireland Under the Penal Laws in the Eighteenth Century, p109.
[72] Patrick Moran – The Catholics of Ireland Under the Penal Laws in the Eighteenth Century, p110
[73] Froude – The English in Ireland, Vol.II, p11.
[74] Patrick Moran – The Catholics of Ireland Under the Penal Laws in the Eighteenth Century, p110
[75] Stephen's Enquiry into The Charter Schools – p107.
[76] Howard – On Prisons, P208.
[77] Patrick Moran – The Catholics of Ireland Under the Penal Laws in the Eighteenth Century, p117.
[78] Patrick Moran – The Catholics of Ireland Under the Penal Laws in the Eighteenth Century, p113.
[79] Patrick Moran – The Catholics of Ireland Under the Penal Laws in the Eighteenth Century, p113
[80] Irish Debates, March 12 1792
[81] Irish Debates, April 12,1797.
[82] Patrick Moran – The Catholics of Ireland Under the Penal Laws in the Eighteenth Century, p124.
[83] Arthur Young – Tour of Ireland, Vol. 1, p76.
[84] Martin Haverty – A History of Ireland Ancient and Modern – p668.
[85] John Davidson – Ireland's Story told to the New Democracy, p181.
[86] Patrick Moran – The Catholics of Ireland Under the Penal Laws in the Eighteenth Century, p180.
[87] Patrick Moran – The Catholics of Ireland Under the Penal Laws in the Eighteenth Century,
[88] Francis Plowden – History of Ireland, Vol 1.
[89] Jonathan Bardon – A History of Ulster, p226.
[90] Madden and Duffy – The United Irishmen, Vol 1, p101.
[91] Patrick Moran – The Catholics of Ireland Under the Penal Laws in the Eighteenth Century, p196
[92] Patrick Moran – The Catholics of Ireland Under the Penal Laws in the Eighteenth Century, p
[93] John Davidson – Ireland's Story told to the New Democracy, p183.
[94] John Davidson – Ireland's Story told to the New Democracy, p183.

[95] John Davidson – Ireland's Story told to the New Democracy, p183.
[96] John Davidson – Ireland's Story told to the New Democracy, p191.
[97] John Davidson – Ireland's Story told to the New Democracy, p191.
[98] John Davidson – Ireland's Story told to the New Democracy, p192.
[99] John Davidson – Ireland's Story told to the New Democracy, p192.
[100] Darrell Figgis - Essay – "The Character of Grattan's Parliament and its Effect on the Nation".
[101] John Davidson – Ireland's Story told to the New Democracy, p193.
[102] John Davidson – Ireland's Story told to the New Democracy, p194.
[103] National Library of Ireland – Folder on Grattan's Parliament, Exhibit 10.
[104] John Davidson – Ireland's Story told to the New Democracy, p195.
[105] Patrick Moran – The Catholics of Ireland Under the Penal Laws in the Eighteenth Century, p191.
[106] Patrick Moran – The Catholics of Ireland Under the Penal Laws in the Eighteenth Century, p191.
[107] Patrick Moran – The Catholics of Ireland Under the Penal Laws in the Eighteenth Century, p192.
[108] Patrick Moran – The Catholics of Ireland Under the Penal Laws in the Eighteenth Century, p192.
[109] Patrick Moran – The Catholics of Ireland Under the Penal Laws in the Eighteenth Century, p193.
[110] Martin Haverty – A History of Ireland Ancient and Modern – p671
[111] Martin Haverty – A History of Ireland Ancient and Modern – p671
[112] Martin Haverty – A History of Ireland Ancient and Modern – p672.
[113] Madden – Life and Times of the United Irishmen, p11.
[114] John Davidson – Ireland's Story told to the New Democracy, p197.
[115] John Davidson – Ireland's Story told to the New Democracy, p197.
[116] Martin Haverty – A History of Ireland Ancient and Modern – p675.
[117] Martin Haverty – A History of Ireland Ancient and Modern – p675.
[118] Edmund Curtis – A History of Ireland From Earliest Times to 1922, p291.
[119] John Davidson – Ireland's Story told to the New Democracy, p199
[120] John Davidson – Ireland's Story told to the New Democracy, p208,209.
[121] John Davidson – Ireland's Story told to the New Democracy, p198
[122] Parliamentary Record of the House of Lords, London, 19/2/1798
[123] John Davidson – Ireland's story told to the New Democracy, p200.
[124] John Davidson – Ireland's Story told to the New Democracy, p183.
[125] John Davidson – Ireland's Story told to the New Democracy, p183.
[126] John Davidson – Ireland's Story told to the New Democracy, p183.
[127] Lord Holland – Memoirs of the Whig Party as quoted in Dr. Maddens "History of the United Irishmen" Chapter XII
[128] Martin Haverty – A History of Ireland Ancient and Modern, p681.
[129] Martin Haverty – A History of Ireland Ancient and Modern, p683.
[130] Nicholas Furlong – Fr. John Murphy of Boolavogue 1753-1798.
[131] Madden – The United Irishmen: their Lives and Times, V4, p491.
[132] Hilaire Belloc – A Shorter History of England, p524.
[133] Martin Haverty – A History of Ireland Ancient and Modern, p688, 689.
[134] Marianne Elliott – Wolfe Tone, Prophet of Irish Independence, p387.
[135] Marianne Elliott – Wolfe Tone, Prophet of Irish Independence, p387
[136] Marianne Elliott – Wolfe Tone, Prophet of Irish Independence, p387
[137] Marianne Elliott – Wolfe Tone, Prophet of Irish Independence, p388.
[138] Marianne Elliott – Wolfe Tone, Prophet of Irish Independence, p388.
[139] Marianne Elliott – Wolfe Tone, Prophet of Irish Independence, p388.
[140] Marianne Elliott – Wolfe Tone, Prophet of Irish Independence, p389.
[141] Marianne Elliott – Wolfe Tone, Prophet of Irish Independence, p390.
[142] Marianne Elliott – Wolfe Tone, Prophet of Irish Independence, p392,393, 394.
[143] Marianne Elliott – Wolfe Tone, Prophet of Irish Independence, p394.
[144] Marianne Elliott – Wolfe Tone, Prophet of Irish Independence, p396, 397.
[145] Marianne Elliott – Wolfe Tone, Prophet of Irish Independence, p399.
[146] Marianne Elliott – Wolfe Tone, Prophet of Irish Independence, p400.
[147] John Davidson – Ireland's Story told to the New Democracy, p208.
[148] John Davidson – Ireland's Story told to the New Democracy, p209.

[149] John Davidson – Ireland's Story told to the New Democracy, p211, also Haverty, p706.
[150] Professor Denis Gwyn – Daniel O'Connell, p68.
[151] John Davidson – Ireland's Story told to the New Democracy, p218.
[152] John Davidson – Ireland's Story told to the New Democracy, p218,219.
[153] John Davidson – Ireland's Story told to the New Democracy, p220.
[154] John Davidson – Ireland's Story told to the New Democracy, p236.
[155] Martin Haverty – A History of Ireland Ancient and Modern, p718.
[156] Martin Haverty – A History of Ireland Ancient and Modern, p728.
[157] Martin Haverty – A History of Ireland Ancient and Modern, p728.
[158] Martin Haverty – A History of Ireland Ancient and Modern, p730.
[159] Martin Haverty – A History of Ireland Ancient and Modern, p732.
[160] Martin Haverty – A History of Ireland Ancient and Modern, p733.
[161] Martin Haverty – A History of Ireland Ancient and Modern, p733.
[162] Martin Haverty – A History of Ireland Ancient and Modern, p733.
[163] Professor Denis Gwynn – Daniel O'Connell, p21.
[164] Denis Gwynn – Daniel O'Connell, p39.
[165] C.J Woods – Was O'Connell a United Irishman, p179
[166] Martin Haverty – A History of Ireland Ancient and Modern, p758.
[167] Denis Gwynn – Daniel O'Connell, p92.
[168] Joe Finn and Michel Lynch – Ireland and England 1798-1922, p18.
[169] Edmund Curtis – A History of Ireland from Earliest Times to 1922, p
[170] Martin Haverty – A History of Ireland Ancient and Modern, p761.
[171] Professor Denis Gwynn – Daniel O'Connell, p92.
[172] Professor Denis Gwynn – Daniel O'Connell, p118.
[173] Professor Denis Gwynn – Daniel O'Connell, p119,120.
[174] Professor Denis Gwynn – Daniel O'Connell, p124.
[175] Professor Denis Gwynn – Daniel O'Connell, p99.
[176] Professor Denis Gwynn – Daniel O'Connell, p100
[177] Professor Denis Gwynn– Daniel O'Connell, p102
[178] Martin Haverty – A History of Ireland Ancient and Modern, p761.
[179] Martin Haverty – A History of Ireland Ancient and Modern, p766.
[180] Professor Denis Gwynn – Daniel O'Connell, p157.
[181] Professor Denis Gwynn – Daniel O'Connell, p158,159.
[182] Professor Denis Gwynn – Daniel O'Connell, p159.
[183] Edmund Curtis – A History of Ireland from Earliest Times to 1922, p309.
[184] Joe Finn and Michel Lynch – Ireland and England 1798-1922
[185] Professor Denis Gwynn – Daniel O'Connell, p167.
[186] Professor Denis Gwynn – Daniel O'Connell, p167
[187] Professor Denis Gwynn – Daniel O'Connell, p167
[188] Professor Denis Gwynn – Daniel O'Connell, p167.
[189] Professor Denis Gwynn – Daniel O'Connell, p169.
[190] Professor Denis Gwynn – Daniel O'Connell, p170.
[191] Professor Denis Gwynn – Daniel O'Connell, p174
[192] Joe Finn and Michel Lynch – Ireland and England 1798-1922
[193] Professor Denis Gwynn – Daniel O'Connell, p1177,178.
[194] Professor Denis Gwynn – Daniel O'Connell, p178.
[195] Professor Denis Gwynn – Daniel O'Connell, p180
[196] Professor Denis Gwynn – Daniel O'Connell, p182
[197] Professor Denis Gwynn– Daniel O'Connell, p185
[198] Professor Denis Gwynn – Daniel O'Connell, p200
[199] Professor Denis Gwynn – Daniel O'Connell, p196.
[200] Professor Denis Gwynn – Daniel O'Connell, p200.
[201] Professor Denis Gwynn – Daniel O'Connell, p200.
[202] Professor Denis Gwynn – Daniel O'Connell, p205,206.
[203] Professor Denis Gwynn – Daniel O'Connell, p209

[204] Professor Denis Gwynn – Daniel O'Connell, p209
[205] Professor Denis Gwynn – Daniel O'Connell, p209,210.
[206] Professor Denis Gwynn – Daniel O'Connell, p210.
[207] Martin Haverty – A History of Ireland Ancient and Modern, p781.
[208] Professor Denis Gwynn – Daniel O'Connell, p213
[209] Cecil Woodham Smith – The Great Hunger, p31.
[210] Professor Denis Gwynn – Daniel O'Connell, p215
[211] Professor Denis Gwynn – Daniel O'Connell, p216
[212] Professor Denis Gwynn – Daniel O'Connell, p219
[213] Professor Denis Gwynn – Daniel O'Connell, p220
[214] Jonathan Bardon, A History of Ireland in 250 Episodes – p367.
[215] Martin Haverty – A History of Ireland Ancient and Modern, p772,773.
[216] Professor Denis Gwynn – Daniel O'Connell, p229.
[217] Professor Denis Gwynn – Daniel O'Connell, p229.
[218] Martin Haverty – A History of Ireland Ancient and Modern, p783.
[219] Professor Denis Gwynn – Daniel O'Connell, p233
[220] Professor Denis Gwynn – Daniel O'Connell, p242
[221] Professor Denis Gwynn – Daniel O'Connell, p249.
[222] Professor Denis Gwynn – Daniel O'Connell, p247.
[223] Professor Denis Gwynn – Daniel O'Connell, p248.
[224] Professor Denis Gwynn – Daniel O'Connell, p248.
[225] Professor Denis Gwynn – Daniel O'Connell, p250.
[226] Professor Denis Gwynn – Daniel O'Connell, p251
[227] Professor Denis Gwynn – Daniel O'Connell, p251
[228] The London Times – October 1847.
[229] Cecil Woodham Smith – The Great Hunger, p27.
[230] Edmund Curtis – A History of Ireland from Earliest Times to 1922, p315.
[231] Jonathan Bardon – A History of Ireland in 250 Episodes, p371.
[232] Jonathan Bardon – A History of Ireland in 250 Episodes, p371.
[233] Jonathan Bardon – A History of Ireland in 250 Episodes, p371.
[234] Jonathan Bardon – A History of Ireland in 250 Episodes, p371.
[235] Jonathan Bardon – A History of Ireland in 250 Episodes, p368.
[236] Jonathan Bardon – A History of Ireland in 250 Episodes, p370,371.
[237] Cecil Woodham Smith – The Great Hunger, p20.
[238] Cecil Woodham Smith – The Great Hunger, p20.
[239] Cecil Woodham Smith – The Great Hunger, p20.
[240] James Godkin – The Land War in Ireland, p290,291.
[241] Jonathan Bardon – A History of Ireland in 250 Episodes, p372.
[242] Cecil Woodham Smith – The Great Hunger, p18.
[243] James Godkin – The Land War in Ireland, p290.
[244] James Godkin – The Land War in Ireland, p291.
[245] Cecil Woodham Smith – The Great Hunger, p31
[246] Cecil Woodham Smith – The Great Hunger, p31.
[247] Cecil Woodham Smith – The Great Hunger, p31.
[248] Jeremiah O'Donovan Rossa – Rossa's Recollections 1838-98, p108,109.
[249] John Davidson – Ireland's Story Told to the New Democracy, p258.
[250] Cecil Woodham Smith – The Great Hunger, p44.
[251] Denis Gwynn – Daniel O'Connell, p244.
[252] Cecil Woodham Smith – The Great Hunger, p44
[253] John Davidson – Ireland's Story Told to the New Democracy, p253.
[254] Chris Fogarty – The Perfect Holocaust And Who Kept it Perfect, p88
[255] Cecil Woodham Smith – The Great Hunger
[256] Robert Kee – Ireland, A History, BBC TV series, episode 4.
[257] Dorothy Macardle – The Irish Republic, p45.
[258] Robert Kee – Ireland, A History, BBC TV series, episode 4.

[259] Robert Kee – Ireland, A History, BBC TV series, episode 4.
[260] John Davidson – Ireland's Story Told to the New Democracy, p258.
[261] Robert Kee – Ireland, A History, BBC TV series, episode 4.
[262] Robert Kee – Ireland, A History, BBC TV series, episode 4.
[263] Robert Kee – Ireland, A History, p87.
[264] Robert Kee – Ireland, A History, p87.
[265] John Mitchel – The Last Conquest of Ireland (Perhaps), Chapter XI.
[266] Robert Kee – Ireland, A History, p88.
[267] Robert Kee – Ireland, A History, p91.
[268] Robert Kee – Ireland, A History, p91.
[269] Robert Kee – Ireland, A History, p88
[270] James Godkin – The Land War in Ireland, p296.
[271] Robert Kee – Ireland, A History, p90
[272] Robert Kee – Ireland, A History, p94.
[273] Robert Kee – Ireland, A History, p94.
[274] Robert Kee – Ireland, A History, p92.
[275] Robert Kee – Ireland, A History, p95.
[276] Robert Kee – Ireland, A History, p96.
[277] Robert Kee – Ireland, A History, p96.
[278] Robert Kee – Ireland, A History, p96.
[279] James Godkin – The Land War in Ireland, p293.
[280] James Godkin – The Land War in Ireland, p293,294.
[281] John Davidson – Ireland's Story Told to the New Democracy, p255,256,257.
[282] Courtesy of Cavan County Museum
[283] Robert Kee – Ireland, A History, p100
[284] Robert Kee – Ireland, A History, p100
[285] Robert Kee – Ireland, A History, p100
[286] Robert Kee – Ireland, A History, p101
[287] John Davidson – Ireland's Story Told to the New Democracy, p253.
[288] John Davidson – Ireland's Story Told to the New Democracy, p253.
[289] A.M Sullivan – The Story of Ireland, p566,567.
[290] Blue Book, No 1,089 as quoted in O'Connor's Parnell Movement, P59.
[291] Robert Kee – Ireland, A History, p97
[292] Hilaire Belloc – A Shorter History of England, p577.
[293] Dorothy Macardle – The Irish Republic, p46.
[294] Martin Haverty – The History of Ireland, Ancient and Modern, p796,797.
[295] Robert Kee – Ireland, A History, p107
[296] Robert Kee – Ireland, A History, p107
[297] Robert Kee – Ireland, A History, p107
[298] Catholic newspaper, Oct. 1865 as quoted in Haverty p818.
[299] Robert Kee – Ireland, A History, p111
[300] Martin Haverty – The History of Ireland, Ancient and Modern, p814,815.
[301] John Davidson – Ireland's Story told to the new democracy, p271.
[302] Martin Haverty – The History of Ireland, Ancient and Modern, p831.
[303] Paul Rose – The Manchester Martyrs, p107-111.
[304] Paul Rose – The Manchester Martyrs, p11
[305] Paul Rose – The Manchester Martyrs, p11.
[306] P.W Joyce – A Concise History of Ireland, p188.
[307] Robert Kee – Ireland, A History, p21.
[308] John Morley – The Life of William Ewart Gladstone Vol II, p293.
[309] John Davidson – Ireland's Story told to the New Democracy, p275.
[310] Martin Haverty – A History of Ireland Ancient and Modern, p836.
[311] John Davidson – Ireland's Story told to the New Democracy, p274.
[312] Martin Haverty – A History of Ireland Ancient and Modern, p836.
[313] John Davidson – Ireland's Story told to the New Democracy, p261.

[314] Martin Haverty – A History of Ireland Ancient and Modern, p837.
[315] John Davidson – Ireland's Story told to the New Democracy, p261.
[316] John Davidson – Ireland's Story told to the New Democracy, p261.
[317] John Davidson – Ireland's Story told to the New Democracy, p280.
[318] Robert Kee – Ireland, A History, p123.
[319] Robert Kee – Ireland, A History, p120.
[320] Jonathan Bardon – A History of Ireland in 250 Episodes, p400.
[321] Moody and Martin – The Course of Irish History, p289.
[322] Robert Kee – Ireland, A History, p124.
[323] Jonathan Bardon – A History of Ireland in 250 Episodes, p400.
[324] Dorothy Macardle – The Irish Republic, p52,53.
[325] Dorothy Macardle – The Irish Republic, p53,54.
[326] Robert Kee – Ireland. A History, p131.
[327] Robert Kee – Ireland. A History, p137.
[328] Jonathan Bardon – A History of Ireland in 250 Episodes, p406.
[329] Robert Kee – Ireland. A History, p132.
[330] Jonathan Bardon – A History of Ireland in 250 Episodes, p407.
[331] Dorothy Macardle – The Irish Republic, p57.
[332] Jonathan Bardon – A History of Ireland in 250 Episodes, p414.
[333] Kevin Kenna – All The Risings 1014 –1916, p153
[334] The Capuchin Annual 1966 – Article on Arthur Griffith by Séan T. Ó Ceallaigh, p137.
[335] Dorothy Macardle – The Irish Republic, p72.
[336] Dorothy Macardle – The Irish Republic, p72.
[337] Dorothy Macardle – The Irish Republic, p65.
[338] Dorothy Macardle – The Irish Republic, p64.
[339] Dorothy Macardle – The Irish Republic, p64.
[340] Dorothy Macardle – The Irish Republic, p83.
[341] Dorothy Macardle – The Irish Republic, p85.
[342] Robert Kee – Ireland, A History, p146.
[343] Dorothy Macardle – The Irish Republic, p86.
[344] Dorothy Macardle – The Irish Republic, p86.
[345] Dorothy Macardle – The Irish Republic, p87.
[346] Dorothy Macardle – The Irish Republic, p89,90.
[347] Dorothy Macardle – The Irish Republic, p89.
[348] Dorothy Macardle – The Irish Republic, p101
[349] Dorothy Macardle – The Irish Republic, p111.
[350] Jonathan Bardon, A History of Ireland in 250 Episodes, p442.
[351] Republican Newspaper "An Phoblacht" April 30th 1926.
[352] Autobiography of Kathleen Clarke, p56.
[353] Dorothy Macardle – The Irish Republic, p136,137.
[354] Jonathan Bardon, A History of Ireland in 250 Episodes, p443.
[355] Dorothy Macardle – The Irish Republic, p148.
[356] Dorothy Macardle – The Irish Republic, p153.
[357] Dorothy Macardle – The Irish Republic, p154.
[358] Dorothy Macardle – The Irish Republic, p159.
[359] Bureau of Military History – Witness statement of Michael Staines (www.militaryarchives.ie)
[360] Bureau of Military History – Witness statement of Michael Staines (www.militaryarchives.ie)
[361] Bureau of Military History – Witness statement of Monsignor Curran (www.militaryarchives.ie)
[362] Robert Kee – Ireland, A History, p165.
[363] Dorothy Macardle – The Republic, p173.
[364] Dorothy Macardle – The Republic, p174
[365] Piaras F. Mac Lochlainn - Last Words. p 107,108.
[366] Piaras F. Mac Lochlainn - Last Words. p 10,11
[367] Robert Kee – Ireland, A History, p169.
[368] Piaras F. Mac Lochlainn - Last Words. P39.

[369] Piaras F. Mac Lochlainn - Last Words. P40.
[370] Piaras F. Mac Lochlainn - Last Words. P40.
[371] Piaras F. Mac Lochlainn - Last Words. P40.
[372] Piaras F. Mac Lochlainn - Last Words. P42.
[373] Peter Berresford Ellis – Eyewitness to Irish History, p214,215.
[374] Peter Berresford Ellis – Eyewitness to Irish History, p215.
[375] Dorothy Macardle – The Republic, p181.
[376] Peter Berresford Ellis – Eyewitness to Irish History, p219.
[377] Piaras F. Mac Lochlainn - Last Words. P71
[378] Dorothy Macardle – The Irish Republic, P192.
[379] Jonathan Bardon – A History of Ireland in 250 Episodes, P450.
[380] Ruán O'Donnell – Patrick Pearse, p272,273.
[381] Piaras F. Mac Lochlainn - Last Words. P60
[382] Piaras F. Mac Lochlainn - Last Words. P63.
[383] Piaras F. Mac Lochlainn - Last Words. P45.
[384] Piaras F. Mac Lochlainn - Last Words. P70.
[385] Piaras F. Mac Lochlainn - Last Words. P79.
[386] Piaras F. Mac Lochlainn - Last Words. P84.
[387] Piaras F. Mac Lochlainn - Last Words. P102,103.
[388] Piaras F. Mac Lochlainn - Last Words. P115.
[389] Piaras F. Mac Lochlainn - Last Words. p 116.
[390] Piaras F. Mac Lochlainn - Last Words. p 135.
[391] Piaras F. Mac Lochlainn - Last Words. p 141.
[392] Piaras F. Mac Lochlainn - Last Words. p 141.
[393] Piaras F. Mac Lochlainn - Last Words. p 122,123.
[394] Piaras F. Mac Lochlainn - Last Words. p 146.
[395] Piaras F. Mac Lochlainn - Last Words
[396] Piaras F. Mac Lochlainn - Last Words
[397] Piaras F. Mac Lochlainn - Last Words. p 172,173.
[398] Piaras F. Mac Lochlainn - Last Words. p 156.
[399] Piaras F. Mac Lochlainn - Last Words. p 157.
[400] Piaras F. Mac Lochlainn - Last Words. P197 – 204.
[401] Piaras F. Mac Lochlainn - Last Words. p 204,208.
[402] Piaras F. Mac Lochlainn - Last Words
[403] Piaras F. Mac Lochlainn - Last Words
[404] Documents Relative to the Sinn Fein Movement, p14.
[405] Dorothy Macardle – The Republic, p192.
[406] Dorothy Macardle – The Republic, p193.
[407] Dorothy Macardle – The Republic, p193.
[408] Dorothy Macardle – The Republic, p201.
[409] Dorothy Macardle – The Republic, p195.
[410] Éamonn Duggan – We Go Into Action Today At Noon, p42
[411] Dorothy Macardle – The Republic, p217,218.
[412] Jonathan Bardon – A History of Ireland in 250 Episodes, P453
[413] Robert Kee – The Green Flag, p607.
[414] Robert Kee – The Green Flag, p607.
[415] Robert Kee – The Green Flag, p607.
[416] Robert Kee – The Green Flag, p609.
[417] Robert Kee – The Green Flag, p609.
[418] Bureau of Military History – Witness statement of Monsignor Michael Curran (www.militaryarchives.ie)
[419] Dorothy Macardle – The Republic, p233.
[420] Dorothy Macardle – The Republic, p233.
[421] Bureau of Military History – Witness statement of Monsignor Michael Curran (www.militaryarchives.ie)

[422] Éamonn Duggan – We Go Into ActionToday At Noon, p46.
[423] Dorothy Macardle – The Republic, p236.
[424] Dorothy Macardle – The Republic, p237.
[425] Michael B. Barry – The Fight for Irish Freedom, p33.
[426] Dorothy Macardle – The Republic, p255.
[427] Dorothy Macardle – The Republic, p261.
[428] Dorothy Macardle – The Republic, p261.
[429] Curtis and McDowell – Irish Historical Documents 1172-1922, p318,319.
[430] Michael B. Barry – The Fight For Irish Freedom, p49.
[431] Curtis and McDowell – Irish Historical Documents 1172-1922, p319,320.
[432] Maire Comerford – The First Dáil.
[433] Michael B. Barry – The Fight For Irish Freedom, p50.
[434] Dorothy Macardle – The Republic, p349.
[435] Bureau of Military History – Witness statement of George Fitzgerald (www.militaryarchives.ie)
[436] Bureau of Military History – Witness statement of Daniel Breen (www.militaryarchives.ie)
[437] Bureau of Military History – Witness statement of Patrick O'Dwyer (www.militaryarchives.ie)
[438] Dorothy Macardle – The Republic, p289,290.
[439] Dorothy Macardle – The Republic, p291.
[440] Joe Finn & Michael Lynch – Ireland & England (1789-1922), p99.
[441] Daily Mail, January 6th, 1920.
[442] Dorothy Macardle – The Republic, p328.
[443] Dorothy Macardle – The Republic, p327
[444] Macready – Annals of an Active Life, Vol 2, p439.
[445] London Daily News, March 29th 1920
[446] Michael B. Barry – The Fight For Irish Freedom, p75.
[447] Keith Jeffrey, Oxford Dictionary of National Biography, p261.
[448] Dorothy Macardle – The Republic, p340
[449] Robert Kee – Ireland A History, Ep. 10.
[450] Dorothy Macardle – The Republic, p356,
[451] Dorothy Macardle – The Republic, p360,361.
[452] Dorothy Macardle – The Republic, p361.
[453] Dorothy Macardle – The Republic, p361.
[454] Dorothy Macardle – The Republic, p361.
[455] Dorothy Macardle – The Republic, p361.
[456] Dorothy Macardle – The Republic, p427.
[457] Dorothy Macardle – The Republic, p427.
[458] Dorothy Macardle – The Republic, p427.
[459] Dorothy Macardle – The Republic, p363.
[460] Thomas Jones – Whitehall Diary Vol III, pp18-23.
[461] Thomas Jones – Whitehall Diary Vol III, pp18-23.
[462] Thomas Jones – Whitehall Diary Vol III, pp18-23.
[463] Dorothy Macardle – The Republic, p380.
[464] Dorothy Macardle – The Republic, p382,383.
[465] London Daily News, August 22nd.
[466] Dorothy Macardle – The Republic, p387
[467] Dorothy Macardle – The Republic, p386,387.
[468] Dorothy Macardle – The Republic, p354.
[469] Freemans Journal, August 18th, 1920
[470] Dorothy Macardle – The Republic, p389
[471] Dorothy Macardle – The Republic, p389
[472] Dorothy Macardle – The Republic, p389, 390.
[473] Dorothy Macardle – The Republic, p390
[474] Dorothy Macardle – The Republic, p390.
[475] Ernie O'Malley – Raids and Ralllies, P87.
[476] Bureau of Military History – Witness statement of Michael Lynch

(www.militaryarchives.ie)
[477] Hansard (online version) for November 22nd 1920
[478] Michael B. Barry – The Fight For Irish Freedom, p170.
Also www.theauxiliaries.com
[479] Michael B. Barry – The Fight For Irish Freedom, p170.
Also www.theauxiliaries.com
[480] Dorothy Macardle – The Republic, p424.
[481] www.bureauofmilitaryhist patrickhiggins
[482] Frank Crozier, Ireland Forever, kindle edition.
[483] Frank Crozier, Ireland Forever, kindle edition.
[484] Irish Press, June 20th 1935.
[485] Dorothy Macardle – The Republic, p466
[486] Dorothy Macardle – The Republic, p471
[487] Dorothy Macardle – The Republic, p542.
[488] Witness statement of Austin Stack
[489] Dorothy Macardle – The Republic, p482
[490] Dorothy Macardle – The Republic, p482
[491] Dorothy Macardle – The Republic, p486, 487.
[492] Witness statement of Austin Stack
[493] Dorothy Macardle – The Republic, p498
[494] Dorothy Macardle – The Republic, p501
[495] Dorothy Macardle – The Republic, p504.
[496] Dorothy Macardle – The Republic, p508.
[497] Dorothy Macardle – The Republic, p524.
[498] Dorothy Macardle – The Republic, p529.
[499] Dorothy Macardle – The Republic, p529.
[500] Dorothy Macardle – The Republic, p529.
[501] Tim Pat Coogan – Michael Collins, Vol 2, p106
[502] Tim Pat Coogan – Michael Collins, Vol 2, p101.
[503] Dorothy Macardle – The Republic, p575.
[504] Curtis and McDowell – Irish Historical Documents 1172 – 1922, p324.
[505] Curtis and McDowell – Irish Historical Documents 1172 – 1922, p324.
[506] Witness statement of Austin Stack
[507] Ó Corráin and Hanley – Cathal Brugha An Indomitable Spirit, p136
[508] Annie Ryan – Comrades, Inside the War of Independence, p268.
[509] Annie Ryan – Comrades, Inside the War of Independence, p268.
[510] Dorothy Macardle – The Republic, p579.
[511] Tim Pat Coogan – Michael Collins, Vol 2 p131
[512] Tim Pat Coogan – Michael Collins, Vol 2 p131
[513] Winston Churchill, The World Crisis
[514] Official Report of Dail Éireann, December 19th 1921
[515] Austen Chamberlain, Down the Years.
[516] David Lloyd George – Is it Peace?, p272,273.
[517] Dorothy Macardle – The Republic, p610
[518] Dorothy Macardle – The Republic, p610
[519] Dorothy Macardle – The Republic, p603.
[520] Dorothy Macardle – The Republic, p603.
[521] Dorothy Macardle – The Republic, p610

www.ingramcontent.com/pod-product-compliance
Lightning Source LLC
Chambersburg PA
CBHW060101170426
43198CB00010B/730